BIOLOGY: PRINCIPLES AND EXPERIMENTS

Mary J Soltay

Longman

To Leslie and to my parents

LONGMAN GROUP LIMITED
London
Associated companies, branches and representatives throughout the world

First published 1976
This edition 1979
ISBN 0 582 33104 8

Printed in Hong Kong by
Wing Tai Cheung Printing Co Ltd.

CONTENTS

Notes on contents

This book is designed to give a comprehensive introduction to the study of living organisms.
The author has taken great care to present the various concepts and principles in a logical sequence that encourages understanding as opposed to memorization. New topics and lines of approach are introduced and developed by means of a sequence of questions that attempt to arouse interest and lead the student to anticipate the information that is to follow.
Plant and animal biology are dealt with together to emphasize common systems and characteristics while pointing out different ways in which various life functions are performed.
Comparative studies are set up between the different levels of complexity among living things. Functions such as transport, sensitivity, movement and reproduction are examined in plants and animal specimens from a unicellular level up to man.
Illustrations have wherever possible been placed alongside the text in order to clarify the points under discussion.

Experiments aim to give students a clear understanding of:
- the information being sought from the experiment
- the design of the experiment and reasons behind its design
- what to look for while the experiment is in progress
- how to examine the results obtained
- what conclusion or new question can be derived from results.

Brief summaries of sections are given at appropriate places. End of chapter exercises were not considered necessary or even desirable as the entire text is developed as a series of questions and answers.
Special care was taken in compiling a comprehensive index to allow quick reference to any of the points covered in the book.

ACKNOWLEDGMENTS

WE ARE GRATEFUL TO THE FOLLOWING FOR PERMISSION TO REPRODUCE SOME OF THE PHOTOGRAPHS:

Cape Engineering Company Ltd, fig. 2.32;
Carolina Biological Supply Company, fig. 5.78 (From *The Science of Biology* by P.B. Weisz. Used with permission of McGraw Hill Book Company.);
D.A. Coult, fig. 2.46;
M.S. Fuller, University of California, Berkeley, figs. 2.49 and 5.77 (From *The Science of Biology* by P.B. Weisz. Used with permission of McGraw Hill Book Company.);
W.J. Garnett, figs. 1.85 and 3.18;
B.J.W. Heath, figs. 1.93, 1.94 and 4.39 (From *Biology: A Functional Approach* by M.B.V. Roberts, published by Thomas Nelson and Sons Ltd.);
A. Ironside, fig. 7.7;
H.B.D. Kettlewell, fig. 7.20;
J. Limbach, Ripon Microslides Incoporated, fig. 2.51 (From *The Science of Biology* by P.B. Weisz. Used with permission of McGraw Hill Book Company.);
Rothamsted Experimental Station, fig. 1.23;
Royal College of Surgeons of England, fig. 2.18 (By permission of the President and Council of the Royal College of Surgeons of England.);
Shell Photographic Unit, fig. 6.22;
Anne Talantire, fig. 5.32;
C.J. Webb, figs. 1.43, 1.62, 1.66, 1.68, 1.71, 1.91, 1.95, 1.103, 2.9, 2.25, 2.27, 3.6, 3.12, 3.35, 4.4, 4.7, 4.11, 4.14, 4.17, 4.19, 4.47, 4.49, 5.4, 5.17, 5.19, 5.24, 5.40, 5.59, 5.64, 5.87, 5.88, 5.90, 5.98, 6.25, 6.26, 6.33, 6.40, 6.49, 7.17, 8.1, 8.2, 8.4, 8.7, 8.9 and 8.10;
Wellcome Museum of Medical Science, fig. 1.47.
D.P. Wilson, fig. 1.100;
World Health Organisation, figs. 1.39, 1.40, 1.41 and 5.100.

FOR PERMISSION TO REPRODUCE THE COVER PHOTOGRAPH, WE ARE MOST GRATEFUL TO Aeronutronic Ford Corporation.

THE PUBLISHERS WOULD ALSO LIKE TO THANK Mr Kong Chuen-wai FOR HIS ADVICE ON THE ILLUSTRATIONS AND Dr Dennis Hill FOR HIS ADVICE ON THE ECOLOGY SECTION OF THE BOOK.

DIAGRAM ACKNOWLEDGEMENTS

The author and publisher are indebted to Mr. D. G. Mackean for the use of the following drawings which are taken from or based on those in *Introduction to Biology; Tropical Edition* ©1969 or *Introduction to Biology; New Tropical Edition* ©1976 published by John Murray Ltd:

Figs 1.44 Action of specialized teeth, 1.46 Section through herbivore's skull to show action of teeth (after J. Maynard Smith), 1.49 Section through herbivore's molar to show how it is worn down, 1.50 Herbivore's molars slide over each other and grind, 1.52 Section through incisor and molar teeth, 1.74 (ii) Stereogram of villus, 2.1 To see if oxygen is taken up by germinating seeds, 2.3 Carbon dioxide production in an animal, 2.42 Association of tracheal system with muscles of insects (after Wigglesworth), 2.50 Section through stem showing lenticel, 3.17 (ii) and (iii) Types of root, 4.15 Function of atlas and axis vertebrae, 4.28 Side view of male cockroach, 4.33 Frog leaping (after Gray), 4.34 Frog crawling (after Gray), 4.35 Tree frog, 5.14 Schematic diagram of human circulation, 5.18 Action of valves in a vein, 5.28 Relation between tissue cells, capillaries and lymphatics, 5.29 Main drainage routes of lymphatic system, 5.31 Distribution of veins from lateral root to leaf, 5.34 To show how vertical columns of cells give rise to vessels, 5.72 Geotropism in root, 5.94 Structure of sympathetic nervous system, 6.20 and 6.21 Metamorphosis in frog, 6.30 Stereogram of *Spirogyra* cell in section, 6.31 Sexual reproduction in *Spirogyra*, 6.41 Female reproductive organs in human, 6.42 Section through ovary, 6.45 Fertilization of starfish egg, 6.46 Development of human embryo, 6.48 Growth and development in uterus, 6.64 (ii) Structure of anther (iii) Pollen sacs split, 6.72 Seed of *Vicia faba*.

Permission to use or adapt any of the above illustrations must be sought from John Murray (Publishers) Ltd, 50 Albemarle Street, London.

The author and publisher are also grateful to Mr. M. B. V. Roberts and Thomas Nelson and Sons Ltd. for the use of the following drawings which are taken from or based on *Biology: a functional approach* (1971): Figs 1.90, 3.13, 3.14, 3.20, 4.24, 4.36, 4.37, 4.45, 4.46, 5.33, 5.35, 5.82, 6.10, 6.11, 6.12, 6.47, 7.22, 7.23; to John W. Kimball and Addison-Wesley, Reading, Massachusetts for permission to reprint the following drawings from *Biology* (4th Edition) © 1978: Figs 1.63, 1.92, 5.37; to V. B. Wigglesworth and Chapman and Hall Ltd. for use of the following drawing from *The Principles of Insect Physiology* (6th Edition): Fig 2.42; to Garrett Hardin and Carl Bajema and W. H. Freeman and Company for use of the following drawings from or adapted from *Biology: Its Principles and Implications*, 3rd Edition, © 1978: Figs 2.29, 3.15, 3.16, 4.10, 4.41, 5.58, 5.60, 5.61, 5.83. to Brocklehurst and Ward and Hodder and Stoughton Educational for use of the following drawings from *A New Biology:* Figs 1.11, 1.64; to Professor Maynard Smith for use of Fig 1.46.

Whilst every effort has been made to trace the owners of Copyright, in a few cases this has proved impossible and we take this opportunity to offer our apologies to any authors whose rights may have been unwittingly infringed.

INTRODUCTORY SECTION

THE STUDY OF BIOLOGY

The approach

Biology as well as other sciences has two phases. First, there is the passive collection of organized knowledge that can be learned from a textbook. Second, but equally important, is the process of finding out new points of knowledge through experimentation.

Obviously we have to learn from the theories derived from experiments performed by others before us. It would be very discouraging indeed if we had to start with the discovery of the basic facts on our own without any help from the work of others. But we can obtain a better and deeper understanding of the subject by performing for ourselves as many experiments as possible. One cannot hope to learn biology by simply reading this book or just listening in class. It is important also to always ask WHY and HOW in learning any science subject.

MAKING NOTES

Making adequate notes on what you are studying is very important, especially in relation to the experiments that you perform. Always start with a clear, concise statement of the aims of the experiment.

Expressing methods, results etc. in the form of a diagram or table is very effective because it gives a general view of the situation at a glance.

Remember that notes should not only be neat and pretty to look at but above all they should be informative.

Making a drawing of something is helpful not only for later reference but because the actual exercise of drawing helps you to learn. In order to draw something you have to really LOOK at the object first, and looking helps you to understand and remember.

All drawings should be accompanied by neat, informative labels.

PREPARATION FOR EXAMINATIONS

The best way to prepare for examinations is to make certain that you thoroughly understand each fact and each experiment at the time that it is first presented to you. Many aspects of biology cannot be simply memorized. They must be understood thoroughly and then remembering becomes easy.

The role of experimentation in Biology

Biology as we know it today is a science based on experimentation. This was not always true of biology. In the Middle Ages, for instance, professors at universities put together elaborate theories on how the human body functioned. They based most of their ideas on the books written by the Greeks many years before. But none of these ideas and theories were ever tested through experiments.

Today experimental proof of every theory is a basic feature of biology as well as all other sciences.

What is a good experiment?

In biology, experiments must be designed in such a way as to meet certain basic requirements as follows:

1. The experiment must be designed to test some theory or observation about the living things around you.
2. The results of the experiment must tell you if the theory is correct or not.
3. Based on the results of the experiment you must be able to make the necessary changes in the theory.
4. The experiment must be reproducible, giving the same result every time.

The need for controls

In order to obtain clear cut, reproducible results from your experiments you must devise suitable controls.

Consider the following example. In mixing 3 components, A, B and C, a certain positive result is obtained. You must ensure that the same result is not obtained if one or more of the components are left out of the mixture.

The exact design of a control experiment depends on the characteristics of the main experiment that you are performing.

As you go through performing the experiments in your biology course you should get a feel for the efficient use of control experiments.

Biology is a dynamic science

During your school years it is very easy to start thinking of biology as something very repetitive to be studied from a book and memorized. Because you spend so much time learning the simple, basic concepts and repeating experiments that many other people have done before, you get the impression that science in general is static, that it is dead. But this is not so.

Scientists working in many research laboratories all over the world are constantly performing new experiments, changing old theories and having active disagreements with one another.

When scientists gather at meetings to present their work to one another and discuss their results, there is a very careful and critical examination of each new theory and new experiment.

The discussions that follow help to improve the theories and experiments on a particular topic.

What can you do to make the study of biology more interesting?

You can, on a smaller scale, do what the research scientists do. Think very critically of each experiment that you perform. Just because it is written down in a book or given to you by your teacher does not mean that you cannot question it. Ask yourself questions like: Is this a well designed experiment?

What do the results tell me?

Is there another even better experiment to test this theory?

Read as much as you can about science, about scientists and their lives. Try to get a feel for the way a scientist thinks and works. Thinking, asking questions and reading along these lines will all help to make the study of biology more exciting and will help you to remember without having to memorize.

The light microscope

In many instances the development of a branch of science is hindered by the lack of necessary equipment for performing certain crucial experiments.

Such was the case in the field of biology before the invention of the microscope. Biologists made as accurate observations as possible with the naked eye and hand lens but many details of the structure of organisms remained hidden to them simply because they were too small to be seen. Since the first microscope was constructed in the middle of the seventeenth century by Robert Hooke better instruments have become available to give higher magnification and clearer images.

The limit of magnification of the **light microscope** (i.e. one using visible light) is about 2000 ×. At this magnification an object appears to be 2000 times as large as in reality. At higher magnifications an object appears as a large but indistinct blur because adjacent points cannot be **resolved** into separate images (i.e. they cannot be distinguished from one another) but become fused into one. This limitation results from the fact that points that are closer to each other than the wavelength of light cannot be resolved.

The electron microscope

The tremendous advance in the field of physics in the early decades of the present century led to the idea of constructing a microscope that would use **electrons** instead of visible light to produce an image.

The object to be examined is soaked or *fixed* by immersing in a metallic solution that does not allow electrons to penetrate.

A narrow stream of electrons is directed onto the object.
The electrons are reflected by the object the same way as a beam of light would be. The reflected beam is focused onto a viewing screen where an image of the object is formed. See Fig. 1 for a comparison of the light microscope and the electron microscope.
The advantage of using electrons is that a stream of electrons has a much shorter wavelength than visible light and therefore the resolving power of the microscope is much greater.
Fig.2 shows the relative sizes of various biological specimens and the limits of resolution of the human eye and various microscopes.
Fig.3 shows the type of microscope you will most likely use in the biology laboratory. In principle all microscopes are the same but there are slight differences depending on the model.

Fig. 1 Comparison of the light microscope and the electron microscope

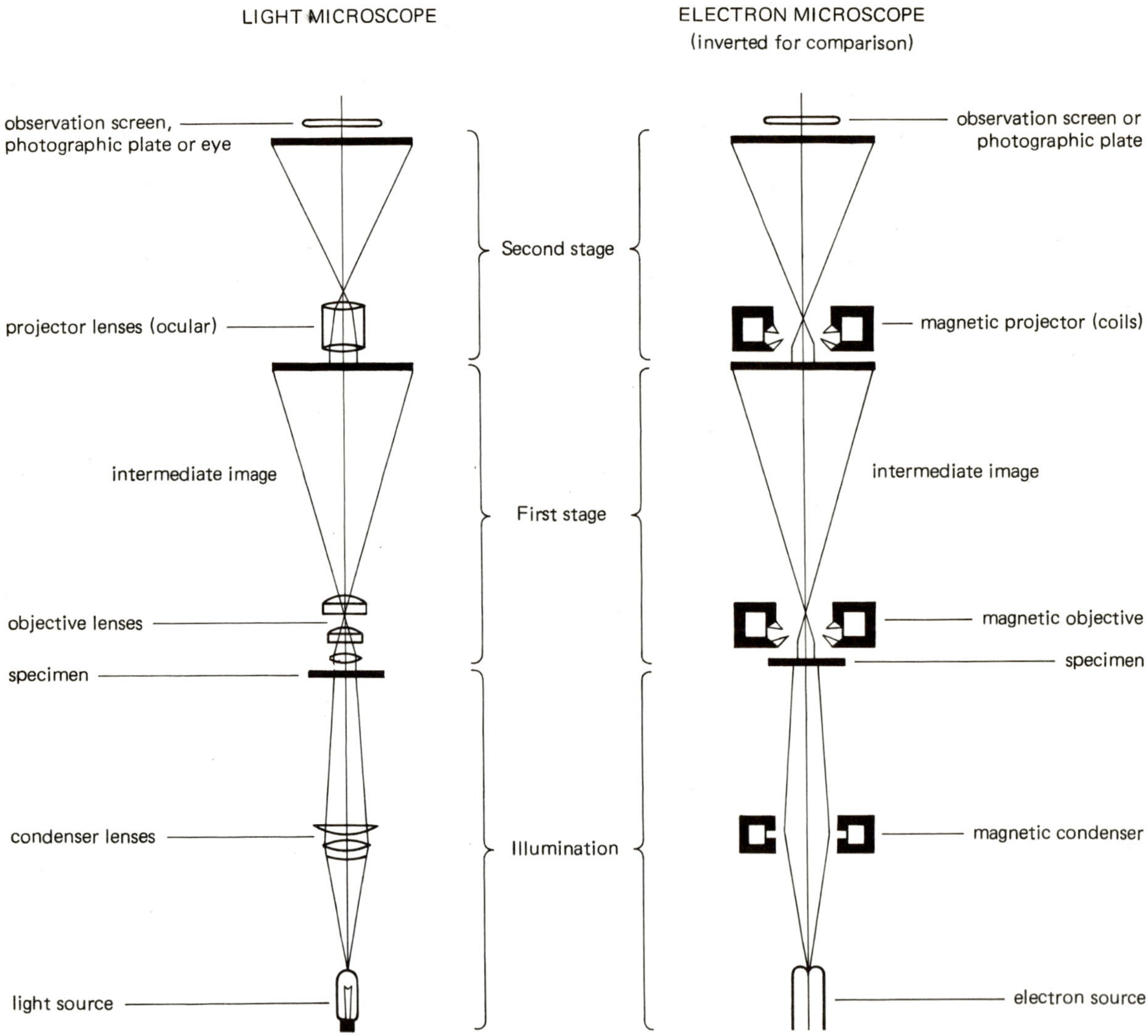

Fig. 2 Relative sizes of some biological specimens

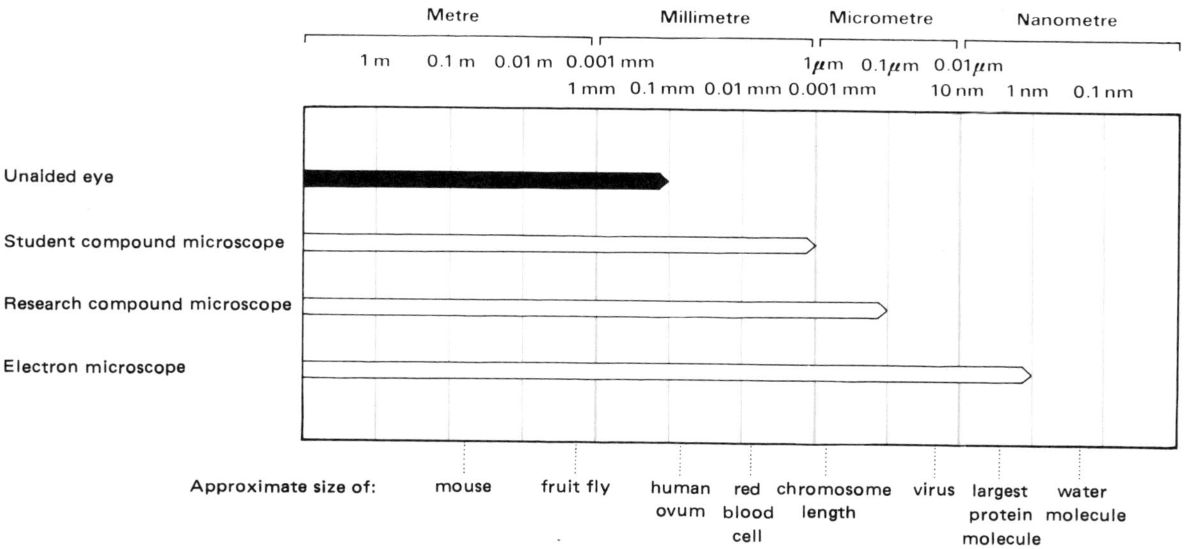

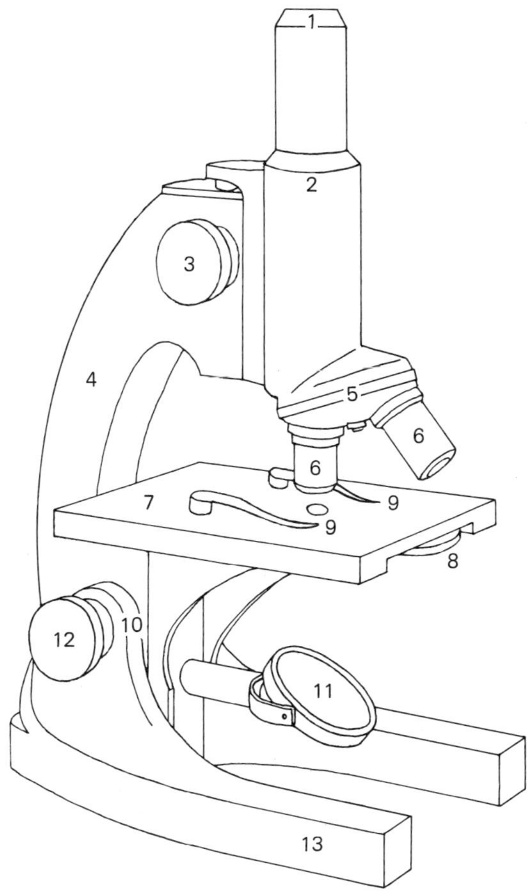

Fig. 3 The compound microscope

1 **Ocular**
contains lenses to increase magnification; it may be replaced with lenses of other magnification power.

2 **Body tube**
holds lenses of ocular and objectives at the proper working distance from each other.

3 **Coarse adjustment**
moves body tube up or down to the approximately correct distance from the specimen for clear observation.

4 **Arm**
supports body tube and coarse adjustment.

5 **Nosepiece**
permits intercharge of low- and high-power objectives.

6 **Objectives**
contain lenses of different magnifications.

7 **Stage**
supports slide.

8 **Diaphragm**
regulates amount of light passing through the specimen.

9 **Stage clips**
hold specimen firmly in place.

10 **Inclination joint**
permits tilting to adjust to eye level.

11 **Mirror**
reflects light upward through diaphragm and hole in stage.

12 **Fine adjustment**
permits exact focusing by moving stage or body up or down

13 **Base**
supports weight of microscope.

Examining your microscope

Place the microscope you are to use on a bench in front of you. Using Fig.3 identify all the parts of the instrument.
A microscope is a very delicate optical instrument. It should always be handled with great care. When carrying it always use both hands.
Always wash your hands before working with the instrument. Never touch the surfaces of the lenses or the eyepiece with your fingers.
When lenses or eyepiece need cleaning, use lens tissue. It is advisable to clean the lenses before and after each use.
Avoid spilling any liquids onto the stage or any other part of the instrument.
If you should accidentally spill something wipe off immediately with clean tissue paper.

How should material be prepared for viewing under the microscope?

Fig. 4

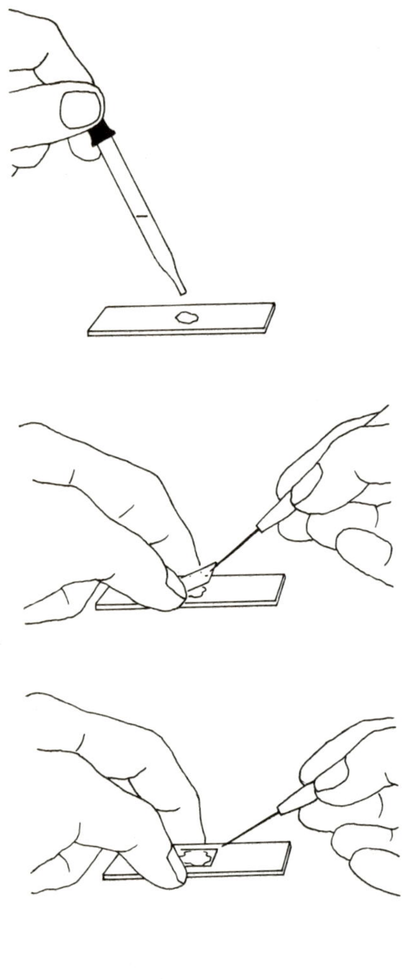

If one is to observe as much detail as possible in a specimen, the specimen also has to be carefully prepared.
One of the most important aspects of preparation of a specimen is the cutting of sections. Sections must be sufficiently thin to allow light to pass through freely: otherwise you will see only a dark shadow.
There are special instruments called **microtomes** that can be used to cut very thin sections. As you are not likely to have one of these instruments you will have to prepare sections manually. Several methods are described in the main text where applicable. (See pp. 133, 211 and 261.)
After sectioning the material should be placed on a *clean* microscope slide, covered with a *single* drop of water and with a coverslip.
It is absolutely essential to ensure that the slide is clean and free from any fingerprints. Slides and coverslips should always be handled by holding at their edges.
The best way to put on the coverslip is to hold it to the slide at an angle of about 45° and gently lower it with the help of a dissecting needle or similar instrument. (See Fig 4.)

Staining procedure

If a stain is to be used to make certain structures more visible a small drop should be placed at one edge of the coverslip, then drawn across the specimen by means of an absorbent paper placed at the opposite edge.
The use of excessive amounts of dye will obscure the object rather than reveal more detail because the object will become too dark and light will not be reflected from it.

EXPERIMENT (A) TO EXAMINE THE CELLS LINING THE CHEEK

Materials
toothpick
eye dropper
slide and coverslip
lens paper
methylene blue

Method
1. Scrape the inside of your mouth gently with a toothpick. This will remove some of the loose cells from the surface of the cheek lining.
2. Place the cells onto a clean microscope slide and spread out to form a thin layer.
3. Add *one* drop of water with an eye dropper.
4. Put on the coverslip.
5. Examine under the microscope.

Note:
When viewing a specimen under the microscope always begin with the lowest power of magnification (the shortest lens).
Looking at the instrument from the side lower the lens as far down as possible without actually touching the slide and breaking it. Then, viewing through the eyepiece, bring the object into focus by slowly moving the lens *upward* with the coarse adjustment knob. Final focusing is done by using the fine adjustment knob.
While using the low power you will probably be able to lower the lens as far as it will go without touching the slide. However, the high power lenses are longer and if you lower them without looking from the side you could easily crush the slide and damage the lens.
Adjust the mirror carefully to let in the correct amount of light. Once you have examined the object with low power, carefully change to the high-power objective. Following the procedure above bring the object into focus again.

EXPERIMENT (B) TO EXAMINE ONION EPIDERMAL CELLS

Materials
onion
microscope slide and coverslip
iodine solution

Method
1. Break an onion scale in half and examine the edges. You will find small sections of delicate epidermal cells protruding at the edges.
2. Gently peel off a small piece of the epidermal layer and place onto the slide.
3. Cover with a drop of water; apply the coverslip.

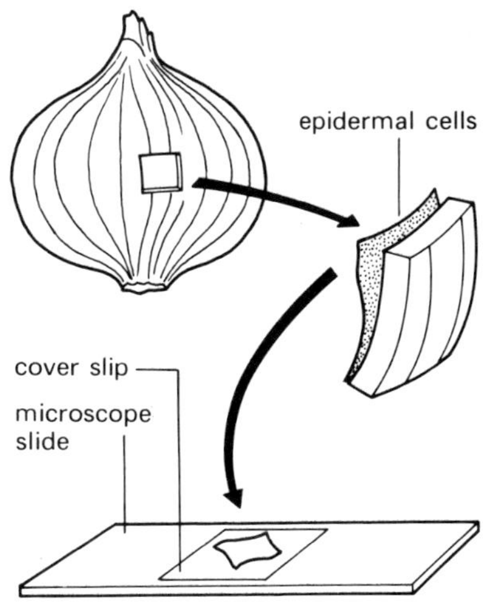

Fig. 5

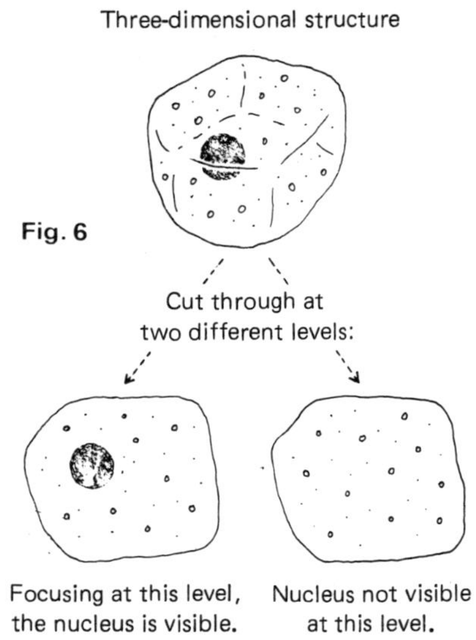

Fig. 6

4. Stain with iodine solution.

Discussion

Cells are three-dimensional structures, that is, they have a definite thickness. When viewing a cell through the microscope it appears to be two dimensional only, because you are only seeing the structures at the level through which you are focusing.

A GENERAL PROCEDURE FOR DISSECTION OF MAMMALS

Materials

1. A dissection tray made of wood or metal and covered with a layer of wax is the best to use.
2. Instruments:

i. Sharp scalpel
ii. Sharp, fine scissors
iii. Large scissors
iv. Blunt probe
v. Large pins
vi. Small forceps
vii. Large forceps

3. A freshly killed animal is the best to use.

For small animals the best method is to place the specimen in a jar containing cotton wool soaked in chloroform or some other anaesthetic.

Larger animals require an injection of an appropriate chemical such as nembutol.

Method

1. Place the animal on its back, spread out the legs and pin securely to the tray.
2. Make the first incision at the midpoint of the abdomen. To make certain that you do not cut through any internal organs lift the skin well away using a pair of forceps.

Fig. 7 Dissecting a mammal – opening the abdomen

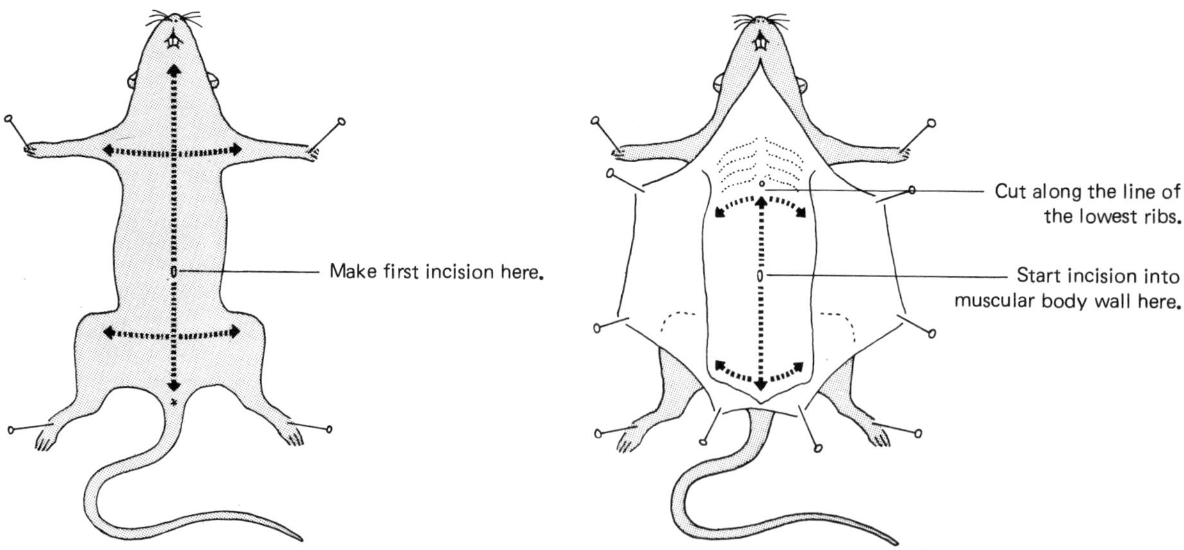

3. Carefully extend the vertical incision up to the throat and then down towards the anal region. (See Fig. 7.)
4. Now make further cuts in a horizontal direction at the level of the front and hind legs.
5. Carefully lift the skin to the side and pin to the board.
6. At this point you may need to cut through some remaining connective tissue to expose the interior of the body cavity.
7. Proceed to further dissection of the abdominal cavity depending on what organ you intend to study. Make as few actual cuts as possible. In most cases organs can be simply moved aside to expose underlying features.
8. To reveal the thorax you need to cut through the ribs up towards the neck. Be careful not to damage any blood vessels or the trachea and oesophagus.

LIVING THINGS

The word biology is derived from the Greek word *bios* meaning life, and *logos* meaning knowledge. It means the 'study of life'.

What is life?

This is a complicated question that scientists and philosophers have been trying to answer for centuries. As yet they have not been able to give a definite answer.
For our purposes it would be much more suitable to ask: What are the characteristics that can be associated with life?

How do we distinguish between a living thing and a non-living thing?

MOVEMENT
The first characteristic associated with life by early man was most probably movement. Although not every living thing is able to move from place to place (e.g. plants), and not every thing that moves is in fact alive, as a general rule movement can be regarded as indicative of life.

SENSITIVITY OR RESPONSIVENESS
The non-living and living environment of an organism is constantly changing. In order to survive the organism must be capable of sensing these changes and responding in an appropriate manner.

METABOLISM
Metabolism includes all the various chemical reactions and processes that take place inside the cells of living organisms. Metabolic processes include nutrition and its associated functions such as digestion, photosynthesis, respiration and excretion to name but a few.

GROWTH AND REPAIR
Many of the metabolic reactions carried on by living cells are directed towards an increase in size and complexity of the organism and/or maintaining the fully developed organism in a healthy condition.

REPRODUCTION
The ability to reproduce is a property that is strictly limited to living things. However, an organism can lack the capacity to reproduce and yet be alive as seen in the case of sterile organisms such as the drones of the honey bee colony.
Through the process of reproduction living things are able to produce others of their own kind. The process also provides a means by which new characteristics can be acquired by a species, that is, it enables evolution of a species to take place.

How many different living things are there in the world?

The answer to the above question is simple—we do not know. A conservative estimate would be two million but there are more being discovered all the time especially in the more remote areas of the world.

Classification

How can biologists hope to keep track of so many different organisms?

Without some system for naming and organization the task would be impossible. No single person could hope to remember even the names let alone information about the structure and habits of each organism if these were not collected into some meaningful system of organization.
In addition there is a need for a universal nomenclature that will be understood by scientists in all countries regardless of language barriers.

The binomial nomenclature

The first system of naming and grouping living things was introduced by the Swedish biologist, Carolus Linnaeus, in 1735. It is called 'binomial' because every name consists of two words. The first word, always written with a capital letter, refers to the **genus** (**generic name)** of the organism and the second word is the **species (specific name)**. The generic and specific names together refer to a distinct organism that is somehow different from all other organisms. Human beings, for example, belong to the group of *Homo sapiens*. (Notice that the scientific name of an organism is either written in italics or is underlined.)

The genus is a grouping of very closely related organisms that differ only in a few minor respects.
As an example we can take the common domestic dog known as *Canis familiaris*. The genus Canis includes other animals closely related to the dog such as the American wolf, *Canis lupus*.
Members of this genus are included in the **family** *Canidae* which also includes wild dogs, jackals and foxes. These all belong to the **order** *Carnivora*. This order includes not only dogs and their relatives but also cats, seals, bears and other animals that have the typical tooth pattern, claw structure, skull and bones attributed to the carnivorous habit.
All carnivores have hair and suckle their young. In these respects they are related to the apes and the rodents such as mice and rabbits and are placed together with them in the **class** *Mammalia*.
Mammals, while they are very different from birds, fish, reptiles and amphibians, share with these groups the common feature of a backbone. For this reason they are all considered to be members of the **subphylum** *Vertebrata*. Vertebrates in turn are members of the **phylum** *Chordata* all of whose members possess a nerve cord that passes along the dorsal part of the body.
As you can see from this example the system of classification does not only serve the purpose of naming and grouping organisms but also provides considerable information about the structure and habits of the particular organism.
The table below shows the complete classification of the domestic dog and of human beings:

Table 1

	Dog	Man
Kingdom	Animal	Animal
Phylum	Chordata	Chordata
Subphylum	Vertebrata	Vertebrata
Class	Mammalia	Mammalia
Order	Carnivora	Primata
Family	Canidae	Hominidae
Genus	Canis	Homo
Species	Familiaris	Sapiens

What are the principles according to which organisms are classified?

According to the early classification schemes similarities and differences were determined on the basis of outward appearance and habits only. For instance, all animals that could swim were considered to be fish. As more became known about the properties and characteristics of organisms, especially their anatomy and embryonic development, the system was revised.

Even today there is by no means general agreement among scientists as to certain details of the scheme of classification. There are bound to be differences in opinion about the significance that is attached to a particular structural feature and to the best method of establishing the classification.
All the names used are derived from Latin, a language that was still commonly used in scientific circles at the time of Linnaeus. The original Latin names have been retained to make the classification universal. If you were to look at an advanced biology book written in Chinese or Japanese, for instance, exactly the same names would be used as in a book written in English or German.

Table 2
PLANT KINGDOM

SUB-KINGDOMS
I. *Thallophyta*
unicellular or if multicellular, little cell differentiation

PHYLA

Chlorophyta	*Euglenophyta*	*Phaeophyta*	*Cyanophyta*	*Myxomycophyta*
mostly fresh water, contains chlorophyll e.g. green algae	fresh water, motile, contains chlorophyll e.g. Euglena	mostly marine, contains pigments other than chlorophyll e.g. brown algae	marine, fresh water chlorophyll and other pigments dissolved in cytoplasm e.g. blue-green algae	terrestrial, naked mass protoplasm, no cell walls, no pigments, saprophytic e.g. slime moulds

Tables 2 and 3 give an outline of the main divisions of the animal and plant **kingdoms** along with some of the basic characteristics of each group.

Some authors prefer to use a separate kingdom called *Protista* to include all species that are neither typical plants nor animals or have some characteristics of both. The group includes protozoa, algae, bacteria, viruses, fungi, lichens and slime moulds.

As far as possible extinct species are also included in the scheme on the basis of information from fossils.

Table 4 gives you some idea of the development of the various types of plants and animals throughout the various periods in the development of the earth.

mycophyta
strial, true cellular
on, no photo-
etic pigments,
phytic
ungi

II. *Embryophyta*
true plants, cellular differentiation, embryo formation

PHYLA

Bryophyta
green plants, diploid and haploid generations
e.g. mosses

Pteropsida
includes all ferns and seed-producing plants

CLASSES

Filicinae
large erect leaves, underground rhizomes, independent diploid and haploid phases in life cycle
e.g. ferns

Gymnospermae
produce seeds mostly on cones
e.g. coniferous trees (evergreens)

Angiospermae
flowering plants, seed protected by outer covering of the fruit
e.g. all familiar flowering plants

ORDERS:

Monocotyledonae
one food storage organ in seed, floral parts in 3's or 6's, parallel veined
e.g. Zea mays

Dicotyledonae
2 food storage organs
floral parts in 4's or 5's, net veined
e.g. broad bean

Table 3 ANIMAL KINGDOM

SUB-KINGDOMS

I. *Protozoa*
single-celled animals usually uni-nucleate.
Examples: *Amoeba*
Paramoecium

II. *Parazoa*
multicellular, aquatic, usually fixed in one spot, thick body wall with a single central cavity, colony made up of many separate individuals
Example: sponges

PHYLA

Coelenterata
radial symmetry, soft body, tentacles
Example: jelly fish

Nematoda
worm-like, unsegmented, no body cavity, mostly parasitic
Example: round worms

Arthropoda
segmented body, exoskeleton, paired appendages, nerve cord

Annelida
segmented worms, body cavity, distinct head, muscular body wall, nerve cord
Examples: earthworm

CLASSES

Crustacea
aquatic with 2 pairs of antennae, gills
Examples: shrimp, crab, barnacle

Myriapoda
long segmented body, trachea for breathing, 1 or 2 pairs of walking legs in each segment
Example: centipede

Insecta
single pair of antennae, 3 pairs of legs on thorax, trachea for breathing
Example: cockroach

Arachnida
biting appendages, four pairs of walking legs
Example: spiders

CLASSES

Agnatha
jaws absent, paired appendages absent
Example: la

III. *Metazoa*
multicellular organism with cellular differentiation and cells dependent on each other, heterotrophic nutrition, sense organs and nervous system

Platyhelminthes
worm-like but unsegmented, no body cavity, may have vascular system
Examples: Planaria, tapeworm

Chordata
segmented body, dorsal nerve cord and a supporting rod or notochord

Echinodermata
radial symmetry in adult, exoskeleton, numerous tube feet
Example: starfish

Mollusca
soft body, unsegmented, often covered by a shell
Examples: snails, oysters, octopus,

DIVISION 1. *Protochordata*
without skull and vertebral column

DIVISION 2. *Vertebrate*

…s
…vith paired …scales, gills, …oduce from
…mple: carp

Reptilia
scales, dry skin, born from eggs, no larval stage, lungs
Example: snakes

Amphibia
moist soft skin, larva with gills, lung in adult
Example: frogs

Aves
warm blooded, wings, feathers, no teeth, eggs
Examples: all familiar birds

Mammalia
warm blooded, hair, mammary glands, young born alive
Example: humans

Table 4 GEOLOGICAL TIME SCALE

Eras and years of duration	Periods and epochs with number of years from the present	Dominant organisms	Plant life	Animal life	Climate
	Quaternary Recent	Herbs and man	Herbs dominant	Civilized man	
	Pleistocene (2,000,000)		Increase in number of herbs	Extinction of great mammals	Periodic glaciation
	Tertiary Pliocene		Rise of herbs[1]	Appearance of man	Cooling
Cenozoic 60,000,000	Miocene	Age of angiosperms, mammals, and birds	Forest reduction; retreat of polar floras	Culmination of mammals	Cool and semiarid
	Oligocene		World-wide distribution of tropical forests	First anthropoids; primitive mammals disappear	Warm Humid
	Eocene (60,000,000)		Sequoias prominent; tropical flora in arctic	Modern birds and marine mammals appear	Cool and semiarid then warm and humid
	Upper cretaceous		Angiosperms dominant, gymnosperms decreasing	First primitive mammals	Fluctuating
	Middle cretaceous		Development of angiosperms	Great reptiles disappearing	Fluctuating
Mesozoic (125,000,000)	Lower cretaceous (125,000,000)	Age of higher gymnosperms and reptiles	Rise of angiosperms, conifers and cycads dominant		Warm
	Jurassic (157,000,000)		First angiosperms, conifers and cycads dominant	Dinosaurs abundant; higher insects	Warm
	Triassic (185,000,000)		Disappearance of seed ferns, gymnosperms (higher) increase	First mammals Rise of giant reptiles	Warm Semiarid
	Permian (223,000,000)		First cycads and conifers	Rise of land vertebrates	Dry, periodic glaciation
	Pennsylvanian (271,000,000)	Age of seed ferns, amphibians, lycopods	Primitive gymnosperms; coal formation		Alteration of marine and terrestrial conditions
	Mississipian (309,000,000)		Horsetails, lycopods, seed ferns dominant, coal deposits	Rise of primitive insects and reptiles	Shallow seas in N. America
Paleozoic (368,000,000)	Devonian (354,000,000)	Age of fish and early plants	Early land plants, horsetails, ferns, seed ferns	Fish dominant, rise of amphibians	Shallow seas in N. America
	Silurian (381,000,000)		First land plants, algae dominant	Scorpions and lungfish	Shallow seas
	Ordovician (448,000,000)	Age of higher invertebrates and algae	Marine algae dominant	Corals, etc. first vertebrates	Shallow seas
	Cambrian (553,000,000)		Algae-marine forms abundant	Trilobites dominant	Warm over earth

Proterozoic (900,000,000)	(1,500,000,000)	Age of primitive marine invertebrates	Algae and bacteria	Worms, brachiopods, crustaceans	Glaciation
Archeozoic (550,000,000 +)	(2,000,000,000)	Age of unicellular life (?)	No fossils known, probably unicellular organisms		?

[1]*herb*—a plant with a non-woody stem.

Assigning living things into their groups

As you can see from the tables each grouping of living things is characterized by a number of common features. By looking for and identifying these features in a particular plant or animal we can decide which group it belongs to.
Scientists have worked out a system of *keys* to help in the identification.
Below is a key to the different classes of vertebrates.

DICHOTOMOUS KEY TO THE PHYLA OF METAZOA

1. Radial symmetry .... go to 2
   Bilateral symmetry .... go to 3
2. Exoskeleton present .... Phylum Echinodermata
   Exoskeleton absent .... Phylum Coelenterata
3. Body segments present .... go to 5
   Body segments absent .... go to 4
4. Shell present .... Phylum Mollusca
   Shell absent .... Phylum Platyhelminthes
5. Central nerve cord present .... Phylum Chordata
   Central nerve cord absent .... go to 6
6. Paired appendages present .... Phylum Arthropoda
   Paired appendages absent .... Phylum Annelida

EXERCISES IN CLASSIFICATION

To which phyla do the following belong?
earthworm, crab, flatworm, oyster, sea urchin, snake, spider, jelly fish, starfish
To assist you in using the key fill in the characteristics of the various animals in the space provided in Table 5. You can obtain the necessary information from your own knowledge of the animals or by examining a specimen.

Table 5

		Earthworm	Crab	Flatworm	Oyster	Sea urchin	Snake	Spider	Jelly fish	Starfish
BODY SYMMETRY	Radial									
	Bilateral	√								
EXOSKELETON	Present									
	Absent	√								
BODY SEGMENTATION	Present	√								
	Absent									
SHELL	Present									
	Absent	√								
CENTRAL NERVE CORD	Present									
	Absent	√								
PAIRED APPENDAGES	Present									
	Absent	√								
PHYLUM		Annelida								

(Header above animal columns: Name of animal)

In a similar way members of the Phylum Chordata can be divided into various classes. Table 6 and the key below will help you to identify these classes.

DICHOTOMOUS KEY TO SELECTED CLASSES OF THE PHYLUM CHORDATA

1. Hair present . . . . Class Mammalia (Mammals)
   Hair absent . . . . go to 2
2. Feathers present . . . . Class Aves (Birds)
   Feathers absent . . . . go to 3
3. Jaws present . . . . go to 4
   Jaws absent . . . . Class Agnatha (Jawless fish)
4. Paired fins present . . . . . . go to 5
   Paired fins absent . . . . . . go to 6
5. Skeleton body . . . . Class Osteichthyes (Bony fish)
   Skeleton cartilaginous. . . Class Chondrichthyes (Cartilaginous fish)
6. Skin scales present . . . . . Class Reptilia (Reptiles)
   Skin scales absent . . . . . . Class Amphibia (Amphibians)

To which class of chordates do the following belong?
dog, mouse, turtle, goldfish, snake, parrot, bat, frog.

Table 6

		Name of animal							
		Dog	Mouse	Turtle	Goldfish	Snake	Parrot	Bat	Frog
SKIN STRUCTURES	Hair present	✓							
	Feathers present								
	Scales present								
	None of above present								
APPENDAGES	Wings present								
	Legs present	✓							
	Fins present								
	None of above present								
SKELETON	Bony	✓							
	Cartilaginous								
TEETH	Present	✓							
	Absent								
JAWS	Present	✓							
	Absent								
	CLASS	Mammal							

The Living Cell

All living matter is composed of basic units called **cells**. With few exceptions the cell can be regarded as the smallest unit that can survive independently.

The name *cell* was first used by Robert Hooke, the English scientist who invented the microscope. He used his microscope to examine the structure of a thin slice of cork. He found a large number of seemingly empty spaces that reminded him of the many tiny rooms found in a monastery building and therefore named them cells. The cells Hooke looked at were no longer alive and were therefore empty. Living cells are filled with a variety of structures.

There is tremendous variation in the internal structure, chemical nature and size and shape of living cells.

On the other hand there are many features that are consistent from one cell type to another.

Protoplasm

The entire living substance contained in the cell is referred to as **protoplasm.**

What does protoplasm consist of?

Protoplasm is a jelly-like, semi-fluid substance containing dissolved chemical substances, visible particles called **organelles** (e.g. nucleus, chloroplast etc.) and other chemical structures such as starch grains, crystals, fat droplets etc.

All essential life processes are carried out by some part of the protoplasm.

How are the activities of the cell regulated?

The **nucleus** is the structure responsible for the overall control of the life processes of the cell. The nucleus contains all the information necessary for regulating the cell and ensuring that it fulfils its role in the greater scheme of the entire organism.

The liquid part of the protoplasm is referred to as **cytoplasm**. It contains many dissolved chemical substances such as enzymes and nutrients. In many cells it has a rather granular appearance and can be seen to move around with a characteristic *streaming* motion.

What are the most common organelles found inside cells?

The **mitochondrion** (pl. mitochondria) is the structure which carries out the energy conversions of the cell. It is inside this organelle that the chemical energy contained in the food is turned into a form that can be used by the living cell.

All green plants have organelles called **chloroplasts.** These contain the green-coloured chemical substance **chlorophyll** that is needed by plants for the conversion of light energy from the sun to chemical energy.

How are the organelles and the cytoplasm separated off from each other?

The nucleus, all the other organelles and the entire cell itself are surrounded by thin **membranes** which act as barriers. Studies with the electron microscope have shown that the membranes contain pores through which exchange of chemicals can take place.
The various membranes are named according to the structures they surround. The **cell membrane** or **cytoplasmic membrane** surrounds the entire cell, the **nuclear membrane** is the one enclosing the nucleus and so on.
Plant cells, in addition to the cell membrane, are surrounded by a **cell wall** made of **cellulose.** In the early stage of its life when the cell is actively growing, the cell wall is flexible and can stretch as growth takes place. When the cell is fully grown, the cell wall becomes rigid and acts as a very important internal support for the plant.

Plants and Animals

So far we have been referring to plants and animals as two basic types of living things.

How do we distinguish between plants and animals?

That is easy, you might say. Plants are green in colour and animals are able to move from place to place. This simple distinction is

Table 7

	Plant	Animal
Organization	variable number of external organs such as leaves and flowers	fixed number of internal organs: heart, liver, kidney etc.
Cell structure	cell membrane—cell wall of cellulose	cell membrane only
Nutrition	make organic food from inorganic components: photosynthesis	must feed on organic food
Movement	usually firmly anchored to the ground	usually able to move freely from place to place
Growth	takes place at fixed growing points—continuous throughout life of organism	takes place all over body for a fixed period of time
Sensitivity	low level of sensitivity and slow responses	high level of sensitivity and quick responses
Excretion	fewer waste material and less obvious methods of excretion	more waste material, visible method of excretion

enough if you are comparing a cabbage with a dog.
But it is not always as easy in other cases.
Differences based on the chemical structure and physiology of the organism are a much more reliable guide.
Table 7 is a summary of the main differences between plants and animals.
At this point you may not fully understand the significance of some of the differences but as you study the different life processes of living organism all these points will become clear.

Section 1. NUTRITION

INTRODUCTION TO MODES OF NUTRITION

If you look up a medical dictionary and find the word **nutrition** the definition given would be something like this: Nutrition is the sum total of the processes by which living organisms receive and utilize the materials necessary for survival, growth and repair of worn out tissues.

All living organisms must take in some raw materials from which they can obtain energy and synthesize the various organic molecules that they need to stay alive. The nature of the raw materials, the means by which they are obtained and the way in which they are used vary from one organism to the next.

The two main modes of nutrition found among living things are **autotrophic nutrition** used by organisms that are referred to as **autotrophs** and **heterotrophic nutrition** used by **heterotrophs**.

Autotrophs are living organisms that are capable of **synthesizing**[1] the various **organic**[2] compounds they need entirely from **inorganic**[3] raw materials. Most autotrophic organisms are able to synthesize organic molecules from carbon dioxide and water through the process of **photosynthesis**, using the energy of sunlight. Other autotrophic organisms called **chemosynthesizers** obtain the necessary energy for the production of organic molecules by oxidizing certain energy-yielding substances in their environment such as sulphur dioxide, iron compounds or ammonia.

How do heterotrophs obtain their nutrients?

Heterotrophs depend on preformed organic molecules for their food. It follows that the nutritional requirements of all heterotrophic organisms are supplied ultimately by autotrophic organisms. All animals, some plants and most bacteria and fungi belong to this group of organisms.

Heterotrophs can be further classified according to the sources from which they obtain their organic materials and the means by which they obtain them.

Holozoic organisms take into their body cavities large amounts of mostly solid organic materials and break them down in their internal digestive systems. Holozoic organisms can be divided into those that

1 *synthesis:* formation of a compound from simpler substances
2 *organic:* compounds that contain carbon other than carbon dioxide and carbonates
3 *inorganic:* compounds that do not contain carbon except carbon dioxide and carbonates

take in only animal flesh (**carnivores**), those that feed only on plants (**herbivores)** and those that feed on either plant or animal material (**omnivores**). Except for a few highly specialized carnivorous plants, all holozoic feeders are animals.

Saprophytic organisms are free living species that obtain their food from dead or decaying organic matter by extracellular digestion. Before a saprophyte can 'eat' a piece of food it must break it down into small organic molecules that can diffuse into its cells.

Symbiosis is the term given to the close association that exists between certain organisms where one organism lives in or on the body of another and obtains its nutrients from the other. If both parties benefit from the arrangement it is termed **mutualism**. If one benefits but the other remains unharmed it is **commensalism**. When one organism lives and feeds at the expense of the other and does some degree of harm to the other, the situation is termed **parasitism**. In the following sections each of the above modes of nutrition will be discussed in greater detail.

Fig.1.1 Summary of modes of nutrition

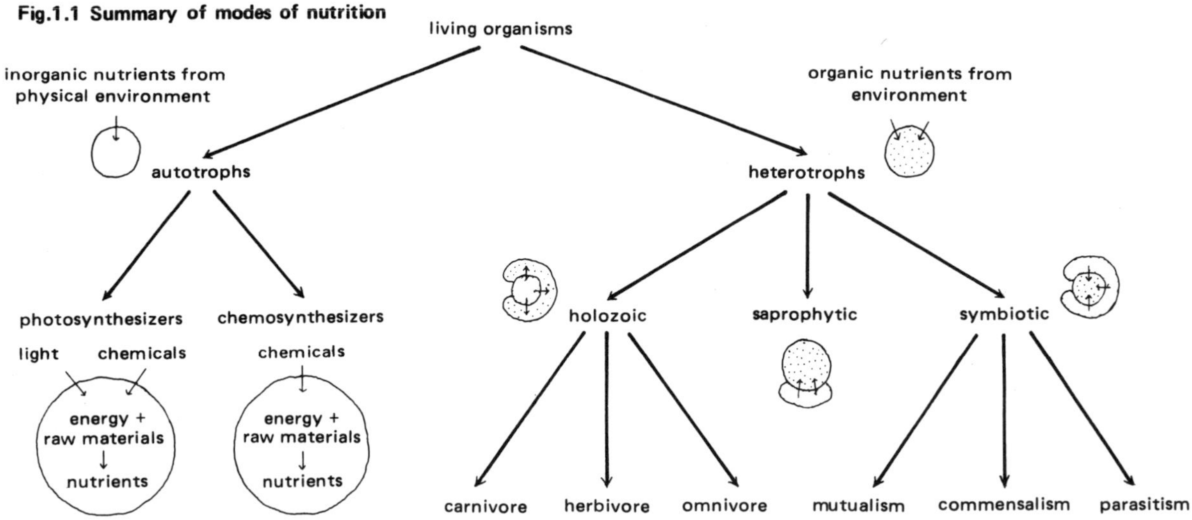

AUTOTROPHIC NUTRITION

Photosynthesis—autotrophic nutrition in green plants. The word photosynthesis is derived from the Greek language. 'Photo' refers to light and 'synthesis' is making or putting together. The entire word, therefore, means 'making with light'.

The sun, at the centre of our solar system, is a gigantic atomic power generator. Nuclear reactions taking place in its interior generate enormous amounts of energy that are radiated away from the sun mostly in the form of infrared radiation called heat and visible radiation called light. Green plants are able to make use of the energy contained in visible light to drive the photosynthetic apparatus inside their cells.

How was photosynthesis discovered?

Perhaps the first experiment performed to explore the nature of photosynthesis was by a Dutch physician called van Helmont in the 1640s. He placed exactly 200 pounds of dry soil in a pot and then planted a five-pound willow shoot in the soil. He placed the pot in the ground, and to prevent soil blowing into or out of it he covered the top with a metal plate that was perforated to allow rain water to reach the soil.

At the end of five years he carefully removed the willow, making certain that no soil adhered to the roots, weighed it and found that it had a mass of 169 lb 3 oz. He then dried the soil and found that it had a mass of 199 lb 14 oz.

Clearly the soil could not be responsible for the increase in mass of the willow and van Helmont concluded that the water was responsible.

Fig.1.2 Van Helmont's experiment

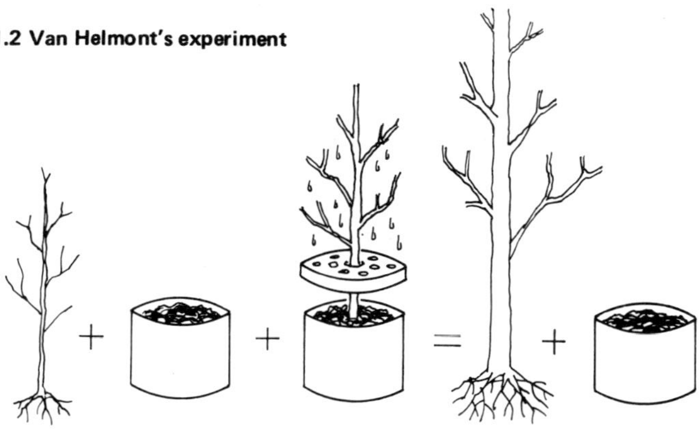

5 lb shoot + 200 lb dry soil + 5 years with only a supply of rain water for growth = 169 lb 3 oz tree + 199 lb 14 oz dry soil

Today we know that in addition to water, photosynthesis involves gases from the air and the energy coming from the sun.

The overall equation that we can write to summarize the process is as follows:

$$\underset{\text{carbon dioxide}}{CO_2} + \underset{\text{water}}{H_2O} \xrightarrow[\text{green plants}]{\text{sunlight}} \underset{\text{basic sugar unit}}{CH_2O} + \underset{\text{oxygen}}{O_2}$$

Fig.1.3

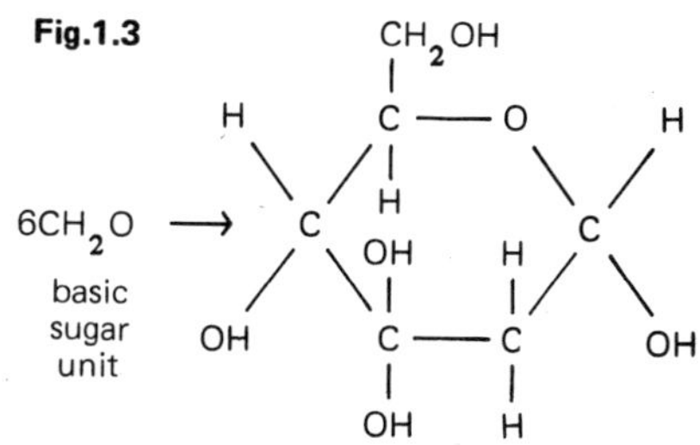

simple sugar: hexose

The CH_2O group can be regarded as the basic sugar unit. To make up a single molecule of a six-carbon sugar or **hexose**, six such units are required. We say that the above is a summary equation because the process does not take place in a single step but in a series of steps.

Fig.1.4

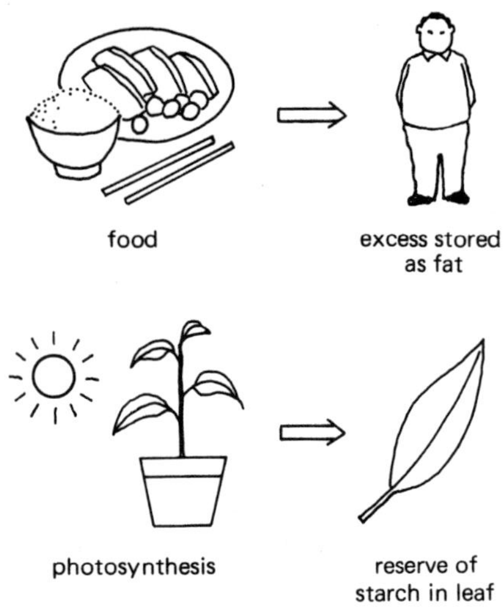

Fig.1.5

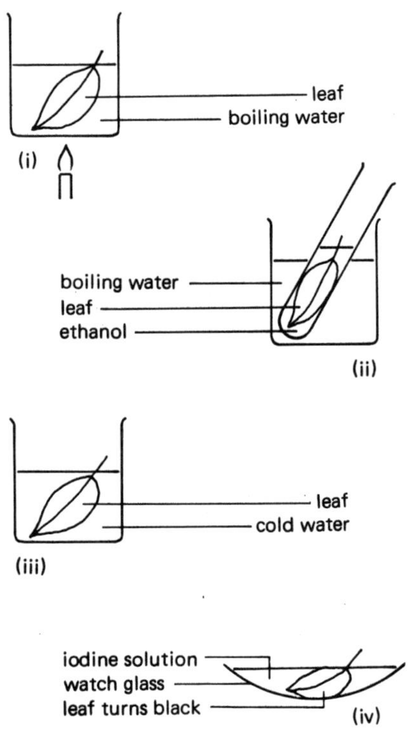

Conditions required for photosynthesis

According to the above equation the requirements for photosynthesis are carbon dioxide, water, sunlight and a green plant. The necessity for these factors can be demonstrated by the following simple experiments.

Production of starch

The simplest experiment would be to set up groups of plants under a series of different conditions, supplying one group with all the necessary requirements and depriving each of the other groups of one of them.

If the plants were observed over a period of time, what would you expect to find?

If our hypothesis[1] is correct the plants that are supplied with all the basic requirements would show healthy growth while the others would eventually die. While this experiment would work well enough it is tedious and takes a long time to complete. A much more convenient assessment of plant growth can be made by examining the production of starch by the leaves.

The immediate products of photosynthesis in green leaves are **monosaccharide sugars.** These sugar units are converted by the plant into starch as a storage product.

Animals turn excess energy-containing molecules into fat while plants store energy-rich molecules in the form of starch. When an overweight person goes on a diet the fat deposits in his body are gradually used up and he becomes thinner. In the same way, if a plant is unable to carry on photosynthesis it will gradually be forced to use up its reserves of starch.

EXPERIMENT TO TEST LEAVES FOR THE PRESENCE OF STARCH

The presence of starch in the leaf of a plant can be detected by the blue-black colour which develops when starch reacts with iodine. Since the green colour of the leaf makes it difficult to see the test colours properly, the green pigment must first be removed.

Materials

freshly picked green leaves from a potted plant
ethanol
iodine solution

Method

1. Dip the leaf into boiling water for 10 seconds to kill the cells.
2. Place the leaf in a tube of ethanol and heat the tube in boiling water until all the pigment has been removed. You may have to change the ethanol after a few minutes if it becomes too saturated with colour.
3. Pour off the ethanol and wash the leaf with cold water.

1 *hypothesis:* a theory that has not yet been proven by experiment

4. Immerse the leaf in a small dish of iodine solution.

What colour does the leaf turn when immersed in iodine solution? What does this indicate?

Discussion

When immersed in iodine solution, the leaf turns blue-black indicating the presence of starch.

Is light required for photosynthesis?

EXPERIMENT (A) TO DEPLETE A GREEN LEAF OF STARCH

Materials

potted plant—if possible, the same one as in the previous experiment
ethanol
iodine solution

Method

1. Keep a potted plant in the dark for 48 hours.
2. Remove one of its leaves and test for the presence of starch as in the previous experiment.

Does the leaf contain starch?
What has happened to the stored starch while the plant has been kept in darkness?

EXPERIMENT (B) TO INVESTIGATE THE NECESSITY OF LIGHT FOR PHOTOSYNTHESIS

Materials

the same destarched potted plant as used in the above experiment
ethanol
iodine solution
aluminium foil

Method

1. Cover part of one of the leaves of the plant with a strip of aluminium foil to prevent any light from getting to that part.
2. Place the plant back in a spot where it will get plenty of light.
3. After 24 hours remove the partially covered leaf and test for the presence of starch as in the previous experiment.

Did you find any difference between the parts of the leaf that were exposed to light and the parts that were covered?
What does this tell you about the production of starch by green leaves?

Discussion

Starch is normally present in the leaves of green plants. When deprived of light the leaves are depleted of starch. When exposed to light starch reappears except in the area that has been covered up by the foil. Since the production of starch in the leaves is a result of the process of photosynthesis we can conclude from these experiments that light is necessary for the process to operate. The areas of the leaf that were not exposed to light did not produce starch because without light, photosynthesis cannot take place.

Fig.1.6
Experiment A

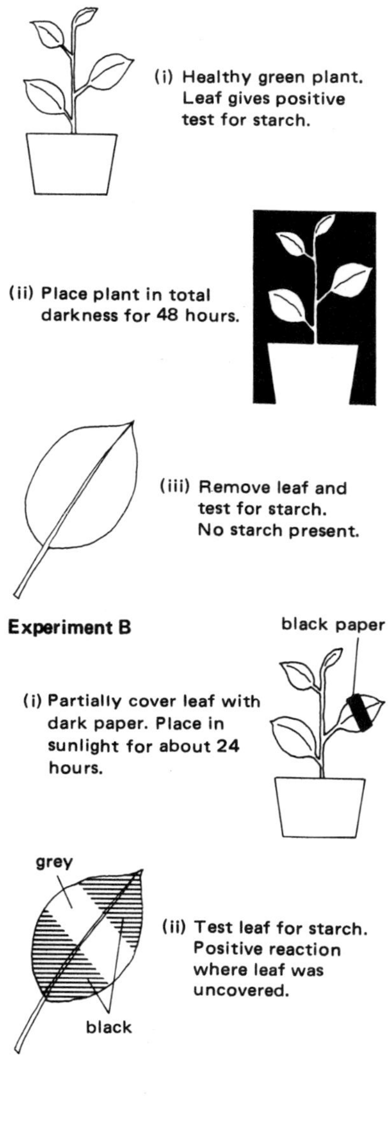

Fig.1.7

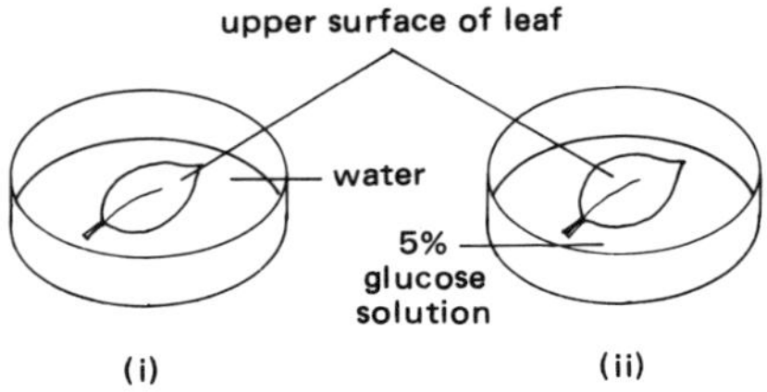

EXPERIMENT TO SHOW THAT GREEN LEAVES ARE ABLE TO SYNTHESIZE STARCH FROM GLUCOSE

Materials

2 destarched leaves
5% glucose solution
ethanol
iodine

Method

1. Float one of the leaves on the surface of water in a small dish and the other on the surface of the glucose solution. In each case make certain that it is the *lower* surface of the leaf that is in contact with the liquid.
2. Place the containers in total darkness for three to four hours.
3. Test the leaves for the presence of starch.

What do you observe?
How do you account for the difference between the leaf that was floated on the glucose solution and the leaf that was floated on water?
What does this tell you about the production of starch in the leaves?

Discussion

You have already proved to yourself that under ordinary conditions leaves cannot make starch in the absence of light. However, if they are supplied with glucose they do have the ability to produce starch in the dark. It seems that light is necessary for the synthesis of sugar through the action of photosynthesis but not for the production of starch from the sugar.

How is the plant able to trap the energy of sunlight?

Throughout the discussion of photosynthesis references made were always to *green* plants. The experiments were carried out using the green leaves, not the roots or the flowers. The colour of a green plant is due to the presence of a pigment[1] called **chlorophyll**.
You know from your physics that white light contains all the colours of the visible spectrum. You can illustrate this by separating out the various colours in white light with the aid of a prism.

EXPERIMENT (A) TO SEPARATE THE COMPONENT COLOURS OF WHITE LIGHT

Materials

light source
piece of black paper with a narrow slit
prism
screen

Method

1. Set up the apparatus as shown in the diagram. To achieve good separation the beam of light must be passed through a narrow slit to make the beam very narrow.

[1] *pigment*: a chemical substance that is coloured

Fig.1.8 Splitting white light into its component colours

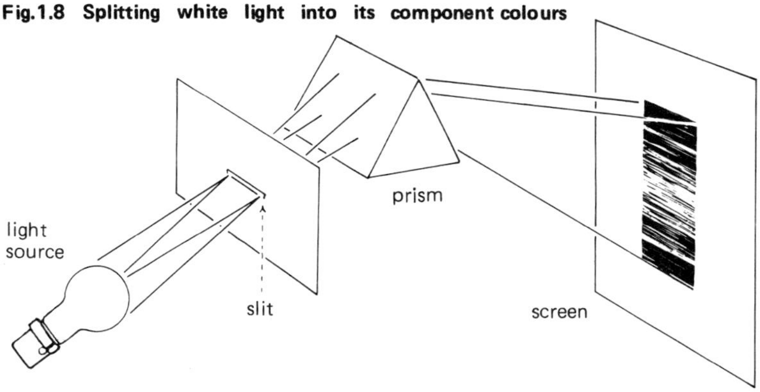

2. Switch on the light source and examine the spectrum.
3. Draw a diagram of what you see indicating all the colours in sequence.

EXPERIMENT (B) TO FIND WHAT COLOURS ARE ABSORBED BY CHLOROPHYLL

Materials

light source
prism
slit
acetone
green leaves (the leaves of a dark green vegetable such as spinach would be best)
cheesecloth
flat-sided glass container

Method

1. Prepare an extract of chlorophyll by grinding up some fresh green leaves in a mixture of 80% acetone and 20% water.
2. Filter out large particles by passing through cheesecloth.
3. Pour the extract into a flat-sided glass container and insert into the path of the light between the slit and the prism.
4. Draw a diagram of the spectrum indicating all the colours.

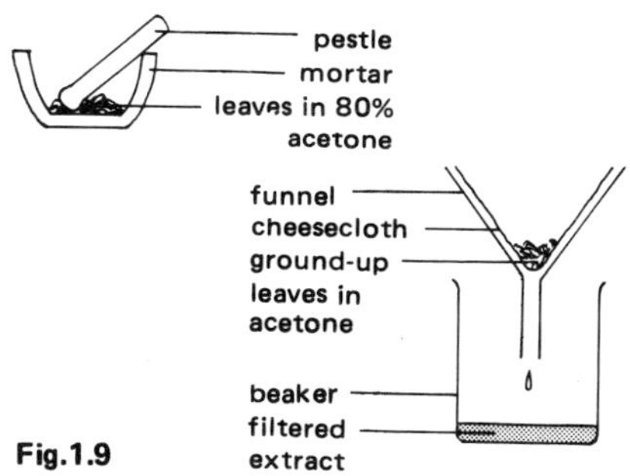

Fig.1.9

What difference do you observe between the normal spectrum of white light and the spectrum obtained when the light is allowed to pass through chlorophyll?
Which are the colours that are missing?
Can you now account for the fact that chlorophyll is green?

Discussion

When white light is broken up into its component colours a continuous spectrum is obtained starting with violet on one side and progressing to red on the other. When a chlorophyll extract is inserted into the path of the light some of the colours are absorbed by the pigment. Most of the colours in the blue and red region are missing from the **absorption spectrum** of chlorophyll. Green and yellow are still present. When white light falls onto chlorophyll the pigment absorbs all the wavelengths in the blue and red region and

Fig.1.10

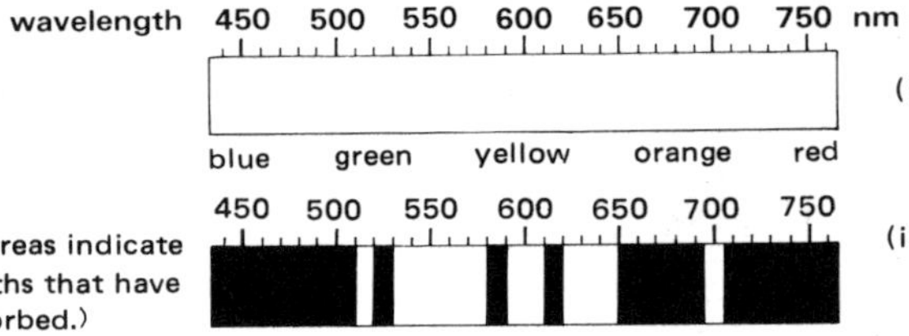

(i) Colours normally present in white light.

(Shaded areas indicate wavelengths that have been absorbed.)

(ii) Colours present after absorption by chlorophyll. Notice that most of the blue, red, and orange wavelengths are absorbed while yellow and green are reflected.

reflects only those in the green and yellow region, thus making the pigment appear green in colour.

Where is chlorophyll to be found in the plant cell?

EXPERIMENT TO OBSERVE CHLOROPHYLL IN THE LIVING CELLS OF PLANTS

Materials

a simple water plant such as *Elodea* or *Spirogyra*
microscope
slides and coverslips

Method

1. Examine the plant material provided first under low power, then under high power.
2. Draw a simple diagram of a cell and label it.

Is chlorophyll dissolved in the fluid of the cell or is it localized in some way?
What are the chlorophyll-containing structures called?
What else do you think they might contain?
Are these structures the same shape and size in all plant cells?

Fig.1.11

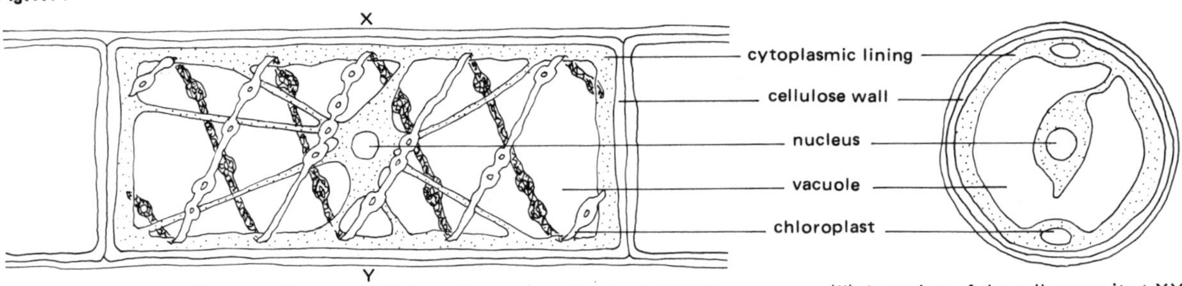

(i) Diagram of one cell from a filament of *Spirogyra* as seen under a microscope

(ii) A section of the cell across it at XY

Fig.1.12

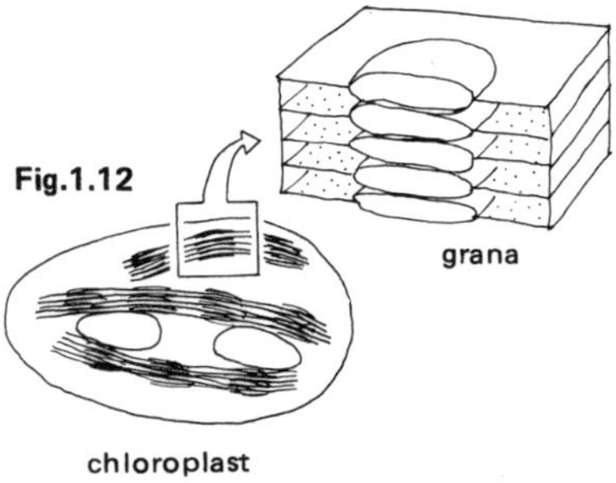

Discussion

The chlorophyll contained in plant cells is localized in structures called **chloroplasts**. Chloroplasts contain all the necessary chemicals for carrying out the reactions of photosynthesis. In higher plants they are usually disc-shaped but in lower plants they assume a variety of shapes from star-shape to spiral.

Electron microscope studies of chloroplasts have revealed that they have a very complex internal structure. The chlorophyll molecules and the enzymes are associated with layers of disc-shaped structures called **grana** that are stacked one on top of the other. The regular

arrangement of the chlorophyll on the membranes of the grana ensures a greater efficiency in trapping light.
Chloroplasts are not rigidly fixed in position inside the cell. Just like the nucleus and other organelles, they are free to move. In fact, as shown in the diagram, their distribution changes in response to varying light conditions.

Fig.1.13

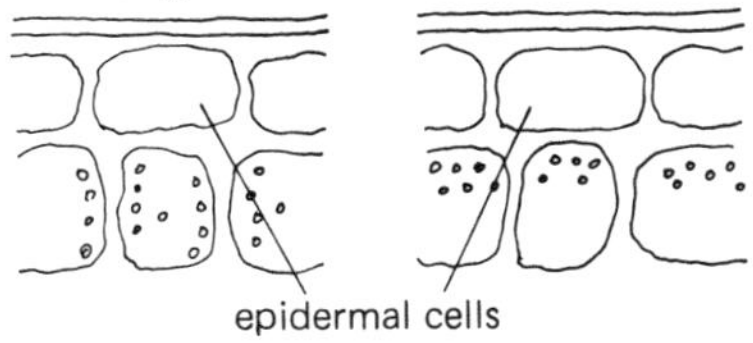

Distribution of chloroplasts

How can we prove that chlorophyll is necessary for photosynthesis?

That chlorophyll is, in fact, necessary for photosynthesis can be shown by studying the distribution of starch in a *variegated* leaf. A variegated leaf is one that has green patches that contain chlorophyll alternating with patches that lack chlorophyll and are therefore yellow, white or pinkish-red in colour, depending on the particular plant.

Fig.1.14

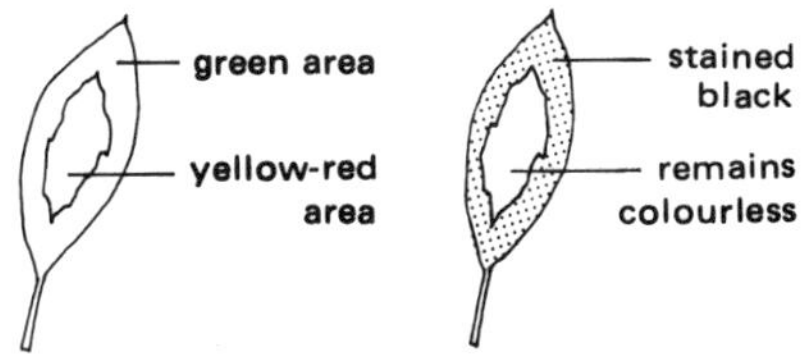

EXPERIMENT TO DEMONSTRATE THAT CHLOROPHYLL IS NECESSARY FOR PHOTOSYNTHESIS

Materials
variegated leaf such as *Coleus*
ethanol
iodine solution
Method
1. Make a drawing of the distribution of colours in the leaf.
2. Test the leaf for starch.
3. Make a drawing of the distribution of starch in the leaf and compare with the first drawing.

How do the distribution of chlorophyll and of starch in the leaf compare?
Is chlorophyll essential for photosynthesis?
Discussion
The distribution of blue-black colour indicating the presence of starch follows the same pattern as the distribution of chlorophyll. Since we have already seen that the presence of starch is indicative of photosynthesis we can conclude that it is only those cells that contain chlorophyll that are able to carry on photosynthesis.

Carbon dioxide

EXPERIMENT TO SHOW THAT CARBON DIOXIDE IS NECESSARY FOR PHOTOSYNTHESIS

Materials
a potted plant that has been destarched
two flasks fitted with split corks
potassium hydroxide
vaseline

Fig.1.15

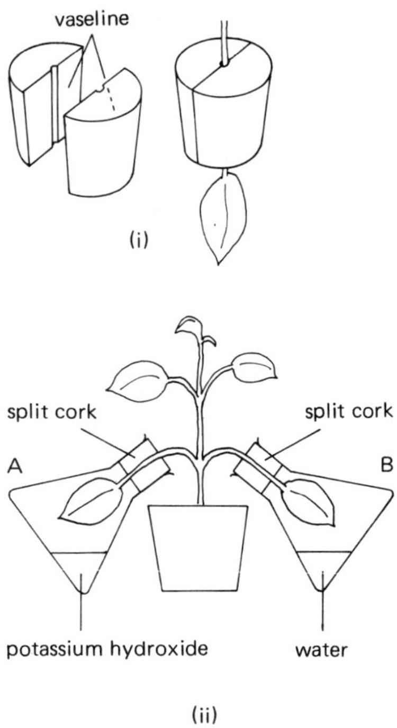

Method

1. Place 10 cm^3 potassium hydroxide in flask A and an equal volume of water into B.
2. Fit one leaf of the plant into each flask by inserting the leaf stem through the split cork as shown in the diagram. To ensure that the flasks are completely airtight, smear the corks with a little vaseline.
3. Leave the plant exposed to sunlight for about six hours.
4. Detach the two leaves and test for starch.

What is the role of the potassium hydroxide in the experiment?
Do both leaves contain starch?
What can you conclude from your observations?

Discussion

The air in flask B contains carbon dioxide and the leaf will probably form a considerable amount of starch during the test period. In flask A the potassium hydroxide absorbs most of the carbon dioxide and the leaf is able to make little or no starch.

Water

There is no simple experiment that can be performed to show that water is necessary for photosynthesis. Depriving a plant of water will kill it, to be sure, but this might not be due to its inability to carry on photosynthesis.
Scientists have investigated the role of water by performing isotope[1] labelling experiments to actually trace the path of water in the plant. According to the overall equation for photosynthesis one of the products is oxygen. Experiments showed that the oxygen liberated comes from water.
Two containers of the unicellular alga *Chlorella* were grown in the presence of light—one in ordinary water and the other in water some of whose oxygen atoms have been replaced by a heavy isotope of oxygen, ^{18}O. Plants in the former group released oxygen containing ^{16}O, that is, normal oxygen atoms. The latter, however, gave off oxygen containing ^{18}O atoms. Through a series of reactions water must have been split up into its component atoms and the oxygen thus produced was released by the plant into the surroundings.

Fig.1.16

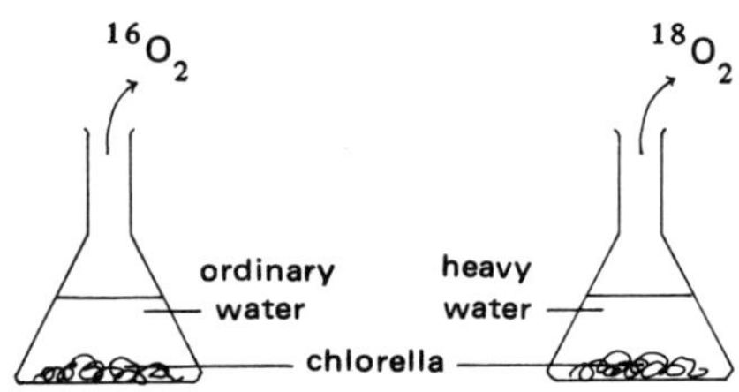

[1] *isotopes*: two or more forms of the same element differing only in atomic weight

The significance of the splitting of water in the process of photosynthesis will be discussed in a later section.

Release of oxygen

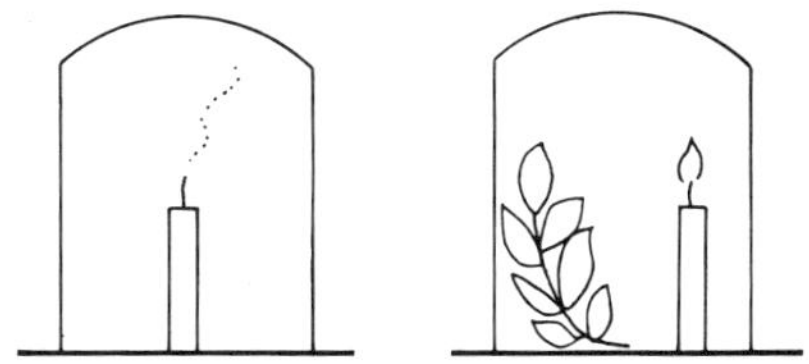

Fig.1.17 Priestley's experiment

The first indication of the fact that green plants give off oxygen was obtained by Joseph Priestley in 1772. He found that if a candle was allowed to burn in a sealed container the flame would soon go out. But, if a sprig of mint was then introduced into the same container after a few days, without letting fresh air into the container, the candle would burn again. Priestley concluded that the mint had restored some factor to the air that was necessary to allow a candle to burn. We now know that this certain factor is oxygen and that it is liberated by green plants through photosynthesis.

EXPERIMENT TO DEMONSTRATE THAT OXYGEN IS GIVEN OFF DURING PHOTOSYNTHESIS

Materials

a water plant such as *Elodea*
3 beakers
3 short-stemmed funnels
3 test-tubes

Method

1. Half fill two beakers with tap water and place a few stems of the plant in the bottom.
2. Invert a funnel over the plant. In order to allow free movement of water between the beaker and the funnel rest the rim of the funnel on a few pieces of plasticine as shown in the diagram.
3. Invert a tube filled with water over each funnel making certain that no air gets in as you do this.
4. Place both beakers by a sunny window. Allow light to get to A but cover B with a piece of dark cloth.
5. Set up a third beaker with the same as A and B but using water that has been boiled to drive off dissolved gases. Expose beaker C to sunlight.
6. Observe for two or three days.

Fig.1.18

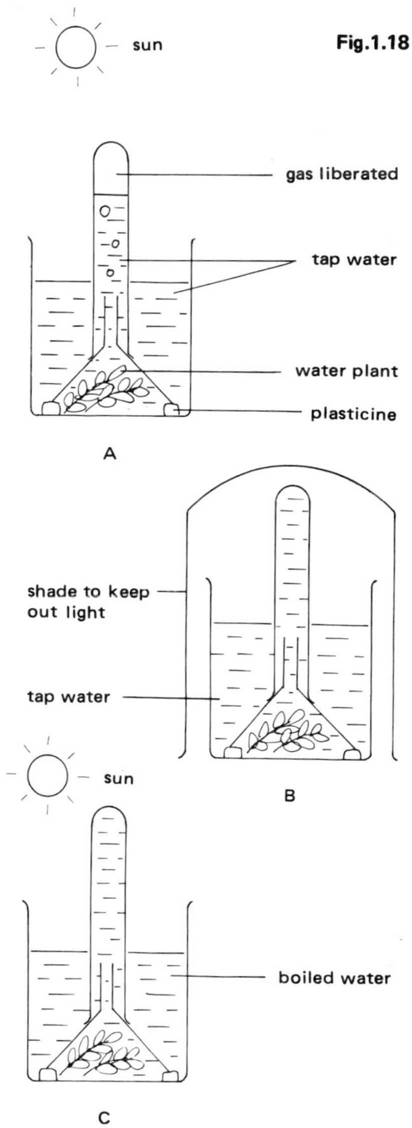

Is there gas being evolved in all three tubes?
Test the gas liberated in A with a glowing splint.
What is the gas?
Why is no gas evolved in B and C?

Discussion

From previous experiments you already know that both light and carbon dioxide are necessary for photosynthesis. The plant in A has access to both of these and therefore it is able to carry on photosynthesis and it liberates oxygen, the gas that rekindles a glowing splint. The plant in B is deprived of light, the one in C is deprived of carbon dioxide. Neither is able to carry on photosynthesis and therefore no oxygen is evolved.

Summary of Experiments

Table 1.1

TESTING FOR	PROCEDURE	OBSERVATION
1. necessity of light	place destarched plant in dark and test with iodine solution	no starch appears
2. necessity of CO_2	place destarched plant in sealed container with potassium hydroxide and test with iodine solution	no starch appears
3. necessity of chlorophyll	test variegated leaf for starch	starch only appears in green areas
4. necessity of water	grow algae in ^{18}O-labelled water	^{18}O-labelled O_2 liberated
5. production of O_2	expose water plant to light and collect gas liberated	gas rekindles a glowing splint
6. production of starch from sugar	float leaf on surface of glucose solution in dark	starch produced
7. production of sugar	expose destarched leaf to light	starch appears

Biochemistry of photosynthesis

The first phase of the reaction is the splitting of water into its component atoms of hydrogen and oxygen. The energy for this reaction is obtained from sunlight trapped and retained by the chlorophyll molecule.

$$2H_2O \longrightarrow 4H + O_2$$

The oxygen is released into the atmosphere and the hydrogen is retained for later use. This phase, since it is dependent on the energy of sunlight is called the **light reaction**. The hydrogen atoms proceed to take part in the second phase called the **dark reaction,** so called because at this stage sunlight is no longer required. It involves the reduction of carbon dioxide to form basic sugar units which are then built up to give hexose sugars. Another term for the reaction is **carbon fixation** since it is in this phase of photosynthesis that sugar is made from inorganic CO_2.

$$CO_2 + 4H \longrightarrow CH_2O + H_2O$$

[1]*fixation*: using individual inorganic molecules to make an organic molecule, i.e. putting together the molecule

[2]*reduction*: removal of oxygen

The reduction of CO_2 is accomplished by the hydrogen atoms that were produced during the light reaction.
The entire process can be summarized as shown in Fig. 1.19.

Fig. 1.19 **Summary of photosynthesis reaction**

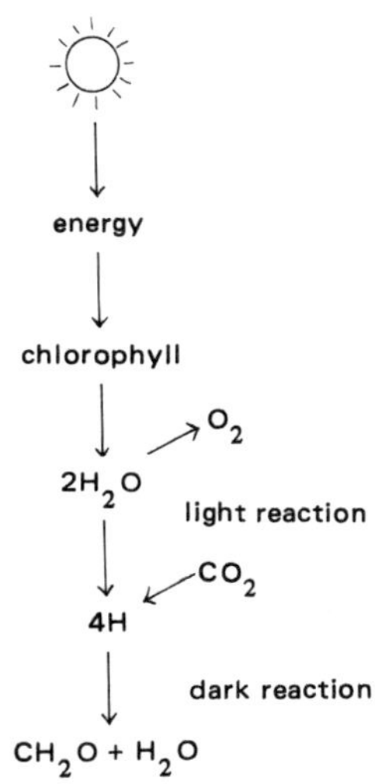

In which cells of the leaf does photosynthesis take place?

If you examine the cross-section of a leaf you will find that it is composed of several different layers of cells. At the top is the **upper epidermis**, a protective layer that does not contain chloroplasts. Under that are two layers of **mesophyll cells**: the **palisade mesophyll** (so named because of its regular appearance) and the **spongy mesophyll** with many air spaces between the cells. These two layers are made up of cells containing chloroplasts and it is in these cells that photosynthesis takes place.

Where does carbon dioxide enter the leaf?

The epidermis of the leaf is equipped with small openings called **stomata** (singular: stoma). Carbon dioxide enters through these openings and passes into the air spaces between the spongy mesophyll cells. From there it diffuses into the cells. Oxygen diffuses out of the cells and passes out through the stomata.
The exchange of gases in plant cells is discussed in detail on p. 130.

Summary

Photosynthesis is the process whereby the cells of green plants synthesize energy-rich organic compounds from inorganic compounds.

Fig. 1.20 Cross-section of a green leaf

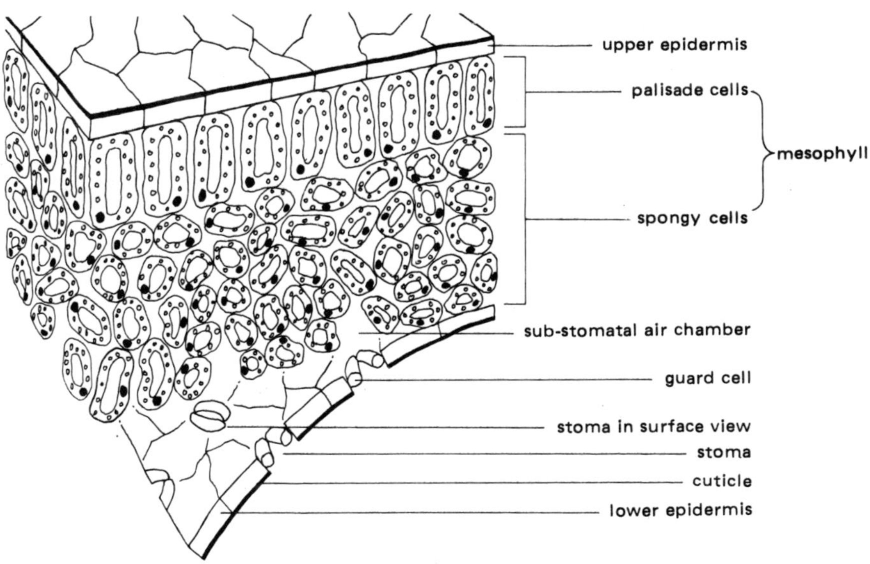

The source of energy for the process is sunlight which is absorbed by a special pigment called chlorophyll found in organelles called chloroplasts.
The essential raw materials are carbon dioxide and water, the products are monosaccharide sugars and oxygen.

Chemosynthesis

The majority of autotrophic organisms are green plants that synthesize organic materials through photosynthesis. Exceptions are a group of **chemosynthetic bacteria.** These organisms possess the basic ability of all autotrophs to manufacture carbohydrates from inorganic materials but they do not use the energy of sunlight. Instead they derive energy from the oxidation of various inorganic substances present in their environment.
Sulphur bacteria found, for instance, in the waters of sulphur springs are able to oxidize hydrogen sulphide.

$$2H_2S + O_2 \longrightarrow 2S + 2H_2O + \text{Energy}$$

Iron bacteria make use of various iron compounds as sources of energy. They are the organisms responsible for the brownish deposits sometimes formed at the bottom of water containers.
Certain **nitrifying bacteria** are able to oxidise the ammonia released by saprophytic organisms into nitrites, usually in the form of nitrous acid (HNO_2). Other members of this group can convert the nitrites to nitrates (NO_3^-).
These activities of the nitrifying bacteria are extremely important in the conversion of the nitrogen compounds released from decayed materials into nitrogen compounds that can be absorbed by other autotrophic organisms. (See p. 351, nitrogen cycle.)

Nitrogen fixation

In addition to the ability to fix carbon dioxide into organic compounds, some autotrophic organisms are able to fix atmospheric nitrogen (N_2) as well. The organisms are referred to as **nitrogen fixers** and are mostly bacteria, algae or fungi. Most autotrophs lack this ability and must obtain nitrogen in the form of nitrites, nitrates or ammonia.

Symbiotic nitrogen fixers:

Symbiosis as a mode of nutrition will be discussed in detail on p. 97.
The term refers to the situation where two organisms live in close proximity sharing certain aspects of the external or internal environment.
The most common group of symbiotic nitrogen fixers are species of the bacterium *Rhizobium.* They are highly specific in their choice of habitat being associated exclusively with the roots of certain

leguminous[1] plants such as peas and beans.
The bacteria penetrate the root hairs of the plants. Nodular enlargements are formed on the roots and the bacteria multiply inside these. The bacteria are able to fix atmospheric nitrogen into nitrogen-containing organic compounds. Some of these are used by the bacteria themselves but some are made available to the host plant. The host in return supplies the bacteria with carbohydrates. When these organisms die, the nitrogenous compounds contained in their cells are made available to other organisms.

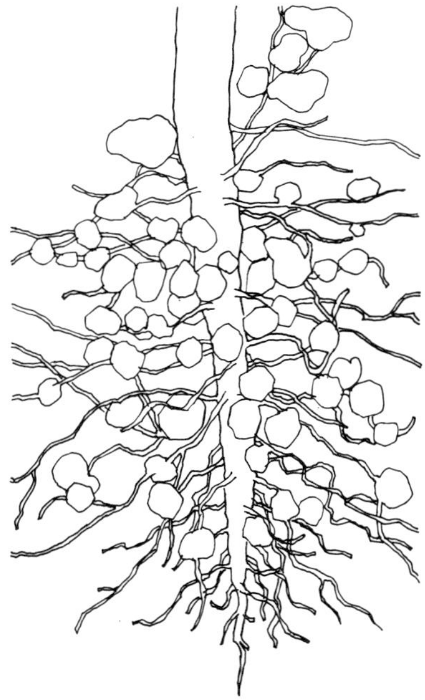

Fig.1.21 Nodules in a root system containing nitrogen-fixing bacteria

Summary

Chemosynthetic organisms are able to obtain energy from the oxidation of inorganic compounds. They then use this energy for carbon fixation.
Nitrogen-fixing organisms are able to convert atmospheric nitrogen into organic molecules.

The mineral requirements of autotrophs

Using either the energy of sunlight, as in the case of green plants, or energy derived from the oxidation of certain inorganic chemicals, autotrophs are able to synthesize simple carbohydrate molecules. These molecules can then be linked up to form more complex organic compounds. Many of the complex compounds contain atoms other than carbon, hydrogen and oxygen and autotrophs must somehow be able to obtain these materials.

What are some of the inorganic substances that autotrophs require?

For the synthesis of proteins plants need nitrogen and sulphur; while for nucleic acids they need phosphorus; and the chlorophyll molecules contain magnesium.
Plants obtain these inorganic substances by absorbing the appropriate salts containing these substances from the soil. To demonstrate the importance of these various mineral elements plants can be grown in **water cultures**. As long as the water contains all the necessary salts and the plant is satisfactorily anchored there is really no need for the presence of soil.

EXPERIMENT TO DEMONSTRATE THE NECESSITY OF INORGANIC SALTS FOR PLANT GROWTH
Materials
bean or wheat seedlings
large test-tubes
culture solutions

[1]*legume*: a group of plants with seeds in pods

Fig.1.22

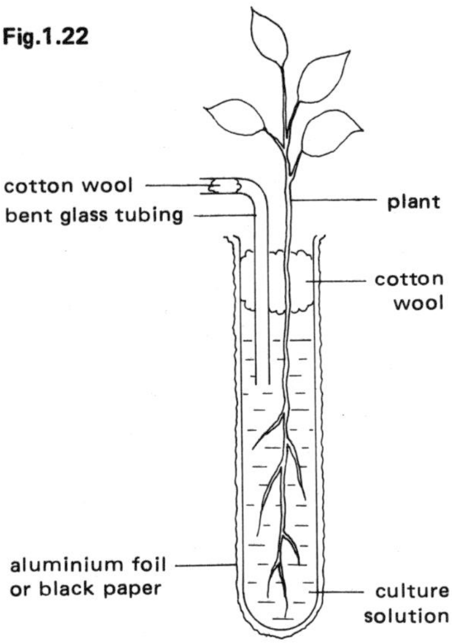

Method

1. Prepare the culture solutions according to the table below.
2. Label nine large test-tubes with names of the solution they are to contain and fill with the culture solution almost to the brim.
3. Select seedlings that are in equivalent stages of development and place one in each of the culture solutions.
4. Carefully seal off the opening with a small wad of cotton wool and insert a small piece of glass tubing to allow air to be blown into the liquid.
5. Cover the tubes with aluminium foil or black paper to keep the roots dark.
6. Set aside in a bright, well ventilated spot. Be sure to blow some air into the tube every few days and top up the solutions with distilled water as required.

What differences do you see between the seedlings grown in the complete culture solution and those grown in the deficient solutions? Watch for variations in the number of leaves, the extent of root development, the colour of the shoot and the height of the plant. Summarize your observations in a table.

In some cases, due to impurities in the chemicals used, results might not be as clear cut as you would hope. If you compare your results with those of your classmates a satisfactory concensus should be obtained.

Discussion

The plant grown in the complete culture solution will be sturdy and vigorous-looking while the ones in the deficient solutions will all show some abnormality in their development. (See Fig. 1.23.)

The one in the distilled water will be the most poorly developed. It will be able to grow and develop only until the mineral salts that it

Table 1.2 Recipes for making up culture solutions in 1000 cm^3 distilled water

Substance / Types of culture	$Ca(NO_3)_2$	$NaNO_3$	$MgSO_4$	$MgCl_2$	K_3PO_4	K_2SO_4	$FeCl_3$	$CaCl_2$	KCl	Na_3PO_4
Complete	2g	0.5g	0.5g	–	0.5g	–	0.1g	–	–	–
Sulphur deficient	2g	0.5g	–	0.5g	0.5g	–	0.1g	–	–	–
Calcium deficient	–	2.5g	0.5g	–	0.5g	–	0.1g	–	–	–
Potassium deficient	2g	0.5g	0.5g	–	–	–	0.1g	–	–	0.5g
Iron deficient	2g	0.5g	0.5g	–	0.5g	–	–	–	–	–
Nitrogen deficient	–	–	0.5g	–	0.5g	–	0.1g	2g	0.5g	0.5g
Phosphorus deficient	2g	0.5g	0.5g	–	–	0.5g	0.1g	–	–	–
Magnesium deficient	2g	0.5g	–	–	0.5g	0.5g	0.1g	–	–	–
Sodium deficient	2g	–	0.5g	–	0.5g	–	0.1g	–	–	–
Distilled water										

Fig.1.23 Results of water culture experiment

has stored in its tissues are all used up. After that, growth will cease. The *nitrogen*-deficient plant shows stunted growth in general. Leaves will be yellowish in colour and very small. Nitrogen is an essential constituent of all proteins, nucleic acids and many vitamins. It is especially important for the development of the leaves. Although the air contains a very large percentage of nitrogen most plants are unable to utilise gaseous nitrogen directly but can only make use of nitrogen in the form of nitrates (NO_3^-), nitrites (NO_2^-) or ammonia (NH_3).

Phosphorus deficiency is characterised by extremely slow growth and small size of both the shoots and the roots. Phosphorus is an essential constituent of nucleic acids and is thus necessary for cell division and growth. It also plays a role in the ripening of fruits.

Calcium is vital for the development of young leaves and shoots. Without it the plant will be extremely small and the young leaves will continually die. The mineral is needed by the plant to lay down cell walls. It also helps to neutralize the effect of certain acid by-products[1] that are toxic[2] for the plant.

[1] *byproduct*: a product of a chemical reaction that is not needed or cannot be used by the cell

[2] *toxic*: poisonous

Magnesium deficiency is characterised by pale yellow leaf colour and slow growth. The most important function of magnesium is as a constituent of chlorophyll.

Without *potassium* the stem of a plant remains very thin, the leaves curl up at the tips and become yellow at first, then brown. This mineral is needed for the processes of photosynthesis and cell division.

Iron deficiency also causes leaves to turn yellow. Iron is needed for the synthesis of chlorophyll although it is not a component of the molecule.

The *sulphur*–deficient plant will show poor root development. It will be yellowish in colour and dead areas will start to appear on the leaves. Sulphur is a constituent of some amino acids and is necessary for the synthesis of chlorophyll.

Small amounts of *copper*, *zinc*, and *manganese* are also necessary for certain chemical reactions.

Fig.1.24

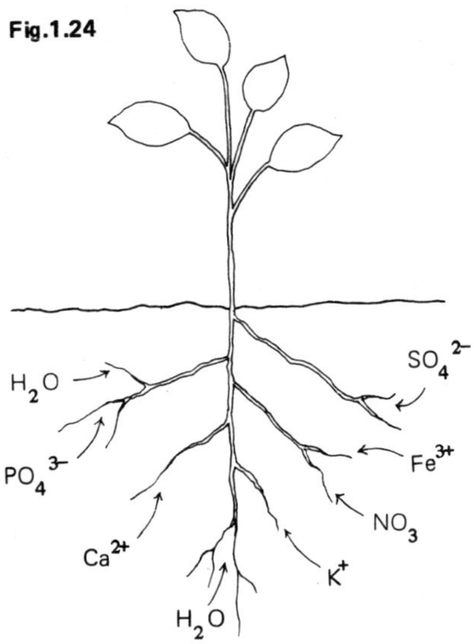

How do plants normally obtain minerals?

In the previous experiments we provided plants with mineral substances in the water that they were growing in. Normally, plants obtain the various minerals they require from the soil through the roots. Mineral salts become dissolved in the moisture contained in the soil and they enter the roots of the plant along with the water molecules. Once inside the root cells the water and mineral salts are passed on to the special transport system of the plant and are taken to all the cells that require them. The process of transport in plants will be discussed fully on p. 210.

Summary

In addition to carbon dioxide and water plants require a series of inorganic substances, the most important of these being nitrogen, phosphorus, calcium, magnesium, potassium, sodium, iron and sulphur. They are necessary for the proper functioning of the plant. Without them a plant will usually show stunted growth of some form and will eventually die.

HOLOZOIC NUTRITION—NUTRITION IN ANIMALS

Holozoic organisms also have a basic need for nutrients in order to stay alive but they are unable to synthesize organic nutrients from inorganic components. They must therefore rely on autotrophs to supply them with these nutrients either by feeding directly on the autotrophs (herbivores) or indirectly by feeding on other holozoic organisms (carnivores). The implications of this dependence on autotrophs, mainly green plants, will be discussed again in the section on ecology (p. 353).

The nature of nutrients

Why do animals require food?

If we examine the molecular composition of an animal cell we find a great variety of complicated organic molecules, some inorganic salts and water. It would be quite difficult if all the organic molecules were to come directly from the diet. In reality, if provided with suitable simple organic molecules cells can synthesize for themselves nearly all the large organic molecules they require.

The molecules contained in food are broken down in the digestive system of the animal, pass into individual cells and the pieces reassembled to make the molecule needed by that particular cell. Holozoic nutrition is in reality a process of recycling of basic organic and inorganic substances.

What are the basic functions of food?

These are: 1. to supply energy; 2. to enable the body to grow and repair defective parts; 3. to supply essential ingredients for the control of body processes and protection against infection.

In order to accomplish the above functions, the food eaten must contain certain substances—the nutrients—that are needed for the synthesis of the necessary organic molecules. The five basic groups of nutrients are **carbohydrates**, **lipids**, **proteins**, **vitamins**, and **inorganic salts**. In a suitably *balanced* diet all these nutrients must be present in the proper proportions to satisfy the needs of the individual. **Water** must also be included.

Fig.1.25 Glucose

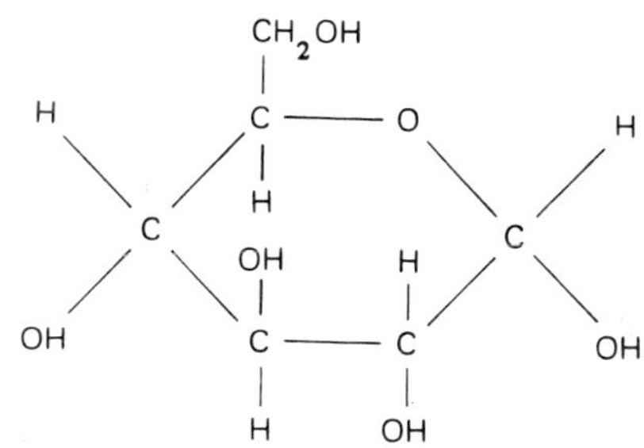

What are the chemical compositions of these nutrients?

CARBOHYDRATE

As the name implies, carbohydrates are made up of the three elements: carbon, hydrogen and oxygen. The basic component of all carbohydrates is the simple sugar molecule.

Fig.1.26 Fructose

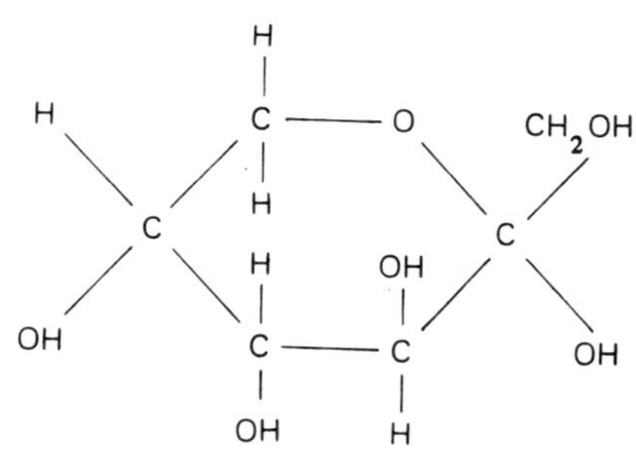

In the language of the chemist sugar does not refer only to the table sugar that we put into our food but to a group of chemical substances with similar properties.

One of the most important groups of sugars are the hexose sugars with the formula $C_6H_{12}O_6$.

Hexoses differ from one another according to the way in which these atoms are arranged relative to one another in the three-dimensional structure of the molecule.

Let us consider as an example the structure of *glucose* since, as we shall see later, it is one of the most important sugars to be found in our bodies. Five carbon atoms and one oxygen atom are joined to

form the basic ring shape of the molecule while the remaining carbon atom and the hydrogens and oxygens are arranged to form side branches to the ring.
Compare the structure of the glucose molecule with that of another hexose sugar, *fructose*. The side groups are arranged in a slightly different way in the two sugars and the properties of the molecules differ accordingly.

Fig.1.27 Condensation of two glucose molecules to give maltose

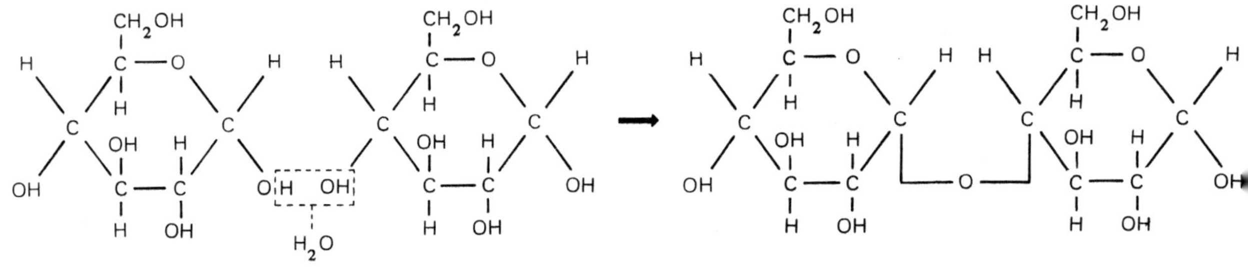

Fig.1.28 Reducing sugar

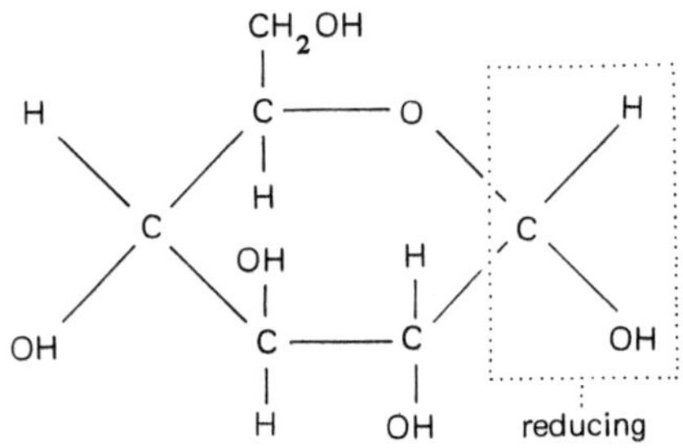

Monosaccharides and disaccharides
Both glucose and fructose consist of a single ring structure and are therefore referred to as single sugars or *monosaccharides*. Two monosaccharides can join together to form a double sugar or *disaccharide*. The chemical reaction that results in the joining of the molecules is called *condensation*—the removal of water. The nature of the disaccharide obtained depends on the two monosaccharides that it is composed of. When two glucose molecules link up with each other they form **maltose**.

Reducing sugar
Any sugar that contains a free H—C—OH group next to the oxygen in the ring is capable of carrying out a *reduction reaction* and is therefore called a **reducing sugar**. This property of sugars is very important in their identification.
Under appropriate conditions disaccharides can further link up to form long chains called multi-sugars or **polysaccharides**. The total number of sugar units in a polysaccharide is variable. Compared with single and double sugars these molecules are very compact, insoluble in water and therefore make ideal storage products. By using sugar molecules to build up polysaccharides the body can store sugars until such time as they are needed.
Table 1.3 is a summary of the most common carbohydrates.

LIPIDS

Lipids can be divided into two main categories: **fats** and **oils,** distinguished by the simple fact that at room temperature fats are solid while oils are liquid. All fats and oils are composed of the basic units **glycerol** and **fatty acids**. Glycerol is a single substance with the formula $C_3H_8O_3$ and structural formula as shown in the diagram.

Table 1.3 The most common carbohydrates

	CONSTITUENTS	SOURCES	PROPERTIES
MONOSACCHARIDES Glucose	—	grapes, honey	sweet, white,
Fructose	—	fruits, honey	soluble,
Galactose	—	not found in food	crystallizable
DISACCHARIDES Sucrose	glucose + fructose	sugar cane, sugar beet	sweet, white,
Lactose	glucose + galactose	milk	soluble,
Maltose	Glucose + glucose	germinating seeds e.g. barley	crystallizable
POLYSACCHARIDES Starch	α-glucose*	stored in plant cells	not sweet,
Glycogen	α and β-glucose*	stored in animal cells	insoluble,
Cellulose	β-glucose	cell walls of plants	uncrystallizable

*α and β glucose are different forms—isomers—of glucose

Fig.1.29 Fatty acids

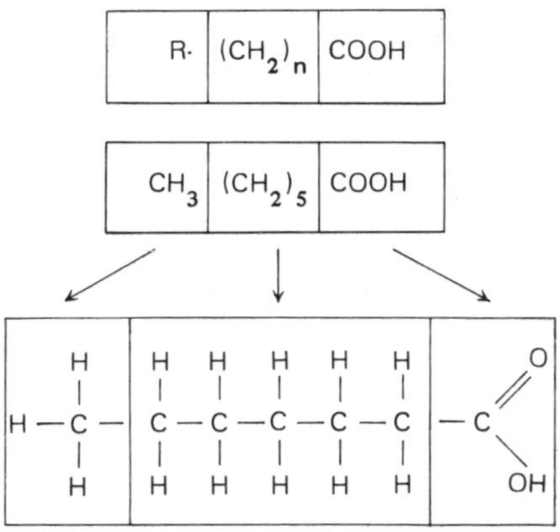

Fig.1.30 Triglyceride

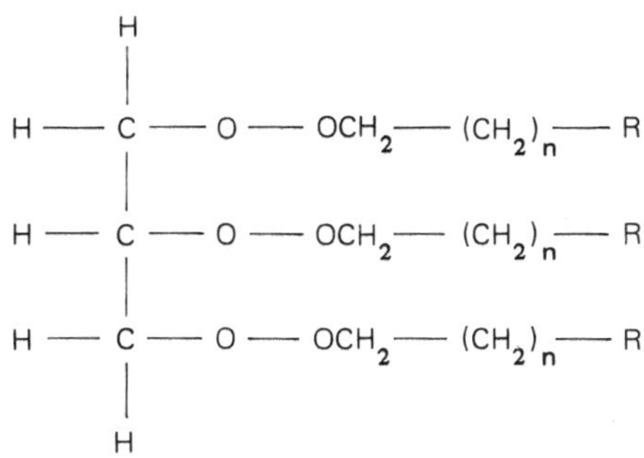

Fig.1.31 Glycerol

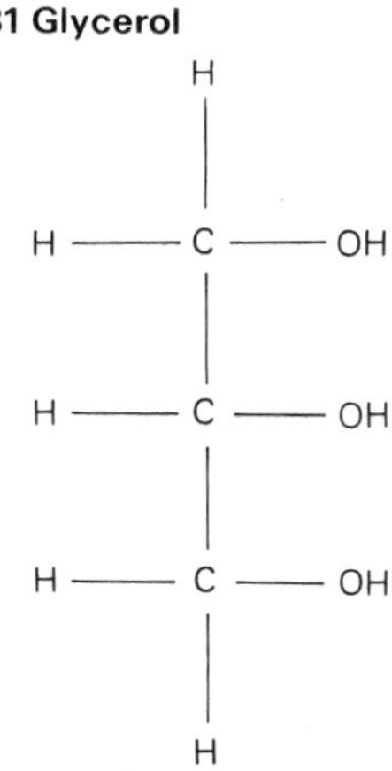

The general formula of a fatty acid is R—$(CH_2)_n$ COOH[1]. R can be a variety of organic groups such as CH_3, C_2H_5, C_3H_7 etc. and *n* can be any number from one to sixteen.

When three molecules of fatty acid combine with one molecule of glycerol, the result is a **triglyceride**, that is, a fat or oil. As in the case of polysaccharides, the exact nature of the substance obtained is determined by the particular basic units involved.

[1] *COOH*: the COOH group refers to an organic acid

PROTEINS

Proteins are considerably more varied in structure than either carbohydrates or lipids. In addition to carbon, hydrogen and oxygen, they always contain nitrogen, and may also contain phosphorus and sulphur. The basic building blocks of the protein molecule are called **amino acids**.

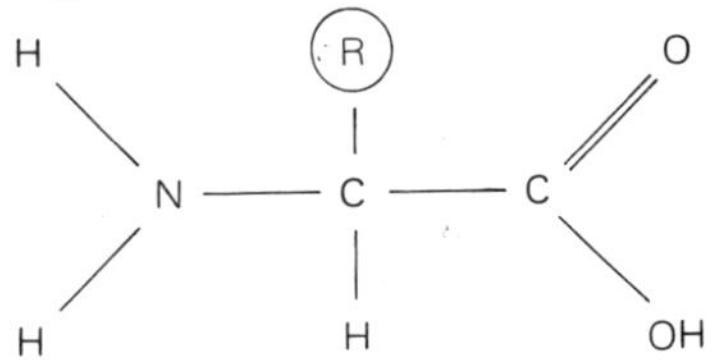

Fig.1.32 Basic structure of amino acid

All amino acids have the same basic structure but their properties differ according to the nature of their side groups (marked R in the diagram).

The simplest amino acid is **glycine**, the R group being hydrogen.

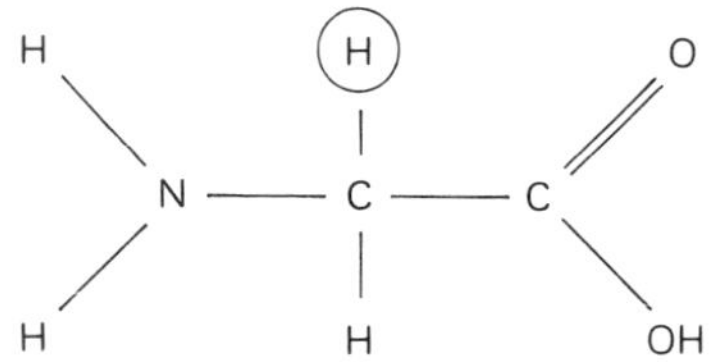

Fig.1.33 Structure of glycine

Under appropriate conditions amino acids can form long-chain molecules. First, two amino acids join to form a **dipeptide**, then further reactions result in a **polypeptide**, in much the same way as polysaccharides are formed from simple sugars. One or more polypeptide chains can then be folded into a complex three-dimensional structure to form the actual protein molecule.

Fig.1.34

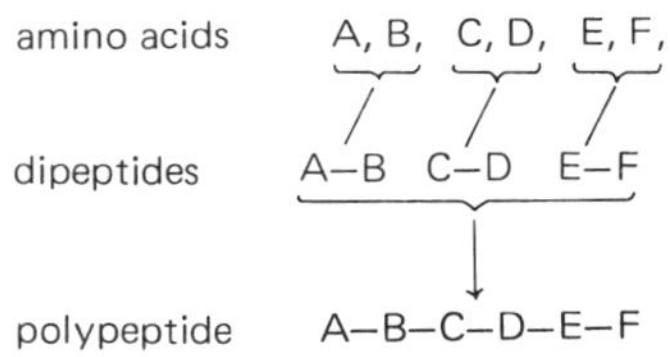

Although there are only twenty amino acids that are commonly found in living organisms the number of ways in which these can combine is very great indeed. When you consider that some proteins contain several hundred or even thousand amino acids it is not difficult to see how each protein can be unique.

Detecting nutrients in food

The main organic components of the food we eat are carbohydrates, lipids and proteins. Individual foods, however, are rarely made up of only one of these nutrients; rather, they usually contain a combination of two or even all three. Scientists studying food and nutrition have provided us with a few very simple chemical tests for the identification of these basic components.

First perform the food tests on material that you know will give a positive reaction, then proceed to test some of the common foods that you eat every day. Dry solid foods should be ground up with a mortar and pestle and dissolved in a small amount of water. Moist solids should be mashed to a fine paste. Perform each test on 1 cm^3 of distilled water to serve as a control.

EXPERIMENT TO TEST FOOD SUBSTANCES TO FIND WHAT NUTRIENTS THEY CONTAIN

Materials

Fehling's solution
dilute hydrochloric acid
sodium hydrogen carbonate
ethanol
Millon's reagent
iodine
sodium hydroxide
copper sulphate

glucose
table sugar
starch powder
cooking oil
egg white
a selection of common foods

Method

1. Fehling's solution test for reducing sugar (for positive reaction use glucose or honey)
Place food in test-tube.
Add 2 cm^3 Fehling's solution.
Heat to boiling and note colour.

2. Test for non-reducing sugar
Note: most non-reducing sugars can be broken down into their reducing sugar components by boiling with dilute acid. (For positive reaction use table sugar.)
Place material in test-tube and add three drops of dilute hydrochloric acid.
Boil for about two minutes and cool under tap.
Slowly neutralize by adding small amounts of sodium hydrogen carbonate until fizzing stops.
Carry out reducing sugar test as above.

3. Starch test
(For positive reaction use starch powder)
Place material in test-tube.
Add a few drops of dilute iodine solution and note colour change.

4. Lipids—spot test
(For positive reaction use cooking oil)
Rub material onto a piece of paper.
Hold up to a light and observe.

5. Lipids—ethanol test
Place food in test-tube.
Add 2 cm^3 ethanol and shake.
Pour off liquid layer into a clean tube and leave behind any solid residue.
Add 2 cm^3 cold water to decanted liquid and observe.

6. Proteins—Millon's reagent test
(For positive reaction use egg white)
Place material in test-tube.
Add two drops of Millon's reagent.
Heat gently and note colour change.

7. Proteins—biuret test
Place sample in test-tube.
Add two drops sodium hydroxide and one drop copper sulphate.
Shake and note colour change.

Summary of food tests

Table 1.4 summarizes the methods for carrying out the food

Table 1.4

Food	Test	Positive Result
Reducing sugar sample: glucose	Add Fehling's solution and heat.	Brick red precipitate.
Starch sample: potato	Add iodine solution.	Blue black colour.
Lipids sample: oil	(i) *Spot test* Rub a drop of oil on paper and observe under light. (ii) *Ethanol test* Add ethanol to a drop of oil and shake. Then add cold water.	Translucent spot. Milky emulsion.
Protein sample: egg white	(i) *Millon's reagent test* Add 2 drops of Millon's reagent and heat. (ii) *Biuret test* Add 2 drops of NaOH and 1 drop of $CuSO_4$.	Red coagulated protein. Purple colour.

tests and indicates the nature of the positive results. After you have tested a variety of foods summarize your results in a table like the one below.

Name of food	Reducing sugar	Starch	Protein	Fat
rice	—	+	+	—

Compare your results with those of your classmates. In some instances, conflicting results might be obtained if a certain component is contained in a particular food in very small amounts. In this case you might get a positive result if you test a rather large sample but a negative result if you use a smaller sample.

How can we determine the energy content of our food?

The energy content of a sample of food can be measured by determining the amount of heat released when the food is burned in an atmosphere of oxygen. The apparatus used for this measurement is called a *calorimeter*. The heat generated by the burning food is used to heat a known volume of water in the outer chamber and the resultant increase in temperature is measured with a thermometer. The units used for the measurement of food and other kinds of energy is the *joule* (J). It is defined as the energy equivalent to the

Fig. 1.35 A calorimeter for use with foodstuffs

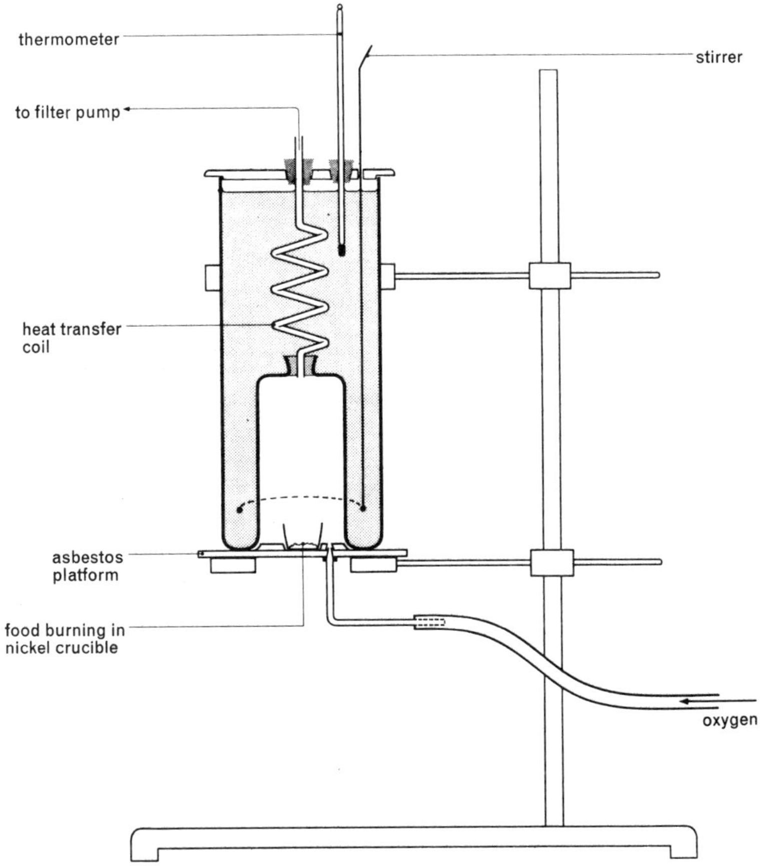

work done by a force of 1 newton acting through a distance of 1 metre. The joule replaced the calorie as a unit of heat energy; 1 calorie = 4.1868 joules.

At this point you might be wondering how accurate this method of measuring food energy is. There are many sources of error in the use of a calorimeter (can you think of some?) and in absolute terms the results obtained are not very accurate. However, since the errors are the same for every food so measured, the apparatus does give valuable information on the relative energy content of the foods we eat.

How much energy does each nutrient make available to the body?

Lipids, such as butter and oil, are the most concentrated sources of energy while carbohydrates and proteins supply a smaller number of calories.

Below is a list of the caloric content of a number of common foods, along with a graphic illustration of some of them for the purpose of comparison.

FOOD	ENERGY (kJ/100g)
Plain biscuits	1800
White bread	1008
Rice	1510
Butter	3320
Eggs	1760
Milk	277
Cooking fats	3860
Fried white fish	840
Tinned salmon	570
Beef	1344
Chicken	570
Pork	1760
Onions	105
Tomato	59
Turnip	76
Apple	190
Banana	323
Orange	147
Raisins	1030
Chocolate	2268
Sugar	1640
Beer	134
Tea	0
Coffee	0

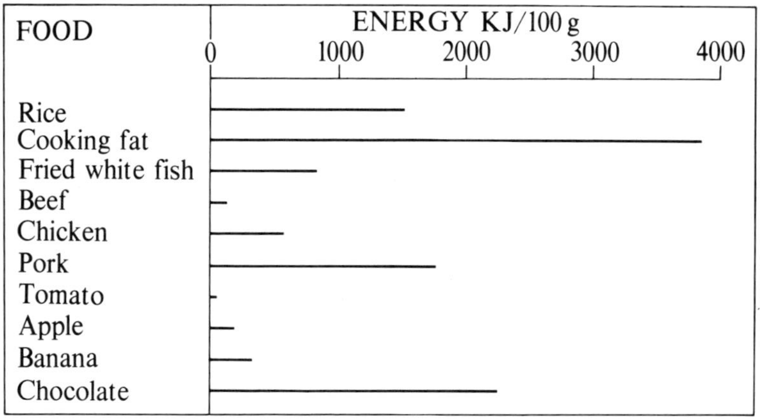

Note that lipids contain more than twice the energy as that in an equal weight of carbohydrate. This is due to the much higher carbon and hydrogen content of lipids.

It is also very interesting to compare the energy content of food with the energy released by various fuels.

FUEL	ENERGY (kJ)
1/3 cup petrol	3360
1″× 22″× 4″ piece of wood	1350
stick of dynamite	1090
1 kg coal	3024

How much energy does the human body require?

Now that you have a rough idea of the energy content of some of the foods you eat, let us find out what the energy requirements of the human body are. The energy needed for basal metabolism in an adult is about 7140 kJ (1700 kcal) per day. The extra energy required above this level depends on the level of physical energy expended by a particular person, this is, it depends on the type of job he or she performs.

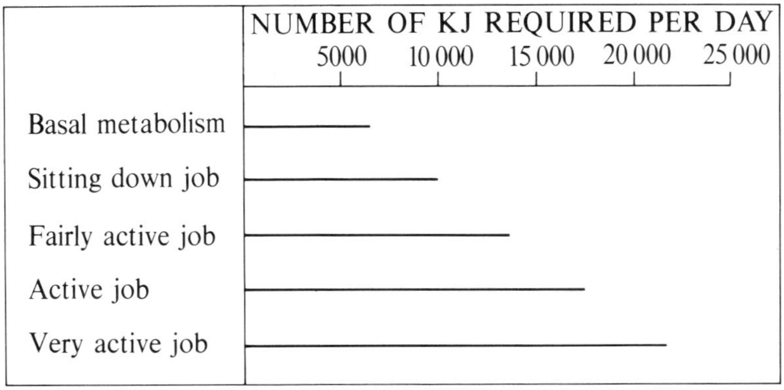

The energy requirements of children must be assessed separately. An actively growing individual needs proportionally more energy than someone who is already fully grown.

AGE	NUMBER OF kJ NEEDED PER DAY
0–1	4200
2–6	6300
7–10	8400
11–14	11 550
15–19	14 700 (male)
	10 500 (female)

The functions of the various nutrients

ENERGY

The main function of lipids and carbohydrates in our diet is to satisfy the body's energy demands. Although in extreme cases proteins can be metabolized to yield energy, normally they fulfil a much more important function as body-building foods—agents of growth and repair.

BODY-BUILDING

Every cell in the human body contains protein and the essential raw materials for synthesizing these proteins must come from the diet. Of the twenty common amino acids making up the proteins of the body, adults require dietary supplies of eight while children require ten. These special amino acids, called **essential amino acids**, cannot be manufactured by the body. What is more, amino acids cannot be stored by the liver the way glucose can (see p. 83) therefore fresh supplies are needed daily.

In the earlier section on proteins we saw that each protein has a unique arrangement of amino acids and that not all twenty amino acids are contained in every protein. The nutrient value of protein foods depends on whether or not it can serve as a source of essential amino acids.

Most protein foods of animal origin—meat, fish, milk, eggs—are of high nutritional value. Most plant proteins, with the notable exception of soya beans, lack at least one of the essential amino acids. Therefore an exclusively vegetarian diet is highly unsatisfactory especially for a growing child unless it contains soya beans or is supplemented by some animal proteins.

Inorganic minerals

Another group of important body-building nutrients are inorganic minerals. Minerals make up an appreciable part of the body of a human adult. A person weighing about 65 kg will have 800 g calcium, 13 g iron, 540 g phosphorus, 100 g sulphur and 130 g iodine in his tissues.

Calcium and *phosphorus* are necessary for healthy growth and maintenance of bones and teeth. Calcium is also important for the proper functioning of nerves, the clotting of blood, and the production of milk by the mammary glands after childbirth.

Iron is an essential part of haemoglobin, the red colouring in the

Fig.1.36 Fate of calcium in body

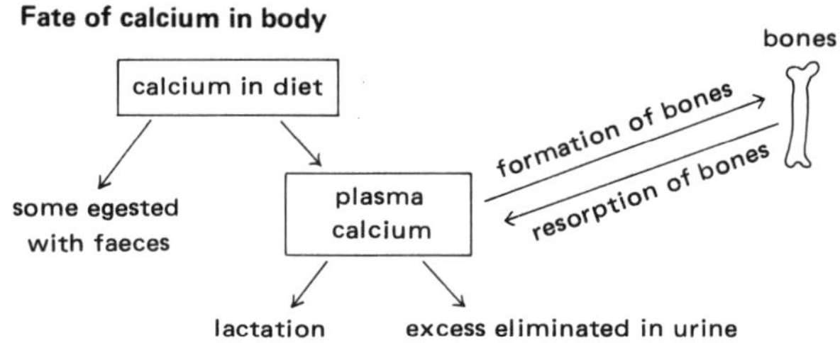

Fig.1.37 Fate of iron in body

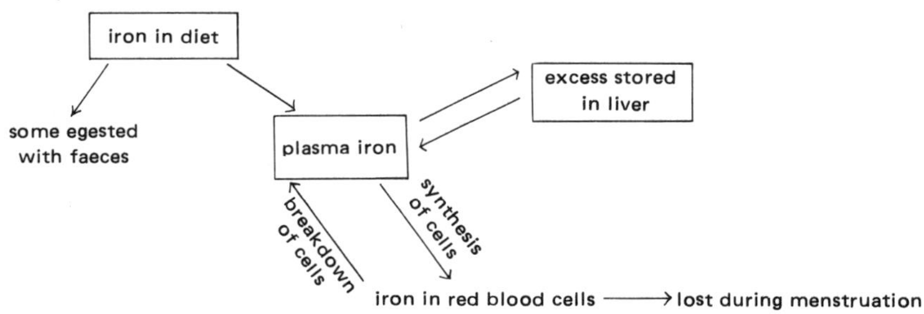

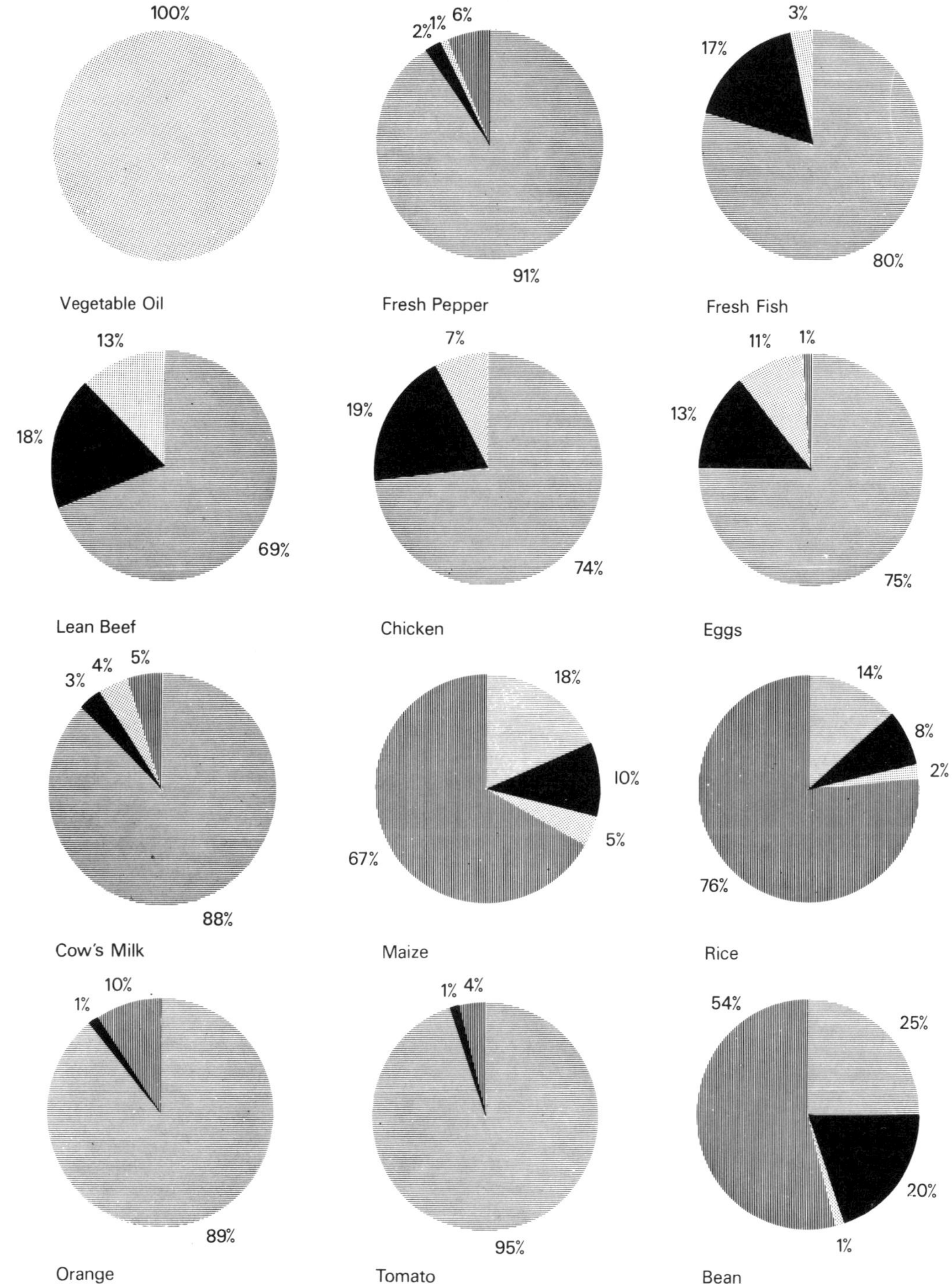

Fig.1.38 Comparison of the proportions of carbohydrates, proteins, lipids and water in some common foods (proportions of minerals and vitamins present are too small to be represented)

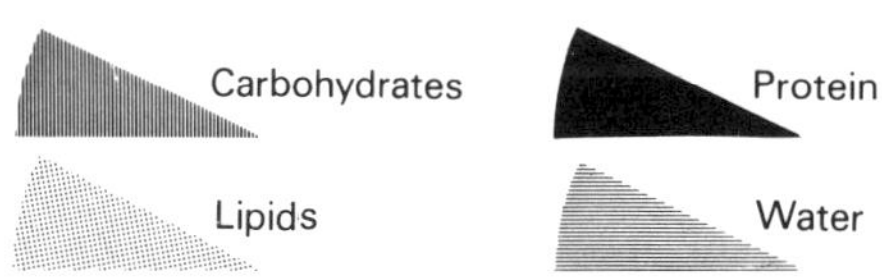

blood. Haemoglobin is responsible for combining with oxygen in the lungs and carrying the oxygen to the various cells of the body where it is required.

The result of iron deficiency is a condition called **anaemia**. The blood of an anaemic person does not contain sufficient levels of haemoglobin and therefore cannot carry enough oxygen to the cells. This leads to fatigue.

The *iodine* contained in our diet is transported to a small gland at the base of the throat, called the **thyroid gland**. There it is used to make **thyroxin**, the hormone responsible for regulating the basal metabolic rate[1] of the body. A person with an overactive thyroid gland—one which synthesizes abnormally high levels of thyroxine—is restless, very active and, since he burns up his food for energy so quickly, he is usually thin. A person whose thyroid gland makes less than normal amounts of the hormone is usually slow and tired looking and is likely to be overweight. (p. 250.)

The amounts of iodine required in the diet are extremely small. Iodine deficiency leads to the development of a **goitre**—an enlarged thyroid gland. The gland, while straining to produce enough hormone to meet the body's normal demands becomes enlarged until it forms a visible swelling at the base of the throat.

Table 1.5

MINERAL	FUNCTION	MAIN SOURCES	MAJOR EFFECT OF DEFICIENCY
Iron	carries oxygen in blood	beef, liver, cocoa, oysters, wheat germ	anaemia
Calcium	bones and teeth, functioning of nerves, clotting of blood	milk, cheese, shrimps, spinach	malformed bones
Iodine	synthesis of thyroxine to control metabolic rate	fish, seaweed, iodized salt	goitre, slow metabolic rate leading to fatigue
Phosphorus	bones and teeth chemicals such as ATP	milk, cheese, liver, eggs	malformed bones
Sodium chloride	constituent of body fluids	table salt	painful cramps, dehydration

[1] *basal metabolic rate*: the minimum rate at which the body uses energy to keep all its functions operating

Vitamins

It was not until the beginning of the present century that the importance of vitamins was realized. In his famous experiment, Francis Gowland Hopkins fed a group of rats on a diet consisting of casein (the protein contained in cheese), starch, sucrose, lard, inorganic salts and water. Instead of showing normal growth the rats began to lose weight rapidly. When Hopkins supplemented the above diet with a very small amount of milk the animals regained their health and started growing.

Hopkins concluded that milk must contain 'accessory factors' that are needed by animals in their diet. These factors are today known as vitamins. The table below shows the most important vitamins, their functions and the effects of their deficiency.

Table 1.6

VITAMIN	RICH SOURCES	GOOD SOURCES	FUNCTIONS	DEFICIENCY DISEASES
A	liver, fish-liver oils, egg-yolk	milk, cheese, leafy vegetables	eyesight	poor night vision, skin diseases
B_1	yeast	whole cereals, liver, lean meat	carbohydrate metabolism	beri-beri: a nervous disease
B_2	yeast	liver, eggs, cheese	enzymes in respiration	skin lesions
B_7	yeast	liver, whole cereals, meat	respiration	pellagra
B_{12}	liver	lean meat, fish, milk	red blood cells	anaemia
C	citrus fruit, green vegetables, potatoes	fresh fruit, liver	formation of collagen, one of the body's proteins	scurvy: sore mouth, teeth fall out
D	fish-liver oils	liver, eggs, cheese, sunlight	absorption of calcium and phosphorus	rickets: poorly developed bones
E	vegetable oil, grains	all foods	reproduction in some animals	
K		green vegetables	blood clotting	slow clotting

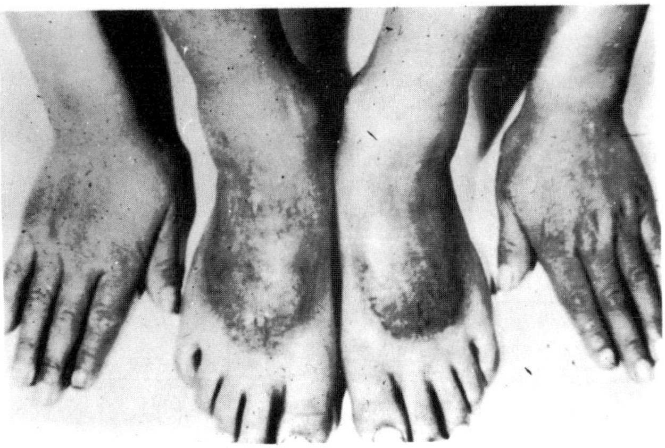

Fig.1.39 Patient with pellagra

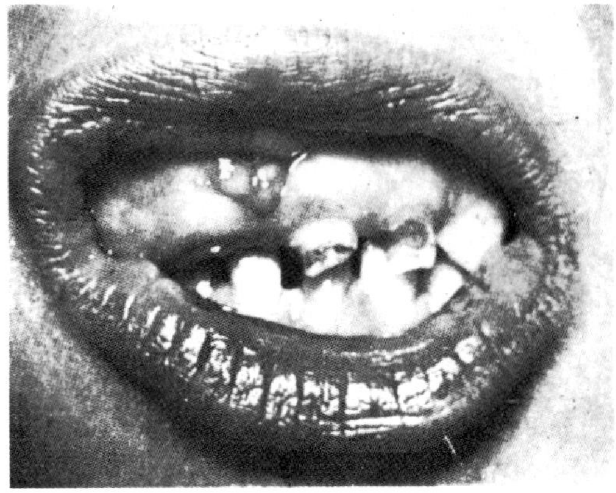

Fig.1.40 Signs of scurvy due to lack of vitamin C

Fig.1.41 Rickets caused by lack of vitamin D

Other components of diet

The main types of nutrients required by the body are carbohydrates, lipids, proteins, vitamins and inorganic salts. In addition to the above, the diet must contain a certain amount of indigestible material termed **roughage** to help move the masses of food along the digestive tract. This material, since it cannot be digested, remains as relatively large molecules or sometimes as visible pieces, and the peristaltic motion of the gut can grip on to them to move the mass of food along. One more important ingredient of a healthy diet is **water**. Water is continually being lost through sweating, in the urine and faeces and must be replaced as required.

BALANCED DIET

To ensure good health and proper growth, a person must have a daily intake of all the necessary nutrients in the correct amounts. One of the best ways to construct a balanced diet is to follow a food guide such as the one shown below.

Fig.1.42 The basic seven groups of food

GROUP 1 Leafy, green and yellow vegetables

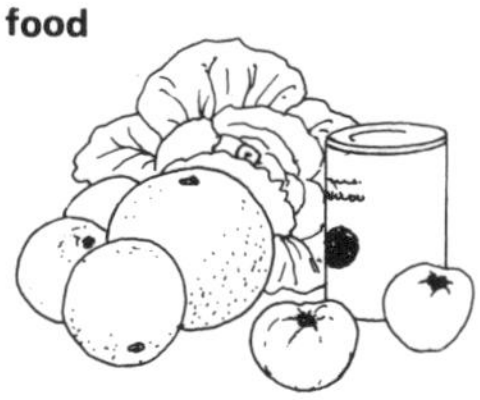

GROUP 2 Citrus fruit, tomatoes, raw cabbage

GROUP 3 Potatoes and other vegetables and fruit

GROUP 4 Milk and milk products

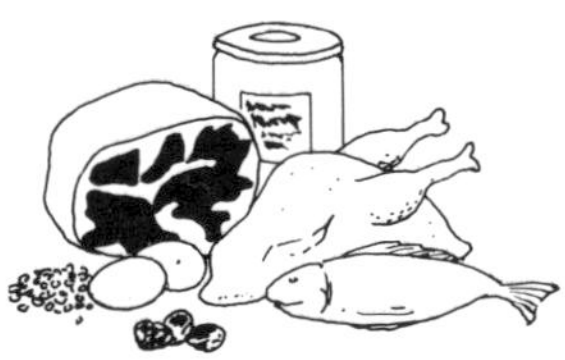

GROUP 5 Meat, poultry, fish, eggs, dried beans, peas, nuts

GROUP 6 Bread, flour, cereals

GROUP 7 Butter, fortified margarine

The diagram shows seven different groups of foods classified according to their basic nutrient content. By eating at least *one* serving per day from *each* of the seven groups the requirements of a balanced diet will be met.

Poor nutrition is commonly called **malnutrition** and results either from eating too little food or not eating the right foods. Large areas of the world today are plagued by starvation and severe malnutrition due to lack of adequate supplies of food. In other areas where food supplies are plentiful, many still suffer from various degrees of malnutrition due to ignorance of the basic principles of nutrition.

Summary

The basic groups of nutrients that must be present in a healthy diet are proteins, carbohydrates, fats, mineral salts and vitamins. The presence of these chemical substances in a particular food can be detected by means of appropriate chemical tests.

In addition, water and a certain amount of indigestible roughage must be consumed.

The main function of proteins is supplying amino acids, the raw materials for the processes of growth and repair.

Carbohydrates and fats serve as sources of energy. Mineral salts and vitamins are needed for a variety of body processes and for keeping our bodies functioning efficiently in general.

In a balanced diet, the above components must all be present in the required daily amounts.

Ingestion in mammals

How does food get into the body?

The process by which animals take food into their body cavities is called **ingestion**.

Mammals being relatively large animals need large amounts of food which they have to find and sometimes actively pursue before they are able to ingest it. Their food consists mainly of large pieces of solid material that need to be cut or ground down to a size that can pass into the body cavity. To accomplish this mammals possess a variety of teeth together making up the **dentition** of the animal.

Since there are considerable variations in the precise nature of the diet of mammals there must be corresponding variations in the types of feeding and dentition.

Carnivores

Meat-eating mammals, or carnivores, have special adaptations[1] such as keen vision, strong limbs for running and claws for catching their

[1] *adaptation*: a characteristic that makes a living organism more suited to its environment or way of life

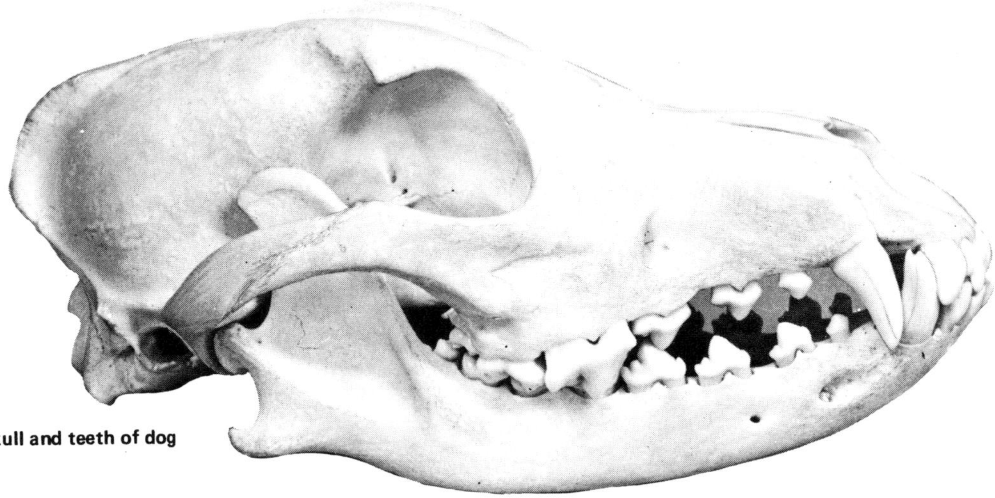

Fig.1.43 Skull and teeth of dog

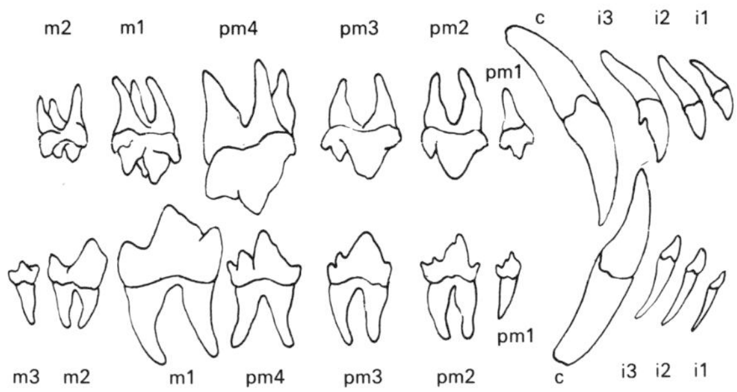

prey. Their dentition is adapted for killing and tearing to pieces the animal flesh they eat.

DOG

Fig.1.44 Action of specialized teeth

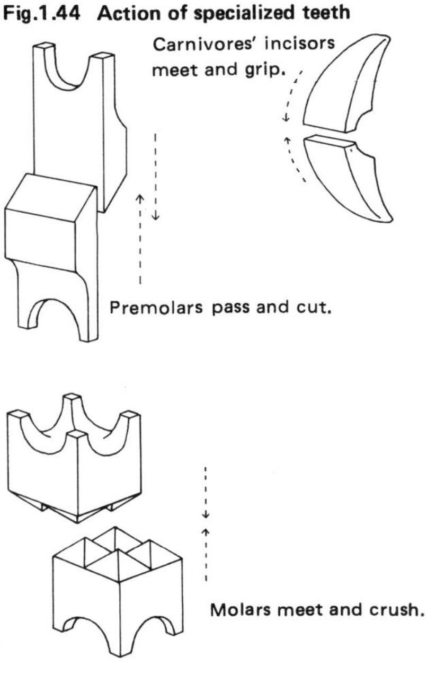

For the purposes of our study the domestic dog will serve as a suitable example of a carnivore. Although living close to man as they do, they do not need to make use of all their skills as carnivores, they do possess all the adaptations of the larger predators that they are related to such as the tiger and the lion.

Examine the skull of a dog and refer to fig. 1.43 to identify the parts of the dentition. Note that the upper jaw, being part of the main section of the skull, is stationary while the lower jaw is a separate piece of bone connected by a hinge-like arrangement below the ears. The front teeth, called **incisors**, are small and pointed like chisels. The **canines** are sharper and narrower, being slightly elongated to form fangs that are used to kill the prey.

The **premolars** and **molars** (together termed the **cheek teeth**) are also sharp and pointed but they are wider and have several separate pointed edges. The ridges along the surface act like the blades of a pair of scissors.

Have you ever tried to cut something with a pair of scissors that have a loose rivet allowing the blade to move sideways? Scissors like that do not cut very well. The same principle can be applied to the dentition of a carnivore. The jaw joint itself and the muscles working the lower jaw allow for only a minimal sideways motion with most of the force concentrated in the up and down motion.

DENTAL FORMULA

In order to simplify the representation of the dentition of an animal, a shorthand system of dental formula is used. The type of tooth is represented by the initial letter of its name, for instance, *i* for incisor. The numbers following slightly above and below indicate the number of that type of tooth present in the upper and lower jaws respectively.

Let us now put together the dental formula of a dog. Starting at the midline it has three incisors in both the upper and lower jaws, therefore we write: i^3_3; one canine: c^1_1; four premolars in the upper jaw and four in the lower jaw: p^4_4; two molars in the upper jaw and three in the lower: m^2_3. The complete dental formula is as follows:

$$^2_3m,\ ^4_4p,\ ^1_1c,\ ^3_3i \qquad i^3_3,\ c^1_1,\ p^4_4,\ m^2_3$$

Normally we would only write the right-hand half of the formula knowing that the other side is the mirror image.

Fig.1.45

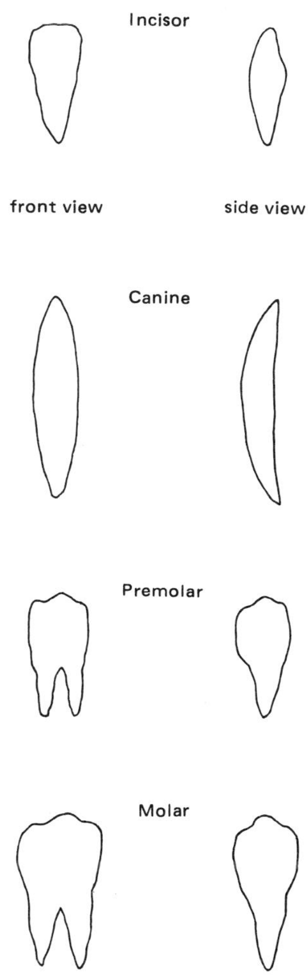

Herbivores

The dentition of herbivores is very different from that of carnivores. Plant material such as grass is particularly tough to cut and grind into small pieces. The next time you are in a grassy area try to tear off portions of a handful of grass blades. More than likely you will end up pulling the plants out by the roots rather than being able to tear the blades.

SHEEP

How does a herbivore such as a sheep manage to cut through the blades of grass?

Herbivores use their long, chisel-like lower incisors that work against a horny pad, rather like a chopping block, that replaces the upper incisors. A single canine in each side of the lower jaw is present. They are very similar in shape to the incisors. Between the incisors and canines and the cheek teeth there is a large gap called a **diastema**.

Fig.1.46 Section through herbivore's skull to show action of teeth

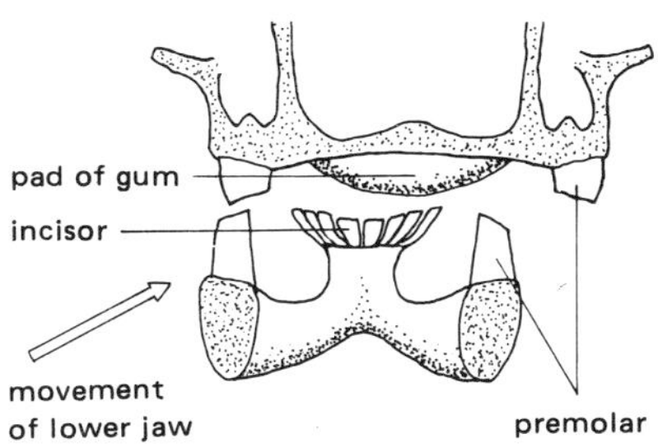

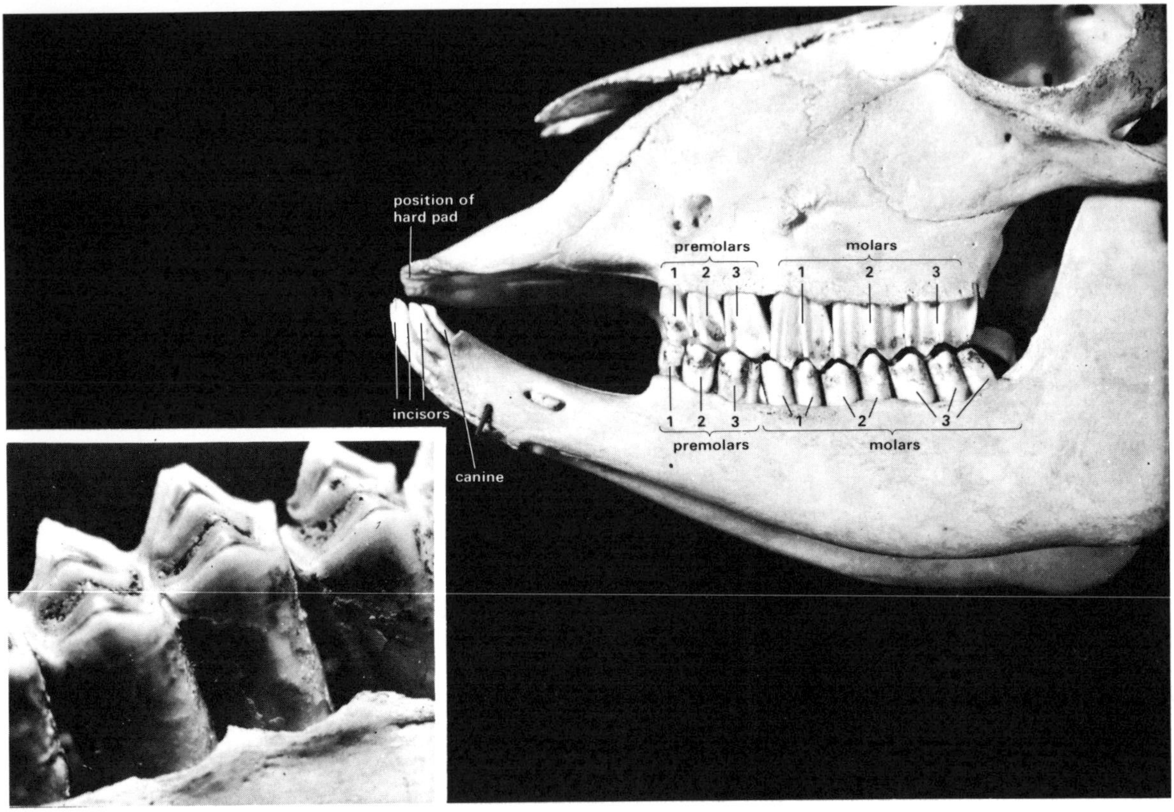

Fig.1.47 Skull of sheep with lower molars showing grinding surfaces

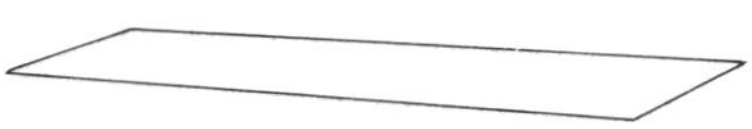

strip of paper

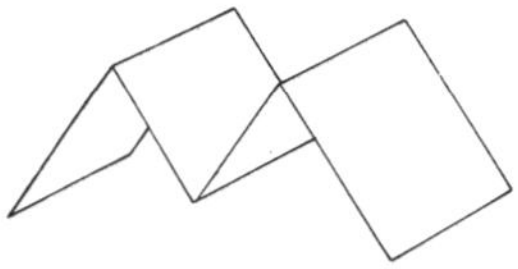

Fold into the shape of the letter M.

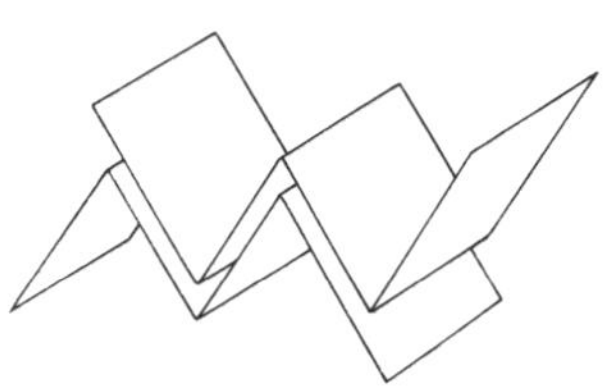

Fig.1.48 Put two together.

Its main purpose is to separate the newly-cropped grass from the material that is already being chewed at the back. The cheek teeth are very broad and have large transverse ridges, with the ridges of the upper teeth fitting exactly into those of the lower teeth. The muscle connections of the lower jaw are such that they allow practically unrestricted movement of the jaw from side to side. As a result the animal is able to reduce plant material to a soft pulp by the effective grinding action of the premolars and molars.

You can demonstrate this grinding action to yourself by making paper models of the cheek teeth of a sheep according to the diagram shown here.

Can you see how effective this arrangement must be for grinding plant material?

Another feature of the cheek teeth of herbivores is the presence of enamel ridges. Enamel, as you will see, is the hardest layer of the tooth. While the other layers wear down very quickly the enamel remains to form jagged edges on the top surface of the tooth. This further helps in the grinding action. Furthermore, the premolars and molars of herbivores continue to grow throughout the animal's life. If this were not so the original teeth would soon be worn completely away.

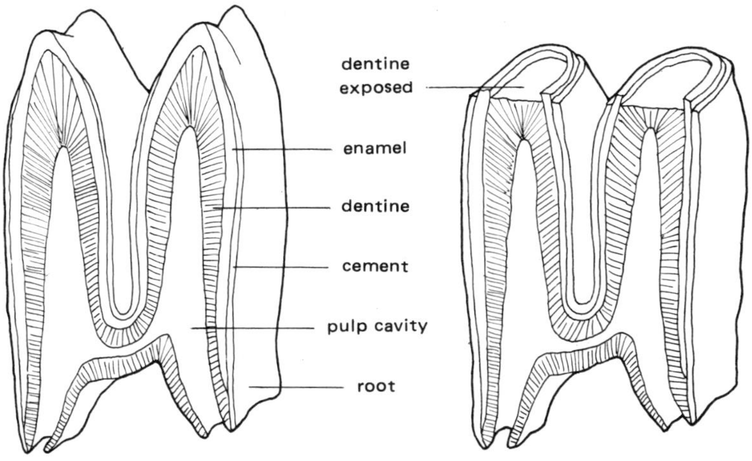

(i) Molar when first formed (ii) Molar after grinding

Fig.1.49 Sections of herbivore's molar to show how it is worn down

Fig.1.50

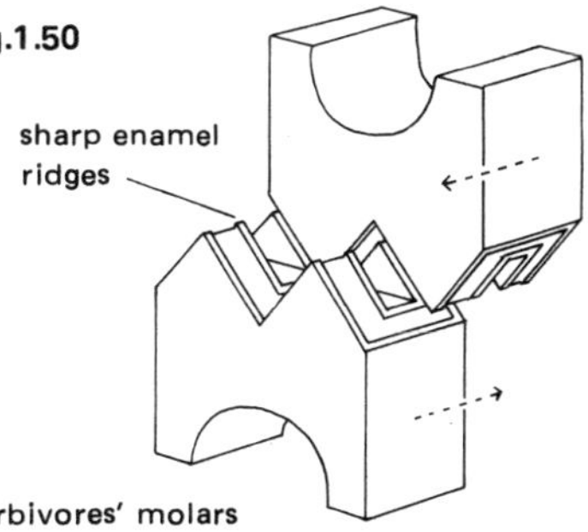

Herbivores' molars
slide over each other and grind.

The dental formula of the sheep is:

$$i^{0}_{3},\ c^{0}_{1},\ p^{3}_{3},\ m^{3}_{3}$$

Omnivores

Man, as an omnivore, has a dentition which is in many ways intermediate between that of a carnivore and that of a herbivore. The dental formula is:

$$i^{2}_{2},\ c^{1}_{1},\ p^{2}_{2},\ m^{3}_{3}$$

This makes a total of 32 teeth in the complete dentition.

The incisors are sharp and chisel-like. The canines are slightly pointed but are not elongated as they are in carnivores. The cheek teeth resemble those of a carnivore but they are not nearly as jagged. Chewing motion is predominantly up-and-down but there is considerable allowance for sideways motion.

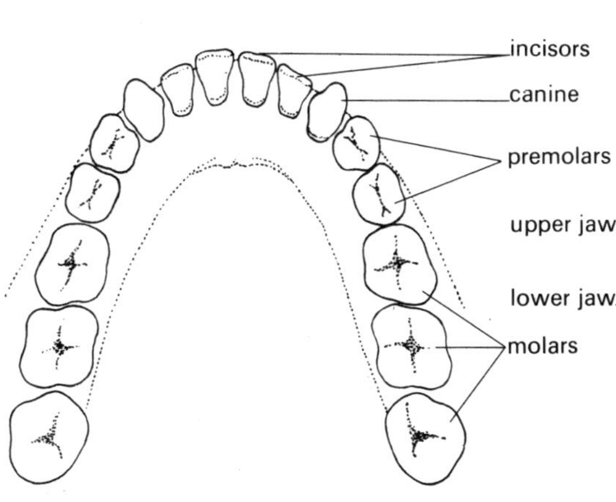

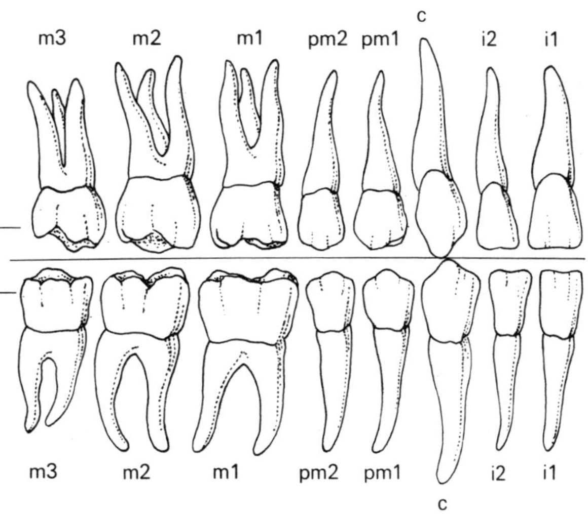

Fig.1.51 Human dentition

Table 1.7 Relationship between the type of food eaten and the type of teeth

Animal	Type of food	Dental formula i c p m	Jaw movements	Special features
Dog	Meat	$\frac{3}{3}\ \frac{1}{1}\ \frac{4}{4}\ \frac{2}{3}$	Up and down only	Carnassials which have scissor-like action and canines for tearing.
Rabbit	Vegetables and grass	$\frac{2}{1}\ \frac{0}{0}\ \frac{3}{2}\ \frac{3}{3}$	Up and down and backwards and forwards	Long curved constantly growing incisors for gnawing. Flat-ridged premolars and molars for grinding.
Black rat	″	$\frac{1}{1}\ \frac{0}{0}\ \frac{0}{0}\ \frac{3}{3}$	″	
Horse	Grass	$\frac{3}{3}\ \frac{1}{1}\ \frac{4}{4}\ \frac{3}{3}$	Side to side	Incisors for tearing grass and broad flat back teeth for grinding.
Sheep, Cow	″	$\frac{0}{3}\ \frac{0}{1}\ \frac{3}{3}\ \frac{3}{3}$	″	Hard pad instead of upper canines and incisors.
Man	Meat and vegetables	$\frac{2}{2}\ \frac{1}{1}\ \frac{2}{2}\ \frac{3}{3}$	Up and down, side to side, backwards and forwards	

The table above summarizes the relationship between dentition and diet that we have discussed, and gives further examples.

STRUCTURE AND DEVELOPMENT OF THE TOOTH

If a tooth is cut in half vertically to reveal the inside structures this is what you see.
The outer covering found only on the part of the tooth protruding above the gum is the **enamel.** It is non-living tissue, very hard and resistant to trauma and decay.

Fig.1.52 Sections through incisor and molar teeth

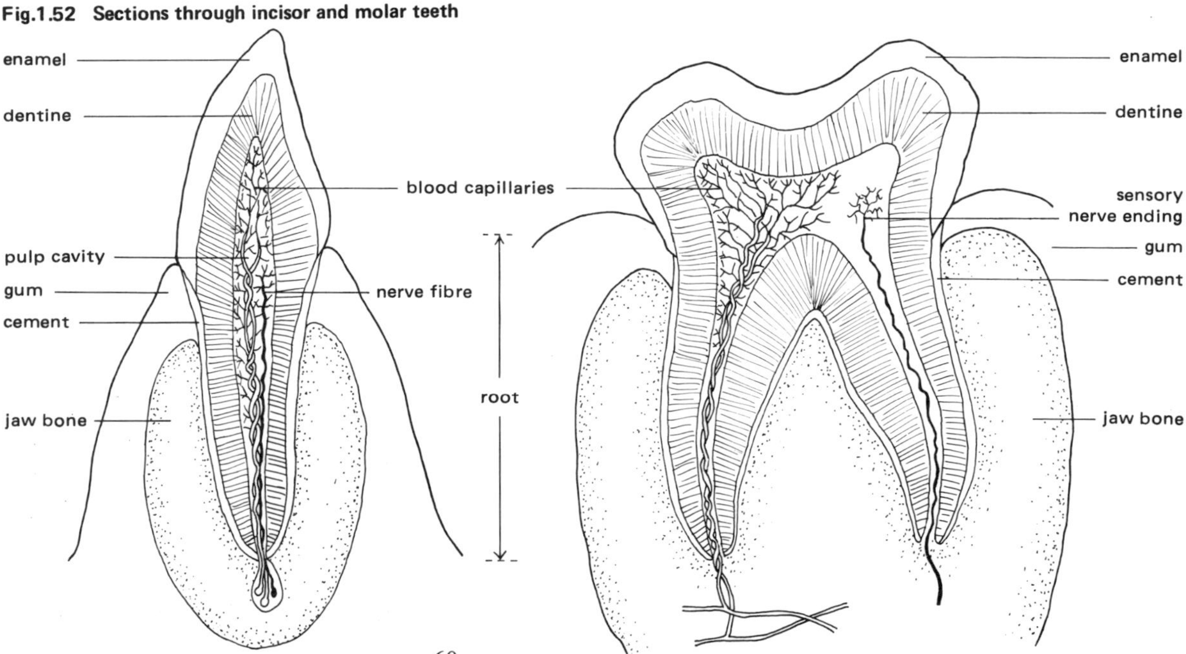

(i) Incisor tooth

(ii) Molar tooth (nerve shown on one side, blood vessels on the other)

The next layer, the **dentine,** is much softer and contains strands of cytoplasm that radiate out from the cells in the interior. It is through these strands that more dentine is added to the inside of the tooth. The innermost layer, the **pulp cavity** contains the living cells, the nerves and the blood supply of the tooth.
The **root** is covered by a thin layer of bony material called **cement**. From the cement supporting fibres pass into the jawbone to anchor the tooth firmly.
In some mammals, including man, two successive sets of teeth develop. The first set of **deciduous** teeth appear between the ages of one and three in human children. From the age of six to about twelve they are progressively replaced by the **permanent** teeth that push their way through the gums to displace the deciduous ones. Molars do not appear as deciduous teeth but only as permanent teeth, erupting usually around the ages of eighteen to twenty. Often there is little room for them to pass through the gums and they remain partly lodged in the jawbone and very little used.

Care of teeth

Permanent teeth can be very easily damaged or lost due to neglect or faulty care allowing the development of tooth decay.

What causes teeth to decay?

Scientists have found that tooth decay is caused by bacteria feeding on carbohydrates lodged between the teeth. Bacteria convert sugars into acids that attack and dissolve the mineral matter of teeth.

EXPERIMENT TO SHOW THAT SUGARY FOODS LODGED BETWEEN THE TEETH WILL LEAD TO THE PRODUCTION OF ACIDS
Materials
glucose
scrapings from your tooth
methyl red, an indicator
Method
1. Place a little debris that has been scraped from your teeth onto two microscope slides.
2. To one sample add a little glucose, and leave for about ten minutes.
3. Set up a third slide with only glucose.
4. Place a drop of methyl red indicator onto the material on each slide.

Fig.1.53

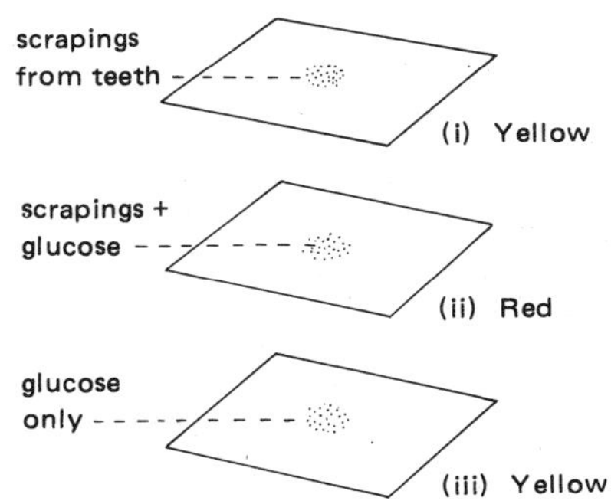

What do you observe?
What causes the reaction?
Discussion
When methyl red is added to a neutral solution it will appear yellow

Fig.1.54

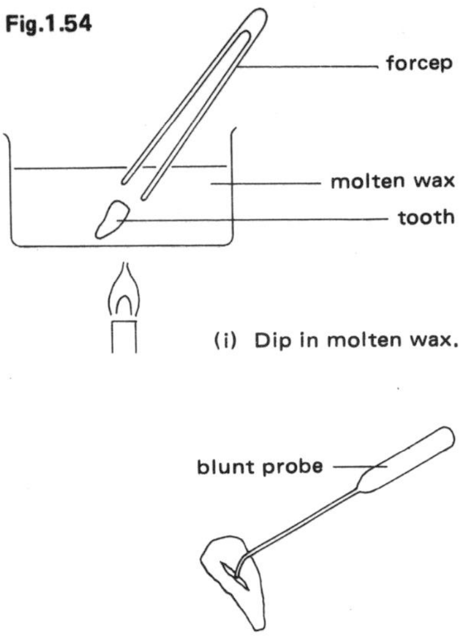

(i) Dip in molten wax.

(ii) Scrape off part of wax coating.

in colour. However, when added to an acid it turns red. Neither the glucose alone nor the scrapings from your teeth alone will cause methyl red to turn to a red colour. But when the two are allowed to come in contact, the micro-organisms contained in the scrapings cause the production of an acid from the glucose and the indicator turns red.

How do we know that acids are responsible for tooth decay?

EXPERIMENT TO SHOW THAT ACIDS CAN DECAY TEETH

Materials

extracted tooth

wax

dilute hydrochloric acid

Method

1. Melt the wax and coat an extracted tooth with the molten wax.
2. Allow the wax to set.
3. Using a blunt instrument scratch away the wax from several spots on the tooth. Be careful not to damage the tooth in any way.
4. Place the tooth in dilute hydrochloric acid and leave for a few days.
5. Take the tooth out of the acid and examine it.

What do you see?

What does this tell you about the role of acids in causing tooth decay?

Discussion

The areas of the tooth that have been left exposed to the acid were eaten away but areas that were protected by the wax were not. This shows us that acids are capable of making holes in a tooth, that is, causing tooth decay.

Fighting tooth decay

Several countries have successfully reduced the incidence of tooth decay in children by adding about one part per million of fluoride to the drinking water. Fluoride seems to act as an antibacterial agent, reducing the number of micro-organisms in the mouth. Strangely enough fluoride does not have much effect in reducing the incidence of tooth decay in adults who have not had fluoride in their water since childhood.

The best defence against tooth decay is brushing one's teeth after every meal or at least rinsing out the mouth after meals and brushing twice a day. The second rule is to avoid eating too many sugar-containing foods such as biscuits and cakes.

Summary

A necessary preliminary to the swallowing of food by most mammals is chewing it.

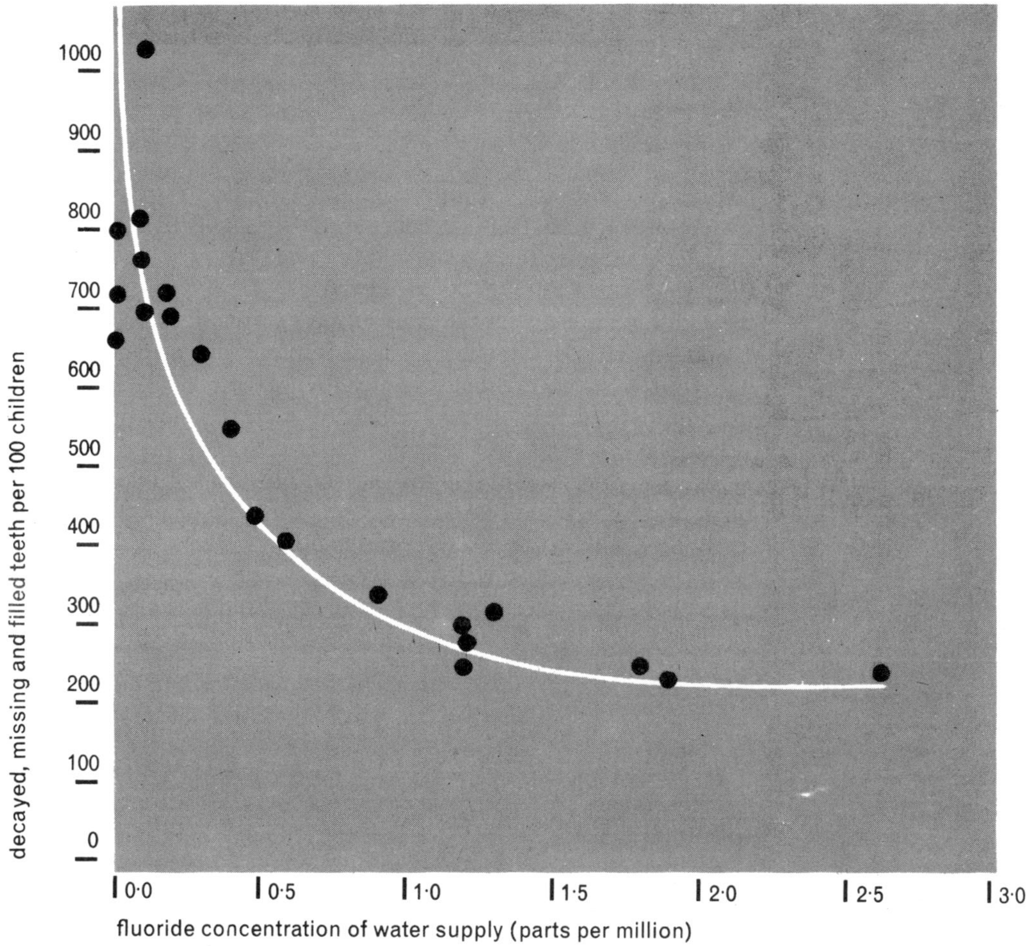

Fig.1.55 Correlation between the amount of dental caries and the fluoride content of drinking water *(From Dean et al (1942), quoted in the Memorandum on the dental health of children (1959) of the British Dental Association)*

The dentition of an animal must be suited to its particular diet. Accordingly, carnivores have teeth that are adapted for biting, tearing and chewing flesh. Herbivores have teeth that are suitable for biting off and grinding plant material.

Omnivores such as man have a dentition which is a compromise between the two.

Chemical digestion

Is there a need for a digestive system in holozoic feeders?

As we have discussed above, the food eaten by animals consists mainly of complex chemical substances, namely proteins, carbohydrates and fats. In the majority of cases this food is eaten in solid form. The complicated system of tubes through which the food passes after entering the mouth of an animal is called the **alimentary canal** or **gut**. If you examine the alimentary canal of an animal more

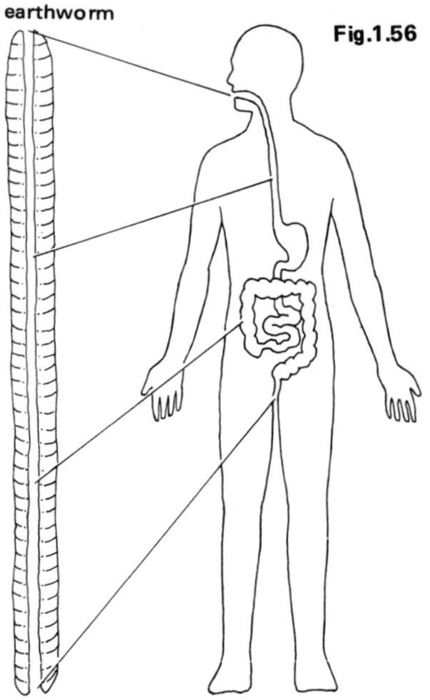

Fig.1.56

closely you will note that substances inside the **lumen**[1] of the canal are not really 'inside' the body.

Perhaps this fact is more obvious in an elongated, worm-like animal such as that shown in fig. 1.56, but it is true of most other animals including man.

The walls of the canal act as a barrier allowing only certain suitable substances to enter the interior of the body.

Clearly, most of the food that enters the gut must be able to pass through the barrier into the cells in the interior of the body, since it is in the cells that the chemicals contained in our food are used. Any food which for some reason cannot pass through the barrier will simply travel the length of the canal and be egested.

The action of the gut wall can be illustrated by a simple experiment using a length of Visking tubing filled with a solution of starch and sugar.

EXPERIMENT TO DEMONSTRATE THE ACTION OF THE GUT WALL AS A BARRIER

Materials

a 6–8 inch piece of Visking tubing
2 beakers or other containers that fit into each other
thermometer
funnel
iodine solution for starch test
Benedict's solution for sugar test
1 % starch solution
1 % glucose solution

Method

1. Place the small container inside the larger one, fill up both with tap water and warm over a flame until the temperature reaches 37°C.
2. Tie a knot close to one end of the Visking tubing. (When working with Visking tubing always remember to keep the tubing moist. If it is allowed to dry out the walls will crack.)
3. Fill up the tubing to about two-thirds full with the starch-sugar solution.
4. Seal off the top with a knot. Rinse the outside of the tubing with water to remove any traces of starch-sugar solution.
5. Place the filled tubing into the smaller container of water (fig. 1.57), and maintain the temperature at 37°C.
6. As soon as you have finished setting up the apparatus withdraw a small amount of the water in contact with the tubing and test it for the presence of starch and reducing sugar. (Do you remember the procedure for performing these tests? If you are not quite sure refer back to p. 45.)
7. After about twenty minutes withdraw a second sample of water and again perform the tests for starch and reducing sugar.
8. If both the tests are negative wait a little longer and repeat.

Fig.1.57

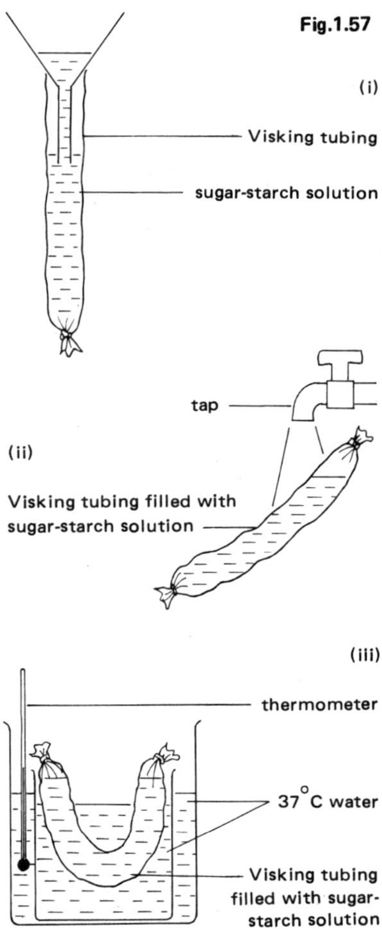

[1] *lumen*: interior cavity

What do you observe?
How can you account for these observations?

Discussion

At the start of the experiment neither sugar nor starch was present in the liquid surrounding the Visking tubing. After about twenty minutes, reducing sugar, that is, glucose, can be detected in the liquid but no starch is present. If you were to leave the experiment set up for several hours, still no starch would leave the Visking tubing.

How can you explain this?

Recall the structure of starch and glucose.

Starch is a polysaccharide, a large chain molecule made up of many sugars joined together. Glucose is a monosaccharide, that is, it consists of only a single unit of sugar.

It seems that the Visking tubing acts as a barrier or a sieve, allowing only molecules below a certain size to pass through the walls.

The walls of the alimentary canal act in the same manner; small, simple molecules can pass through them into the blood stream but large ones such as starch or protein cannot pass through. Large molecules must first be broken down into their basic components through the process of digestion.

Is this the sole function of digestion?

The net result of the process of digestion is not simply a reduction in size but a chemical alteration as well. The chemical properties of the foods that we take into our mouth are not suitable for entry into the body.

If we were to take a piece of meat, mince it up into minute particles and inject it into the blood stream of an animal the process would almost certainly prove fatal. Before food can be safely allowed to enter the body it must be chemically modified and all toxic components must be taken out of it.

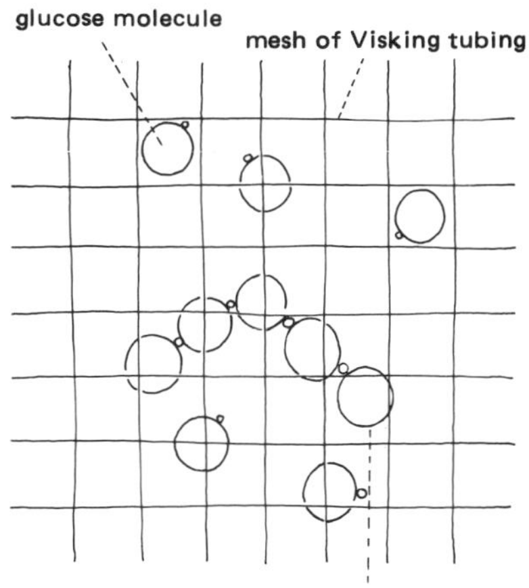

Fig.1.58

Chemical breakdown of nutrients

There are various chemical methods available for breaking down complicated organic molecules.

Can you think of some methods?

In the section on food tests you observed that sucrose, a disaccharide, can be split into its component monosaccharides by boiling with dilute acid. Starch can be broken down using the same method.

EXPERIMENT TO DIGEST STARCH WITH HYDROCHLORIC ACID.

Materials

a 1% starch suspension
dilute hydrochloric acid (HCl)
sodium bicarbonate
boiling water bath
iodine solution
Benedict's solution

Fig. 1.59 Hydrolysis of starch

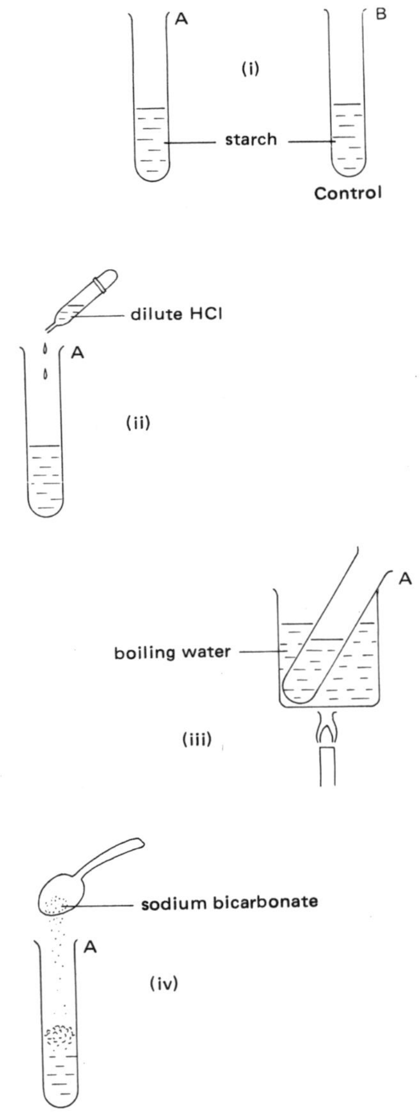

Method

1. Place 2 cm^3 starch suspension in each of two test-tubes. Place one tube aside as a control.
2. To the other (tube A) add five drops dilute hydrochloric acid, bring to the boil and place in the boiling water bath for fifteen minutes.
3. Cool the boiled solution and neutralize it by adding solid sodium bicarbonate until the fizzing stops.
4. Test each of the two solutions for starch and reducing sugar.

What do you observe?
What has the acid done to the starch solution?
Do you think this method of digestion would be suitable for living organisms?

Discussion

The solution in tube A gives a positive reaction for reducing sugar and a negative reaction, or weak positive reaction, for starch. Tube B is negative for sugar and positive for starch. The hydrochloric acid has therefore broken down most of the starch in tube A into glucose. Most chemical reactions, if they are to proceed at an appreciable rate, require rather high temperatures or pressures—conditions that are incompatible with life.

Living organisms can carry on countless chemical reactions at atmospheric pressure and at much lower temperatures with the help of specific catalysts called enzymes. These catalysts speed up chemical reactions without actually taking part in the reactions.

How were enzymes first discovered?

In the late nineteenth century knowledge of the chemical reactions taking place inside living cells was widening. One of the reactions that was studied in great detail was alcoholic fermentation by yeast cells. (See p. 115.) The chemical equation for the reaction is:

$$\underset{\text{sugar}}{C_6H_{12}O_6} \longrightarrow \underset{\text{ethyl alcohol}}{2C_2H_5OH} + \underset{\text{carbon dioxide}}{2CO_2}$$

Scientists at the time believed that some mysterious *life force* inside living cells was responsible for making this and other chemical reactions possible. A biologist called Edward Buchner was studying the possible therapeutic[1] effects of an extract of yeast cells. To do this he had to grind up the tiny yeast cells to yield what he called a *yeast broth*. In order to preserve his broth he decided to add sugar to it. As soon as he added the sugar he observed something unexpected; the yeast juice began to froth and foam and carbon dioxide was

[1] *therapeutic*: suitable for curing a disease

given off. Buchner realised that he was observing alcoholic fermentation *outside a living cell.*

It seemed that there was no mysterious life force at work after all. Yeast cells must contain some chemical substance that can cause fermentation to take place either inside or outside the living cell. Buchner's chemical substance became known as an enzyme, meaning 'in yeast'.

What do we know about the properties and the action of enzymes?

All enzymes are protein molecules.

The smallest enzyme known has a molecular weight of about 10 000 (that is, 10 000 times as heavy as a hydrogen atom); the largest have molecular weights in the millions.

For every single chemical reaction carried out by a living organism, be it a plant cell or an animal, there is a specific enzyme that catalyses the reaction Expressed in the form of a chemical equation we can write:

$$A + B + \text{Enzyme} \longrightarrow AB + \text{Enzyme}$$

Because enzymes are not consumed by the reactions they catalyze they can be used over and over again.

Where are enzymes made in a living organism?

Enzymes are made by the individual cells of an organism. Most of the enzymes are used right inside the cells that make them but some are *secreted*[1] by the cell and they act outside the cell. For example, the enzymes that are active in digestion are made by various cells lining the alimentary canal but they act inside the lumen of the canal.

Although there are many, many different kinds of enzyme catalyzing many different reactions, all enzymes have certain basic characteristics in common. We can illustrate some of these characteristics through the following simple experiments.

A convenient enzyme for you to use is **salivary amylase**, produced by the **salivary glands** and secreted into the mouth. The function of salivary amylase is to initiate the digestion of starch into sugar as the food is being chewed in the mouth. A simple way to illustrate the action of this enzyme is to chew a piece of bread or biscuit which does not contain sugar. After a short time a sweetish taste will be noticeable, indicating that some of the starch contained in the food has been converted into sugar.

[1] *secreted*: passed out of the cell

EXPERIMENT TO ILLUSTRATE SOME OF THE PROPERTIES OF ENZYMES

Materials
elastic band
distilled water
starch powder
Benedict's solution
iodine
teat pipettes
37°C water bath

Note: the following experiments are fairly complicated and they require fast and accurate work on your part. The best thing to do is to divide the various tasks among the members of your group. One person can be the timer, another can remove the samples for testing and the third can perform the tests and record the results.

Method

a. Collection of saliva

1. Rinse out your mouth with distilled water to eliminate any food particles.
2. Chew on a clean elastic band for a few minutes to promote the flow of saliva, then collect as much saliva as you can. Rinse your mouth with a small amount of distilled water and add to the saliva.
3. Transfer the saliva to a test-tube and place it in a 37°C water bath.

b. Preparation of starch suspension

1. Dissolve 1 g starch powder in 100 cm^3 boiling water. Allow to cool to 37°C.

c. Digestion of starch by saliva

1. Label two tubes A and B and place 1 cm^3 starch in each. Into a third tube, labelled C, put 1 cm^3 distilled water.
2. Prepare nine tubes each containing 1 cm^3 Benedict's solution and nine tubes containing a few drops of iodine solution. Set these aside.
3. Add 1 cm^3 saliva to tubes A and C prepared in step 1, and 1 cm^3 distilled water to tube B. Mix well by hitting the tubes against the palms of your hand. Note the time.
4. Immediately after mixing, that is at time 0, remove five drops from each of samples A, B, and C (using a separate teat pipette for each sample) to test for sugar using the prepared tubes of Benedict's solution. At the same time remove five drops of solution to test for starch using the iodine you have prepared.
5. Repeat the tests after 30 seconds and 60 seconds.
6. Enter your results in a table such as the one on p. 69. You can arbitrarily indicate the amount of sugar present in your samples on the basis of the colour obtained in the Benedict's test.

clear blue —— no sugar —— –
greenish, slightly turbid —— some sugar —— +
emerald green —— more sugar —— + +
orange-green —— more sugar —— + + +
bright orange —— more sugar —— + + + +

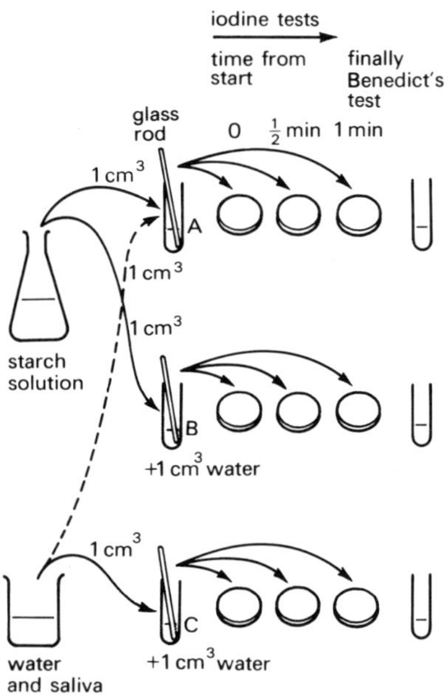

Table of results

	STARCH				SUGAR		
	Time	0time	2min	5min	0time	2min	5min
Tube Contents							
A starch + saliva							
B starch + water							
C water + saliva							

Why do you need to set up tubes B and C?
What conclusion can you reach on the basis of this experiment concerning the action of saliva on starch?

Discussion

At the end of the five-minute period a considerable amount of sugar can be detected in tube A while no sugar can be detected in either tubes B or C. It seems that saliva contains some agent which is able to break down starch into glucose. The negative results obtained in sample B indicate that starch would not change into glucose simply by being heated to 37°C and the results in sample C assure us that the saliva used did not contain any glucose.
The agent contained in saliva is, of course, salivary amylase. The efficiency of the enzyme in breaking down starch is shown by the speed with which the reaction takes place. Recall that in order to split starch with hydrochloric acid you had to boil the mixture for fifteen minutes. The enzymes, however, started to act within two minutes at 37°C.

EXPERIMENT TO DEMONSTRATE THE EFFECT OF DIFFERENT TEMPERATURES ON THE ACTION OF AN ENZYME

Materials

saliva
starch suspension (prepared as in the previous experiment)
Benedict's solution
iodine solution
water baths at 25°C, 37°C and 60°C
ice bath at approximately 4°C

Method

Since the controls containing saliva and water and starch and water were already shown to give negative results in the previous experiment, you need not repeat them. The work could be split up among the class so that each group performs the experiment at only one or two temperatures.

1. Prepare 15 tubes containing Benedict's solution and 15 tubes containing iodine and set them up in separate racks as shown in the flow chart.
2. Label 5 tubes A, B, C, D, E.
3. Into each tube, place 1cm^3 starch suspension.
4. Place tube A into the ice bath, tube B into the 25°C water bath,

tubes C and E into the 37°C water bath and tube D into the 60° water bath.

5. Boil about 2cm³ saliva for 10 minutes.

6. To tubes A, B, C and D add 1cm³ fresh saliva. To tube E add 1cm³ saliva that has been boiled.

7. Mix the solutions in the tubes and note the time.

8. Test each sample for sugar and starch at time 0, 2 minutes and 5 minutes using the tubes of solutions you have set aside. Make certain that you use the same number of drops of sample in each case.

9. Summarize your results in a table like the one below.

Table of results

	SUGAR	STARCH
Temperature	0 time 2min 5min	0 time 2min 5min
4°C		
25°C		
37°C		
60°C		
boiled saliva at 37°C		

What can you conclude from the above results concerning the effect of temperature on the reactivity of an enzyme?

What is the effect of boiling?

Discussion

Salivary amylase, like other enzymes, seems to act best in a narrow temperature range around 37°C. Boiling destroys the activity of the enzyme.

The effects of enzyme concentration and pH

Experiments similar to the two you have just performed can be devised to illustrate the effect of enzyme concentration and pH on the activity of enzymes. The speed of an enzyme-catalysed reaction increases as more and more enzyme is added to the reaction mixture. That is, if it takes 1cm³ saliva 10 minutes to turn a sample of starch completely into glucose then by adding 2cm³ enzyme the process will be completed in half the time. Most enzymes seem to act best within a narrow pH range around pH 7, that is, in the neutral range. Both a lower pH (acid medium) and a higher pH (alkaline medium) reduce the efficiency of most enzymes. Lowering the pH to 3 or 2 for prolonged periods of time permanently destroys the activity of most enzymes.

One exception to this rule is the group of digestive enzymes found in the mammalian stomach. These act most efficiently at an acid pH of around 2. (See p. 75.)

Summary

Holozoic feeders are in need of a digestive system both to break down the particles of food eaten into small enough units for entry into the body proper and for the elimination of toxic substances from the food.

The breakdown of the complicated organic molecules contained in the food is achieved through the action of biological catalysts called enzymes. Enzymes are protein molecules synthesized by living cells. Their function is to catalyse biological reactions so that they can take place at the relatively low temperatures and pressures found inside living organisms. Most enzymes act best at a temperature of around 37°C and a pH of 7. As the concentration of an enzyme increases the speed of the reaction it catalyses also increases up to a certain limit.

Most enzymes will be inactivated by very high temperatures.

The mammalian digestive system

As with the other systems of the body, the best way to gain an understanding of the individual structures of the digestive system and their relation to each other is to study a dissected specimen.

Fig. 1.60 shows a diagrammatic view of the digestive system of a rabbit and fig. 1.61 is a corresponding diagram of the human digestive system. Fig. 1.62 shows a dissected rat.

Even at first glance you can see that, except for variations in relative size, the organization of the digestive systems in rabbits and in humans is very similar.

Food is taken into the **mouth**, is chewed and mixed with saliva and then passes down the **oesophagus** into the **stomach**. At intervals of two or three hours food is allowed to pass from the stomach into the **small intestine** through the **pyloric sphincter**. Ducts leading from the **gall bladder** and the **pancreas** are situated at the upper part of the small intestine.

After food has passed along the length of the small intestine it enters the **large intestine**. At the junction of the small and large intestines is a blind pocket called the **caecum** ending in a short extension, the **appendix**.

The small and large intestines are held in place against the dorsal body wall by a membrane called the **mesentery**. The final parts of the system are the **rectum** and the **anus**, controlled by the **anal sphincter**.

The **alimentary canal** can be thought of as a very efficient assembly line. As food passes from one part to the next, changes take place at every point until all useful chemicals have been extracted and have passed into the body. Waste materials pass through the entire length of the system to be egested.

Now let us look at the parts of the digestive system in more detail.

The mouth

While within the mouth, the food is chewed and mixed with saliva. Saliva is secreted by pairs of **salivary glands** (fig. 1.63) and passes into the mouth through a system of ducts.

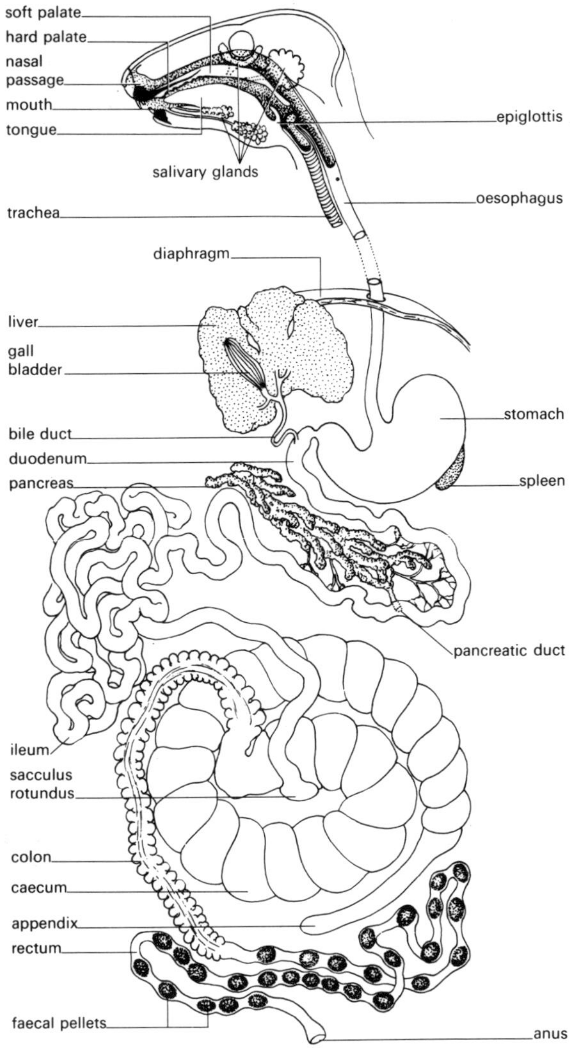

Fig.1.60 Alimentary canal of rabbit

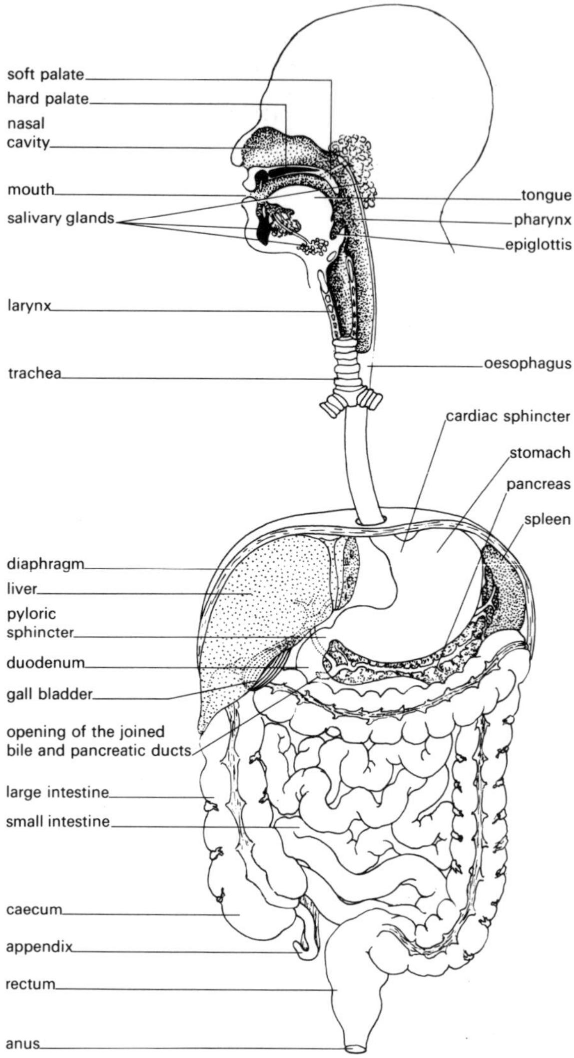

Fig.1.61 Alimentary canal of human

The salivary glands are under the control of the nervous system. The taste, sight, smell, or even the mere thought of food can trigger the passage of saliva into the mouth.

You have already performed a series of experiments to illustrate that saliva contains an enzyme called amylase (sometimes referred to as **ptyalin**) which catalyses the breakdown of starch into sugar. Saliva also acts as a lubricant to facilitate the swallowing of solid food. It contains a slimy carbohydrate-protein called **mucin** which forms the food into a compact mass or **bolus**.

As the bolus of food reaches the back of the mouth it has two passages open to it: the oesophagus and the trachea. To ensure that food does not pass into the trachea, swallowing involves a complex series of movements that result in the closing off of this passage.

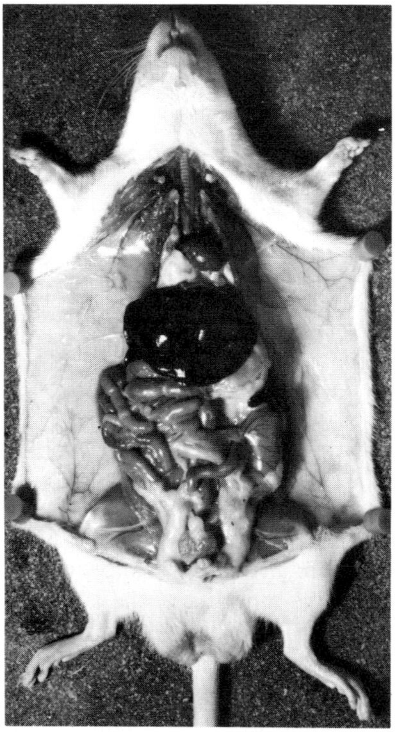

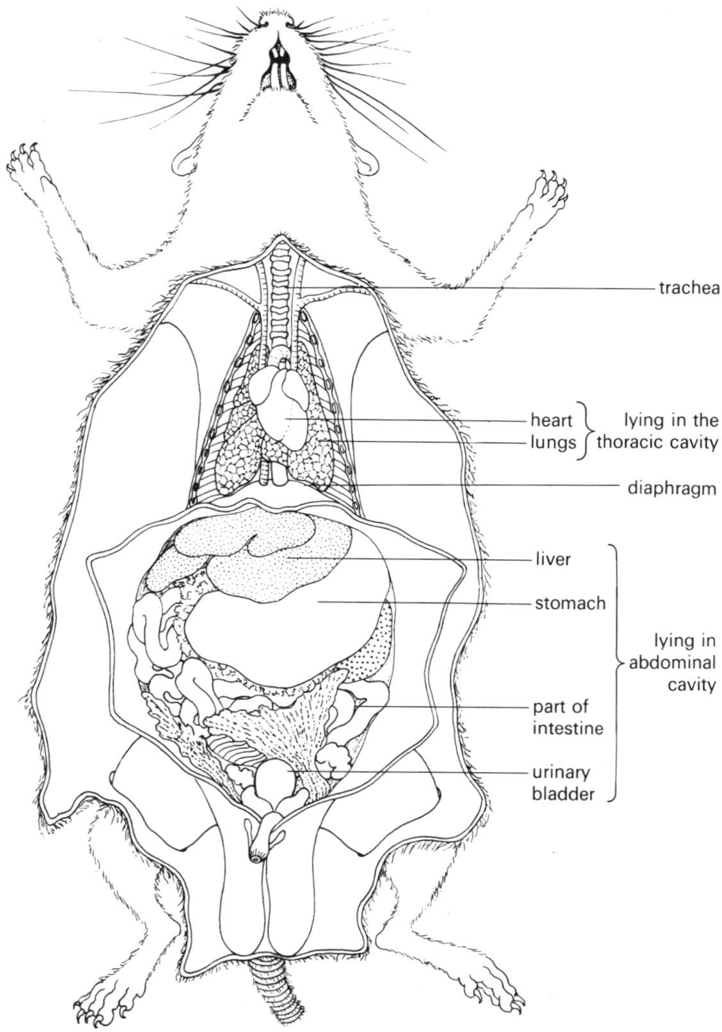

Fig.1.62 Some principal organs seen in a ventral dissection of the rat

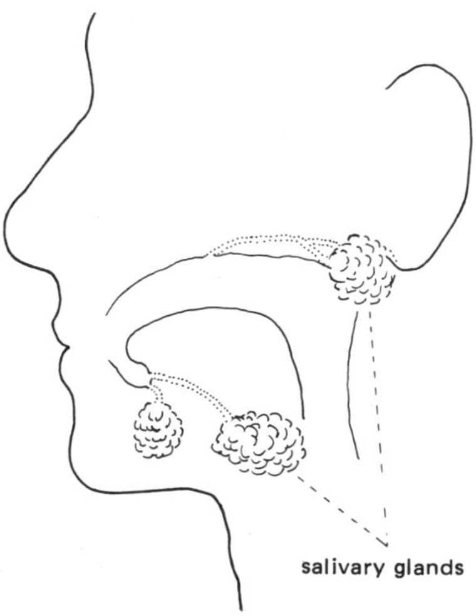

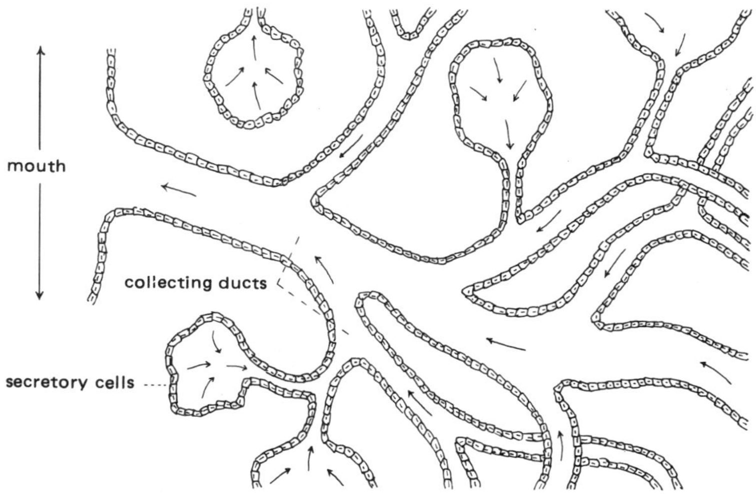

Fig.1.63 Organization of human salivary glands

Fig.1.64

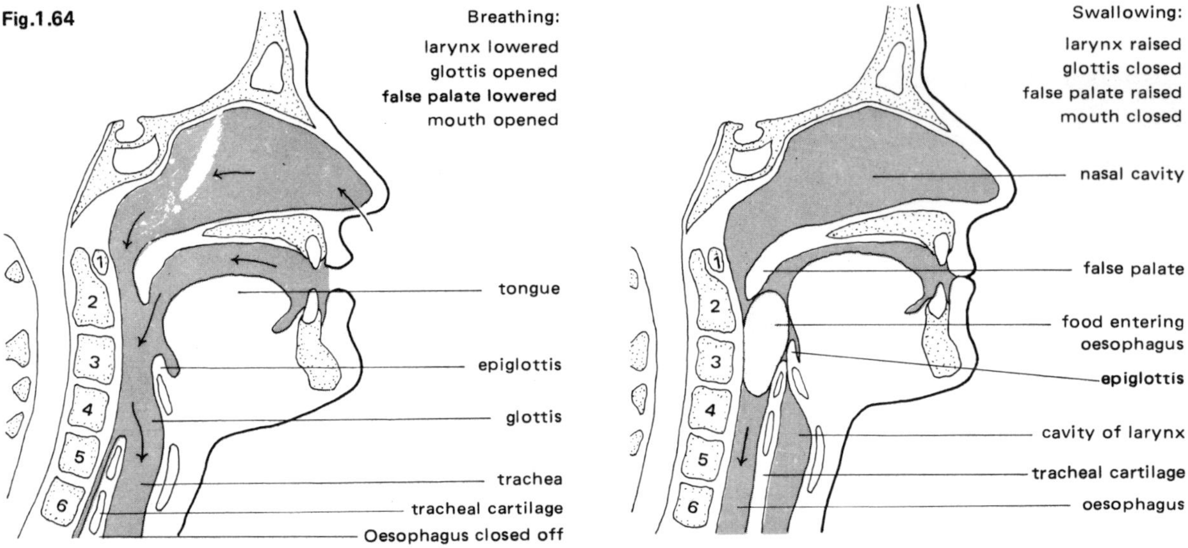

Examine fig. 1.64. The drawing on the left shows the relative positions of the two passages during breathing. During swallowing the tongue is pressed against the roof of the mouth and the larynx is raised so that the opening of the trachea is forced against the **epiglottis** (see right-hand drawing). The result is that the food has to pass down the now widened oesophagus. (If you place your hand on your throat at the spot commonly referred to as the Adam's apple you can feel the up-and-down movements of the larynx during swallowing.)

How does the food pass down the oesophagus?

Once in the oesophagus the food rapidly passes down into the stomach. It does not simply slide down the passage but is helped along by a series of muscle movements called **peristalsis**.

Peristalsis is essentially a wave of muscular contraction and relaxation of the circular muscles lining the oesophagus. The wave of relaxation is just ahead of the bolus of food, while the wave of contraction is just behind. The result is that the food is moved along the passage into the stomach.

The process of peristalsis is initiated by the presence of food in the lumen (passageway) of the oesophagus. The bolus of food exerts a pressure on the walls and this stimulates the nerve endings present.

What happens to the food in the stomach?

The stomach is located in the upper part of the abdominal cavity immediately beneath the diaphragm. The walls of the organ are lined with three separate layers of **involuntary muscle**. These muscles are responsible for churning the contents of the stomach to produce a semi-liquid substance called **chyme**.

Fig.1.65 **Peristalsis**

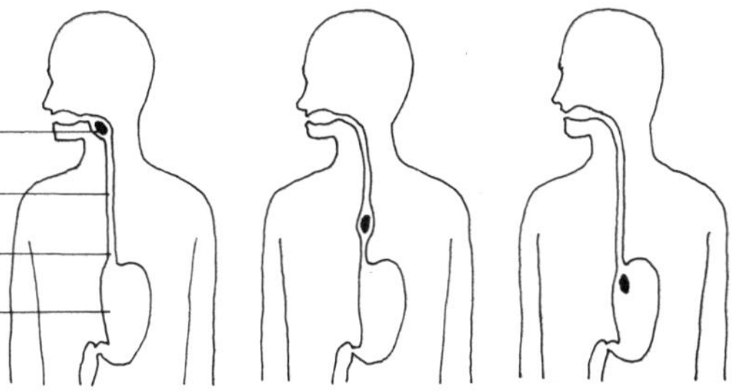

As food enters the stomach it becomes arranged in layers around the walls, with the latest entry in the middle. The stomach wall contains glands that produce and secrete a dilute solution of hydrochloric acid; as a result the pH of the stomach contents is in the region of 1 or 2.

A second set of glands secretes gastric juice, containing two proteases[1], namely **pepsin** and **rennin**. In the acidic medium of the stomach pepsin is able to catalyse the splitting of large protein molecules into smaller polypeptide fragments known as **peptones**. The action of rennin is to *coagulate* casein, the protein found in milk products.

The connection between the stomach and the small intestine is controlled by a ring of circular muscle called the pyloric sphincter.

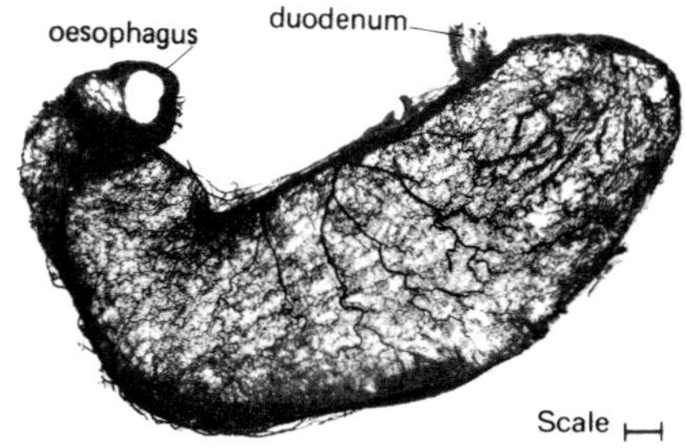

Fig.1.66 Stomach of man

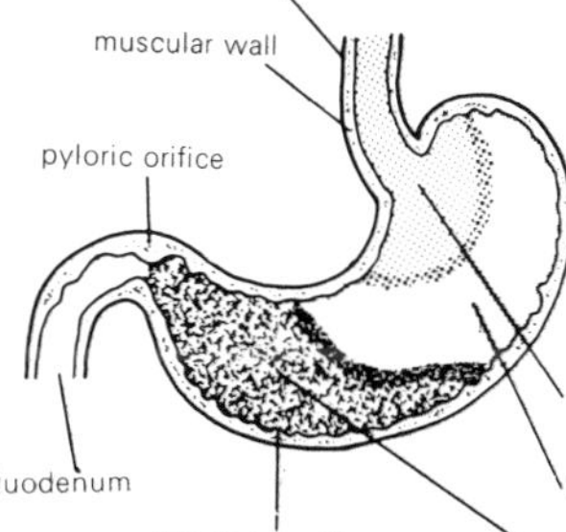

Fig.1.67 Digestion in the stomach

Why is the pyloric sphincter necessary?

If this passage at the lower end of the stomach were open all the time, due to the vigorous churning action of the stomach, food would be continually leaking out into the small intestine. Chances are that most of the food would leave the stomach before the process of digestion was completed.

When the muscles of the pyloric sphincter are in a contracted state, however, the opening is completely sealed off so that leakage is not possible. Every few hours the ring of muscle relaxes and a certain amount of partially digested food is allowed to pass into the small intestine.

The pancreas

The pancreas is an elongated structure situated directly beneath the stomach. The gland serves two distinct functions and, correspondingly, contains two distinct types of cell.

One group of cells synthesizes and secretes the hormones **insulin** and **glucagon** into the blood stream. These two hormones are important in the regulation of the sugar content of the blood. (See pp. 83, 162.)

The second group of cells secretes **pancreatic juice**, a digestive liquid that is passed into the upper part of the small intestine through the

[1] *protease*: an enzyme that catalyses the breakdown of protein

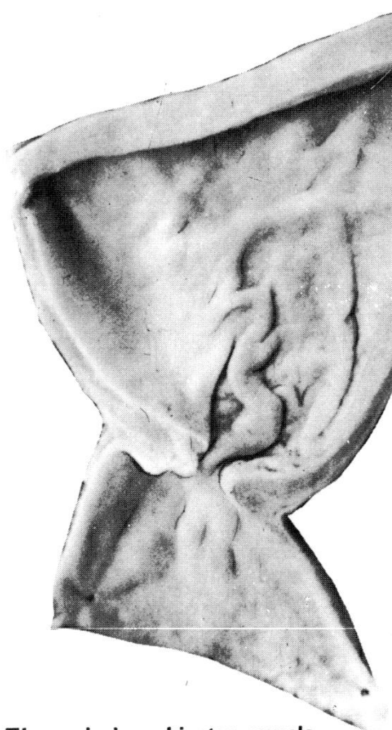

Fig.1.68 The pyloric sphincter muscle

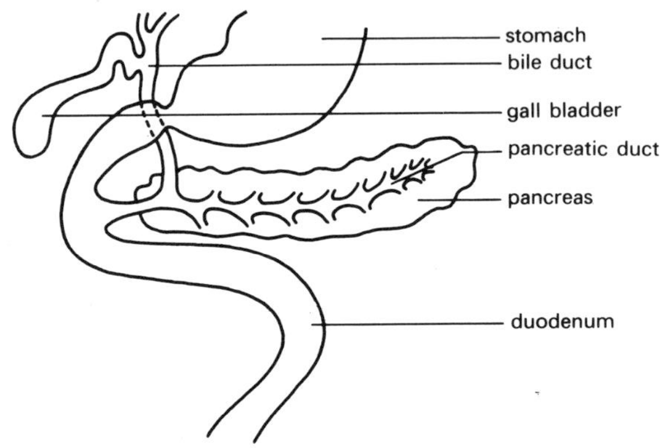

Fig. 1.69 Duodenum and pancreas

pancreatic duct. Pancreatic juice contains the following substances.
1. **Sodium bicarbonate**. Due to the presence of hydrochloric acid in the stomach, the chyme passing into the small intestine is highly acidic. Since the enzymes acting in the small intestine cannot function in an acid medium the chyme must be neutralized by sodium bicarbonate.
2. **Pancreatic amylase** to digest starch into the disaccharide maltose.
3. A **lipase** to digest fatty substances into fatty acid and glycerol. Lipase can only act after the fats have been emulsified[1] by the bile salts (see below).
4. **Proteases**. Two different proteases are found in pancreatic juice to continue the digestion of proteins and peptones.
5. **Nucleases**. These enzymes are able to digest any nucleic acids that might be found in the food.

The secretion of pancreatic juice is stimulated by the entry of food into the small intestine.

The liver

The liver, strictly speaking, is not an organ concerned with digestion but its secretion of **bile** does play a vital role in the digestion of lipids. Bile is continually being produced by the liver; when not

[1] *emulsify*: to make a substance that cannot be dissolved into a suspension

needed it is stored in the gall bladder. The entry of chyme into the small intestine stimulates the gall bladder to release the bile, which then passes into the small intestine by way of the **bile duct**. Bile contains important substances called **bile salts** that are able to emulsify lipid molecules into particles small enough for the pancreatic lipases to act on. It also contains bile pigments that are the waste materials from the breakdown of haemoglobin in the liver. The characteristic brownish colour of faeces is due to the presence of these bile pigments.

The action of bile salts can be demonstrated in the following way: Fill a jar with water and add some oil. Shake the liquid to mix the water and oil. You will find that the oil always separates to the top. Now add a little liquid detergent and shake again. This time the oil will be broken up into small droplets that are suspended in the water. The liquid detergent has emulsified the oil.

The liver acts as a storage organ for the digested material and distributes this material to the rest of the body as required. Without this action of the liver the circulatory system and the cells of the body would be flooded with digested food material immediately after a large meal but would be lacking vital materials if no food was eaten for several hours.

What are the functions of the small intestine?

The main function of the upper part of the small intestine, the **duodenum**, is digestion; that of the lower part, the **ileum**, is absorption.

The duodenum receives the secretions of bile and pancreatic juice and in addition its walls secrete a third digestive component called

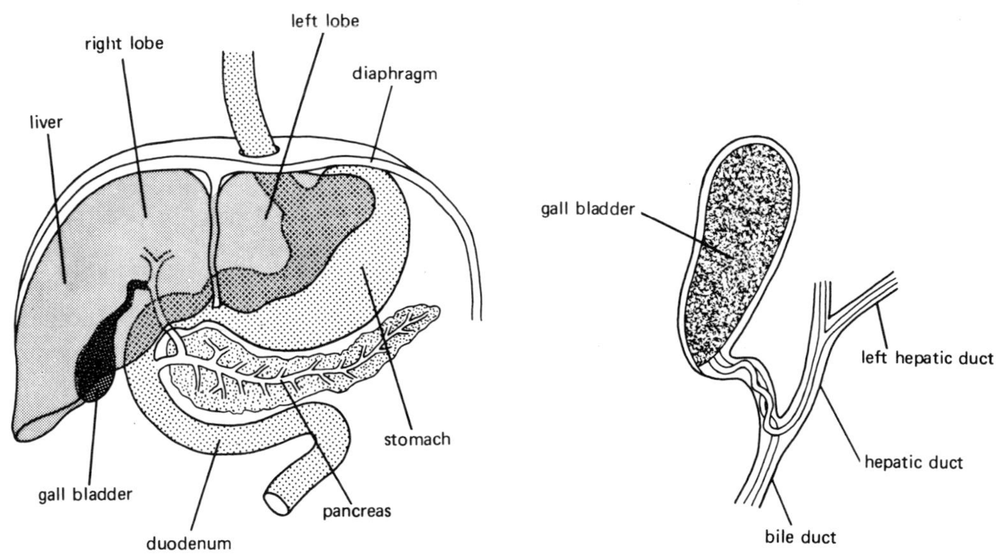

Fig.1.70 Liver and gall bladder

intestinal juice. It contains enzymes that break down disaccharides to monosaccharides and an enzyme to hydrolyse any remaining peptide bonds to yield single amino acids. By the time the food has passed the length of the duodenum digestion is complete and the food is ready to pass into the body proper. Of course there is no fixed point along the small intestine where digestion stops and absorption begins; the two functions overlap to a great degree.

The inner wall of the small intestine is covered with countless finger-like projections called **villi** (singular: **villus**). They give the surface an appearance similar to that of a thick pile rug. If you examine the intestinal wall of a freshly killed mammal with a hand lens you will be able to see the villi.

What functions do these strange projections serve?

The cells secreting intestinal juice are located at the base of the villi and the enzymes act on and between the structures.

An even more significant function is that of increasing the surface area of the small intestine to make the process of absorption faster and more efficient. As a result, the average total surface area of the

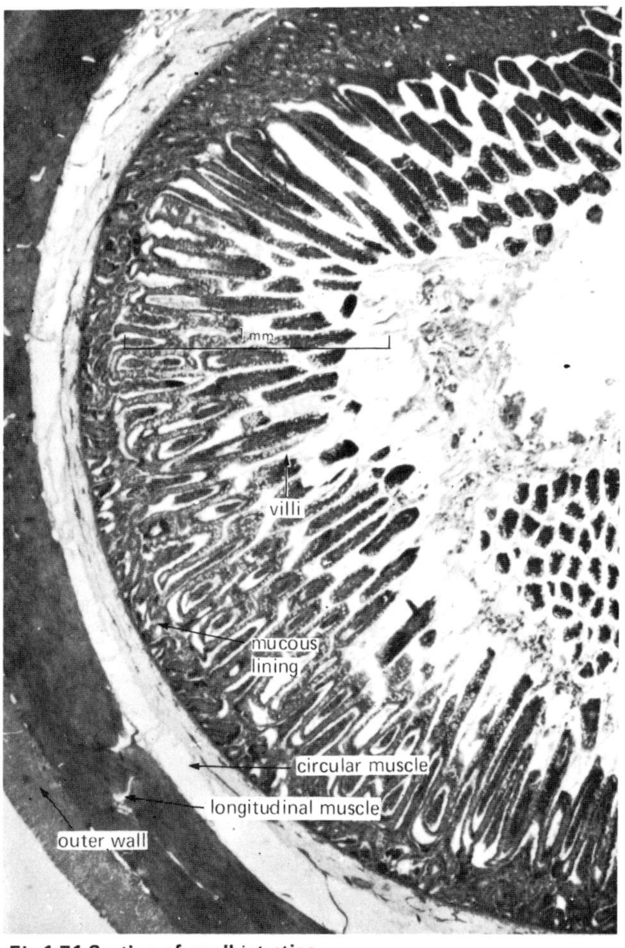

Fig.1.71 Section of small intestine

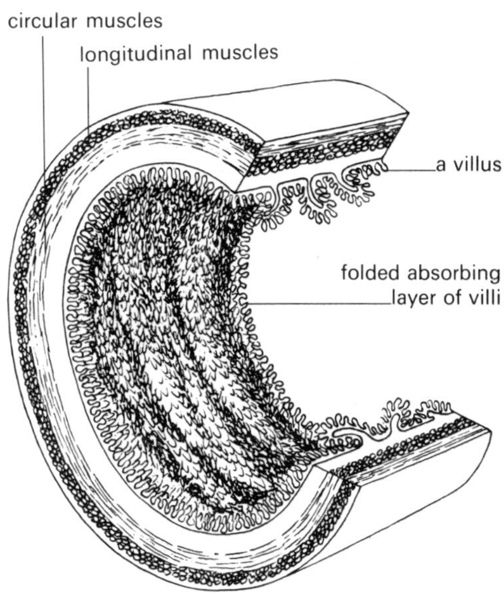

Fig.1.72 How the surface area of the gut wall is increased

small intestine in an adult human is $10 m^2$, that is, approximately five times the entire body surface area.

Why is a large surface area important for efficient absorption?

To help you understand this, consider fig. 1.73.

If the walls of the lumen were smooth as in (i) there would only be a very limited amount of space for molecules to pass through the walls. However, by having the villi projecting into the lumen the area available is greatly increased and there are many more spots where food can pass through the walls.

Each villus is supplied with an abundant network of blood capillaries and a **lymph lacteal**. Blood that has flowed into the villus through the artery is dispersed through the system of capillaries. The products of digestion—sugars, amino acids, vitamins, salts and some water—pass into the capillaries and are carried away by the blood through the outgoing vein to be taken to the liver. Fat droplets do not enter the capillaries; instead they pass into the lacteals of the lymphatic system. Since the regular blood circulatory system and the lymphatic system are connected, fatty substances too, eventually end up in the blood. (Details of the lymphatic system are discussed on p. 208.)

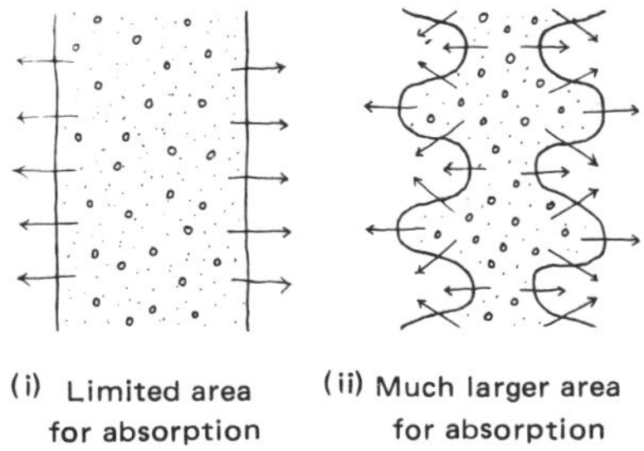

Fig.1.73

How do the food molecules get into the capillaries?

Absorption is accomplished for the most part by a simple process of diffusion. Again, using Visking tubing as a model of the gut wall will help you to understand the process.

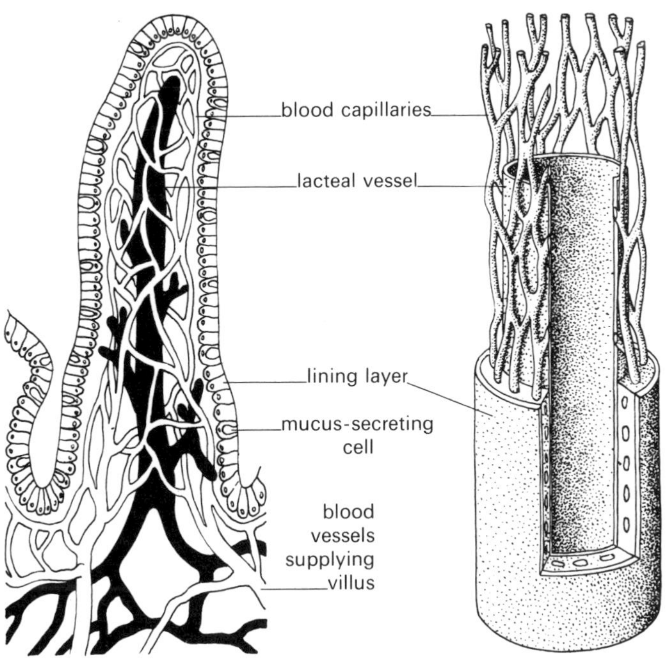

Fig.1.74 Vertical section through villus and stereogram

Fig.1.75
Simple diffusion

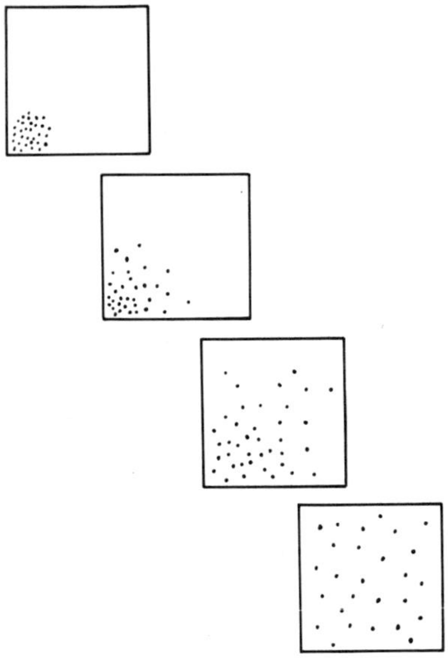

Diffusion across a membrane

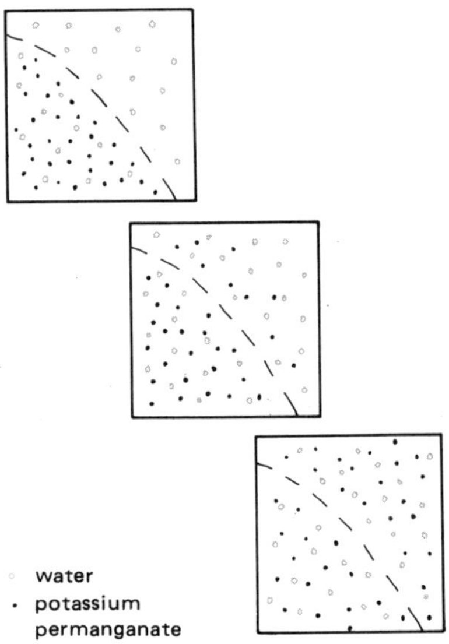

If you were to place some water that had been coloured with potassium permanganate inside the tubing and tie off the end and place the tubing in a beaker of clean water, what would you observe? Try it and see.

Diffusion is defined as the movement of particles from an area of high concentration to an area of low concentration. In your experiment, at the outset there was a high concentration of potassium permanganate inside the Visking tubing and none outside. With the passage of time more and more of the material passed through the walls until the concentrations inside and outside became approximately equal.

We can apply the same principle to the situation at the surface of a villus. Whenever there is a high concentration of a certain nutrient in the intestine and a lower concentration in the blood flowing through the vessels in the area, the nutrient will diffuse from the intestine into the bloodstream in much the same way as the potassium permanganate diffuses through the Visking tubing in the experiment described above.

Large intestine

The small intestine leads into the large intestine. At the junction of the two is the caecum, a blind pocket, and leading from it is the appendix.

The appendix is a vestigial organ, thought to have played a role in cellulose digestion in our prehuman ancestors. Its only significance in humans today is a negative one—the appendix can become seriously inflamed causing appendicitis.

Fig.1.76 Large intestine

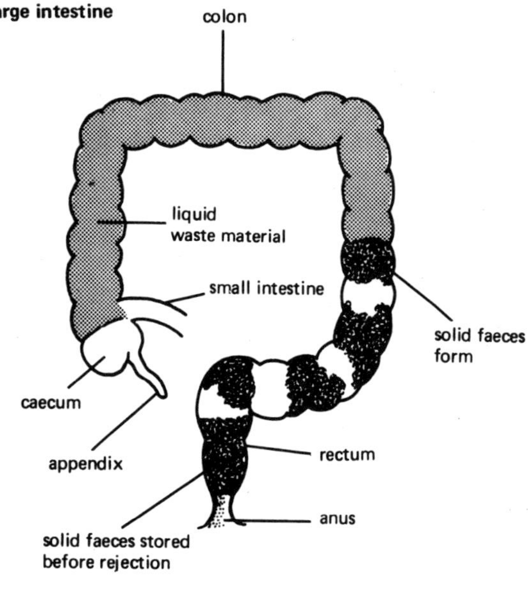

What is the content of the material that reaches the large intestine? It is residual material, left over after digestion has been completed and all useful chemical substances have been absorbed through the walls of the small intestine. It contains a large amount of water, indigestible substances such as cellulose and insignificant amounts of unabsorbed food material.

The main function of the large intestine is to reabsorb water. The various digestive juices secreted into the gut contain large amounts of water which the body cannot afford to lose or continual thirst and dehydration will result.

Irritation of the large intestine may cause discharging of waste materials before the reabsorption of water has been completed. This condition is known as **diarrhoea** and is characteristically accompanied by increased thirst.

The solidified waste material called faeces finally passes into the rectum from where it is periodically discharged from the body through the anus. This process is referred to as **egestion**. The large intestine of man and most other mammals provides a home for an enormous number and variety of micro-organisms that feed on the residual food material found in the organ. Normally, these are entirely harmless; indeed some are very useful due to their ability to

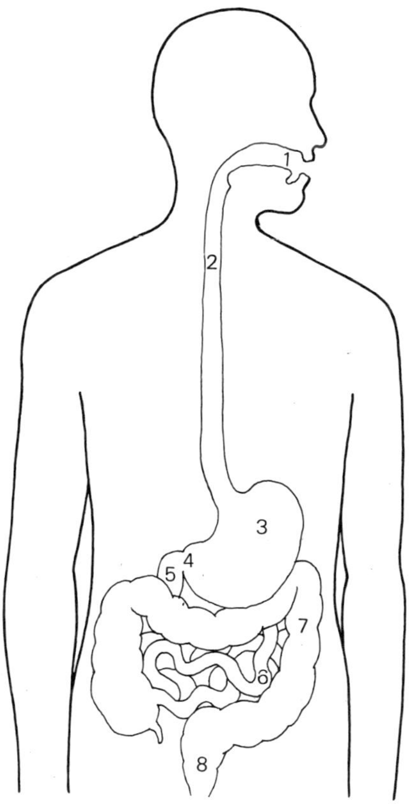

1. Mouth – taste
   chew
   mix with saliva
   starch → sugar
2. Oesophagus – passage to stomach (peristalsis)
3. Stomach – churning
   mix with gastric juice (acid)
   proteins → peptones
   casein coagulated
   cooked starch → maltose
   alcohol absorbed
4. Pyloric sphincter
5. Duodenum – acid neutralized
   pancreatic juice: proteins and peptones → amino acids
   carbohydrates (except cellulose) → simple sugars
   bile salts emulsify fats: lipase →
   fatty acids + glycerol
6. Ileum – soluble food molecules pass into blood stream
   left over fats pass into lymph
7. Large intestine – cellulose and other undigested materials
   pass through
   water is reabsorbed
8. Rectum – waste stored and periodically egested

Fig.1.77 Summary of parts of the digestive system

manufacture certain vitamins, most notably vitamin B_{12}.
At times harmful organisms may appear in the large intestine causing a variety of disease conditions ranging from simple diarrhoea to typhoid fever.

Summary

In this section we have traced the path travelled by the food we eat from the time it enters the mouth through the various stages of digestion culminating in the absorption of all usable chemical nutrients and water, and the egestion of unusable wastes.
Digestion starts in the mouth while the food is being chewed and continues in the stomach and the upper part of the small intestine.
Digestive enzymes are secreted by the cells lining the stomach and the small intestine and by the cells of the pancreas. In addition, the liver makes and secretes bile to assist in the digestion of fats.
Absorption of the digested food takes place in the lower parts of the small intestine.
The large intestine reabsorbs most of the water that has passed into the gut along with the various enzyme secretions.
Egestion takes place by way of the rectum and the anus.

Assimilation

After soluble food particles have been absorbed into the bloodstream they are ready to be transported to all the body cells to be assimilated.

Blood vessels

Fig.1.78 Relationship of blood vessels to small intestine

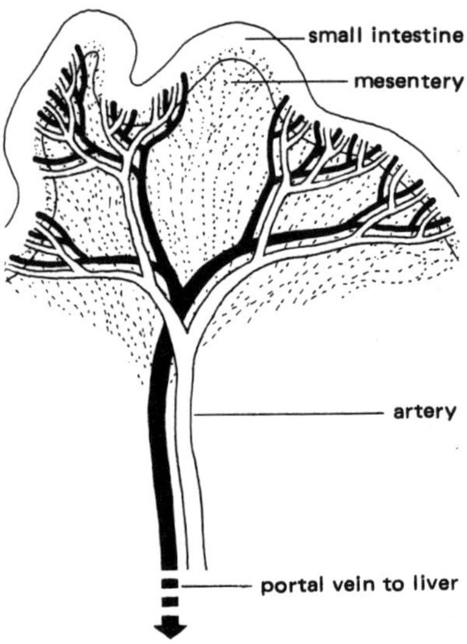

When we examined the digestive system of the mammal we observed the presence of a membrane, the mesentery, that joins the loops of the intestines and holds them in place. The blood vessels found in the mesentery are the ones through which most absorbed nutrients leave the abdominal area. The mesenteric blood vessels from the small intestine join to form the **portal vein** going to the liver.
Glucose, amino acids, mineral salts and vitamins are carried to the liver by the portal vein. From the liver they are distributed to the rest of the body and any excess can be stored by the liver for future use.
The only nutrients that cannot be stored by the body for any length of time are amino acids. Any unused amino acids are transported back to the liver and are broken down or *deaminated* by the liver cells.

Deamination of amino acids

Deamination is the removal of the amino group of the acid to yield the carbohydrate part and ammonia.

$$
2\,NH_2-\overset{\displaystyle R}{\underset{\displaystyle H}{\overset{|}{\underset{|}{C}}}}-COOH+O_2 \longrightarrow 2\,\overset{\displaystyle R}{\underset{\displaystyle O}{\overset{|}{\underset{\|}{C}}}}-COOH+2NH_3
$$

amino acid — oxygen — carbohydrate residue — ammonia

Since ammonia is extremely toxic to living cells even in small quantities it is immediately changed into a less toxic substance, **urea**. Urea is then taken to the kidneys to be eliminated from the body in the urine. The action of the kidneys in relation to the excretion of urea and other waste products is discussed in greater detail on p. 145.

The carbohydrate residue of the amino acid is utilized as a source of energy.

Storage of glucose

Glucose is the immediate source of energy for the body. In order to make glucose readily available to the body cells at any given moment the blood always contains a certain level of glucose. The cells are continually removing glucose from the blood, and the liver, under the regulatory action of the hormone *insulin* (see pp. 75, 162), releases glucose into the blood to replenish the supply.

The liver does not store glucose in its monosaccharide form but builds it up to the polysaccharide glycogen. Muscle cells too, are capable of storing small amounts of glycogen.

Fig.1.79 Distribution of amino acids by the liver

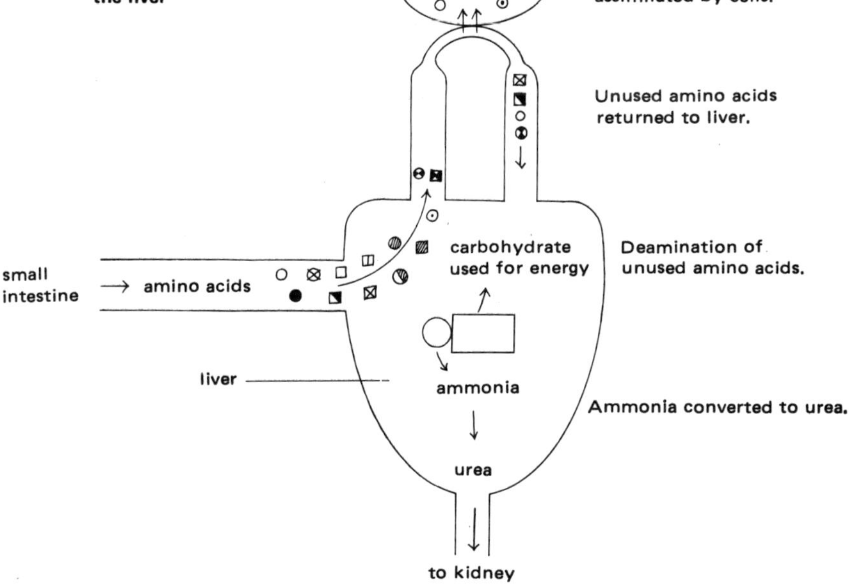

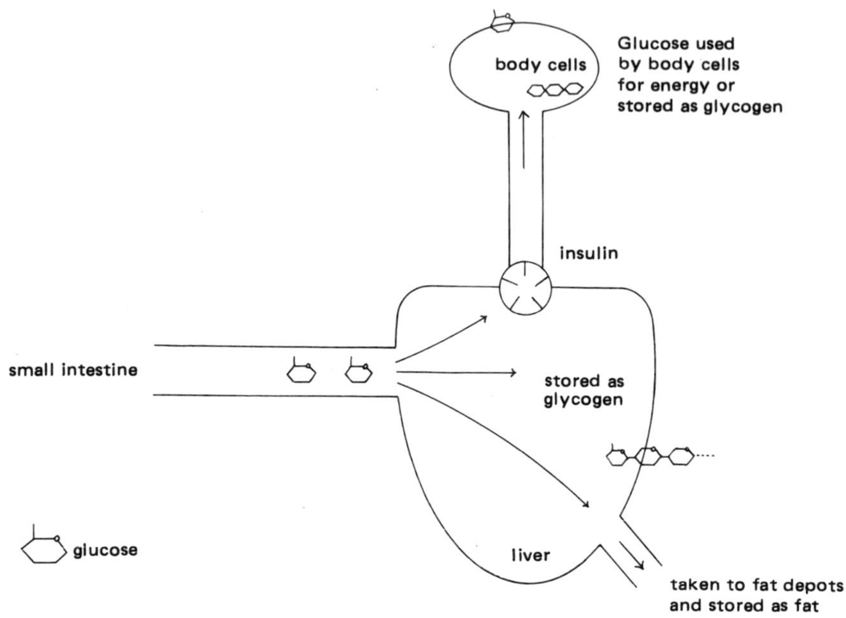

Fig.1.80 Storage and distribution of glucose

When the supply of glucose far exceeds the immediate demand leading to the problem of storage the excess is converted into fat and stored in the various fat deposits around the body.
Most inorganic salts and vitamins are stored in the liver as well.

Lipids

Lipids reach the liver by a more circuitous route. The fatty acids and glycerine that are absorbed by the small intestine pass into the lacteals of the lymphatic system. They eventually pass into the blood circulation and end up in the liver. Excess fatty substances are stored in the body's fat depots.

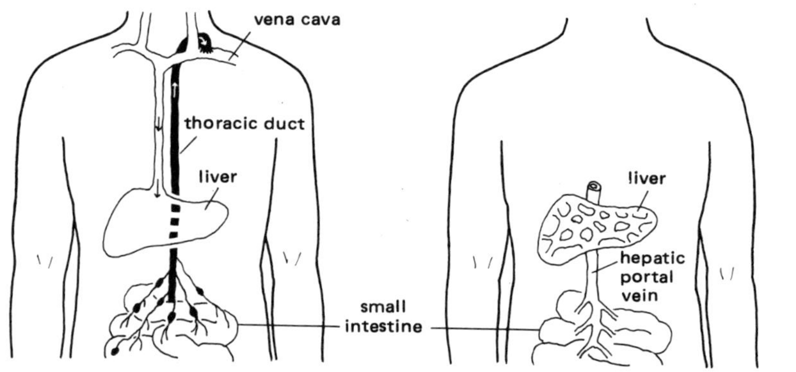

Fig.1.81 (i) Path of lipids (ii) Path of amino acids and carbohydrates

The utilization of nutrients

The energy-containing molecules are oxidized by individual cells through the process of respiration (see Section 2) and the energy released is used for various cellular processes, such as muscle contraction, carrying of nerve impulses and the synthesis of complex organic molecules.

From the absorbed nutrients cells are able to synthesize the various proteins, polysaccharides, lipids and nucleic acids that they require. As a result of this synthesis cells are able to increase in size and number—in other words, to grow. Synthesis of organic molecules, termed **anabolism**, is catalysed by enzymes.

How does anabolism take place?

When performing the various food tests in the section on nutrients you no doubt found that one of the foods that is very rich in starch is the potato. It stands to reason that if the potato tuber contains starch, its cells must contain all the necessary enzymes to assemble starch molecules from glucose. The first step in the synthesis of starch from glucose is turning the glucose into an activated form called **glucose-1-phosphate**.

EXPERIMENT TO DEMONSTRATE THE SYNTHESIS OF STARCH BY ENZYMES FROM POTATO CELLS

Materials

potato
liquid agar
glucose-1-phosphate
iodine solution
mortar and pestle

Method

a. Preparation of agar plates

Agar is a carbohydrate extract from seaweed. It is liquid at temperatures above 50°C but solidifies to form a jelly at room temperature.

1. Mix 20cm^3 liquid agar with 2cm^3 glucose-1-phosphate solution and pour onto two sterilized petri dishes. Quickly replace the cover and set aside to solidify.
2. Using a small cork borer or the end of a teat pipette punch four small holes in the agar. (If you connect a teat pipette to a suction pump you will be able to suck up small pieces of agar.)

b. Preparation of the potato extract

1. Pare a small potato and cut it into pieces. Grind it up with a mortar and pestle or mash it up with a fork. The addition of a small amount of clean sand will help to break up the tissue.
2. Add enough water to make a runny mixture.
3. Either drain the liquid into a pair of centrifuge tubes and centrifuge at high speed for five minutes or filter through a double layer of fine cheesecloth.

Fig.1.82

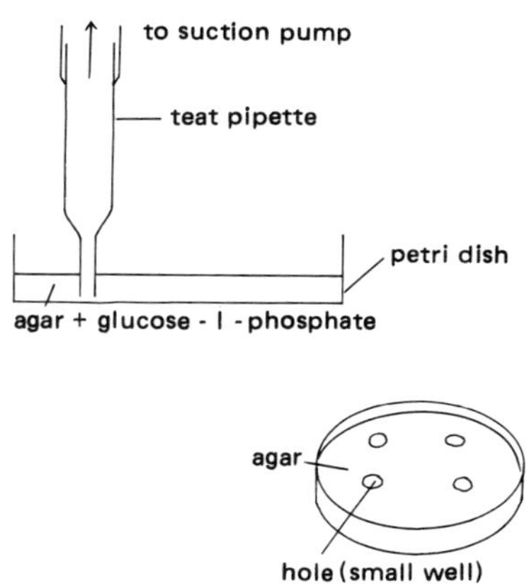

Fig.1.83

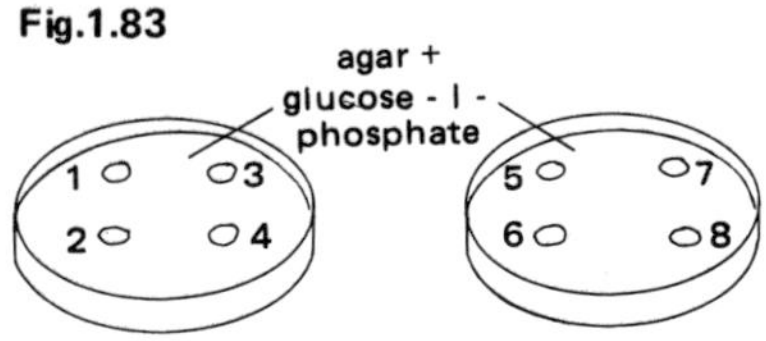

Well 8 contains water — control
Wells 1 to 7 contain potato extract

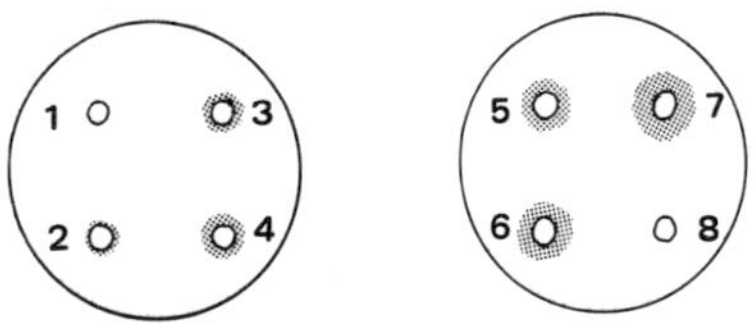

The rings of blue colour get increasingly larger showing that more and more starch has been produced
No starch is produced in 8.

4. Test the clear solution obtained with iodine to ensure that no traces of starch remain. If starch is present repeat step 3.

c. Synthesis of starch

1. Place the two agar plates in front of you. Number the wells as shown in the diagram. Into well number 8 place a drop of distilled water.
2. Into wells 1 to 7 place drops of starch-free potato extract. Fill the wells as quickly as possible and note the time.
3. At required time intervals as set out in the table below place a drop of iodine solution into each well and look for any colour change that might take place.

Well no.	1	2	3	4	5	6	7	8 (Control)
Time (min.)	1	2	5	10	15	20	25	25

Do you get a blue colour developing in any of the wells? What is the length of time required?
Why might the timing differ from one group of students to the next?
Draw a diagram of the appearance of the agar plates at the conclusion of the experiment.

Discussion

Enzymes from living cells are able to act on glucose-1-phosphate, an activated form of glucose, to build up macromolecules of starch. As shown by your control in well 8, without enzymes no starch is formed. As the enzyme preparation in the other wells diffuses through the agar and encounteres the molecules of glucose-1-phosphate more and more starch is synthesized.
The length of time required for the appearance of the first signs of starch production depends on factors such as the concentration of the enzyme preparation, that is, the amount of water you used in the preparation of the potato extract, and the amount of extract that was put into each well.
In a way similar to the synthesis of starch, cells are able to make other complex molecules such as hormones, haemoglobin for carrying oxygen in the blood, proteins for building up muscles and so on.
Some products are made for the exclusive use of the cell in question while others are made in the cell and then secreted to fulfil a function outside the cell. Some of the cells belonging to this latter group are the salivary glands that secret saliva, the cells in the walls of the stomach that secrete gastric juice and the special cells in the liver that make and secrete bile.

Excretion

Although most living organisms are very efficient in utilizing chemical substances that enter their bodies, unwanted by-products do

accumulate as a result of the various processes of synthesis and breakdown. These substances must be eliminated from the body through the process of **excretion**.
The main excretory organ of the body is the kidney (see p. 145). In addition, certain waste substances are chemically altered in the liver before being released into the bloodstream to be taken to the kidneys and some are passed into the intestine and become part of the faeces.
Most substances eliminated in the faeces, however, are indigestible materials that have never entered the body proper. These cannot be regarded as excretory products but as materials that are being egested. (See p. 81.)

Summary

Molecules of sugars, amino acids, vitamins and inorganic salts pass into the blood capillaries in the villi and are eventually taken by the portal vein to the liver.
Lipids reach the liver by way of the lymphatic system. The liver is responsible for regulating the distribution of the absorbed nutrients to the various cells. The only nutrients that cannot be stored by the body are the amino acids.
Assimilated nutrients are used by the cells either as a source of energy or as raw materials for the synthesis of complex organic compounds.
Unwanted products are eliminated by the excretory system.

Ingestion in other holozoic organisms

There are more than a million species of animal ranging in size from microscopic single-celled species to the largest mammals such as the whale. Their methods of feeding are equally varied. Some

Fig.1.84 Recycling of nutrients by holozoic organisms

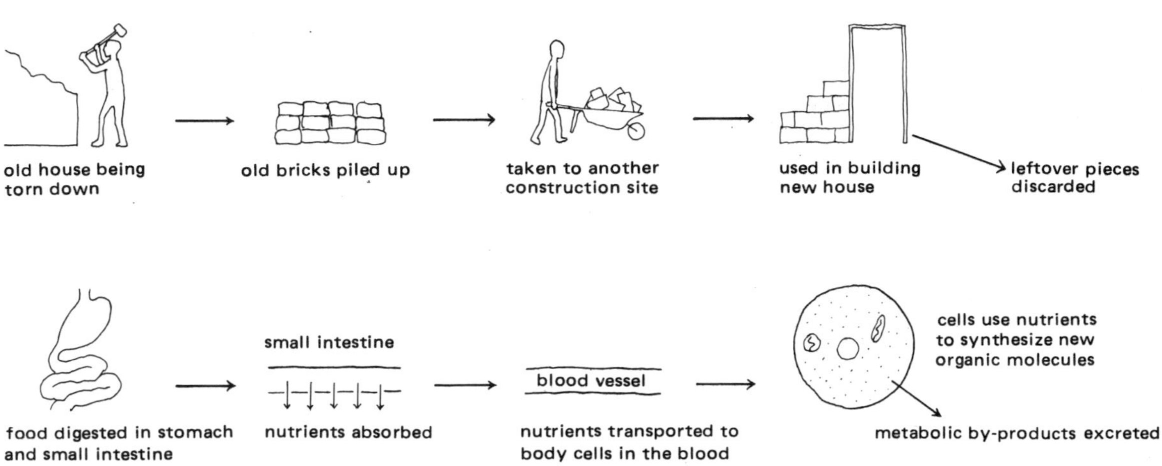

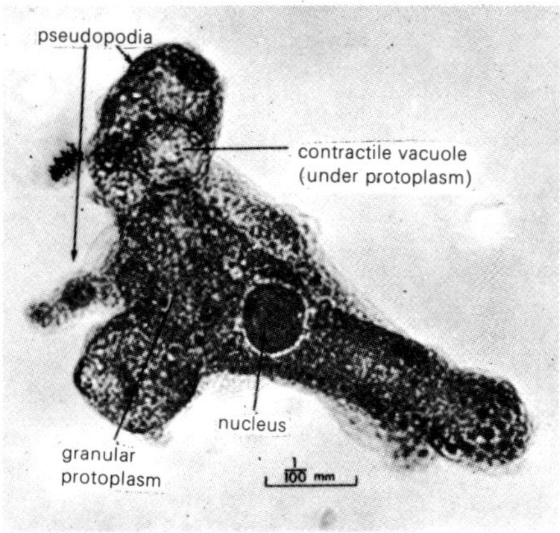

Fig.1.85 An amoeba

have no special organs for taking in food or even for digesting it. They simply float around in their watery medium and wait for particles of food to float by, which they then engulf. Large predators on the other hand pursue their prey actively, they catch it and kill it before ingesting it. We have already discussed feeding and digestion in mammals. Now let us examine some of the methods used by other organisms.

Protozoa

These are structurally the simplest animals alive. They are unicellular, that is, all life processes including respiration, feeding and reproduction are carried out by their single cell.
The most familiar example of a protozoan is the **amoeba**. The amoeba is bounded on the outside by a membrane; the interior is filled with cytoplasm and contains a single nucleus.

How does an amoeba feed?

The amoeba is able to move about by extending projections called **pseudopodia** in the direction it wants to go and flowing along as illustrated in the diagram below. When it encounters an edible food particle it simply flows around it and engulfs[1] it. You must remember that the organism is three-dimensional therefore it is able to enclose the particle from all sides. The process is called **phagocytosis**.
Once inside the cell the food is kept away from the cytoplasm by the membrane around it forming what is called a **food vacuole**. The food is digested by enzymes that are passed into the vacuole and the soluble molecules then diffuse into the cytoplasm. Indigestible parts are discharged to the outside by emptying out the food vacuole.
The food vacuole of the amoeba fulfils the same function as the much more elaborate digestive system of mammals.

Insects

Insects are one of the most varied and most numerous of all living organisms. Here we will discuss only three of the many types of feeding methods that are used by insects.

Fig. 1.86 Phagocytosis of amoeba

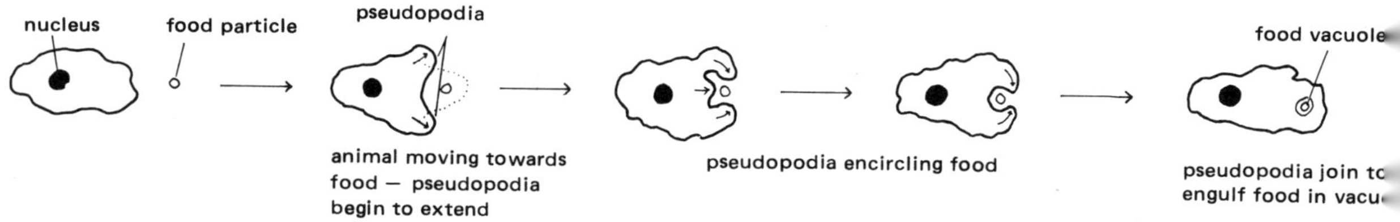

[1] *engulf*: taken inside the body, swallow

Herbivorous and omnivorous insects

Can you think of some examples of insects that feed on plants? Examples include grasshoppers, cockroaches, various beetles and so on. Plant material is usually rather tough and resistant and must be reduced to small pieces before the insect is able to ingest it.

To accomplish this many insects have very complicated mouth parts that are designed to manipulate and chew the plant material they feed on. The structures are made of protein and a hard resistant substance called **chitin**.

There are over one thousand different species of cockroach in the world. The American cockroach, *Periplaneta americana* is probably the one you are familiar with. It is an omnivore and will eat leftover bits of food, the remains of dead insects and even paper and clothing.

Examine fig. 1.89 of the cockroach. Notice the long antennae. They are sensitive to vibrations, touch and smell and play a role in finding and testing food as well as in protection. Notice also the position of the mouth parts shown in detail below. They consist of an upper lip (**labrum**), two **mandibles** equipped with teeth for cutting, two **maxillae** bearing special feelers and a lower lip (**labium**). The lower lip also bears a set of feelers that are used for testing food before ingestion.

The food is crushed and cut into pieces by the powerful mandibles while the rest of the mouth parts hold the food and help to push it into the mouth.

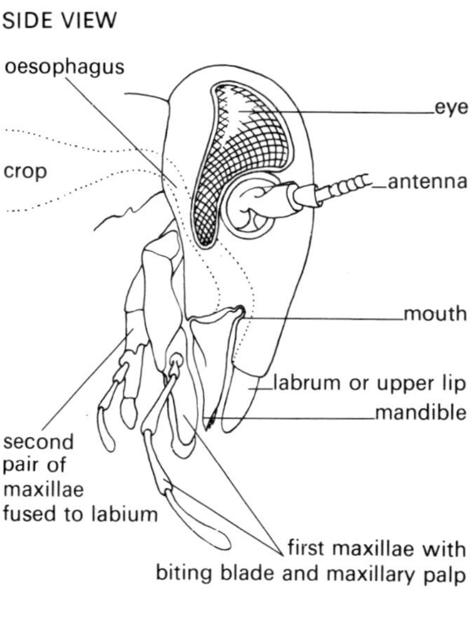

Fig.1.87 Head of a cockroach

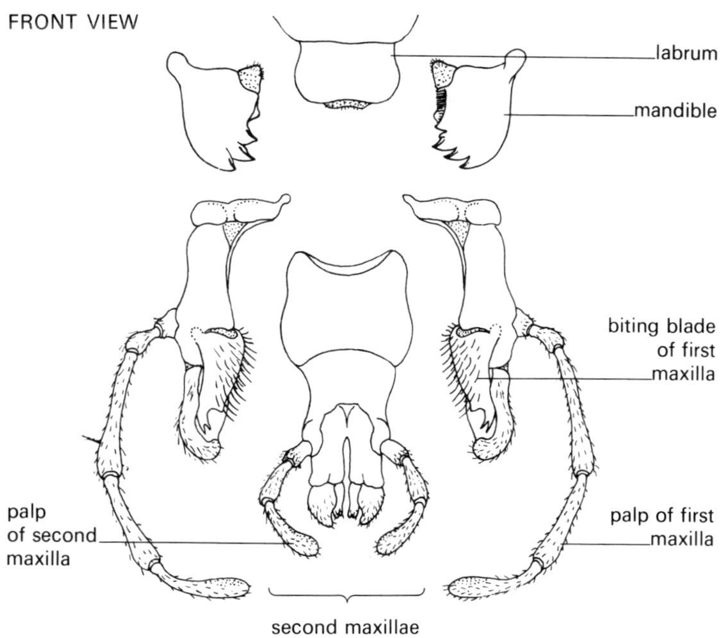

Fig.1.88 Mouth parts of a cockroach

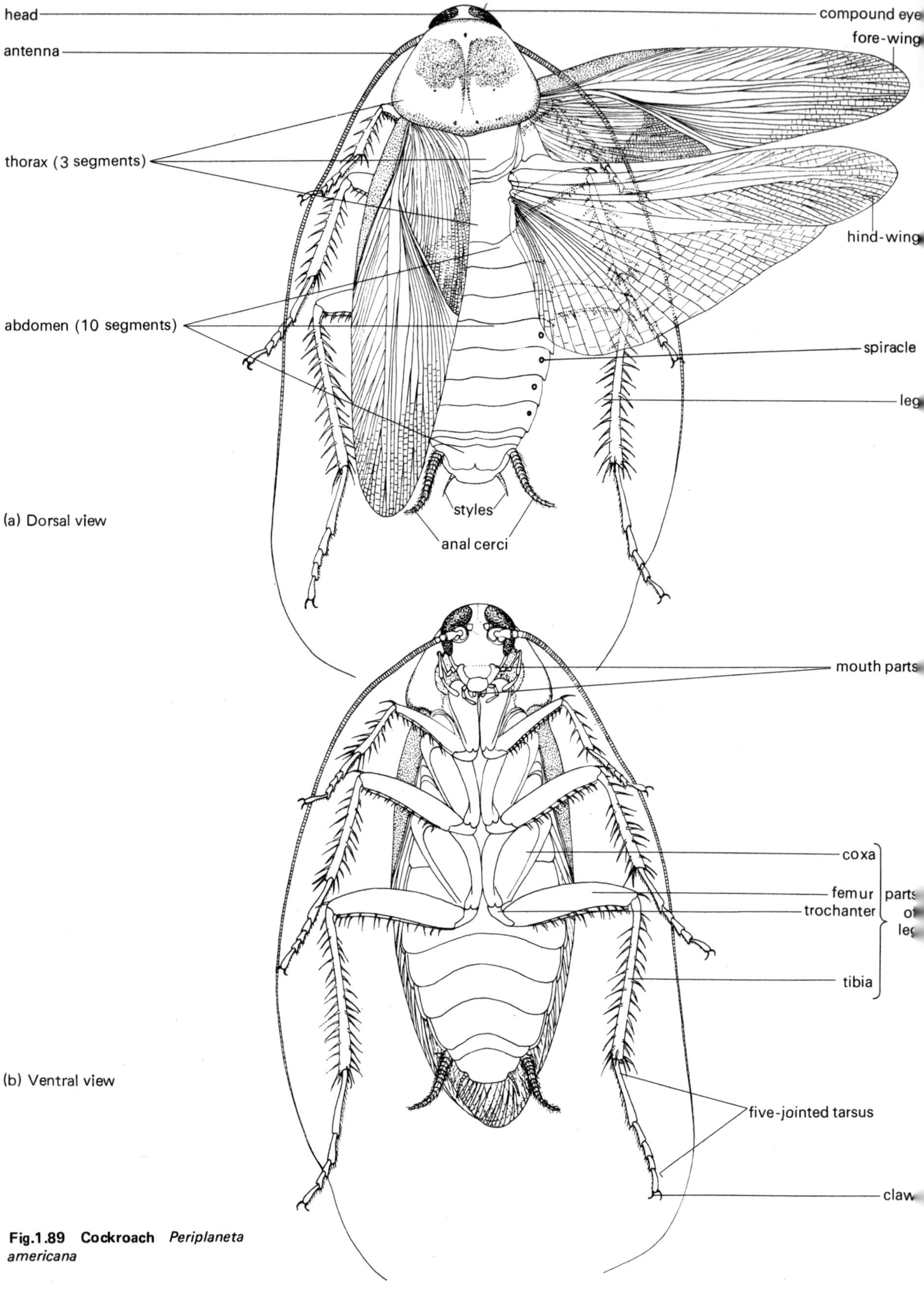

Fig.1.89 Cockroach *Periplaneta americana*

EXPERIMENT TO EXAMINE THE MOUTH PARTS OF A COCKROACH

Materials

freshly killed or preserved cockroach
dissecting needle
hand lens

Method

1. Place the insect on its back with its head pointing away from you.
2. Starting from the front end, locate the upper lip, mandibles, maxillae and the lower lip. Carefully examine with the help of the needle and the hand lens.
3. Examine the cutting edges of the mandibles.
4. With the help of fig. 1.88 examine and identify the various mouth parts.

Sucking insects

Sucking insects feed either on the blood of higher animals or on plant juices. In either case they require special adaptations for the ingestion of liquid materials.
To accomplish the sucking action necessary to remove the liquid from either the animal or the plant their mouth parts include a sharply pointed **proboscis**.

The Mosquito

In the mosquito the actual suction tube is surrounded by a group of sharp stylets that pierce the skin of the prey and a tube through which the insect's saliva flows down. The saliva contains a chemical substance that prevents blood from clotting. It is the chemicals in the saliva that are responsible for the itching and the swelling that appear at the site of a mosquito bite. Notice that, although in a greatly altered form, all the mouth parts of the cockroach are found in the mosquito as well.
It is interesting to note that only the female insect feeds on mammalian blood since some constituent of the blood seems to be necessary to enable it to lay fertile eggs. The male lives exclusively on plant juices. Since both blood and plant juices are rich in the organic substances that an animal needs to stay alive they make an ideal diet in many ways. For one thing, there is no need for a complicated digestive system because all the organic substances are present in a soluble form.

Are mosquitoes harmful to man?

In many areas of the world mosquitoes constitute a great health hazard because certain species of the insect spread malaria, yellow fever, and various other infectious diseases.

Fig.1.90 Mouth parts of a mosquito

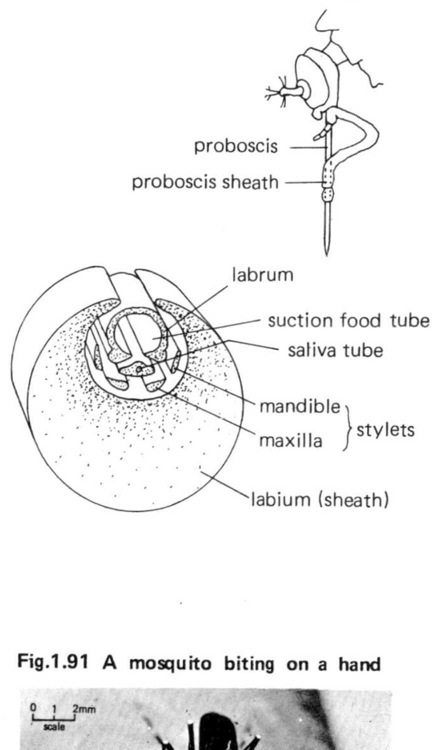

Fig.1.91 A mosquito biting on a hand

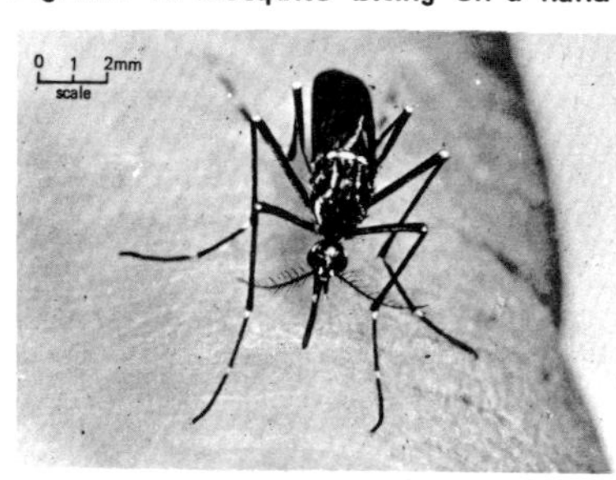

Malaria is caused by a tiny micro-organism that invades the circulatory system and destroys the red blood cells.
Yellow fever is caused by a virus that attacks the liver and the kidneys.
Both micro-organisms are spread by mosquitoes. When a mosquito bites an infected person some micro-organisms enter the body of the insect. After a period during which they multiply, the organisms pass into the salivary gland and are injected, along with the saliva, into the blood of any person that the mosquito bites.
The female mosquito lays its eggs in the water of stagnant pools and drains containing microscopic food particles. Therefore the best protection against the spread of mosquitoes is a proper drainage system and spraying streams and pools with a thin layer of oil to make them unsuitable as breeding grounds.
Although prevalent in the past, malaria has been entirely eliminated in Hong Kong, mostly through the use of stringent control measures especially in the rural areas.

Honey bee

The honey bee is one of the few insects that is not only *not* harmful to man but is of considerable value because it produces honey and also because of the role it plays in the pollination of various crops. More will be said of the habits of the honey bee as a social insect in a later section (p. 256). Here, we will restrict the discussion to its methods of feeding.

What do bees feed on?

The nectar from flowers serves as the main source of carbohydrate and water and protein is obtained from the pollen[1]. Food is collected by the female workers for the entire colony. The mouth parts of the workers are well adapted for sucking nectar. Like the mosquito, they are equipped with a proboscis with which the liquid is sucked up. When not in use, the proboscis is folded back under the head to expose the mandibles that are very much like those of the cockroach and are used for chewing pollen and manipulating the wax needed to build the hives. Only part of the nectar taken in passes down into the gut of the particular bee. Most of it is stored in the **honey stomach** from where it is regurgitated[2] when the bee gets back to the hive.
In order to assist in gathering food bees have good vision and sense of smell, as well as an extremely accurate sense of direction that enables them to return repeatedly to sources of food.

[1] *pollen*: male reproductive cell of plants see p.298

[2] *regurgitate*: bring back up from the stomach

Fig.1.92 **Food-manipulating structures of the honey bee**

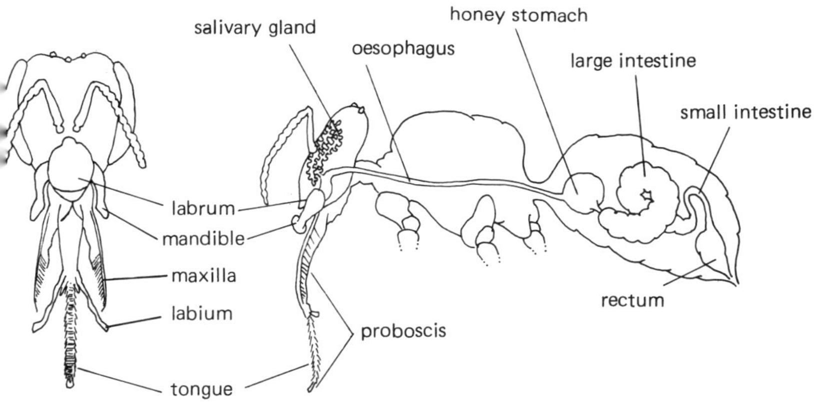

Carnivorous plants

As you already know most green plants are autotrophic organisms that can synthesize all their necessary organic molecules from raw materials obtained from the air and the soil. An exception to this rule is formed by about four hundred known species of **carnivorous plant**.

Do carnivorous plants carry out photosynthesis?

Carnivorous plants do contain chlorophyll and they are able to obtain carbohydrates through photosynthesis. However, since they all inhabit areas where the soil is deficient in nitrates their nitrogen requirements are met by feeding on small animals, mostly insects. Insects are attracted to the plants by their bright colours or the

Fig. 1.93 Venus fly trap

(a) Open

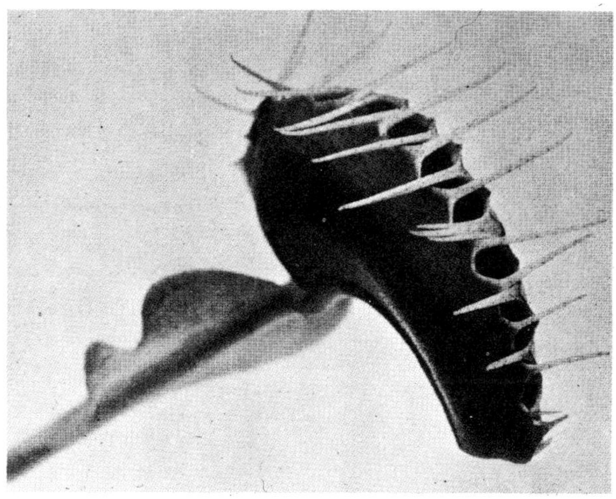

(b) Shut

Fig.1.94 Pitcher plant

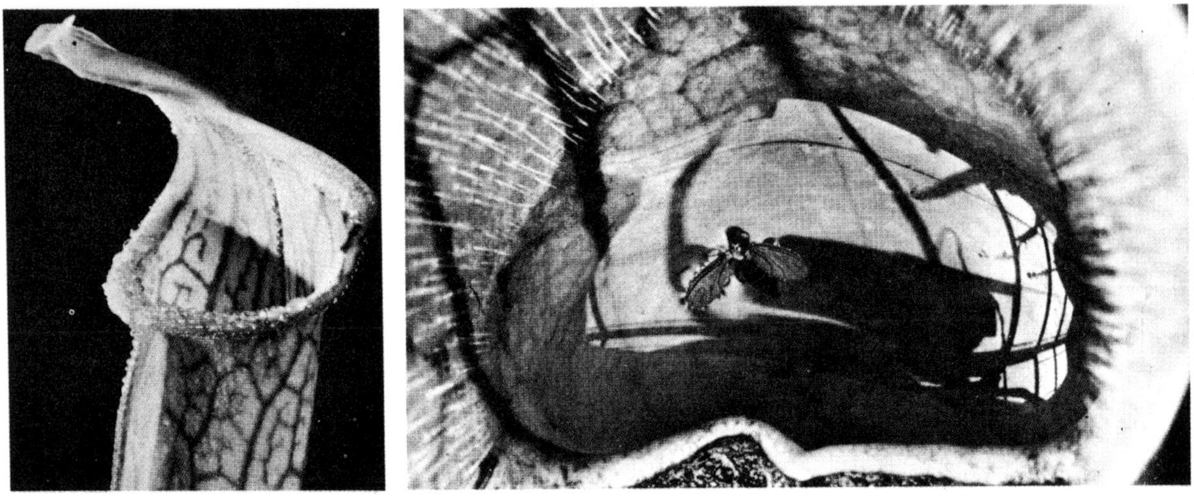

(a) The plant (b) An insect that has fallen into the pitcher

sweet-scented nectar they secrete. Once they land on the plant they are doomed.

The Venus fly-trap has interlocking leaves with long, slender spikes along the free edges. When an insect alights on their surface the two halves snap together trapping the unfortunate victim.

Digestive juices secreted by the plant kill the insect and digest its components. The amino acids released are absorbed by the plant as raw material for its protein synthesis.

Another species, the pitcher plant, has modified leaves in the form of a sac resembling a pitcher. Insects are attracted by the nectar secreted at the rim of the sac. In trying to get to it they fall into the pitcher to be digested by the pool of liquid containing digestive enzymes.

Summary

The feeding apparatus and method of catching and ingesting food by an organism is usually well adapted to the type of food eaten. Herbivorous insects have strong mandibles for chewing and grinding food while insects that feed on liquids have a proboscis for sucking. Carnivorous plants have a variety of ways for catching their prey. Simple organisms such as the unicellular protozoa have no separate digestive systems but take food into tiny food vacuoles where it is digested and the usable molecules absorbed.

Saprophytes

Saprophytic organisms take in organic materials derived from other organisms by feeding on dead and decaying organic matter. As an example of saprophytic feeders we can use the fungus *Mucor*, the common bread mould.

Fig.1.95 *Mucor* on bread

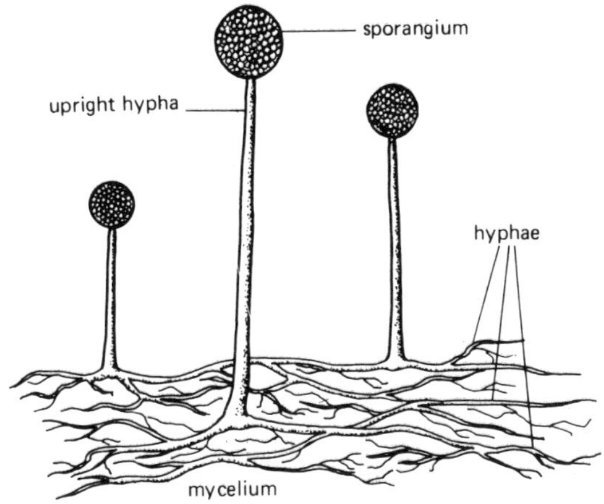

Fig.1.96 Diagram of *Mucor*

EXPERIMENT TO GROW AND EXAMINE THE FUNGUS *MUCOR*

Materials

piece of bread
covered glass dish
hand lens

Method

1. Leave bread out in the air for about a day.
2. Moisten it with a little water and place it in a covered glass dish.
3. Look for any growth that appears on the bread after a few days.
4. Examine carefully with a hand lens.
5. Make a drawing of as much of the detail as you can.

Is the growth on the surface of the bread all one colour?
Do you think there is only one or several types of fungus growing?

Discussion

You will probably find that several types of fungus are growing on the surface of the bread, some greyish and some green. If you pick out an area of greyish growth to examine you will see that the fungus is composed of delicate, thread-like **hyphae** some of which end in a short stalk supporting a spherical, black head.

How does a fungus obtain its nutrients?

The hyphae (singular: hypha) penetrate beneath the surface of the food material forming a tangled mass called a **mycelium**. These are the feeding parts of the organism. They produce and secrete onto the food enzymes that are able to break it down into soluble form that can be absorbed through the walls of the hyphae.
Waste materials diffuse out by the same route. Oxygen for respiration is also obtained by diffusion through the walls of the hyphae.

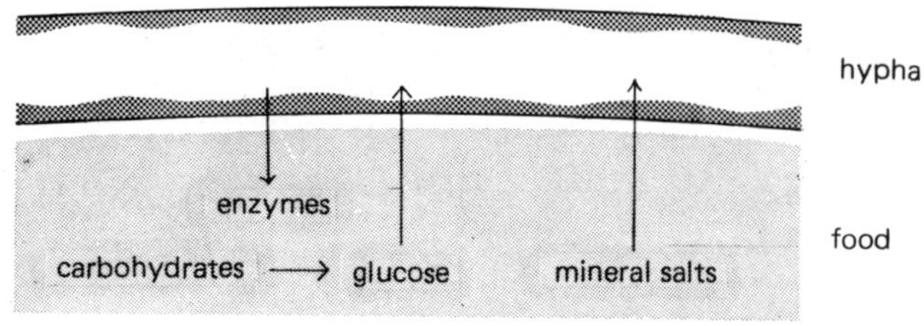

Fig.1.97 Digestion and absorption by saprophytes

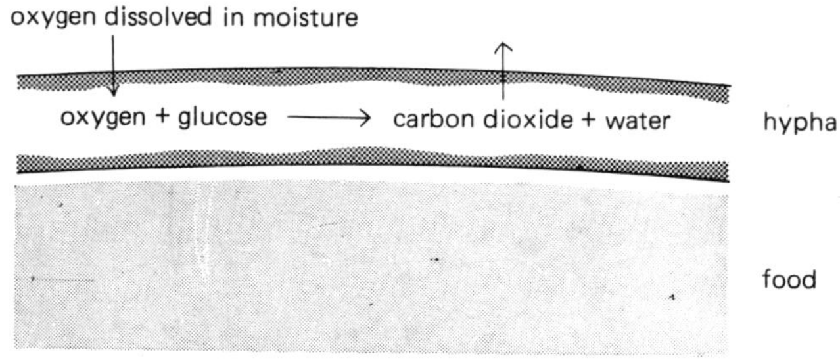

Fig.1.98 Gas exchange and respiration by saprophytes

Since oxygen supplies are vital to the organism the hyphae cannot penetrate too deeply into the food material where oxygen is no longer available.

There are many other species of saprophytic fungus including toadstools, puffballs, mushrooms and the penicillium mould, the source of the well known antibiotic penicillin.

There are also numerous species of saprophytic bacteria. All saprophytic organisms perform a very vital function in that they are the agents of decomposition of dead organic material. The chemical substances they release are then made available for re-use by other organisms.

It is important to understand that the decay of dead material cannot occur without the presence of these organisms. The final products of the collective action of the saprophytes are carbon dioxide, water, ammonia and some gaseous nitrogen.

The role of saprophytic organisms as the decomposers in food chains and in particular in the nitrogen cycle is discussed in the section on ecosystems (pp. 351, 356).

Summary

Saprophytic organisms belong to the plant kingdom but are heterotrophic in their feeding habits. They feed on the organic materials of dead organisms and in the process bring about the decay of the remains of these organisms. Most saprophytes are either bacteria or fungi. An example is the fungus *Mucor*, commonly known as bread mould. The hyphae of *Mucor* penetrate the surface of the food material, secrete digestive enzymes to render the food soluble and the solute molecules then diffuse into the cells of the mould.

Symbiosis

The term symbiosis means living together. At times the term is used according to its narrower definition to describe the mutualistic relationship that exists for instance between the nitrogen-fixing bacteria and leguminous plants.
In a wider context it can be used to refer to any situation where one organism lives in close association with, in or on another organism. There are three types of symbiotic relationship depending on whether the association is of benefit to both or only one of the partners, or is in some way harmful to one but of benefit to the other.

Mutualism

Mutualism describes the situation where the relationship is to the benefit of both partners. One of the best examples is the mutualistic arrangement between nitrogen-fixing bacteria and leguminous plants (see p. 36). Although each organism is capable of survival on its own the relationship that exists between them is clearly to the benefit of both.
A much more intricate form of mutualism exists between certain species of ant and a particular fungus that the ants cultivate in their underground nests. The ants collect leaves, take them underground and chew them into a pulp[1] suitable to serve as food for the fungi. The fungi in turn act as food for the ants.
Another interesting instance of mutualism exists between the hermit crab and the sea anemone. Hermit crabs inhabit discarded snail shells in order to protect the soft parts of their bodies. The anemone establishes itself on top of a snail shell and gives the crab inside the advantage of protective camouflage. The sting of the anemone is a further means of protection for both organisms. In return the crab offers its guest free transportation and bits of food that are scattered while it is feeding.

Fig.1.99 Leguminous plant

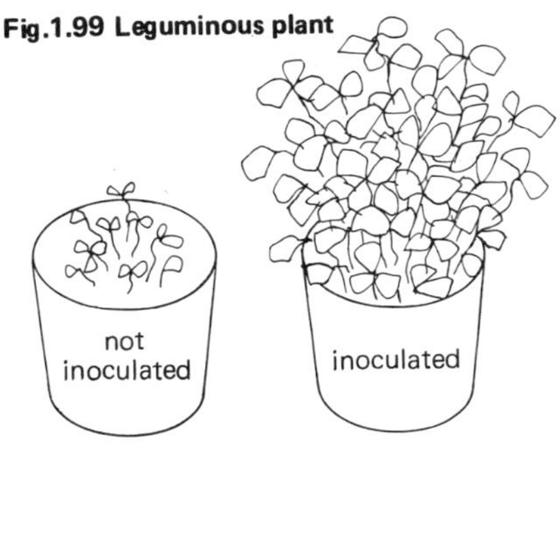

Fig.1.100 Sea anemone living on shell of hermit crab

[1]*pulp*: a soft mass

Commensalism

Commensalism is used to describe the situation where one organism feeds on the unconsumed food of the other organism called the host, without causing any harm to the host.
Many of the bacteria living in our digestive systems belong to this category. They feed on undigested materials such as cellulose and generally do not harm us in any way.
In fact, there is evidence that some of the bacteria produce vitamin B which our bodies can absorb, indicating that our relationship with these particular bacteria is mutualistic.

Parasitism

Parasitism is the term applied to the situation where the parasite derives nourishment from the tissues of the host thereby causing the host various degrees of injury, or in rare cases, death.
The relationship between parasite and host can differ both with respect to spatial and temporal conditions. Some parasites only come in contact with the outer surface of the host while others live inside the body cavity or even within the individual cells of the host.
Some parasites only attach themselves to the host during the short period that they are actually feeding while others, once established, never leave the host. The two main benefits gained by the parasite through its association with the host are shelter and food.
Parasites can invade both plants and animals. They can cause damage by:

1. consuming the food and the tissues of the host;
2. releasing toxic substances as by-products of their metabolism;
3. blocking vital organs or passages, for example, the intestine or lymph passages.

Tapeworm

Tapeworms live inside the digestive system of the host. Adult forms are found in the intestines of many mammals including humans,

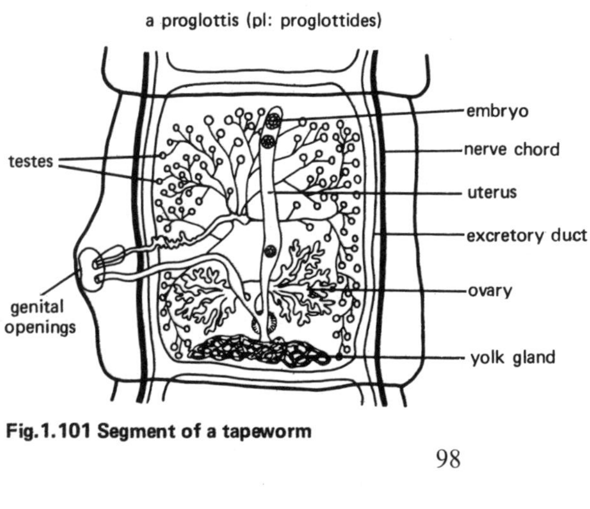

Fig.1.101 Segment of a tapeworm

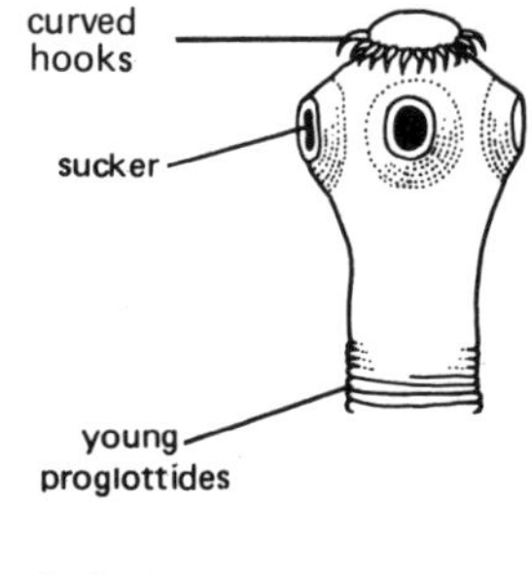

Fig.1.102 Head of a tapeworm

dogs, cats, pigs and fish. The body of the tapeworm consists of nothing but an endless string of segments, each filled with a complete set of both male and female reproductive organs.

Living inside the body of the host as it does, the tapeworm has no need for sense organs or a means of locomotion. It has no digestive system because soluble nutrients can diffuse into the individual cells. It attaches itself to the host by means of suckers and hooks located on its head. Segments are continually growing out of the head so that the overall length can reach as much as 10 metres.

As a means of protection against the digestive juices of the host it has a thick cuticle.

As stated before, the tapeworm has both a male and a female reproductive system in each segment; that is, it is a **hermaphrodite**. Each segment can therefore produce both sperm and eggs. The eggs can be fertilized by:

1. sperm from the same segment;
2. sperm from an adjoining segment of the same worm; or
3. sperm from another tapeworm.

The fertilized eggs develop in the uterus into embryos with individual protective coats. By the time a given segment becomes older it is near the posterior end of the organism and ready to break away and be expelled from the body through the faeces. Embryos, after they are excreted, retain their power of infection for up to one year.

If they find their way into human food and are eaten they will not develop into worms. However, if eaten by an appropriate intermediate host—a pig in the case of a pork tapeworm—the embryos are released and they burrow through the intestinal wall of the animal to enter the bloodstream. They eventually find their way to the muscles where they develop, in about three months, into **bladderworms**. The name is derived from the small, fluid-filled sac enclosing the worm's head. If a piece of pork containing bladderworms is well cooked the worms will die. If not, they enter the intestine of the person eating the meat and there develop into new tapeworms.

The presence of pork or beef tapeworms in the intestine does not normally lead to severe disability: in fact a great many people have worms and are not even aware of the fact until segments begin to appear in the faeces.

The usual symptoms are anaemia, loss of weight and general weakness. If tapeworms should somehow find their way into the circulatory system of the host, as they do at times, they can develop into bladderworms. These can very easily become lodged in the liver, lungs or brain, and lead to quite serious problems.

Infection by tapeworms can be avoided by:

1. making sure that all pork, beef, or fish is thoroughly cooked;
2. disposing of faeces in a way that domestic animals and fish do not have access to infected material;
3. in the case of dog tapeworms, safeguards include washing one's hands after handling dogs, and not allowing a dog to lick one's face

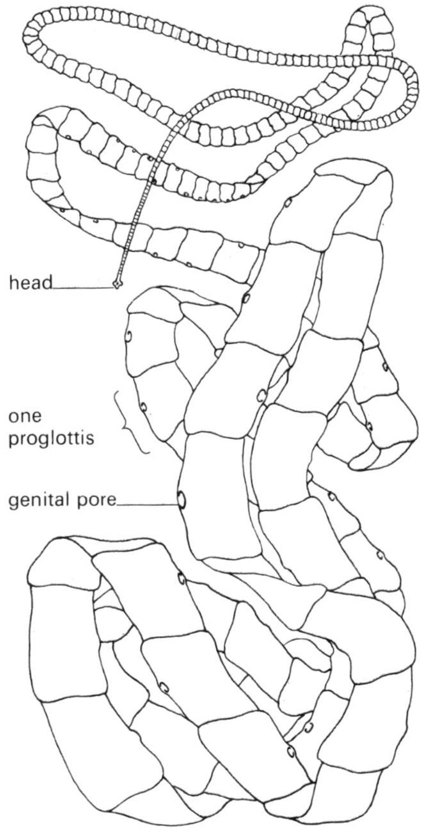

Fig.1.103 Diagram and photo of a tapeworm

Fig.1.104 Cycle of tapeworm infestation

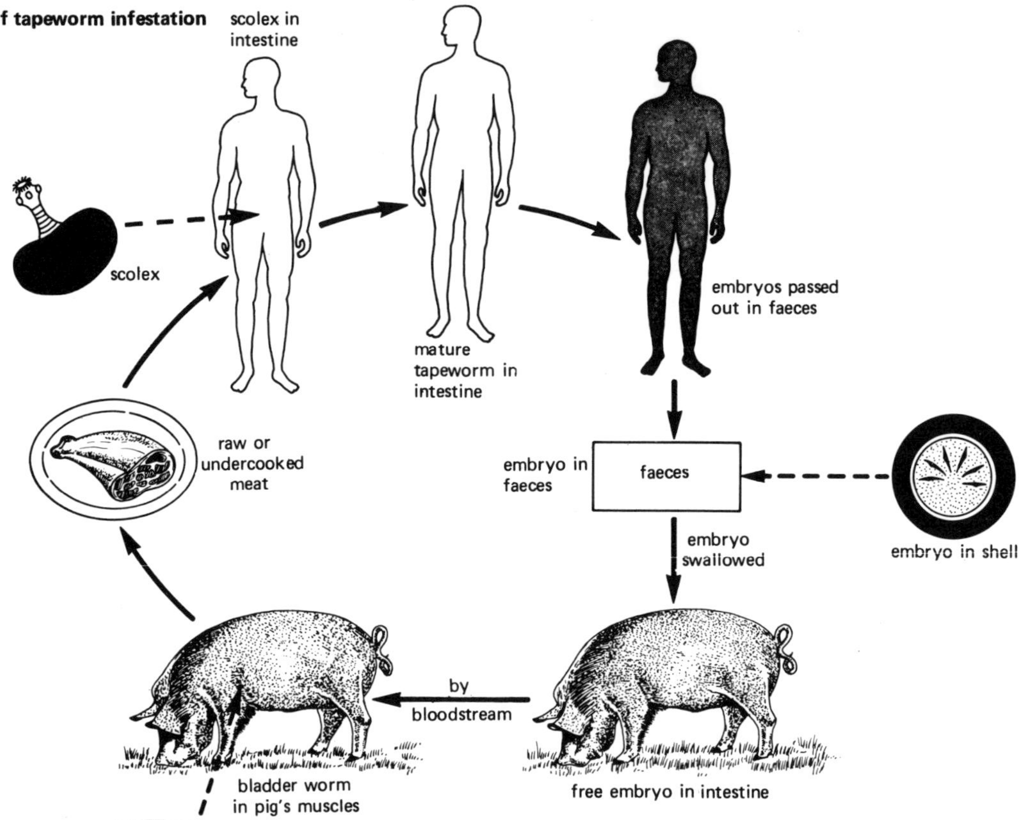

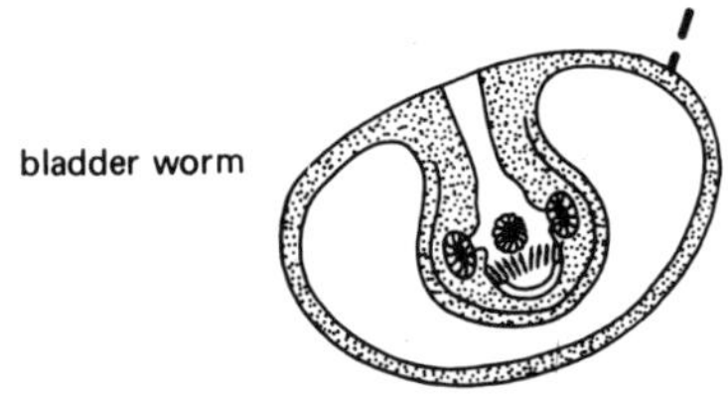

and keeping the dog's food dish away from contact with human food.

In many countries stringent inspection of all meats sold has considerably cut down on the incidence of tapeworm infections.

Cuckoo

A very highly developed form of parasitism is that practised by the cuckoo. The female bird lays its eggs in the nests of other birds whose eggs are about the same size and colour as its own. She lays only one egg per nest and to keep the total number of eggs the same, she removes one of the eggs of the host. In all she lays four or five eggs, each in a different nest.

The young cuckoo is usually the first to hatch and although blind and feeble, without feathers, it immediately sets about pushing the unhatched eggs of the host out of the nest. When not the first to hatch it tries to do the same to the other young nestlings[1].

The instinctive urge of the foster parents to feed their young is so great that they continue to satisfy the parasite's incessant demands for food even when greatly weakened by the exertion and at the expense of their own nestlings.

[1] *nestlings*: newly-hatched birds

Dodder

An example of a plant parasite is the dodder which can be found growing coiled around the stem of the nettle plant. The parasite has no roots and its small scale-like leaves do not contain chlorophyll. The stem of the dodder is very thin, pink in colour and is equipped with small suckers at intervals which penetrate the stem of the host plant. The suckers, called **hastoria** (singular: **hastorium**) reach into the vascular bundles of the nettle from where the dodder obtains the water and organic materials necessary for its survival.
Dodder reproduces from seeds developing from clusters of tiny pink flowers borne on the plant in late summer. The seeds are dispersed by the wind and water and remain dormant until the following spring.
The tiny seedling does not even begin to develop roots, only a wiry shoot that grows upwards until it encounters a suitable plant and begins to coil around its stem. Once permanently attached to the stem of the host the lower parts of the parasite's stem wither and die.

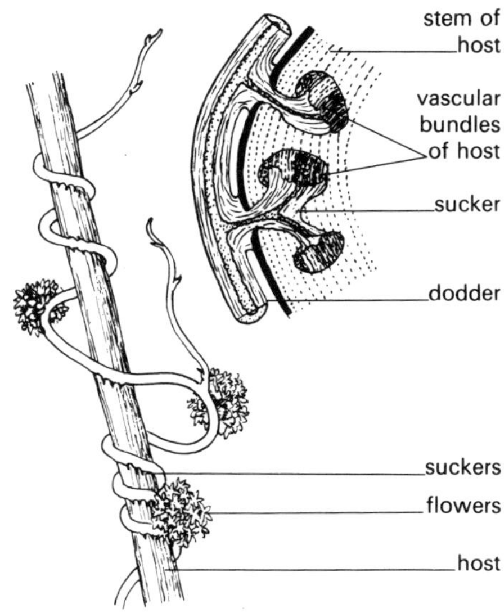

Fig. 1.105 Dodder growing on a host plant and section through dodder and host

Crop parasites

Many other plant parasites such as wheat rust and corn smut devastate countless acres of crops all over the world causing enormous losses of food supplies.

Summary

Three different forms of symbiosis can be distinguished. Mutualism is of benefit to both the organisms; commensalism is beneficial for the guest organism but does not confer any particular advantages on the host; and parasitism always implies some degree of harm to the host.
Note that according to the old terminology, still partially in use and found in many texts, the word symbiosis is used only to mean a mutualistic arrangement between guest and host as exists in the case of the nitrogen-fixing bacteria and leguminous plants. However, the real meaning of the words 'living together' encompasses all three categories of association as described above.

Section 2. THE RELEASE OF ENERGY FROM NUTRIENTS

RESPIRATION AND ENERGY RELEASE

Respiration

One of the reasons why a living organism needs to take in food is to supply energy for its various activities such as muscle contraction, protein synthesis and other energy-requiring processes.

How is the chemical energy locked up in the nutrients released and made available to the cells in our bodies?

The way to determine experimentally the energy content of a food substance is to burn it in a calorimeter in the presence of oxygen. The process of oxidation releases the chemical energy locked up in the organic molecules and this energy manifests itself in the form of heat.

Can the cells of other living organisms release energy from their food in the same way?

They certainly can and do. Most living cells have the ability to oxidize organic molecules to release the chemical energy they contain. The process is called **aerobic respiration** (or internal respiration) and may be summarized by the following equation:

$$C_6H_{12}O_6 + 6O_2 \longrightarrow 6CO_2 + 6H_2O + \text{energy}$$

$$\text{sugar} + \text{oxygen} \longrightarrow \text{carbon dioxide} + \text{water} + \text{energy}$$

The breakdown of organic molecules represented by sugar in the above equation is achieved through a series of chemical reactions each catalysed by an appropriate enzyme. The process is one of oxidation of carbon atoms. In a sugar molecule the ratio of carbon to oxygen is one to one, while in carbon dioxide the ratio is one to two. Therefore the conversion of sugar to molecules of carbon dioxide involves the addition of oxygen. If the above equation is correct we should be able to find evidence of oxygen consumption, production of carbon dioxide and water, and the release of energy in both plants and animals during respiration. The most convenient plant specimen to use in illustrating the action of respiration is the germinating seed. The use of a green plant is impractical due to the fact that in the presence of light green plants take up carbon dioxide for use in photosynthesis and release oxygen.

EXPERIMENT TO ILLUSTRATE THE UPTAKE OF OXYGEN BY GERMINATING SEEDS

Note: Since there is no change in pH when oxygen dissolves in water the presence or absence of oxygen in solution cannot be detected by an indicator the way the presence of carbon dioxide can. We therefore have to look for a change in volume of gas in the container with the aid of a manometer. If the volume of gas in container A in fig. 2.1 is reduced water will rise up the glass tubing to replace the gas.
To eliminate the effect of the liberation of carbon dioxide by the seeds it is necessary to absorb this gas with soda-lime.

Materials

Ten or twelve germinating seeds such as pea or bean
disinfectant solution such as formalin
soda-lime
two flasks
two pieces of narrow tubing as shown in the diagram
beaker containing water

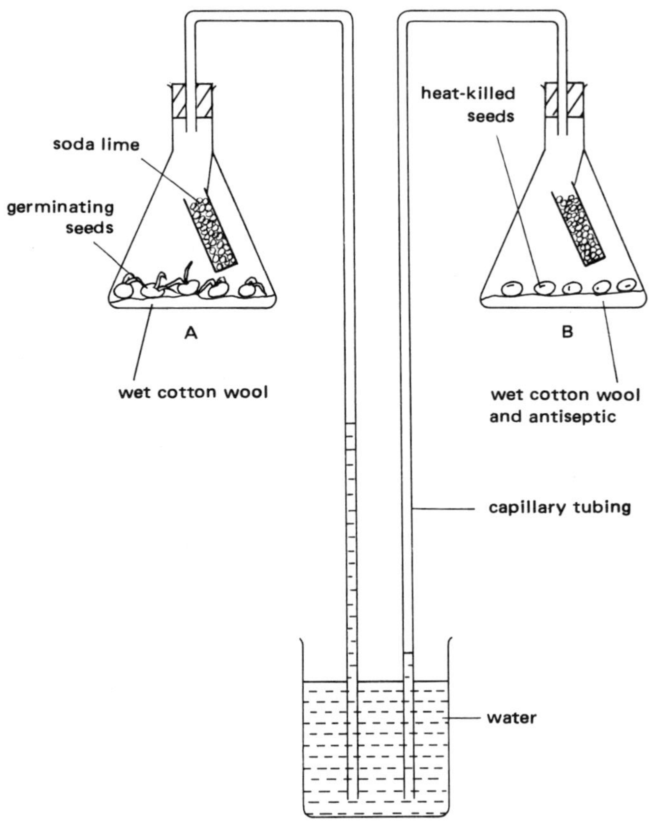

Fig. 2.1 **To see if oxygen is taken up by germinating seeds**

Method

1. To start the seeds germinating soak in water for about twelve hours then keep between layers of moist filter paper until germination begins.
2. Kill half the seeds by plunging them into boiling water for ten minutes.
3. Set up the apparatus as shown in fig. 2.1. Mark the level of water in the tubes.
4. Place in a spot where the influence of outside temperatures will be the same on the two flasks. (Why is this important?)
5. Observe the level of the liquid in the two tubes over a period of three or four days.

What do you observe?
What does a change in the level of liquid indicate?
Is there a marked difference in levels between the two tubes?
How might you test for the presence or absence of oxygen in the two flasks?

Discussion

Fluctuations in temperature can cause the gas in the flasks to expand or contract but if the two are under identical conditions this will not cause a difference in water level in the two glass tubes.

As the experiment proceeds, however, you will observe a very marked difference in the two liquid levels, the level in A being considerably higher than that in B. This indicates that gas has been removed from flask A but not from B. Since the flasks are sealed the gas could only have been removed by some activity of the seeds. The change in level cannot be caused by liberation of carbon dioxide because it is absorbed by the soda line.

If the air in the two flasks is tested with a burning taper the flame will immediately go out in A but will stay alight for a few seconds in B. The germinating seeds therefore have consumed oxygen while the heat-killed seeds have not.

The purpose of the disinfectant is to prevent bacterial or fungal growth on the heat-killed seeds.

Production of carbon dioxide

EXPERIMENT TO ILLUSTRATE THAT SMALL ANIMALS PRODUCE CARBON DIOXIDE

Experiment a

Materials

a variety of small animals such as insects or worms
wire mesh (about 2 cm^2 pieces)
bicarbonate/indicator

Method

1. Pour about 2 cm^3 bicarbonate/indicator into each of two test-tubes.
2. Fit one of the tubes with a wire mesh platform as shown in the diagram.

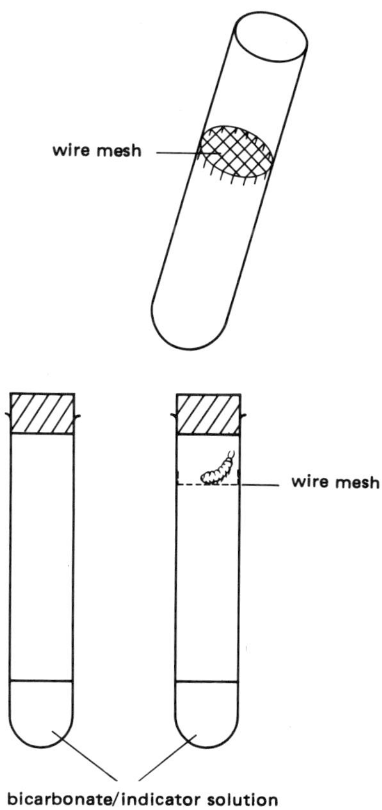

Fig. 2.2 Testing for the production of carbon dioxide

3. Place your animal on top of the platform and seal both tubes with a bung.
4. Set aside and observe over a period of twenty to thirty minutes.

What happens to the indicator solution in the two tubes?
What does this tell you about the animal you used?

Experiment b
A more elaborate experiment using a larger animal can be set up as shown below. With this apparatus we can also illustrate the uptake of oxygen by the animal used.
Materials
a mouse or other animal of similar size
soda-lime
bicarbonate/indicator
bell jar
containers for indicator and soda-lime
Method
1. Pour equal volumes of indicator into the two containers A and C.
2. Place your animal into the bell jar B.
3. Connect the three containers as shown in the diagram. The purpose of the soda-lime is to ensure that no atmospheric carbon dioxide passes into the container.
4. Connect the apparatus to a filter pump and observe for thirty to forty minutes.
Note the arrows on the diagram indicating the pathway of air in the system.
5. Disconnect the containers one at a time and test the air inside A and C with a burning taper.

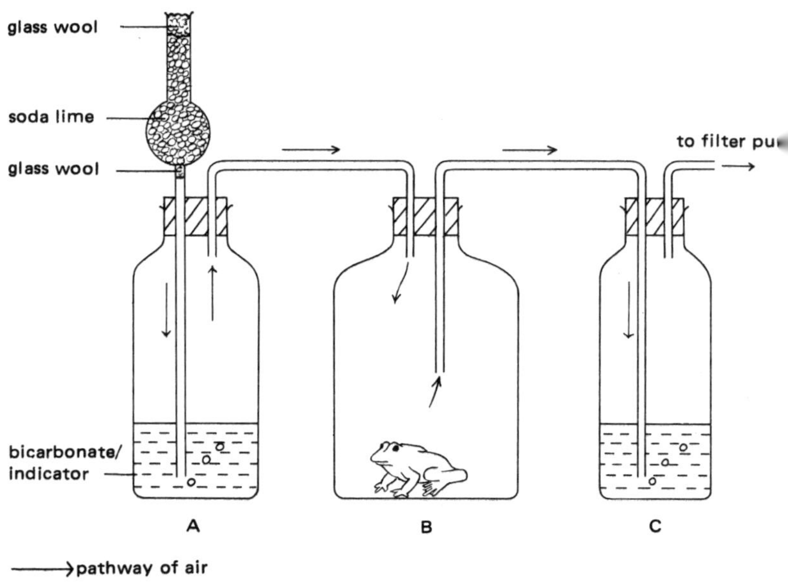

Fig. 2.3 Carbon dioxide production in an animal

What happens to the indicator in container A? What does this tell you about the air inside?
Why does the colour of the indicator in C change?
What do you observe when you test the air in the containers A and C with the burning taper?

Discussion

The bicarbonate/indicator in A turns a purplish colour indicating that the concentration of carbon dioxide in the container is less than that in atmospheric air. This is due to the presence of the soda-lime.

In both the above experiments the air exhaled by the animal caused the indicator to turn yellow showing the presence of carbon dioxide in concentrations higher than that in atmospheric air.

When the air in the containers is tested with the burning taper the flame immediately goes out in C but stays alight for a few seconds in A showing that the animal has removed some of the oxygen from the air. Some process in the body of the animal must be removing oxygen from and releasing carbon dioxide into the surrounding air.

EXPERIMENT TO ILLUSTRATE THAT GERMINATING SEEDS PRODUCE CARBON DIOXIDE

Materials

two tubes fitted with a wire mesh platform
ten or twelve germinating seeds such as peas or beans
bicarbonate/indicator
cotton wool
disinfectant such as formalin

Method

1. To start the peas germinating they should be soaked in water for about twelve hours then kept between moist layers of filter paper until germination begins.
2. Kill half the seeds by heating them in boiling water for ten minutes.
3. Place equal amounts of bicarbonate indicator in two tubes.
4. Fit the wire mesh into the tubes and arrange the living seeds on the mesh in tube A and the heat-killed seeds in tube B as shown in fig. 2.4.

Moist cotton wool or paper towel that has been soaked in mild disinfectant solution is placed under the seeds to prevent them from drying out. (The purpose of the disinfectant in tube B is to prevent bacterial or fungal growth from interfering with the experiment.)

5. Observe for two or three days.

What happens to the indicator in the two tubes?
How do you account for the difference between tube A and tube B?
What can you conclude from the above experiment?

Discussion

The indicator in the tube containing live seeds turns yellow showing that the seeds produce carbon dioxide. In the control tube containing

heat-killed seeds no carbon dioxide is detected.
The above experiments have shown that living things do indeed produce carbon dioxide in their bodies. But how do we know that the carbon dioxide produced does indeed come from the oxidation of sugar molecules?

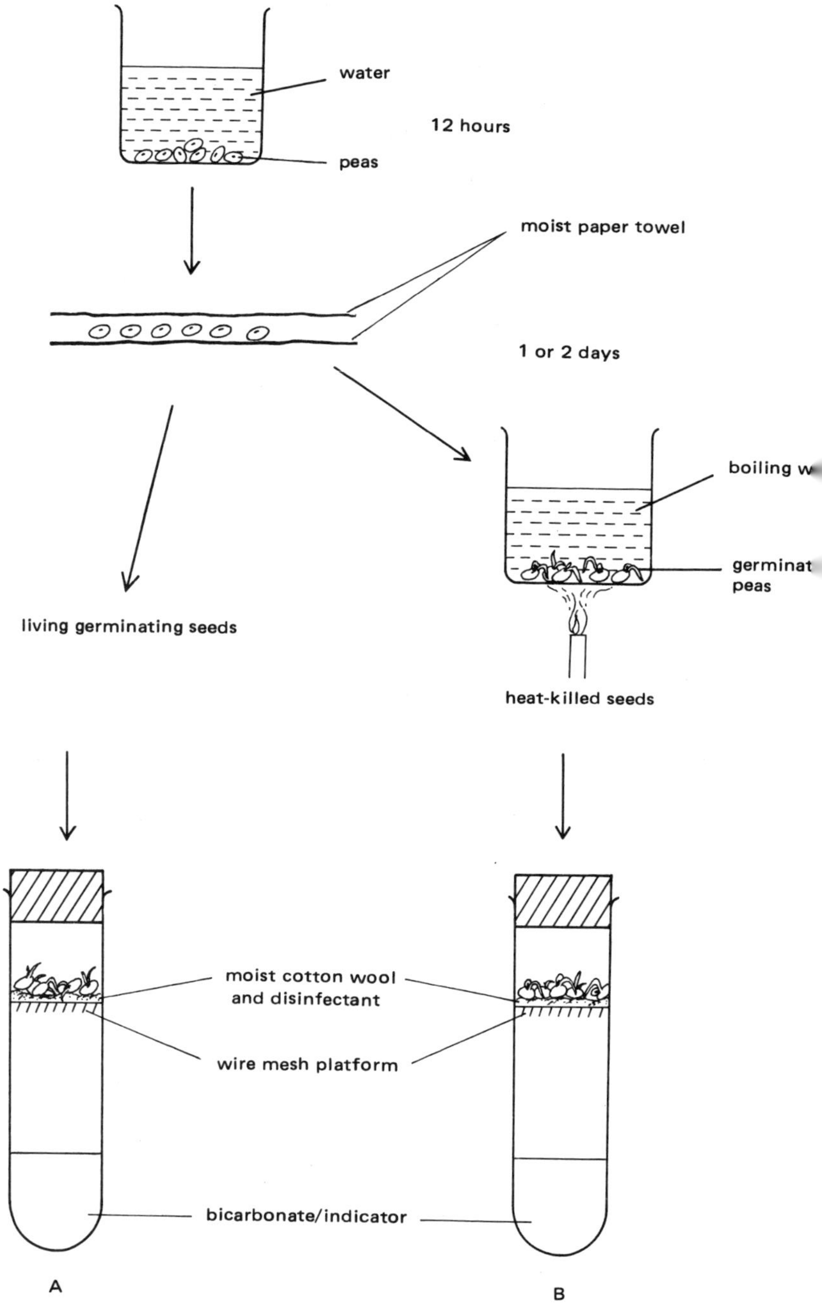

Fig. 2.4

Scientists have been able to demonstrate that the carbon atoms appearing in the carbon dioxide exhaled by an animal do come from the oxidized food by performing the following experiment.
A group of experimental animals was given glucose that had been *labelled* by including a small proportion of sugar containing radioactive carbon, ^{14}C. A similar group of animals was fed with ordinary unlabelled glucose. The exhaled air from the two groups of animals was collected and analysed in a radioactive counter.
Results showed that the animals fed with ^{14}C-glucose exhaled ^{14}C-carbon dioxide. This is a direct illustration of the fact that the carbon atoms of the carbon dioxide exhaled come from the food, in this case sugar, that is oxidized in respiration.

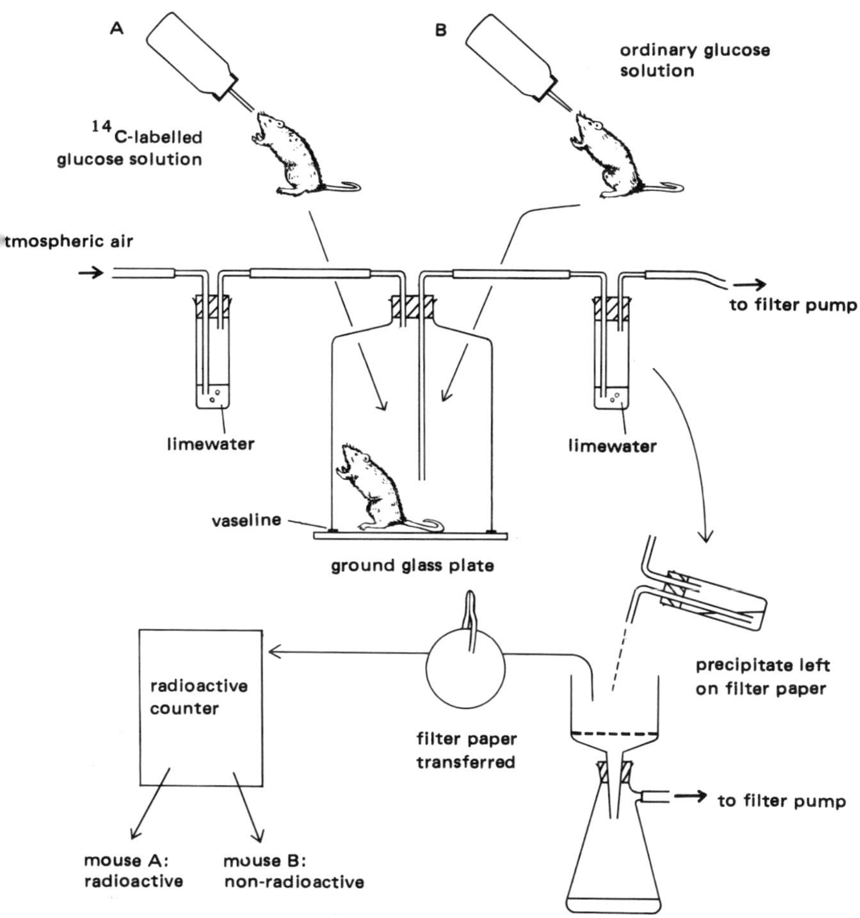

Fig. 2.5 **Feeding rats with ^{14}C-labelled glucose and testing their exhaled CO_2 for radioactivity**

Production of water

The second product shown in the equation for respiration is water. This is more difficult to demonstrate conclusively since non-living things as well as living things are capable of releasing moisture into the atmosphere.

Scientists have been able to demonstrate the production of water during respiration by performing radioactive labelling experiments similar to the one described above. They have found that if an animal or plant is given glucose in which some of the hydrogen atoms have been labelled, these same labelled hydrogen atoms can be detected in the water passing out of the organism.

Production of energy

Although living organisms produce various forms of energy the most convenient form for us to look for in experiments is heat energy.

Fig.2.6

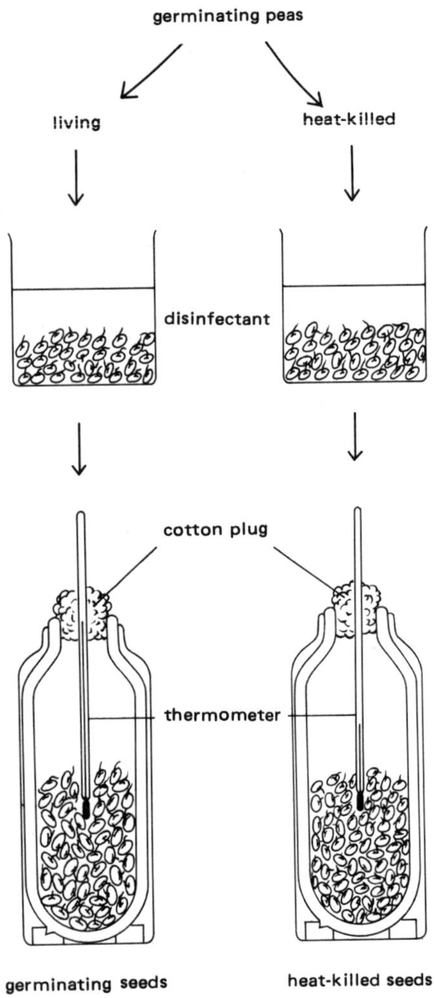

EXPERIMENT TO DEMONSTRATE THE PRODUCTION OF HEAT BY GERMINATING SEEDS

Materials

living and heat-killed germinating seeds in equal amounts
two insulated flasks
thermometers

Method

1. The germinating seeds are prepared as described on p. 105.
2. Both sets of seeds should be rinsed in a mild disinfectant solution to prevent the growth of micro-organisms on their surface.
3. Place the seeds in identical insulated flasks and insert a thermometer into each through a cotton plug.
4. Check the temperature inside the containers several times a day for three to four days.
5. Plot the temperatures on a graph.

Do you find that there is a difference in temperature between the two containers?

How do you account for this difference?

On the basis of this experiment what can you conclude regarding the production of heat by plants?

Discussion

The temperature in the flask containing living seeds gradually rose showing that the seeds were liberating heat energy. The temperature of the control remained steady throughout the same period showing that heat-killed seeds cannot produce heat energy.

There are various other types of energy produced by living things in addition to heat.

Muscular movements of any kind are examples of mechanical energy. Some organisms, for example, glow-worms and some bacteria, produce energy in the form of light.

Summary

The above series of experiments has provided some evidence for the existence in the cells of living organisms of an oxidation process called respiration which releases energy. The overall equation for the process is:

organic matter + oxygen ⟶ carbon dioxide + water + energy

The release of energy

In the previous section it was stressed that the equation given for respiration is the *overall* equation. When food is burned in a calorimeter the oxidation of the organic material is a direct, one-step process. It requires very high temperatures and is essentially an uncontrolled reaction. Energy is liberated in the form of heat and can then be used to perform useful work in heating water, for instance.

The oxidation of organic material in living cells is an enzyme-catalysed process requiring many steps. The reaction takes place at the relatively low temperature of 37°C. It is a very precisely controlled reaction catalysed by enzymes. Only a small portion of the total energy liberated is in the form of heat, the rest being harnessed by the cell for its functioning.

How do living cells harness the energy liberated in respiration?

The energy is used for the synthesis of a special organic molecule called **adenosine triphosphate** or **ATP** for short. ATP consists of a complex molecule called adenosine with three phosphate units attached to it. ATP is a very unstable compound which will very easily break down into **adenosine diphosphate (ADP)** and then to **adenosine monophosphate (AMP)**.

In order to synthesize ADP or ATP from AMP large amounts of energy are necessary. This energy becomes stored in the bonds between the phosphate groups. When ATP breaks down the energy is released again.

AMP + phosphate + energy ⇌ ADP

ADP + phosphate + energy ⇌ ATP

Why is the cell's energy stored in the ATP molecule?

While the energy stored in other organic molecules is not immediately available to the cell, requiring the complex process of respiration in order to release it, the energy stored in ATP is immediately available for use.

When a muscle cell, for instance, requires energy for contraction the ATP molecule is broken down to ADP and the energy stored in the bond is immediately released. ATP can be compared to the money a person earns by working. It takes a long time to actually

earn the money to buy something but once you have the cash in your hands you are able to walk into a store and immediately exchange it for something you wish to buy.
For a living cell to make ATP it must obtain the necessary energy-containing nutrients. These must be oxidised through the process of respiration and the energy released must be used to form the energy-containing bonds of the ATP molecule. Once this is done the energy is available to be used in whatever cellular process it is required.
To illustrate the action of ATP in supplying energy for muscle contraction the following simple experiment can be performed.

EXPERIMENT TO ILLUSTRATE THE ROLE OF ATP IN MUSCLE CONTRACTION

Materials

small piece of fresh lean meat (muscle)
ATP solution
glucose
distilled water
syringe

Fig.2.7

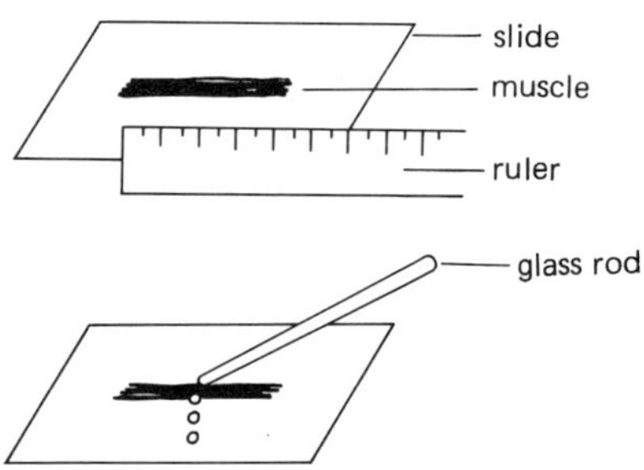

Method

1. Place a fresh piece of meat on a glass slide and carefully measure its length.
2. Put a few drops of distilled water on the muscle, wait for a few seconds and measure the length again.
3. Now place a few drops of glucose on the muscle and repeat your measurement.
4. Allow the glucose to drain off the muscle and rinse with a small amount of distilled water.
5. Place a few drops of ATP solution on the muscle and again measure.
6. Record your results in a table.

original length	
after distilled water	
after glucose	
after ATP	

Can an isolated piece of muscle obtain energy for contraction from glucose?
Can it obtain energy from ATP?
How can you account for these observations?

Discussion

ATP can, on its own, provide all the necessary energy for the contraction of muscle. It can very easily diffuse into the cells of the muscle, be converted to ADP and release the energy locked up in its energy bond. Glucose is also an energy-containing molecule but this energy can only be released through the complicated process of respiration.

Where does respiration take place in the cell?

Respiration takes place in special organelles called **mitochondria** that are found in most living cells. The energy-containing organic molecules that are to be oxidized, together with oxygen, diffuse into the mitochondria. The interior of the organelle is filled with a liquid that contains all the enzymes necessary for respiration, and ADP.

ATP and the by-products carbon dioxide and water diffuse out into the rest of the cell.

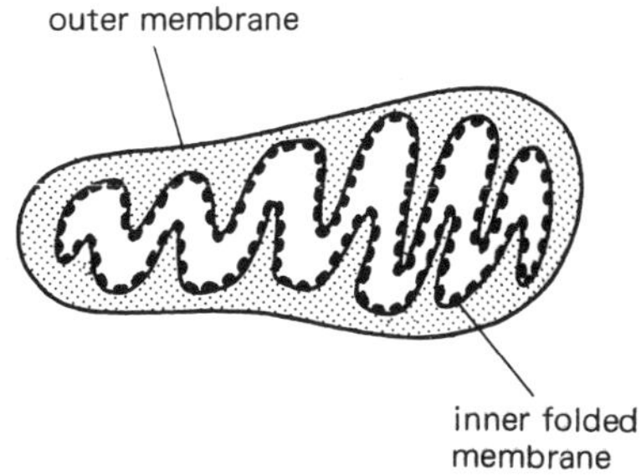

Fig. 2.8 The structure of a mitochondrion

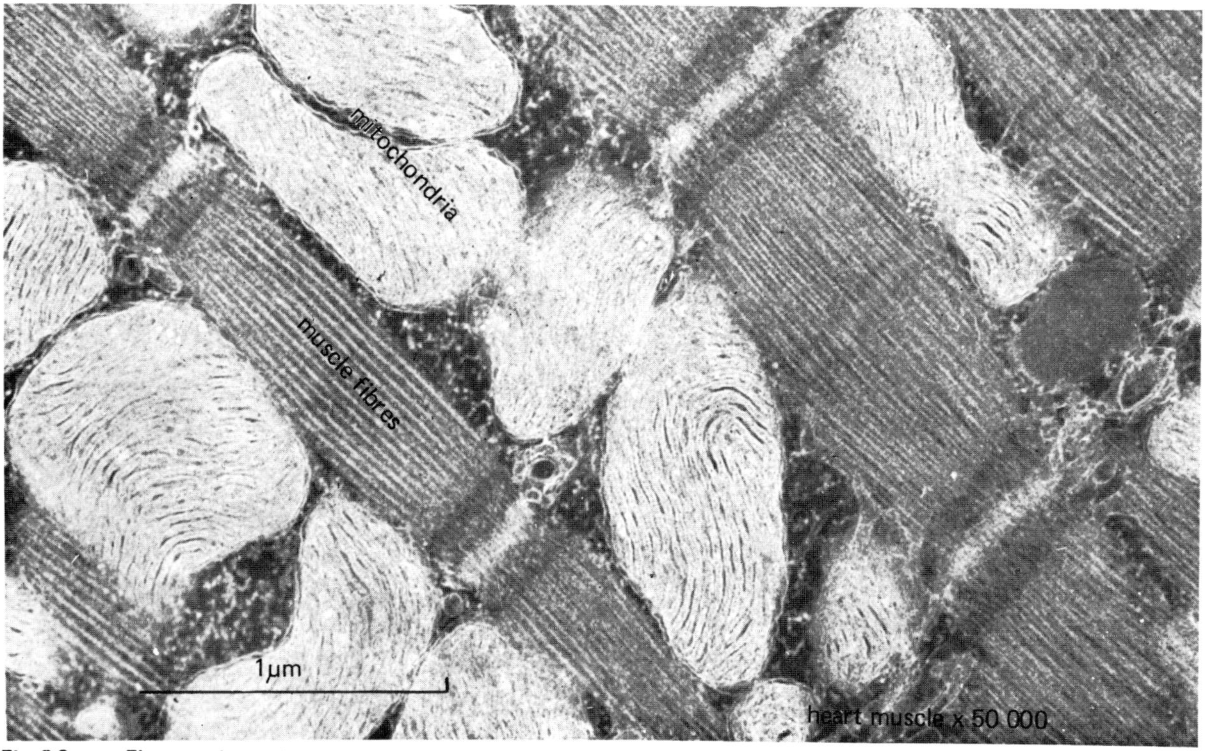

Fig. 2.9 Electron photomicrograph of a mitochondrion

Summary

Food + oxygen ⇄(a) ADP + phosphate ⇄(b) contracted muscle

$CO_2 + H_2O$ ATP relaxed muscle

(a) Energy released from food is stored in ATP molecules.
(b) Energy released from ATP is used for muscle contraction.

Anaerobic respiration

The respiratory process we have discussed so far is an oxidation process requiring oxygen.

Is release of energy possible in the absence of oxygen?

When supplied with sugar and kept at a suitable temperature yeast cells will grow and multiply even in the absence of oxygen.

EXPERIMENT TO FIND OUT IF YEAST CELLS CAN RESPIRE WITHOUT OXYGEN

As before, we can regard the production of heat energy and carbon dioxide as indicative of respiration.

Materials

glucose solution
dried yeast
thermometer
liquid paraffin
bicarbonate/indicator

Method

1. Place about 200cm^3 of glucose solution into each of two flasks. To drive off any oxygen that might be dissolved in the solution boil it for a few minutes and allow it to cool undisturbed.
2. Put one teaspoon of dried yeast into flask A, but not into B which will serve as a control.
3. Prepare a second control by dissolving one teaspoon of yeast in 200cm^3 of boiled water in flask C.
4. To stop oxygen from getting in during the experiment pour a thin layer of liquid paraffin onto the top of the liquid in each flask.
5. Very quickly, before the paraffin hardens, insert the thermometer and glass tubing as shown in fig. 2.10.
6. Connect each flask to a test-tube containing 5cm^3 of bicarbonate indicator. Wrap the flasks in a piece of cloth for insulation.
7. Observe the temperature in each flask and the colour of the indicator over a period of thirty to forty-five minutes.

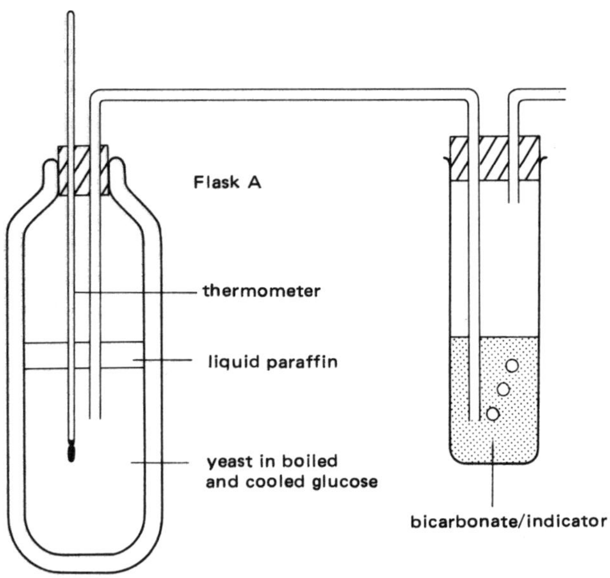

Fig. 2.10 **Testing for the production of heat and carbon dioxide under anaerobic conditions**

What happens to the temperature inside the flasks?
What happens to the indicator?
Why are the two controls necessary?
What can you conclude from this experiment about energy release by yeast cells in the absence of oxygen?

Discussion

In flask A the temperature increases showing that the yeast cells are releasing energy and the indicator turns yellow showing that carbon dioxide is given off. Neither heat nor carbon dioxide production is observed in the control flasks.

Yeast cells seem to have the ability to release energy from glucose without the presence of oxygen. If flask A were allowed to stand without oxygen for a few days an additional product, ethanol, would accumulate.

The two by-products of anaerobic respiration by yeast cells are then carbon dioxide and ethanol. The by-products produced during aerobic respiration, that is, respiration in the presence of oxygen, are carbon dioxide and water.

Clearly in anaerobic respiration glucose is not completely oxidized but is only partially oxidized to give a molecule that still contains stored energy. You can prove this by putting a small amount of ethanol on a watchglass and lighting it with a match. You will find that ethanol burns releasing heat and light energy as it does so. It must therefore be an energy-rich molecule, an intermediate or partially oxidized product of respiration.

Anaerobic respiration by yeast is known also by the alternative name of **alcoholic fermentation.** The process is of great commercial importance as the basis for the production of alcoholic beverages such as wine and beer (see p. 336).

Are animal cells also able to carry on anaerobic respiration?

Do we ever find ourselves in a situation where our cells cannot get sufficient supplies of oxygen?

The rate at which respiration is going on and thus the rate at which oxygen is used up in an animal depends on the changing energy requirements of the particular animal. During sleep or moderate activity energy demands can be met very easily and the necessary oxygen can be supplied by normal breathing.

What about in instances of strenuous activity such as a game of soccer or swimming?

In order to meet the increasing demand for energy the rate of respiration and the rate of oxygen uptake must be increased.

What would happen if the requirements for oxygen became so high that even at maximum rates of gas exchange they could not be met?

Under these conditions animal cells are capable of anaerobic respiration for a limited period of time.

What are the products of anaerobic respiration in animals?

The product formed is not the same as the products in plant cells; in animal cells the partially oxidized product is **lactic acid**. Lactic acid contains almost as much energy as glucose. Whereas complete oxidation of glucose to carbon dioxide and water yields thirty-eight molecules of ATP, anaerobic breakdown to lactic acid only yields two molecules of ATP.
High concentrations of lactic cannot be tolerated by animal cells and therefore anaerobic respiration can only be used for a limited length of time.

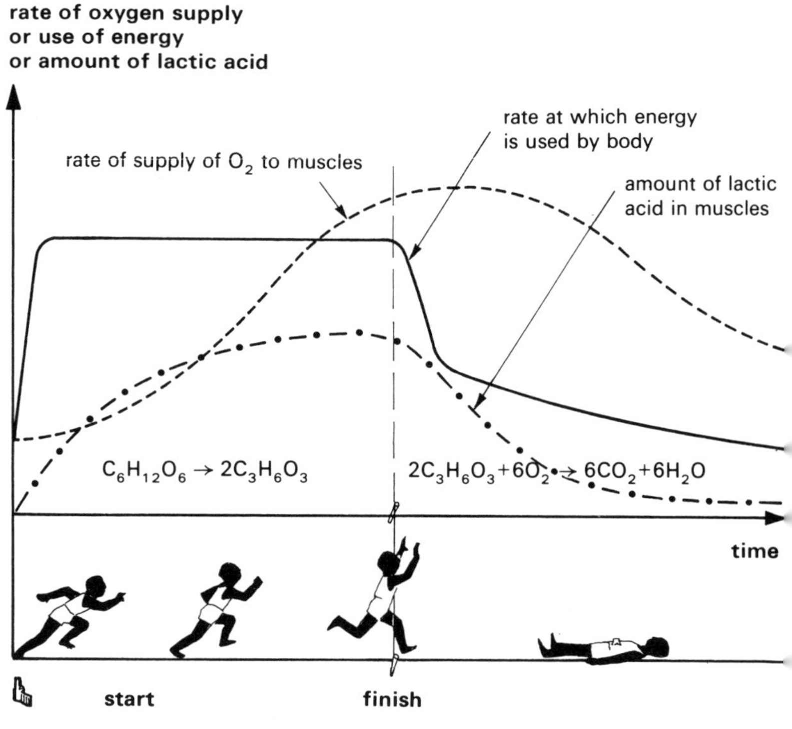

Fig. 2.11 **Lactic acid production during vigorous physical activity**

Fig. 2.12

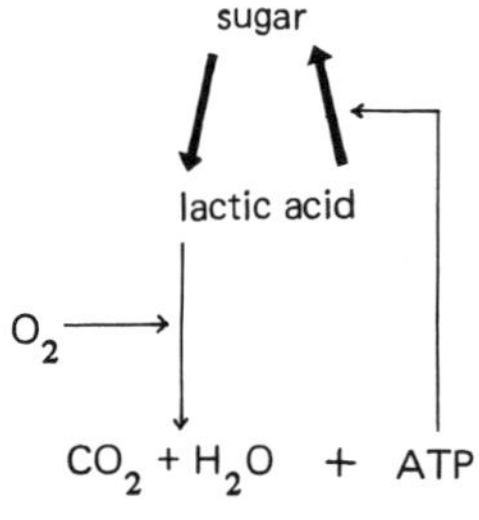

It is the inability of our breathing apparatus to supply adequate amounts of oxygen to the muscle cells during vigorous exercise that causes muscle fatigue. After exercise is stopped the high concentrations of lactic acid that have accumulated in the muscle cells and in the blood must be eliminated. For the lactic acid to be simply excreted from the body would be an extremely wasteful process, since it still contains so much energy. Instead a small part of it is oxidized to carbon dioxide and water and the ATP produced is used to convert the rest back to glucose. (See fig. 2.12.)

Respiration and photosynthesis

While performing the experiments and reading about the details of respiration you must have been struck with the idea that in many ways it is the opposite of photosynthesis.
Can you make a list in your book comparing the two processes?

Photosynthesis	*Respiration*
reduction	oxidation
requires carbon dioxide and water	produces carbon dioxide and water
produces oxygen	requires oxygen
energy consumed	energy released
in green plants only	both plants and animals
requires chlorophyll	does not require chlorophyll

Fig. 2.13

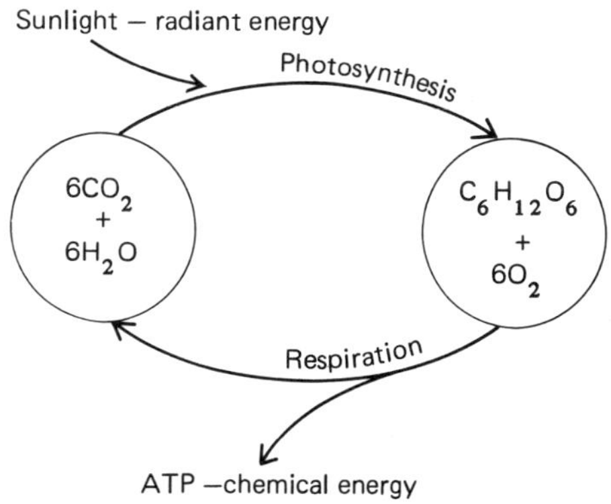

Summary

Although under normal conditions most living organisms obtain energy from organic molecules through the process of aerobic respiration both plants and animals are able to use anaerobic respiration for shorter periods of time when sufficient supplies of oxygen are not available. The table below gives a comparison of the two processes and fig. 2.14 is a diagrammatic illustration of the relationship between the two processes.

Aerobic	*Anaerobic*
uses oxygen	without oxygen
products are carbon dioxide and water	products are carbon dioxide and ethanol in plants, lactic acid in animals
complete oxidation releasing all the energy in the molecules (38 ATP molecules)	incomplete breakdown releasing only a small part of the energy in the molecule (2 ATP molecules)

Fig. 2.14

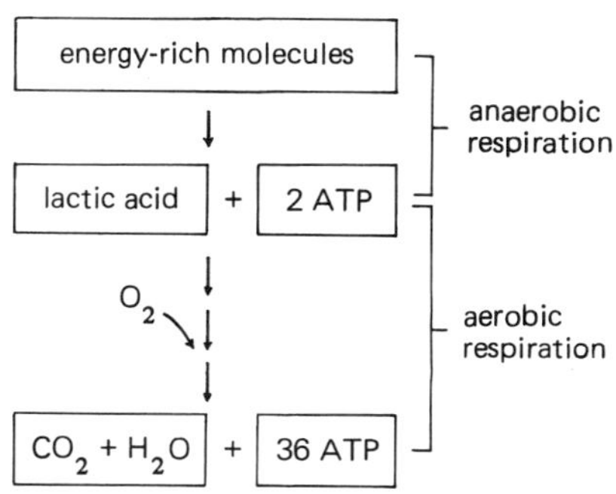

GAS EXCHANGE

Why is gas exchange necessary?

In the previous sections dealing with photosynthesis and respiration we have already established that during photosynthesis green plants consume carbon dioxide and liberate oxygen; and in respiration both plants and animals consume oxygen and liberate carbon dioxide. Clearly there must be some way for the necessary gases to get into the cells where they are required and for the waste gases to get out into the atmosphere.

Gas exchange in animals

Breathing

The mechanism of gas exchange in animals is commonly referred to as **breathing**.
Breathing consists of two phases, namely sucking air in **(inhalation)** and blowing air out **(exhalation)**. Atmospheric air contains more oxygen and less carbon dioxide than exhaled air.
If we were to measure the levels of the other gases comprising air we would find that they are present in approximately the same amounts in both atmospheric and exhaled air.

SUMMARY OF THE APPROXIMATE PERCENTAGE OF VARIOUS GASES IN ATMOSPHERIC AIR AND EXHALED AIR FROM A TYPICAL HUMAN SUBJECT

Gas	% in atmospheric air	% in exhaled air
Nitrogen	77.62	76.90
Oxygen	20.85	15.30
Carbon dioxide	0.03	3.60
Other gases	1.00	1.00
Water vapour	0.50	4.20

By what route does inhaled air get into the body of mammals?

One way to find out the route of inhaled air is to dissect a small mammal such as a rabbit or a rat. Instructions for performing the dissection have been given on p. 8.
If the dorsal body wall is opened up to reveal the interior structures you will find two cavities divided horizontally by a muscular, dome-shaped partition called the **diaphragm**. The upper cavity, the **thorax** contains the heart and the lungs. The lower, **abdominal cavity** with which you are already familiar contains mainly the

digestive organs. If you expose the area at the base of the neck you will find a large tube leading from the throat to the lungs. By inserting a piece of flexible plastic tubing from the mouth of the animal you can follow the passage right down into the lungs. If you blow air into the tube you will find that the lungs inflate.

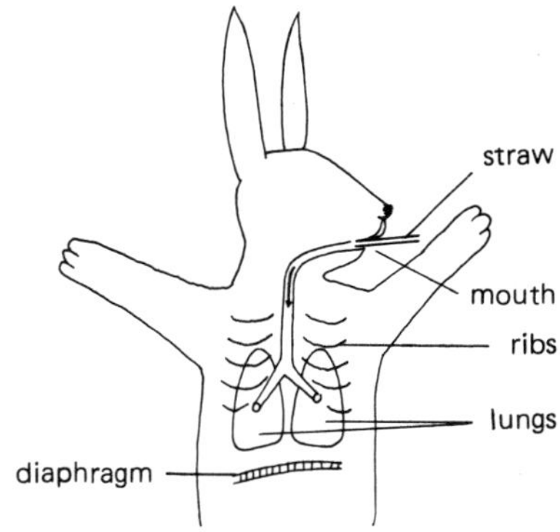

Fig. 2.15 **Blowing air into lungs of dissected rabbit**

Air entering through the nose or the mouth can pass down this tube called the **trachea** and enter the lungs by way of the left and right **bronchi** (singular **bronchus**). The second tube leading down from the back of the mouth is the oesophagus leading to the stomach. Refer back to the diagram on p. 74 to recall the relative positions of the various structures during breathing as opposed to swallowing.

The trachea is surrounded by rings of cartilage that help to maintain its shape. Without these rings to support it the wall of the trachea might collapse and stick together closing off the air passage.

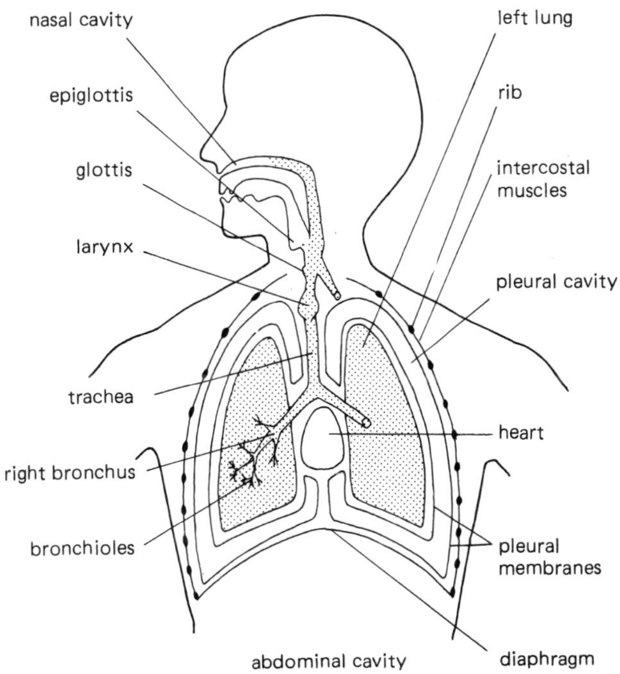

Fig. 2.16 Respiratory tract and associated structures of human

Both the two lungs and the side of the thorax are covered by a thin membrane called the **pleural membrane**. There is a very small space between the membrane covering the lungs and that covering the body wall and this space is filled with a fluid to reduce the friction that might develop as the two move relative to each other.

There is a longitudinal partition down the middle of the thorax dividing it into two independent, airtight cavities. The ribs form a protective cage around the lungs and the heart.

What causes air to go down these passages to the lungs? The action of the ribs

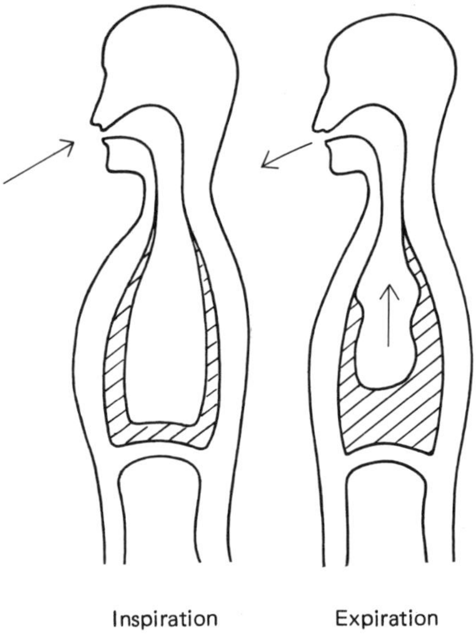

Fig. 2.17 Diagrammatic view of lungs during inspiration and expiration

Place your hands on the two sides of your body above the waist. Inhale as slowly and as deeply as you can. Can you feel your rib cage move out and your thorax get larger as you inhale? Try to position your fingers so you can feel the individual ribs. You will feel that the bones not only move out but slightly upwards as well. When you exhale the ribs fall back to their resting position.

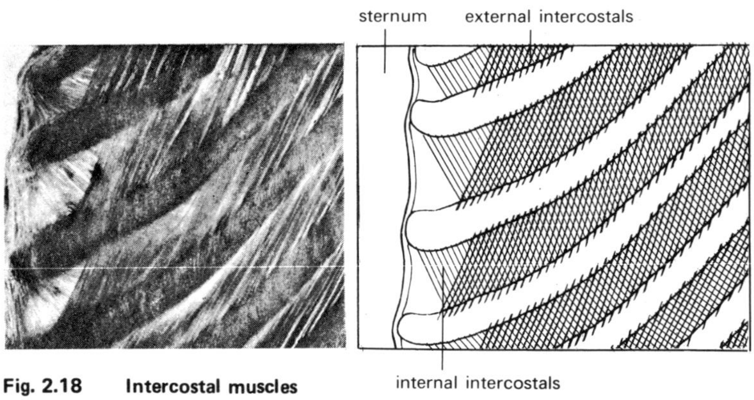

Fig. 2.18 Intercostal muscles

The movement of the ribs is caused by the alternate contractions of the **intercostal** muscles that run at an angle of about 40° between adjacent ribs. The contractions of the exterior intercostal muscles are responsible for raising the rib cage while the interior intercostals help to lower it. The alternate action of these two sets of muscles can be illustrated using the following model.

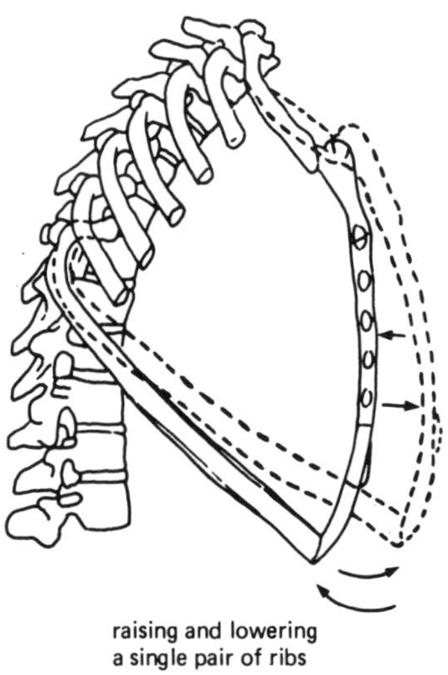

Fig. 2.19 Action of ribs in breathing

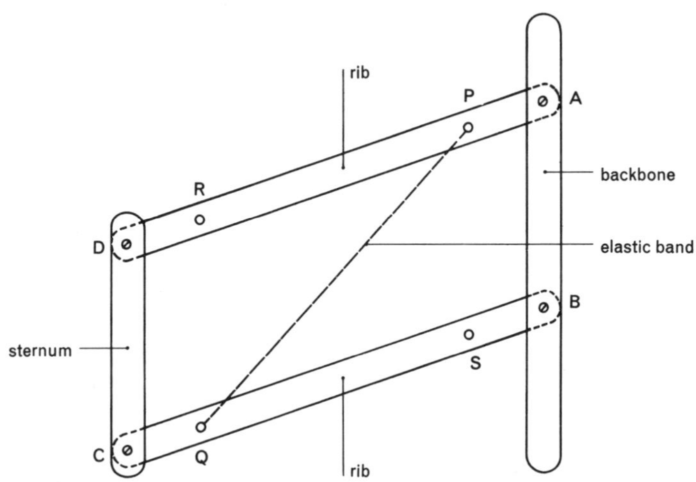

Fig. 2.20 Model of the action of intercostal muscles

Connect four small sticks (lollipop sticks are ideal) using drawing pins as shown in the diagram. Place additional pins at points P, Q, R and S.
Connect P and Q with an elastic band.
Then, keeping the 'backbone' rigid by bracing it against the top of your desk pinch the elastic band together. What happens to the 'ribs'?
Let go of the elastic band. What do you observe?
Now place a second elastic band between points R and S and pinch together. What happens this time?
By making the two elastic bands alternatively 'contract' and 'relax' you can raise and lower the lollipop sticks representing the rib cage. Note however, that during the actual breathing process relaxation of the external intercostal muscles is sufficient to allow the rib cage to be lowered to its resting position and air to be forced out of the lungs. Contractions of the internal intercostals only occur during forced expiration such as when coughing.

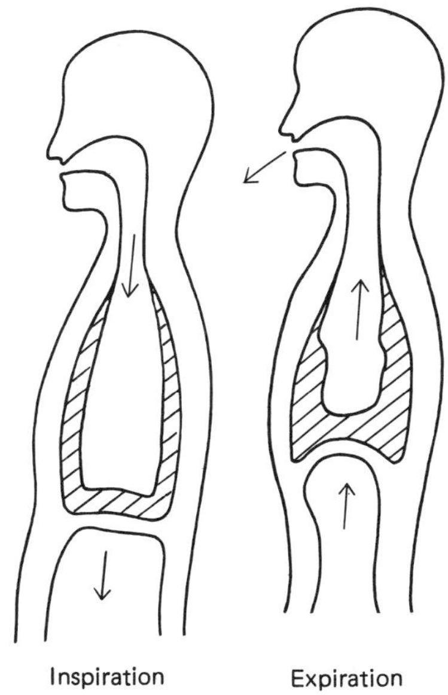

Fig. 2.21

The action of the diaphragm

Fold your arms tightly across your chest, pressing down on your rib cage.
In this position the breathing movements of the ribs are hindered.
Breathe in and out as slowly and as deeply as you can.
Can you feel the walls of your abdomen moving in and out?
This is due to the action of the muscles of the diaphragm contracting and relaxing.
Fig. 2.22 shows the position of the diaphragm in the contracted and relaxed states.

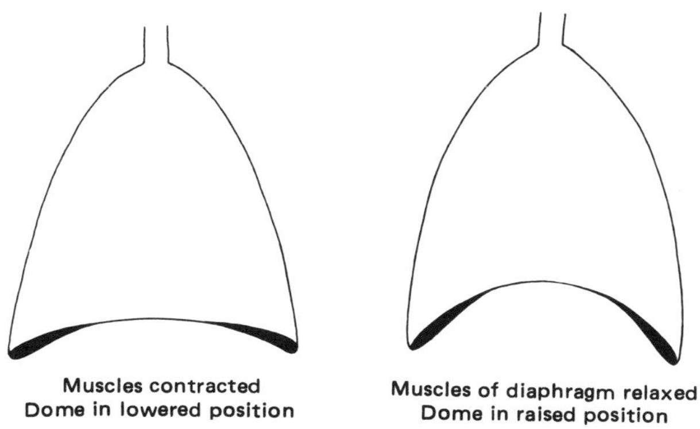

Fig. 2.22

Bell jar model

The action of the diaphragm can be illustrated using the bell jar model shown in fig. 2.23. When the rubber sheet is pulled down, due to the increase in volume inside the jar the air pressure decreases and air is drawn in through the opening and the balloons become

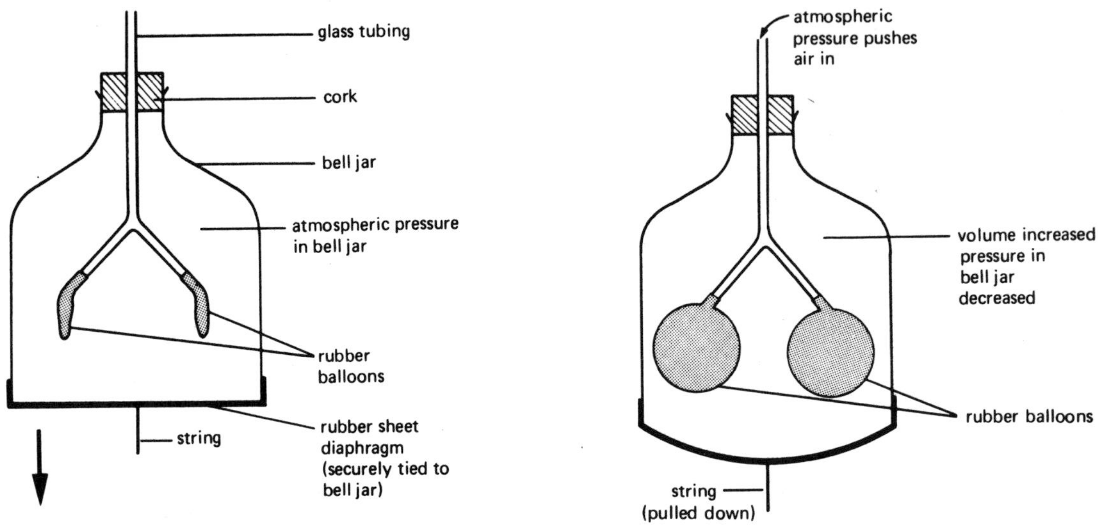

Fig. 2.23 **Bell-jar model**

filled. When the rubber sheet is released air is forced out of the balloons.

The action of the diaphragm in the body produces similar results. When the muscles contract the size of the thoracic cavity is increased. The internal pressure is lowered so that air is drawn in through the nose. The action of the ribs produces the same results as well. When the ribs are raised there is a slight increase in the thoracic volume. When the muscles of the diaphragm and the ribs relax the thoracic volume is decreased and air is forced out of the lungs.

There are several discrepancies between the bell jar model and the diaghragm that are worth noting.

1. In the body the diaphragm moves from a dome-shaped position to a more flattened position while the rubber sheet of the model is lowered from a horizontal position.
2. The chest wall is flexible and can move in and out as the volume inside is increased or decreased but the bell jar has rigid sides.
3. The lungs are surrounded by a thin layer of fluid which makes them adhere to the body wall whereas the balloons in the model are surrounded by air.

While breathing at rest mammals tend to use the action of the diaphragm more than that of the intercostal muscles. For efficient inhalation during physical activity both sets of muscles are necessary.

What causes air to rush into the lungs when the thoracic cavity is increased in size?

When the size of the cavity is increased the pressure of the air inside the cavity goes down because the amount of air that was in there originally has now been distributed in a larger volume. The pressure inside will be lower than the atmospheric pressure outside. To equalize the pressures air comes rushing into the lungs.

Summary

The sequence of events taking place during breathing in a mammal is:

1. Intercostal muscles contract raising the ribs.
2. At the same time the muscles of the diaphragm contract.
3. As a result of 1 and 2 the volume of the thoracic cavity is increased causing the pressure to decrease.
4. In order to restore the pressure air rushes in through the nose down the trachea and bronchi into the lungs.
5. The intercostal muscles and the muscles of the diaphragm relax and air is forced out of the lungs.
6. The sequence is repeated from 1.

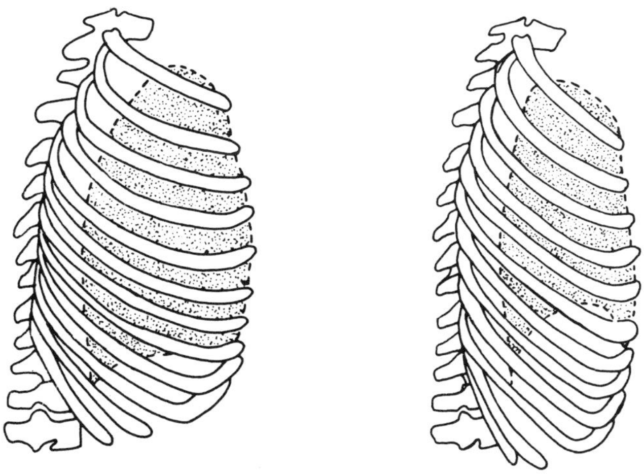

Inspiration — ribs are raised, diaphragm lowered

Expiration — ribs are lowered, diaphragm relaxed

Fig.2.24 Breathing in mammals

The structure of the lungs

If you cut in half the lungs of a dissected animal to reveal the internal structure or study fig. 2.25 you will realize that the passages through which air passes are arranged in a way that is very similar to the branches of a tree.

The trachea branches to form the left and right bronchi which in turn branch into smaller **bronchioles**. At the end of each passage is a tiny sac called an **alveolus**. Upon inhalation the alveoli become inflated with air; with expiration they collapse again.

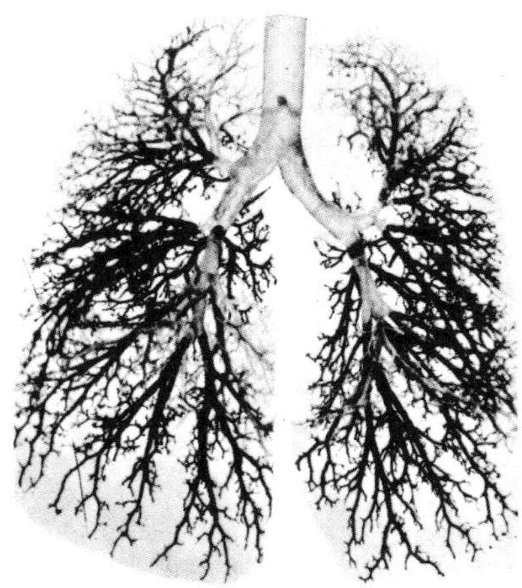

Fig.2.25 Bronchioles in lungs

Gas exchange

The walls of the alveoli are surrounded by numerous blood capillaries. Oxygen from the alveoli diffuses into the capillaries while carbon dioxide diffuses in the opposite direction.

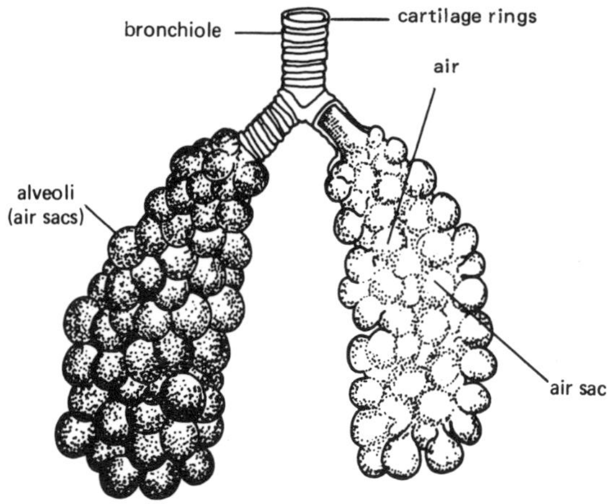

Fig.2.26 Diagram of lung with alveoli filled with air

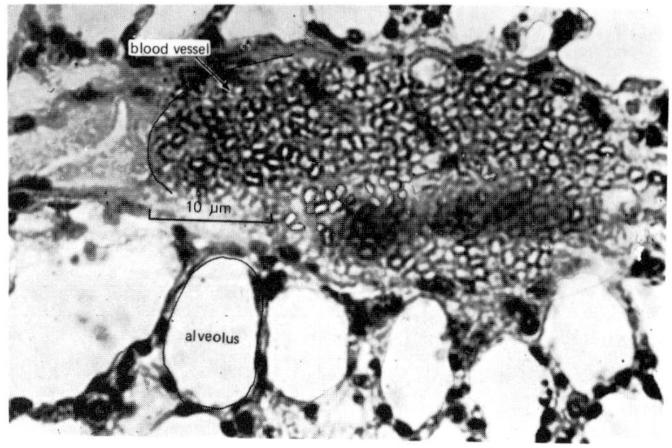

Fig.2.27 Magnified view of alveoli

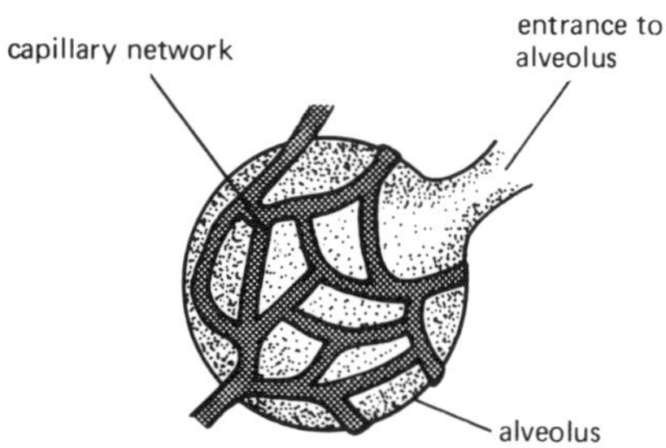

Fig.2.28 Relationship of capillaries with alveolar sac

You are already familiar with the process of diffusion as the mechanism responsible for the passage of soluble nutrient molecules from the small intestine into the blood stream at the surface of the villi. (See p. 80.) In order for diffusion to occur there must be a difference in the concentration of gases between the alveolus and the capillary. We can express the concentrations of the gases present by their pressure in millimetres of mercury (Hg).

Gas \ Partial pressure mm Hg	alveolus	capillary
Oxygen	100–110	40
Carbon dioxide	40	46

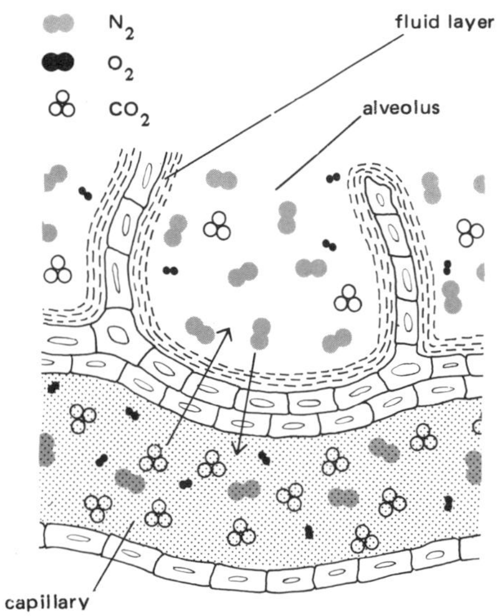

Fig.2.29 Gas exchange at surface of alveolus

Some of the oxygen in the alveolus dissolves in the fluid that moistens the lining of the sac. From there it diffuses into the blood of the capillaries. In the same way carbon dioxide diffuses from the capillaries into the alveoli.

It is therefore at the surface of the alveoli that the actual process of gas exchange takes place.

Once inside the capillaries most of the oxygen combines with the haemoglobin in the red blood cells and is carried around the body to all the cells that require it.

Rate of breathing

Oxygen is required in the body for respiration, the burning of organic molecules to release the energy they contain. As the energy requirements of the body change depending on whether we are at rest or doing vigorous exercise the rate of respiration and therefore the oxygen requirements change as well.

EXPERIMENT TO INVESTIGATE THE RATE OF BREATHING AND THE AMOUNT OF AIR INHALED WITH EACH BREATH

Materials

stop watch
bell jar
large container of water
rubber tubing

Method

1. Set up the apparatus as shown in the diagram. Be sure that the top opening of the bell jar is tightly sealed.
2. Ask your partner to determine with the aid of a stop watch the number of times you breathe per minute and the average volume of air that you inhale.
3. Breathe through the rubber tubing at your normal rate.
4. Perform a predetermined sequence of vigorous exercises such as running up and down several flights of stairs or stepping onto and down from a chair twenty-five times.
5. Repeat the measurements of breathing rate and volume of air inhaled.
6. Compare the results obtained before and after the exercises. Is there any difference between the two?

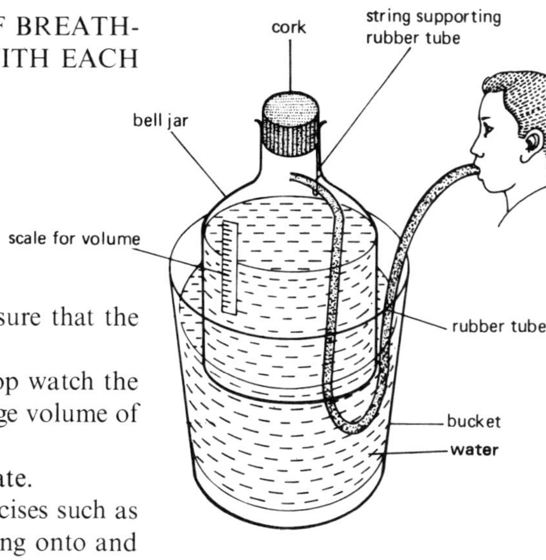

Fig.2.30 Measuring lung capacity

Discussion

You will probably find that both breathing rate and volume of inhaled air increase due to vigorous exercise. The usual rate of breathing in adult humans is between eight and twelve per minute when at rest but the rate can increase to sixty or more per minute with vigorous exercise.

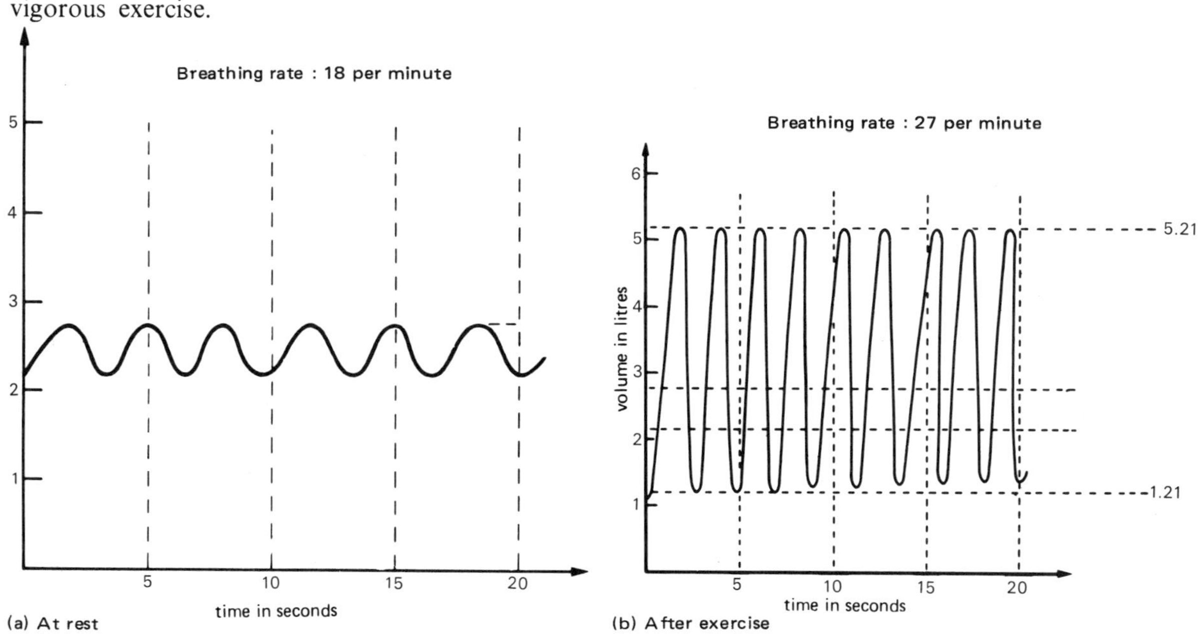

Fig.2.31 Graph showing rate of breathing and amount of air inhaled

How is the rate of breathing controlled?

The crucial factor in the regulatory mechanism is the level of carbon dioxide in the circulating blood. When the rate of cellular respiration increases such as in the case of vigorous exercise when there is a great demand for energy there is a corresponding increase in oxygen requirements and in carbon dioxide production. The blood carbon dioxide level is constantly being monitored by the brain. Impulses from the brain control the contractions of the intercostal muscles and the muscles of the diaphragm. Therefore when carbon dioxide levels increase the brain speeds up the rate of breathing, and when there is little carbon dioxide in the blood the brain slows down the breathing rate. If you put your head inside a large paper bag for only a few seconds so that you are inhaling exhaled air you would soon find an appreciable increase in your rate of breathing. The increase would be due to the body's efforts to eliminate excess carbon dioxide and to obtain sufficient supplies of oxygen. You may decide to test this idea but do not attempt to do it unless a teacher is present to supervise you and under no circumstances should you keep your head in the bag for more than about twenty seconds.

Fig. 2.32 **An iron lung in action**

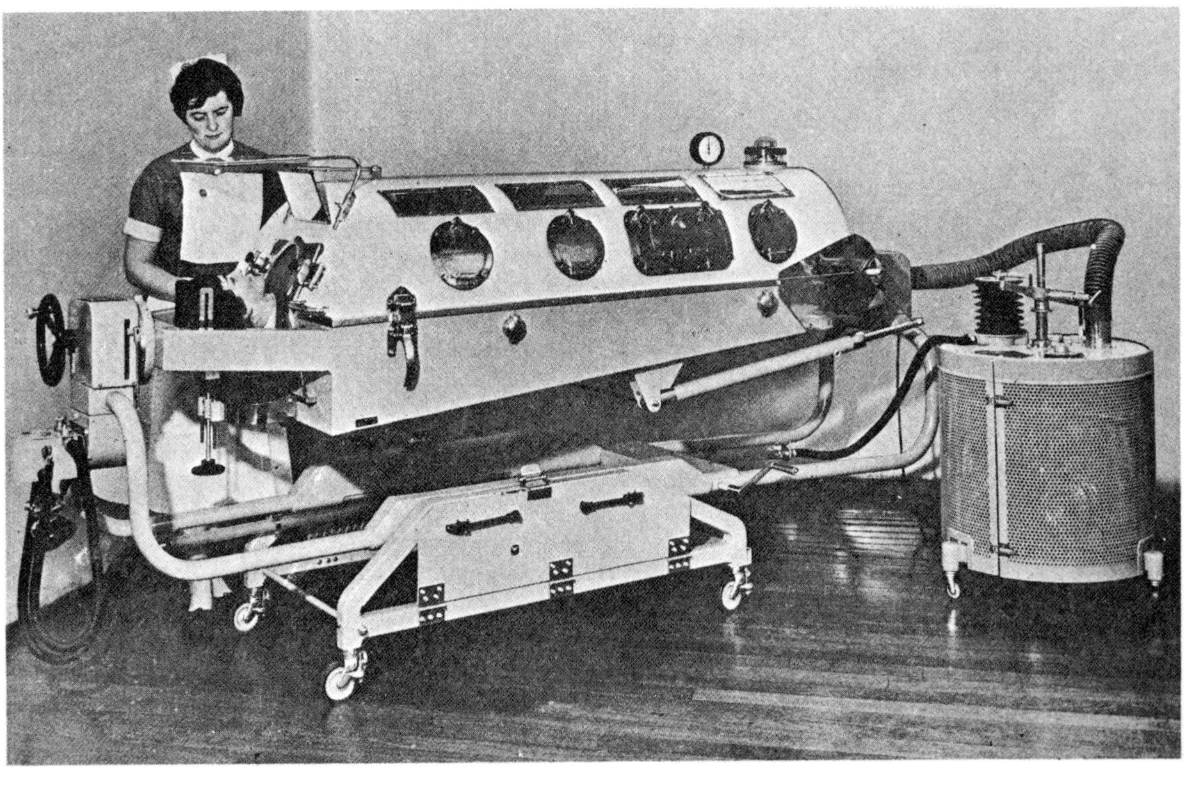

Abnormalities in breathing

We have said that the thorax is essentially an airtight box divided into two pleural sacs by a longitudinal partition.
Why does the thoracic cavity have to be air-tight?
It has to be air-tight to make possible the pressure changes needed for breathing.
What if, as a result of an accident, one of the pleural sacs was punctured?
Since the punctured pleural sac will be open to the atmosphere, the necessary pressure changes will no longer take place and the lung on that side will not be able to function.
A person's ability to breathe can also be lost as a result of other diseases, for example, poliomyelitis. In cases like this the patient can be made to breathe artificially with the help of an *iron lung*. He is placed inside a metal cabinet from the neck down and the air pressure inside the cabinet is alternately decreased and increased. When the air pressure inside the metal cabinet is decreased it causes a lowering of the pressure inside the lungs and air will flow in, as if the person were breathing normally. When the pressure is increased the air is forced out of the lungs.

Lung cancer[1]

In recent years more and more evidence has been accumulating to indicate that impurities in the air can cause serious irritation of the lung passages. Workers in coal mines, for example, breathe in air that contains fine particles of coal dust which become deposited in the membrane surface of the alveoli damaging the surface.
Scientists have also pointed out that more heavy smokers die from lung cancer than persons who do not smoke. Research work is still being done to find out if smoking can cause lung cancer. (See figs. 2.33 and 2.34.)

Summary

Gas exchange takes place at the surface of the alveoli in the lungs. Carbon dioxide diffuses from the blood capillaries into the alveoli while oxygen diffuses from the alveoli into the capillaries.
Both the rate of breathing and the amount of air inhaled in each breath increase during exercise.
Rate of breathing is controlled by the brain according to the level of carbon dioxide in the blood.
In recent years evidence has been found for a connection between smoking and lung cancer.

[1] *cancer*: uncontrolled growth of cells leading to serious damage of the affected organ

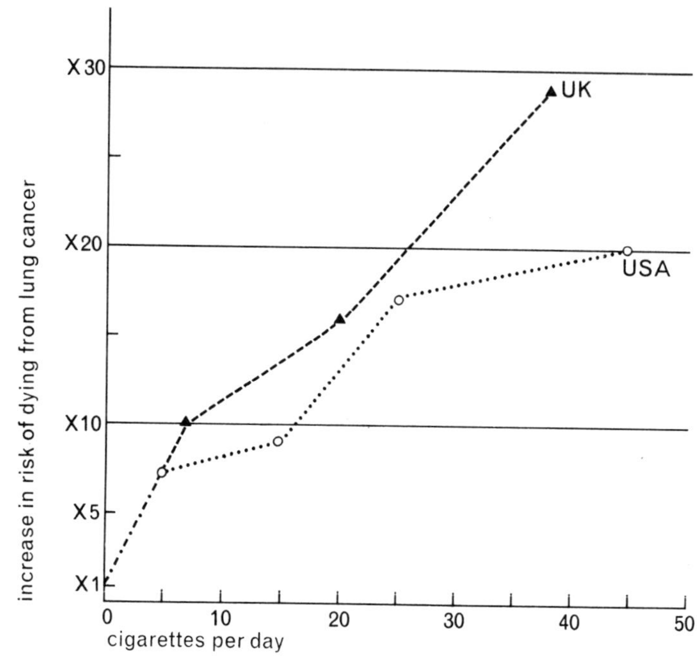

Fig.2.33 Relationship between number of cigarettes smoked per day and risk of lung cancer ***(From Smoking and Health, 1962)***

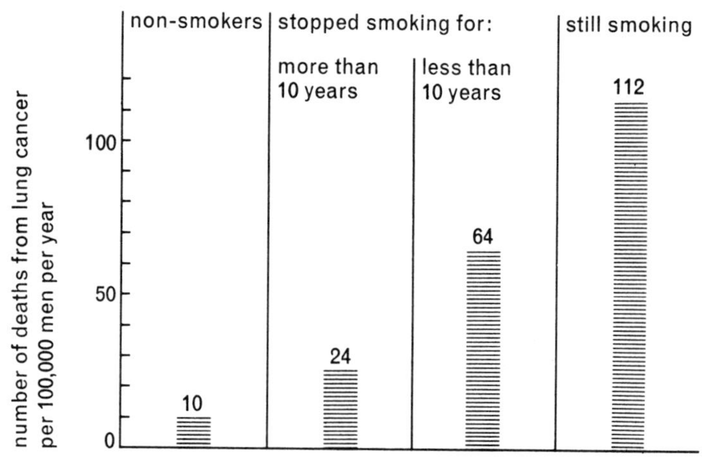

Fig.2.34 Relationship between smoking and number of deaths from lung cancer ***(From Smoking and Health, 1962)***

Gas exchange in other animals

The mechanisms of breathing and gas exchange described in the previous section apply only to mammals. Non-mammalian species have other ways of obtaining oxygen and eliminating carbon dioxide.

Aquatic and land invertebrates

In aquatic invertebrates and some terrestrial invertebrates gas exchange takes place by diffusion through the surface of the skin. The ratio of surface area to volume of these animals is sufficiently high so that the amount of oxygen diffusing in through the surface can satisfy the needs of the organisms. Most of their body cells are sufficiently close to the surface that oxygen can reach them by diffusion, or if not, a simple system of capillaries may exist such as that in the earthworm.

Oxygen dissolves in a thin layer of moisture covering the outer surface of the body and from there diffuses into the interior in much the same way as oxygen diffuses into the capillaries of a mammal from the alveoli. In the case of land invertebrates, therefore, a moist body surface is essential.

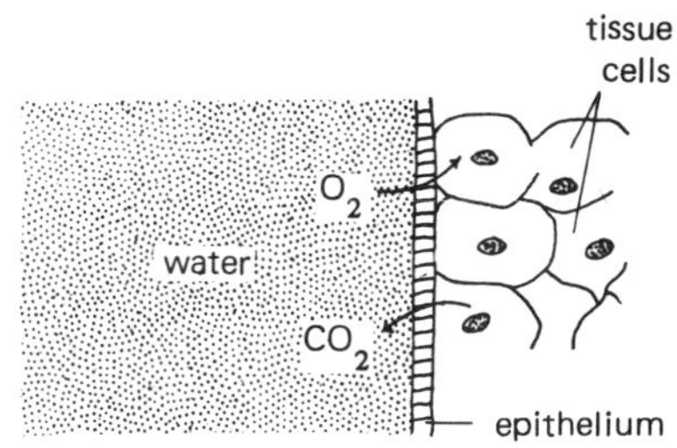

Fig.2.35 Body wall of aquatic invertebrate

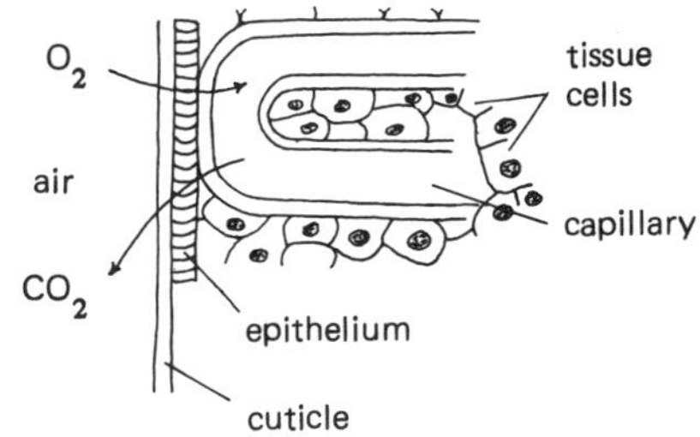

Fig.2.36 Body wall of earthworm

Fish

In larger aquatic animals such as the fish the ratio of surface to volume is much smaller. Many of the cells are located deep within the body of the animals and diffusion alone cannot satisfy their needs. The efficiency of the diffusion process is further limited by the low solubility of oxygen in water. These animals therefore need a circulatory system of some sort to carry oxygen to their cells and remove carbon dioxide from them.

In fish gas exchange takes place with the help of **gills**. The **gill filaments**, feather-like pieces of tissue, have a very rich blood supply, and they provide a sufficiently large surface area for adequate diffusion to take place.

Water passing through the mouth of the fish is forced over the gills where gas exchange takes place and is then forced out through the **operculum**.

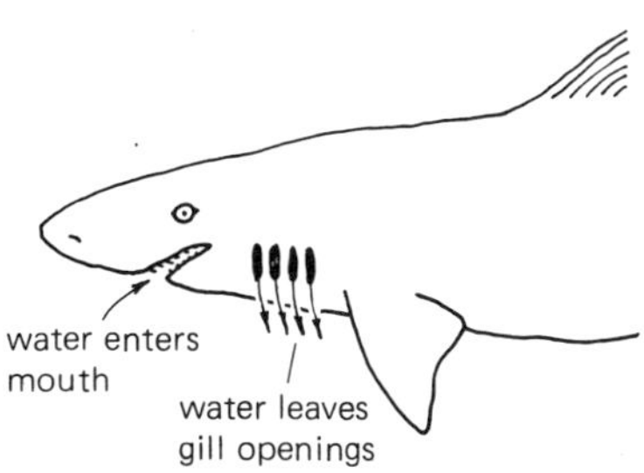

Fig.2.37 Head of fish

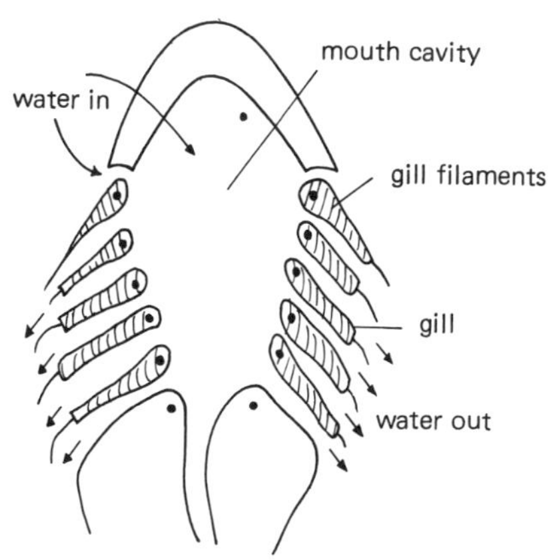

Fig.2.38 Water circulation in mouth and over gills

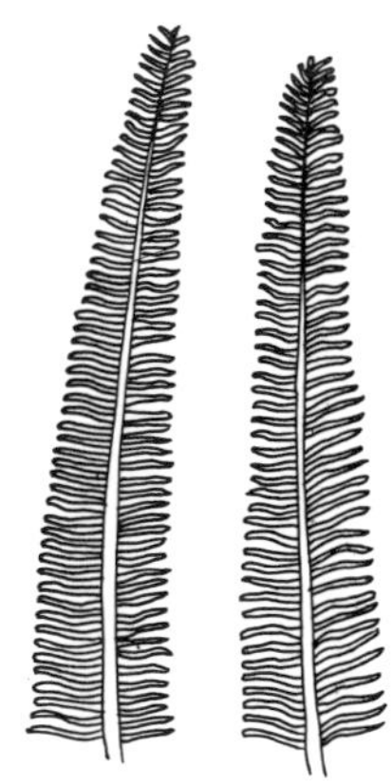

Fig.2.39 Gill filaments

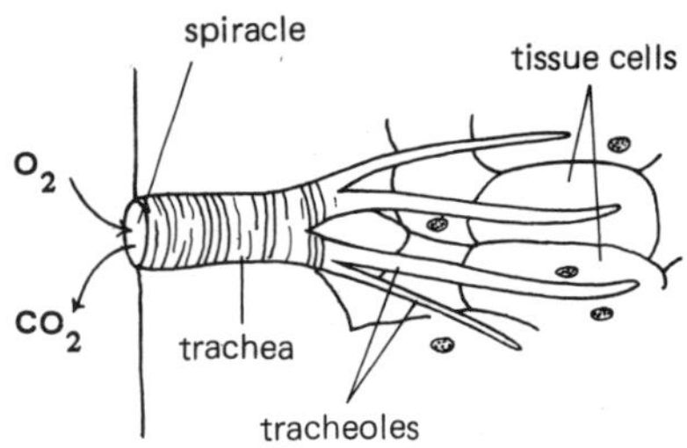

Fig.2.40 Trachea of insect

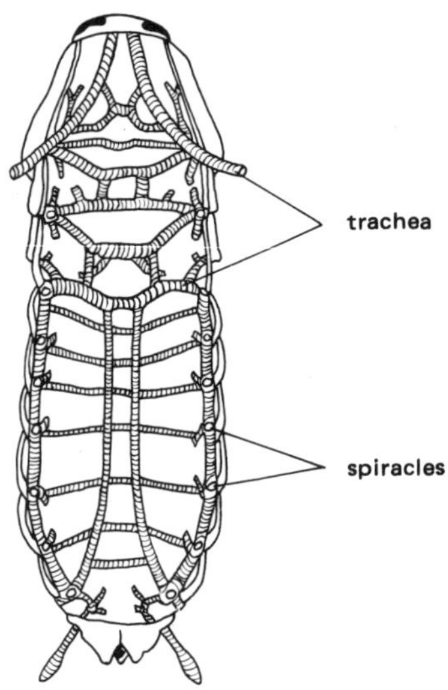

Fig.2.41 Main tracheal system of cockroach

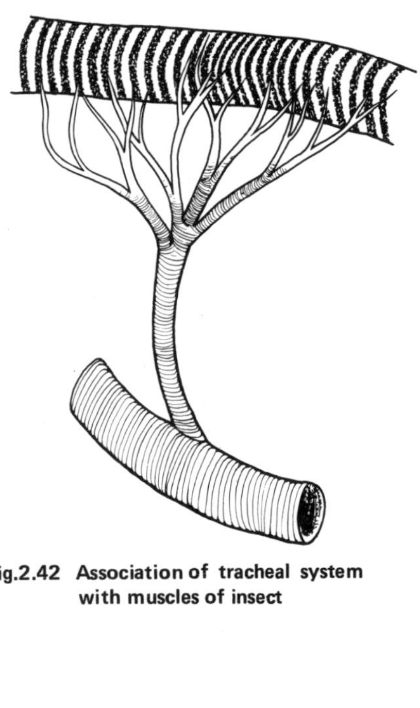

Fig.2.42 Association of tracheal system with muscles of insect

Insects

Many insects have a complicated system of tubules leading from the surface of the body to the cells in the interior for the purpose of gas exchange. Air enters the tiny pores called **spiracles**, then passes along a complicated branching system of **trachea** and **tracheoles.** The tracheal system of the cockroach shown in fig. 2.41 is a typical example.

The tiny endings of the tracheoles deep inside the body of the insect are filled with fluid. Oxygen dissolves in the fluid and diffuses into the adjacent cells. Carbon dioxide diffuses out.

Among smaller or less active insects there is no need for special means of ventilating the system of spiracles. In larger, more active insects such as the cockroach, contractions of the abdominal muscles force air into and out of the trachea.

Land vertebrates

Most land vertebrates possess lungs whether consisting of merely a simple sac or a complicated system such as that of the mammals. In species such as the frog, however, lungs are secondary in importance and are used only when the animal is extremely active. At rest, about fifty percent of the gas exchange takes place through the skin of the frog. Oxygen from the air dissolves in the moisture on the skin and diffuses into the capillaries. The lining membrane of the mouth is also rich in capillaries and gas exchange takes place through its surface.

Summary

All aquatic invertebrates and some land invertebrates exchange gases through the surface of their skin without need for any specialized respiratory organs.

Fish accomplish gas exchange by the use of gills.

Insects have a complicated system of tubules to carry gases throughout their bodies.

Most land vertebrates possess lungs.

Gas exchange in plants

Gas exchange in green plants is a seemingly more complex process than that in animals since in photosynthesis carbon dioxide is consumed and oxygen is liberated while in respiration the reverse is true. (See fig. 2.43.)

How are these two opposing reactions kept in balance?

Since photosynthesis can only take place in the presence of light perhaps the degree of illumination has an influence on the balancing of the two processes.

EXPERIMENT TO INVESTIGATE GAS EXCHANGE IN GREEN PLANTS UNDER VARYING LIGHT CONDITIONS

Materials

bicarbonate/indicator
soda-lime
freshly picked leaves
muslin or cheesecloth
aluminium foil or black paper

Method

1. Pour equal amounts of indicator (about 3cm^3) into each of four test-tubes.
2. In each of tubes 1, 2 and 3 place a green leaf taking care that it does not come into contact with the indicator.
3. Cover tube 1 with aluminium foil.
4. Cover tube 2 with a layer of muslin or cheesecloth.
5. Seal all four tubes with rubber bungs. Place the tubes in a water bath at room temperature to keep the temperature inside as constant as possible.
6. Place the water bath by a sunny window or about two feet away from an incandescent lamp.
7. Every five minutes or so shake the tubes gently to make better contact between the indicator and the air.

Note: Be sure to use absolutely clean tubes and do not breathe over them as you are setting up the experiment.

Fig.2.43

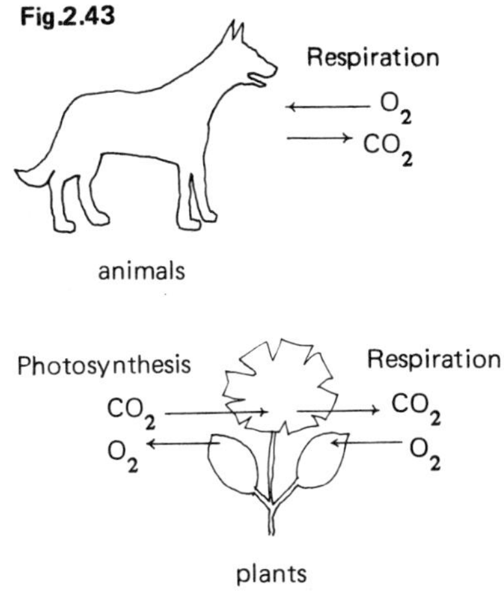

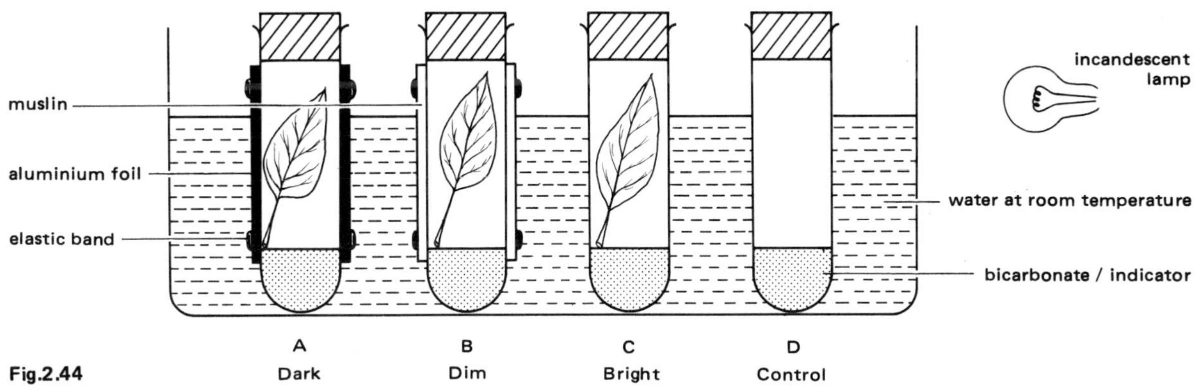

Fig.2.44

What happens to the indicator solutions in the four tubes?
Compare your results with those of your fellow students. Do they agree?
Why might there be considerable variation in the colour of the indicator in tube B?
How can you relate the amount of carbon dioxide in a given tube to the light conditions?

Discussion

The results of this experiment can be summarized in a table as shown below.

Tube	Light conditions	Colour of indicator	Amount of carbon dioxide
1	dark	yellow	more than in atmospheric air
2	dim	red*	same as in atmospheric air
3	bright	purple	less than in atmospheric air

*The colour obtained in tube 2 depends on exactly how much light is able to get through the tube. If the muslin used is fairly thick and little light gets through the indicator will tend to turn yellow. If the reverse is true the indicator will tend to turn purple.

The above results suggest that green plants consume carbon dioxide in bright light and release carbon dioxide in the absence of light. What is actually happening is that plants respire at more or less the same rate all the time, just as animals do. In other words, plants consume oxygen and release carbon dioxide continuously.

Fig.2.45

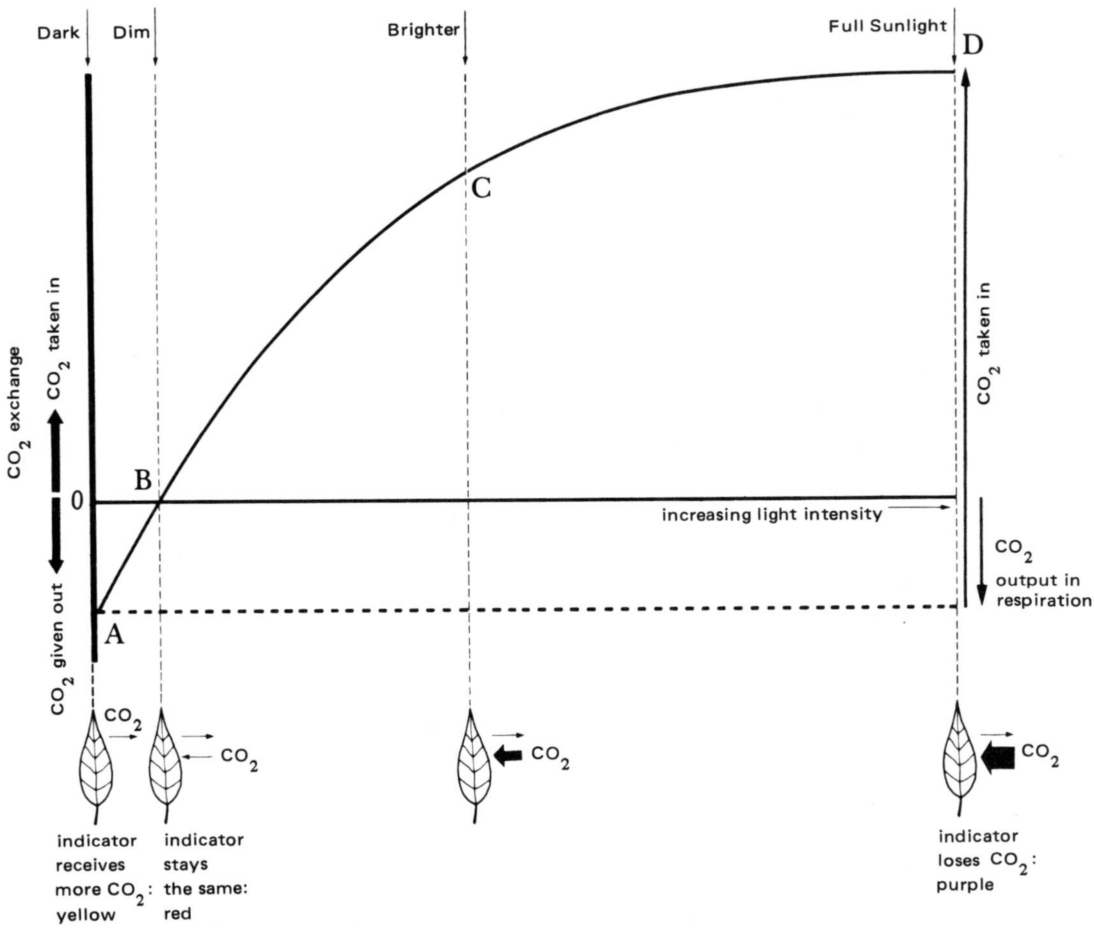

In addition, when exposed to light they consume carbon dioxide and liberate oxygen due to photosynthesis. The rate at which photosynthesis proceeds depends in part on the intensity of light. In very bright light the carbon dioxide consumed far exceeds the amount liberated with the result that the plant removes carbon dioxide from the atmosphere. In dim light the rate of respiration and the rate of photosynthesis are just about equal and no net exchange of gases takes place. The amount of carbon dioxide liberated in respiration is just enough to balance the amount needed for photosynthesis. Therefore the indicator stays red. Fig. 2.45 helps to illustrate what is happening.

How do gases get into and out of the cells of green leaves?

Gas exchange in green leaves occurs through pores called **stomata** (singular **stoma**) in the leaf surface.

EXPERIMENT TO PREPARE A SECTION OF LEAF EPIDERMIS TO OBSERVE THE STOMATA

Materials

freshly picked leaf
coloured nail varnish
microscope
slides and coverslips

Method

1. Paint a small portion of each leaf surface with a single coat of nail varnish.
2. After the varnish has dried peel it away from the surface of the leaf.
3. Mount the peels in a drop of water on a clean microscope slide. Make certain you remember which surface each has come from.
4. Observe the imprint of the leaf epidermis that has been left on the varnish peel.

Are the epidermal cells arranged in a regular fashion?
Are they tightly packed everywhere or are there some gaps?
Look for oval-shaped structures that may be interspersed among the epidermal cells. These are the stomata.
Are stomata found on both surfaces of the leaf?
Draw a simple sketch of the two leaf surfaces.

Discussion

The cells of the upper and lower epidermis of a leaf form a regular array that acts as a protective layer. Scattered among the cells are the special openings called the stomata. In some plants they are found only on the upper surface, in some, only on the lower surface and in still others on both surfaces. Note that the actual shape of the cells differs depending on the plant used and will not be identical with fig. 2.46.
The two oval-shaped cells on either side of the actual opening are the **guard cells**, so called because they are able to control the opening

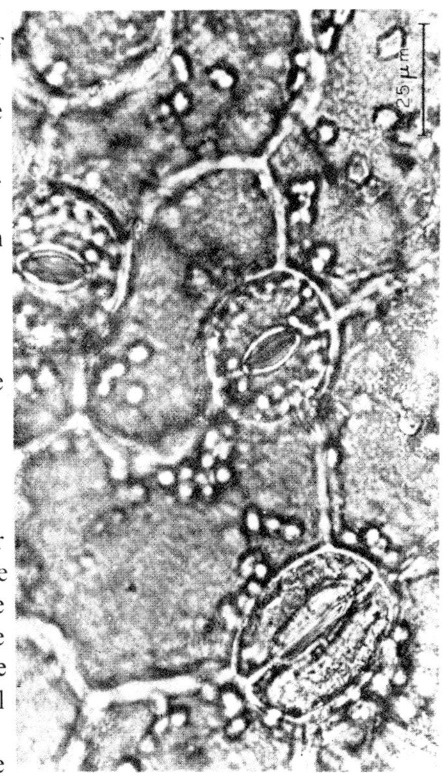

Fig.2.46 Stomata on surface of leaf

and closing of the pore. In general, guard cells are shaped like a pair of sausages. Due to changes in turgidity inside the cells, they assume either a crescent shape whereby the stoma opens or a straight line so that the opening becomes closed.
Stomata are usually open during the day when a lot of light is falling on the leaves and remain closed at night when no light falls on them.

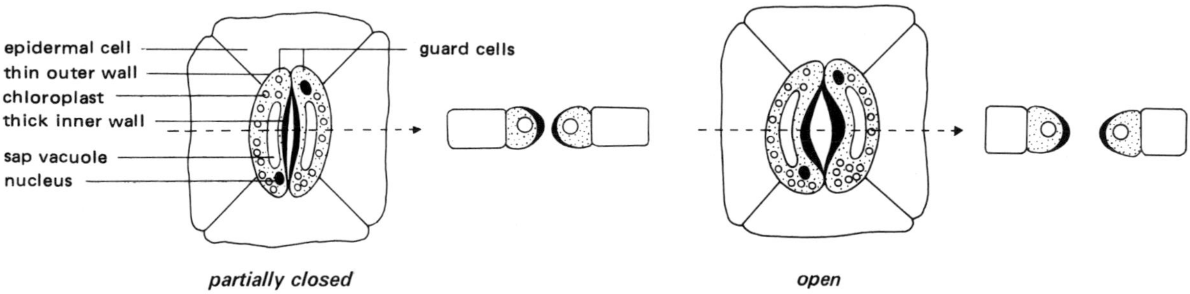

Fig.2.47 A stoma in surface view and section

In addition to their role in gas exchange stomata are also responsible for controlling the amount of moisture that leaves the plant through **transpiration**. This aspect of stomatal activity is discussed in detail on pp. 148 to 156.

What happens to the air that enters the leaf through the stomata?

The air that enters the leaf through the stomatal opening passes into the air spaces between the spongy mesophyll cells (fig. 2.48). Gases

Fig.2.48 Gas exchange in air spaces in leaf

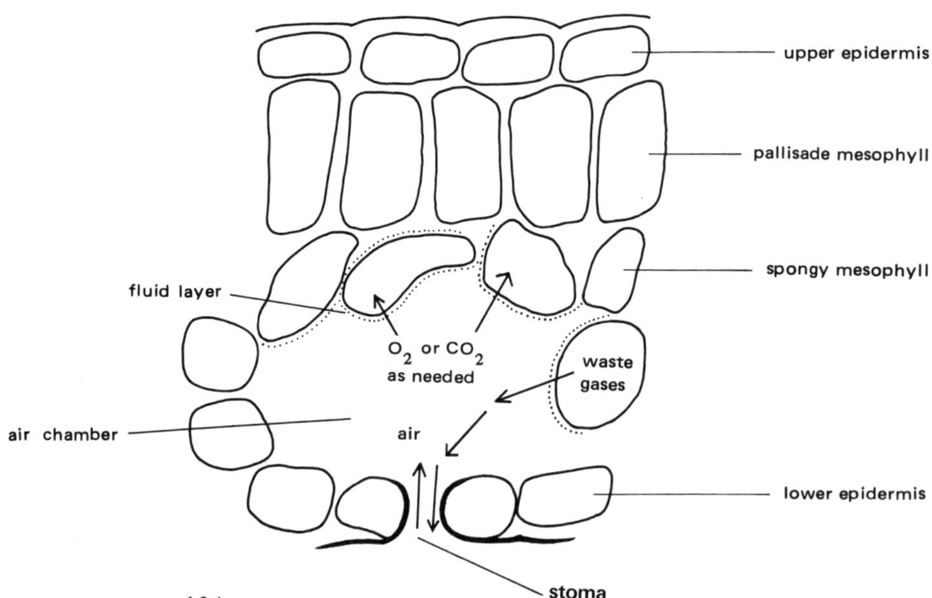

can dissolve in the layer of moisture found on the surfaces of these cells and diffuse into their interior.
Waste gases from the cells diffuse out into the intercellular[1] spaces and leave by way of the stomata.

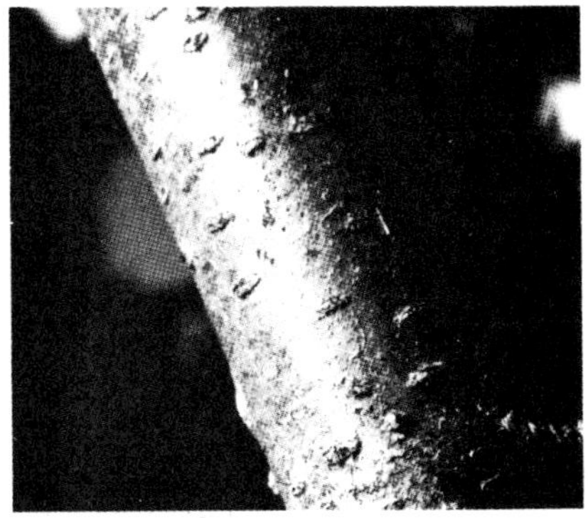

Fig.2.49 Lenticels on a stem

Does gas exchange take place in the plant stem?

The cells in the stem of a plant require oxygen for respiration even though non-green stems do not require carbon dioxide for photosynthesis. In young green stems where photosynthesis is still proceeding actively gas exchange takes place through stomatal openings in the same manner as in the leaves. In older stems where a protective bark has already formed special gaps in the bark called **lenticels** are present.

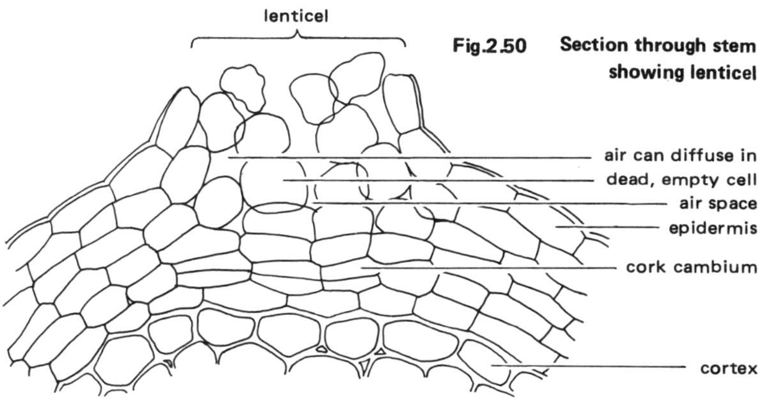

Fig.2.50 Section through stem showing lenticel

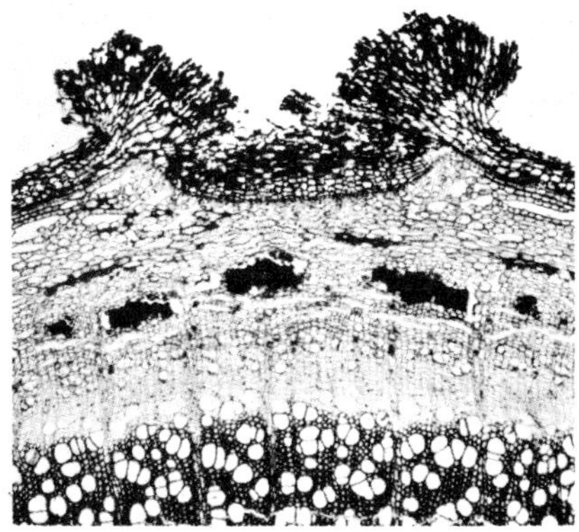

Fig.2.51 Section through a lenticel

The opening of a lenticel is usually round or oval and it is raised slightly above the surface of the surrounding tissues. Air passes into the spaces between the surface cells and from there diffuses into the surrounding cells in the deeper layers.

Gas exchange in roots

The oxygen needs of roots are not very great and are generally met by diffusion of air into the cells from the air spaces in the surrounding soil. Some oxygen is always found dissolved in the film of water on the surfaces of soil particles and from there enters the root hairs by diffusion. From the root hairs it can pass into the cells of the interior. In the thick, older portions of the root where root hairs are not present gas exchange takes place through lenticels.
If the soil is soaked through with water so that there is no air in the spaces between the particles the roots will not be able to obtain oxygen. If exposed to such water-logged conditions for prolonged periods most plants will die. Some plants that live in very swampy

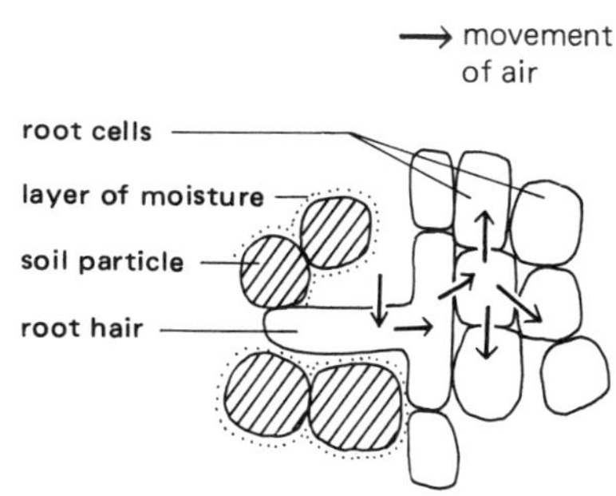

Fig.2.52 Diffusion of oxygen into roots

[1] *intercellular*: between the cells

habitats have acquired a special adaptation to overcome this problem. The mangrove tree for instance has special **breathing roots** that project out of the ground and absorb air from the atmosphere.

Gas exchange in seeds

In seeds and young seedlings gas exchange takes place through simple diffusion through the epidermis. Until the stomata of the seedling start to develop no special structures for gas exchange exist.

Summary

Green parts of plants such as the leaves, need carbon dioxide for photosynthesis, while all plant cells need oxygen for respiration.
In cells that carry on photosynthesis, requirement for gas exchange depends on light conditions.
In leaves and green stems gas exchange takes place through the stomatal openings.
In woody stems and roots the lenticels provide openings for gas exchange.
In seedlings and young roots gas exchange takes place by diffusion through the surface cell layers.

Section 3. OTHER ASPECTS OF METABOLISM

WATER RELATIONS

Osmosis

EXPERIMENT TO ILLUSTRATE THE EXISTENCE OF OSMOTIC PRESSURE IN PLANT AND ANIMAL CELLS

a. Osmosis across a non-living semi-permeable membrane

Materials

two thistle funnels
selectively-permeable membrane eg. cellophane, Visking tubing
ten percent solution of sucrose in water
distilled water
dilute hydrochloric acid
Benedict's solution

Method

1. Cover the wide end of the thistle funnels with the membrane making certain that there is no possibility of leakage.
2. Fill funnel A with sugar solution to about 1cm from the bottom of the narrow part. Mark the level.
3. Attach to a stand and lower into a container of distilled water. Note the time.
4. In exactly the same way, set up a second thistle funnel, B, containing distilled water only.
5. Find and mark the levels of the liquid in the two funnels, five, ten and twenty minutes after the start of the experiment.
6. At the end of the twenty-minute period test the water in the two outside containers for the presence of sugar (see p. 45).

What do you observe?
Is there any difference in liquid levels between the two funnels?
How do you account for the difference?
Why has sugar not passed into the outside container?

b. Observing osmosis across living tissue

Materials

two raw potatoes
one potato that has been boiled for five minutes to kill the cells
ten percent sucrose solution
distilled water

Method

1. Remove the skin and slice off one end of each potato to make a flat bottom.

Fig.3.1

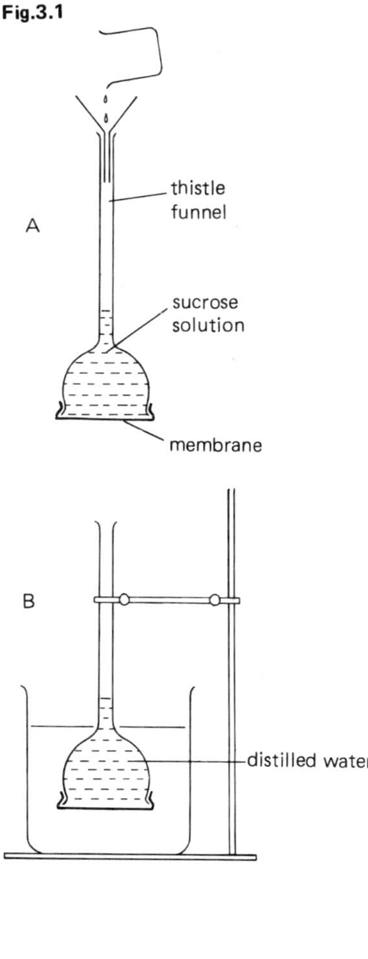

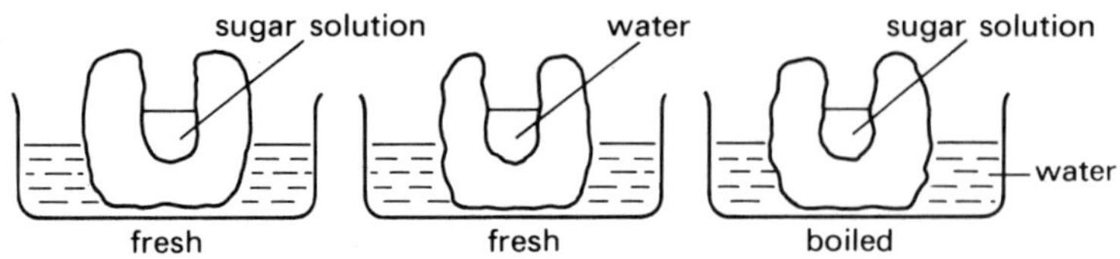

Fig. 3.2

2. Scoop out the centre from the top with a knife or cork borer to leave a deep cavity.
3. Pour in sucrose solution to fill two-thirds of the cavity of the boiled potato and one of the fresh ones.
4. Pour an equal amount of distilled water into the second fresh potato.
5. Stand all three in separate containers of distilled water and set aside until the next day.
6. Test the distilled water in the containers for the presence of sugar.

Fig.3.3 Mechanism of osmosis

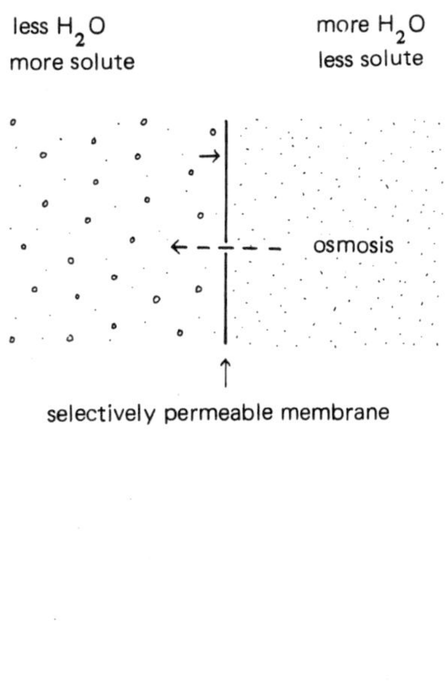

What do you observe in this experiment?
Do the observations agree with those of experiment *a*?
How do you explain the results obtained in the case of the boiled potato?

Discussion

From experiments carried out on diffusion we know that substances tend to move from a place of high concentration to one of low concentration. This is a purely mechanical process requiring no energy. It is due to the constant motion of all molecules, whether solid, liquid or gas, and results in an equal distribution of these molecules in the space available.

Consider a system such as the one in experiment *a* where two solutions of unequal strength are separated by a *selectively permeable* membrane. One can either say that the thistle funnel contains a higher concentration of sucrose or that it has a lower concentration of water; whereas the container has a lower concentration of solute or a higher concentration of water. If the two were separated by a *freely permeable* membrane the differences in concentration would be equalized by the combined effect of water diffusing into the funnel and sugar diffusing out.

Since the selectively permeable membrane does not allow sugar molecules to pass through it, equalizing of the two concentrations has to be achieved solely by water moving into the thistle funnel. This movement of water across a selectively permeable membrane is called **osmosis**. The pressure causing the water to move across the membrane is called **osmotic pressure.** In experiment *a* water flowed across the selectively permeable membrane into the funnel containing the sugar solution but not into the one containing water. There was no trace of sugar leaking out through the membrane. In experiment *b* water entered the sugar-filled cavity of the fresh potato but the sugar was not able to get out. The living cells of the potato must therefore be acting as a selectively permeable membrane.

What is happening in the case of the boiled potato?
Boiling has killed the cells of the potato and they are no longer able to act as a barrier to solute molecules. The system becomes freely permeable. Water moves into the cavity and at the same time some sugar moves out into the outside container.

Is the amount of water passing through a selectively permeable membrane affected by the difference in the concentrations on the two sides?

It certainly is. The greater the difference between the solute concentrations the higher the osmotic pressure. More water will be required to pass through the membrane to equalize the concentrations.
You can illustrate this by having different members of the class set up experiment *a* using a variety of sugar concentrations from, say, one percent to twenty-five percent. You could also try putting sugar solution in both the inside and the outside containers. You will find that the determining factor in osmosis is the *difference* in concentrations between the two sides of the membrane.

Terminology relating to osmosis

If a cell is placed in a solution whose osmotic pressure is the same as that of the cell contents the solution is said to be **isotonic** with the cell. If the external solution has a lower osmotic pressure the solution is referred to as **hypotonic**; if higher, the solution is **hypertonic**.

Fig.3.4

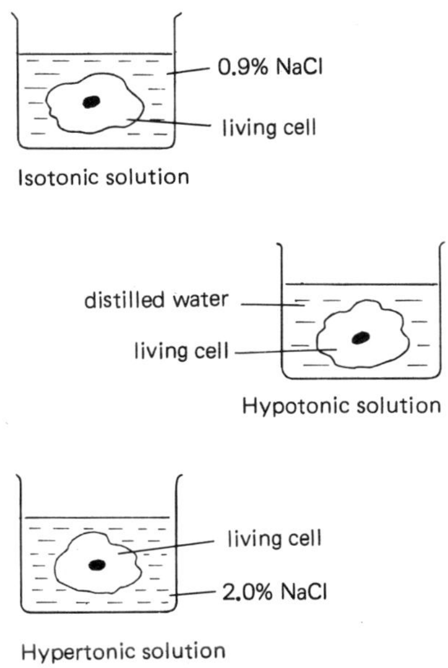

EXPERIMENT TO INVESTIGATE THE EFFECT OF HYPERTONIC, ISOTONIC AND HYPOTONIC SOLUTIONS ON LIVING CELLS

a. Simple demonstration using an animal cell.
Materials
Solutions: A—isotonic saline—0.9 percent sodium chloride
B—hypertonic saline—2.0 percent sodium chloride
C—hypotonic saline—0.1 percent sodium chloride
drops of fresh blood
microscope, slides, coverslips
alcohol
sterilized pipette
Method
1. Prepare three slides labelled A, B and C and place a drop of the corresponding solution on each.
2. Sterilize the tip of one of your fingers and prick it with a sterilized needle or ask your partner to prick it for you.
3. Draw up some blood into a sterilized pipette and place a drop into the solution on each slide. Mix with a toothpick.
4. Carefully put on the coverslips and observe under the microscope.

Fig.3.5

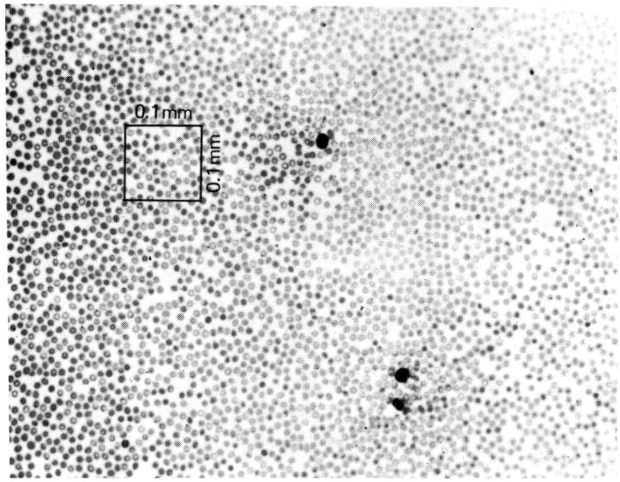

Fig.3.6 Blood cells under the microscope

What changes do you observe?
What are the changes due to?
Draw a simple diagram to show the appearance of the red blood cells on each of the slides.

b. Simple demonstration using a plant cell
Materials
strips of raw potato about 1cm wide
ten percent sucrose solution
distilled water
Method
1. Weigh and measure the length of the potato strip.
2. Place into a small container of distilled water for about twenty minutes.
3. Remove, weight and measure length.
4. Place into the sugar solution for twenty minutes.
5. Remove, weigh and measure the length.

What happens when living cells are placed in a hypotonic solution (water)? In a hypertonic solution (sugar solution)?
What is responsible for the changes you observe?
Draw a simple diagram to illustrate your observation using arrows to indicate the direction of water movement.

c. The effect of salt solution and distilled water on Spirogyra or epidermal tissue
Materials
Spirogyra or a thin layer of an onion scale
five percent sodium chloride
microscope, slides, coverslips
iodine solution
Method
1. Place some of the tissue on a microscope slide. If you are using

Fig.3.7

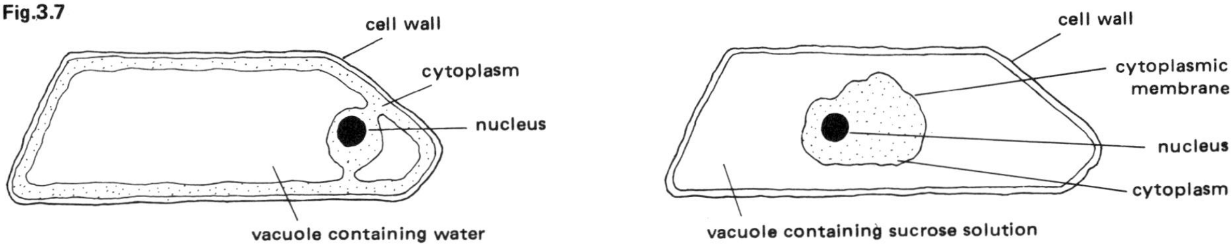

(i) Surface view of typical onion epidermal cell

(ii) Plasmolysed onion epidermal cell (position of the nucleus varies)

onion scales staining with a drop of iodine will make the cells more visible. Carefully blot off all excess stain.

2. Place a drop of salt solution on your material, put on a coverslip and blot off excess solution.

3. Observe under the microscope for five to ten minutes or until a definite change can be seen in the cells.

4. Replace the salt solution by water. You can do this by touching a piece of absorbent paper to one side of the coverslip and placing drops of water next to the opposite edge. Gradually, as the liquid is drawn over the slide the salt solution will be washed away and be replaced by water.

5. Observe under the microscope again until a definite change can be seen.

What happens to the cells when they are in the salt solution?
What can you conclude about the differences between the cellulose cell wall and the protoplasmic membrane? Is the process you observe reversible?

Discussion

Experiment *a* showed that when red blood cells are placed into an isotonic solution no changes are apparent since the solute concentration inside and outside is the same.

In a hypotonic solution the osmotic pressure inside the cell is higher than that outside and water will tend to flow into the cell by osmosis. As a result the protoplasmic membrane will expand and the cell will swell up. If the difference in osmotic pressures is very great so much water will enter the cells that they will burst, much the same way as a balloon with too much air forced into it will burst. The bursting of the red blood cells under these conditions is called **haemolysis**.

If the cells are in a hypertonic solution the osmotic pressure is higher outside and water will leave the cell. The cell will shrink perceptibly and the protoplasmic membrane will assume a characteristic 'crinkled' shape.

Experiments *b* and *c* dealt with plant cells. In the former you were able to observe that plant material will lose weight and shrink slightly if placed in a hypertonic solution. Clearly, water must be leaving the cells.

Fig.3.8 Red blood cells

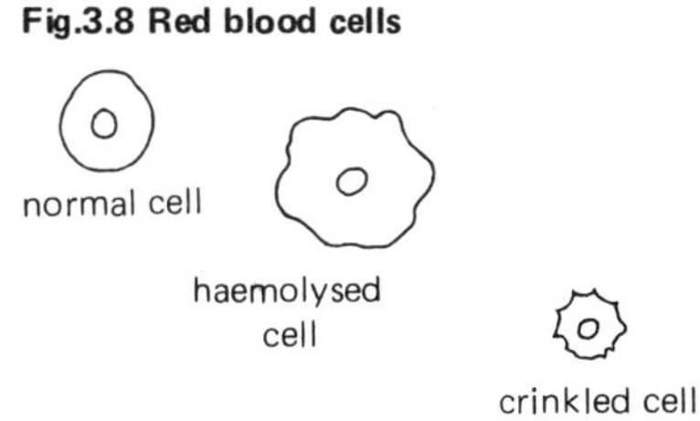

Experiment *c* indicates that the situation is more complex. Plant cells are surrounded not only by a protoplasmic membrane but by a wall of cellulose. While the former is selectively permeable, the latter is freely permeable. When a plant cell is placed in a hypertonic solution the difference in osmotic pressure will cause the water to move out through the protoplasmic membrane and the membrane will gradually shrink away from the cell wall towards the interior of the cell as more and more water is lost. The cell wall, being completely rigid, will maintain its original position. Since it is freely permeable a small amount of sugar solution will pass into the space between the cell wall and the protoplasmic membrane. This state of the plant cell is called **plasmolysis**.

If a cell remains **plasmolysed** for a short time only, upon replacement of the hypertonic solution with an isotonic or hypotonic one, water will enter the cell and the protoplasmic membrane will return to its original position.

When placed in a hypotonic solution water will enter, the cell will expand and become **turgid**. However, it will not burst because the rigidity of the cell wall will prevent more water from entering. **Turgidity** is a very important factor in relation to support in plants (see p. 175).

Summary

The differential movement of water across a selectively permeable membrane from the side containing a lower solute concentration to the side with a higher concentration is called osmosis.

The pressure that develops as a result of the unequal concentrations is called osmotic pressure and its value depends on the difference in the concentrations.

If a living cell is placed in a hypotonic solution water will move into the cell causing the cell to expand. A cell placed in a hypertonic solution will lose water and shrink. When a cell is isotonic with the surrounding solution no net movement of water will occur.

Water and the organism

The importance of water in the various processes carried on by living organisms cannot be emphasized too much. The chemical processes of respiration and photosynthesis cannot proceed without water. The only way chemical substances of any kind can pass through the membrane barriers in living organisms is by dissolving in water and passing through by diffusion. Oxygen dissolves in a thin film of liquid on the walls of the alveoli in order to be able to pass through into the capillaries. Food particles have to be in a soluble form before they can be absorbed in the small intestine.

Of the numerous compounds and elements found in living organisms water is the most abundant. The actual percentage of water varies. In some organisms water makes up ninety percent of the total body weight. In humans it makes up about seventy percent of the body weight.

Most of this water is contained in the cytoplasm of the cells and in the intercellular spaces. The rest is found in the circulatory system, the digestive system and so on.

How do living organisms obtain the water they need?

Many plants and animals live in a liquid medium and therefore have no problems obtaining water. In fact their problem is, on the contrary, to keep excess water out. Among terrestrial animals, the ones that live in damp surroundings are able to take in water through the skin. Some, for example snails, have a special body covering to prevent the loss of excessive moisture. Most other animals replenish their water supply by eating foods that contain a large percentage of water and by drinking water.

Plants obtain water from the soil through their roots.

Osmoregulation in animals

The maintenance of the correct intracellular concentration of water in the face of varying extracellular conditions is called **osmoregulation** and the process is of vital importance to every living organism.

Amoeba

Among unicellular amoebae, there exist both marine and freshwater species. Since sea water is approximately isotonic with their protoplasm, marine species need no special adaptations for water regulation.

The freshwater species are surrounded by a medium that is markedly hypotonic. As a result water is continually entering the cell through osmosis. Recall from your experiments on osmosis what happens if a living animal cell is placed in a hypotonic solution. Up to a certain point the cell is able to cope with the influx of water by expanding but eventually the membrane will not be able to take the strain and the cell will burst.

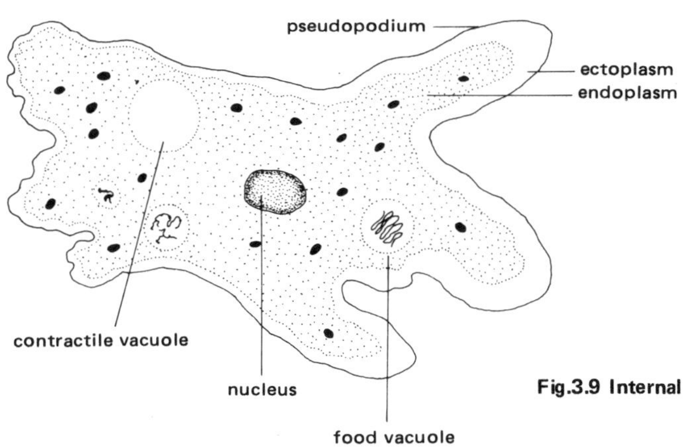

Fig.3.9 Internal structure of an amoeba

How does the amoeba prevent itself from bursting?

The freshwater amoeba collects all the water entering its cell in a special membrane sac called the **contractile vacuole**. When the vacuole is filled its contents are discharged into the surroundings. Through this continual pumping process the osmotic pressure inside the cell is kept constant and the cell is prevented from accumulating excessive amounts of water.

Higher animals

In higher animals osmoregulation is a dual process. In order that the body fluids be kept at a constant osmotic pressure both the amount of water and the amount of dissolved solutes must be strictly regulated, and there must be a balance between the amount of water lost and the amount gained.

How is water lost from the body?

Water is constantly lost from our bodies through a variety of ways. The exhaled air we breathe out is saturated with moisture taken from the alveoli. Since the surfaces of the alveoli must be covered with a film of water in order for gas exchange to take place the moisture lost must be continually replaced by water from the blood in the adjacent capillaries.

A significant quantity of water is lost through the skin by **sweating**. The rate of loss depends on the temperature of the surroundings and on the temperature of the body. Sweating is one of the prime means available to the body for regulating its temperature (see p. 159).

Small amounts of fluid are lost through the faeces and other lost body fluids such as tears or vomit.

Loss of water through the above means is completely beyond the control of the body as far as osmoregulation is concerned. The main way of water loss that can be, and is, very rigidly controlled is that that occurs through the **urine**.

Fig.3.10

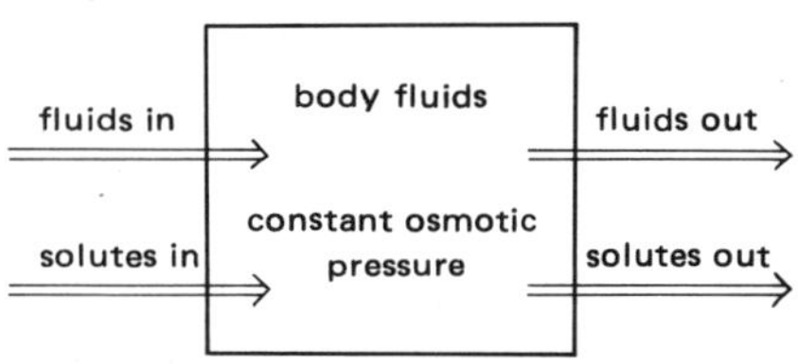

Solutes entering the body must either be used by the cells, converted to a storage form or excreted to prevent excess buildup in blood. There must also be a balance between water taken in and water used or excreted.

How is the output of urine controlled by the body of mammals?

The amount of solutes and water leaving the body in the urine is controlled by the kidneys.

Composition of urine

Urine normally contains various metabolic wastes such as *urea* derived from the break-down of excess amino acids. In various diseases it may also contain other organic molecules that have accumulated in abnormally high concentrations in the blood stream. In addition it contains inorganic salts, and of course water.

Principles of regulation

The general principles on which the functioning of the kidney is based are very simple. If the amount of water leaving the body is more than the amount going in, the kidneys will form a smaller volume of more concentrated urine to conserve water. If the opposite is true the kidneys will produce a larger amount of more dilute urine. In instances where there is an unusually high concentration of a particular solute in the blood stream and body cells the kidneys will eliminate some of the solute in question. In order to make this possible the volume of urine also has be to increased. This in turn means loss of fluid which will have to be replaced. This is why eating extremely salty food causes one to be thirsty. If the concentration of a solute is lower than desirable the kidneys will not allow any of the substance to leave the body.

The structure of the kidney

In order to understand fully the osmoregulatory action of the kidneys we must be familiar with the basic structure of the kidney. The kidneys in man are a pair of dark red, bean-shaped organs attached to the back of the abdominal cavity just below the stomach (fig. 3.11).

Each kidney is covered by an outer layer of protective cells called the **capsule** and consists of two inner cell layers, the **cortex** and the **medulla**. The functional unit of the kidney is the **nephron**, of which each kidney contains more than one million. The structure of a nephron and its position in relation to the kidney as a whole is shown in fig. 3.13.

The action of the kidney

Blood flowing to the kidney enters a system of tiny capillaries known as the **glomerulus.** From the capillaries most of the blood contents are filtered through the capillary wall into the **capsular space** around each glomerulus. The only constituents that normally stay behind in the circulation are the blood cells and the large protein molecules that, due to their size, cannot pass through the membranes. This filtration process is entirely mechanical with no regard for the body's requirements for conserving some substances and excreting other. As the **glomerular filtrate** flows along the kidney tubules of the nephron certain useful substances are reabsorbed into the capillaries surrounding the tubules while others are left behind.

Normally all the glucose is reabsorbed and a certain amount of inorganic salts and water are also reabsorbed, depending on the osmotic state of the body cells. If there is a tendency towards excess

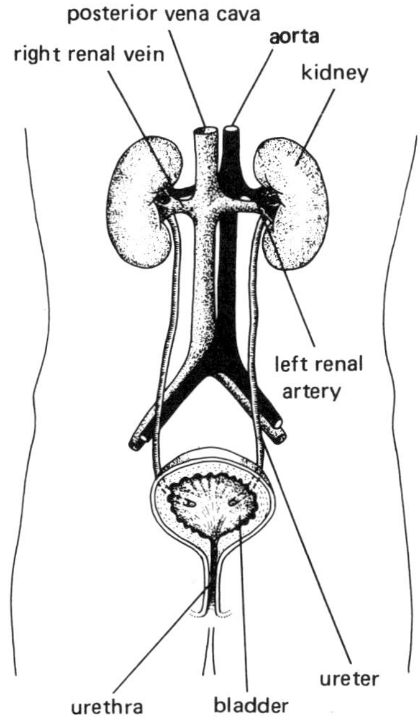

Fig.3.11 Position of kidneys relative to other structures

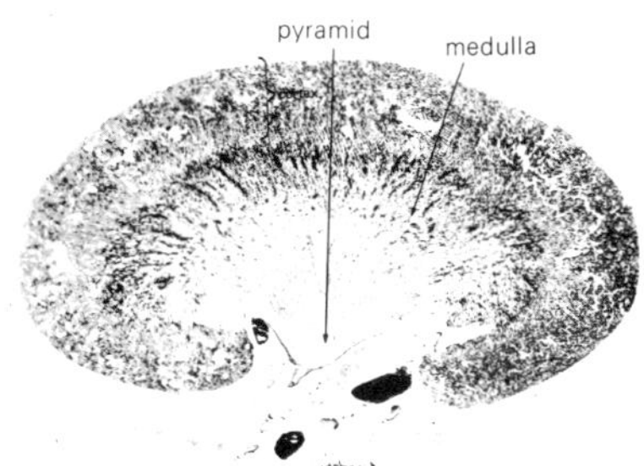

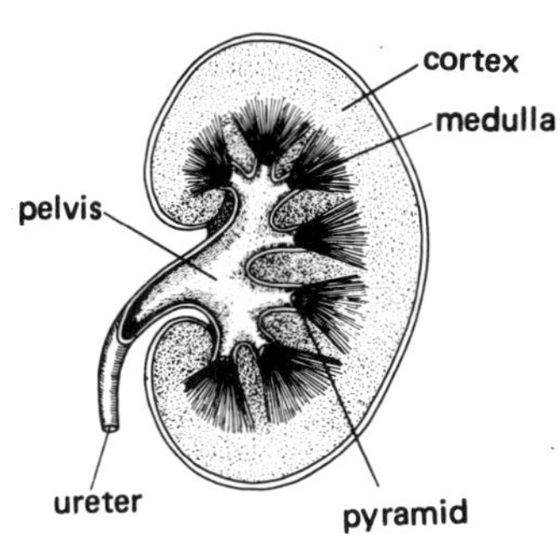

Fig. 3.12 Section of a kidney

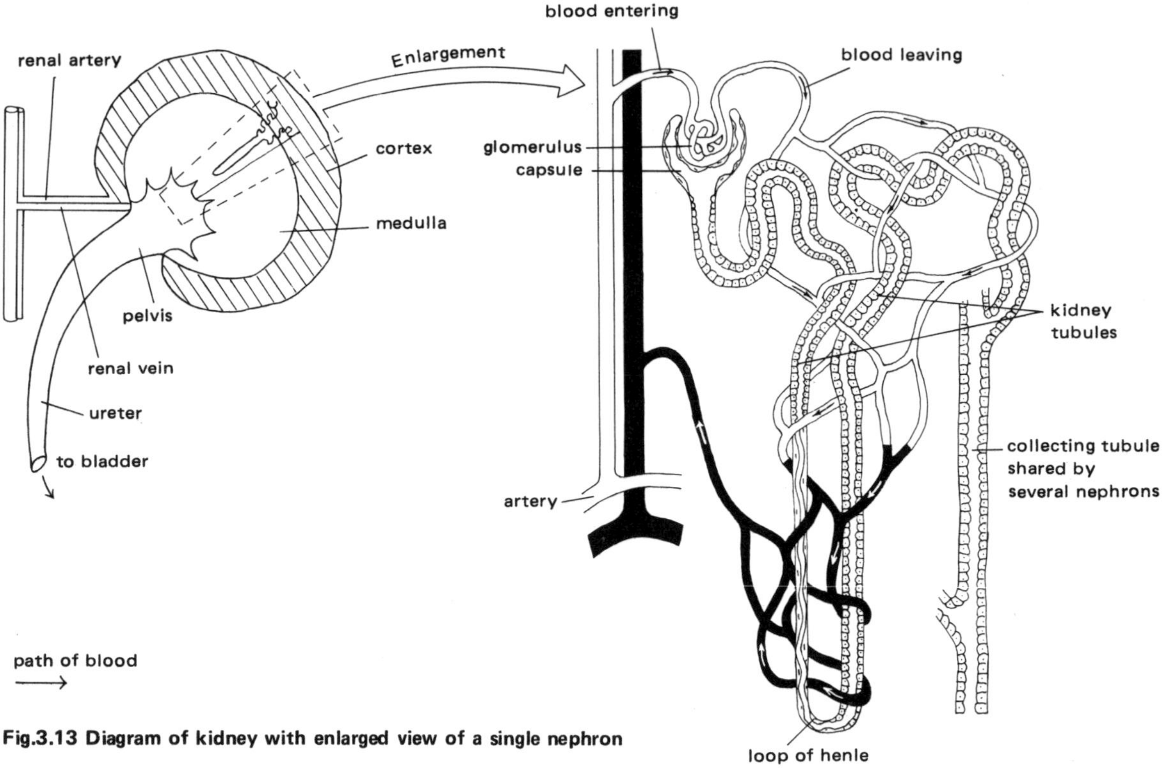

Fig.3.13 Diagram of kidney with enlarged view of a single nephron

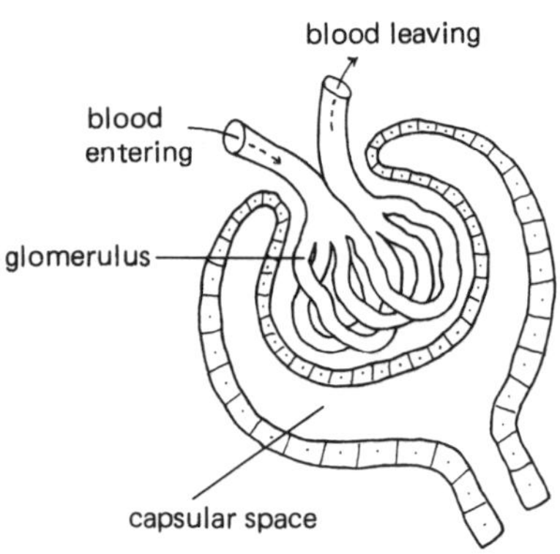

Fig.3.14 Structure of glomerulus

water being present, the kidneys will reduce their reabsorption of water and a larger volume of urine will be produced. If there is danger of dehydration most of the water will be reabsorbed. Metabolic wastes such as urea are *never* reabsorbed.

By the time the liquid reaches the end of the tubules and passes into the **collecting duct** its composition has been suitably altered by reabsorption and it is ready to be taken to the bladder in preparation for leaving the body by way of the **urethra**.

The reabsorption of solutes is an active process requiring energy. Some water is reabsorbed along with the solutes through osmosis. A large proportion of water, however, has to be actively reabsorbed through the action of the cells lining the kidney tubules. These cells 'push' water into the blood capillaries while holding back the molecules of waste products that are to be excreted. The active reabsorption of water is controlled by the activity of **antidiuretic hormone** secreted by the **pituitary gland**. (See p. 161.)

Rates of kidney activity

To give an idea of the enormous task performed by the kidneys, consider the fact that all the nephrons working together are capable of filtering 120cm^3 of water per minute, giving a total rate of 170 litres per day. Of the 120cm^3 of water filtered in a minute, 119cm^3 are reabsorbed and only 1cm^3 becomes urine. Since the average

Fig.3.15 Reabsorption of water in kidney tubules

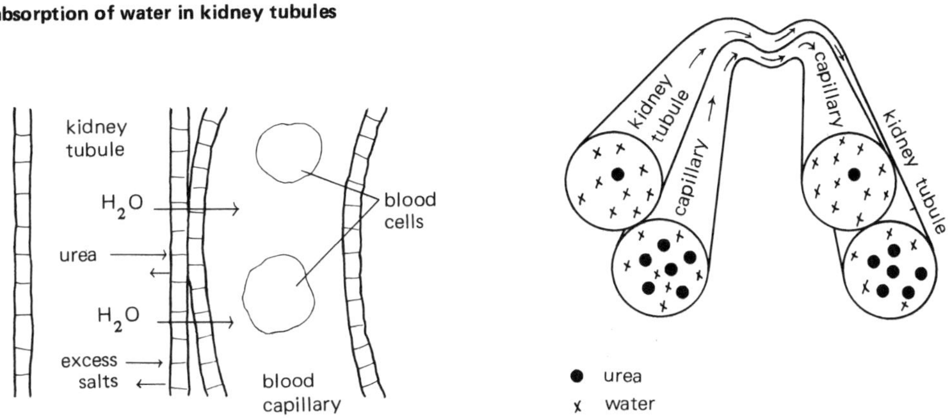

volume of blood in the human body is only about three litres and the total volume of body water only forty to forty-five litres this means that all the water in the body is filtered through the kidney about four times daily.

Kidney disorders

The functioning of the kidneys is vital to the health of the body. Malfunctioning leads to the accumulation of harmful waste products in the blood stream or loss of valuable organic materials due to failure of the reabsorption process. In either case severe illness and eventual death will result.

Since glomerular filtration occurs as a result of the pressure of the blood in the circulatory system 'pushing' the fluid into the glomerulus any alterations in blood pressure will affect the work of the kidneys. Low blood pressure will lead to a reduction in the volume of the filtrate thus reducing the efficiency of the system. Increase in blood pressure leads to an increased volume of filtrate so that the kidney tubules will be overloaded. Furthermore, due to the excess pressure protein molecules that are normally held back in the capillaries will be forced through the capillary walls and be excreted along with the rest of the urine.

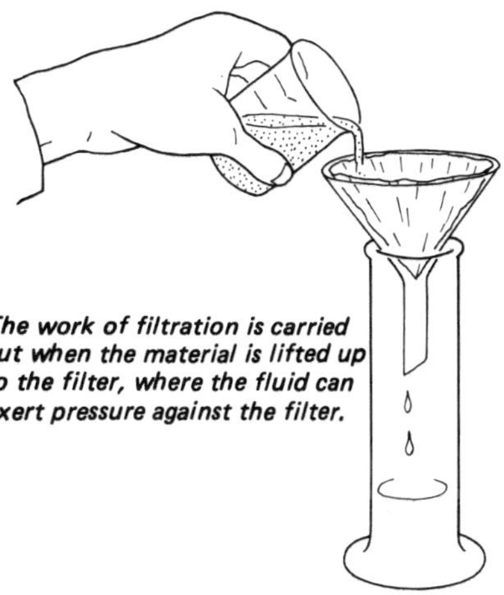

The work of filtration is carried out when the material is lifted up to the filter, where the fluid can exert pressure against the filter.

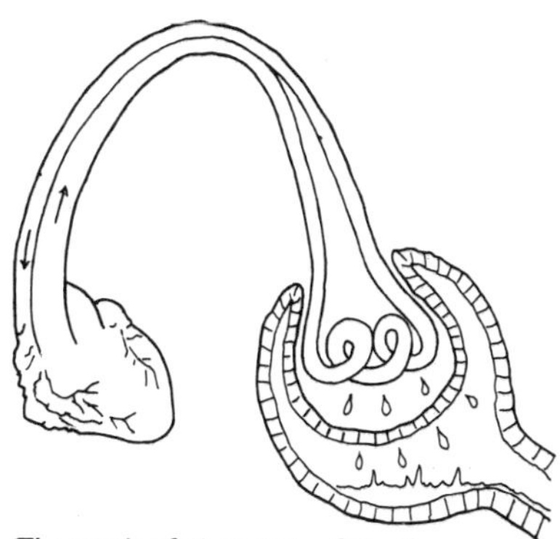

The work of glomerular filtration is performed by heart creating blood pressure.

Fig.3.16 How the work of glomerular filtration is accomplished

Summary

Osmoregulation, the control of the amount of water and solutes in the cells and extracellular fluid of an animal, is a vital process. In mammals it is achieved through the action of the kidneys.

Through a mechanical filtration process water and solutes pass from the capillaries into the glomeruli of the kidneys. As the liquid travels along the kidney tubules all the substances required by the body are reabsorbed while those not required are excreted in the urine. Through the action of the kidneys the water uptake of an animal and its total water loss are precisely regulated and kept in balance.

Fig.3.17 Types of root

Fig.3.18 Photograph of small root with root hairs

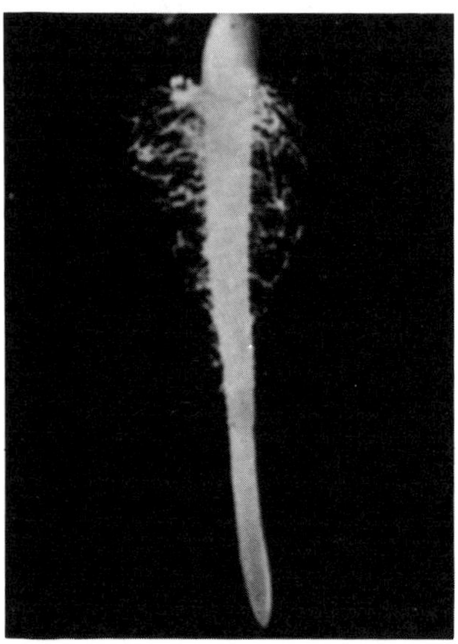

Water relations in plants

We have already discussed the ways in which animals obtain and get rid of water. How about plants? You know that when it rains water drains into the soil and when you water your potted plants it is the soil that you are really watering. Plants must somehow be able to take in water from the soil through their roots.

To understand how roots are able to take in water we must know something about the structure of roots.

The structure of roots

Although the root structures of different plants vary to a considerable degree most fall into one of the following categories.

In a **tap root** system the main root develops directly from the **radicle** of the seed and the various **lateral roots** arise from the main root. The main root normally grows straight downward while the lateral roots branch out obliquely[1]. The degree of branching depends on the particular needs of the plant and the availability of water in the soil. Tap roots are characteristic of dicotyledonous plants.

In a **fibrous root** system the main root derived from the radicle is not well developed. Instead a number of **adventitious roots** are given off in clusters from the base of the stem. (Any root that does not derive from the radicle directly is considered to be an adventitious root.) Fibrous roots are characteristic of monocotyledonous plants[2].

In addition there are many different types of modified roots such as the adventitious roots originating from the stems of clinging plants such as the ivy, the suckers of parasitic plants, and the aerial roots of maize that develop from the part of the stem above the ground.

Details of root structure

Root hairs

The epidermal cells of roots produce numerous unicellular hair-like extensions that project laterally into the soil. These are called **root hairs** and they occur in clusters a short distance above the region of the root tip.

The development of root hairs can be very easily observed by growing a seedling pinned to the cork of a small transparent vial that contains a little water, as seen in fig. 3.19. The root hairs can be examined with a hand lens without removing them from the vial.

Root hairs serve the dual purpose of anchoring the plant in the soil and participating in the uptake of water and minerals.

[1] *oblique*: at an angle

[2] *monocotyledonous* plant: see pp.13, 301

Fig.3.19

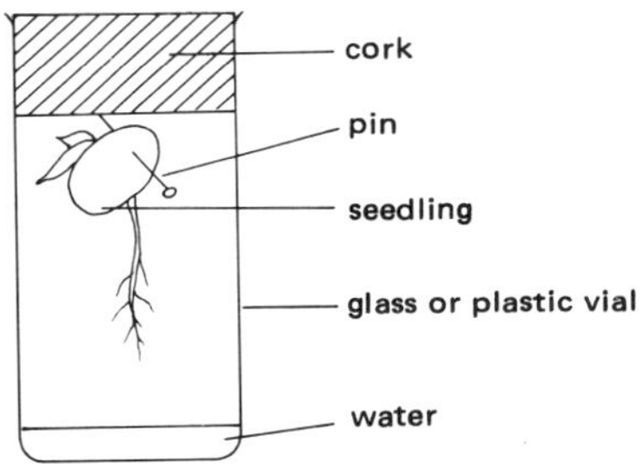

Fig.3.20 Passage of water into root

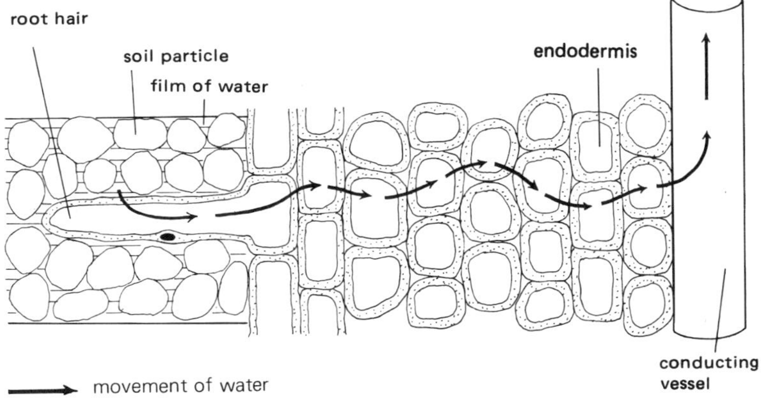

How does water pass into the cells of the roots?

Soil particles are normally covered by a thin film of water on the outside. The small, flexible root hairs are able to penetrate the spaces between the soil particles and water can enter the cells freely.
The numerous projecting root hairs are reminiscent of the microvilli of the small intestine in that they both greatly increase the surface area over which exchange of materials can take place.
Water is drawn up into the roots by osmosis and also by an active process. Active uptake of water means that cells are able to take in water even if the solute concentration of the soil is higher than that of the cells and osmosis would normally proceed in the opposite direction.
From the root hairs water passes through the outer cell layers of the main part of the rootlet to the conducting elements on the inside through which it is transported to the stem and leaves. There is considerable experimental evidence to indicate that water may be actively secreted by the root cells into the conducting elements. You may have noticed that when the stem of a plant is severed water is seen to exude from the top of the stump. This is due to the pressure of the roots pushing water into the stem.

EXPERIMENT TO DEMONSTRATE ROOT PRESSURE
Materials
potted plant
glass tube about the thickness of the plant stem
rubber tubing
Method
1. Cut off the stem of the plant about two inches from the soil and discard the shoots.
2. Using a short piece of rubber tubing attach the stump to the glass tubing and seal the joint to make it airtight.
3. Pour water into the tube to bring the water level up past the level of the rubber tubing. Mark the liquid level.
4. Observe for twenty to twenty-five minutes.

Fig.3.21

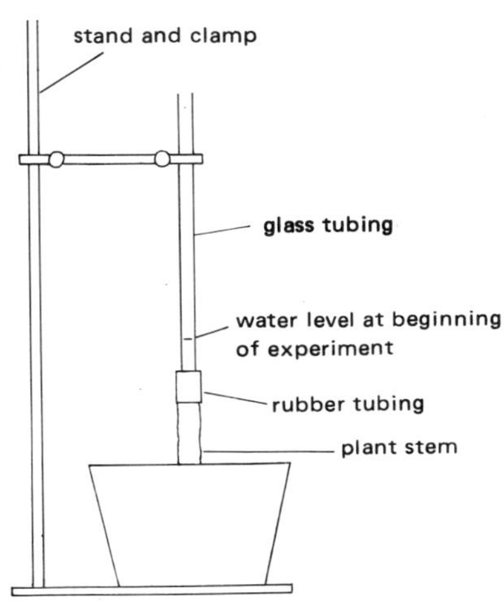

What do you see?
How far does the water level rise?
How can you account for this?

Discussion

About ten minutes or so after the start of the experiment water will be seen to rise up the glass tubing. The only place this water can come from is the roots and the only way it can go up the tubing is by being forced up by the roots. The pressure is believed to be due to active transport of water in the cells of the endodermis (fig. 3.20). The removal of water at this point causes a chain reaction of water movement by osmosis throughout the outer layers of the root. As the removal of water from a cell causes a loss in turgidity water will tend to move into it from the adjacent cell on the outside. The latter in turn will pull water in from the cell adjacent to it and so on. The net result is a movement of water from the soil, through the cells of the root and up the stem. Water will rise up the stem as a result of root pressure to a certain maximum level only. After this point the atmospheric pressure forcing the liquid down will balance the root pressure forcing it up and no further movement will take place. The movement of water up to the tip of a tall plant is accomplished by additional factors.

The above experiment seems to suggest that there is a continual movement of water from the roots of a plant to the upper regions.

What happens to all the water taken in by plants?

Fig.3.22

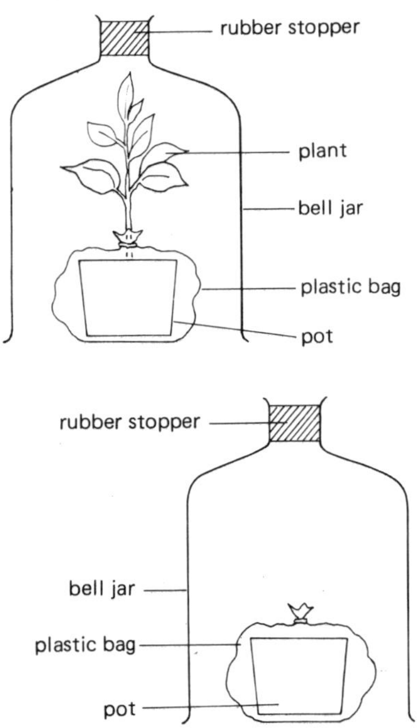

EXPERIMENT TO DEMONSTRATE THE LOSS OF WATER FROM PLANTS

Materials

small potted plant
two bell jars
two large plastic sheets
a pot of soil with no plant in it

Method

1. Cover the surface of the soil of both pots with a plastic sheet.
2. Place them in bright sunlight and cover each with a bell jar as shown in the diagram.
3. Take a look at the pots every few minutes through a fifteen-minute period.

What do you observe?
Where has the moisture come from?

Discussion

Within a short time the inner surface of the bell jar containing the plant is covered with a layer of moisture while no moisture appears on the control jar. It is clear that the moisture has come from the plant.

The process whereby plants lose water to the atmosphere is called **transpiration**.

EXPERIMENT TO DEMONSTRATE TRANSPIRATION FROM LEAVES

Materials

dry cobalt chloride paper

potted plant

Note: cobalt chloride paper is blue in colour when dry but turns pink when it comes in contact with water.

Method

1. Place a small piece of dry cobalt chloride paper on each surface of a leaf of the plant. Cover it with cellophane to protect from atmospheric moisture and fix into position with paper clips.
2. Observe for ten to fifteen minutes.

Fig.3.23

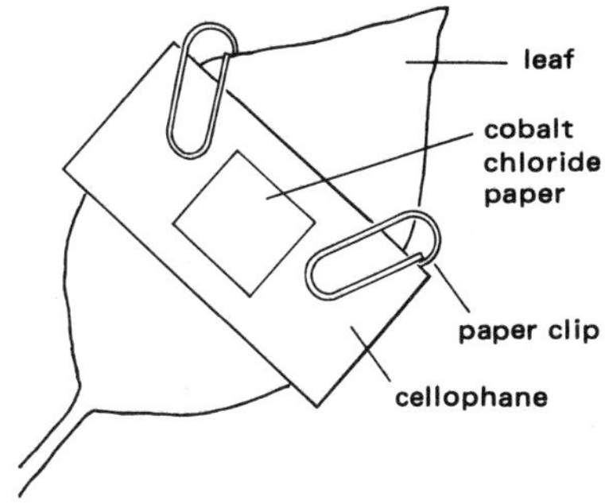

What do you observe?

Is there any difference between the two surfaces of the leaf?

Discussion

With time the blue cobalt chloride paper gradually turns pink indicating that moisture is coming out of the leaf. Depending on the species of plant used there may be a difference in the amount of moisture that can be detected on the two surfaces. In some instances the lower surface will show significantly more moisture.

Why do you think there might be a difference between the two surfaces?

How do you think water is getting out of the leaf?

In the previous section you have already observed that the regular arrangement of epidermal cells in the leaf is interrupted by openings called stomata through which gas exchange takes place. The stomatal openings are also responsible for the loss of water from the leaves.

EXPERIMENT TO SHOW THAT TRANSPIRATION OCCURS MAINLY THROUGH THE STOMATA

Materials

three leaves which have stomata on the lower surface only e.g. hibiscus

petroleum jelly

beakers

cardboard

Method

1. Smear the lower surface of leaf A and the upper surface of leaf B with petroleum jelly. Leave leaf C untouched.
2. Prepare three beakers containing enough water for the petiole of the leaf to reach down into.
3. Punch a small hole in the centre of three pieces of cardboard that are large enough to cover the tops of the beakers.
4. Insert the petiole of each leaf through a piece of cardboard and place on top of the water-filled beakers as shown in fig. 3.24.
5. Seal the openings in the cardboard around the petiole with petroleum jelly to prevent water vapour escaping from the beakers.

Fig.3.24

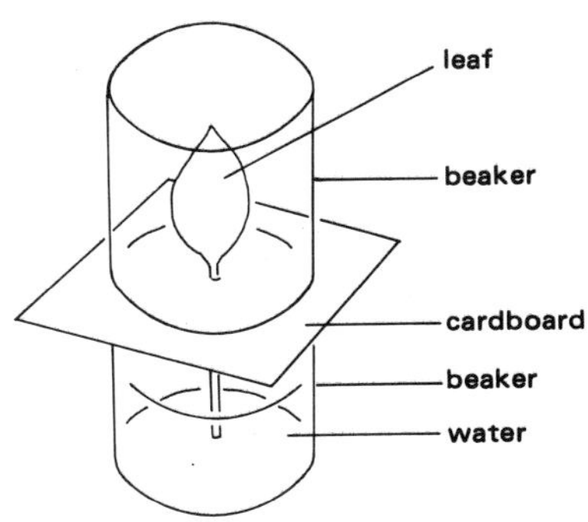

A Vaseline on lower surface of leaf
B Vaseline on upper surface of leaf
C No vaseline

6. Cover the leaves with a second beaker as shown in the diagram and leave in bright light for several hours.

What do you observe?
How can you account for these observations?
What does this tell you about the mechanism of transpiration?

Discussion

The inner walls of the beakers covering leaves B and C gradually become covered with moisture showing that the leaves have been losing moisture. Leaf A whose underside was covered with vaseline does not appear to lose water. Since all the stomata of the leaves are on the lower surface it is clear that blocking the stomata prevents transpiration.

Although a tiny amount of water does escape through the epidermal cells this is insignificant compared with the amount evaporating through the stomata. Water loss from the epidermal cells is prevented by the presence of the cuticle which forms a waxy covering.

The rate of transpiration from plants can be measured using an instrument called the **potometer**.

Fig.3.25 Potometer

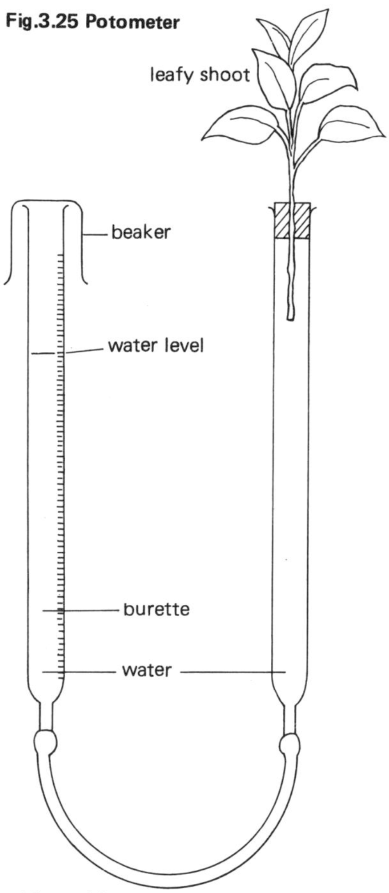

EXPERIMENT TO CONSTRUCT A SIMPLE POTOMETER TO MEASURE THE RATE OF WATER LOSS FROM A PLANT

Materials

two glass burettes—one narrow and graduated, the other wider
rubber tubing
a potted plant with plenty of leafy shoots
petroleum jelly

Method

1. Connect the narrow ends of the two burettes with a piece of rubber tubing.
2. Fill the apparatus with water.
3. Cut off a leafy shoot from the plant under water to prevent air from entering the stem.
4. Fit the branch through a stopper and still working under water fit into one of the burettes. Seal the space around the stopper with petroleum jelly.
5. Set aside the apparatus for about ten minutes to ensure that all the cells are fully turgid.
6. Cover the second burette with a small beaker as shown in the diagram and mark the level of the water. Place the apparatus in a bright place.
7. Observe the apparatus at regular intervals looking for changes in the water level in the burette.

Record your measurements in a table.
Draw a graph of the change in water level with elapsed time.

Are you surprised to find such a high rate of water loss from the plant?
Do you think the rate of transpiration is always the same or does it depend on external conditions?

EXPERIMENT TO MEASURE THE RATE OF TRANSPIRATION UNDER VARIOUS EXTERNAL CONDITIONS

Note: the materials and the basic method for this experiment are the same as for the previous one. The varying external conditions can be achieved as described below. When changing from one set of conditions to the next allow about twenty minutes to ensure that the plant has become equilibrated with the environment.

1. *Higher temperature* can be obtained by placing the plant near an electric heater or bunsen flame.
2. *Light conditions* can be varied by placing the plant in full sunlight, dim light or complete darkness.
3. *Strong air currents* can be obtained by placing the apparatus in front of an electric fan.
4. *A humid environment* can be obtained by covering the shoots with a plastic bag and placing wet paper towels inside.

Compare the standard rate of transpiration as obtained in the previous experiment with the rate of transpiration observed under altered conditions. You can record your results in a suitable table and plot them on a histogram.

Discussion

The rate of transpiration increases with

a. rise in temperature
b. increasing air movement
c. decrease in relative humidity
d. increasing light

The first three conditions listed above exert a purely physical effect on the plant, the same way as they influence evaporation from any non-living surface. Clothes, for instance, dry faster on a warm, dry, windy day. Variation of transpiration with light intensity, however, is a biological response on the part of the plant. The opening and closing of the stomata is influenced by the amount of light available. Since stomata are the sites of gas exchange and it is vital that gas exchange proceeds efficiently during the daylight hours, stomata tend to open under strong illumination and close in the absence of light. It follows that transpiration too, increases in bright light and decreases in dim light.

What causes the stomata of a plant to open and close in response to light?

This is one of the questions that biologists, even after years of research, are not able to answer precisely.

The immediate cause of stomatal movement is a change in the turgidity of the guard cells. An increased turgidity causes the guard cells to swell up. Since the inner walls of the cells, adjacent to the opening, are much thicker than the outer walls, expansion of the outer edge is much greater. This causes the cell to assume a sausage shape, and creates an oval opening between the two cells. You can demonstrate this effect to yourself by putting a layer of plastic tape

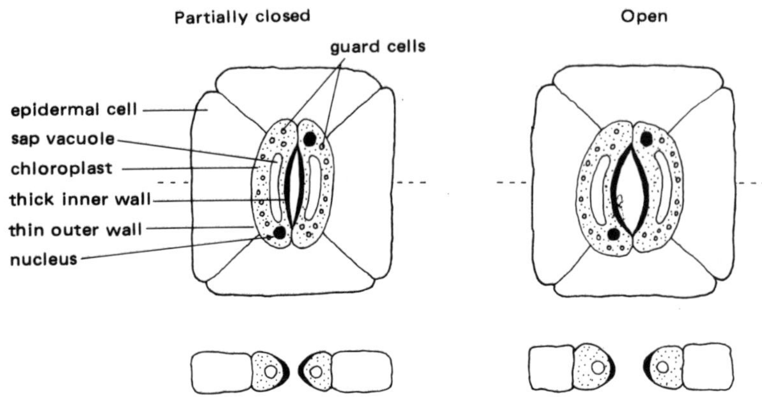

Fig.3.26 Stoma in surface view and section

Fig.3.27

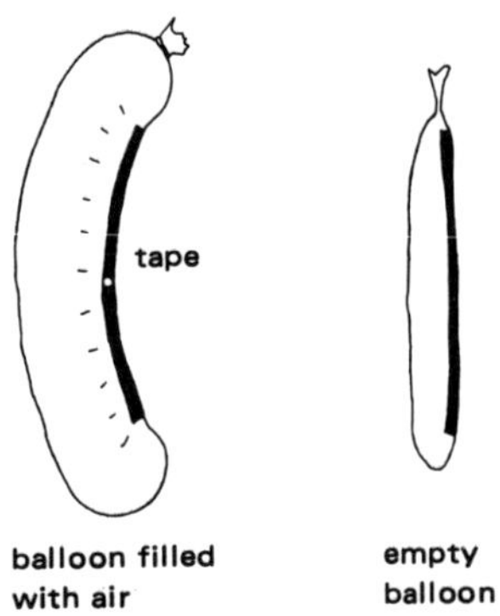

along one side of a cylindrical balloon and blowing up the balloon. The disproportionate expansion of the two sides will cause the balloon to assume a sausage shape. As you allow the air to escape the balloon returns to its normal shape. The same happens with the guard cells. As they lose turgidity the guard cells assume their resting shape and the opening disappears. (See fig. 3.26.)

The connection between guard cell turgidity and light conditions is not known. It is, however, apparent that the guard cells are able to close in response to excess transpiration since this will cause a reduction in their turgidity.

How are plants able to protect themselves against excess water loss through transpiration?

Since excess transpiration can be very dangerous to the plant a variety of adaptations exist to guard against this.

The cuticle, a layer of impermeable, waxy substance covering the epidermis of most leaves and stems effectively cuts down water loss through the epidermal cells. In some plants epidermal water loss is further reduced by the existence of a cork layer, the **bark**, on the surface of the stem.

The number of stomata per unit area and their distribution is related to the conditions of moisture in the environment of a particular plant. Desert plants, for instance, have much fewer stomata than plants that inhabit tropical regions. Embedding the stomata in small grooves **(sunken stomata)** also cuts down on the rate of transpiration.

Plants in dry habitats have a reduced leaf surface area. Cacti, for example, do not have the usual leaf structure of plants found in wetter regions. By reducing the leaf area transpiration is also reduced.

The above discussion has indicated that the existence of transpiration causes plants many problems.

Fig.3.28 Epidermal

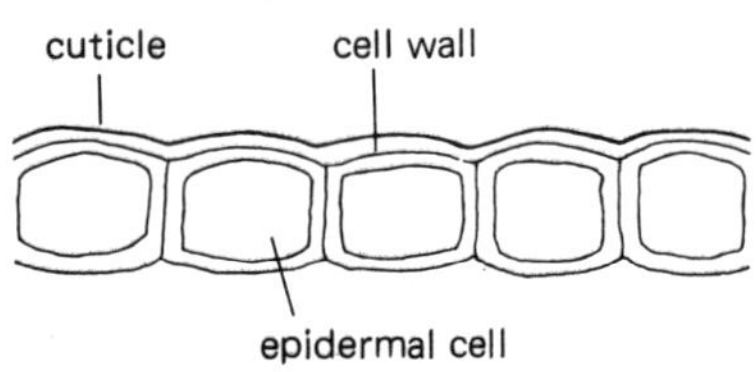

Fig.3.29 A sunken stoma in section

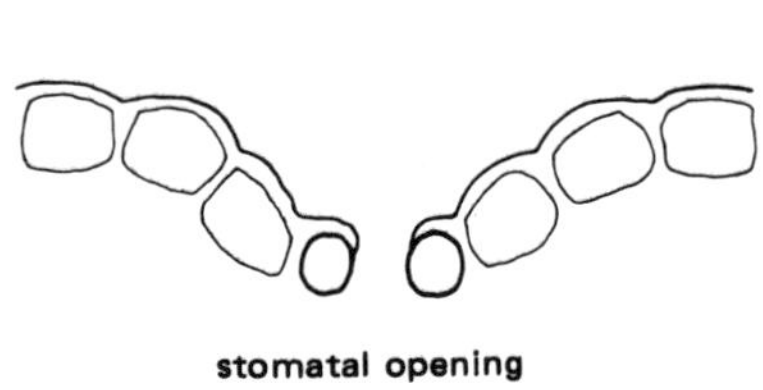

Why does transpiration occur? What is its significance to the plant?

The importance of the process of transpiration lies in the movement of water from the root to the higher regions of the plant. Recall the experiment to demonstrate root pressure (p. 149). One of the conclusions of that experiment was that there is a limit to the height to which root pressure can force water up the stem of a plant. The answer to how water gets to the tips of a tall plant lies in the process of transpiration. The continual removal of water from the plant at the level of the leaves exerts a suctioning effect on the liquid in the conducting elements of the plant. As long as the conducting channels are all filled with liquid and there is a continual loss of water from the leaves there will be a steady movement of liquid from the roots of the plant all the way up to the leaves. The effect is referred to as **transpirational pull** and is very similar to the action of sucking up a liquid through a straw. The role of transpirational pull in the transport of materials through the plant will be discussed in greater detail on p. 214.

Transpiration also serves as a means for regulating the temperature of plants since evaporation of water from the surface exerts a cooling effect. Excess transpiration can lead to *wilting* of the plant. Since there are few or no supporting tissues in leaves and young shoots, support is achieved through the turgidity of the cells (see p 174). If too much water is lost the leaf will become limp and droop down, thereby turning away from the direct rays of the sun.

Summary

Plants obtain water from the soil through the tiny unicellular root hairs that penetrate the spaces between the soil particles. Water is forced part of the way up the plant through an active transport

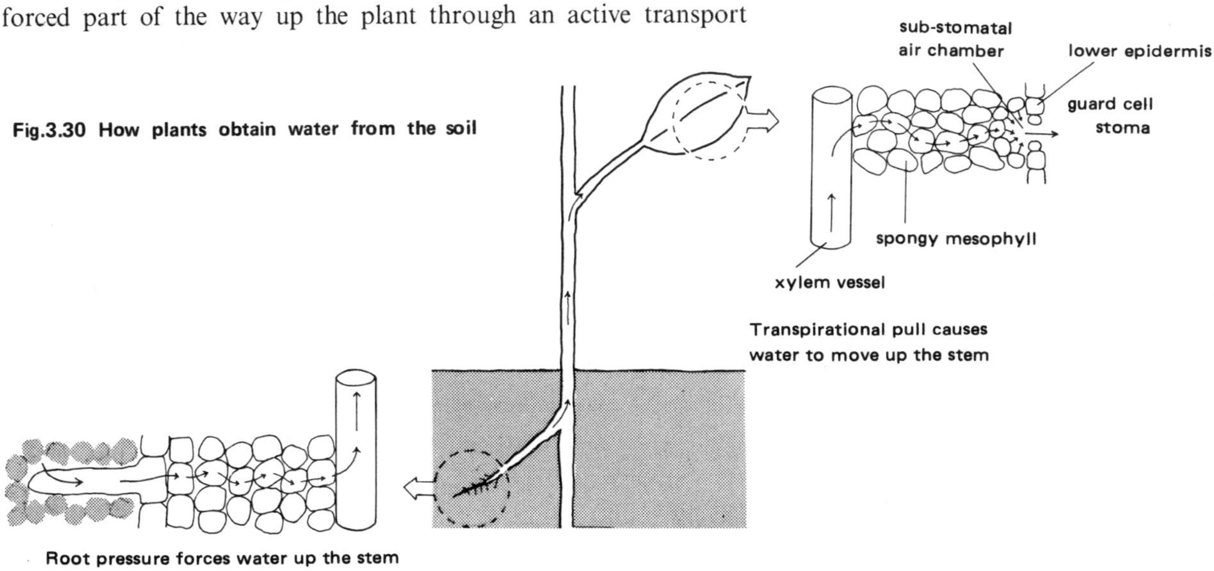

Fig.3.30 How plants obtain water from the soil

phenomenon called root pressure, and partly by the process of transpiration.

Transpiration is the loss of water through the stomata of the leaves by evaporation. The rate of evaporation is influenced by a number of physical environmental factors such as light, humidity, temperature and air movement. Plants possess a number of adaptations that are directed towards reducing excessive water loss through transpiration.

Homeostasis

The word **homeostasis** is derived from Greek—*homo* meaning *like* and *stasis* meaning *standing*. The two words together can be translated to mean 'steady state'. The expression refers to the tendency of living organisms to maintain a constant internal environment in the face of changing external or internal conditions.

The more complex and highly developed the organism the greater the task of maintaining homeostasis and the more elaborate the means of maintaining it. The operation of an effective control mechanism requires a number of factors. First the external or internal change that is to be compensated for must be detected, recognized and evaluated in relation to the current state of the organism. The appropriate action must then be taken to counteract the change. Most control mechanisms operate through a **feedback system** as illustrated diagrammatically in fig. 3.31.

Fig.3.31 Feedback system

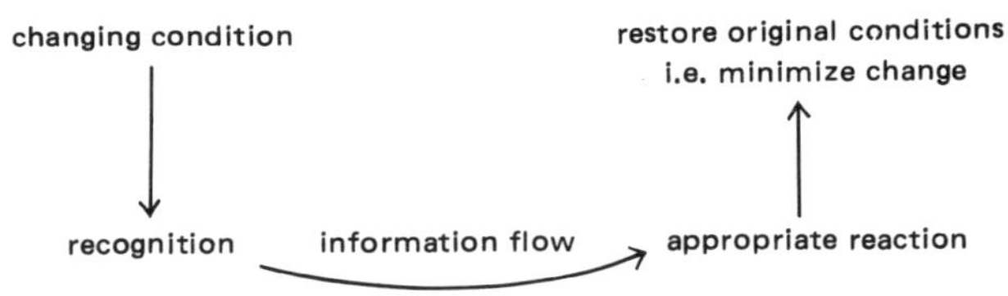

The simplest example of a mechanical feedback system is the thermostat used in our heating and air conditioning systems. The system is adjusted to a certain 'set point'. If the temperature deviates from the set point the machine switches on to restore it back to normal. In the case of the air conditioner, when the temperature in the room rises above the set point an electric contact in the system is completed and the motor switches on. As soon as the temperature reaches the set point again the system is automatically switched off.

Fig.3.32 Operation of a thermostat

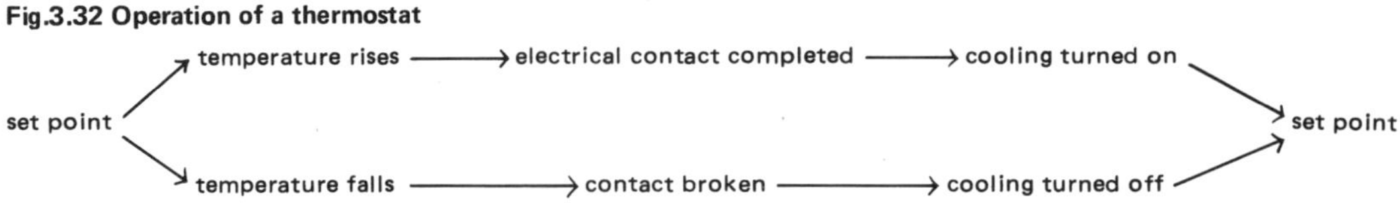

Fig.3.33 Fluctuation of temperature during negative feedback

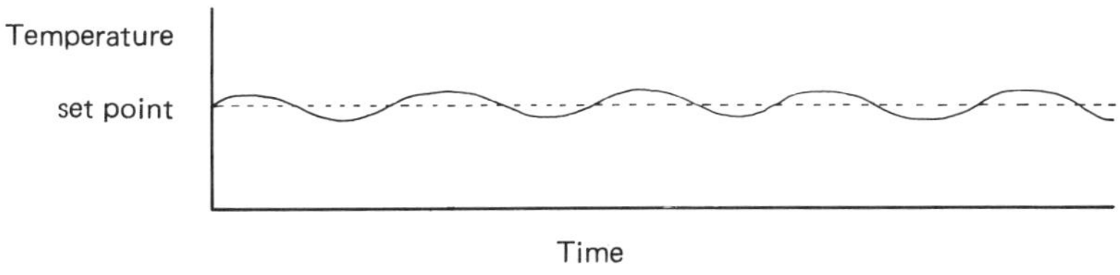

The temperature of the room is constantly being compared to the set point and adjustments are made as necessary. The full name of the process is **negative feedback** because the adjustment is always in the opposite direction to the change detected. The temperature is not kept absolutely constant but is allowed to fluctuate between narrow limits on either side of the set point.

Negative feedback in the human body

Negative feedback operates in many of the body's systems. One example is the control of body temperature in warm blooded mammals. The cells of the human body are adjusted to a temperature of about 37°C, with differences of the order of a few tenths of a degree from one individual to the next. It is at this temperature that the enzymes of the body work most efficiently. When the temperature gets much higher many organic molecules become inactivated. At extremely low temperatures the enzymes work very slowly.

Sources of heat gain

Fig.3.34

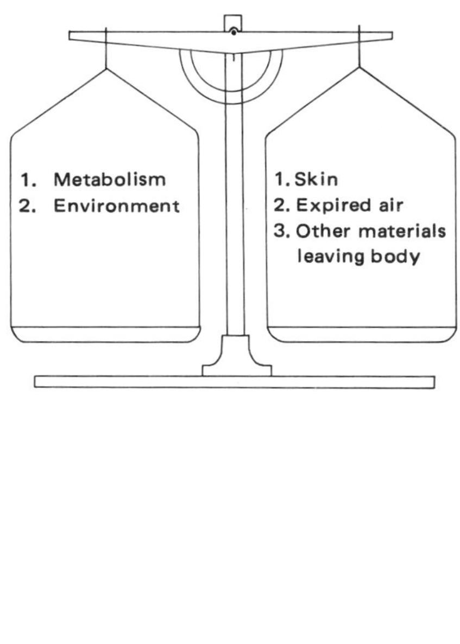

The two principle sources of heat for the body are the heat gained from the environment and heat produced as a byproduct of metabolism. It is probable that you have all experienced the effects of the hot summer weather and the problems of keeping comfortably cool. You also know that your body heats up when you are performing vigorous physical activity such as running. This is heat coming from the increased rate of metabolism required by the body during exercise.

Sources of heat loss

Some heat is lost from the body through the exhaled air passing out from the lungs and from other materials leaving the body such as urine and faeces. These losses are completely beyond the control of the body. But, by far the most important source of heat loss occurs through the skin. Regulating the amount of heat lost by this route is the principal means of temperature control available to mammals.

How does the skin act in regulating body temperature?

Fig. 3.36 shows a diagram of a human skin section. Fig. 3.35 is a photograph of a skin section. Notice the numerous heat and cold re-

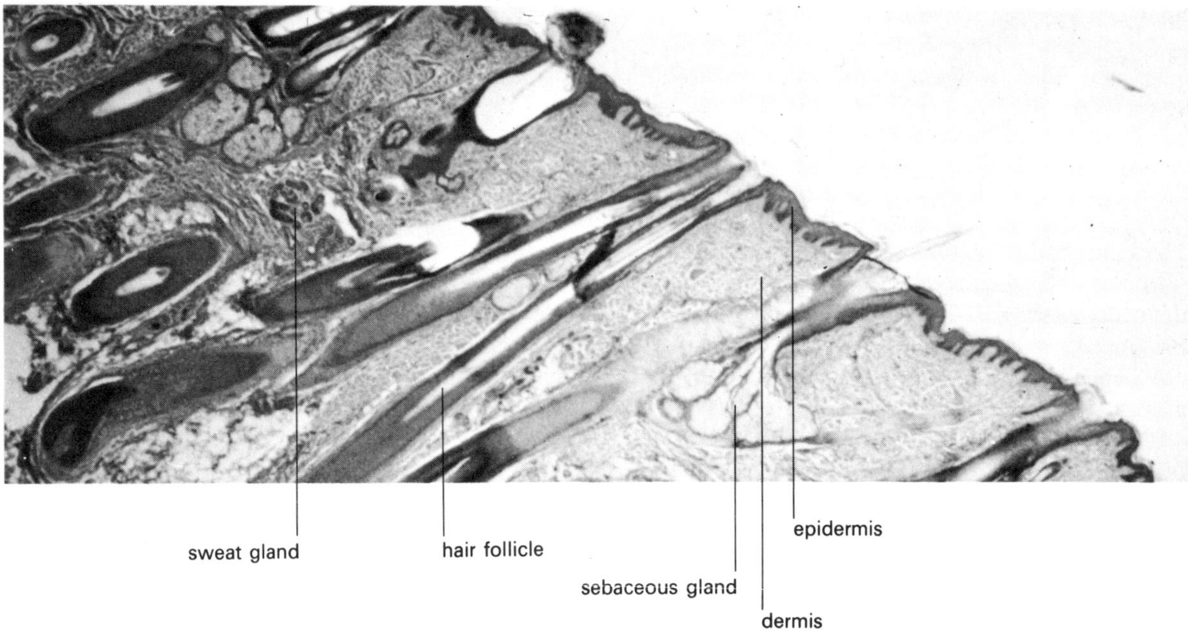

Fig.3.35 Photo of vertical section of skin (x50)

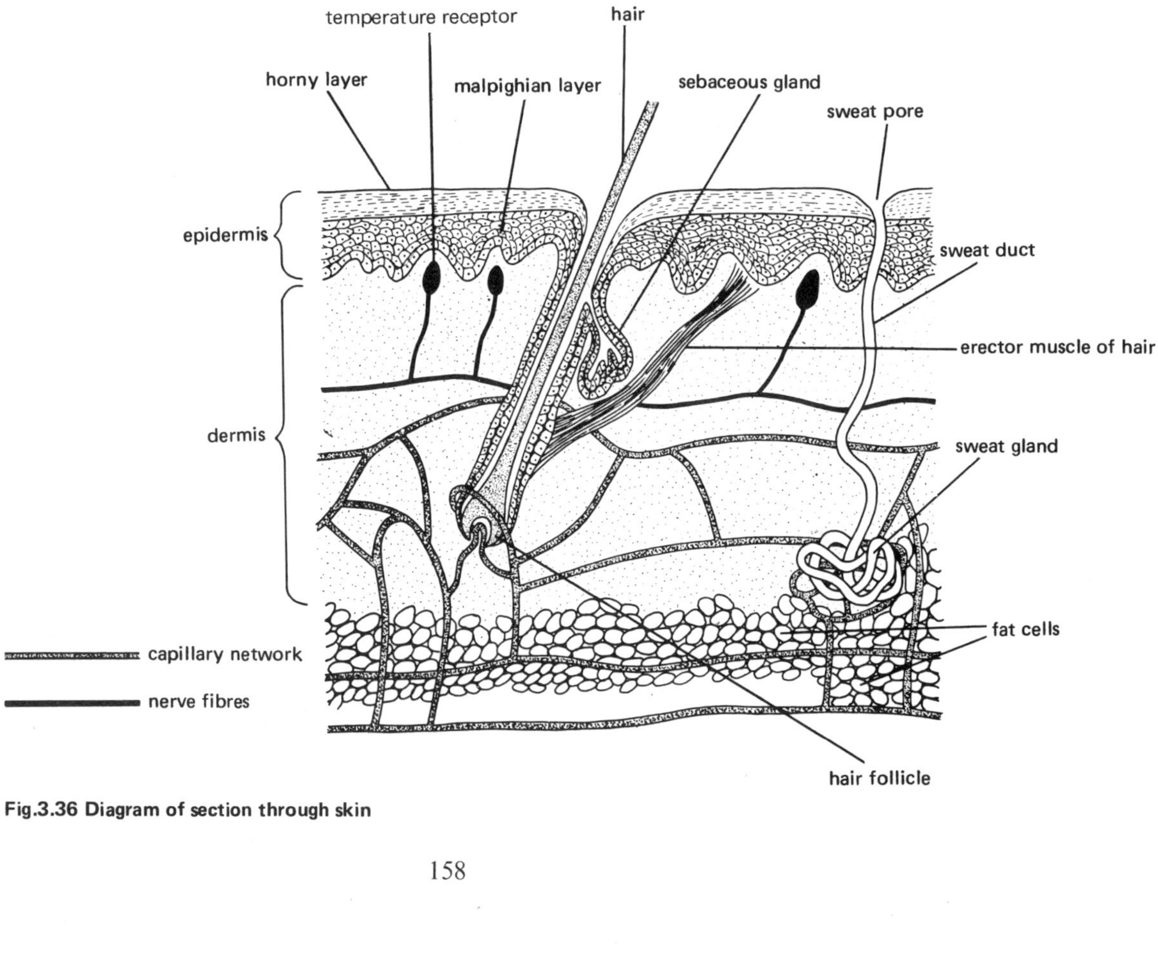

Fig.3.36 Diagram of section through skin

located just beneath the epidermal layer. These receptors are constantly sending messages to the **temperature regulating centre** of the brain concerning the temperature at various points along the surface of the body. The temperature regulating centre itself is capable of sensing the temperature of the blood flowing past it. The centre therefore acts as the thermostat for the body, and sends out appropriate instructions to increase or decrease heat loss from the body surfaces.

Fig.3.37 Diagram of blood circulation under skin surface

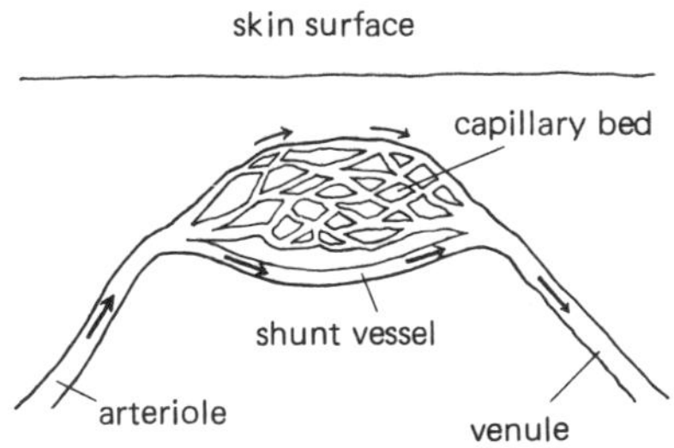

INCREASED FLOW

Whenever the body temperature exceeds the set point the superficial blood vessels of the body, that is, those found in the skin, dilate so that more blood is brought close to the surface and heat can be lost to the surrounding atmosphere by radiation. When body temperature is low the opposite happens. As much blood as possible is diverted from the surface to minimize heat loss. In certain areas **shunt vessels** connect the **arterioles** and the **venules** bypassing the capillaries so that most of the blood can be diverted to deeper layers of the skin. You can easily demonstrate this response to yourself by placing one hand in a container of hot water, as hot as you can stand, and the other into ice water. After a few minutes withdraw your hands and examine them. The one that was in the hot water will appear red due to the increased blood flow while the other will appear bluish-white because blood flow has been reduced. (See p. 193.)

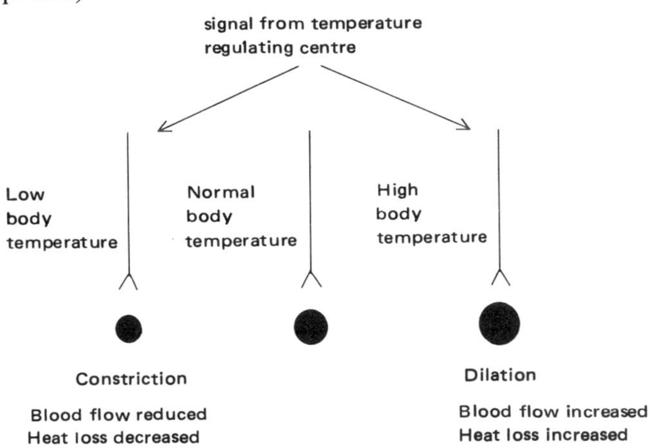

Fig.3.38 Control of heat loss from skin surface

SWEATING

Sweating increases when the body temperature is high and decreases when it is low.

You know from your knowledge of physics that to change a substance from a liquid to a gas requires heat energy. When sweating occurs water is evaporating from the surface of the skin and the heat required for the evaporation is taken from the skin. The overall

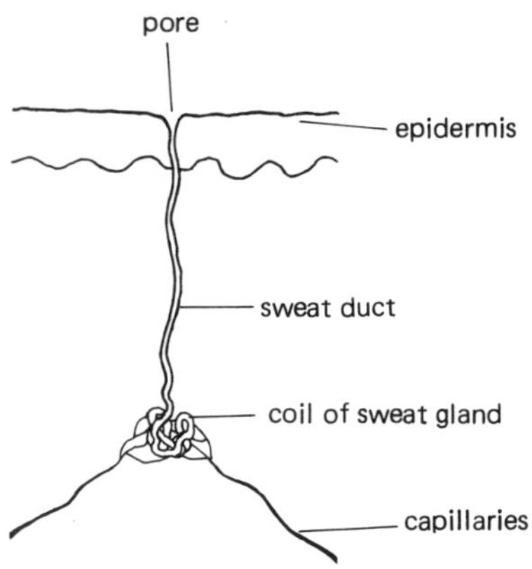

Fig.3.39 Diagram of skin section showing sweat gland

effect is one of cooling the skin and the blood flowing through it. The efficiency of the cooling effect depends on the atmospheric temperature and on the relative humidity. When the humidity is high evaporation is much slower and it is much more difficult to keep cool.
How does evaporation from the skin take place?
Moisture is secreted by the **sweat glands** found in the deeper layers of the skin. It is brought to the surface of the skin by special structures called **sweat ducts** connecting the deeper layers of the skin with the surface. The coiled inner end of the duct is usually surrounded by a network of blood capillaries. A watery fluid passing out of the dilated capillaries diffuses into the duct and is passed to the surface of the skin where evaporation can take place.
A second type of sweat gland, the **sebaceous gland**, usually associated with hair follicles, exudes sweat of a different composition at times when the body is under some physical or mental stress. Bacterial activity on the surface causes this liquid to acquire an unpleasant odour.
Why are sweat glands necessary?
Special glands for passing liquids to the surface of the body are necessary because the rest of the skin is an unbroken layer of tissue that provides an effective barrier against the environment preventing substances from either entering or leaving the deeper layers. The skin is in fact one of the most important protective structures of the body.

SLOWER METABOLIC RATE

A further reaction to excess body heat is the reduction of the metabolic rate. Human beings and most other animals are usually less active during the hot humid season. In colder weather the rate of metabolism is increased to provide extra heat for the body. At times muscular activity is increased voluntarily by walking, rubbing the hands or waving the arms around in an attempt to keep warm. In some instances involuntary muscle contraction leading to shivering will be instituted by the body.
The diagram below summarizes the basic mechanism of temperature control of the human body.

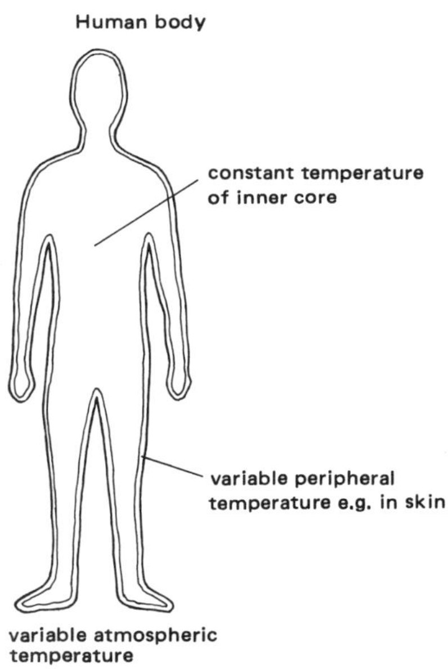

Fig.3.40 Summary of temperature control mechanisms

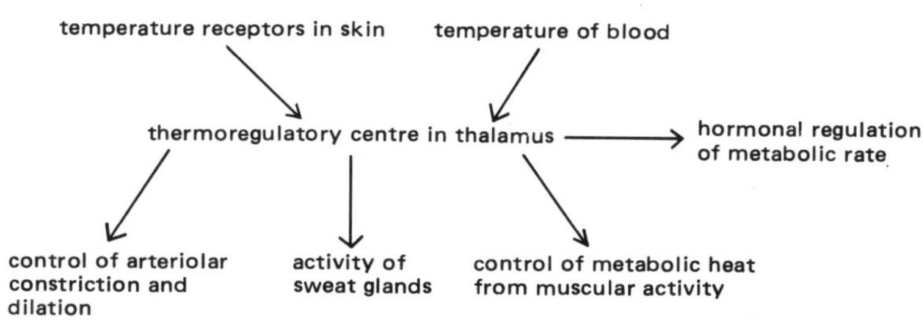

FEVER

An unusual and persistent rise in body temperature is called a **fever**. A fever is a common feature of many bacterial infections. Toxic substances liberated by bacteria can influence the temperature regulating centres of the brain altering the set point to a higher level. In order to conserve heat and maintain the body core at the altered temperature the blood vessels in the skin contract and the patient feels cold and starts to shiver.
When the temperature starts to drop either of its own accord or as a result of drug treatment the skin vessels dilate causing the patient to feel warm and to start to sweat.

The functions of the kidneys

Another example of a homeostatic mechanism in the body is the regulation of water and mineral salt concentrations by the kidneys. This mechanism has already been discussed in considerable detail from p. 145 on.
The mammalian kidney fulfils a function as the organ of excretion of organic wastes such as urea and the organ of osmoregulation. Both functions are accomplished by the production of the aqueous fluid called urine.
Urine is normally about ninety-five percent water by weight. The rest of the weight is made up of the various waste products such as urea and excess salts such as sodium chloride that need to be eliminated in order to maintain the correct osmotic pressure in the blood.
Metabolic wastes are always eliminated through the urine as quickly as possible and are never retained in the body for the purposes of osmoregulation. However, the concentration of other urine components is changed.
When a person drinks unusually large amounts of water, for example, the urine will become more dilute and more of it will be produced until the excess liquid has been eliminated. If very salty food is eaten the excess sodium chloride must be eliminated in the urine.
The reabsorption of both water and salts and therefore the regulation of the final concentration of the urine are under the control of hormones secreted under the direction of the **osmoreceptor cells** of the brain. These sensory cells are continually monitoring the osmotic pressure of the blood and secreting quantities of hormone accordingly. The hormone secreted is called **antidiuretic hormone** and its action is to decrease the volume of urine produced and increase its concentration.
If the osmotic pressure of the blood is higher than normal, more hormone will be produced causing the reabsorption of more water in order to lower the osmotic pressure. If the osmotic pressure is too low hormone production will decrease and consequently the volume of urine will increase. (See fig. 3.41.)

Fig.3.41 Summary of action of ADH

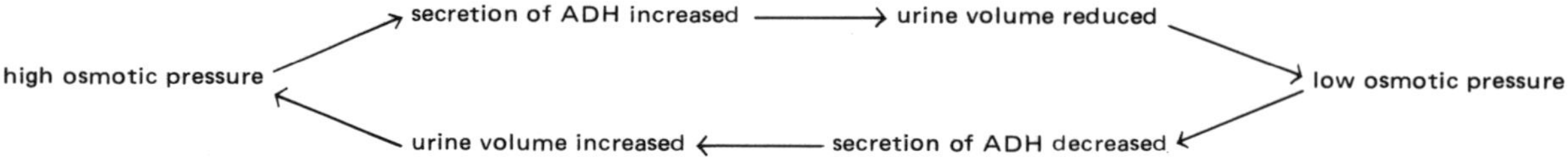

Hormonal control

Many of the homeostatic mechanisms of the body are mediated by the action of hormones.

A hormone is a chemical messenger produced in one part of the body that has the ability to influence and regulate a particular metabolic process at some point away from its site of production.

In the section above we briefly mentioned the role of antidiuretic hormone in osmoregulation. This is but one example.

Hormonal control of blood sugar levels

The end product of carbohydrate digestion is the simple sugar glucose which is then absorbed into the blood stream from the small intestine. Glucose is used as a source of energy by all the cells of the body. Most cells are able to use alternative sources such as fats and, in extreme cases, even proteins so that shortage of readily available glucose does not pose an immediate threat to their survival.

One notable exception to this rule is the brain which must have glucose as an energy source. If the level of glucose in the circulation falls below the normal range of between 70 and 100 mg per 100 ml of blood to about 40 mg the brain will cease conscious functioning and a **hypoglycemic coma** will result. Hypoglycemia simply refers to a lower than normal level of blood glucose.

How is the level of glucose in the blood controlled?

Some of the glucose absorbed from the small intestine stays in the blood stream to be used by the cells immediately. A much greater portion is taken to the liver where it is converted into the storage product glycogen. Whenever necessary glycogen stores are turned back into glucose and released into the circulation.

The liver cannot fulfil this homeostatic function unaided but does so under the direction of the hormone **insulin** secreted by the pancreas.

Fig.3.42 What happens to the sugar we eat

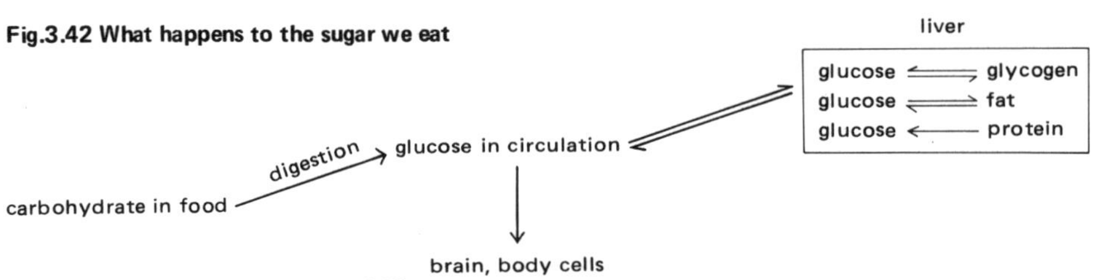

It is believed that the pancreas itself is able to monitor the amount of sugar dissolved in the blood and compare it to the normal set-point level of 70 to 100 mg per 100 ml.

Whenever there is too much sugar in the circulation the pancreas secretes insulin into the blood stream. Upon reaching the liver insulin brings about three different changes that are all directed towards lowering the glucose level.

1. It promotes the oxidation of glucose into carbon dioxide and water.
2. It increases the rate of conversion of glucose into glycogen and fat.
3. It inhibits the formation of glucose from other non-carbohydrate sources such as fat and protein.

As soon as the pancreas senses that there has been a sufficient drop in glucose levels the secretion of insulin is slowed down and brought to a halt.

In the absence of insulin the reverse of the above processes takes place in the liver. The oxidative breakdown of glucose and its conversion into glycogen and fat are inhibited, glycogen stores are converted into glucose and if these have been exhausted glucose is formed from non-carbohydrate sources. These result in increasing the blood sugar level. If the level should again surpass the set point insulin production is resumed.

This feedback control mechanism is shown diagrammatically in fig. 3.43. If, for some reason, the pancreas regularly fails to produce sufficient insulin a disease called **diabetes mellitus** results. Blood sugar levels increase to such a degree that some begins to spill over into the urine. If untreated more serious symptoms will result and eventually lead to death.

Diabetes can be kept under control by the continual administration of insulin. Since the hormone is a protein it cannot be taken by mouth as it would be broken down by the digestive system. It must be injected directly into the blood stream.

Summary

Homeostasis refers to the action of maintaining a 'steady state' condition in the face of changing external and internal conditions affecting an organism.

Fig.3.43 Summary of control of blood sugar

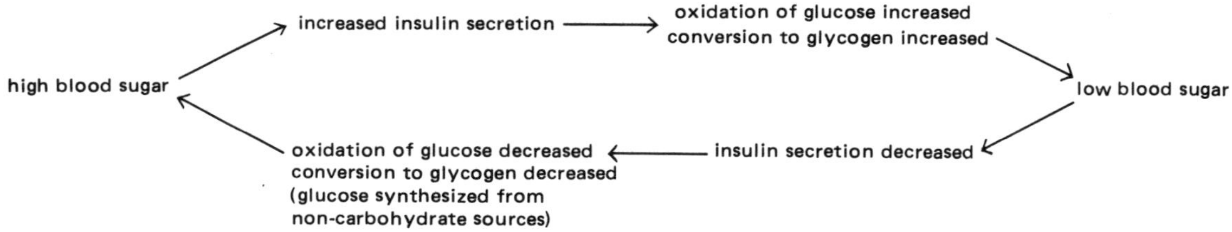

The mechanism of homeostasis frequently involves the operation of a negative feedback system.

Body temperature of mammals is controlled by regulating the heat lost from the skin through radiation and sweating.

Regulation of the water and mineral salts of the body is achieved through the action of the kidneys.

Hormones are chemical messengers that are able to influence various metabolic functions of the body. They are therefore important agents in the homeostatic mechanisms of the body.

The hormone insulin secreted by the pancreas controls the glucose level of the blood. An increase in circulating insulin lowers the blood glucose level while a decrease allows it to be raised.

Section 4. SUPPORT AND MOVEMENT

SUPPORT

Higher plants and animals are made up of a cell mass of considerable size and they are faced with the task of maintaining this cell mass in a definite shape and with a certain orientation relative to their surroundings.

Support in animals

Animals, since they move around, are more in need of support than plants that are stationary. Aquatic animals are better off because the water buoys them up and gives a large measure of support. As a result these animals can reach quite a large size without the need for any special support tissues.

The simplest supporting mechanism, found in soft-bodied invertebrates such as the earthworm and sea anemone, is the **hydroskeleton** (sometimes called a **hydrostatic skeleton**). The system consists of a fluid layer in the interior of the body that is surrounded by layers of muscle tissue that contract against the fluid. The action of the muscles keeps the fluid at high pressure and this in turn helps to maintain body shape somewhat the same way as the shape of a balloon is maintained by the air inside it.

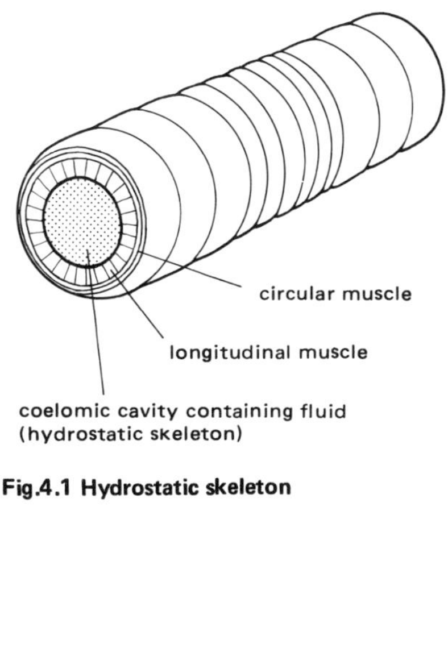

Fig.4.1 Hydrostatic skeleton

Support in higher animals

If you wanted to build a clay or paper model of an animal, how do you think you could support it? Would you build a rigid form around the outside or would you put, say, a metal rod on the inside and build your model around it?

Both the above methods of support are in fact found in the animal world. The **Arthropods**, a group of animals including insects, spiders and crabs are supported from the outside by an **exoskeleton**. Vertebrates have a rigid internal skeleton or **endoskeleton**. The very name 'vertebrate' is derived from the main component of the skeleton, the backbone or **vertebral column**.

Exoskeleton

Exoskeletons consist of a material called **chitin**. The material is basically very thin and pliable so as to allow movement around the joints. Around the main parts of the body the chitin is reinforced by additional protein secretions that result in thick, hard covering sheets. A thin layer of wax deposited on the outside of the

entire exoskeleton makes it impermeable to water.
Muscles are attached to the inside of the exoskeleton to effect movement.

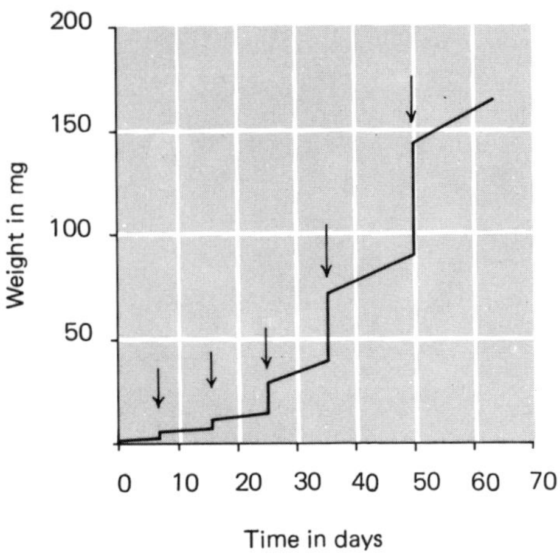

Fig.4.2 Graph showing increase in weight of an arthropod

Fig.4.3

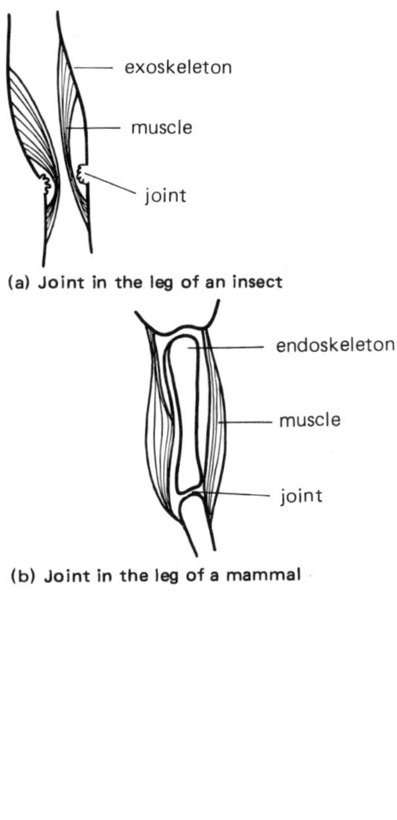

What are the advantages and drawbacks of an exoskeleton?

An exoskeleton has the advantage that, in addition to providing body support, it also protects the soft parts of the body from mechanical injury. However, it presents problems when it comes to increase in size. By nature a skeleton is inflexible and therefore must be shed periodically to allow growth. This process is called **moulting** or **ecdysis**.
Since the volume and weight of an animal increase much more rapidly than the surface area the only way for an arthropod to continue to support its mounting bulk is to increase the thickness of the exoskeleton. This, however, further adds to the body weight and results in the animals being extremely sluggish as indeed large arthropods such as lobsters and crabs are. The exoskeleton therefore severely limits the size of arthropods.

Endoskeleton

Vertebrates have a complete internal skeletal system of bone and cartilage. In order to allow for movement the bones are attached to one another at joints that are held together by flexible **ligaments**. The movement of the body is effected by the action of muscles. (See p. 186.)

Mammalian skeleton

During the course of the present discussion we will use the human skeletal system as an example of the typical mammalian structure. The main features of the skeleton are the **backbone** and the **skull**. These together with the ribs are referred to as the **axial skeleton**, since they form the main axis of the body.

THE BACKBONE

The backbone is made up of thirty-three bones called **vertebrae** (singular vertebra) connected to each other by means of **cartilage discs**. The backbone is rigid enough to support the entire weight of the trunk, yet flexible enough to allow for considerable scope in movement. If you have ever watched the performance of a highly skilled dancer or acrobat you have witnessed a demonstration of what a marvellous structure the human backbone is.
Viewed from the side, it is curved into an S shape. It can arbitrarily be divided into five sections along its length, corresponding to the position they occupy along the axis of the body. Although the basic structure of each individual vertebra is roughly the same there are

differences depending on the particular location of each.
The upper twenty-four vertebrae, that is, those in the **cervical**, **thoracic** and **lumbar** regions are free to move individually. The **sacrum** is made up of five vertebrae that are fused together and the **coccyx** consists of four smaller fused units representing the remnant of the tail found in lower animals.
Fig. 4.4 shows the structure of an individual vertebra as seen from above and from the side. The **centrum** is a solid cylinder of bone that

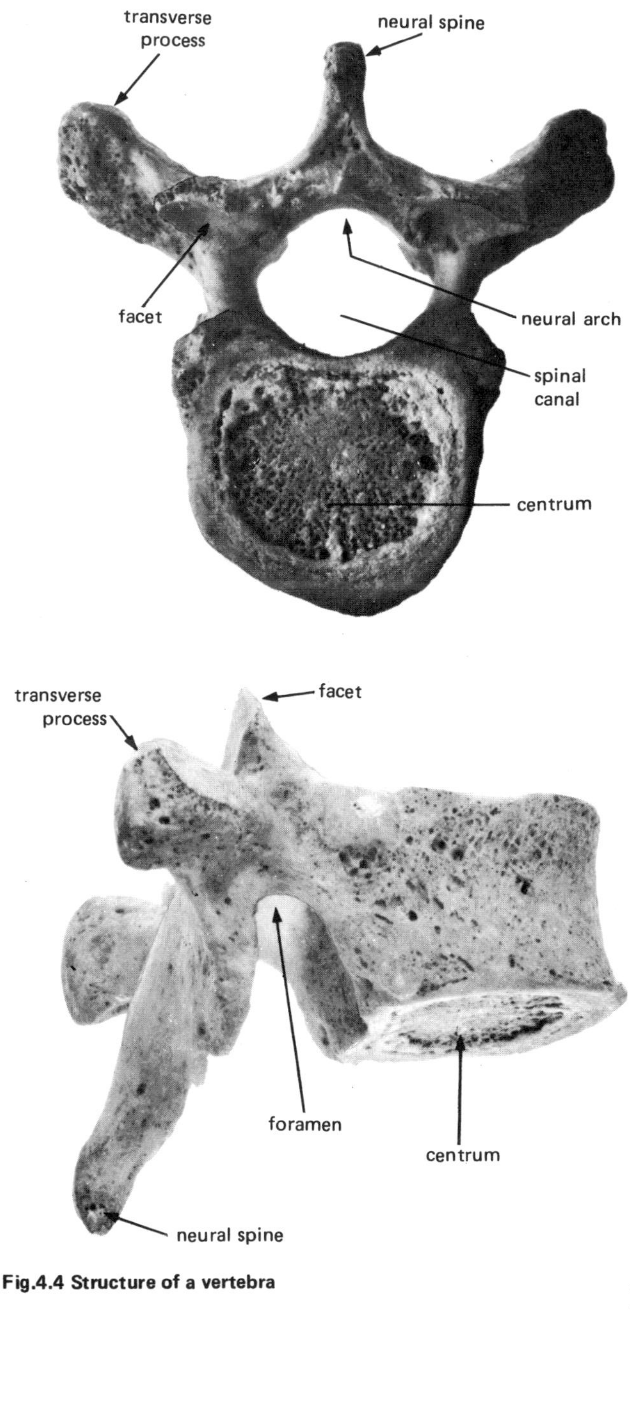

Fig.4.4 Structure of a vertebra

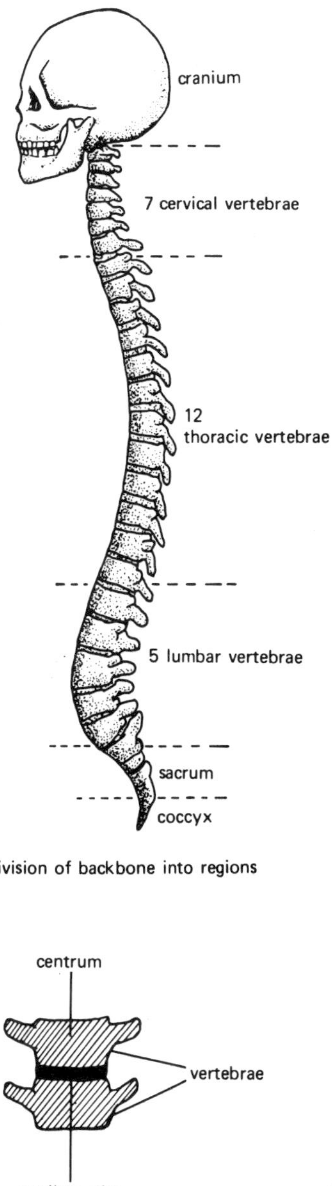

(b) connection between vertebrae

Fig.4.5 The human vertebral column

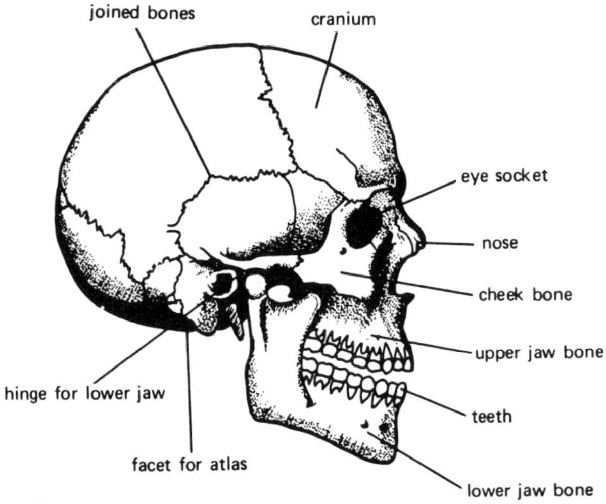

Fig.4.6 Side view of the human skull

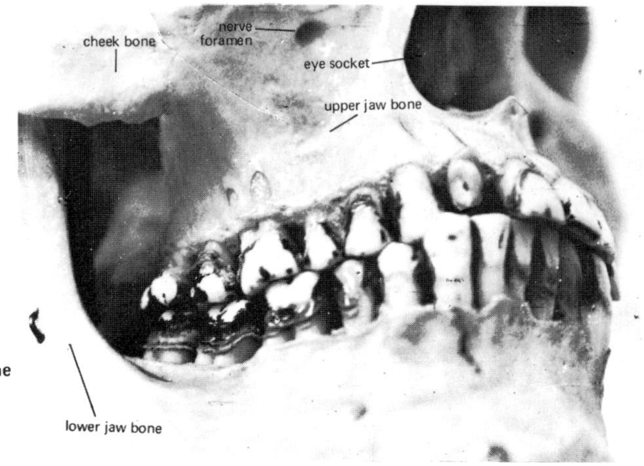

Fig.4.7 Front view of the human skull

forms the main support of the vertebra. The **neural canal** is the passage through which the nerves of the spinal cord pass. (See p. 242.)

Each vertebra has four **facets**, that is, surfaces against which movements between adjacent members are possible. The **neural spine** and the **transverse process** serve as points of attachment for muscles and ligaments.

THE SKULL

Fig.4.8 The brain case develops from separate bones which fuse as they grow

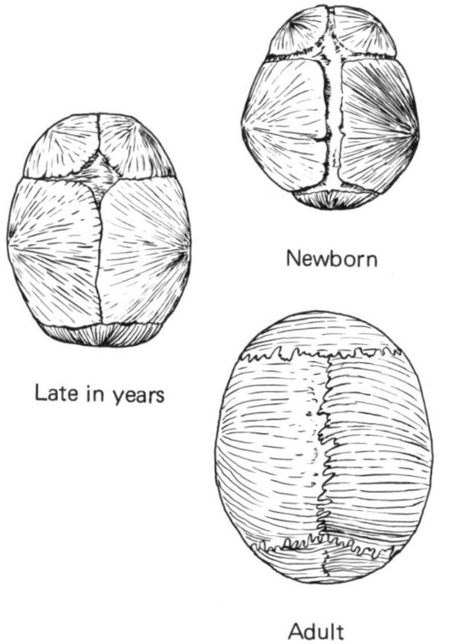

The function of the skull is to enclose and protect the brain. It is essentially a spherical, hollow casing made of bone.

In order for the brain to fulfil its function as co-ordinator of the activities of the body it must be connected to the nerve networks and the various sense organs. Accordingly the skull possesses numerous openings for these connections, such as the one where the spinal cord passes through and the openings for the optic and auditory nerves.

The upper jaw is part of the main structure of the skull while the lower jaw is hinged on to the upper part on either side of the head just behind the cheek bone. If you place your hands on the side of your head just in front of the ears and open and close your mouth you will be able to feel the **articulation**[1] at these hinges.

At the point of attachment of the skull to the vertebral column there are two special vertebrae called the **atlas** and the **axis**. These have special articulations with the skull to permit nodding and rotary movements of the head.

During the development of the embryo the skull is formed from a number of plate-like bones of various shapes. As the head enlarges,

[1] *articulation*: movement of one bone surface relative to another

these bone plates enlarge as well until they are touching each other in most regions. At the time of birth the skull is still quite pliable permitting easier passage of the head down the birth canal. After birth the individual bone plates gradually become rigidly and permanently fused together along their serrated edges. The process is usually completed by about the age of twenty.

THE RIB CAGE

The rib cage forms a loose protective casing for the heart and the lungs. The structure is made up of twelve pairs of bones that form the ribs and the **sternum**, the breast bone, along the front of the body. The upper seven pairs of ribs are directly attached to the backbone at the back and to the sternum at the front through pieces of connecting **cartilage**. The next three pairs are attached to each other and the sternum indirectly through the cartilage while the remaining two pairs have no front attachment at all and are therefore referred to as the **floating ribs**.

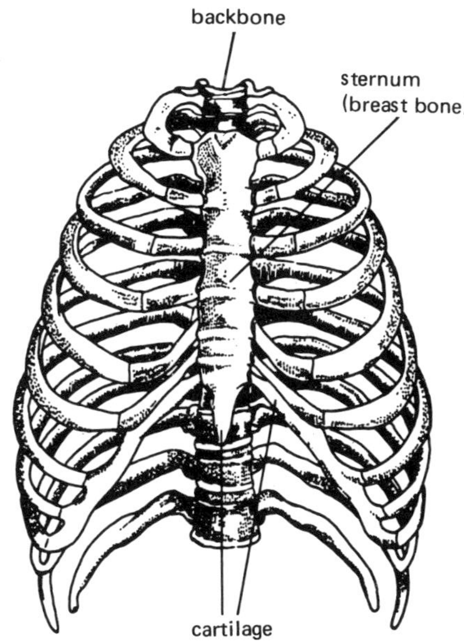

Fig.4.9 The rib cage

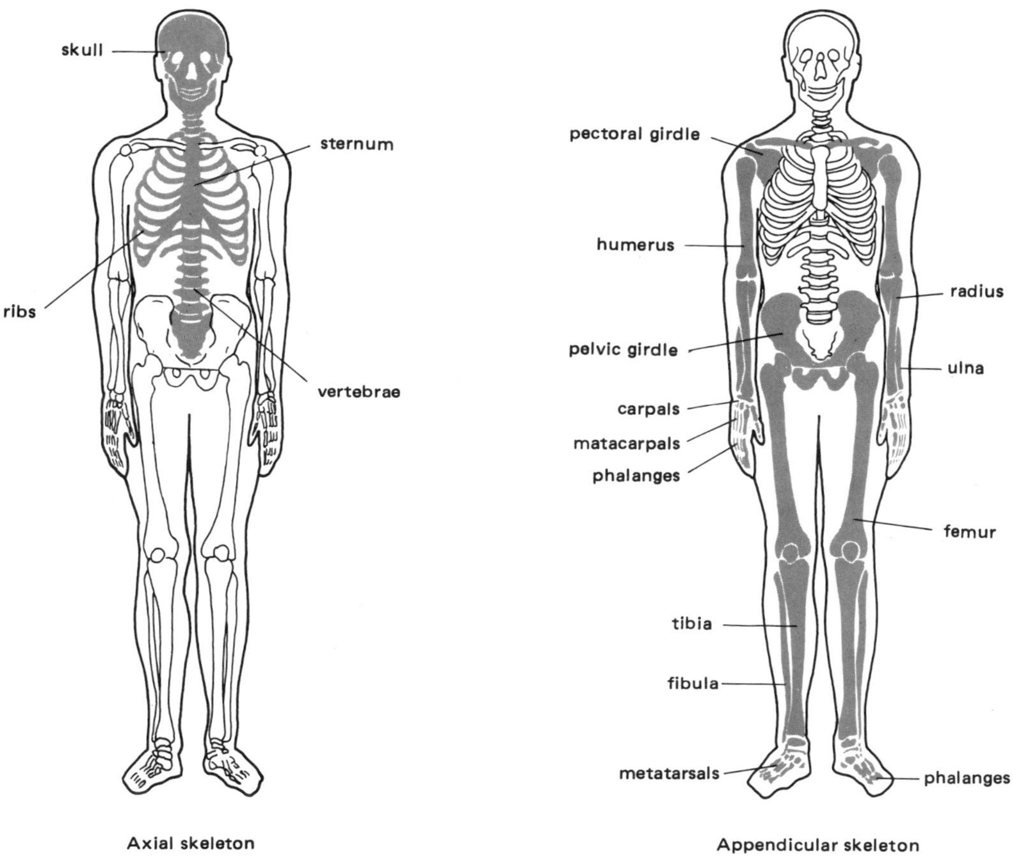

Fig.4.10 The human skeleton divided into axial and appendicular components

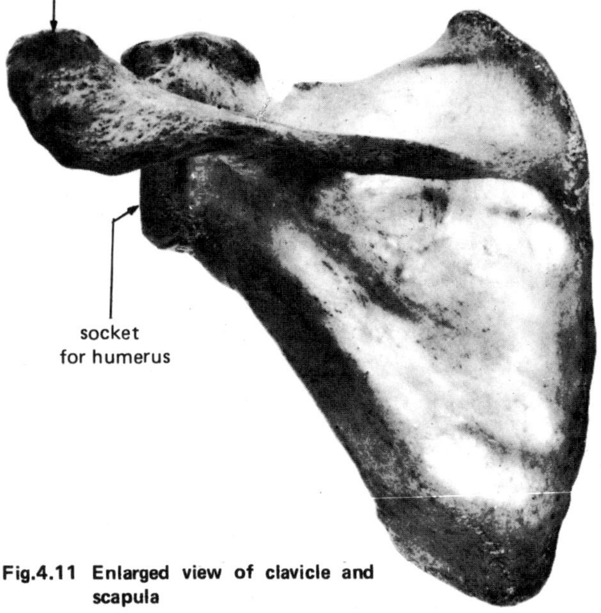

Fig.4.11 Enlarged view of clavicle and scapula

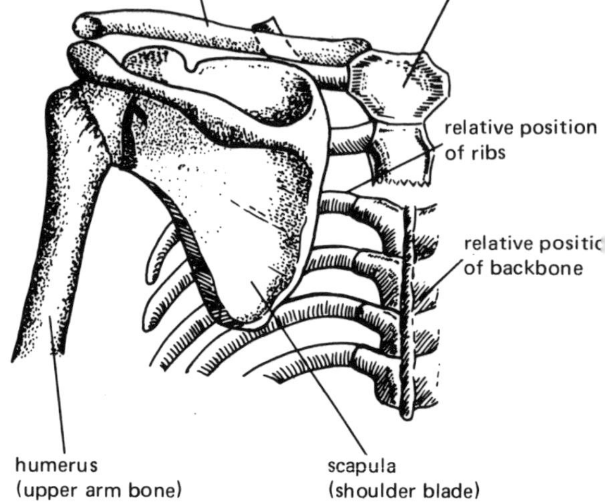

Fig.4.12 The pectoral girdle in relation to the rib cage

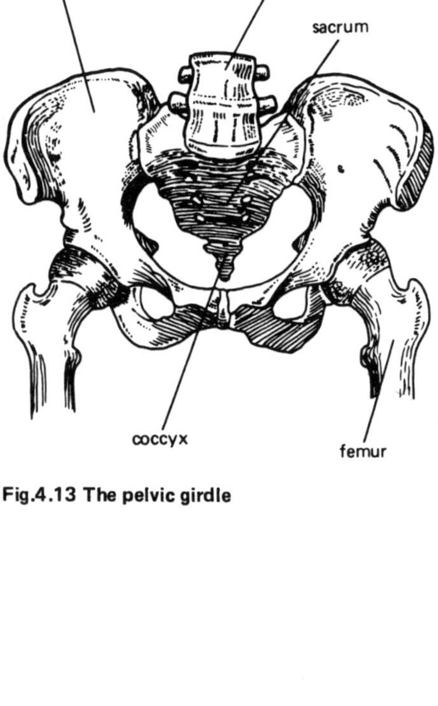

Fig.4.13 The pelvic girdle

The skull, backbone and rib cage are collectively referred to as the axial skeleton, since they form the central axis of the body. Attached to the axial skeleton is the **appendicular skeleton** consisting of the four limbs and their attachments.

APPENDICULAR SKELETON

The fore limbs, that is, the arms in the case of humans, are attached to the axial skeleton by means of the collar bone **(clavicle)** and the shoulder blade **(scapula)**, the two together forming the **pectoral girdle**. Fig. 4.12 shows the attachment in detail. Notice that the scapula is not rigidly fixed to the spine. This arrangement permits considerable flexibility of movement in the shoulders and greater mobility for the upper arm. In contrast to the pectoral girdle, the **pelvic girdle** consists of a ring-shaped mass of bone that is firmly attached to the backbone. The force exerted on the lower limbs in walking, jumping and so on and even by the mere weight of the body at rest, is thus transmitted to the vertebral column. As a result some of the strain is removed from the limbs themselves. Refer to the diagram of the human skeleton (fig. 4.14). Notice that the upper part of each limb is supported by a single bone called the **humerus** in the case of the upper limb and the **femur** in the case of the lower limb.

The lower part of the arm is formed by the **radius** and the **ulna**, joining the humerus at the elbow. The lower part of the leg consists of the **tibia** and the **fibula**, joining the femur at the knee.

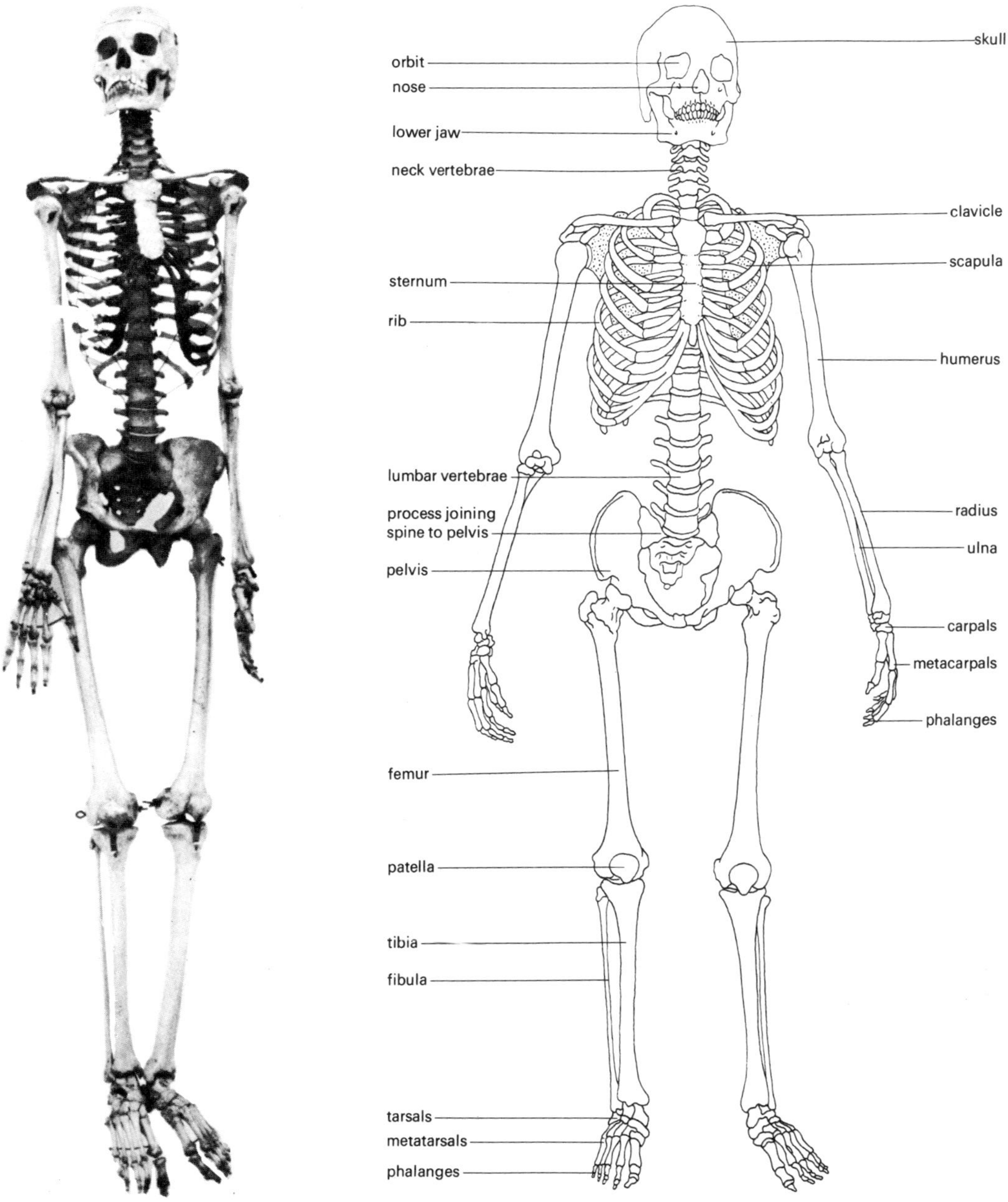

Fig.4.14 Photo and diagram of the human skeleton

How are bones connected to each other at the joints?

At various points along the skeletal system there are **movable joints** that allow for movement of two bones relative to each other. The type and scope of movement permitted depends on the precise nature of the joint.

Gliding joints are the kind found between the individual vertebrae of the backbone. These joints allow bones to slide over one another in one direction only.

Fig.4.15 Function of atlas and axis vertebrae (pivot joint)

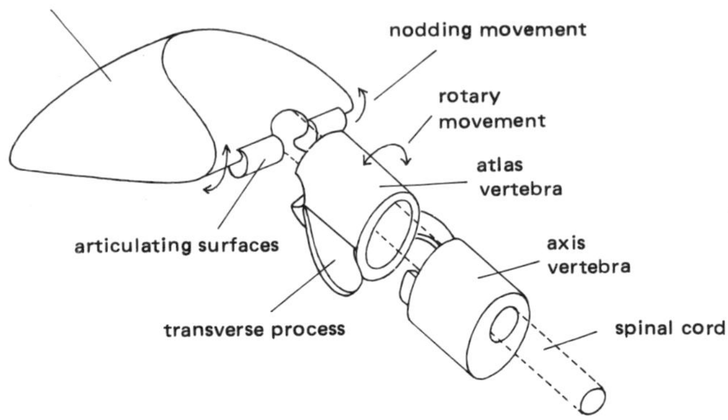

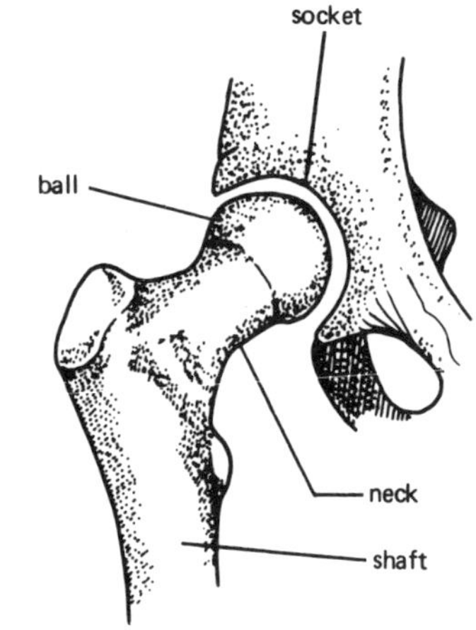

Fig.4.16 Ball and socket joint

Pivot joints allow rotatory motion. The joint between the atlas and the axis at the top of the vertebral column is a pivot joint allowing circular movement of the head.

Ball and socket joints are much more versatile and allow movement in all directions. They are found at the attachments of the limbs.

Hinge joints are found at the knee and elbow and allow movement only along a single plane.

In addition, the body has some immovable or **fixed joints**. At these points there is a complete fusion of the bones concerned with no allowance for any movement whatsoever.

The ends of two given bones forming a movable joint are covered with a layer of smooth cartilage and are surrounded by a **capsule** of connective tissue. The capsule is filled with a sticky **synovial fluid** that acts as a lubricant, facilitating the movements of the bones.

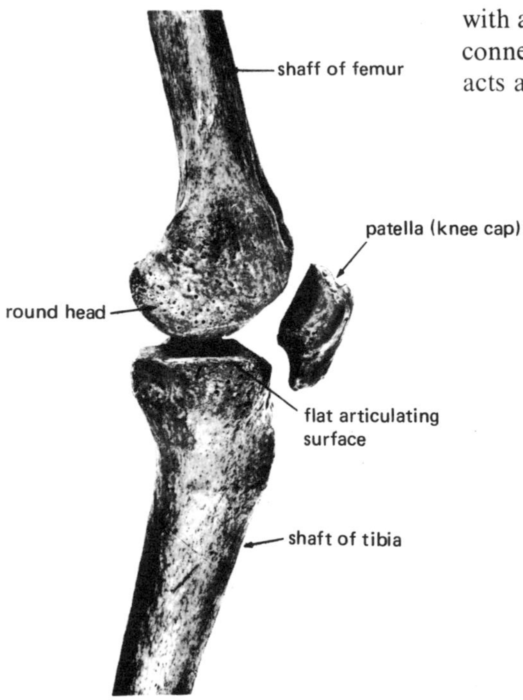

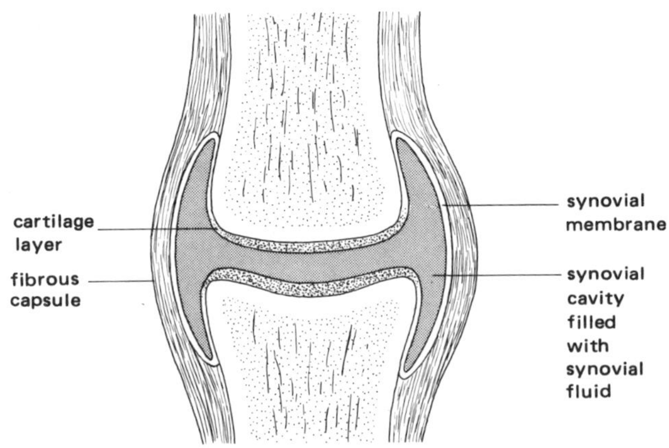

Fig.4.17 Hinge joint at knee

Fig.4.18 Structure of a movable joint

What are the various functions of the skeletal system?

In addition to the basic function of providing support and maintaining the body shape the skeletal system has various other functions. It permits the protection of delicate organs such as the brain and spinal cord. Bones provide an effective lever system against which the muscles of the body can act to produce movement. Cells in the interior of the bony parts of the skeleton play an important role in the production of blood cells.

The structure of bone

Bone belongs to a particular type of tissue of the body called **connective tissue**. The characteristic feature of connective tissue is that the cells are widely separated from one another and therefore there is an increased amount of inter-cellular substance. Bone is the hardest of all the connective tissues. It is composed of only twenty-five percent water, thirty percent organic material and the rest is inorganic salts.

Bone cells are arranged in a pattern of concentric circles around the small canals that carry blood vessels and nerves to the tissue.

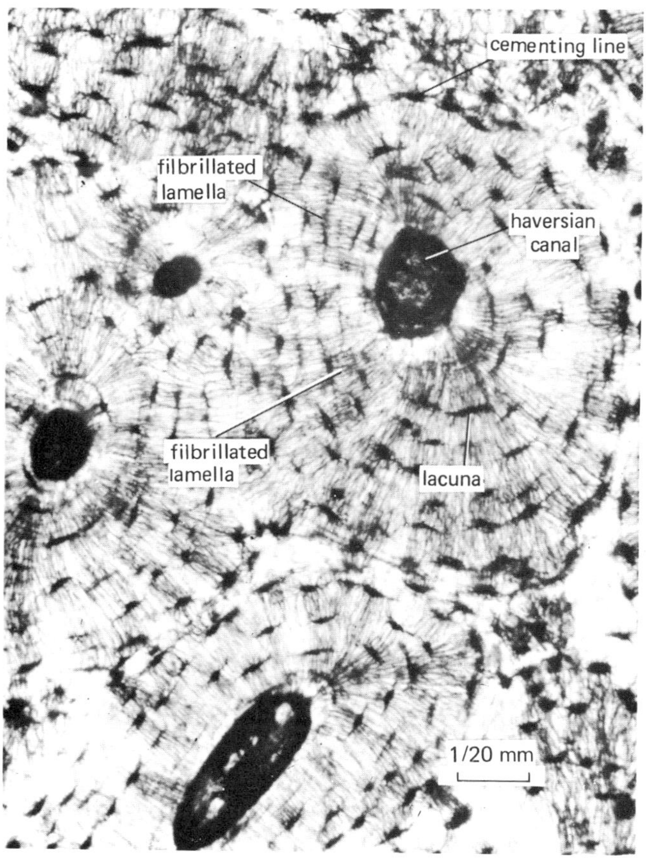

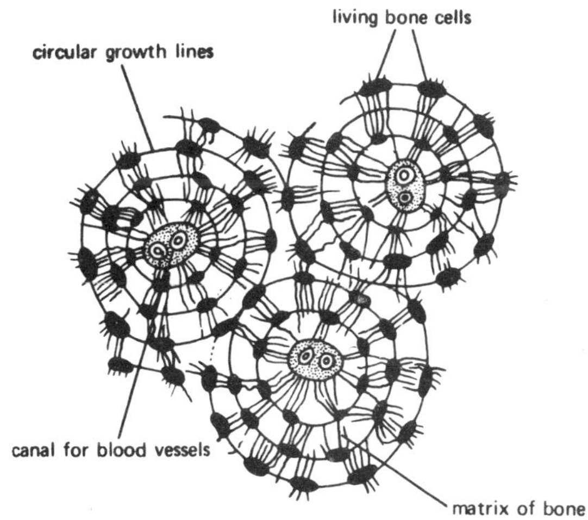

Fig.4.19 Photo and diagram of bone cells

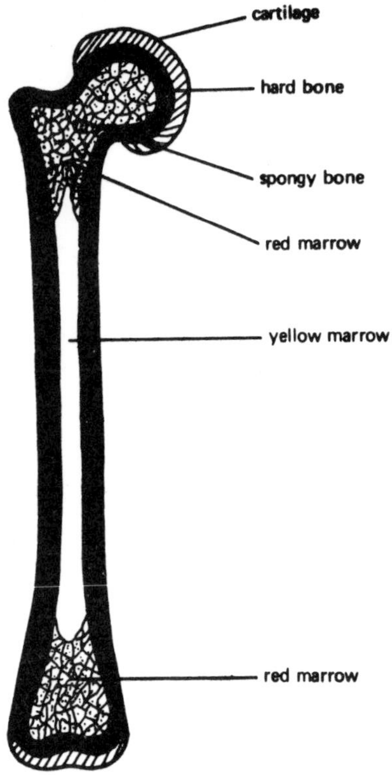

Fig.4.20 A long bone

The intercellular matrix which is really the essence of bony tissue consists mainly of calcium carbonate and calcium phosphate. As more and more matrix is secreted the cells get forced increasingly further apart. Fine processes radiating out through the matrix connect up with the canals and provide a pathway for getting nutrients to the cells.

Fig. 4.20 shows the interior structure of a **long bone**, that is, a limb bone, in this case the femur.

The outside layer, called **hard bone**, has the structure shown in fig. 4.19. The two extremities are filled with **spongy bone**, which is similar to hard bone except that it contains many cavities between the individual cell units. These cavities are filled with **red marrow** where red blood cells are made.

The shaft is hollow, the interior being filled with **yellow marrow** consisting mainly of fat cells.

What is cartilage?

Cartilage is a more elastic form of connective tissue that is of considerable importance in the skeletal system.

There are two types of cartilage found in humans. One is present only in embryonic and very early life and then gradually turns into bone, that is, it becomes **ossified**. The second type persists through adult life at points in the skeletal system where a more flexible type of support is required.

The lower ribs, for example, are connected to each other and to the sternum by means of cartilage to facilitate greater freedom in movement. This area of the rib cage is under considerable strain during the regular breathing movements of the body and if made of the more inflexible bone, there would be danger of the bones breaking.

Summary

The three types of support system found in animals are the hydroskeleton, the exoskeleton and the endoskeleton.

The mammalian endoskeleton consists of the skull housing the brain, the backbone giving support along the axis of the body and connecting it to the limbs, the rib cage that protects the lungs and the four limbs. Individual bones are connected at the joints to facilitate the relative movement of different parts of the skeleton.

The skeletal system consists mostly of bone tissue and a small amount of cartilage.

Support in plants

In the section dealing with osmosis and turgidity we already noted that the accumulation of water in the vacuoles of its cells provides a plant with a certain amount of rigidity. This is especially true in the

case of young leaves and growing tips where support tissues have not yet fully developed. This is the reason why plants that do not receive adequate moisture lose their rigidity and wilt.
When it is first formed, a plant cell is enclosed by a thin, elastic cell wall that is capable of expanding as the cell increases in size. As soon as maximum size is reached the cellulose wall thickens and flexibility is lost.

Fig.4.21

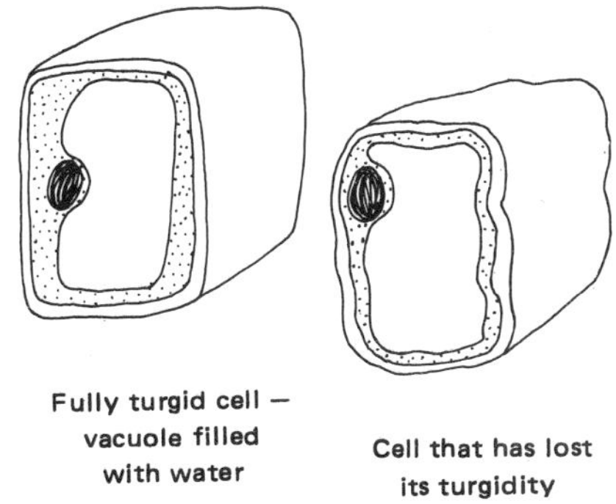

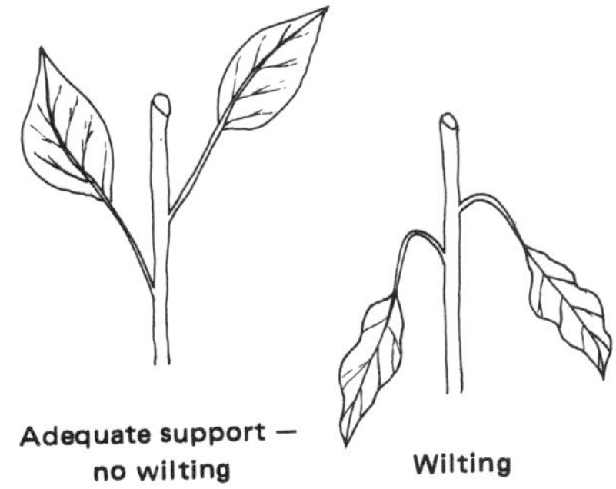

Do plants have any specialized support tissue?

The walls of some cells become especially thickened to serve as aids in support. One of the tissues whose specific purpose is to provide strength and rigidity while maintaining flexibility and elasticity is the **sclerenchyma**. Sclerenchyma (scleros—hard) consists of very long, narrow, thick-walled cells that are usually pointed at the ends. These cells sometimes occur in definite patches or individually dispersed among other types of cell. In a mature plant the cells of the sclerenchyma are no longer alive. The thickenings of the walls consist of **lignin**, a hard waterproof substance.
Sclerenchyma is found in the stems and associated with the veins in the leaves of dicotyledonous plants. Many natural textile fibres such as hemp, jute and flax are in fact derived from the sclerenchyma fibres of the plants in question.
The most commonly found means of support in rapidly growing areas of the plant such as leaf petioles is called **collenchyma**. The

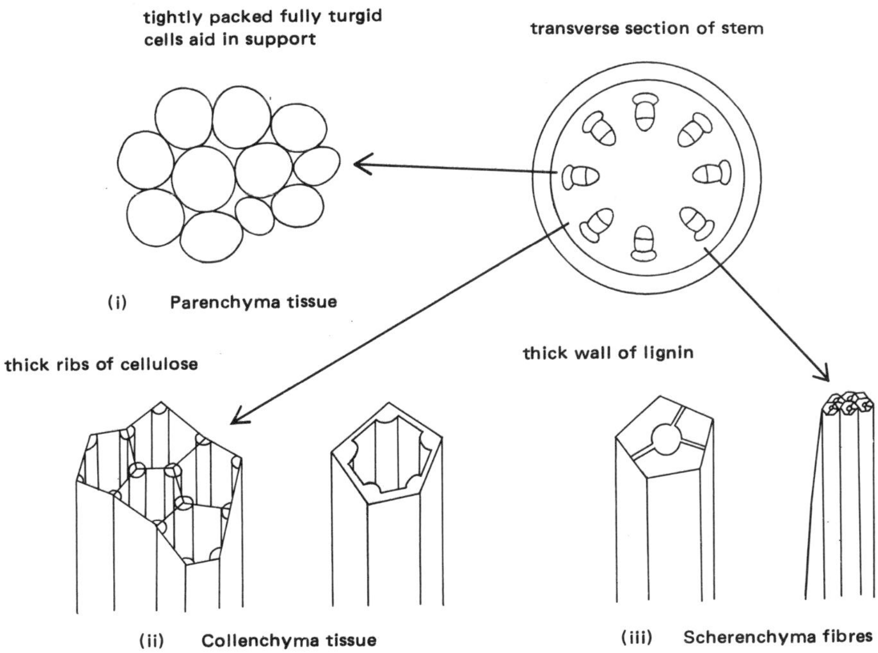

Fig.4.22 The principal support tissues found in the stem of a flowering plant

special feature of this tissue is that thickenings of cellulose occur at the corners of the cells and the tissue remains alive. In the stem of herbaceous[1] dicots[2], collenchyma is found forming a discrete ring immediately outside the ring of the sclerenchyma. (Fig. 4.22.)

Collenchyma and sclerenchyma are sometimes referred to as **mechanical tissues** since their function is fulfilled not as a result of any biological activity but simply by being present in a particular area of the plant. They are roughly analogous to the skeletal tissue of animals. Mechanical tissue is usually not found in roots since the anchoring action of the root hairs and rootlets is adequate as a means of support.

Fig.4.23 Stone cells

An even more specialized type of support tissue is the **stone cell**. Stone cells are non-living cells of no definite geometric shape. Their thick walls are laid down in layers forming a marked concentric pattern. Stone cells are found scattered among the **parenchyma cells** of the leaves and stems of many dicotyledonous plants, in the outer covering of hard seeds and in the flesh of some fruits such as the pear.

The unspecialized parenchyma cells contribute to support functions by way of their turgidity. Their primary function is the storage of

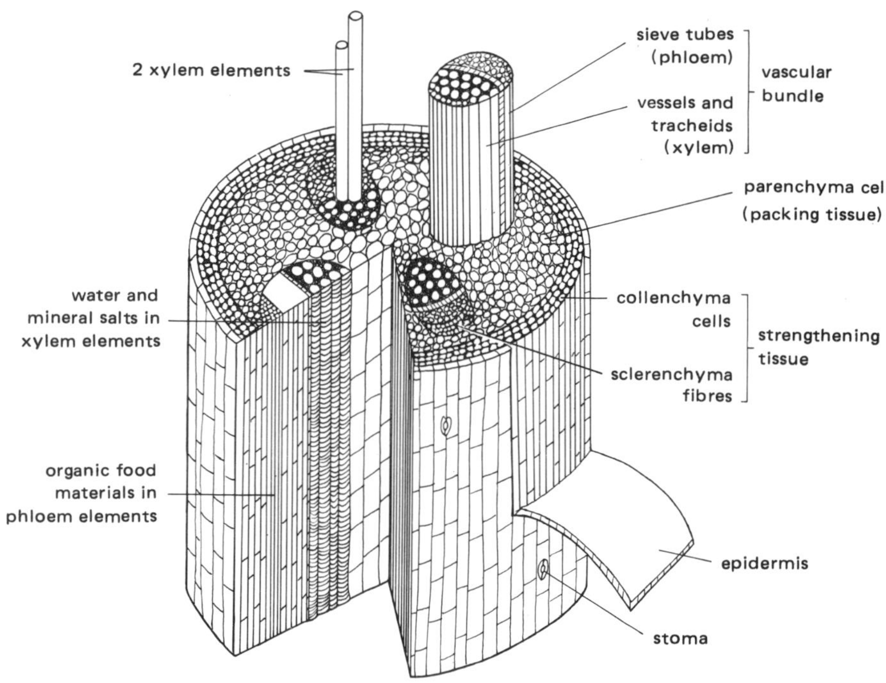

Fig.4.24 Stereogram of part of a dicotyledonous stem

[1]*herbaceous:* a plant that does not have woody tissues

[2]*dicots*: see p. 301

organic nutrients. **Xylem** vessels and tracheids, although their primary function is transport, (see p. 212) contribute to support by way of their thickened cell walls. Fig. 4.24 shows the distribution of tissues in a dicotyledonous plant stem.

Summary

Plants derive support from the turgidity of their cells and the branching structure of the roots that grip into the ground.
In addition they have special support tissues in the stem and leaves. Sclerenchyma consisting of dead cells is found in older parts of the plant while the living collenchyma is found mainly in the rapidly growing areas.

MOVEMENT

In the introductory section we made the point that one of the basic characteristics of all living organisms is movement. Since plants and different types of animal vary tremendously in their outward appearance it is not surprising that their methods of locomotion are equally varied.

Movement in animals

Even a casual glance at individual species of the animal world helps to convince us of the tremendous variation in the types of locomotion used by these animals. Some animals in fact do not move from place to place at all. Sponges, for instance, are attached to one spot and are able to move only their tentacles in order to aid them in capturing food.
In considering locomotion in any animal three basic requirements must be kept in mind.

1. The animal must somehow be propelled in the appropriate direction.
2. The body of the animal must have some form of support against the forces exerted on it by the medium it lives in, such as air pressure on land and the pressure of the surrounding water if in an aquatic medium.
3. The animal must have some means of maintaining its stability as it moves.

Amoeboid movement

Amoeboid movement is named after the unicellular protozoan called the amoeba with which you are already familiar. An amoeba is able to move from place to place by constantly changing its shape due to the streaming motion of its cytoplasm. The streaming of the cytoplasm can easily be observed under a microscope. Watching the motion of the liquid and the granules will convince you that cytoplasm is indeed a living entity.

What are the characteristics of amoeboid movement?

Small extensions called **pseudopodia** (singular: **pseudopodium**) are repeatedly sent out by the animal in the direction in which it is moving while others are slowly withdrawn on the opposite side. The extensions are formed as a result of changes in the physical nature of the cytoplasm.

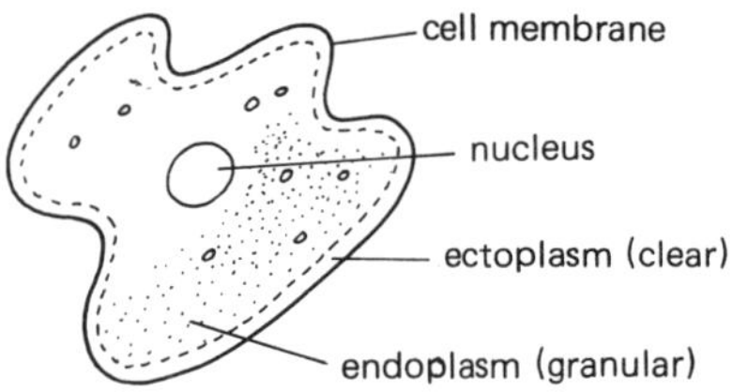

Fig.4.25 Diagram of an amoeba

The cytoplasm in the interior of the cell, called **endoplasm**, is quite watery in consistency and is very granular. On the outside is a layer of **ectoplasm** which is clear and jelly-like. The fluid endoplasm starts to stream out in the direction in which the animal wants to move. As it comes in contact with the exterior of the cell it changes to ectoplasm. At the other extremity of the cell the opposite change is taking place. Ectoplasm is being changed to endoplasm as the pseudopodium is withdrawn. Through a continual streaming motion of this type the animal gradually 'flows along' in a given direction.

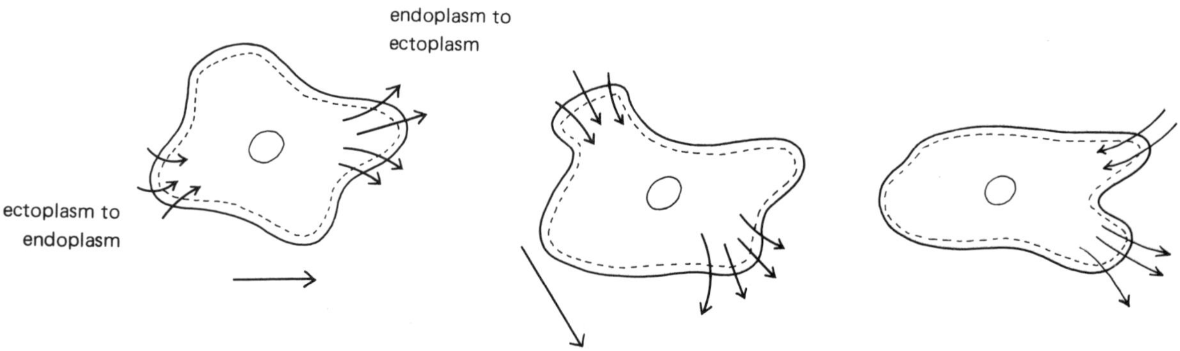

Fig.4.26 Movements of amoeba

Scientists have shown that energy in the form of ATP is necessary for the motion and have also detected the presence of certain proteins that have the ability to contract in the presence of ATP. However, the exact mechanism by which the movement is brought about is not known.

Amoeboid animals have no special problems as far as support and stability are concerned. Since they are extremely small and light they are buoyed up by the watery medium in which they live and they do not have to worry about maintaining a definite shape.

Is amoeboid movement found in higher animals?

Amoeboid movement is found not only in protozoans but in certain cells of higher animals as well. It is the type of motion exhibited by the white blood cells of mammals when they squeeze through the capillary walls and pass into the surrounding intercellular spaces to fight infection. (See p. 333.)

Movement in higher animals

As the degree of complexity of an animal increases there is a corresponding increase in the complexity of its locomotion and support.

In almost all multicellular animals, movement is accomplished through the action of a special tissue called **muscle**. The characteristics of this tissue will be discussed in detail on pp. 186 to 192. At this stage let us just make one point about the action of muscles. Contraction of a muscle causes the fibres to become shorter so that the two ends of the muscle are brought closer together. Relaxation restores the muscle to its original, resting length. Thus it follows that whatever structures may be attached to the two ends of a muscle are correspondingly brought closer together or further apart as the muscle contracts and relaxes.

Soft-bodied invertebrates

Soft-bodied invertebrates such as the sea anemone and the earthworm have a special kind of support system called a hydroskeleton, consisting of a fluid under pressure. (See p. 165.) The fluid is surrounded by layers of muscle that contract against it.

In an earthworm, for instance, there are layers of muscle whose fibres run in a circular direction and others whose fibres are arranged longitudinally. By alternate contractions of the longitudinal and circular muscles the animal can move forward as shown in fig. 4.27.

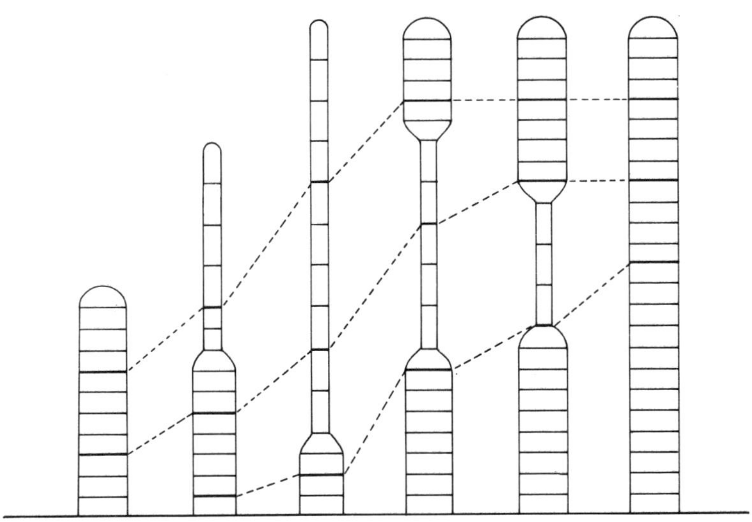

Fig.4.27 Movement in earthworm

Movement in insects

Insects are the most successful animal group; insect species make up nearly three quarters of the animal world. The great majority of them are terrestrial and they show a high degree of specialization for life on land as far as locomotion is concerned. The insect body is divided into three distinct regions. The **head** bears a pair of compound eyes, antennae and specialized feeding appendages (see p. 89). The antennae are sensitive to touch, smell, vibrations and air movements.

The head is connected by a short neck portion to the **thorax** which consists of three separate segments. Each segment bears a pair of legs and one or two of the segments bear wings.

The posterior region, called the **abdomen**, is also segmented. The entire body is covered by an exoskeleton of chitin (p. 165).

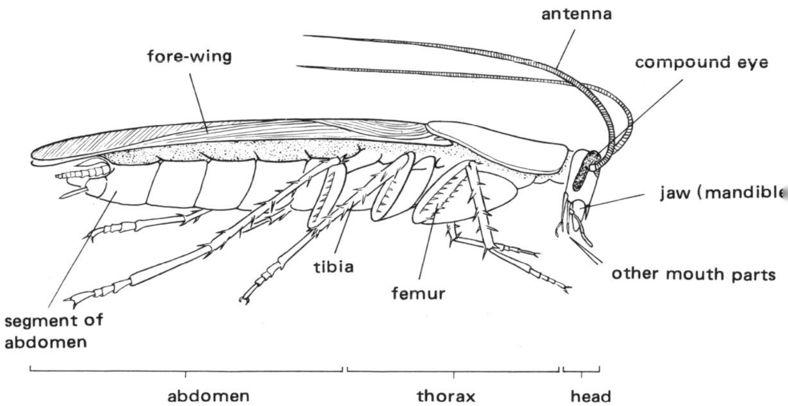

Fig. 4.28 Side view of male cockroach

How do insects move?

Movement is accomplished by the action of opposing pairs of muscle attached to the interior of the exoskeleton. Although the presence of the exoskeleton limits the amount of movement possible the fact that the cuticle is much thinner and more flexible at the joints means that relative movement of various body parts is possible.

Fig. 4.29 shows the pattern of muscles in the insect leg. The contraction of muscle A would result in movement of the lower leg segment to the left, whereas contraction of muscle B would have the opposite effect.

The **flight muscles** serving the wings are attached to the walls of the thorax rather than being attached directly to the wings. Contraction of the muscles changes the shape of the thorax causing the wings to move up and down. The tension set up in the thoracic wall results in forty or more wing beats for every nerve impulse of the flight

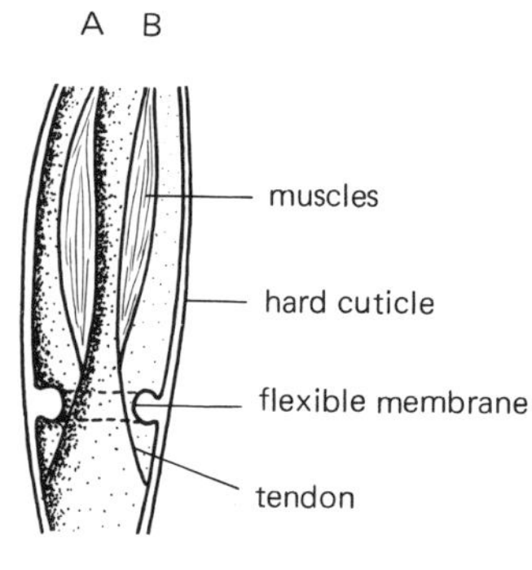

Fig.4.29 Muscle-skeleton arrangement in limb of crustacean

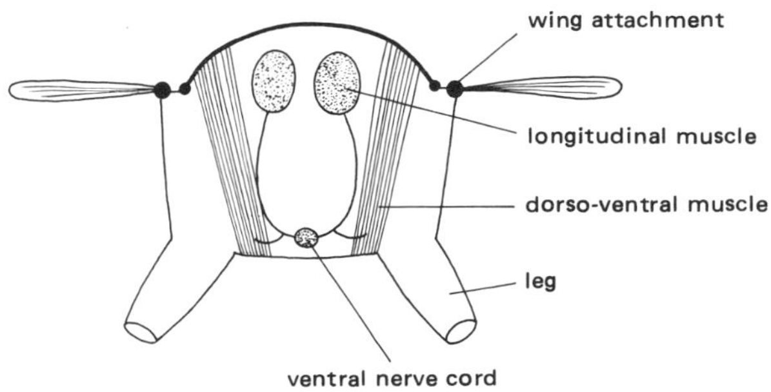

Fig.4.30 Cross-section of thorax of an insect

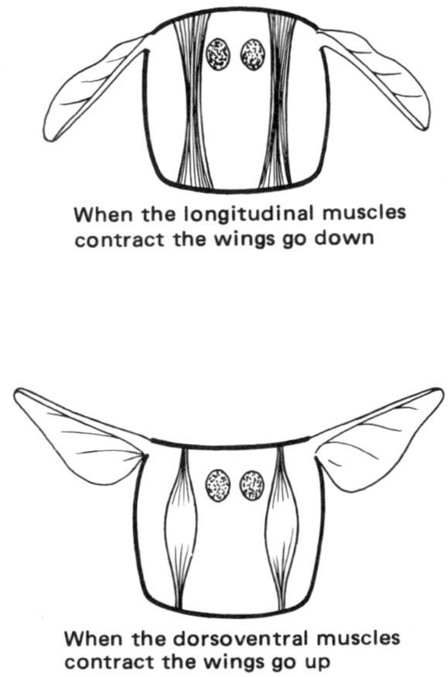

Fig.4.31 Flight muscles of an insect

muscles. This makes possible frequencies of wing beats ranging from the relatively slow rate of fifty per second in butterflies and dragonflies to the incredible rate of six hundred per second in mosquitoes. There is no doubt as to the high degree of efficiency of insect flight due to this unique system of muscle arrangement.

On land the three pairs of legs ensure that the insect is propelled along at a fast rate and has adequate stability at all times.

Claws at the ends of the legs help the animal to drag itself forward on uneven ground while pads located on the surfaces of some insect legs aid in movement on wet or extremely smooth surfaces.

Movement in amphibians

Amphibians inhabit both land and water at some stage of their life cycle. The body form and muscle arrangements of the purely aquatic larval form is distinctly different from that of the adult which is usually equally at home both on land and in water.

The amphibian that you are probably most familiar with and one whose development will be discussed in detail (p. 271) is the frog. The larval form, called the *tadpole*, has an elongated muscular tail. Alternate contractions of the tail muscles on the right and left sides of the body propel the animal forward.

As illustrated in fig. 4.32 rapid contraction of the tail muscles on the right side gives the animal a shape like that shown in *b*. Contraction

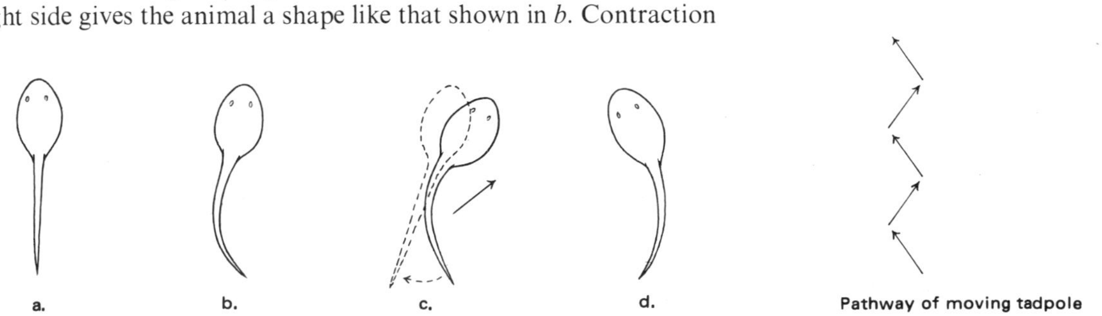

Fig.4.32 Movement of tadpole

of the muscles on the opposite side causes the tail to sweep towards the left and in doing so press against the water in its path. This gives the animal a slight forward and sideways thrust as shown in *d*. Contraction of the right muscles and sweeping the tail to the right gives a slight thrust forward and to the left. Repeated contractions move the animal forward with a kind of wriggling motion.
Even after the hind legs have fully developed the tadpole still employs the swimming motions of the tail to propel itself. It is not until the front legs have emerged and the tail starts to be reabsorbed in the last stages of metamorphosis[1] that the adult type of movement is adopted.

How does the adult frog move?

The body shape and muscle patterns of the adult frog make it possible for it to move about with equal ease both on land and in the water. The amount of time spent in one habitat or the other depends on the species. Some spend a considerable amount of time in the water especially in the dry season while others live almost exclusively on land. Some tree frogs return to the water only for the purposes of spawning and some not even then.

MOVEMENT ON LAND

The greatly enlarged muscular hind legs of the frog provide the propellant force for its movements both on land and in the water. Normally the hind legs are tucked in close to the body.

Fig.4.33 Frog leaping

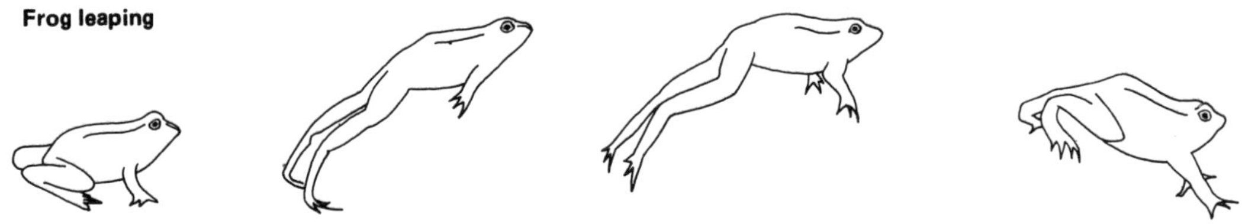

(i) At rest: hind legs flexed

(ii) Hind legs extended pushing frog forward and upward

(iii) Front legs being extended: beginning to draw up the hind legs

(iv) Front legs extended to take first shock of landing: hind legs drawn up

In leaping, the strong extensor muscles of the thighs contract, the legs are extended and pressed against the ground giving a forward thrust to the entire body. The thrust is transmitted to the pelvic girdle and then to the entire body causing the frog to soar up into the air. The motion is somewhat similar to that of a person standing with knees slightly bent and then leaping up into the air such as in the act of diving into the water for a swim.
In preparation for landing the frog again folds up its hind legs and

[1] *metamorphosis*: see p. 271

Fig.4.34 Frog crawling

uses the much smaller front ones to cushion itself as it hits the ground. Crawling motions are also possible by extending one of the back legs along with the corresponding front leg. Again it is the back leg pushing against the ground that provides the forward impetus.

Fig.4.35 Tree frog

MOVEMENT IN THE WATER

In swimming the frog is aided by its webbed feet. The webs increase the surface area with which the feet can push back on the water. The motions of the hind legs in swimming are very similar to those in jumping. From a tucked-in position the legs are thrust into a fully extended one, thereby pushing back on the water. This results in a considerable amount of forward thrust. The front legs are used in steering and in helping to stabilize the animal.
Tree frogs have a further adaptation, namely the presence of padded suckers at the tips of their toes. These aid the frog in clinging to leaves and branches. The webs on the feet of tree frogs are very small or entirely absent since they do not spend a great deal of time in the water.

Fig.4.36 **Arrangement of muscles around the vertebral column of a dogfish**

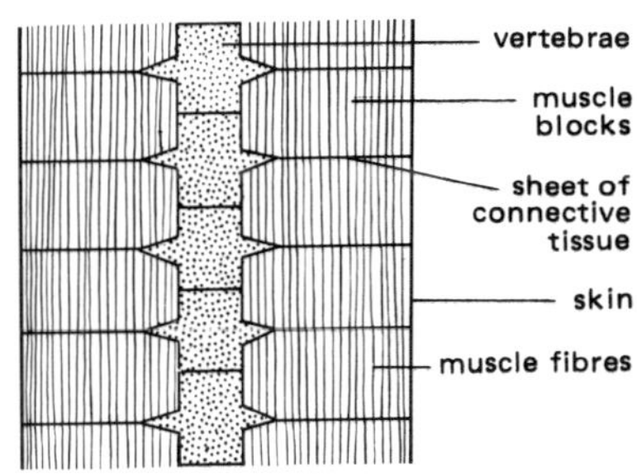

Movement in fish

About eighty percent of the body weight of a fish is made up of its muscles, attached symmetrically to the two sides of the vertebral column. The vertebral column itself is flexible enough to allow for considerable lateral movement.
Fig. 4.36 shows the way the muscles are attached to the vertebral column separated in a transverse direction by sheets of connective

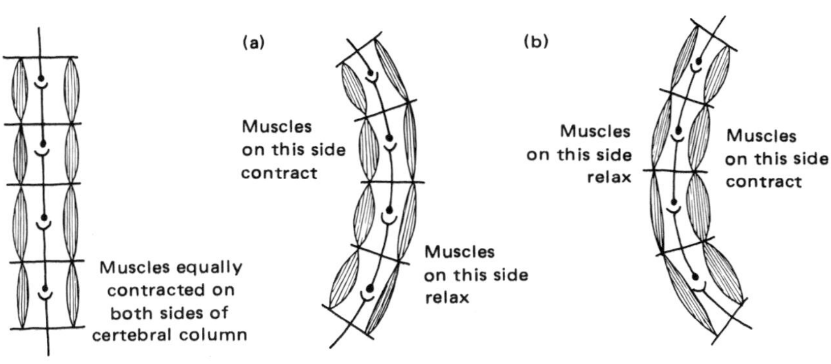

Fig.4.37 Movement in fish

tissue arising from their processes of the individual vertebrae.
Fig. 4.37 is a schematic illustration of the muscular apparatus. Notice that when the muscles on the left side of the body contract as in *a*, the vertebral column is bent to that side. When the opposite muscles contract bending takes place in the opposite direction as in *b*. The alternate contraction of the muscles causes the tail to sweep across from one side of the animal to the other pushing against the water as it does so. This tends to cause movement both towards the front and towards one side, as in the case of the tadpole. Fish, however, are able to reduce the sideways motion by the stabilizing effect of their **dorsal** and **ventral fins**. As shown in fig. 4.38 these project in a vertical direction from the back and the abdomen of the animal. They tend to act in the same manner as the keel of a boat in reducing sideways motion.
The **caudal fin** attached to the tail increases the surface area with which the tail can sweep through the water.

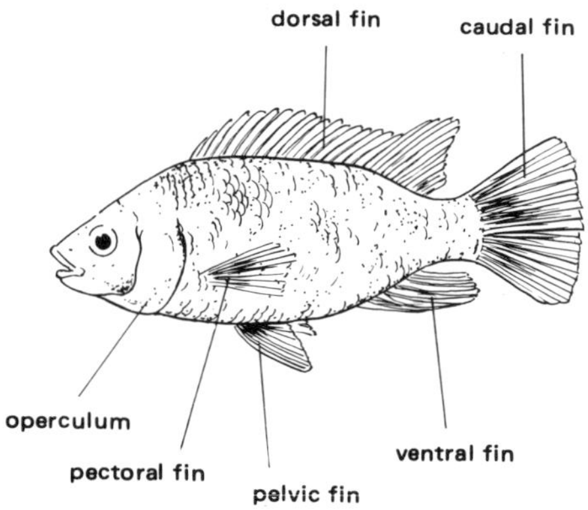

Fig.4.38 Fins of a fish

How can fish stabilize themselves as they swim through the water?

One means of gaining stability has already been mentioned above, namely the action of the dorsal and ventral fins in keeping the animal moving in a straight line, and preventing it from rolling sideways in the water.
The best way to acquire a feeling for the way in which fish move is to watch them swimming in an aquarium that you may have at your school or in a nearby pet shop.
As fish tend to be heavier than the surrounding water they need special adaptations to stop them from sinking to the bottom. While actively swimming the pressure of the water against the **pectoral fin** tends to give an upward thrust. In some fish the caudal fin is also attached at such an angle as to give additional upward impetus.
Cartilaginous fish such as the dogfish do not have any means of staying at the surface of the water unless they are actively swimming. Bony fish such as the cod have an air-filled sac called a **swim-bladder**. When at rest the fish can control the depth at which they stay by increasing or decreasing the amount of air that they have in the swim bladder.
Air can enter the structure either through the mouth by the fish having to swim to the surface and gulp in air or by a more sophisticated method of special gas glands that obtain carbon dioxide from the capillaries and actively secrete it into the swim bladder.
The more air there is inside the swim bladder of the fish the more buoyant it will be and the higher up it will be able to stay in the water. The principle used in submarines is the same.
It is thought that the swim bladder developed from a primitive lung possessed by some ancestors of these fish. In present-day fish the structure does not have any function as an accessory breathing organ.

Movement in birds

The predominant form of movement in most birds is flight.
The requirements of flight are so specialized that they impose a rather set body form which does not deviate very much from one species of bird to the next.
Examine fig. 4.39 which shows a photograph of the skeleton of a pigeon. Notice that the bones are very slender to minimize the mass of the animal yet give adequate support. The head is smooth and streamlined with no outside appendages. The predominant feature of the skeleton is the sternum. It is very large and powerful in order to support the wings and provide a place of attachment for the powerful flight muscles. Feathers located on the wings and the tail feathers are necessary for flight whereas the downy feathers covering the rest of the body serve as insulation to retain body heat.

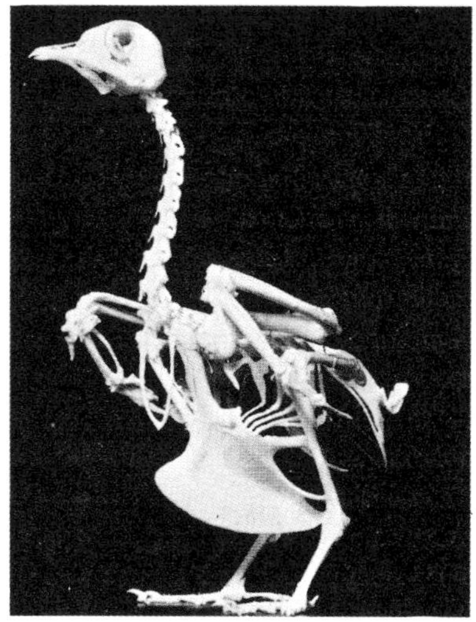

Fig.4.39 Skeleton of a pigeon

What enables a bird to fly?

The mechanism of flight depends on the presence of the wings which act as *aerofoils* enabling the bird to rise up in the air. If you look at a section cut through the wings of a bird the shape will be similar to that in fig. 4.40. In fact, due to the effect of the stream-lining the shape of the entire body from the side is quite similar to this pattern.
Now let us consider the situation where the bird has been flying in the direction indicated by the arrow and then starts to glide. The forward motion of the birds creates a flow of air over the wings. As the streams of air encounter the forward edge of the wing they are deflected upwards and the resulting swift air movement across the top of the wings causes a suction-type effect on the wings which lifts them in the air. As a result the bird does not drop down through the air but glides along at a downward angle.
If there is a wind blowing the speed at which the air rushes past the wings will be greater resulting in a corresponding increase in the upward lift and the bird will be able to glide along horizontally. When the wind hits a vertical obstruction such as the side of a mountain it is deflected upwards with considerable force causing upward currents. Birds are able to make use of these currents to lift them higher up in the air.

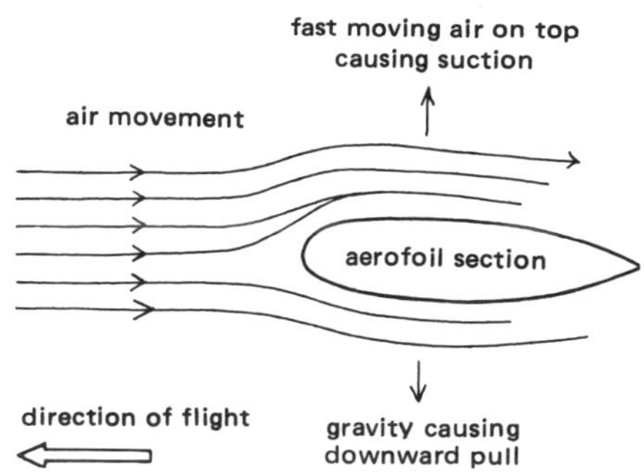

Fig.4.40 Forces acting on the wing of a bird or aeroplane in flight

How can birds fly in the absence of upward air currents?

At times when little or no lift can be derived from upward air currents a bird can create its own current by flapping its wings, to create much the same type of airflow as in gliding.
The large quantities of oxygen necessary for the respiration of the flight muscles are supplied with the aid of a series of air sacs that open out from the lung greatly enhancing the efficiency of that organ.

Summary

Amoebae move by extending pseudopodia in the direction of travel and withdrawing them from the opposite direction.
Soft-bodied invertebrates possess a system of muscles that contract against the hydrostatic skeleton of the animal.
Insects are highly adapted for both running and flying.
Most amphibians are adapted for movement in water during their larval stage and on land in the adult stage.
Birds are highly specialized in body structure to meet the requirements of flight.
Fish, also, are highly specialized in structure enabling them to swim.

Movement in mammals

The highest degree of complexity and organization in the animal world is found in mammals. These animals are not only able to move from one place to another very efficiently but many can move individual parts of their bodies with great precision.

How are muscles able to move the bones?

Each muscle of the mammalian body is connected to two different bones, one at either end of the muscle, so that contraction of the muscle causes the two bones to move relative to each other. The upper attachment of the muscle is called the **origin** and the lower attachment the **insertion**.
The muscles of the body are attached to the bones of the endoskeleton by means of **tendons** made of a tough connective tissue called **collagen**. The tendons act as cables in transmitting the pull of the contracting muscle to the bone. Thus the muscle is able to act a considerable distance away from its ends. The figure below illustrates this point by comparing the actual appearance of the human hand with a picture of what it would be like without tendons.

Fig.4.41

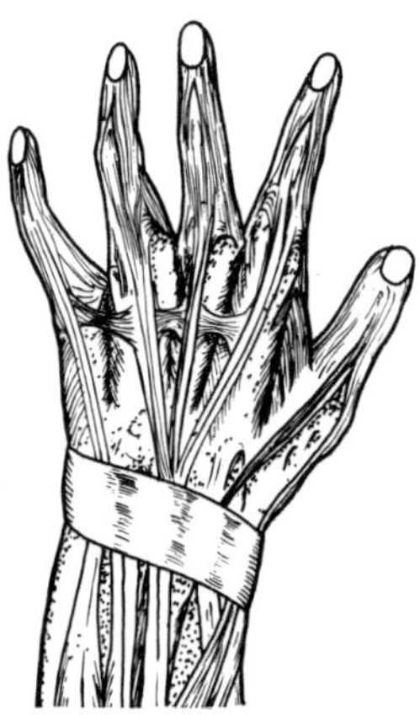

(i) How tendons enable muscles to act at a distance in the hand

(ii) What the hand would be like if muscles had to be attached directly to the bones they move

In order for the system of muscles to provide a complete range of movement there must be different sets of muscles that oppose each other. If there is a muscle that enables the arm to be raised there must also be an **antagonistic**[1] muscle that enables it to be lowered again.
One example of antagonistic muscle pairs are the **extensors** and the **flexors**. The contraction of a flexor muscle results in two parts of a limb being moved closer to each other while the contraction of the extensor pulls the parts further away from each other. The **biceps** and **triceps** muscles of the human arm will serve as a good example. The biceps is attached to its origin, the **scapula**, by two tendons and to its insertion, the **radius**, by a single tendon as shown in fig. 4.42. Contraction of the biceps moves the elbow joint causing the upper and lower arms to come closer together. The biceps is therefore the flexor muscle of the pair.
The triceps is attached to its origins by three tendons, one to the scapula and two to the **humerus**. It is attached by a single tendon to the ulna. The triceps is an extensor. When it contracts it causes the lower arm to straighten out. When the biceps muscle is used, to lift a load for instance, the triceps also contracts slightly and helps to steady the arm.
If you extend your arm along the top of your desk and while raising and lowering a weight with the hand, feel your upper arm muscles with the other hand. You will notice that there is considerable tension in both muscles at all times.

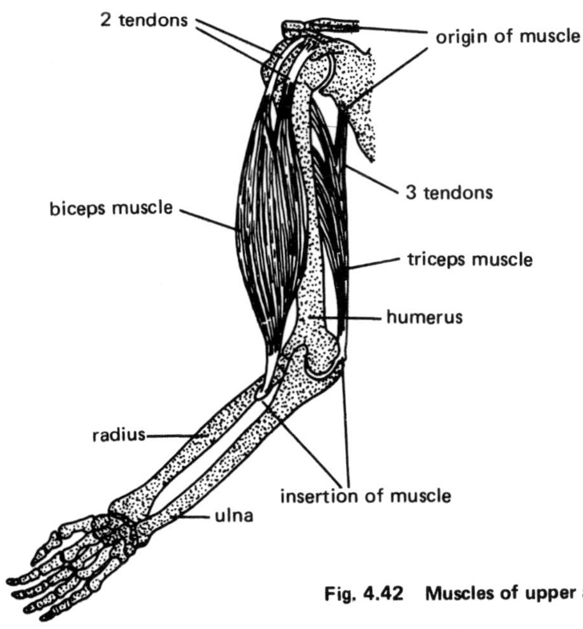

Fig. 4.42 Muscles of upper arm

[1] *antagonistic*: acting in an opposing direction

The action of muscles as levers

Pairs of extensor and flexor muscles act as levers in moving the bones relative to each other at the joints and in supporting loads. Fig. 4.43 is a diagrammatic illustration of what is actually happening when the biceps and triceps muscles are contracting.

Fig.4.43

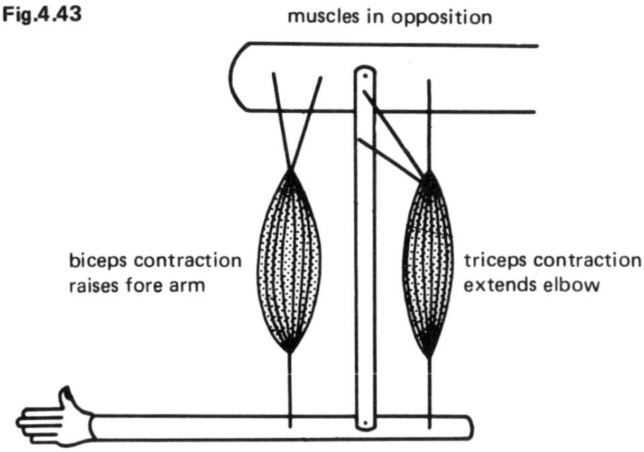

Consider a load being placed on the hand. The load is supported by the biceps muscle. Fig. 4.44 is a diagrammatic representation of the forces at work in the arm while supporting the weight and compared with a *third order lever*. In both cases F represents the *fulcrum*, the point around which movement takes place. E represents the *effort*, that is, the force applied to lift the *load*, L.

In both the case of the arm and of the mechanical lever, raising E a very short distance causes the load to be lifted through a much longer distance. In other words, a relatively small contraction of the biceps muscle causes the load to be lifted high in the air.

The same principle applies in the case of other joints such as the knee, hip and shoulder. A small contraction of the appropriate muscle causes the corresponding limb to move through a much longer distance.

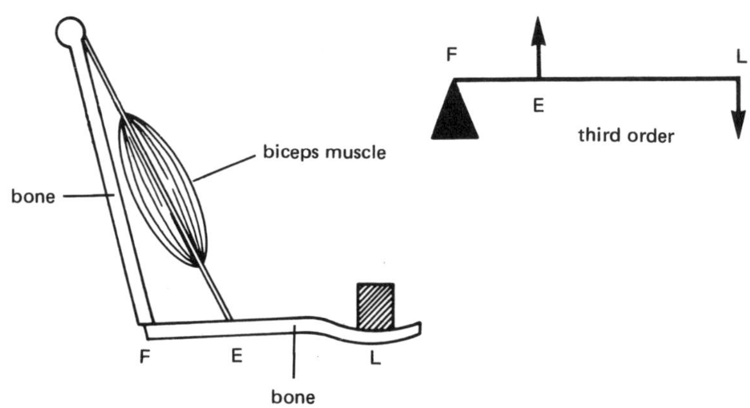

Fig.4.44 Biceps muscle compared to a lever

Other types of muscle

There are several other types of muscle in the body such as **rotator** muscles that cause circular motions of the arms and legs, **retractors** and **protractors** that allow the base of a limb to be moved. Fig. 4.45 shows the various muscles in the mammalian leg indicating the type of motion they bring about and fig. 4.46 explains some of these more clearly.

In addition, the linings of many internal organs such as the oesophagus, stomach and the blood vessels contain layers of muscle cells.

Fig.4.45 Muscles found in the hind leg of a mammal and the actions they produce

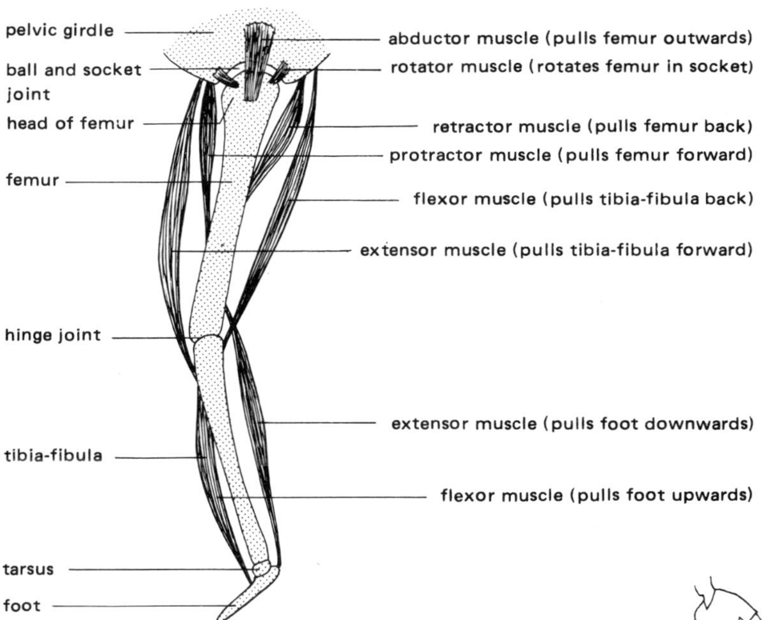

Fig.4.46

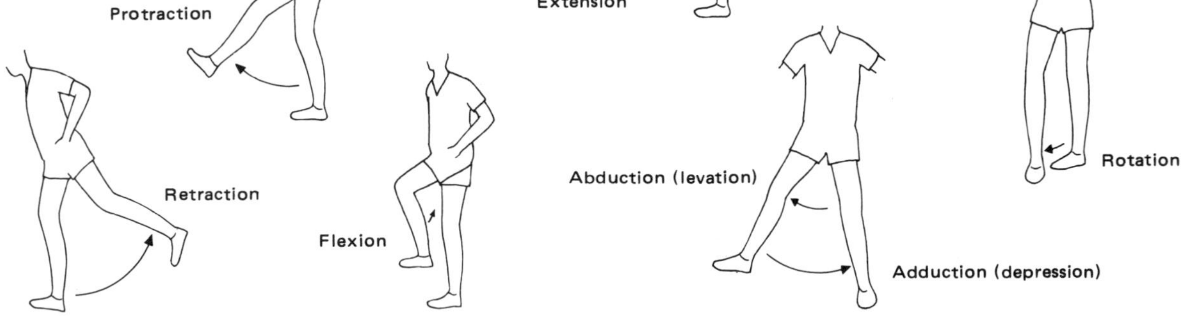

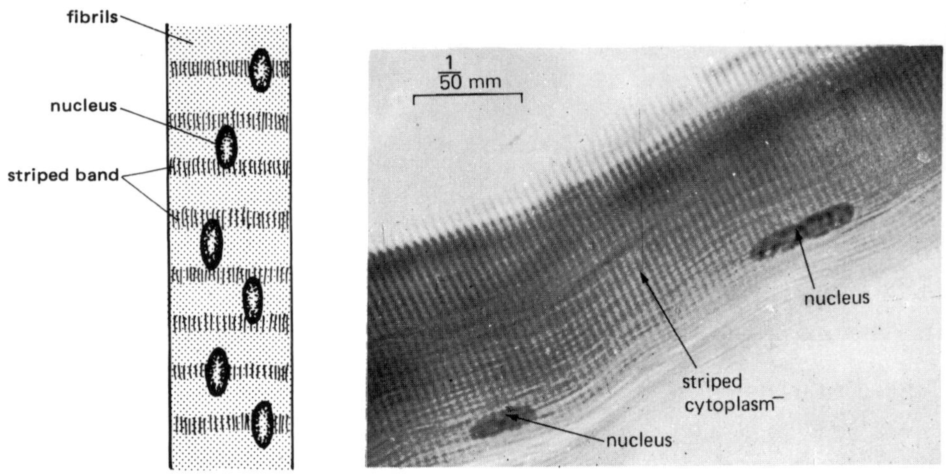

Fig.4.47 Striated muscle

Are there different types of muscle tissue in the human body?

There are three different types of muscle tissue in the body. They have different properties and perform different tasks. The musculature attached to the skeletal system and which receives impulses from the voluntary nervous system (p. 245) is referred to as **skeletal muscle** or, owing to its distinctly striped appearance, as **striated muscle.**

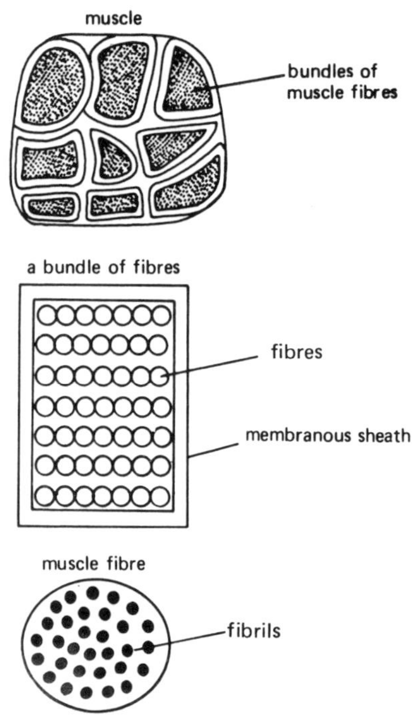

Fig.4.48 Components of a muscle

What is the structure of striated muscle?

Striated muscle is made up of many individual muscle **fibres** that run along the length of a given muscle. Each fibre is surrounded by a membrane and has numerous nuclei but is not divided into separate cells. The striped appearance is due to the regular arrangement of muscle **fibrils** in each fibre. The ability of a muscle to contract is due to the unique elastic properties of these fibrils. (Fig. 4.47.) Bundles of muscle fibres are surrounded by a membrane sheath and several bundles are joined by connective tissue to form the actual muscle. The red colour of striated muscle is due to the presence of a very rich blood supply needed to bring the necessary oxygen and nutrients to the tissue. (Fig. 4.48.)

There are over six hundred separate skeletal muscles in the human body. The precise number varies from one individual to the next. Smaller, insignificant muscles may be present in some people and absent in others, while there can be variation in the origin and insertion of the larger muscles.

An interesting feature of skeletal muscle is that it needs constant stimulation and activity to remain healthy. Muscles that are not used for a period of time, for instance due to prolonged illness in bed, will shrink in size and become weak, that is, they will **atrophy**.

Smooth muscle

The internal organs such as the stomach, intestines and the walls of the blood vessels are lined with layers of **smooth muscle**. These muscles are under the control of the **autonomic nervous system** (p. 245) and perform functions that are not under the conscious control of the individual.

Smooth muscle is composed of spindle-shaped muscle fibres that are smaller than those of striated muscle. They do not show striations and have a single nucleus per fibre. Fig. 4.49 shows a section of smooth muscle as well as a diagram of the muscle cells.

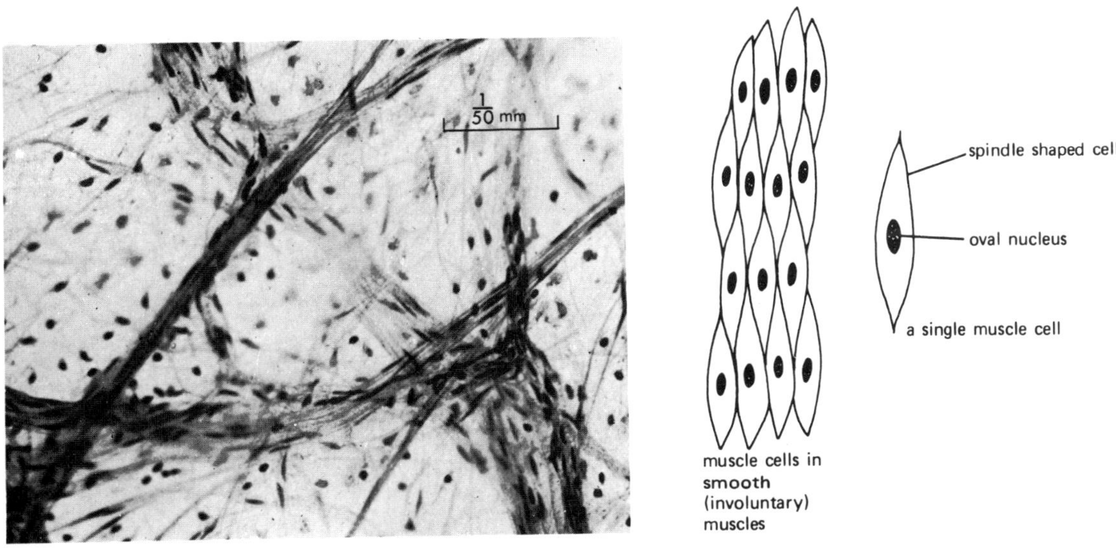

Fig.4.49 Smooth muscle

Cardiac muscle

As the name implies, **cardiac muscle** is the type found in the heart. It consists of striped fibres similar to those of striated muscle but there are numerous cross-connections between fibres. Fibres are divided into individual cells each with a single nucleus.

Contractions of the muscle are governed partly by the autonomic nervous system and partly by the heart's own pacemaker (p. 199). The cross connections between the fibres ensure a smooth and rapid excitation of the entire organ with each contraction of the heart.

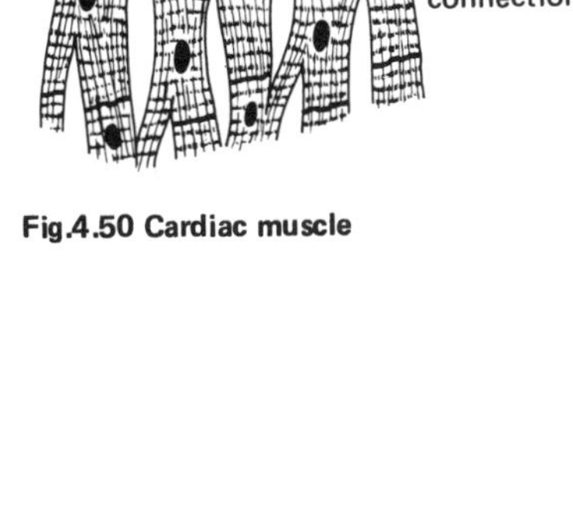

Fig.4.50 Cardiac muscle

What is the reason for having three different types of muscle tissue?

The three types of muscle tissue fulfil distinctly different functions and possess characteristics to meet the specific requirements of these functions.

Skeletal muscle must be able to contract quickly and with considerable force and relax quickly as required. However, under normal circumstances it does not need to act for prolonged periods of time. Skeletal muscle fatigues easily due to the build-up of lactic acid (p. 116).

Smooth muscle has a much longer reaction time, that is, it contracts and relaxes with a slow, undulating motion. Completion of a single contraction may take several seconds for smooth muscle compared to less than one second for striated muscle. On the other hand smooth muscle does not fatigue nearly as quickly and, in fact, may remain in a contracted state for several hours.

Cardiac muscle is the most active of all three types. The heart beats continuously throughout the life of an individual whether awake or sleeping. The only rest the muscle gets is between each successive contraction.

Energy requirements of muscle

The activities of the muscles of the body require an enormous amount of energy. As discussed previously in the section on respiration, this energy is supplied to the muscle in the form of the high energy compound ATP. ATP in turn is derived from the respiration of organic nutrients.

Summary

The human musculature is built up of pairs of antagonistic muscles that cause movement about the joints and muscles that line the various internal organs. The extensor-flexor muscle pairs act as levers in moving the limbs and supporting loads.

The three types of muscle tissue found in humans are striated muscle, smooth muscle and cardiac muscle. They each have different properties and different functions.

Energy for muscle contraction is obtained from ATP, the end product of respiration.

Movement in plants

Plants in general are not capable of self-induced movement from place to place. Most are firmly rooted in the ground and others such as the microscopic plankton in the seas are swept along by the currents. Plants, however, are capable of certain growth movements in response to various external stimuli such as light, gravity and water. A full discussion of these is given on p. 230.

Section 5. TRANSPORT AND COMMUNICATION

TRANSPORT

Fig.5.1

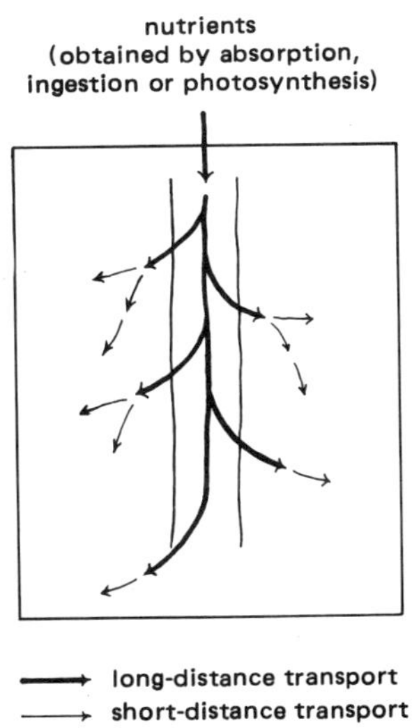

In the case of unicellular or simple multicellular organisms all the cells are in close proximity and exchange of materials between adjacent cells does not present a problem. The processes of diffusion, osmosis and if necessary, active transport are adequate to supply all the needs of the organism.
In higher plants and animals where specialization of tissues has reached more sophisticated levels, where the place of entry or of synthesis of a substance might be a considerable distance from the site of storage or utilization, a system of long-distance conduction is necessary.
The generalized pattern of relations between short- and long-distance transport in living organisms is illustrated in fig. 5.1.

Transport in animals

In animals long-distance transport is carried on by the **blood vascular system (circulatory system)** and to a lesser extent by the **lymphatic system**.

What does the mammalian vascular system consist of?

The basic units of the vascular system arc the **heart**, a muscular organ that pumps a liquid, the **blood**, through a one-way system of **blood vessels** through the body and back to the heart.
The pathway of circulation through the body is referred to as the **systemic circulation**. There is a separate system connecting the heart and the lungs that is called the **pulmonary circulation**.

Fig.5.2

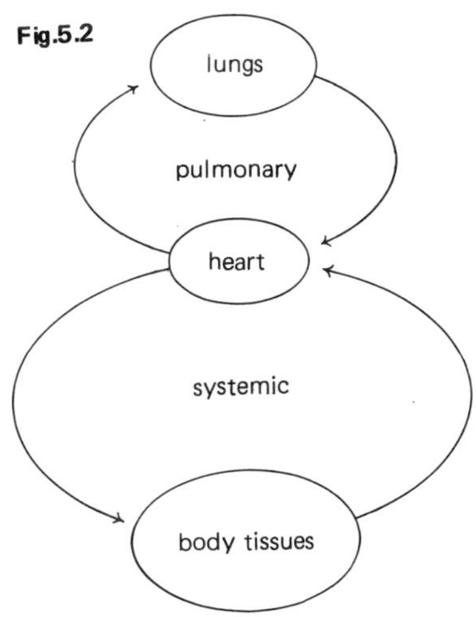

Discovery

The existence of a circulatory system was first realized by a physician, William Harvey, in the 17th century. He was able to demonstrate that blood flows away from the heart through certain vessels **(arteries)** and returns by way of different vessels **(veins)**. He was not, however, able to find any connection between the arteries and the veins and therefore could not explain how transfer of blood between the two systems of vessels occurred.
Capillaries were first observed by Marcello Malpighi and were shown by him to form the connection between the arteries and veins.

Functions

Essentially the function of the vascular system is to pick up materials from one part of the body and deliver them to other parts. Oxygen, for instance, is picked up at the alveoli of the lungs and distributed throughout the cells of the body. Carbon dioxide is picked up at the cells and transported to the lungs.

Details of the structure of the vascular system
The heart

The heart is a cone-shaped organ situated in the thoracic cavity next to the lungs. In humans it is about the size of the clenched fist and weighs around two hundred grams.
The mammalian heart is divided into a right and a left half with no direct connection between the two sides. Each side has an upper chamber called the **atrium** and a lower chamber called the **ventricle**. The two chambers are divided by **atrio-ventricular valves** that allow the blood to flow in one direction only, namely from the atrium to the ventricle.

EXPERIMENT TO EXAMINE AND DISSECT A MAMMALIAN HEART
Materials
the heart of a pig or sheep with the trunks of the blood vessels intact
dissecting instruments
Method
1. Examine the appearance of the exterior of the heart and draw a

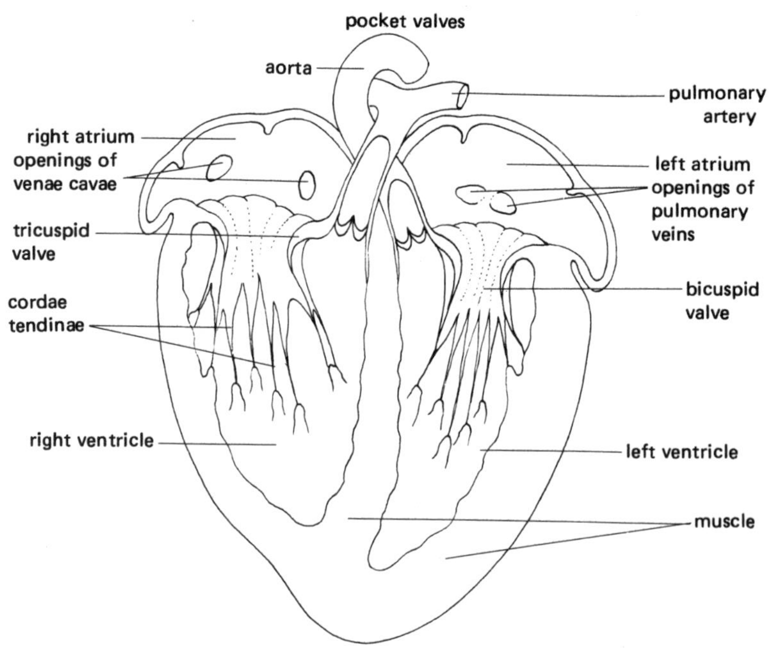

Fig.5.3 Internal structures of the heart

simple sketch of each side.

2. With the aid of fig. 5.3 identify the parts of the heart. Note that this is a schematic view of the general structures of the mammalian heart and may not look precisely like your specimen.

3. Place the heart in front of you on the dissecting tray so that the point where the large blood vessels leave the heart is facing you. In this position the right side of the heart is to your left and the left side to your right as shown in the diagram.

Discussion

The top one third of the heart is the atrium and the lower two thirds, the ventricle. The diagonal deposit of fat usually found along the lower portion of the organ marks the division between the right and left sides. Notice that the left side of the heart is thicker and more muscular. The reason for this will become apparent when we discuss the functions of the two halves.

Find the two thin-walled blood vessels that enter the right atrium. The **superior vena cava** is the pathway by which the venous blood from the head and neck regions returns to the heart and the **inferior vena cava** returns blood from the rest of the body.

The thicker-walled vessel leaving the right ventricle and branching into two is the **pulmonary artery** that takes blood to the lungs.

Oxygenated blood returns to the heart from the lungs by way of the **pulmonary vein**. The very large thick-walled vessel leaving the left ventricle is the **aorta**, the route by which oxygenated blood is pumped to the entire body. To explore the points of origin of the various blood vessels you can use a blunt probe.

Note: a vessel going *to* the heart is a vein; one going *away* from the heart is an artery.

Heart valves

The junctions of the various blood vessels with the heart, and of the atria with the ventricles are guarded by valves.

Cut off the free end of the aorta at the level where it leaves the heart to reveal the valve. Notice that it consists of three cup-shaped flaps that can be forced apart from the inside but not from the outside. Because of its crescent shape it is also referred to as a **semi-lunar valve**.

With a rubber hose direct a jet of water into the left atrium through the pulmonary vein. Soon you will see water coming through the valve in the aorta. What would happen if you tried to squirt water in through the aorta? The pockets of the flaps simply fill up with water and the opening is closed off.

Starting at the lower tip of the ventricle carefully slice open the heart to expose the interior chambers. If you are careful the atrio-ventricular valves will remain intact. Notice that the valve on the right side has three cups whereas the one on the left has only two. The function of the valves is to ensure a one way flow of blood from

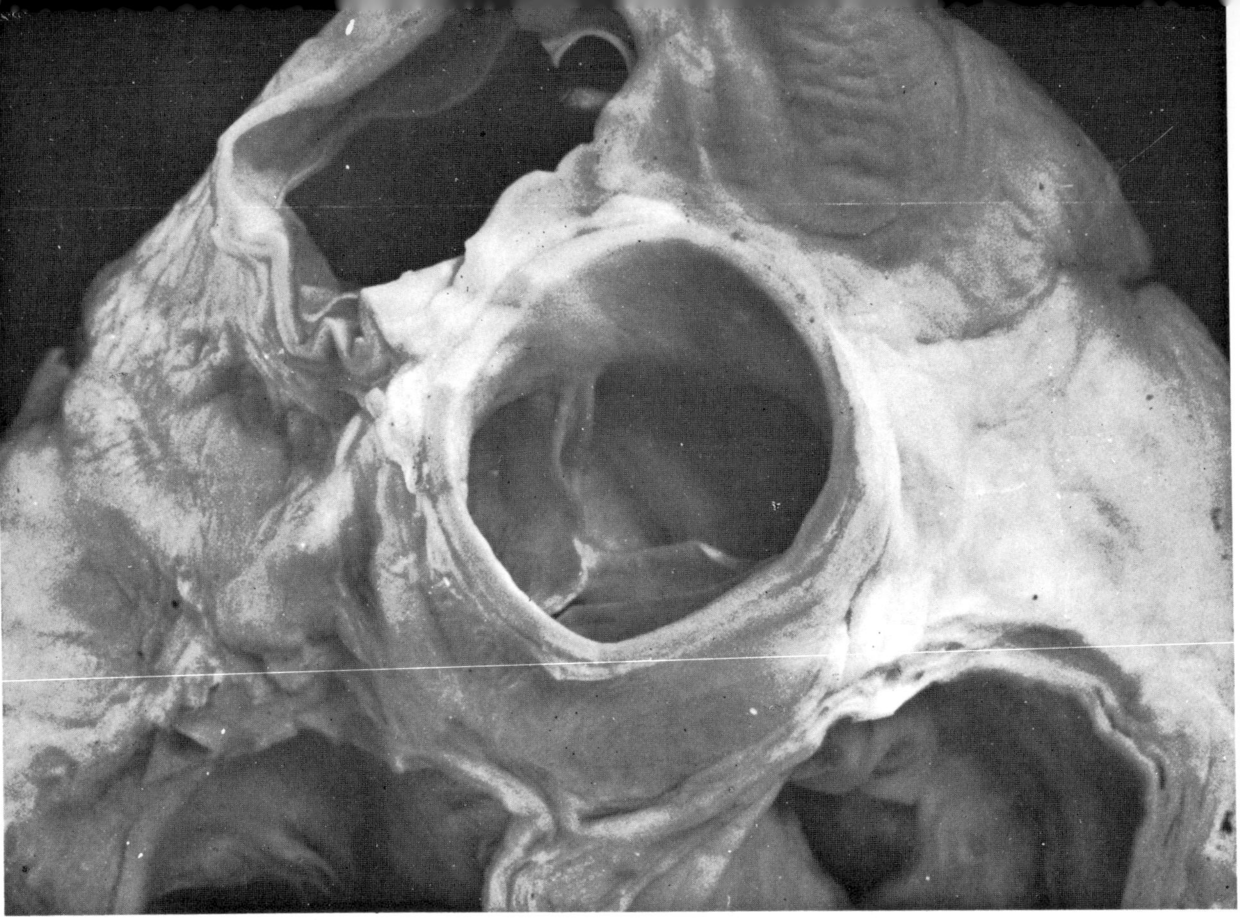

Fig.5.4 Valves in heart

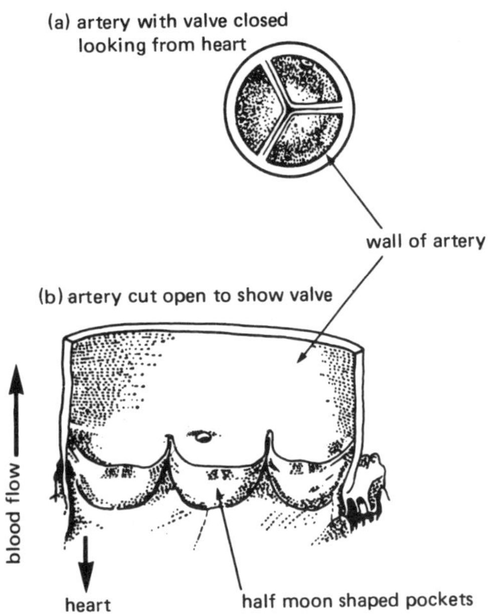

Fig.5.5 Semi-lunar valves

the atria to the ventricles and to prevent regurgitation from the latter to the former.

Blood flow through the heart

Referring to your dissected specimen trace the path of blood flow through the vessels and chambers of the heart.

A. Venous blood enters the right atrium and is forced by the contraction of that chamber into the right ventricle.

B. Contraction of the right ventricle forces blood out through the pulmonary artery to the lungs. The atrioventricular valve prevents leakage back to the atrium. From the lungs, oxygenated blood returns via the pulmonary veins to the left atrium.

C. Contraction of the left atrium forces the blood into the left ventricle.

D. Contraction of the left ventricle sends oxygenated blood through the aorta to the arterial system throughout the body.

Note that the right side of the heart is concerned exclusively with venous blood and the left side with arterial blood. Both sides of the heart are in operation at the same time and the systemic and pulmonary circulations operate simultaneously.

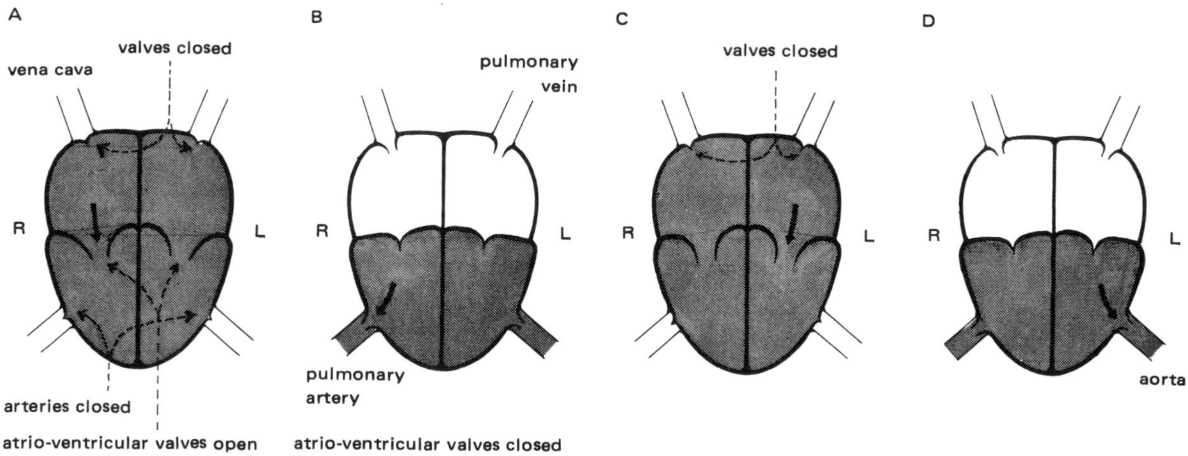

Fig.5.6 Action of the heart

Are the blood vessels filled with blood all the time or are they sometimes empty?

The blood vessels of the body are constantly filled with blood. The volume of blood that is in the heart at any given time is only a fraction of the entire blood volume. Thus when the contraction of the left ventricle pushes blood into the already full aorta the walls of the vessel become greatly distended and blood is forced along the length of the artery. The next contraction of the ventricle sends a further supply of blood out of the heart and the content of the artery is pushed along further. Thus blood is moved from the heart along the arteries in a series of spurts.

For a simple illustration of this pumping action connect a long transparent plastic hose to a tap. Hold the hose so that its free end is above the level of the tap. Now repeatedly open and close the tap for short spurts of one or two seconds. Observe how the water is moved up the hose.

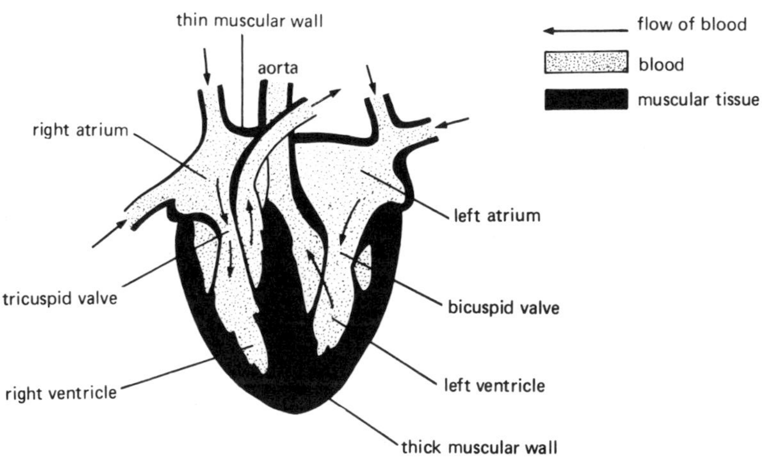

Fig.5.7 Blood flow in heart

Referring again to your dissected specimen notice the difference in thickness between the muscular walls of the atria and the ventricles. Since the contractions of the atria need send the blood only to the ventricles the force required is not very great and therefore the layer of muscle does not have to be very thick. The ventricles, on the other hand, especially the left ventricle that serves the systemic circulation, must squirt blood out with considerable force to reach the lungs or the systemic arteries. The ventricles therefore have much thicker muscular walls.

Heart rate and blood volumes

In a healthy adult human the heart contracts or 'beats' about seventy times every minute. Each contraction of the left ventricle forces about 70cm^3 of blood into the aorta. Since the total volume of blood in the body is around 3000cm^3 it takes about forty-three beats for the entire volume to circulate through the body and back to the heart.

The action of the heart can be observed in a dissected anaesthetised frog. *Note*: the same animal can be used to observe capillary circulation (see p. 203).

EXPERIMENT TO OBSERVE THE ACTION OF THE HEART IN VIVO[1]

Materials

live frog

0.5 percent chloretane solution

dissecting tray and instruments

Ringer's solution made up of the following:

Potassium chloride	—0.14g
Sodium chloride	—6.50g
Calcium chloride	—0.12g
Sodium bicarbonate	—0.20g
Distilled water	—1 litre

Method

1. Anaesthetize the animal by immersing in a solution of one part chloretane and four parts Ringer's solution for fifteen to twenty minutes depending on the size of the frog.
2. Carefully open up the thoracic cavity to expose the heart.
3. Bathe the heart with Ringer's solution at all times.
4. Observe the beating of the heart.
5. When you finish, kill the animal by putting it back into the chloretane solution.

Can you see that the left and right sides of the heart contract together?

Observe the alternate contractions of the atria and ventricles.

[1] *in vivo*: in a living organism

What causes the heart to contract?

Most muscles contract as a result of nerve impulses coming from the motor nerve supplying them (see p. 238). The heart is an exception—it continues to contract rhythmically even after its nerve supply has been cut and for a considerable length of time even after it is removed from the body as long as it is nourished and kept moist. The rhythmic contractions of the heart are governed by a special group of fine muscle fibres located in the wall of the right atrium. The fibres are referred to as the **sinu-atrial node** and they act as the **pacemaker** for the heart.
There are times, however, when the contraction of the heart must speed up or slow down in response to special demands of the body.

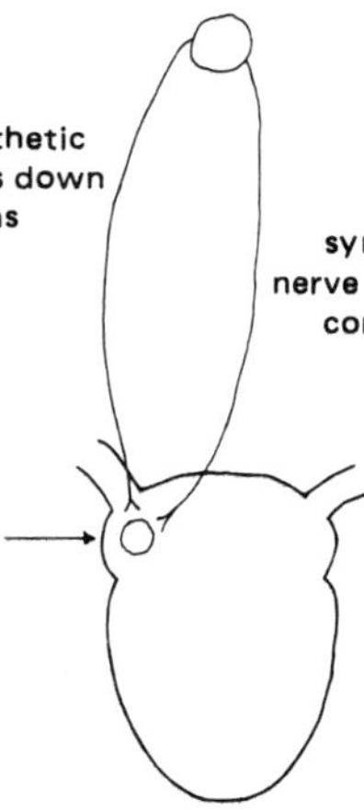

Fig.5.8 Control of heart rate

How is the speed of contractions regulated?

The heart is supplied by branches of the autonomic nervous system. These nerves modify the activity of the pacemaker to either speed up or slow down the heart. The antagonistic action of the sympathetic and parasympathetic nerves keeps the rate of the heart at an acceptable level. (The sympathetic nervous system is discussed on p. 246.) Heart rate can also be influenced by the hormone **adrenalin**, secreted by the **adrenal glands** (p. 252), under instructions from the brain, and mediated by the autonomic nervous system.

Summary

The heart is a small muscular-walled organ that is responsible for pumping blood throughout the body. It is the powerhouse that drives the circulatory system.
There is a clear separation of functions between the right and left sides of the heart, the right side being concerned with the pulmonary circulation and the left side the systemic circulation.
Valves located between the atria and ventricles and at the origin of the arteries and veins keep the circulation flowing in one direction only.
The heart is capable of maintaining its rhythmic contractions under the influence of the sinu-atrial node. Heart rate can be regulated by the action of the autonomic nervous system.

Circulation of the blood

Pulmonary circulation

After the pulmonary artery leaves the heart it branches into two and proceeds directly to the lungs. Upon reaching the lungs the branches of the artery break up into smaller and smaller vessels ultimately terminating in the tiny capillaries that are found adjacent to the alveoli, forming a dense network on their surfaces. Gas

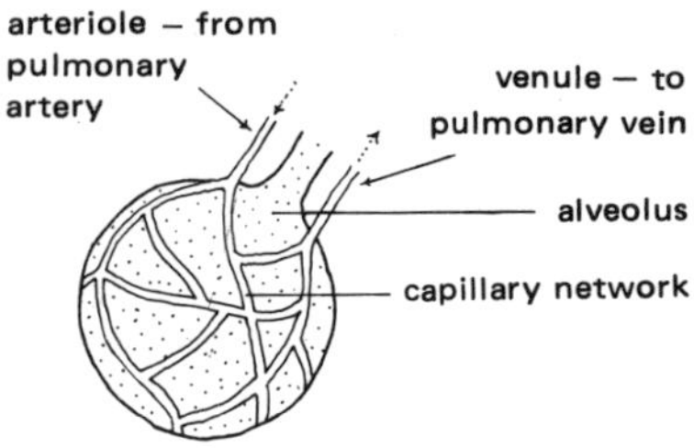

Fig.5.9 Relationship between alveolus, arterioles and venules

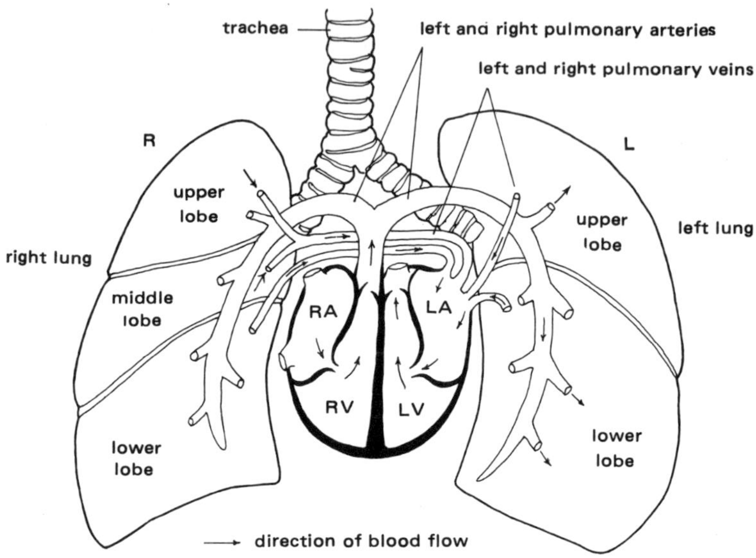

Fig.5.10 Pulmonary circulation

exchange takes place through the alveolar and capillary membranes. The capillaries join up again, eventually forming two large pulmonary veins in each lung. The veins pass back to the heart independent of each other and enter the left atrium as shown in the diagram above.

Systemic circulation

The aorta leaves the left ventricle and after passing upward for a very short distance it descends behind the heart and leaves the thoracic cavity through an opening in the diaphragm.

At the level of the **aortic arch** immediately above the heart it gives off further branches to the organs in the abdominal cavity and to the two lower limbs. The general pattern of branching of the aorta and the names of the vessels are indicated in fig. 5.12.

The main arteries continually branch to form smaller and smaller vessels, the **arterioles**, and finally the tiny capillaries that penetrate among the individual cells. At the outset blood flows along the vessels very quickly propelled by the force of the contraction of the heart. By the time it reaches the level of the individual tissues, the flow has slowed down considerably. At the level of the capillaries exchange of materials between the blood and the cells takes place. The capillary network then joins up to form larger and larger vessels of the venous system. Veins from adjacent areas join up and blood is finally collected by the two venae cavae. (Fig. 5.13.)

If you pry apart the strands in the central section of a piece of hemp cord you will get a good idea of the way arterioles break up into capillaries which in turn join up again to form veins. (Fig 5.11)

Fig.5.11

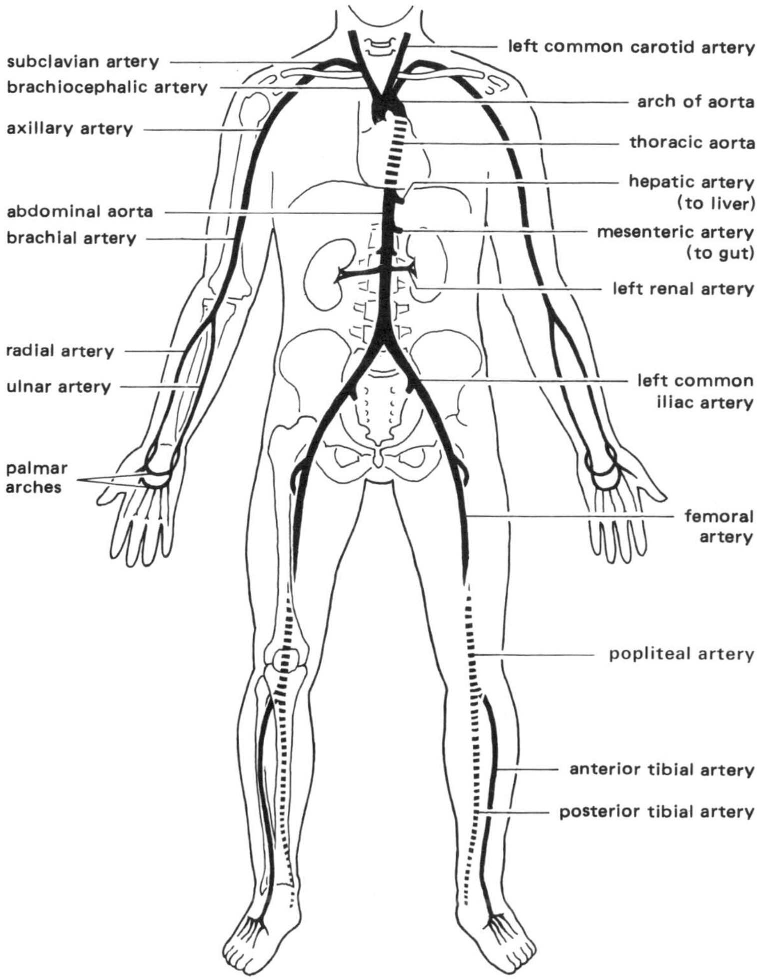

Fig.5.12 General impression of the aorta and main arteries of the limbs

Observation of blood circulation in vivo

The best places to observe circulation in a living animal are in the webbed toes of the frog or the tail of a goldfish.

EXPERIMENT TO OBSERVE CIRCULATION IN VIVO

Materials

a small goldfish or a frog
microscope, binocular if available, glass slides
0.5 percent chloretane
Ringer's solution (see p. 198)

Method

a. Goldfish

1. Wrap the fish in wet paper towels or place in a very shallow dish of water so that the tail is hanging onto the stage of a microscope.

2. Secure the animals into position with a piece of sellotape.
3. Place a glass slide over the tail and press gently to flatten as much as possible.
4. Observe the thin edge sections of the tail under the lowest power of your microscope.
b. Frog
1. Anaesthetize the frog in a solution of one part 0.5 percent chloretane and four parts Ringer's solution for fifteen to twenty minutes depending on the size of the animal.
2. Wrap the animal in moist paper towels and secure on a cork board so that one leg is hanging over the edge.
3. Place the cork board level with the stage of the microscope and pull the foot under the lens.
4. Spread the toes apart and observe the webbed skin under the lowest power of your microscope.

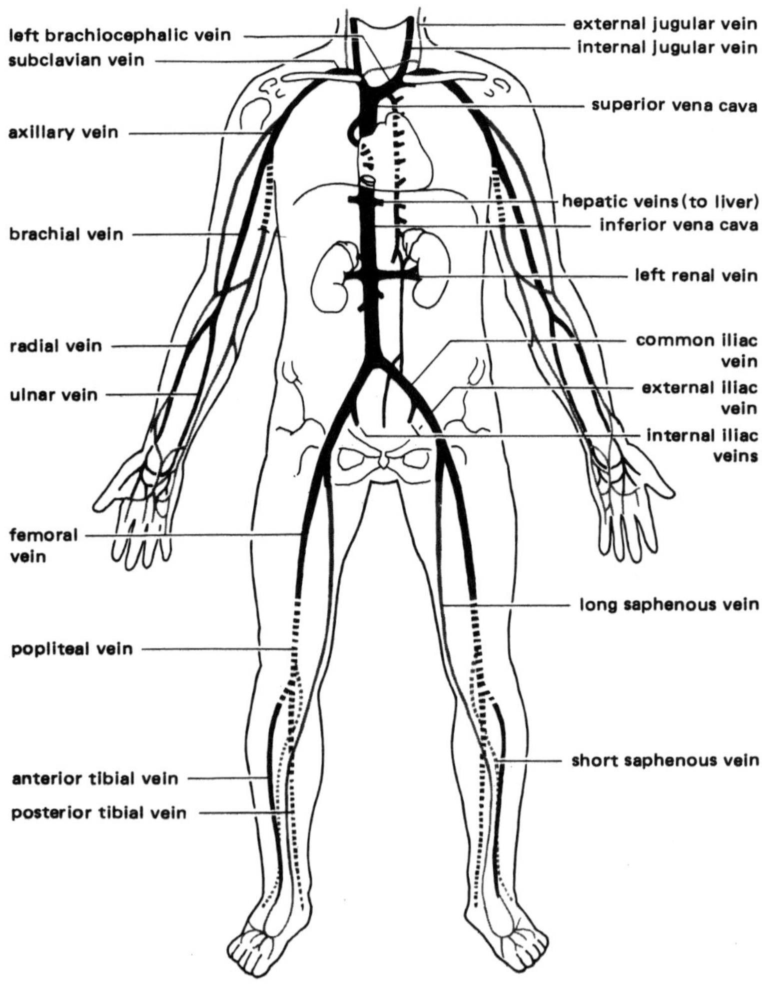

Fig.5.13 General impression of venae cavae and veins of the limbs

Note: in both instances make certain that the animals are kept moist at all times. Observe the capillaries and arterioles and venules under the microscope.

Make a simple drawing of what you see, indicating the direction of blood flow. Observe the movement of the cells in the blood. We will return to a discussion of these a little later.

The structure of veins and arteries

The walls of both the veins and the arteries are made up of an inner lining of **endothelial cells** surrounded by a layer of elastic tissue and finally an outer layer of fibrous tissue.

The arteries in general contain more muscular elastic tissue arranged in a circular pattern around their opening. The muscles contain nervous connections that are able to cause the walls of the arteries

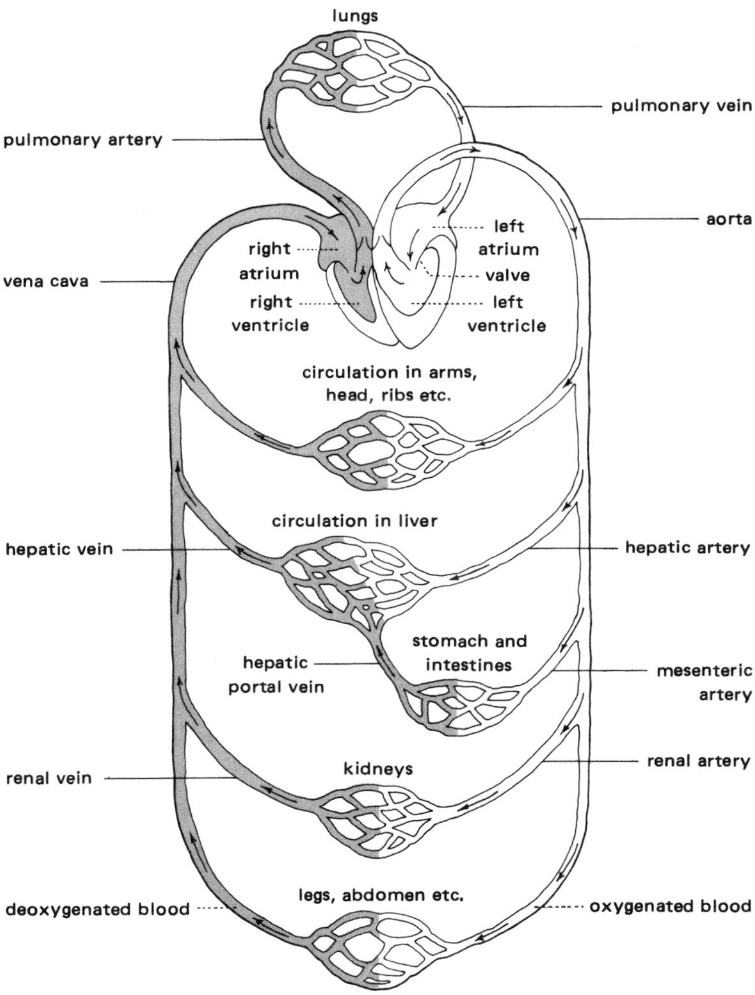

Fig.5.14 Schematic diagram of human circulation

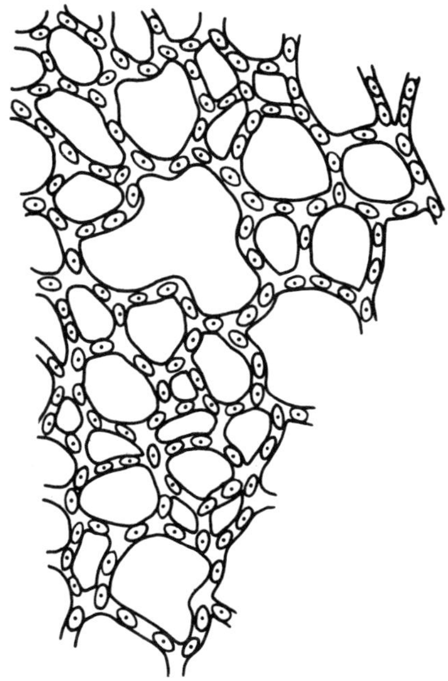

Fig. 5.15 Capillaries with blood cells in web of frog

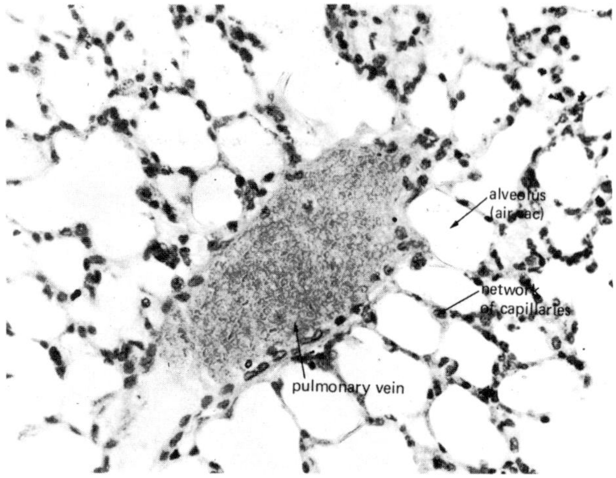

Fig.5.16 Veins and capillaries

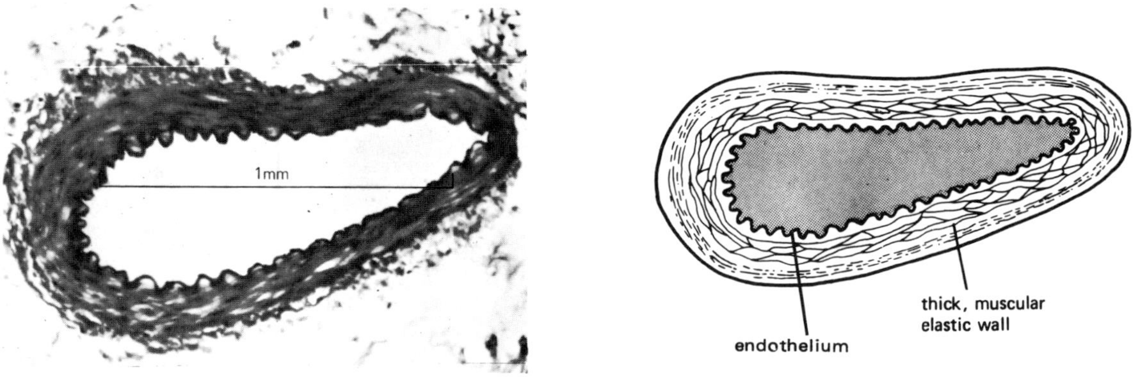

Fig.5.17 Photo and diagram of section of an artery

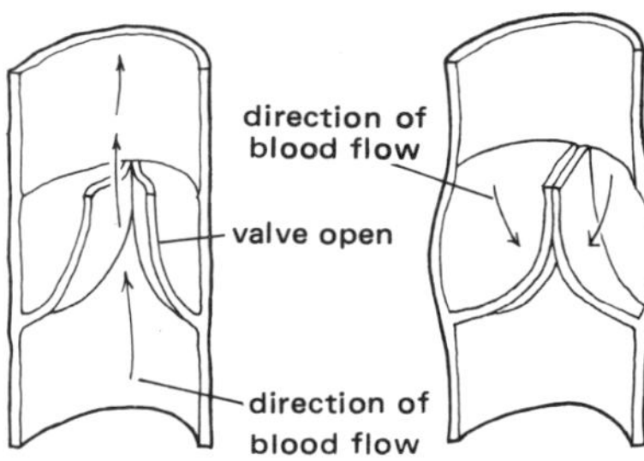

Fig.5.18 **Action of valves in a vein or the semi-lunar valves in the arteries leaving the heart**

to contract or relax thereby regulating the size of the opening and the amount of blood flowing through.

The reason for the greatly thickened elastic walls of the arteries is, of course, the fact that they have to withstand the pressure of the heart pumping the blood along them.

By the time the blood reaches the veins the pressure is greatly reduced and therefore these vessels have much less muscular and elastic tissues in their walls. Veins are equipped with simple valves at various points along their length. These valves ensure that blood in the veins flows only in one direction towards the heart. Whereas in the arteries the pressure of the blood is sufficient to keep it flowing in the right direction, the lower pressure in the veins and the squeezing action of the muscles might result in venous blood leaking backwards in the circulation without the valves.

The structure of capillaries

Capillary walls consist of only a single layer of cells with no elastic or muscle layers at all. This facilitates the exchange of materials between these vessels and the surrounding cells.

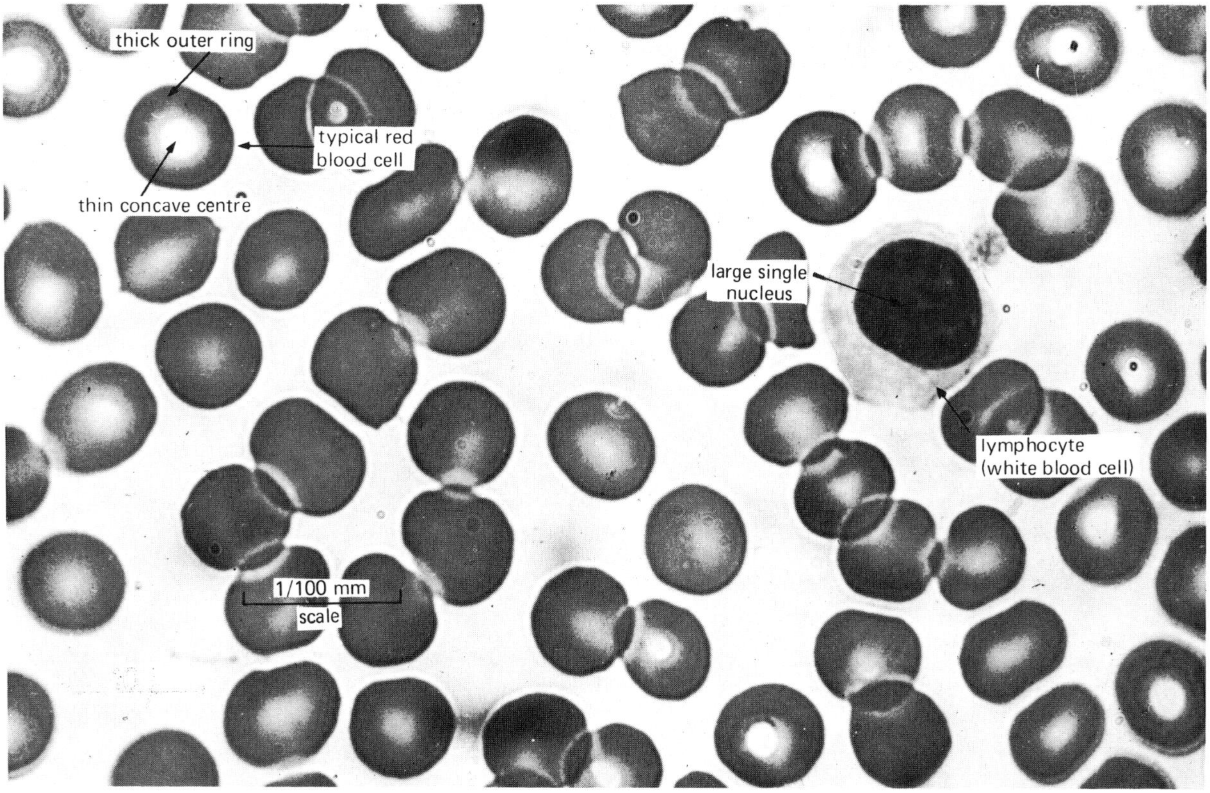

Fig.5.19 Red and white blood cells

Blood cells

One of the most important functions of the blood is to carry oxygen to the body cells.
How is oxygen carried in the blood? Is it simply dissolved in the liquid?
Although oxygen is soluble in watery solutions such as the blood, the solubility is very low and the amounts dissolved would not be sufficient to supply the demands of the body.
The great oxygen-carrying capacity of the blood is due to the presence in the **red blood cells** of the chemical substance called **haemoglobin**, which gives the cells their red colour. The small spherical cells that you saw in the capillaries of the goldfish or the frog are red blood cells.

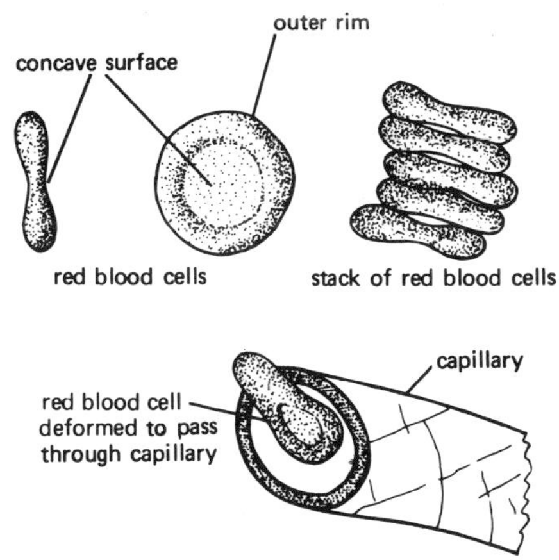

Fig.5.20 Red blood cells

What is haemoglobin?

Haemoglobin is a protein that has the capacity to reversibly combine with oxygen. When oxygen concentration is high, haemoglobin tends to combine with oxygen; when the reverse is true haemoglobin will release the oxygen that it is carrying. In the lung capillaries the

Fig.5.21

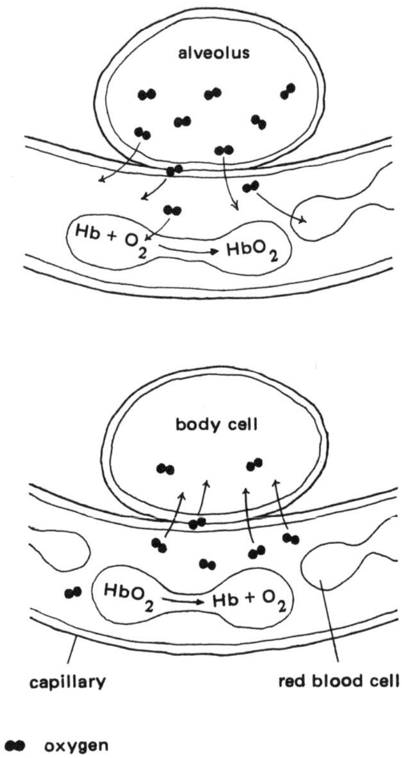

Fig.5.22

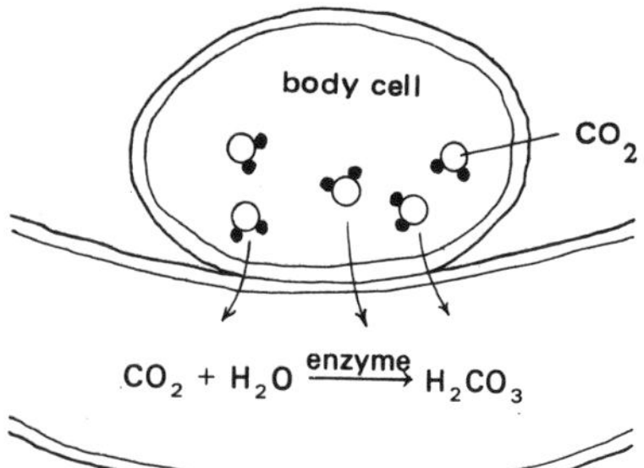

oxygen concentration is high and therefore the reaction taking place is:

$$\underset{\text{haemoglobin}}{Hb} + \underset{\text{oxygen}}{O_2} \longrightarrow \underset{\text{oxyhaemoglobin}}{HbO_2}$$

In the cells surrounding the capillaries throughout the body the oxygen concentration is very low and the opposite reaction takes place:

$$HbO_2 \longrightarrow Hb + O_2$$

The oxygen that is released is then free to diffuse into the cells.

Can carbon dioxide combine with haemoglobin?

Although carbon dioxide can combine with haemoglobin the efficiency of the process is not very high. In fact, most of the carbon dioxide is carried back to the lungs in the form of carbonic acid (H_2CO_3).

Another gas that can combine with haemoglobin is carbon monoxide. This combination, however, is *not* reversible. If a person inhales large amount of carbon monoxide, for example, from car exhaust fumes, the carbon monoxide molecules will combine with more and more of the haemoglobin molecules thereby reducing the amount that is available for carrying oxygen. Death will soon result due to oxygen deprivation of the tissues of the body.

Where do red blood cells come from?

Red blood cells are continually being made in the bone marrow. The average life span of a given cell is about one hundred and twenty days. Old cells are deposited in the spleen and are destroyed. Some of their constituent components such as iron are used over again in the manufacture of new cells.

An insufficient number of red blood cells in the circulation or a low level of haemoglobin in the cells will result in anaemia, due to

Fig.5.23 How red blood cells are made

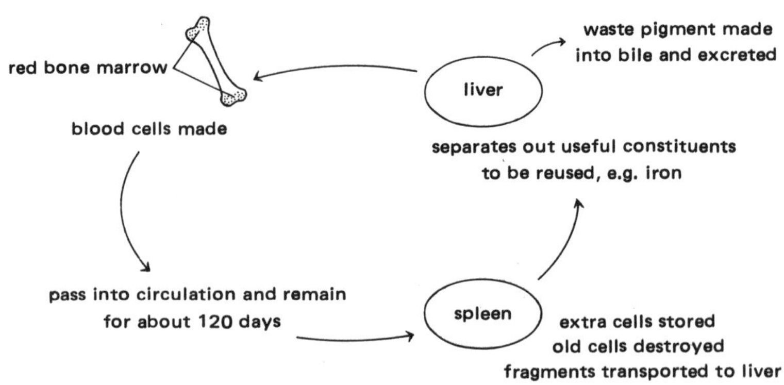

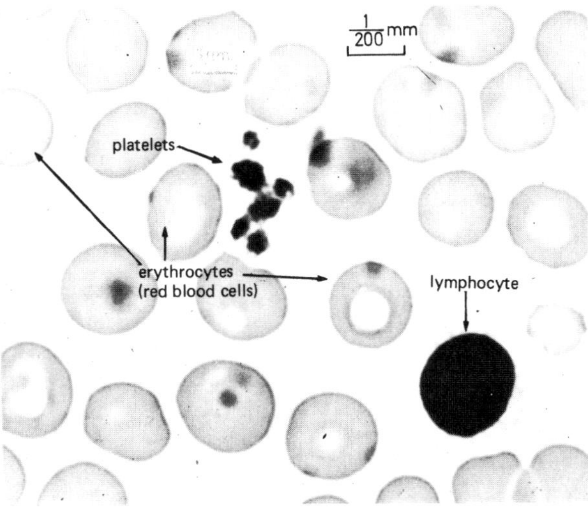

Fig.5.24 Platelets

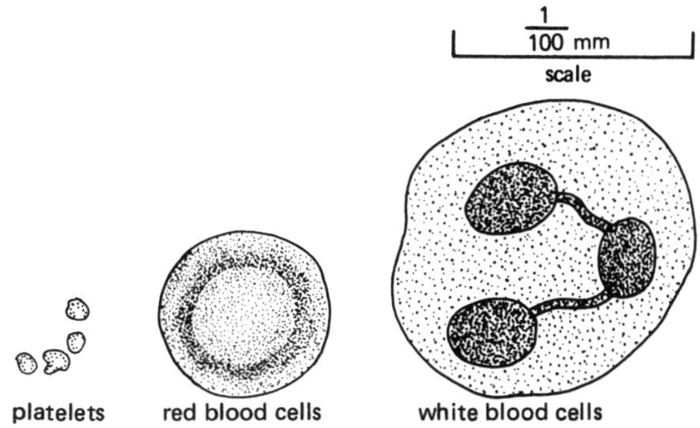

250 000	5 000 000	5 000 – 9 000	quantity in 1 mm^3 blood

Fig.5.25 Relative sizes of the blood corpuscles

inadequate supplies of oxygen in the cells. As you will recall from the section dealing with nutrition, low haemoglobin levels can be caused by inadequate iron in the diet.

Are there any other kinds of cell in the blood?

In addition to red blood cells the circulation also contains **white blood cells**. These cells are important in the body's defence against invading foreign substances such as bacteria. (See p. 333.)

Platelets are cell fragments formed in the bone marrow, about one-third of the size of the red blood cells. Their function is to aggregate at sites where there is a break in the wall of a blood vessel and form a **platelet plug** to stop blood from escaping into the surrounding tissues before clotting can take placc.

The relative sizes and numbers of red cells, white cells and platelets are summarized in fig. 5.25.

What are the constituents of the liquid part of the blood?

The liquid part of the blood is called **plasma**. If a sample of blood is centrifuged at medium speed the red cells will settle out on the bottom, the white cells will form a thin layer on top of them and a clear yellowish liquid, the plasma, will remain at the very top.

Plasma is an aqueous solution containing all the dissolved chemical substances carried by the blood. These include:

1. organic nutrients such as glucose and amino acids,
2. inorganic salts such as sodium chloride, sodium bicarbonate, calcium phosphate and iron sulphate,
3. hormones and vitamins,
4. waste products such as carbon dioxide, urea, that are being carried away from the body cells,

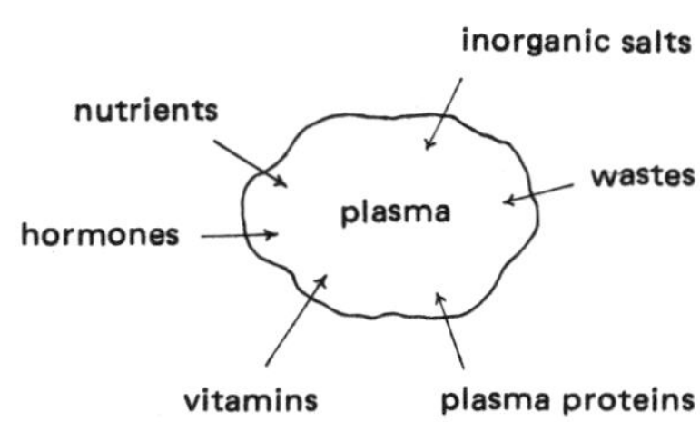

Fig.5.26 Constituents of plasma

Fig.5.27 Summary of functions of circulatory system

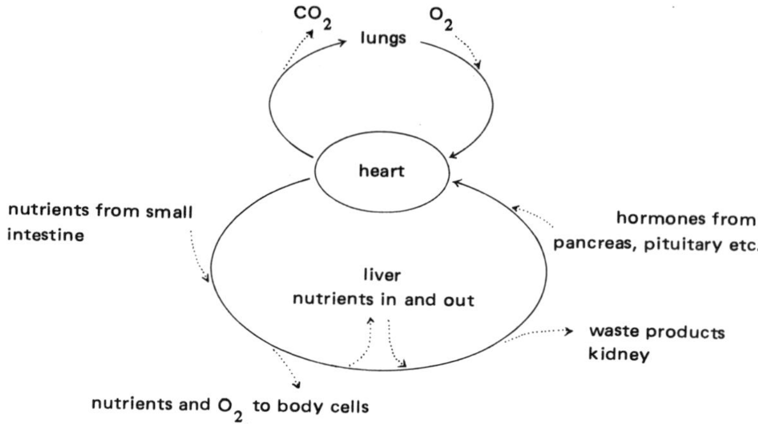

5. plasma proteins necessary for the clotting of blood and for various immunological reactions that form part of the body's defences against injury.

Osmotic pressure of the blood

The osmotic pressure of the blood must be kept at a steady level at all times. The task of osmoregulation is carried out by the kidneys (see p. 161). If the osmotic pressure of the blood is too high water will be drawn into the blood vessels from the intercellular spaces resulting in dehydration of the tissues. If the liquid content of the circulation is too great large amounts will leak out into the intercellular spaces causing a fluid swelling known as **oedema**. An increase in blood volume also puts severe strain on the heart since it increases the blood pressure.

Summary

One can think of the circulatory system as a continuous moving belt like the ones used in factories. At just about every point along its flow some substance is added to or removed from the blood.
The pulmonary circulation connected with the right side of the heart operates between the heart and the lungs. The systemic circulation serves the rest of the body.
Arteries carry blood away from the heart, veins carry blood to the heart.
Exchange of materials between the blood and the surrounding tissues takes place by diffusion through the walls of the capillaries.
Blood is an aqueous solution containing various organic and inorganic components, red and white blood cells and platelets.

The lymphatic system

The lymphatic system is very closely associated with the vascular system. It consists of a network of tiny **lymph capillaries** that are continuous with the intercellular spaces.

The fluid circulating in these capillaries is known as **lymph**. Its composition is very similar to that of the blood plasma except that the components are present in different concentrations.

Where does the lymph fluid come from?

As blood circulates in the capillaries of the blood vascular system some of the plasma filters out through the walls of the vessels. White blood cells also squeeze through the walls to travel to sites of infection. Some of the lymph filters back into the capillaries at the venous end of the network but the rest of the liquid and the cells are collected in the lymph capillaries. The lymph capillaries join up to form thin-walled ducts that flow towards the heart.

How does liquid move in the lymphatic system?

There is no pumping apparatus for the lymphatic system. The liquid is moved along by the squeezing action of the muscles

Fig.5.28 Relation between tissue cells, capillaries, and lymphatics

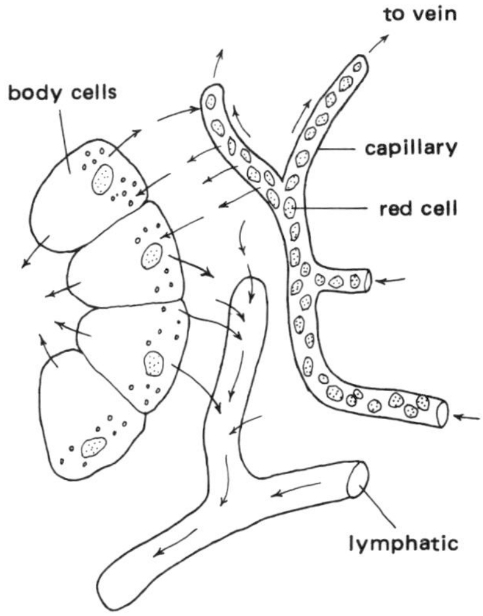

a. Plasma diffuses out through capillary walls
b. Used and excess fluid drains into capillary (90%)
c. Used and excess fluid drains into lymphatic (10%)

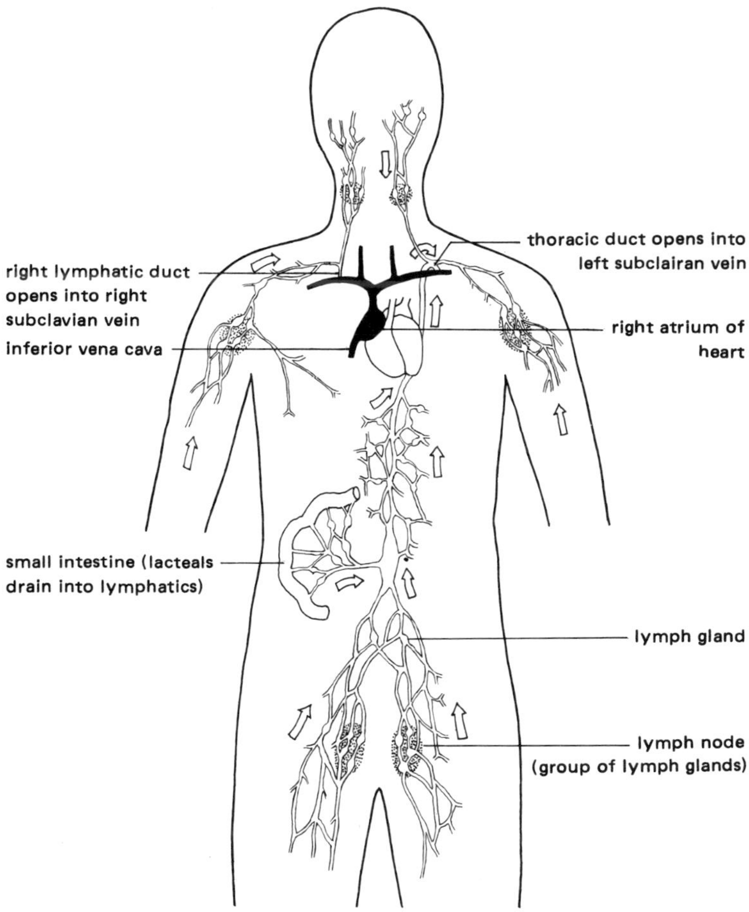

Fig.5.29 Main drainage routes of lymphatic system

surrounding the channels. Back flow is prevented by a series of valves such as the ones found in the major veins. The **thoracic duct** which collects lymph from the lower part of the body also carries the lipids that have passed into the lacteals from the microvilli of the small intestine (p. 79). The duct enters the subclavian vein of the blood vascular system.

Fig. 5.29 shows the main vessels of the lymphatic system. Notice that at various points along the system there are structures called **lymph nodes**. The lymph nodes produce special white cells called **lymphocytes** that are important in the production of antibodies to fight infections (p. 333).

Due to the intense activity of the nodes during times of infection these points may undergo considerable swelling. The swelling of the **tonsils** at the back of the throat is an example.

The body's defence against infection and the role of the lymphatic system in this respect will be discussed again in Section 8.

Another function of the lymphatic system is to filter out certain poisons, waste products and bacterial debris from the body cells and destroy them before they enter the blood vascular system.

Summary

The lymphatic system is a backup system that operates in parallel with the blood vascular system. It collects and drains from the tissues any liquid and organic materials that have leaked out of the circulation. It also transports white blood cells that have left the circulation to sites of infection.

Transport in plants

It is obvious that plants do not have a heart and a circulatory system of the type possessed by animals. If you examine the leaves, however, a definite pattern of lines called **veins** can be seen. The stems of some plants such as the celery have obvious tubular structures running along their length. Could these have some function in the transport of materials in plants?

EXPERIMENT TO SHOW TRANSPORT IN PLANTS

Materials

a length of celery stem with leaves
sharp razor
methylene blue
microscope, slides and coverslips

Method

1. Prepare a dilute solution of methylene blue.

2. Place the cut end of the celery stalk into the solution and leave for a few hours. Observe from time to time.
What happens to the celery stem and the leaves?
How does the colour move up?
3. With a sharp razor cut sections of the stem. Slice at a slight angle so that the edge of the section becomes as thin as possible.
4. Examine under the microscope.

What do you see?
Make a simple drawing of the structures.

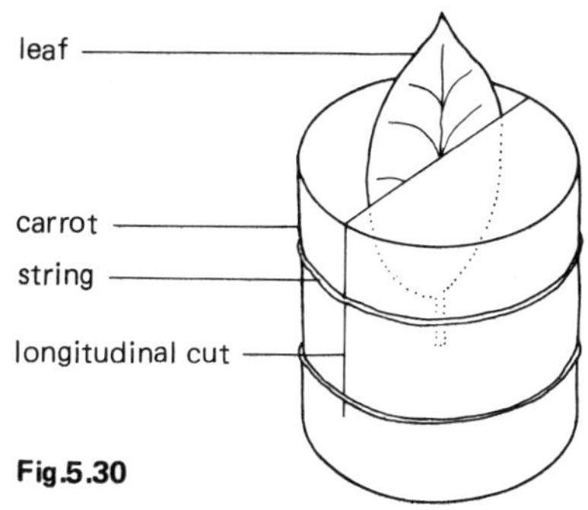

Fig.5.30

EXPERIMENT TO EXAMINE THE VEINS OF A GREEN LEAF

If prepared sections are available examine those. If not, sections can be prepared using the following method.

Materials
freshly picked green leaves
four-centimetre lengths of carrot tissue
methylene blue for staining

Method
1. Make a longitudinal cut in the middle of the carrot tissue through about three-quarters of its length.
2. Sandwich a leaf between the two halves as shown in fig. 5.30. Bind the carrot tissue together very tightly with string and soak in water for several hours until the cells become fully turgid.
3. With a sharp razor cut slices at a slight angle to the horizontal and float the cut sections on water to keep them from curling up or drying out. Place on a microscope slide in a drop of water.
4. Examine under the microscope. It might be helpful to stain the sections with a little methylene blue. You can do this by placing a drop of the stain at the side of the coverslip and drawing the stain through with a filter paper from the other side.

What do you observe?
Make a simple drawing of the section.
Identify the various structures you see in your section.

Discussion
The vertical conducting elements of a plant are called **vascular bundles**. They are found in the roots, stems, leaves and flowers. All the vascular bundles along the length of the plant are interconnected so as to form a continuous channel from the roots to the tips of the shoots.
The conducting elements of the lateral roots converge in the main root and continue up through the stem side by side as shown in fig. 5.31. From the main stem elements pass into the side branches and then into the leaves. The main vein of the leaf further divides into side branches that penetrate almost to the edges of the leaf.

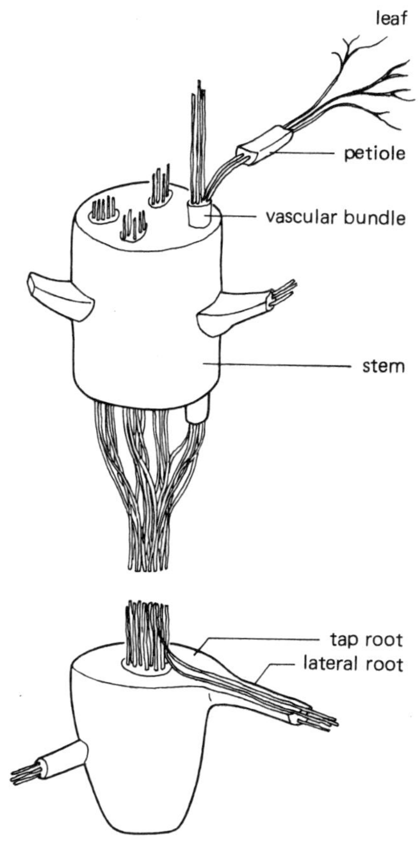

Fig.5.31 Distribution of veins from lateral root to leaf

Fig.5.32 Diagram and photo of transverse section of young root

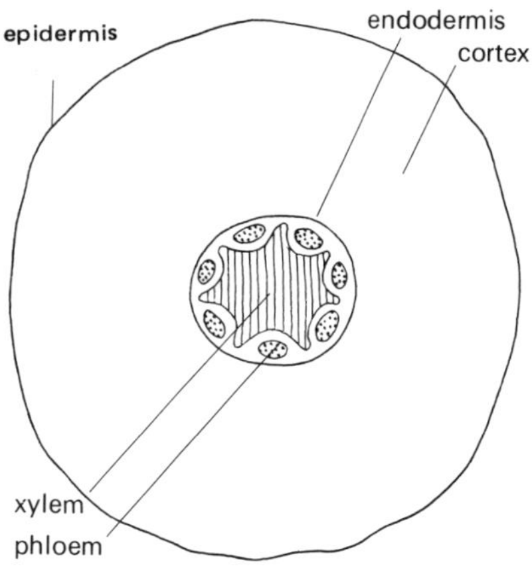

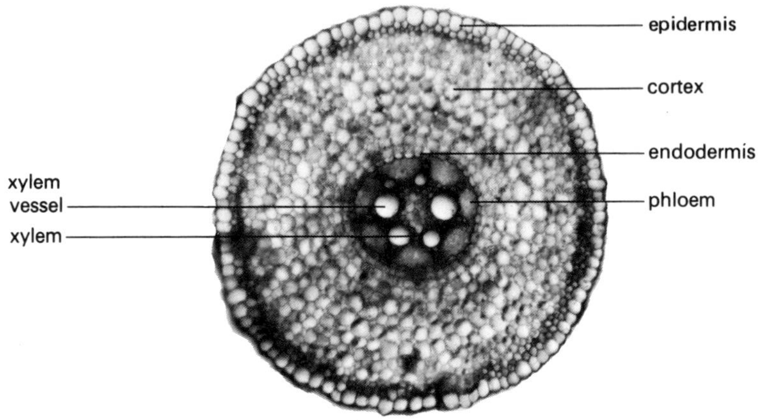

Arrangement of vascular bundles

In the root and stem of many plants the vascular bundles are arranged more or less in a cylindrical pattern although there are variations depending on the type of plant.

What kinds of tissues are found in the vascular bundles?

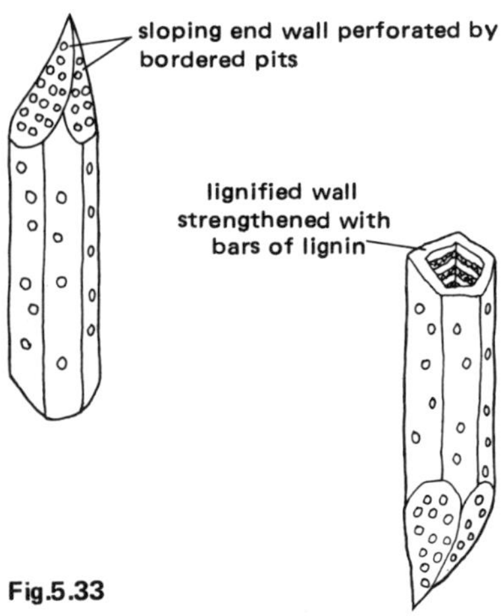

Fig.5.33

There are two distinct kinds of tissue found and they are called the **xylem** and the **phloem**.
The xylem in turn is composed of two distinct types of conducting element called **vessels** and **tracheids**. Vessels consist of chains of elongated cylindrical cells placed end to end so as to form a continuous channel. The end walls of the mature xylem vessels have disappeared so that free passage of materials from cell to cell is possible. The lateral cell walls of the vessels become thickened with deposits of an impregnable[1] material called **lignin**. The lignin is sometimes laid down in a complex spiral pattern to provide extra strength. The side walls also contain openings called **pits** through which water can enter and leave the vessels.
Tracheids are very similar to vessels except that communication between adjacent cells is by means of pits located in the intact end walls of the cells.

What is the function of xylem?

The function of xylem is to conduct water and mineral salts from the roots to the rest of the plant. Water and salts enter by way of the root hairs and by diffusion pass into the xylem of the roots and are then carried up the stem.
The 'wood' of a tree is made up largely of xylem elements.

[1] *impregnable*: forming a barrier through which nothing can pass

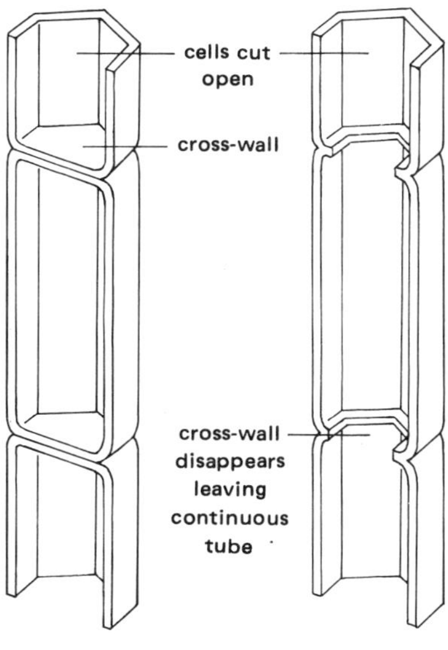

Fig.5.34 To show how vertical columns of cells give rise to vessels

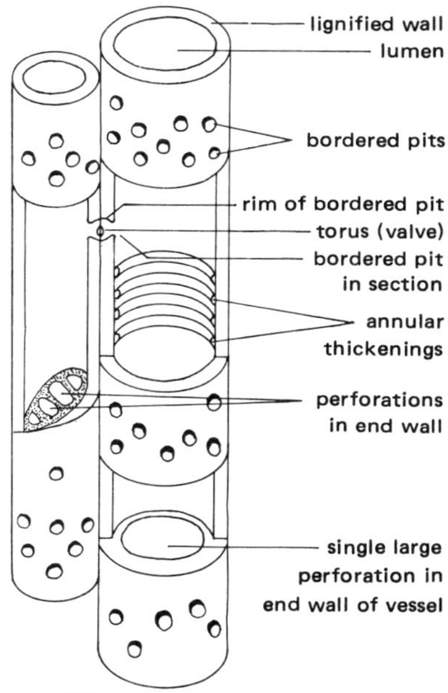

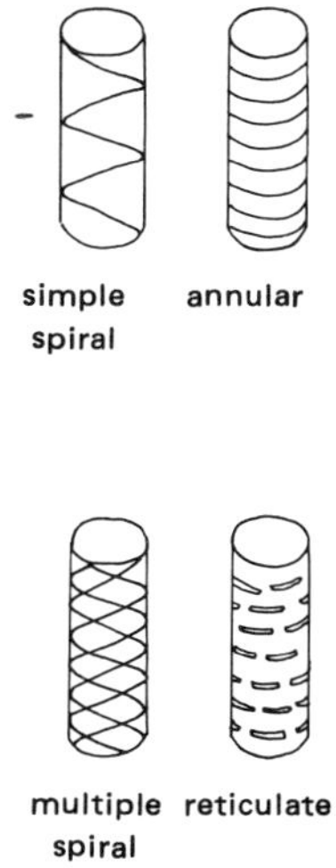

Fig.5.35

What causes the water to move up the stem?

Recall the experiment on p. 149 to illustrate the existence of root pressure. Water rose up in the tube connected to the severed stem until it reached a certain level and stopped. Root pressure is obviously not the complete answer because it cannot be responsible for causing water to move up the stem of a forty- or fifty-foot tree. However, it provides the original impetus for the movement.

The rest of the movement takes place due to the *cohesion* of the water molecules, that is, the force of attraction between individual molecules of water.

The effects of cohesion can be illustrated by watching water rise in a capillary tube.

When the plant is still very young and the distance between the roots and the stem is not very great all the conducting elements of the plant become filled with water. As the leaves lose water through transpiration water is continually being drawn from the xylem vessels into the intercellular spaces to replace the lost water.

This in turn causes a small amount to be drawn up through the stem and in through the root hairs. We can compare the system to a person drinking a liquid through a straw. Once he has sucked up enough liquid to fill the entire length of the straw, as he is removing liquid from the top it is automatically replaced at the bottom from the container. As long as the column of liquid is not broken by any air bubbles the straw will stay permanently filled with water. Fig. 5.36 shows the analogy in diagrammatic form.

The effect exerted by the process of transpiration in keeping the

Fig.5.36

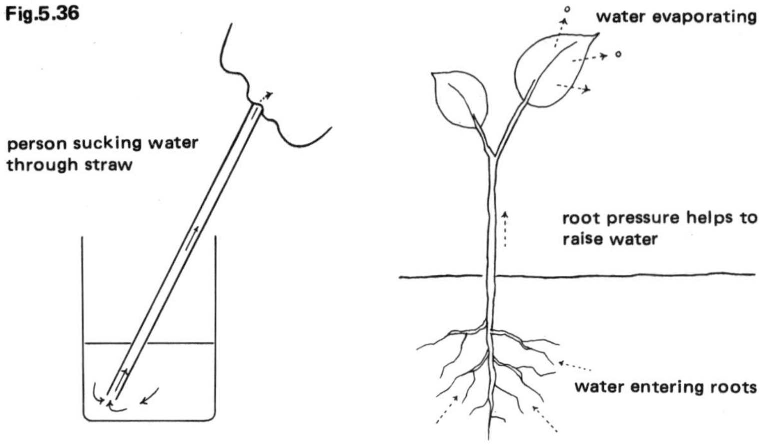

xylem elements filled with water is called **transpirational pull**. As the plant grows in height the length of the water column gradually increases as well. The system does not require the action of living tissue but is purely mechanical in nature. However, root pressure, which is an active process, does supply added impetus to the process.

The transport of the organic substances synthesized in photosynthesis

These are transported by the second type of tissue, the phloem. The organic materials manufactured in the cells of green leaves diffuse from cell to cell until the vascular bundles are reached. Once they enter the phloem the materials can be transported to other parts of the plant that cannot satisfy their demands for nutrients through photosynthesis.

What are the properties of phloem?

Fig.5.37 The structure of phloem

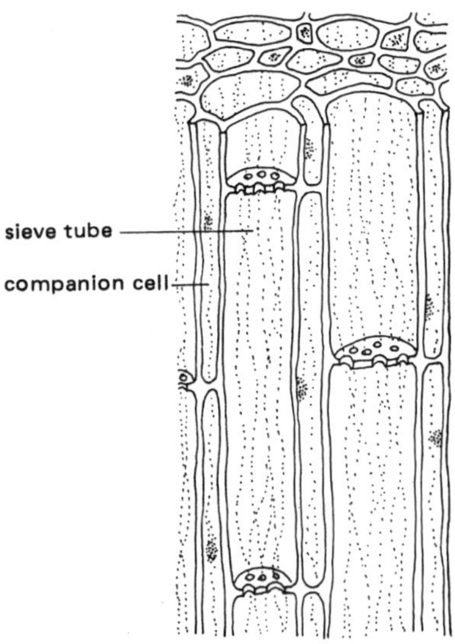

Phloem consists of elongated, living cells called **sieve elements** that are stacked up end to end to form long **sieve tubes**. The end walls of the cells are called **sieve plates** and they are perforated with small pores which allow movement of materials from cell to cell and the passage of cytoplasmic strands from one cell to the next.
Although sieve elements are living cells they have neither a nucleus nor cell organelles and are probably not capable of obtaining their own energy through respiration. Adjacent to each sieve element is a **companion cell** whose function is to satisfy the metabolic needs of the sieve cell.

What experimental evidence is there for this theory of transport?

The earliest evidence for the division of labour between xylem and phloem has been obtained from so called *ringing experiments*.

In a mature tree trunk the outer layer of tissue is made up almost exclusively of phloem, whereas the non-living inner tissue is xylem. If all the living tissue is cut away from the trunk in a narrow ring the conduction of water and mineral salts continues unhindered. However, conduction of organic materials ceases.
More precise investigations have been carried out using radioactive tracers. If a plant is provided with carbon dioxide that is labelled with radioactive ^{14}C, the radioactive atoms will be incorporated into the sugar made by the plant. If sections of the stem of such a plant are placed in contact with photographic film the areas where the radioactivity is concentrated will be outlined on the film. These areas correspond exactly with the position of the phloem tissue.
The experiments described above indicate that water and mineral salts are conducted in the xylem while organic materials are conducted in the phloem.

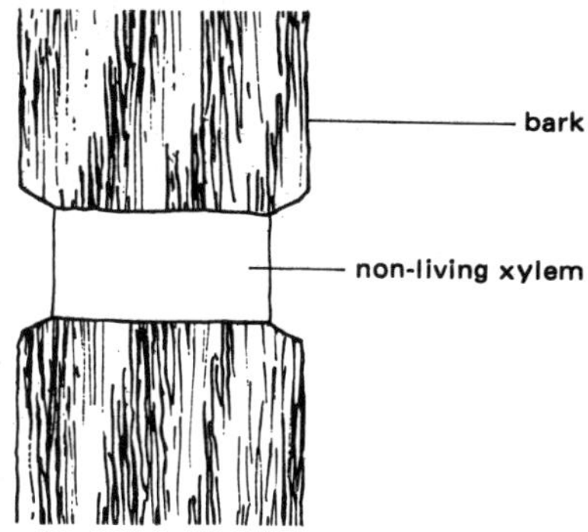

Fig.5.38 Ringing experiment

Summary

The task of transporting materials in plants is shared by two types of tissue called the xylem and the phloem. The former is non-living tissue while the latter is living tissue.
Both are found in all parts of a plant from the roots up the stem to the leaves.
Xylem is responsible for conducting water and mineral salts. The passage of water up to the top of very tall plants is made possible by the effect of transpirational pull and by the cohesion of water molecules.
Phloem conducts organic nutrients from the green leaves to the rest of the plant.

Sensitivity—Detecting changes in the environment

As in the case of many of the other properties of living things sensitivity to the external environment varies to a large degree from one species to the next. Plants in general are more limited in their ability to detect changes in their external environment, their sensitivity being limited to changes in light intensity and temperature, to the presence of water, some chemical substances and gravity and in some instances to touch. Animals are able to respond to a much greater variety of things including light, sound, gravity, chemicals, touch, temperature, hunger, thirst and so on.
There are three phases in the response of an organism to environmental changes. First of all, the change usually referred to as a **stimulus** must be detected by an appropriate sensory device. Secondly it must be interpreted with reference to the current state of the organism and finally a suitable response must be made. In the following sections we will investigate the processes of sensitivity among both animals and plants.

Fig.5.39

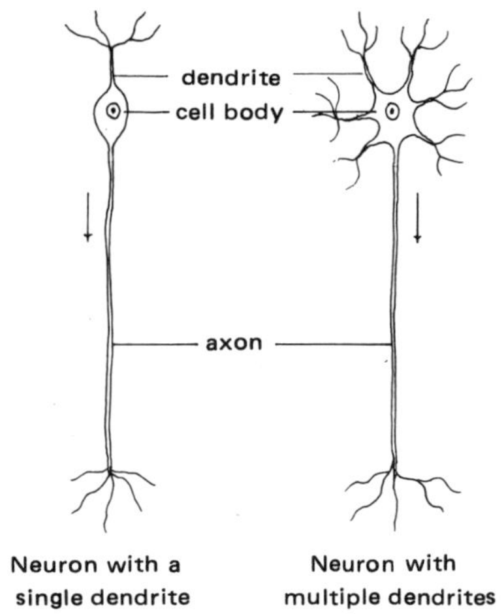

Sensitivity in animals

In animals environmental stimuli are received by special **sensory receptor** cells that form part of the nervous network of the organism. There is a considerable range in complexity among receptors. Some are merely individual sensory cells scattered over the body such as the temperature receptors in the skin of mammals, while certain sensory organs such as the eye are extremely complex in their structure.

Before discussing the nature of sensory receptors in detail it is important to have some knowledge of the basic functional unit of the **nervous system**, namely the nerve cell or **neuron**.

Neurons are specialized for carrying messages called **nerve impulses**. A simple neuron consists of a **cell body** with a nucleus from which **nerve fibres** extend in one or more directions. A nerve fibre along which the impulse travels towards the cell body is called a **dendrite** while the one along which impulses travel away from the cell is the **axon**. As a rule each nerve cell has only one axon but can have more than one dendrite. The axon is usually much longer than the dendrite; it is sometimes up to about a metre in length.

A **nerve** consists of bundles of nerve fibres surrounded by a layer of connective tissue which serves as a means of protection and insula-

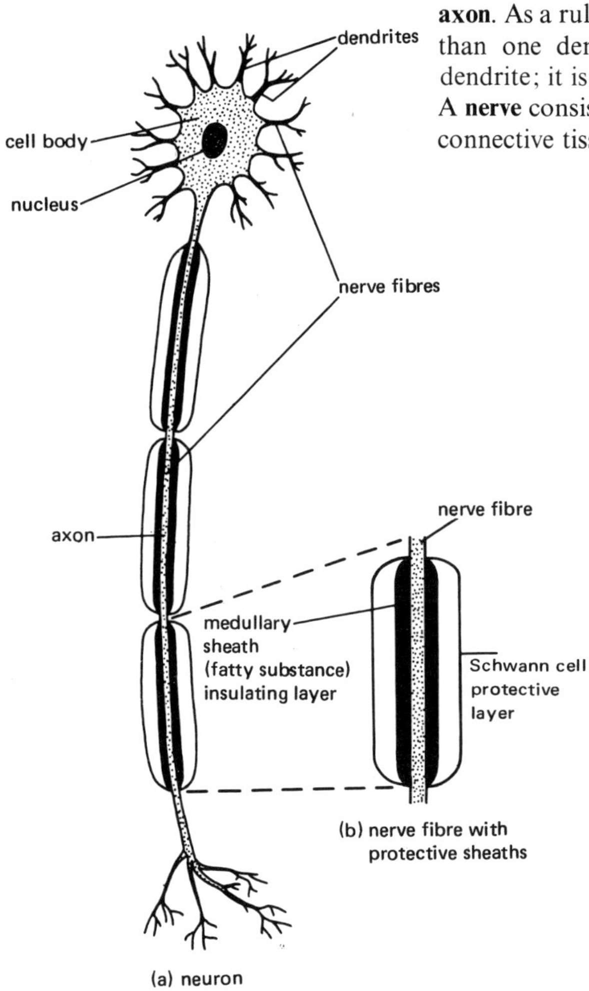

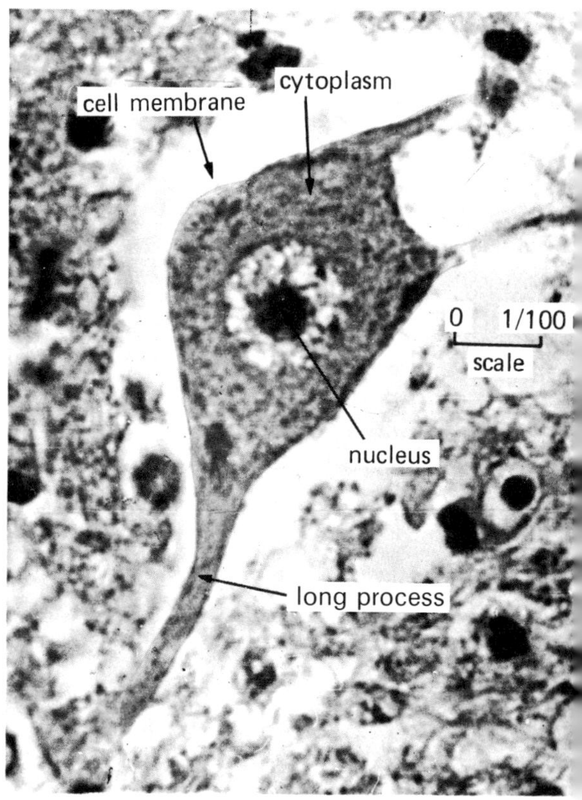

Fig.5.40 Diagram and photo of a neuron

tion. In addition axons are surrounded by a fatty **myelin sheath** and an accessory cell called a **Schwann cell** as shown in fig. 5.40.
Neurons can be classified on the basis of whether they carry information towards or away from the neural centres of the nervous system. Those carrying information towards the centres are called **afferent** or **sensory neurons**, while the latter are **efferent** or **motor neurons**.

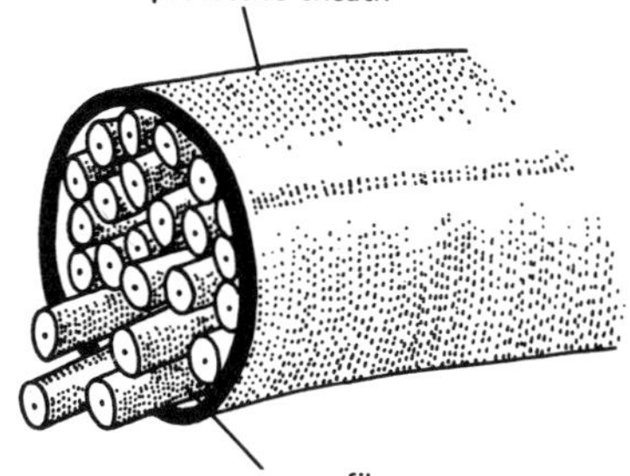

Fig.5.41 A nerve

What is the nature of sensory receptors and how do they function?

Two types of sensory receptor are found in vertebrates.
A **primary** or **neural receptor** is a sensory neuron whose dendrite ending is specialized to initiate a nerve impulse in response to a particular stimulus.
A **secondary** or **epithelial receptor** is a separate sensory cell which has the ability to perceive a particular stimulus and transmit it to an associated neuron.
Most receptors are highly specific with respect to the type of stimulus they are able to receive. A light receptor in the eye is sensitive only to light, a temperature receptor to temperature and so on. There are occasional exceptions however—for instance, gentle pressure exerted on the eyeballs by the hand elicits a sensation of light even if the eyes are closed.

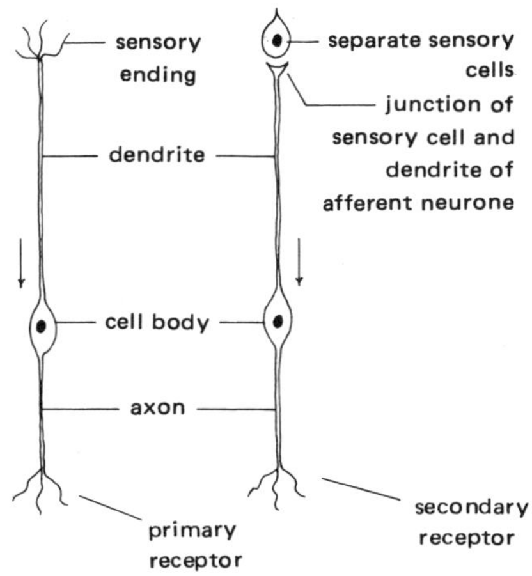

Fig.5.42

How many different types of sensory receptors are there?

There are four main classes of receptor present in most vertebrates.
1. **Chemoreceptors** respond to the presence of various chemical substances. Examples are the sense of taste, the sense of smell and receptors that register the carbon dioxide content of the blood.
2. **Mechanoreceptors** respond to such things as pressure, sound and displacements of the body with respect to gravity.
3. **Photoreceptors** are sensitive to light.
4. **Thermoreceptors** are stimulated by warmth and cold.

The action of a sensory receptor alone does not result in perception of the particular sensation in question. The receptor is only capable of initiating a nerve impulse; the impulse has then to be passed on to the **central nervous system** where it is registered as a sound or a pattern of lights and so on. Eyes by themselves cannot see; it takes the interrelationship of the eyes and the brain to produce the effect of sight.

Characteristics of sensory receptors

ADAPTATION

When continuously stimulated for a certain length of time most sensory receptors gradually cease to transmit nerve impulses. That is, they become **adapted** to a state of continuous stimulation.

The adaptation time is different for each receptor cell or organ. Some adapt very quickly, others more slowly. To illustrate the point think of what happens when you walk into a room that is filled with a strong odour of some type. The sensation is very strong when you first enter, then gradually fades until you are not aware of it at all.

FREQUENCY

If a sensory cell is stimulated at very frequent intervals the repetitive stimuli merge so that they produce one continuous impulse. The electric current which operates the lights in our homes is an alternating current that flickers on and off at a frequency of fifty cycles per second. Our eyes, however, are not able to detect the flicker but sense only a continuous sensation of light.

Fig.5.43

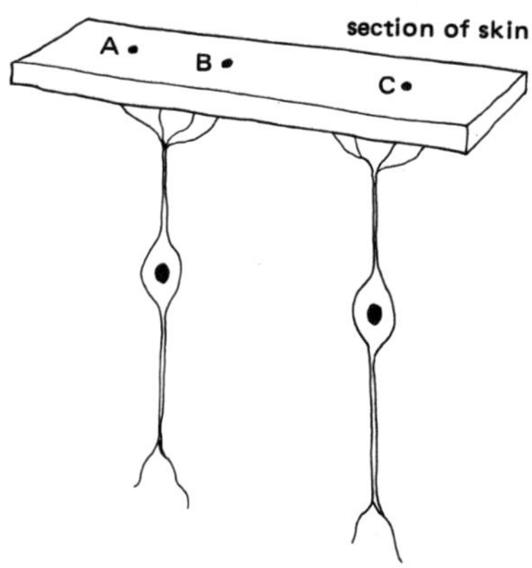

A and B used as one impulse
C distinguished as separate

PRECISION

In order to distinguish two adjacent stimuli as separate entities they must fall on the receptive fields of two separate neurons. If, for instance, two needle pricks are applied to the skin on the arm they will only be distinguished as separate pricks if they are sufficiently far apart. Otherwise only a single sensation will be registered. (Fig. 5.43.)

SENSITIVITY

The sensory receptors of vertebrates, especially mammals are extremely sensitive to the various stimuli they receive. For instance, the human ear is capable of distinguishing between an astonishing 340 000 different tones of sound, and the human eye can detect over 15 000 different hues of colour.

Summary

Animals are able to perceive external and internal stimuli through the action of sensory neurons.
The four classes of sensory neurons are chemoreceptors, mechanoreceptors, photoreceptors and thermoreceptors. In order for a stimulus to be perceived the nerve impulse from the receptor must travel to the central nervous system where it is interpreted and registered.

Sensory organs

The points we have discussed so far are general characteristics relevant to all types of sensory cell. Let us now turn to a detailed discussion of some of the sensory organs.

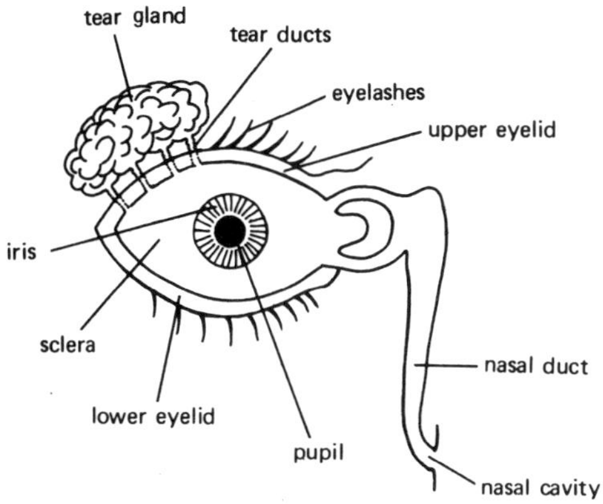

Fig.5.44 The eye

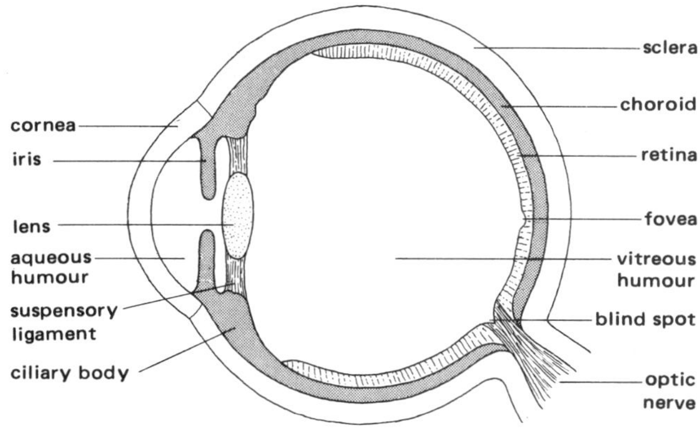

Fig.5.46 Section through eye

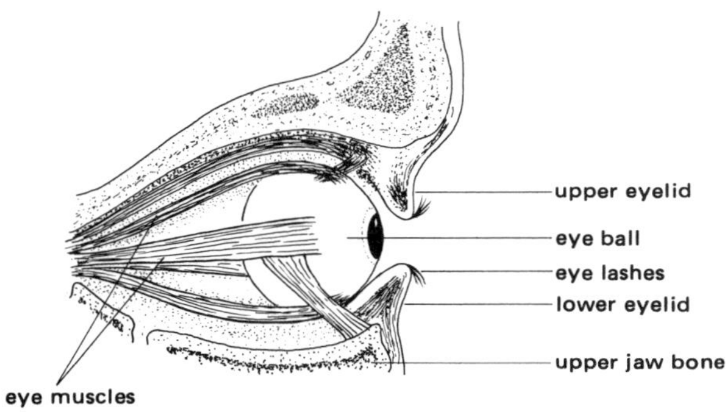

Fig. 5.45 Eye socket

The eye

The eye is an organ that is specialized for light reception. The structure of the mammalian eye is shown in fig. 5.46 and the functions of the various parts are discussed briefly below.

The **eyelids** serve to protect the eye from mechanical injury while the action of blinking distributes the thin film of **tears** over the eye to wash away any foreign bodies that might get in. Closing the eyelids also protects the eyes from excessive stimulation caused by too much light.

Tears are secreted by special **tear glands** located around the eyes. The liquid is a clear solution that has anti-bacterial properties. The front of the eye is covered with a thin transparent protective membrane called the **conjunctiva**.

The **sclerotic** (or **sclera**) is the tough, opaque layer of connective tissue that encloses the back portion of the eyes that is surrounded by the socket. The front portion of the eyeball is covered by the **cornea**, a transparent disc through which light passes and is refracted into the interior of the eye.

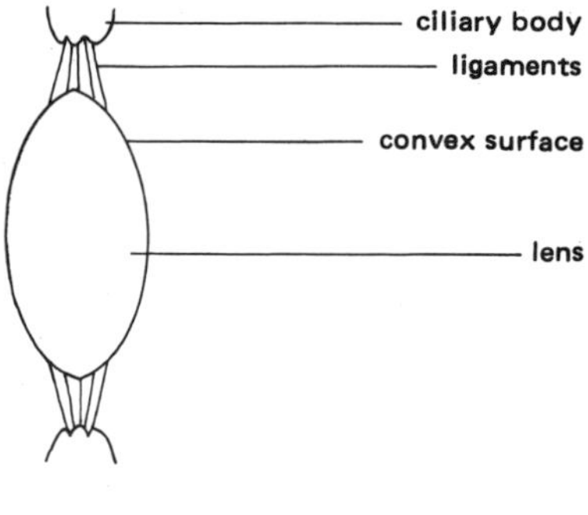

Fig.5.47 Attachment of lens

The inner side of the sclerotic is lined by the **choroid**, a pigmented tissue layer that reduces reflections inside the eye and contains the blood vessels needed to supply the needs of the eye.

At its front ends, the sclerotic expands into a thickening called the **ciliary body**, containing muscles that surround the lens and hold it in place.

The pigmented **iris** covers part of the anterior of the eye. It is composed of the pigment cells and muscle fibres radiating out towards the edges of the eye. In the centre of the iris is a circular aperture, the **pupil**, through which light enters the interior of the eye. Through contraction and relaxation of the radial muscle fibres the iris can control the size of the opening of the pupil and thus the amount of light that enters.

The **lens** is transparent, circular and bi-convex, that is, it has two convex surfaces. (Fig. 5.47.) It is attached to the ciliary body and is held in place by muscles and ligaments originating from the body. The lens is composed of tightly packed living cells. It is elastic in nature so that its curvature can be changed by contraction and relaxation of the ciliary muscles. Changes in the curvature of the lens are very important in focusing and we will return to them again.

The **retina** is the innermost layer of the eye and is composed of layers of nerve cells and fibres. The **optic nerve** enters the eyeball at the lower end of the retina. The large interior chamber of the eye between the retina and the lens is filled with a transparent, jelly-like substance called **vitreous humour**. It supplies nutrition to the lens which does not have its own blood supply, and plays a role in the refraction of light entering the eye.

The smaller chamber between the lens and the cornea is filled with **aqueous humour**, a fluid that is more watery in consistency.

Fig.5.48 Connection of nerve fibres

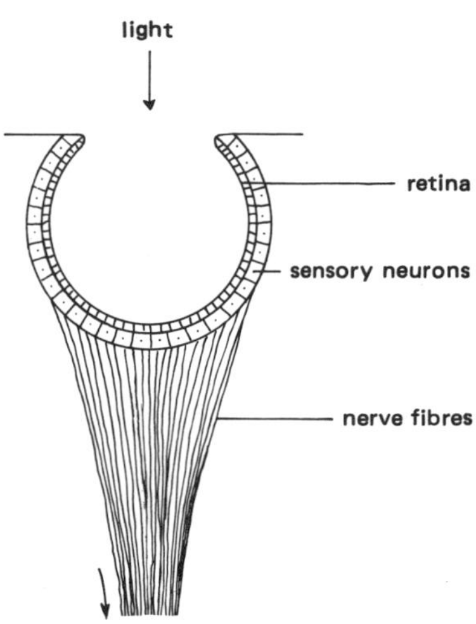

How does the mammalian eye function?

Light rays striking the eye are focused by the curved surfaces of the cornea, by the lens and by the vitreous humour, onto the retina so that points of light coming from an object are registered as points of light on the retina. The image formed on the retina is upside down, the same as the image formed by the lens of a camera. The reason for this is illustrated in fig. 5.49.

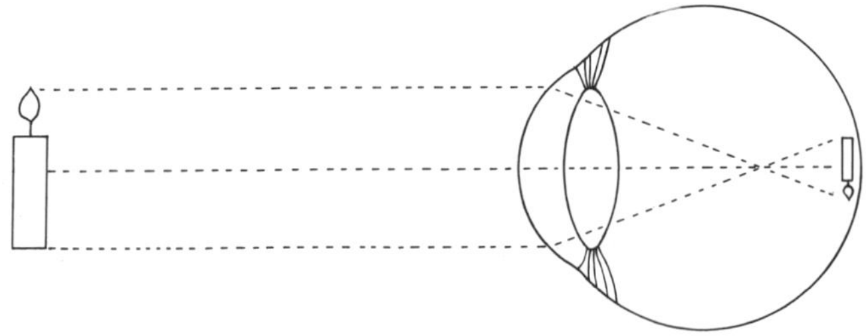

Fig.5.49

The light-sensitive cells of the retina initiate nerve impulses in response to the light that falls upon them. These impulses are transmitted by the optic nerve to the brain where the actual impression of an upright object is perceived.

What are the characteristics of the light-sensitive cells?

Due to their respective shapes, the sensory cells of the retina are called **rods** and **cones**.

The cones are responsible for reception of light under favourable conditions of illumination. The central portion of the retina called the **fovea** contains only cones. It is on this area that light is focused when we are examining something at close range like, for instance, when we are reading.

Rods are more sensitive than cones and are stimulated by light of lower intensity. They are more abundant in the periphery of the retina. For this reason our eyes are more able to see an object in the dark if we do not stare directly at it. Try this out tonight. Pick out an object that you can barely discern in the darkness while looking straight at it. Then turn your head slightly so that you are looking at the object from a slight angle. Can you see it more clearly? By turning your head away slightly you are causing the image of the object to be formed at the periphery of the retina where there are many rods rather than at the centre where there are mostly cones.

Colour vision

Light is a form of electromagnetic radiation. The electromagnetic spectrum is composed of radiation of various wavelengths from the very short cosmic rays to the extremely long radio waves. The human eye is able to respond to radiation only within a small range of wavelengths referred to as the visible spectrum. Within the visible spectrum the wavelength of the light determines its colour as shown in fig. 5.52.

It is believed that there are three different types of cone in the retina and that they are sensitive to three distinct wavelengths of light,

Fig.5.50 Structure of light-sensitive cells and retina

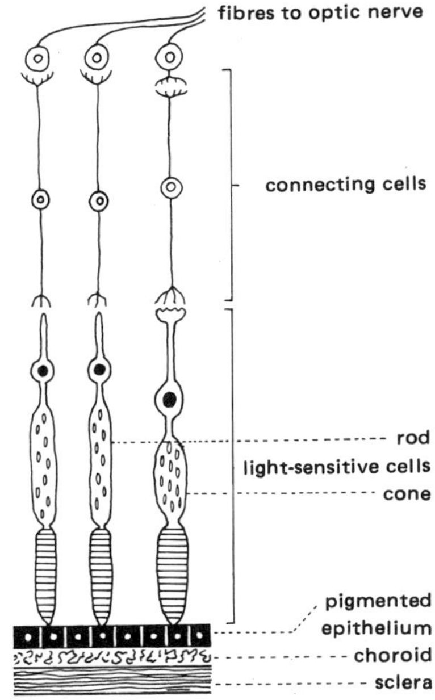

Fig.5.51

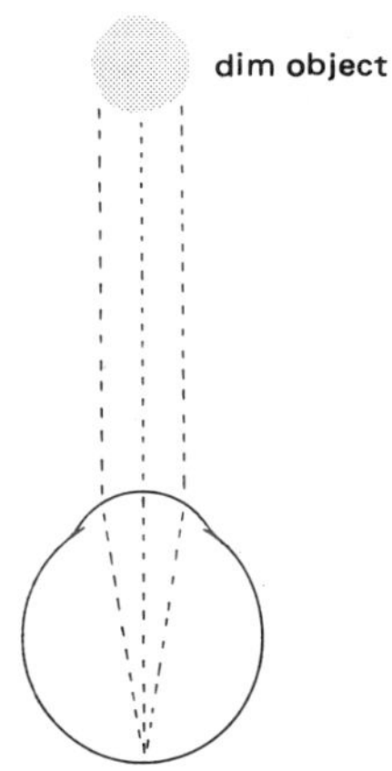

Looking directly at it image is focused on fovea where cones are more numerous

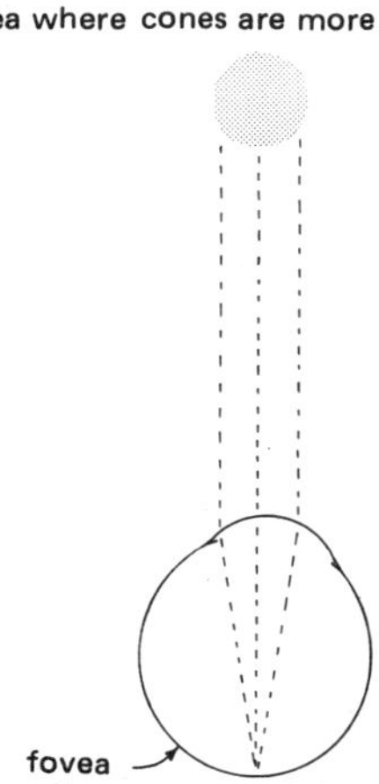

Image focused on peripheral areas where rods are more abundant

Fig.5.52

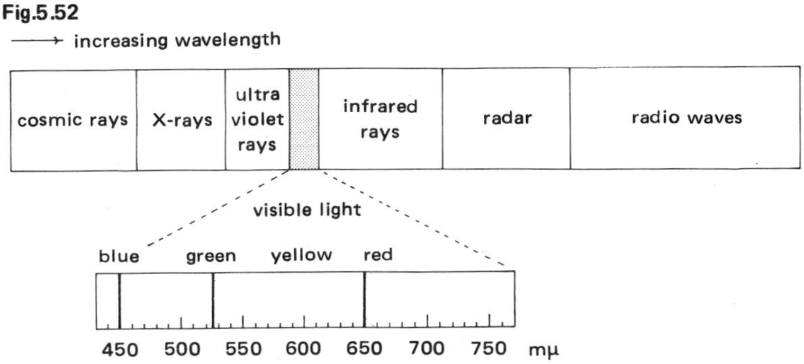

corresponding to the blue, green and red colours. The colour 'seen' by the eye depends on the relative level of stimulation of one, two or all three types of cone.

Individuals who have a certain hereditary defect in their cone structure are unable to distinguish between some or all of the colours of the spectrum.

Rods, responsible for night vision, are not sensitive to differences in wavelength and therefore in the dark we do not see colours.

Binocular vision

When we are viewing a particular object with both the eyes open an image of the object is formed on each retina but the image is focused at slightly different parts. In fig. 5.53 the lines from the object represent the pathways of rays of light coming from it.

Since there is a space between the two eyes each eye sees a slightly different aspect of the object. If you pick out a certain object in your field of vision and look at it alternately with the right eye and then the left eye you will notice that the object seems to be slightly displaced as you switch from one eye to the other. It is this displacement of the two images with respect to each other that leads to a three-dimensional perception of the objects around us.

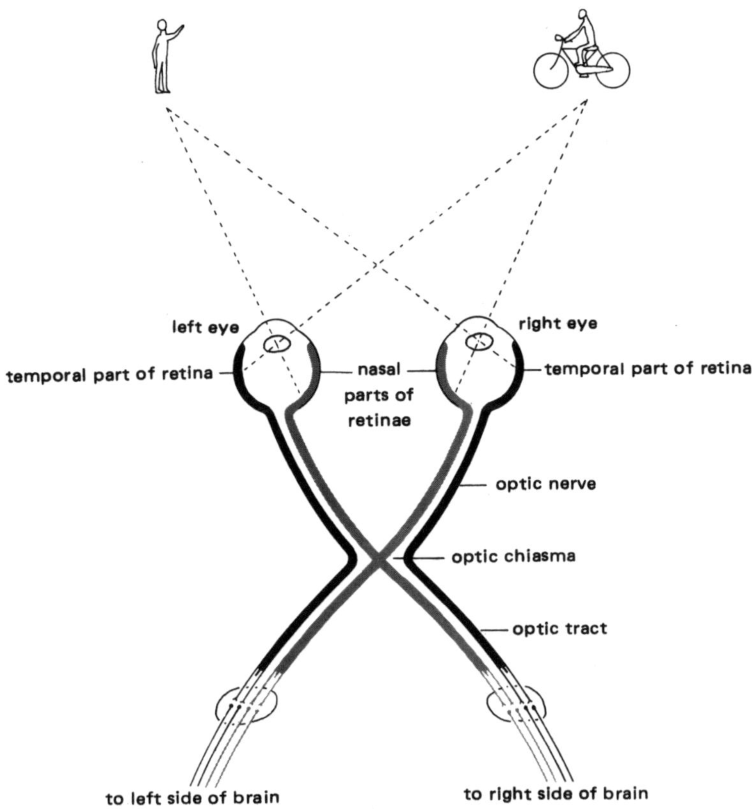

Fig.5.53 Diagram illustrating binocular vision

Fig.5.54 Accommodation

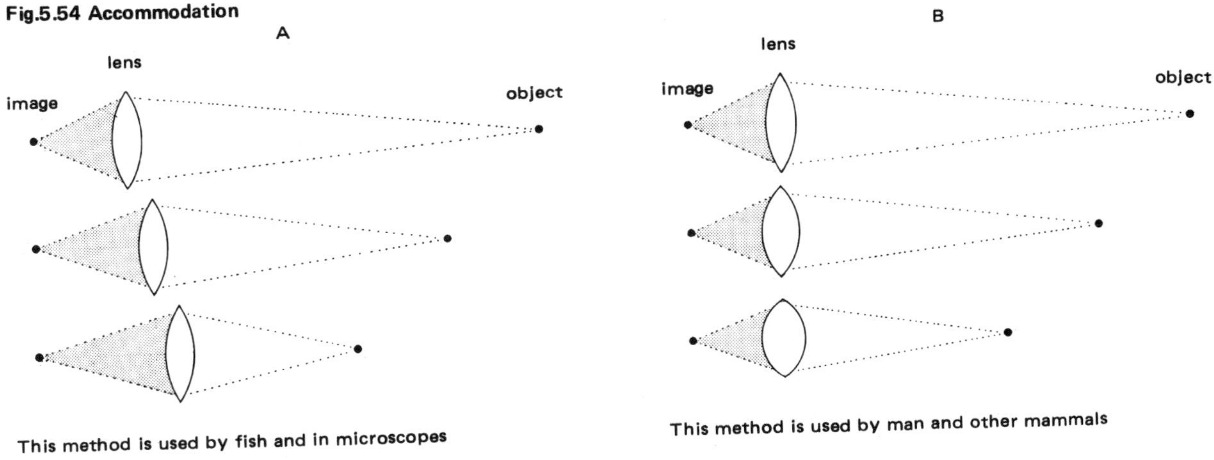

Fig. 5.53 shows the pathways of the optic nerves from the two eyes. While the nerve fibres from the part of the retina that is towards the nose cross over at the optic chiasma, the fibres from the outside do not cross over. Thus the nerve impulses reaching the brain enable the brain to perceive a composite image of the object as seen by the two eyes together.

Accommodation

When you are using a hand lens or a microscope the image you see will be in sharp focus only if the magnifying lens is at the correct distance from the object. Our eyes, however, can focus objects that are on the distant horizon just as well as objects that are only a few inches away.
How is this possible?
There are two different ways that an object can be brought into focus. One is to change the distance between it and the lens and the other is to change the focal length of the lens.
The former method is used in focusing a microscope. It is also used by some animals such as fish that have the ability to move their eyeballs forward and backward in their sockets. The mammalian eye uses the latter method. Through the action of the ciliary muscles the lens of the eye can be made thinner for observing more distant objects or thicker for viewing near objects. **Accommodation**, as this is called, is achieved by changing the shape of the lens which changes the focal length and thus brings the object into focus.

The blind spot

At the point where the optic nerve enters the eyeball the retina does not contain any light-sensitive cells. Objects focused on this **blind spot** of the retina therefore cannot be seen. Fig. 5.55 is a diagram for a blind spot exercise. Hold the book directly in front of you at arm's length. Close the left eye and with the right eye look at the

Fig.5.55 The blind spot exercise

cross. Slowly bring the book closer and closer. For a while you will be able to see the dot out of the corner of your eye, then it will suddenly disappear. At that point the image of the dot is being focused on the blind spot.

Defects of the eye

The two most common defects of the eye are long and short sightedness.

A long-sighted person can focus on objects that are far away with no problem at all but he cannot clearly see near objects. The reason is that due to an incompatibility between the lens and the size of the eyeballs, when viewing near objects the image is focused at a point behind the retina instead of on it. The defect can be corrected by placing a *convex* or converging lens in front of the eye. The effect of the lens is to shift the images of near objects onto the retina. (See fig. 5.56.)

A short-sighted person has an eyeball that is too long for the lens so that when viewing distant objects the image is focused some distance in front of the retina. As the distance of the object viewed decreases the image is brought closer to the retina so that near objects can be seen clearly. A *concave*, or diverging lens is used to shift the image of far away objects onto the retina as shown in fig. 5.57.

Care of the eyes

The ability to see is so basic to our everyday lives that it is difficult to imagine what life would be like without it. If we want to ensure good vision and healthy eyes the following simple rules should be

Fig.5.56 Long-sightedness and its correction

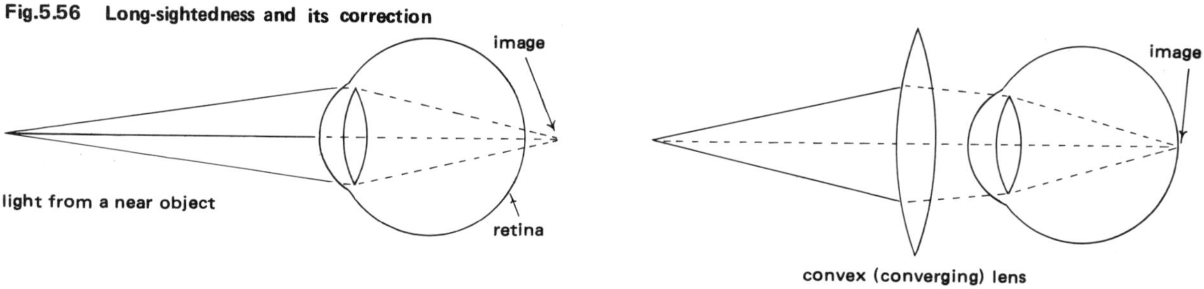

Fig.5.57 Short-sightedness and its correction

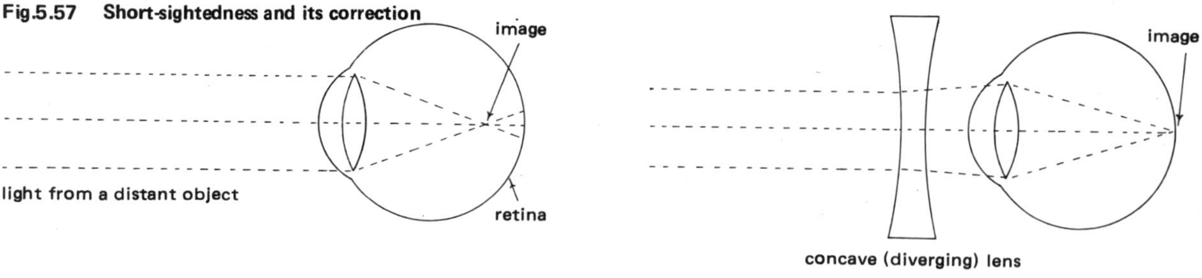

observed at all times.

1. Never read or work in an area where there is no proper illumination as this puts a severe strain on the eye.
2. Never look directly at very bright objects such as the sun or hot glowing metals.
3. If you have difficulties with your vision be sure to seek medical aid and get corrective lenses if necessary.
4. Eat a properly balanced diet and get adequate rest to ensure good health in general.

Summary

The eye is a specialized organ for light perception. Rays of light striking the eye are focused on the light-sensitive cells of the retina which then send nerve impulses to the brain via the optic nerve.
Cones are the light-sensitive cells used under favourable light conditions. They are also responsible for colour vision. Rods are stimulated by light of lower intensity.
Objects are focused on the retina by changing the thickness and as a result the focal length of the lens.

The mammalian ear

The mammalian ear serves the dual purpose of an organ of hearing and an organ of equilibrium. Since the majority of the structures are concerned with the former function let us discuss it first.
Sound consists of successions of vibrations of the molecules in the air setting up a sound wave. The waves travel at a speed of 330 metres per second. Hearing consists of concentrating these vibrations and transmitting them to the sensory cells that are able to respond to the vibrations with appropriate nerve impulses that are then carried to the brain by way of the **auditory nerve**.

The structure of the ear

For convenience in discussing the various structures the ear can be divided into three regions: the **outer**, **middle** and **inner ear**.

The outer ear

The outer ear consists of a flap of skin called the **pinna** and an **external auditory passage** leading to the middle ear.
In some animals the pinna is mobile and when turned towards the source of sound acts as a sound-gathering device. Very few of us have retained the capacity to move the ears. In humans, the pinna is predominantly a decorative device.
The auditory passage is covered with hair and is lined with special glands that secrete a wax. Both of these help to eliminate dust and dirt from the ear.

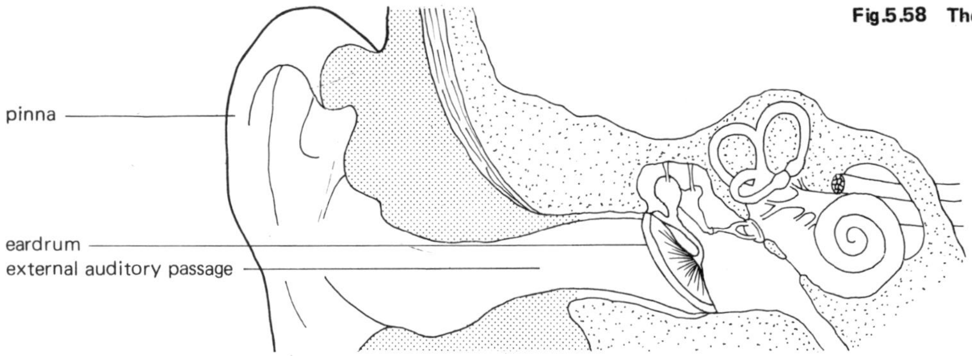

Fig.5.58 The parts of the outer ear

Sound waves travel down the auditory passage and strike the **ear drum** at the end of the passage setting up vibrations in its membrane. That is, the wave motion of the sound wave is translated into mechanical vibrations of the membrane.

Fig.5.59 The middle ear

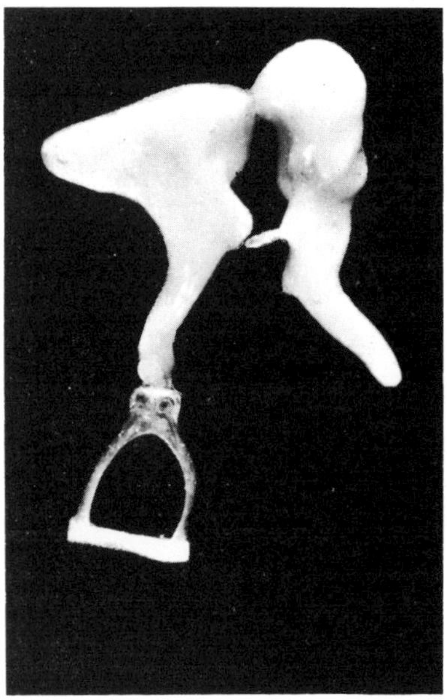

The middle ear

The middle ear is a cavity bounded at one end by the ear drum and on the other end by another membrane called the **oval window**. The space itself contains three small bones called the **hammer**, **anvil** and **stirrup** owing to their resemblance to these objects (fig. 5.59). These three bones pass on the vibrations of the ear drum to the oval window causing it to vibrate.

The middle ear magnifies the pressures caused by the vibrations of the ear drum and thereby increases the efficiency of the ear. It also acts as a safety device, protecting the inner ear against very loud noises.

The interior space of the middle ear is connected to the pharynx by means of an air passage called the **Eustachian tube**. Through the tube air can enter the middle ear so that the pressure on the two sides of the ear drum can be equalised. The heavy, congested feeling you experience when travelling down a steep road or when you are diving is due to unequal pressure on the two sides of the ear drum. As you are travelling downward pressure is steadily increasing. Although this is only a minute change our ears are

Fig.5.60 The parts of the middle ear

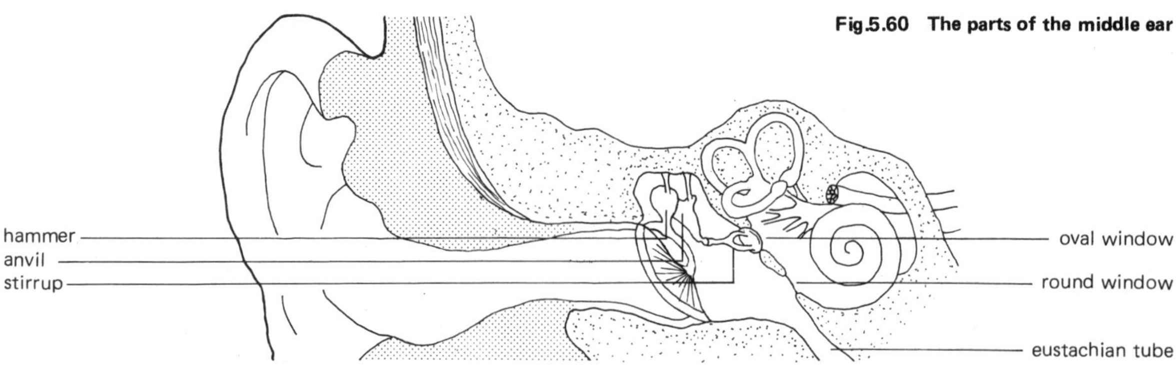

Fig.5.61 The inner ear structures concerned with hearing

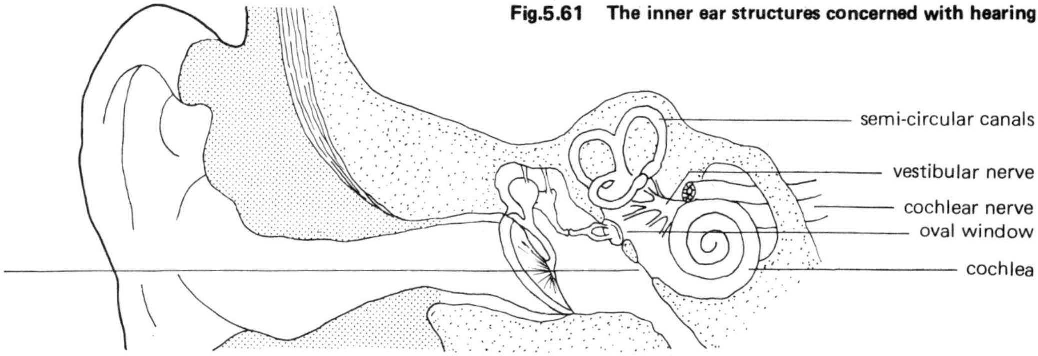

sensitive enough to notice it. When you 'blow out' your ear what you are doing is forcing air through the Eustachian tubes to the middle ear to increase the interior pressure and make it equal to the pressure on the outside.

The inner ear

The inner ear is a fluid-filled bony space connected to the middle ear by the oval window. The inner ear is the true site of hearing, the outer and middle ears being only accessory parts needed to convey the sound to the inner ear. Vibrations of the oval window cause the liquid inside the **cochlea** to vibrate. The cochlea (Latin: snail) is a coiled, fluid-filled tube. If we were to uncoil and straighten it out it would measure about 4 cm. Fig. 5.62 shows a cross-section of the organ.

Stretched out along the length of the cochlea are the **basilar membrane** and the **tectorial membrane**. The chambers formed by these two membranes are filled with a fluid. Attached to the basilar membrane are numerous tiny hair cells equipped with sensory nerve endings.

Fig.5.62 Section of cochlea

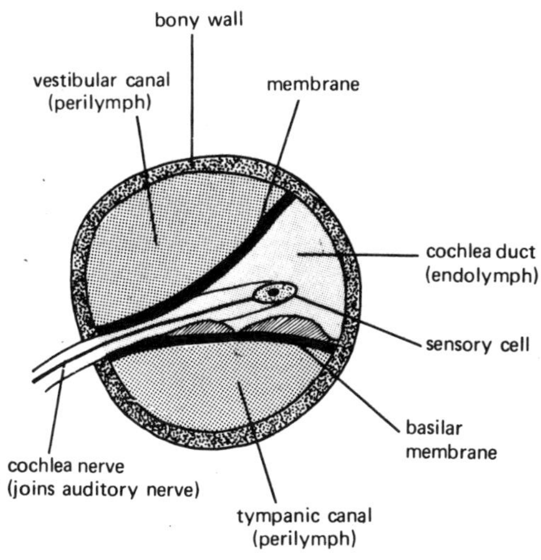

How are the vibrations reaching the ear able to set up nerve impulses?

Vibrations of the oval window set up corresponding vibrations in the fluid of the cochlea as well as in the basilar membrane. These vibrations cause movements of the tiny hair cells and these in turn set up nerve impulses that are transmitted by the auditory nerve.
The point along the membrane at which the vibrations reach their maximum amplitude is determined by the frequency of the sound. The human ear is able to detect sounds of frequencies ranging from sixteen to twenty thousand cycles per second. The sense of hearing is, therefore, a highly complicated form of touch. The hair cells in the basilar membrane respond to being moved in the same way as the hairs along your arm respond if you touch them very gently without actually touching your skin.

The ear as an organ of balance

An additional structure found in the inner ear is a system of three **semi-circular canals** which are placed at right angles to each other and filled with fluid, and two membrane sacs, the **utricle** and the **saccule**.
Movements, changes in direction and changes in the speed of movement of the head cause corresponding movements in the fluid of the canals. The liquid flow stimulates the sensory hair cells located in the **ampulla**, a swelling at the end of the semicircular canals. The nerve impulses set up in these cells are carried to the brain where they are analysed to determine the position of the head

Fig.5.63 Semi-circular canal

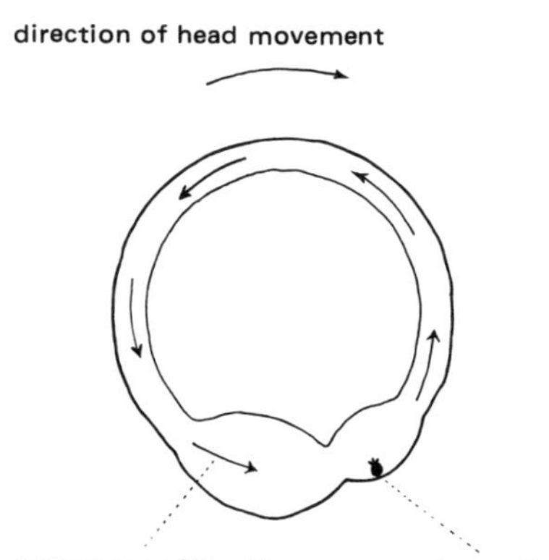

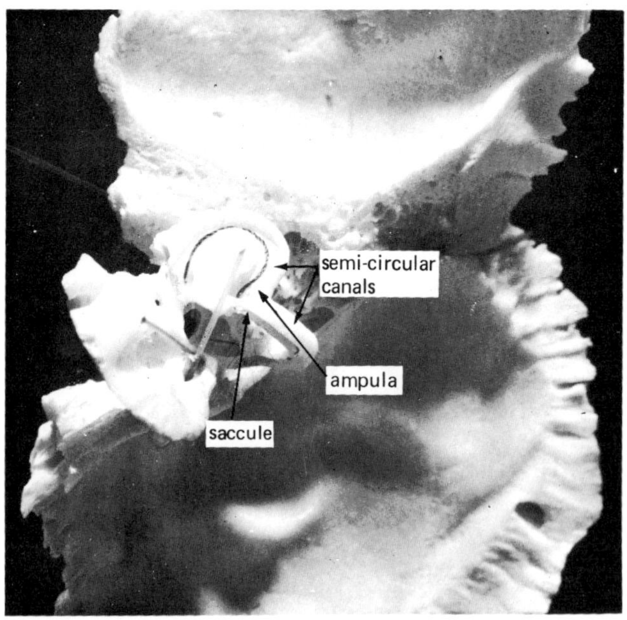

Fig.5.64 Organs of balance in inner ear

and changes in the speed of movement of the body.
Due to the effect of inertia the flow of liquid in the canals lags slightly behind the movements of the head. Thus it takes a few seconds after the termination of vigorous movements for the motion to stop. If you touch your toes rapidly ten times in a row, at the end of the exercise you will still feel apparent movement for a second or two due to the lag time in the response.
For maintaining balance at rest the impulses are provided by the utricle and the saccule. The interior of these sacs is also lined with sensory hair cells and in addition contain small particles called **ear stones**, made of calcium carbonate. As the head is moved from side to side the stones also move around and stimulate the sensory cells at various parts of the structures. The exact location of the stimulations enables the brain to determine the exact position of the head with respect to the rest of the body and to the direction of the force of gravity.

The other senses

Taste and smell

Both taste and smell are chemical senses. That they are closely associated is illustrated by the fact that both senses are impaired when the nasal passage is blocked due to a cold.
Sensory cells called **taste buds** located on the tongue are able to respond to chemical substances that are in solution in the saliva. When the mouth is completely dry the sense of taste cannot function. There are four basic taste sensations; sweet, sour, bitter and salty. Different areas of the tongue are able to respond to different tastes according to the pattern shown in fig. 5.65. The sensory receptors stimulated by the chemical substance send nerve impulses to the brain and, depending on which area of the tongue the impulse is coming from, it is interpreted as a different taste sensation.

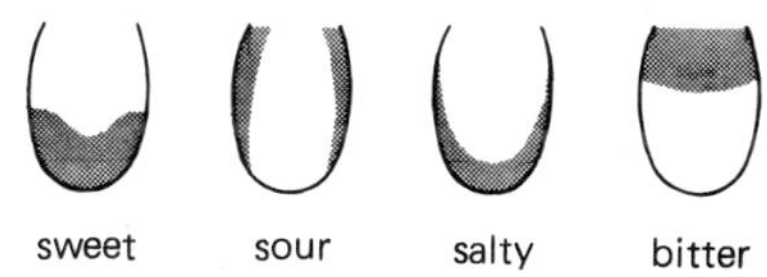

Fig.5.65 Distribution of taste buds in the tongue

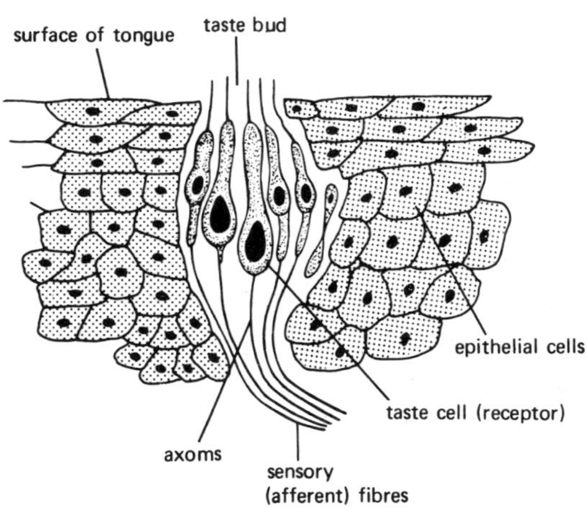

Fig.5.66 a taste bud

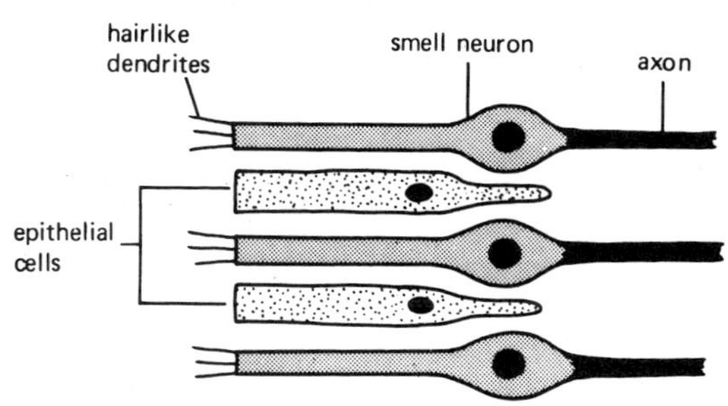

Fig.5.67 Smell receptors

The nose contains receptor cells with hair-like dendrites that are sensitive to chemical substances in the air. The sense of smell in humans is not nearly as acute as in some other animals and is easily fatigued.

Touch

The sense of touch is mediated directly by sensory receptors in the skin. There are separate receptors for pressure, pain and temperature. Depending on which type of receptor is being stimulated and in which area, the brain can interpret, for instance, that there is a slight feeling of pain in your left toe.

Proprioceptors

In contrast to the senses such as sight and hearing that give us information about the external world there are other senses that tell us about the state of our own bodies. (Proprius—Latin, meaning 'one's own'.)
One of the proprioceptive senses is the **muscle sense**. A muscle is equipped not only with motor nerves that tell it to contract but with sensory receptors that give information about its degree of contraction and its exact position. Continuous reports being sent to the brain keep us aware of the position of each part of our bodies. As a result of muscle sense you can move your head, arms or legs into various positions with your eyes closed and still be aware of exactly where they are. Without it you would have to look directly at each part of your body as it is moving to determine how far it should be moved. Although we have discussed the sense of balance along with that of hearing it really belongs to the group of proprioceptors since it tells us about the position of our bodies.

Summary

The outer and middle portions of the mammalian ear serve to collect and amplify sound while the inner ear sends out nerve impulses in response to the vibrations that reach it.
The semi-circular canals of the inner ear act as the organ of balance.
Taste and smell are both chemical senses. Sensory cells on the tongue respond to chemicals in solution. Sensory hairs in the nose respond to chemicals in the air.
Proprioceptors such as the ones in our muscle cells provide information about the position of our bodies at any given time.

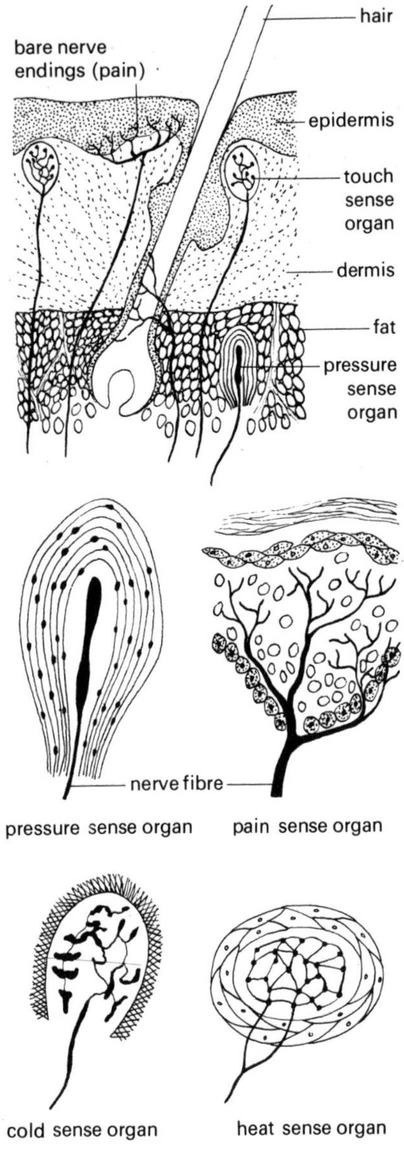

Fig.5.68 Touch receptors in skin

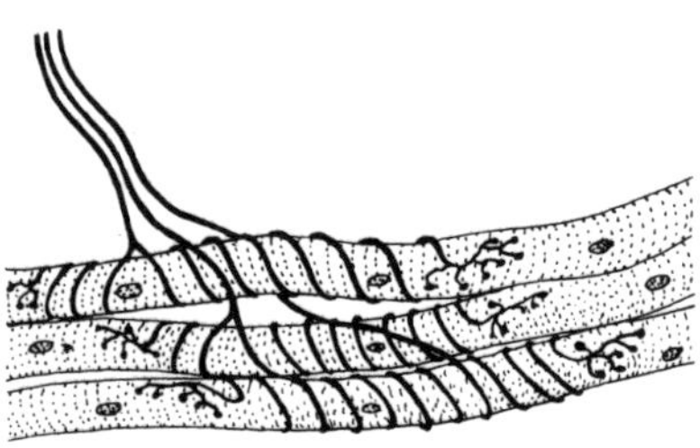

Fig.5.69 Stretch receptor in a muscle

Sensitivity in plants

Being living organisms, plants also exhibit a certain measure of sensitivity to their environment although the scope of their responses is quite limited compared to that of animals.

Plants do not have a nervous system and they do not have specific sensory cells or sense organs. Their response to the environment is limited to a number of so called **tropic responses**. The word 'tropic' is Greek in origin and it means 'turning'. Since a tropic response quite often takes the form of a change in the direction of growth of the plant it is also referred to as a **growth movement**.

Response to light

As you have already found in the section on photosynthesis light is an extremely important external factor in the growth of green plants. One of the most prominent responses shown by plants is their response to the presence and direction of light called **phototropism**.

EXPERIMENT TO DEMONSTRATE PHOTOTROPISM IN PLANTS

Materials

pea or bean seedlings
two small dishes
two cardboard boxes

Method

1. Place the germinating seeds in two small dishes of earth and allow to grow until several inches high.
2. Prepare two cardboard boxes. Box A should have a slit along one side while B should have slits on all four sides as shown in the diagram.
3. Place the pea seedlings inside each box and observe for a week or so. Keep in a spot where the boxes will receive equal illumination from all sides.

Do you observe any difference between the seedlings in boxes A and B?
What could be the cause of the difference?
Draw a diagram of the seedlings in boxes A and B.

Discussion

Seedlings A received a small amount of light from one direction only, that is, through the single opening in the box. The stems after a few days showed an unmistakable bending towards the source of light. If kept in the box long enough the stems would eventually grow through the opening into the light. The effect is one of **positive phototropism**.
The young root on the other hand would grow in a direction away from the source of light showing **negative phototropism**. The bending movement of the shoot is much more marked than that of the root. This is not surprising since roots are not normally exposed to light.
Since the control seedlings B were equally illuminated from all sides no bending at all is observed.

Fig.5.70

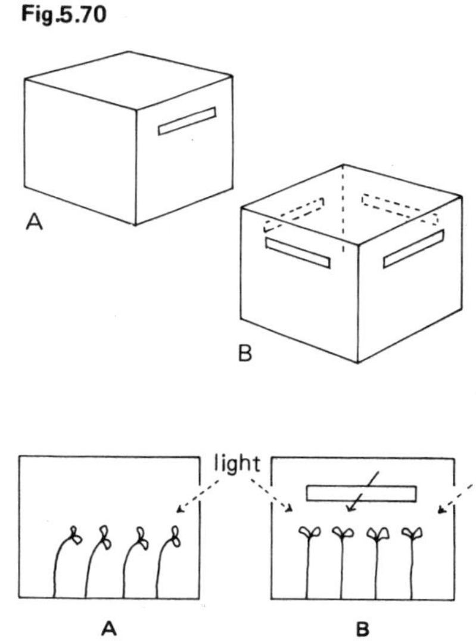

Seedlings bending towards light sources

No bending

Fig.5.71

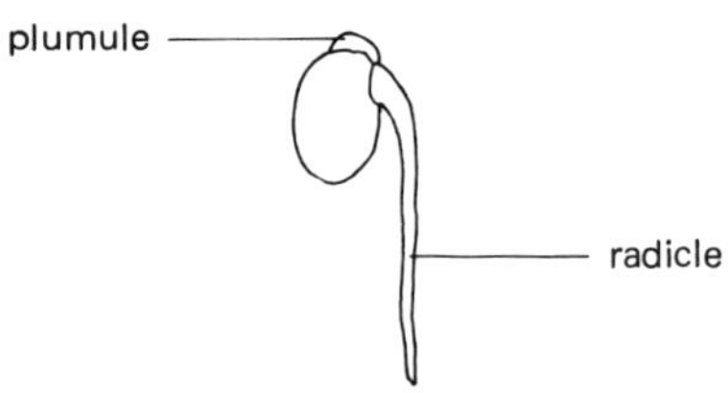

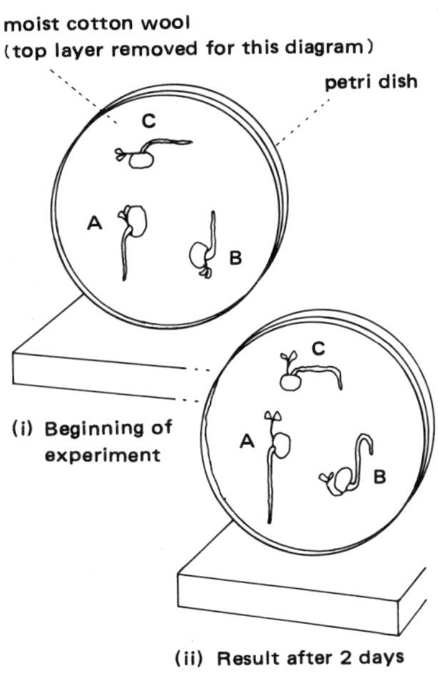

Fig.5.72 **Geotropism in roots**

The importance of phototropism

The positive phototropic response of the shoot ensures that a plant gets sufficient light energy to carry on photosynthesis. If a seed happens to germinate in a spot where the light is blocked off by surrounding plants the phototropic response will direct its growth in such a way as to receive as much light as possible.

Response to gravity

When a seed falls on the ground and starts to germinate or when it is planted in the ground it is not necessarily oriented in such a way that the shoot is up and the roots are down. Yet one never sees a seedling developing horizontally on the ground, or upside down. Clearly there must be some mechanism directing the orientation of the seedling with respect to the ground to ensure a proper **geotropic** response.

EXPERIMENT TO ILLUSTRATE GEOTROPISM IN SEEDLINGS

Materials
pea or bean seedlings
filter paper
shallow dish such as a Petri dish

Method
1. Line the bottom of the dish with a thick layer of moist filter paper.
2. Attach three germinating seeds to the dish as follows:
A—right side up, that is, the plumule of the shoot pointing upwards and the radicle pointing downward
B—upside down, that is, the reverse of A
C—horizontally
3. Place the dish on its side as shown in the accompanying diagram. Observe for several days.

Describe what happens to the shoot and rootlet of each plant.
Does the shoot show positive or negative geotropism?
What about the root?

Discussion
Seedlings show a definite geotropic response that ensures that tney will grow upright with relation to the ground. Roots are positively geotropic, that is, they bend down towards the ground while shoots are negatively geotropic and bend up away from the ground.
The predominant factor responsible for keeping plants upright is the force of gravity.
This can be investigated using an apparatus known as the *klinostat*. Various models are available. Some are suitable for an entire potted plant, others are suitable for seedlings. The apparatus is set up as in fig. 5.73 along with the controls. The motor of the klinostat is switched on so as to rotate at a fast rate.

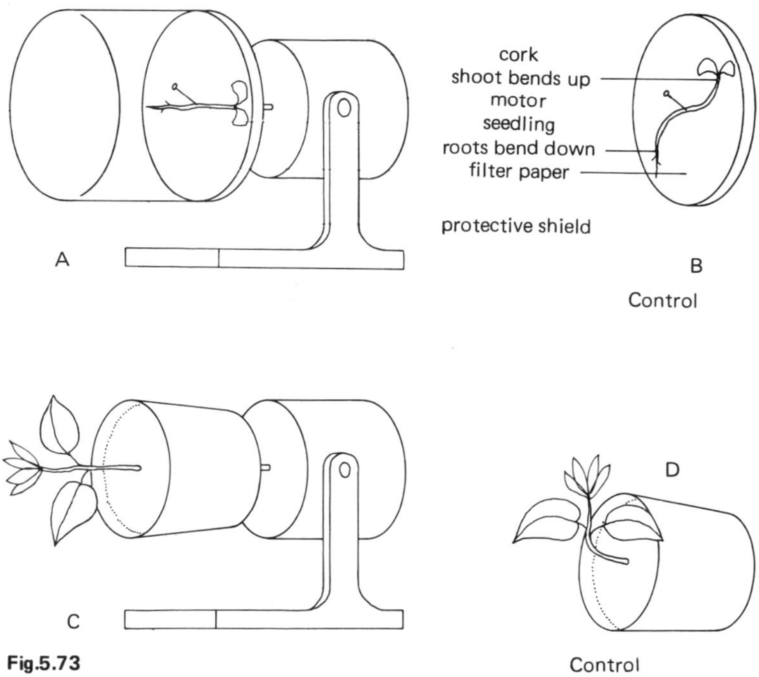

Fig.5.73

Even after several days no geotropic response is observed in A. If a seedling is set up under similar conditions but is not rotated, after a day or two there is a noticeable downward curvature of the rootlet and an upward curvature of the shoots.

As the direction from which gravity is acting on the seedling that is being rotated is constantly changing the force of gravity cannot influence the seedling to grow in any particular direction. Clearly the effect of gravity has to be constant from a particular direction before the geotropic response will be exhibited.

In a similar manner the negative geotropism of shoots can be demonstrated by placing a small potted plant sideways at rest and placing another plant sideways on the klinostat as in C. The shoots of the plant at rest will start to grow in an upward direction in a few days' time. The shoots of the plant being rotated on the klinostat will remain pointing in a sideways direction.

Response to water

In addition to sunlight another important substance needed by plants is water, which they obtain from the soil through the roots. The amount of water in the various sections of soil around the roots of a plant can and usually does vary considerably.

Are the roots of a plant able to actively seek water or does it have to stay in a fixed position waiting for water to come to it?

We can find the answer to this question by performing the following experiment.

Fig.5.74

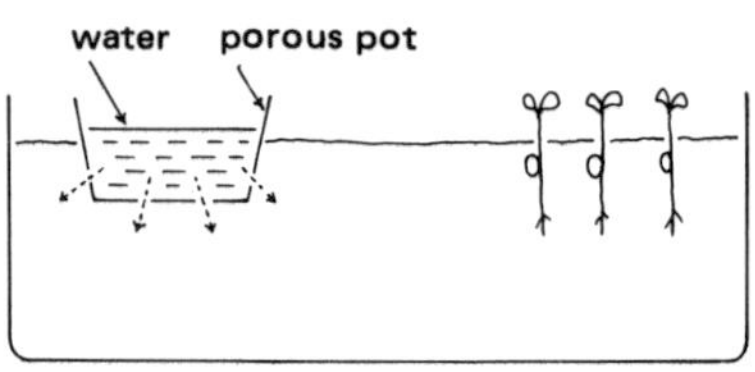

EXPERIMENT TO FIND OUT IF ROOTS SHOW HYDROTROPISM, THAT IS, RESPONSE TO THE PRESENCE OF WATER

Materials

pea or bean seedlings
porous pot
planter with soil

Method

1. Plant the germinated seeds in a layer of soil in the planter.
2. Water regularly until the shoots appear above the ground.
3. Stop watering and wait for two or three days.
4. Pull out one of the seedlings and examine the root structure. Make a drawing of it.
5. Into one corner of the soil insert a porous pot containing water and leave the planter undisturbed for a few days.
6. Carefully expose the roots of the remaining seedlings. Be sure that you do not rotate them as you pull them out of the ground.

Fig.5.75

Appearance of seedling when watered regularly

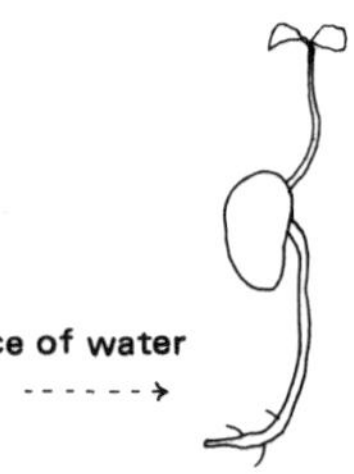

Appearance at end of experiment

Describe the appearance of the roots of these plants.
Make a drawing of one of them.
Compare with the appearance of the original seedling that you examined in step 4.
How can you account for the difference?
Do roots show positive or negative hydrotropism?

Discussion

When the seeds are first planted and are watered regularly the young roots grow straight down according to the laws of the geotropic response. When water is supplied at only one specific area of the soil the roots begin to show a marked bending towards the direction from which water is diffusing. That is, they show positive hydrotropism. Furthermore, it seems that the effect of the hydrotropic response is stronger than that of the geotropic one. We can illustrate this point better by setting up the following experiment.

Fig.5.76

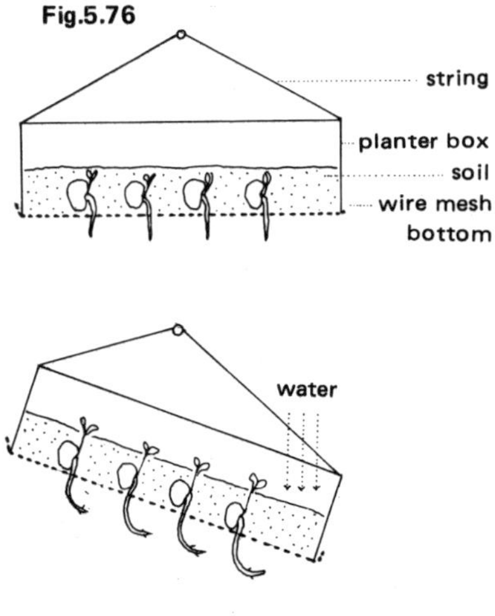

EXPERIMENT TO INVESTIGATE THE RELATIONSHIP BETWEEN THE HYDROTROPIC AND GEOTROPIC RESPONSE IN PLANTS

Materials

planter with perforated bottom—this can be a wooden or metal container with wire mesh fitted at the bottom
pea or bean seedlings
soil

Method

1. Plant the germinating seeds in a thin layer of soil on the bottom of the planter. Keep the planter suspended in a horizontal position.
2. Water regularly until the rootlets appear through the wire mesh on the bottom.
3. Stop watering for two or three days.
4. Suspend the planter so that it is inclined at an angle of about

thirty degrees. Supply water only at the lower edge of the container as shown in the diagram.

What do you observe?
Which of the two responses is stronger?
Discussion
As observed in the previous experiment when seedlings receive an equal amount of moisture on all sides the roots grow vertically downward in response to the pull of gravity. When moisture is supplied only on one side the roots curve in the direction of the source of moisture even though this may be at ninety degrees or more from the direction dictated by the geotropic response. Hydrotropism is therefore a stronger response than geotropism.

Response to chemicals

The response of a plant to the presence of certain chemical substances is called **chemotropism**. The response usually directs the growth of the plant towards the source of the particular chemical substance. Chemotropism is involved in bringing about the growth of the pollen tube into the embryo sac to make fertilization possible. (See p. 299.)

Common characteristics of tropic responses

All tropic responses have one important characteristic in common, namely, the direction of growth elicited by the response is either towards or away from the direction of the external stimulus causing it. The precise mechanism by which these movements are brought about will be discussed in the section dealing with plant hormones (p. 254).

Do plants exhibit any other responses to the environment?

There are other types of growth response that although brought about by external stimuli, are independent of the direction of the given stimulus. Changes in light intensity for instance can cause either the opening or the folding up of flowers and leaves depending on the characteristics of the particular plant.
Many flowers will also open and close in response to changes in heat intensity.
Stomata open and close in response to the changing turgidity of the guard cells. (See p. 154.)
A more dramatic response to external stimuli occurs in some plants in which contact with an external object causes the leaves to close very rapidly. The best example of this response is shown by the Mimosa plant (shown in fig. 5.77) whose leaves fold up if one of the tips is pinched with the fingers. This response is very like the nervous response exhibited by animals but it is probably mediated

Fig.5.77 Mimosa plant before and after being touched

by the passage along the vascular bundles of a chemical substance. The response could be set off by a sudden drop in turgidity in the pinched leaf tip.

Carnivorous plants exhibit a very special form of response to the stimulus of a small insect landing on their leaves. The Venus fly-trap will instantly snap shut trapping the insect within its spiked leaves. The response is triggered by touching the sensitive hairs on the inner leaf surface. The stimulation is probably carried to the effector cells by the diffusion of a chemical substance. The details of the reaction are as yet not understood by scientists.

Fig.5.78 Venus fly trap 'catching' a fly ***(Courtesy of Carolina Biological Supply Company)***

Summary

The sensitivity of plants to external stimuli is considerably more limited than that of animals. The majority of responses are in the form of growth movements frequently with one part of the plant growing more rapidly than other parts. A tropic response is a growth movement whose direction is determined by the direction of the external stimulus. Other types of movement are independent of the direction of the stimulus.

NERVOUS CO-ORDINATION

In the previous section we have discussed the various senses of the body through which we become aware of the changing environment around us. We mentioned that the sensory receptors were nerve cells and that they belonged to a special system of the body called the **nervous system**. The function of the nervous system is to interpret, co-ordinate and respond to the sensory impulses coming from the various parts of the body, to monitor the actions of the various parts and in general make certain that each part of the body is in as near perfect harmony as possible with every other part of the body. Without co-ordination in both space and time the human body would be nothing more than a collection of haphazardly functioning isolated organs, incapable of collective existence.

The nerve impulse

Communication between various parts of the body via the nervous system takes place by means of nerve impulses.

What is a nerve impulse?

A nerve impulse is an electrical phenomenon somewhat similar to the electric current we use to provide power for our machines. A simple electric current in a copper wire consists of a flow of electrons. A nerve impulse carried along a nerve fibre consists of waves of alterations of the charges along the surface of the nerve fibre.

How does a nerve impulse originate?

Fig.5.79 Wave of depolarization passing along nerve fibre

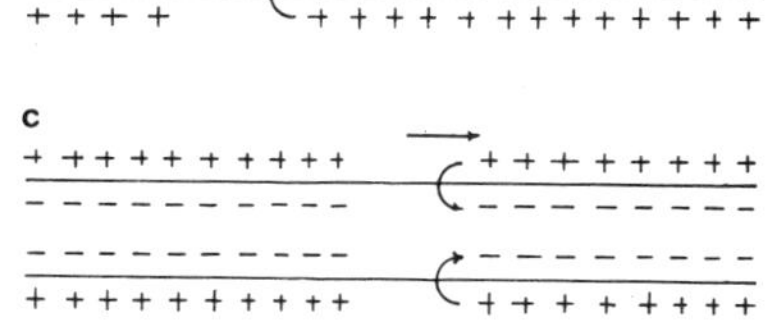

When at rest, that is, when not conducting an impulse, the outside membrane of a nerve fibre is positively charged while the inside is negatively charged. The nerve fibre in this state is said to be **polarized**. Certain chemical changes taking place in the interior of the cell are able to reverse this balance of charges and **depolarize** the cell membrane.
An appropriate stimulus can cause waves of depolarizations to pass along the length of a nerve fibre. The duration of the depolarized state in any one spot is only about one *milli-second* and the speed at which it travels is about one hundred metres per second.
As soon as the wave passes the normal polarized state of the membrane is restored and it is capable of carrying the next nerve impulse.

What happens when a nerve impulse reaches the end of a nerve fibre?

Adjacent nerve cells are able to communicate, that is, pass impulses from one to the other at a special junction called a **synapse**. The impulse is transmitted across the microscopic space of the synapse

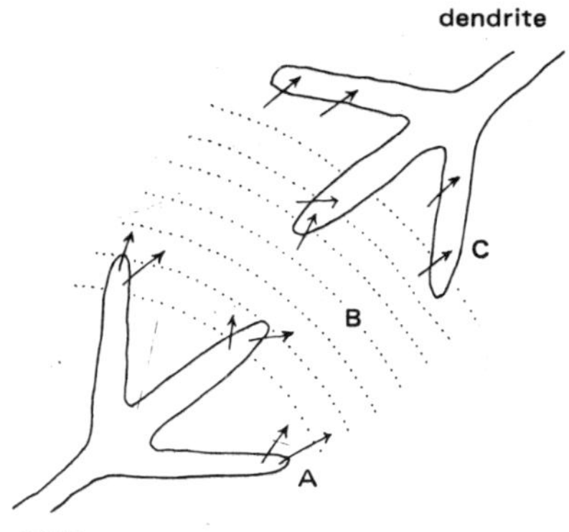

Fig.5.80

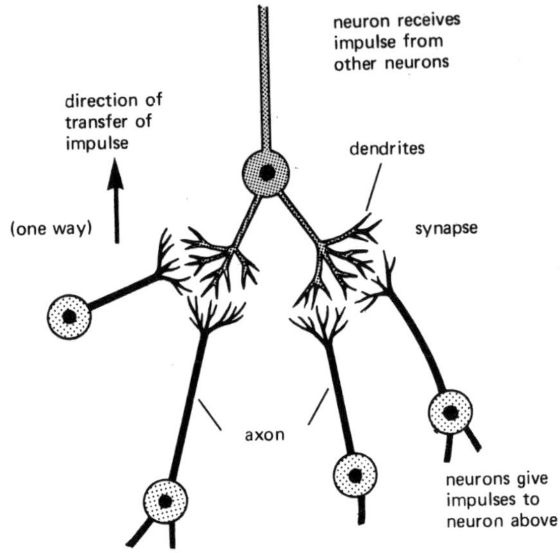

Fig.5.81 Synapses

by a chemical substance released from the axon ending of the cell that the impulse is coming from. This substance diffuses across the space to the dendrites of the adjacent cell.

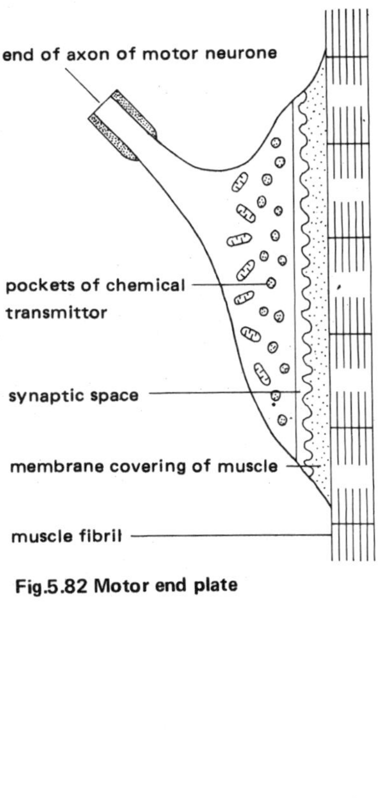

Fig.5.82 Motor end plate

Sensory impulses and motor impulses

Nerve impulses at the various sites around the body are initiated in response to sensory stimulation. These are carried by the afferent nerves to the central nervous system. Instructions from the central nervous system are transmitted back to the appropriate parts by way of the efferent or **motor neurons**. Motor neurons are essentially identical with sensory neurons except for the fact that the former do not have any specialized sensory endings. The junction of the motor neuron and the muscle to which it transmits its instructions is very similar to a synapse. The axon ending is equipped with a **motor end plate**. When a nerve impulse arrives at the end plate a chemical transmitter substance is released by the plate. This diffuses across a small gap to the muscle fibres and causes them to contract.

How are the various units of the nervous system integrated to form a coherent whole?

The term **central nervous system** (CNS) has already been mentioned several times but has not been defined precisely. As the name implies, the CNS is the main co-ordinator of the nervous system. The two components of the CNS are the brain and the spinal cord. The neural pathways connecting the rest of the body with the CNS are referred to as the **peripheral nervous system** (fig. 5.83).

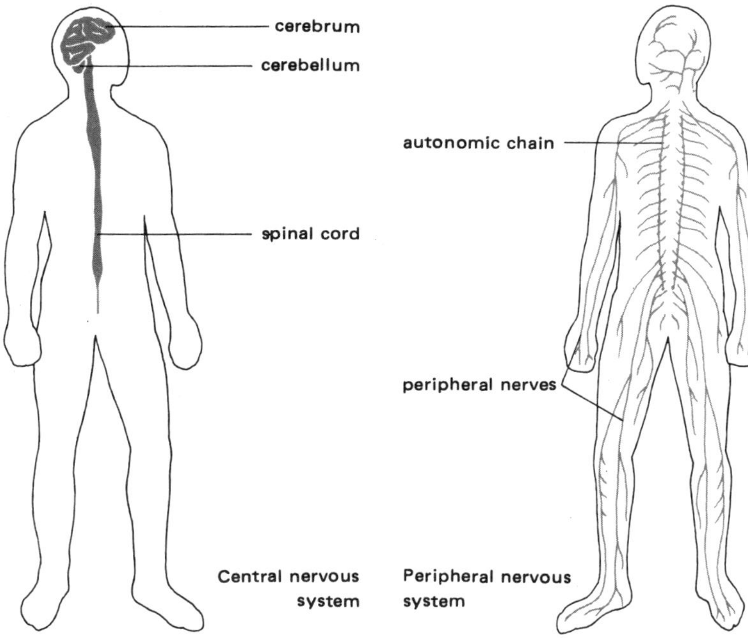

Fig.5.83 Principal divisions of the nervous system

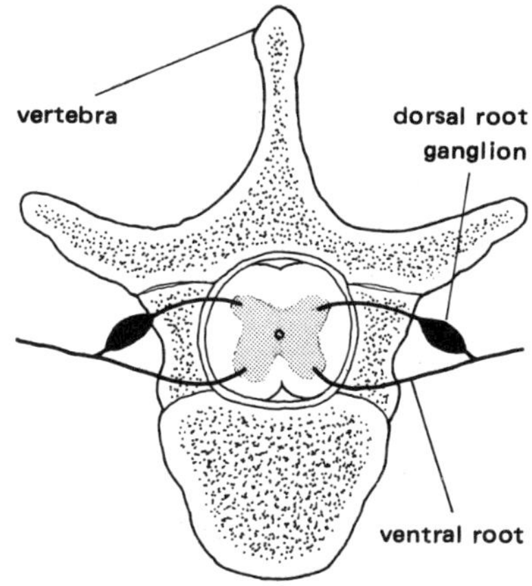

Fig.5.84 Spinal cord and backbone

The central nervous system

The spinal cord is enclosed within the neural canal of the vertebral column while the brain is encased inside the skull for protection. In addition, the tissues are covered by three separate layers of membrane called the **meninges**. The two inner layers are divided by a tiny space containing cerebrospinal fluid which helps to cushion

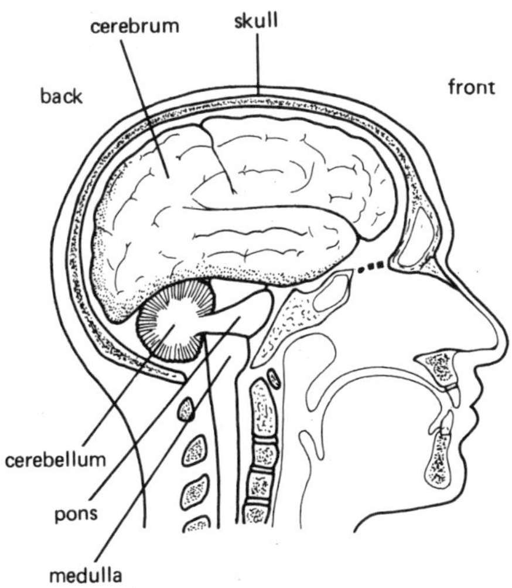

Fig. 5.85 Relationship of brain to skull and spine

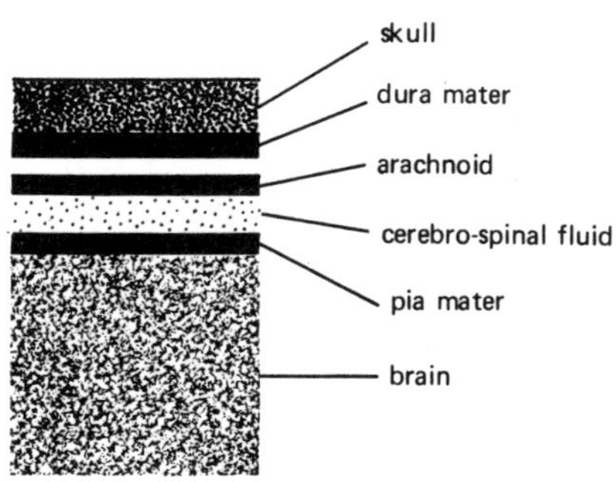

Fig.5.86 Protective layers of the brain

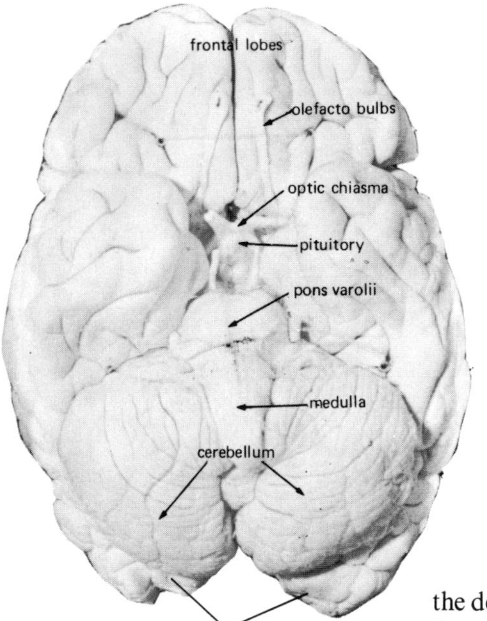

Fig.5.87 Ventral view of brain

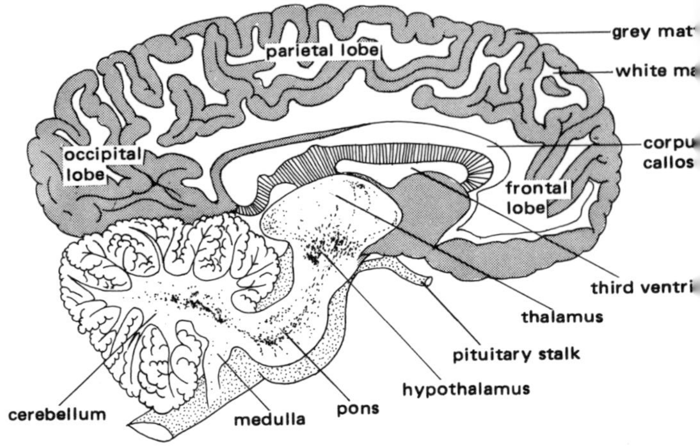

Fig.5.88 Parts of brain in section

the delicate tissues and facilitates the passage of oxygen and nutrients to the cells.

There are two types of nervous tissue found in the CNS, namely, **grey matter**, consisting of cell bodies of neurons and **white matter** made up of axons. The white colour of the tissue containing the axons is due to the presence of the protective **myelin sheaths.**

The brain

The brain is specialized for the enormous task of co-ordinating the activities of the entire body both on the level of conscious action and unconscious responses of the type we will refer to later.

The organ is divided into three sections called the **fore-**, **mid-**, and **hind-brain**. These are not actual structural divisions but serve for convenience in discussing the various parts.

THE FORE-BRAIN

The fore-brain includes the small, paired **olfactory lobes** that interpret sensations coming from the nose and the **cerebrum**.

The cerebrum is the largest single area of the brain. It consists of two cerebral hemispheres separated by a deep fissure[1]. The thin, outer cortex consists of grey matter, while the inner regions consist of white matter. The grey matter of the cortex contains several billion individual cells.

All conscious, voluntary activities connected with intelligence such as the ability to reason and to retain memories originate in this section of the brain.

Particular areas of the cerebral hemispheres are connected by

[1] *fissure*: opening

nervous pathways to different parts of the body for receiving sensory messages while other parts are the source of motor connections to diverse parts of the body.

Establishing the localization of the functions in the cerebrum is a difficult task and is by no means complete, although much information is already available. Fig. 5.89 shows the major sensory and motor centres in the cerebrum of a human. Information has been gained through animal experimentation, from the study of diseases that destroy parts of the brain and through the course of brain operations such as the removal of tumours.

A very interesting fact is that the two cerebral hemispheres have an inverse relationship with the two sides of the body, the right hemisphere controlling the left side and vice versa. In addition, sensations from the lower part of the body arrive at the top of the hemispheres and those from the upper part at the lower hemispheres. The two hemispheres are connected by a mass of white matter known as the **corpus callosum** located in the fissure between the two. It has been shown that up to a certain maximum level, intelligence is directly related to the brain size of an animal and in particular to the proportion of the brain made up by the cerebrum.

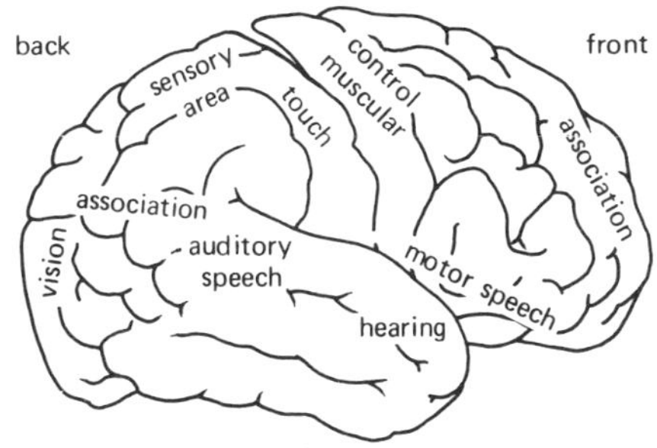

Fig. 5.89 **Localisation of function in cerebrum**

OTHER STRUCTURES IN THE FOREBRAIN

Other structures in the forebrain are the **pituitary gland** concerned with hormonal co-ordination (see p. 249) and the **thalamus** which controls such diverse activities as sleep, feeding, drinking, body temperature, osmoregulation and sexual behaviour.

THE MID-BRAIN

This is a very small area joining the fore- and hind-brains. Attached to it is the **pineal body** thought to be the remnant of a third eye that was once present in vertebrates. The **optic lobes**, below the thalami control the movements of the eyeballs and interpret the sensations of sight coming from the retina.

THE HIND-BRAIN

The hind-brain contains the **medulla oblongata**, the **cerebellum** and the **pons**. Paired nerves leading from the medulla to the pacemaker centres of the heart control the rate of heart beat. Other connections control the respiratory rate, and the constriction and dilation of blood vessels.

The cerebellum is responsible for the maintenance of posture, equilibrium and the co-ordination of the actions of individual muscles to produce complex activities such as walking, running and doing delicate work with the hands. The common symptoms of alcoholic intoxication result from the effects of alcohol on the cerebellum.

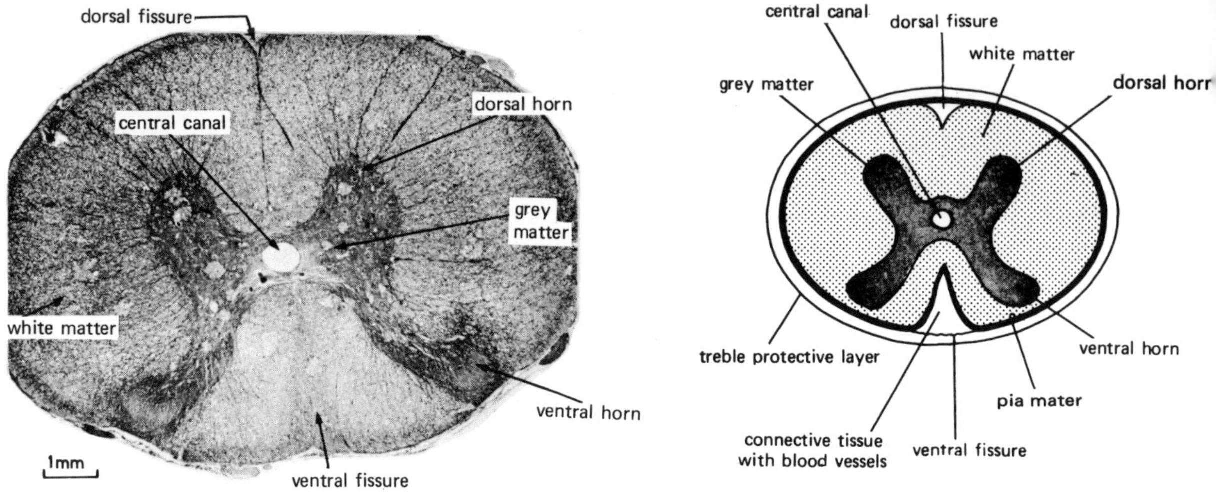

Fig.5.90 Photo and diagram of section of a spinal cord

The pons is a connecting area that is made up mainly of nerve fibres connecting the two halves of the cerebellum.

The spinal cord

The internal structure of the spinal cord is shown in fig. 5.90. The central canal is filled with **cerebrospinal fluid**. The distribution of grey matter and white matter is also shown diagrammatically. Paired spinal nerves join up with the spinal cord at regular intervals along its length. The point of junction of a nerve is called a **root**.
Each nerve has a **dorsal root** where the afferent nerves enter and a **ventral root** where the efferent nerves leave. Dorsal refers to the side of the spinal cord that is closest to the back.
After leaving the spinal cord the two roots join up to form a single mixed nerve.
The cell bodies of the sensory neurons are located in an oval thicken-

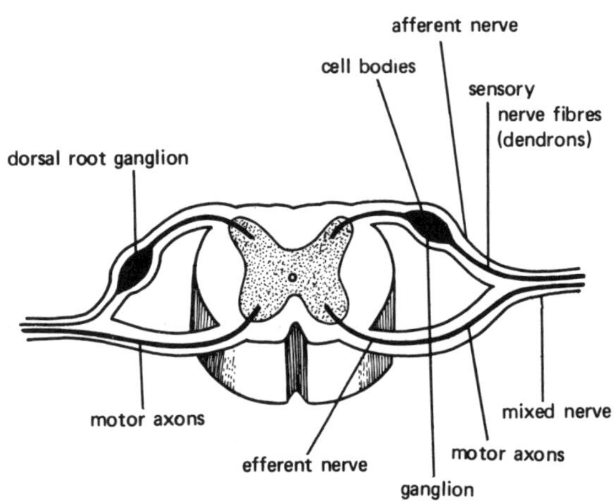

Fig.5.91 Connections of nerves to spinal cord

ing of the dorsal root called the **dorsal root ganglion**. From the ganglion the axons pass to the dorsal horns of the grey matter in the spinal cord. From there synaptic connections are made with the motor neurons in the ventral region through the **intermediate neurons**.

The reflex arc

The primary neural centre that all impulses in vertebrates travel to is the spinal cord, a continuous column of nervous tissue from the brain to the bottom of the backbone. In most cases impulses travel up the spinal cord to the appropriate reception centres in the brain. In some cases a response to a stimulus is initiated as soon as the impulse arrives at the spinal cord, before it even reaches the brain. This is called a reflex response and the pathway of nerve action is called the **reflex arc**.

What is the organisation of the reflex arc?

Fig. 5.93 is a diagrammatic representation with the arrows indicating the direction in which nerve impulses travel and fig. 5.92 is a schematic diagram of the reflex arc.

The sensory receptor detects a certain stimulus such as that of extreme heat when a finger comes in contact with a very hot object. In the spinal cord the information is passed on through an intermediary neuron to a motor neuron which transmits a message to the arm concerned to withdraw the finger from the hot object. At the same time the message travels along the spinal cord in both directions and to the brain. Along the way additional motor neurous might be stimulated to initiate a further reaction. For instance, not only might the arm be withdrawn from the hot object but the person might also take a quick step backwards if the sensory stimulus is strong enough. All these responses take place within a matter of split seconds. Even before the sensation of pain is consciously realized, that is, before the sensory message has arrived at the brain, the hand has already been withdrawn.

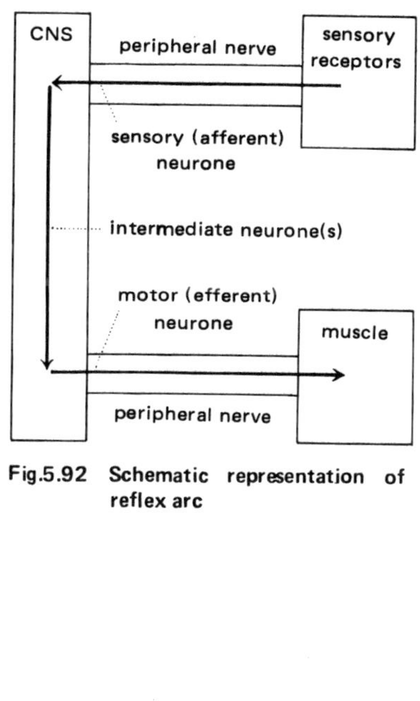

Fig.5.92 Schematic representation of reflex arc

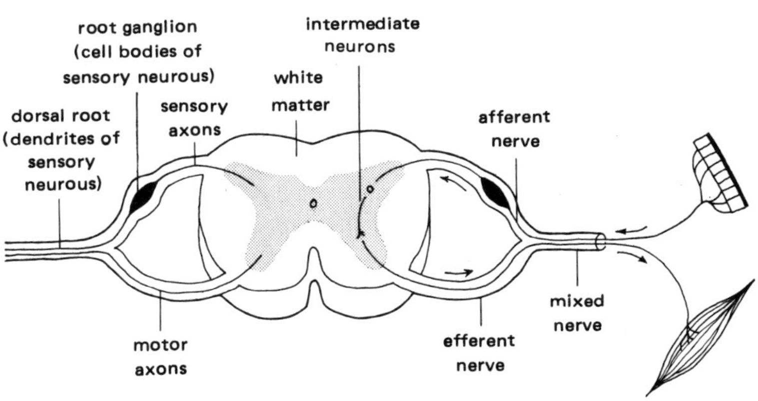

Fig.5.93 The reflex arc

Fig.5.94 Structure of sympathetic nervous system

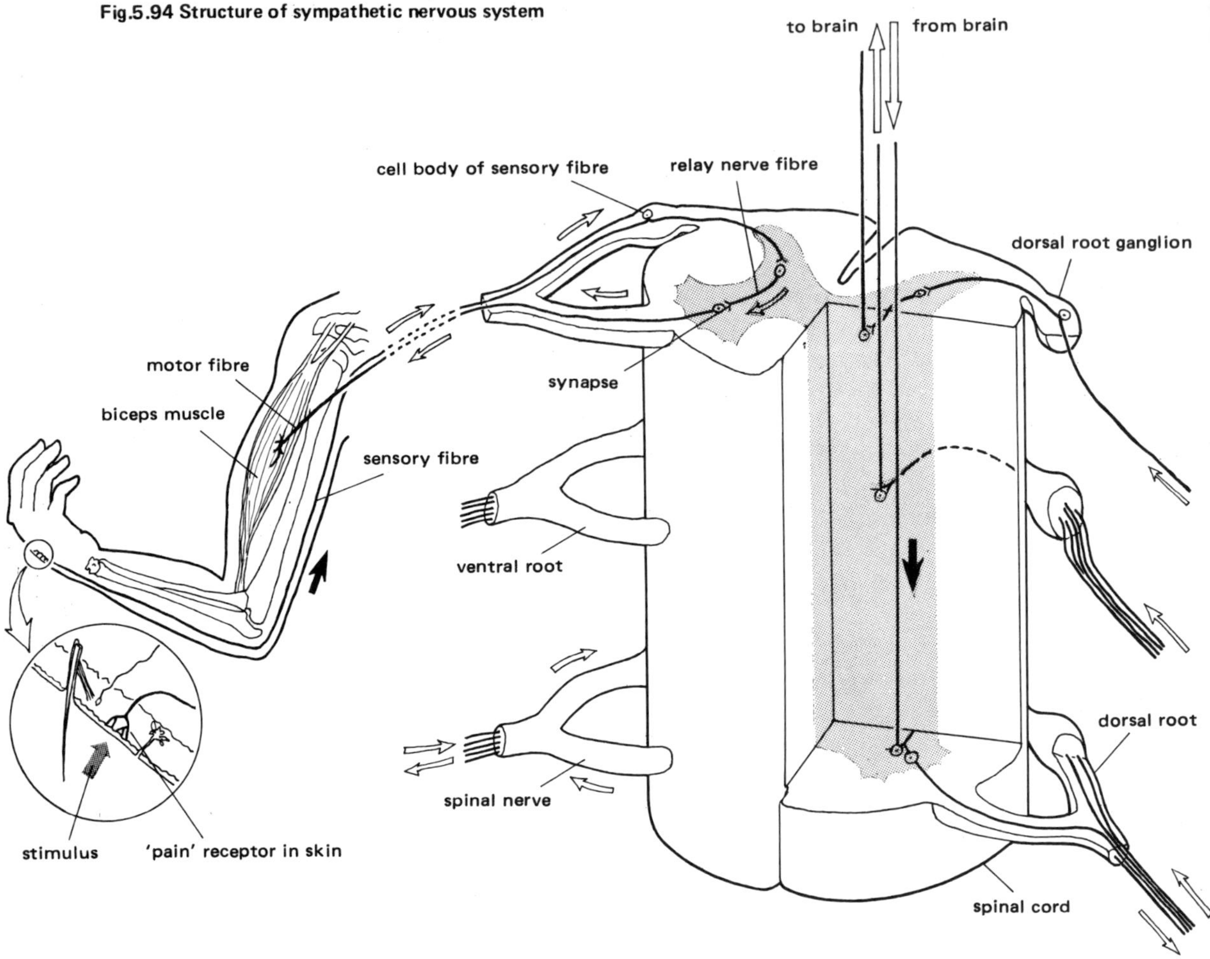

What are the advantages of reflex actions?

The most obvious advantage of the operation of the reflex arc is the speed with which responses are brought about and the fact that it takes no conscious effort of the will to mount the appropriate response. If a person were asleep at the time the response would take place just the same. Reflex actions of this type take place in all animals that have a central nervous system, not just in mammals. In most instances, especially if the sensory stimulus is not extremely strong, instructions from the brain can override the effects of the reflex arc. If you are carrying a hot liquid in a container, even though reflex action would cause you to drop the container the conscious control of the brain can cause you to keep on carrying it all the same.

Summary

Impulses are transmitted along the nerves by waves of depolarization passing along the membranes.
Impulses are transmitted across the gaps between adjacent nerve

cells and between motor neurons and muscles by a chemical transmitter substance.
The central nervous system consists of the brain and the spinal cord. The brain contains various sensory and motor areas that interpret sensory information and initiate motor responses. The spinal cord itself is able to initiate motor responses in answer to sensory stimulation. These are called reflex responses.

The peripheral nervous system

The peripheral nervous system is formed by the thirty-one pairs of **spinal nerves** and their branches that form a complicated nerve network that reaches all parts of the body.
At its proximal end, that is, close to the spinal cord, each nerve is a mixed nerve containing both afferent and efferent neurons. At the distal ends each mixed nerve splits into its sensory and motor components and connects the appropriate spots it is meant to service.

Cranial nerves

In addition to the spinal nerves, twelve pairs of **cranial nerves** arranged in an irregular pattern connect the brain to the head and neck regions, and a single cranial nerve called the **vagus nerve** connects to the abdominal region and the heart. Some of the cranial nerves form connections with the sense organs located in the head: the optic nerves to the eyes, the olfactory nerves to the nose, auditory nerves to the ears.
Motor nerves connect to the muscles responsible for speech, head movements, and facial expressions and so on. The cranial nerves cross over in the brain so that the right side of the head is serviced by the left cranial nerves.

Parts of the peripheral nervous system

On a functional basis the peripheral nervous system can be divided into two parts: the **voluntary** system and the **autonomic** system. The latter can be further subdivided into the **sympathetic** and the **parasympathetic**.

Voluntary nervous system

The part of the peripheral nervous system mediating conscious or voluntary actions is referred to as the voluntary nervous system. It is the voluntary nervous system that innervates all the skeletal muscles of the body (see p. 190) and is responsible for directing actions such as movements of the limbs, head, eyes and so on.

Autonomic nervous system

The system of nerves that controls the unconscious, involuntary activities of the body is the autonomic nervous system. It is composed of two largely antagonistic nerve networks called the **sympathetic** and the **parasympathetic systems.** Each contains both sensory and motor neurons and every organ of the body is supplied by both systems.

Structurally the sympathetic nervous system consists of a pair of nerve cords, the sympathetic tracts that run parallel to the spinal cord and originate from it by way of the mixed nerves. The nerve cords extend from the skull to the pelvis and have associated with them a series of **sympathetic ganglia** as shown in fig. 5.95. The ganglia contain the synapses between the sympathetic nerves from the spinal cord and the nerves serving the various organs.

Groups of nerve fibres from the ganglia pass through a structure called a **plexus**, a collection of cell bodies and synapses of the nerves that serve several organs with related functions. For example, all the nerves serving the digestive system pass through the **solar plexus** while the **cardiac plexus** contains nerves going to the heart and the lungs. The effects brought about by the action of the sympathetic nervous system are shown in fig. 5.96.

In general the system steps into prominence at times of excitement, danger or adverse environmental conditions such as extremes of temperature. At such times the functioning of the digestive and excretory systems are inhibited while heart rate, respiratory rate and blood flow are increased. The pupils become dilated, and lacrimal and salivary glands are stimulated. The aim is to prepare the body for strenuous physical activity in order to avoid whatever danger has been sensed.

The parasympathetic system is much simpler in its organization. Most of the fibres originate from four of the cranial nerves. Impulses to the body organs are carried by the **vagus nerve** and its branches and by branches arising from the lower section of the spinal cord.

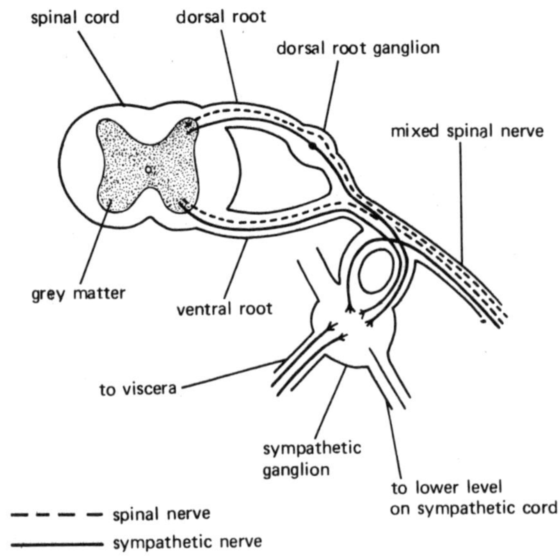

Fig.5.95

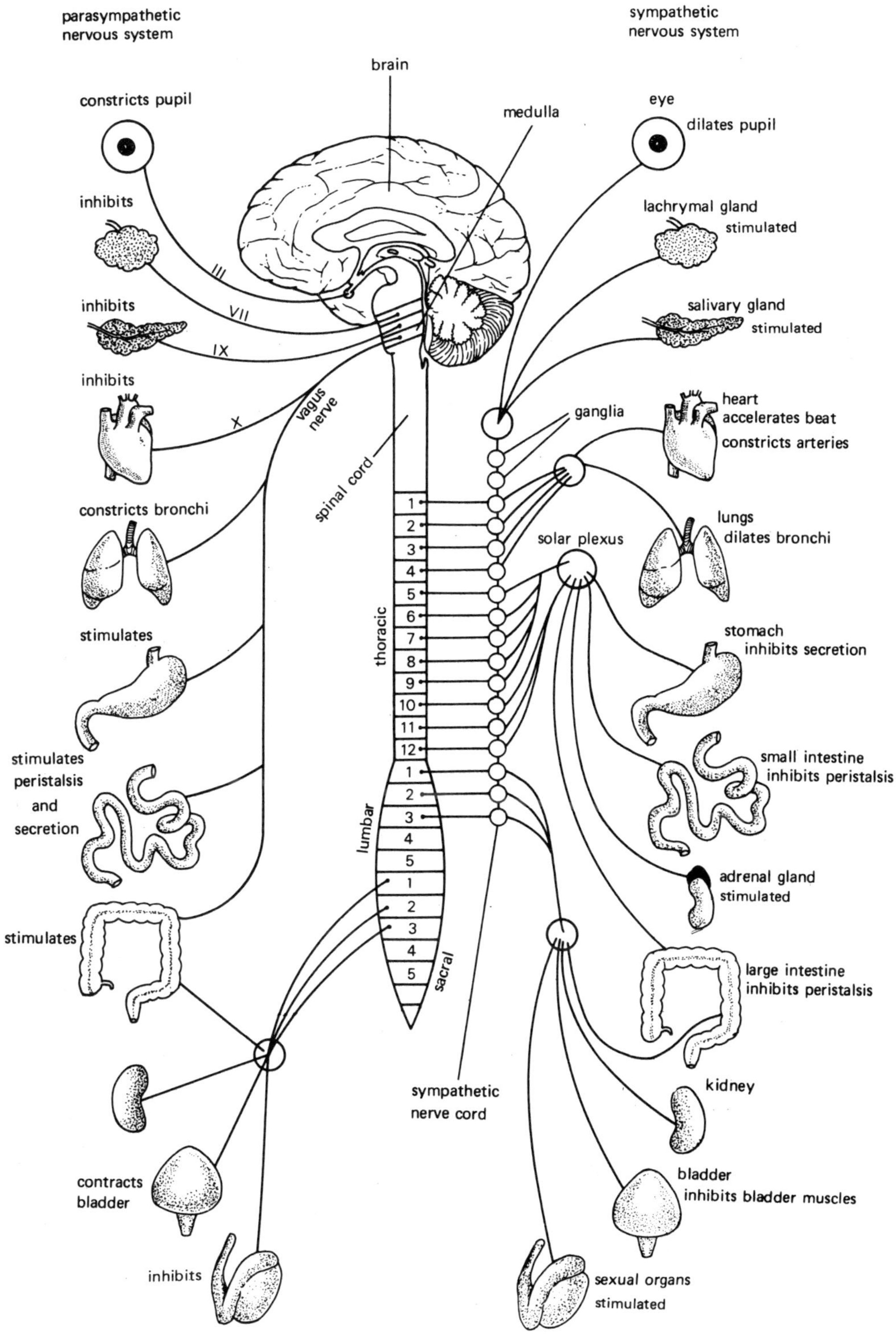

Fig.5.96 Autonomic nervous system

This system promotes the activity of the digestive system while moderating the action of the cardiovascular and respiratory systems. Its operation signals a time of rest and recuperation when the various processes of restoration and repair can take place.

How is the balance kept between the two systems?

Normally both the sympathetic and the parasympathetic systems operate simultaneously to keep heart rate, respiratory rate and the overall internal environment at a balanced level. In emergencies the sympathetic system steps up its activity while at times of rest such as in sleep the parasympathetic is the one in predominant control.
One final point should be made concerning the relationship between the various systems of nerves. Even though, for purposes of discussion we have regarded them as entirely separate from each other, in reality neurons belonging to the various systems frequently share the same mixed nerve fibres and travel from the spinal cord to the peripheral parts of the body by the same pathway. However, since they are connected to different parts of the brain and spinal cord, they bring about distinctly different effects. The neural transmitter substances for the two systems is also different and this eliminates interference between them.

Overall control by the brain

Although many of the activities of the body are unconscious, involuntary ones, the overall control of body activities still rests in the brain. Every single sensory input, as long as its intensity is above the minimum threshold, is transmitted to the brain to be sorted out and acted upon as required. However, we are consciously aware only of the sensory input that goes to the cerebral hemispheres but are unaware of nerve impulses travelling to other parts of the brain.
Even in the case of impulses to the cerebrum, under certain conditions sensations can be screened out from the consciousness. A very simple example is when you are reading an extremely interesting book you will often be completely unaware of music playing over the radio or someone calling you. The brain is concentrating all its conscious faculties on the book and even though the ear is functioning normally the messages sent to the brain by way of the auditory nerve are screened from the consciousness because at that moment they are only secondary in importance.

Summary

The peripheral nervous system consists of the cranial nerves and the spinal nerves.
Voluntary actions are mediated by the voluntary nervous system serving the skeletal muscles.

The autonomic nervous system, mediating all involuntary actions is divided into the sympathetic and the parasympathetic parts. The sympathetic steps into action in times of danger and stress while the parasympathetic operates in times of rest and recuperation. The overall direction of all nervous responses both sensory and motor is the brain.

CHEMICAL CO-ORDINATION

The preceeding section has emphasized the great importance of nervous co-ordination of the activities of the body in order to ensure that the organism as a whole functions smoothly and efficiently. An equally important need is the control of the chemical processes of the organism to ensure that there is harmony between the various parts of the body as far as metabolic activity is concerned. In both plants and higher animals chemical co-ordination is achieved through the action of special substances called **hormones**.

The endocrine system and hormones in animals

By definition a hormone is a chemical substance produced in one part of the organism that affects the actions of the cells in a different part. The organs producing the hormones are called the **endocrine glands** and the entire system is called the **endocrine system**.
An endocrine gland is a structure which synthesizes and secretes the substance it makes directly into the blood stream to be distributed throughout the body. All the chemicals synthesized by endocrine glands are considered to be hormones.
In addition there are other glands called **exocrine glands**. These secrete the chemical substance that they synthesize into a duct to be delivered to a definite location. The glands secreting the digestive enzymes are all exocrine glands. (See p. 75.)

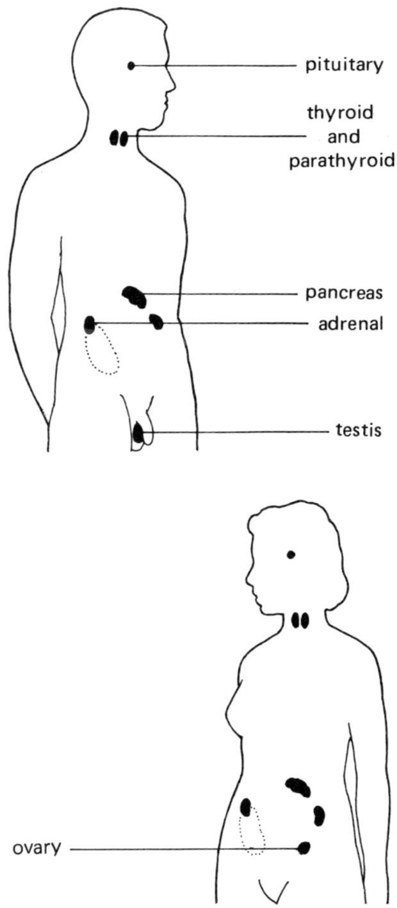

Fig.5.97 Principal endocrine organs of vertebrates

What are the principal endocrine organs in the human body?

Fig. 5.97 shows the locations of these various glands in humans. The most important hormone secretory gland of the body is the **pituitary gland**. It is located under the middle section of the brain and is connected to the hypothalamus (see p. 241).
The gland is divided into the **anterior pituitary** and the **posterior pituitary**. During embryonic life the two sections develop separately and later fuse to form a single organ. The anterior pituitary secretes a group of hormones referred to as the **tropic hormones**. These hormones are carried by the blood stream to specific **target organs** where they in turn induce the production of yet another hormone.
The process can be illustrated by taking the example of **thyrotropic hormone**. The thyrotropic hormone synthesized in the pituitary is released into the circulation and carried to all parts of the body.

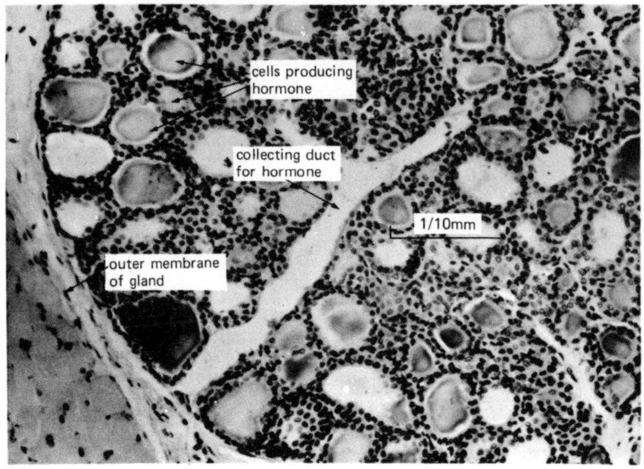

Fig. 5.98 Thyroid gland

The specific effect of the hormone, however, is only felt on the target organ itself, in this case the **thyroid gland**.

The thyroid gland consists of two lobes of tissue on either side of the larynx and its function is the secretion of the hormone **thyroxin** which regulates the basal metabolic rate of the body. An increase in the level of thyrotropic hormone in the circulation is sensed by the thyroid gland and is interpreted as an instruction to increase the rate of production of thyroxin. A decrease in the level of thyrotropic hormone is a signal to decrease the rate of thyroxin production.

How does the pituitary gland regulate the production of thyrotropic hormone?

Fig.5.99 Regulation of metabolic rate

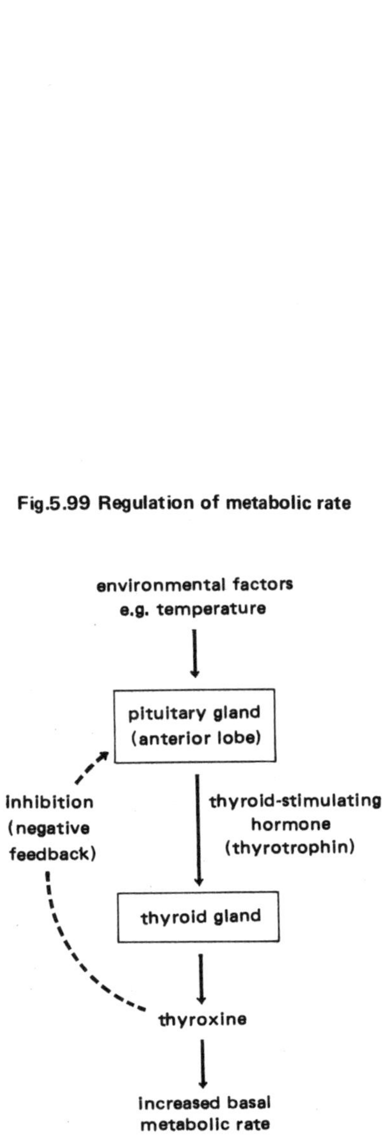

The activity of the anterior pituitary is controlled by the hypothalamus of the brain. The brain is constantly monitoring both the external and internal environment of the body and on the basis of the information it receives it establishes a certain set-point for the metabolic rate.

Both the centres of the hypothalamus and the anterior pituitary also monitor the level of thyroxin in the blood. If the level is too low to achieve the desired metabolic rate the hypothalamus sends a specific **releasing factor** to the pituitary telling it to secrete more thyrotropic hormone. The tropic hormone in turn increases the production of thyroxin which then increases the metabolic rate. As soon as the level of thyroxin has reached the desired set-point secretion of tropic hormone ceases. The process is a more sophisticated form of the negative feedback system that you are already familiar with. It is shown diagrammatically in fig. 5.99.

Abnormalities in thyroxin production

Since one of the chemical components of thyroxin is iodine, insufficient dietary iodine can lead to irregularities in thyroxin production. In an effort to produce adequate amounts of thyroxin in response to the instructions of the tropic hormone the thyroid gland greatly enlarges producing a characteristic swelling called a **goitre**. Since the problem lies not with the inadequacies of the cells themselves but with the supplies of iodine this attempt by the body to put things right is completely futile. The condition can easily be corrected by administration of iodine. In most countries today the use of *iodized* table salt ensures an adequate intake of iodine.

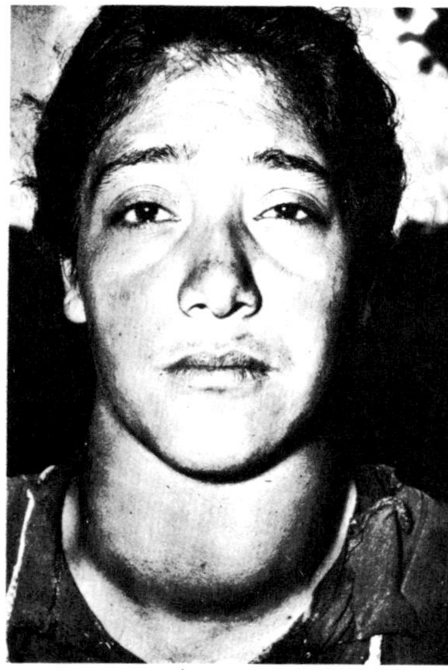

Fig.5.100 Patient with goitre

Defects in the feedback system resulting in the release of insufficient amounts of thyrotropic hormone can have much more serious results. Since the metabolic rate of the body indirectly controls the rate of growth, abnormally low thyroxin levels in children will lead to a condition called **cretinism** characterised by stunted growth both mentally and physically.

In adults the condition is termed **myxoedema** and involves the lowering of the heart rate and body temperature, puffiness of the face and eyelids and a general weakness and lethargy.

Both cretinism and myxoedema can be treated by the administration of thyroxin by mouth.

Overactivity of the thyroid gland causes a corresponding increase in metabolic rate. Heart rate increases and body temperature rises so that the skin becomes hot and sweaty and the patient is generally highly excitable and usually unable to sleep. **Thyrotoxicosis**, as the condition is called, can be caused by overactivity of the anterior pituitary or hypothalamus or as a result of a tumour in the thyroid gland itself.

What other hormones does the anterior pituitary secrete?

The anterior pituitary produces two other tropic hormones namely **adrenocorticotropic hormone** controlling the activities of the **adrenal glands** and **gonadotropic hormone** regulating the release of sex hormones by the ovaries in females and the testes in males.

The anterior pituitary is also responsible for the secretion of **growth hormone**. This hormone has no specific target organ but acts to promote growth all over the body. Insufficient growth hormone in the early stages of life leads to a condition known as **pituitary dwarfism** characterised by very short stature but normal mental development. Oversecretion leads to excessive growth, that is, **gigantism**.

The anterior pituitary also secretes **lactogenic hormone** to stimulate milk production by the mammary glands after the birth of a baby.

The posterior pituitary secretes **oxytocin**, the hormone responsible for the uterine contractions necessary to bring about the birth of a baby. Fig. 5.101 summarizes the actions of the various pituitary hormones. As in the case of thyrotropic hormone, the synthesis of other pituitary hormones is also regulated by releasing factors from the hypothalamus.

Fig.5.101

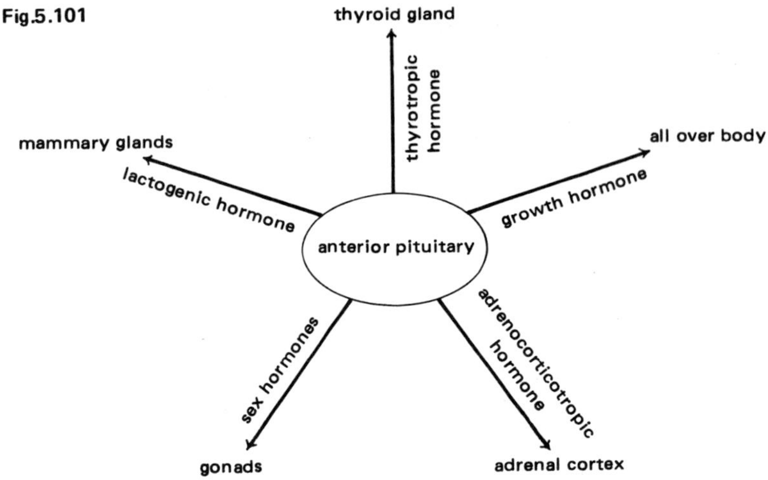

The adrenal glands

The adrenal glands are located just above the kidneys on either side of the body and are about the size of a large bean. The outer part of the gland, the **cortex**, secretes several hormones that control the metabolism of various organic nutrients and the preferential retention of some salts in the body. The actions of these hormones are so vital for health that destruction of the adrenal cortex quickly leads to death.

The inner region known as the **medulla** is under the control of the sympathetic nervous system and secretes a hormone called **adrenalin**. It is the hormone adrenalin that brings about all the characteristic effects of the sympathetic nervous system such as an increase in heart rate, dilation of the pupils and so on in response to external or internal stress. Adrenalin also speeds up the conversion of glycogen stores to glucose in the liver to ensure that adequate energy resources are available for the cells of the body in such times of danger.

Table 5.1 is a summary of the endocrine organs of the body and the hormones they secrete. Some of the hormones included in the table have not been specifically discussed in the text. For a discussion of the action of insulin see p. 162 under the heading of homeostatic mechanisms.

Summary

Chemical co-ordination achieved by the action of hormones in animals functions in parallel with and sometimes in conjunction with nervous co-ordination.

While the latter is directed mainly towards the control of muscular activities hormones exert a vital controlling influence on the metabolic activities of the body. They act as chemical messengers synthesized in response to particular stimuli and carried to their

Table 5.1 Endocrine glands and their related hormones

GLAND	HORMONES	CHIEF FUNCTIONS	EFFECTS OF DEFICIENCY OR EXCESS
pituitary, anterior lobe	thyrotropic	stimulates thyroid	
	adrenocorticotropic	stimulates adrenal cortex	
	gonadotropic	stimulates ovary (follicle) stimulates testes in male, corpus luteum in female	
	lactogenic	stimulates milk secretion, parental behavior	
	growth	promotes cell metabolism	dwarfism; gigantism
pituitary, posterior	at least five distinct fractions	controls water metabolism, blood pressure, kidney function, smooth-muscle action	increased or reduced water excretion
thyroid	thyroxine	stimulates respiration; inhibits TTH secretion	goiter; cretinism; myxedema
parathyroid	parathormone	controls Ca metabolism	nerve, muscle abnormalities; bone thickening or weakening
adrenal cortex	cortisone, other steroid hormones	controls metabolism of water, minerals, carbohydrates; controls kidney function; duplicates sex-hormone functions	Addison's disease
adrenal medulla	adrenaline	alarm reaction, for example, raises blood pressure, heart rate	inability to cope with stress
pancreas	insulin	glucose → glycogen conversion	diabetes
testis	testosterone, other androgens	promote cell respiration, blood circulation; maintain primary and secondary sex characteristics, sex urge;	atrophy of reproductive system; decline of secondary sex characteristics
ovary:	estrogens progesterone	promotes secretions of oviduct, uterus growth in pregnancy;	abortion during pregnancy

sites of action through the circulation.

All vertebrates have a distinct endocrine system no matter how simple. Among invertebrates only arthropods possess specific hormone-secreting cells.

Chemical co-ordination in plants

Plants do not have the benefit of the complex nervous system that most animals possess. Co-ordination of the activities of the various groups of cells and responses to the environment therefore have to be achieved entirely by chemical means, through the action of the plant hormones. Three groups of substances called **auxins**, **gibberellins** and **kinins** constitute the main hormones found in plants.

Of these the first to be identified and perhaps the most significant are the auxins.

How were auxins discovered?

The effects of auxins were first observed by Charles Darwin in the course of his study of the responses of plants to light. By covering the growing tips of plants with light-proof paper he was able to demonstrate that the light-sensitive area of a plant stem was not the part where the actual bending towards the light took place but it was the growing tip. Darwin's experiment is shown diagrammatically in fig. 5.102. The plants whose tips are covered do not bend in response to light whereas the uncovered ones do.

Later experiments showed that if the tip of a seedling was cut off, again no bending took place. If the tip was cut off then replaced with a layer of gelatin interposed between the stem and the tip the response was unimpaired. If the cut tip was attached to the plant not at the tip but along one side of the stem as shown in fig. 5.103 bending occurred at the point of contact even if the plant was kept in the dark.

These and other experiments led to the conclusion that the response to light known as phototropism was caused by the migration of a chemical substance from the tip of the plant down the stem. The chemical substance is a growth-promoting hormone. If one side of the stem receives more hormone than the other the first side will grow more quickly resulting in the bending of the stem.

What is the precise mechanism of the phototropic response?

A particular type of auxin is synthesized by plant tips in response to exposure to light. However, even though it is produced in response to light, its effect is somehow inhibited by light. The auxin migrates down all sides of the plant at a uniform rate but its action is less effective on the side of the stem that faces the source of light. Growth will therefore be more rapid on the side away from the light, resulting in bending of the shoot towards the light. (See fig. 5.104.)

Fig.5.102 Darwin's experiments

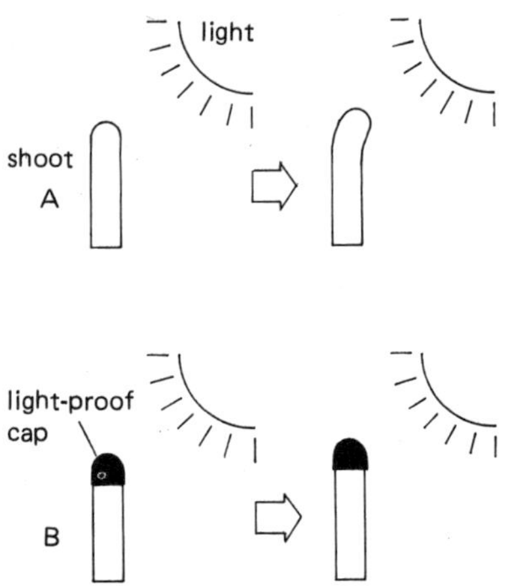

Fig.5.103

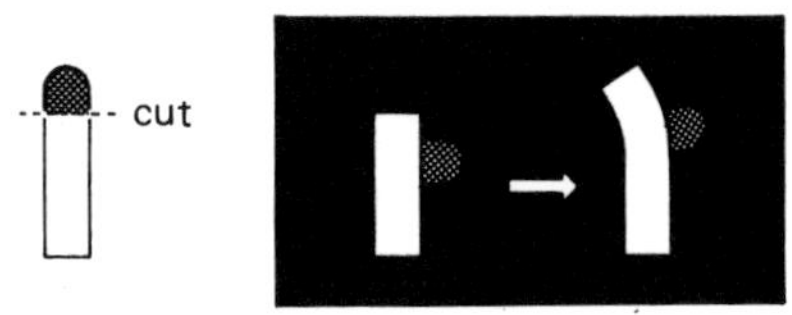

Fig.5.104

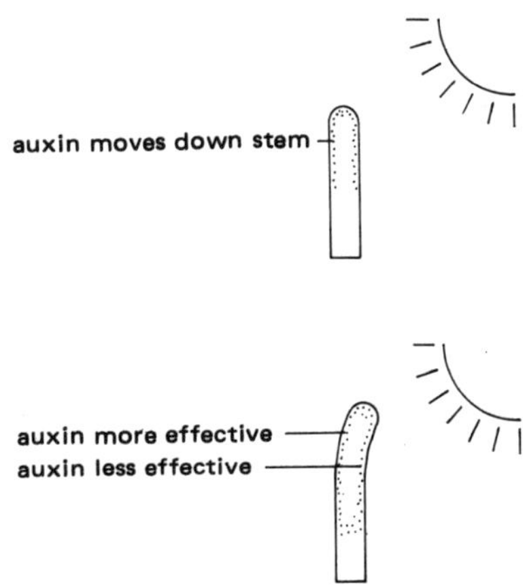

Geotropism (see p.232) can also be explained on the basis of hormone action. Due to the action of gravity on the young seedling auxin tends to accumulate on the lower side rather than on the upper side of the central axis. In fig. 5.105 the shaded areas represent the presence of auxin.

The presence of auxin on the lower portion of the stem will cause more rapid growth on that side resulting in an upward curvature of the stem.

Curiously enough, it has been demonstrated experimentally that auxin inhibits the growth of roots. Root growth will therefore be more rapid on the side containing no auxin. The total effect will be a downward curvature of the root.

The precise metabolic mechanism by which this paradoxical action of plant auxin is achieved is not known.

Fig. 5.105

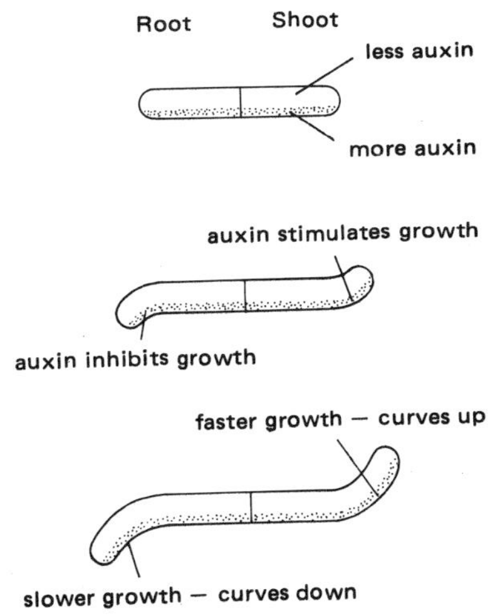

Do auxins produce any other effects?

In addition to their role in promoting photo- and geotropism auxins have many other effects. Auxins produced by the apical bud[1] of a plant inhibit the formation of side branches from the lateral buds immediately below. Side branches will readily develop if the apical bud is removed. If, however, auxin is applied to the lateral buds again no side branches will grow. This phenomenon is known as **apical dominance**.

In association with other plant hormones auxins play a role in the ripening of fruit, in the initiation of secondary growth (see p. 267) and they promote the growth of adventitious roots.

Where are auxins produced?

Auxins are produced by all the actively growing regions of the plant including shoot tips and the cambia. Specialised hormone-secreting organs such as those found in animals are absent in plants.

What is the significance of the other types of plant hormone?

Gibberellins are concerned with elongation of the main stem. Dwarf varieties of certain plants such as peas are thought to be the result of a genetically inherited deficiency of gibberellins. Unlike auxins these hormones are not associated in any way with the tropic responses of plants.

Kinins are important for their role in promoting cell division. They are able to do this only in conjunction with certain auxins.

The concentrations in which a particular plant hormone is present in the plants are very critical. The same hormone may exert quite widely differing influences depending on the concentrations

[1] *apical bud*: the bud at the top of the main stem

involved. Excessive amounts of hormone can easily lead to the death of the plant.

Summary

Plant hormones play a vital role in promoting the growth of plants and controlling their responses to environmental factors such as light and gravity.
In many instances the combined action of at least two hormones is needed to bring about a particular effect.

SPECIAL ASPECTS OF ANIMAL BEHAVIOUR

In previous sections we have looked at some of the ways in which animals are made aware of the environment around them, the way they move, ingest food and so on. All these can be considered as aspects of the behaviour of an animal. In this section we will consider some special types of behaviour.

Social organization

As a rule individuals of a given animal species have little contact with one another except for their association during and immediately after the breeding season. There are exceptions of course and one of the more interesting of these is the high degree of social organization found among some species of insect, referred to as the **social insects**.
Honey bees live in elaborate colonies where each individual has a certain function, a certain job to perform, depending on its age and **caste**. The term caste refers to the different types of individual that can be distinguished on the basis of both physical appearance and function.
The laying of the eggs is the sole responsibility of the **queen**, the only fertile female of the colony. The eggs are fertilized by sperms from the **drones**, the fertile males.
A queen usually mates only once in her lifetime. Sperms are transferred from the drone to the sperm sac of the queen where they are stored until needed for fertilizing the eggs.
Over ninety-nine percent of the members of the colony belong to the caste of **workers**, whose duties include gathering of food, caring for the developing larvae and keeping the hive in order. The workers are sterile females. They possess special adaptations for collecting pollen and nectar and special glands that secrete food substances for feeding the larvae, the queen and the drones.

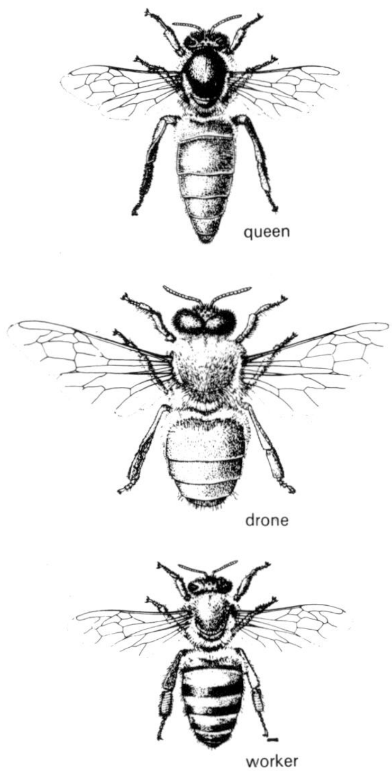

Fig.5.106 Types of honey bee

How do these various castes arise?

Fertilized eggs laid by the queen can develop into either new queens or workers. The crucial difference is the food that the larvae

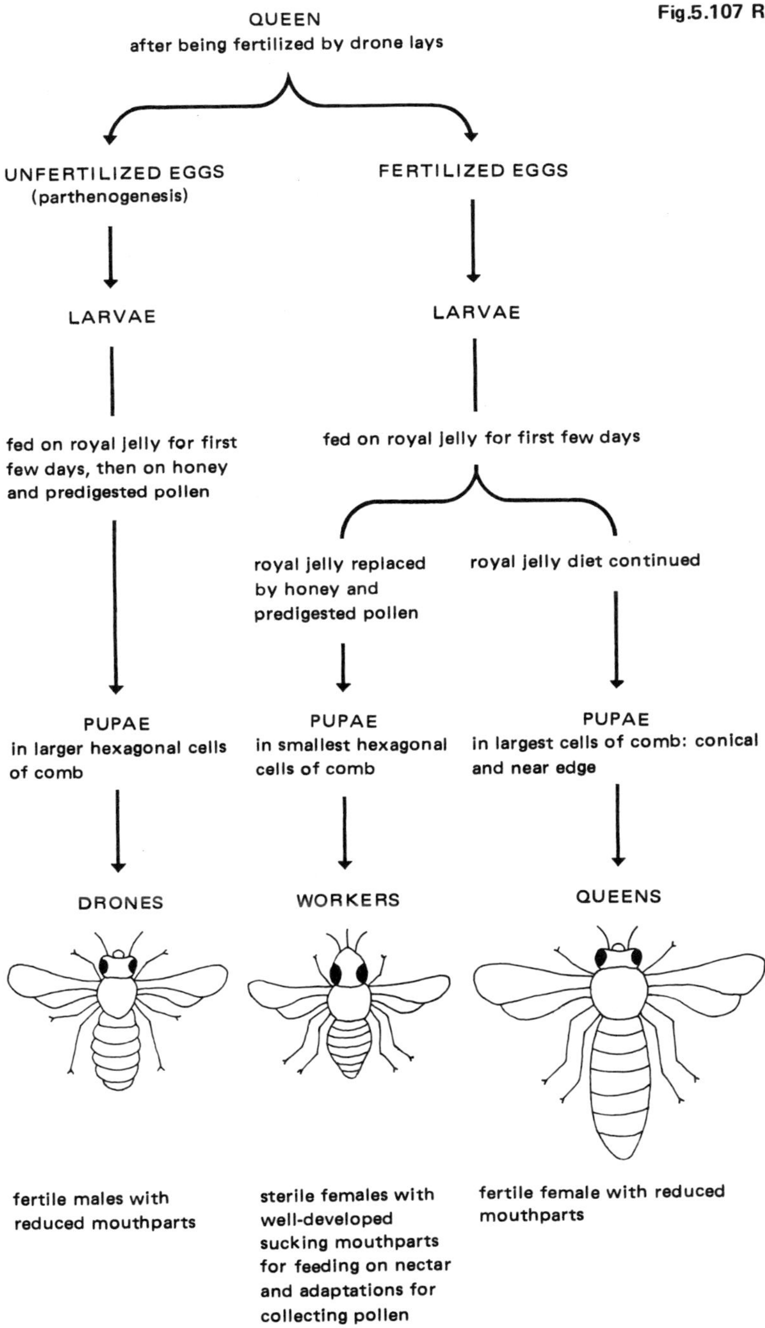

Fig.5.107 Reproduction in honey bee

are given to eat. The ones destined to be queens (usually five or six) are fed on a special substance called **royal jelly** while those destined to be workers are fed on honey mixed with predigested pollen. As yet scientists have not been able to explain how a difference in diet can help to bring about such a marked difference in physical characteristics and instinctive behaviour such as that existing between the honey bee queen and worker.

The first queen to emerge from its larval form kills off all her competitors. If there is already a fertile queen in the colony the new queen will fly off with some of the members of the colony to establish a new hive. She mates with one of the drones and begins her reproductive duties. In addition to laying fertilized eggs the queen also lays unfertilized ones that develop into the drones (parthenogenesis, see p. 282).
The drones are the free loaders of the colony, for apart from the one that succeeds in mating with the queen they serve no useful function. Among most species of bee, therefore, the drones are driven out of the hive at the end of each summer and new ones are reared for the next year. Social organization of this type is also found in many species of ant and termite.

Social behaviour in higher mammals

Among higher mammals interactions between individuals are more elaborate. Whereas among the social insects roles are rigidly defined and emphasized by an actual physical difference, among mammals roles are much less rigid. In many instances roles are established on a temporary basis, the most powerful individual of a group being the leader and the others subordinate to him only until he is over-powered by another stronger than himself. Division of labour frequently occurs but again only on a temporary basis. The most advanced and most flexible form of social behaviour is, of course, found among human beings.

Migration

One of the most unusual and fascinating animal habits is that of **migration**.
Some species of bird that nest in the temperate regions of Europe and North America migrate to the southern hemisphere for the winter. Eggs are laid and the nestlings are reared in the north between April and September. During the last few days of September these birds gather in large groups and begin their journey of several thousand miles to the southern hemisphere for the southern summer. It is believed that the migratory habit evolved due to lack of food during the winter months in the colder regions of the northern hemisphere. The immediate cause of migration is the secretion of a certain hormone by the sexual organs of the birds. With the arrival of colder weather in the southern hemisphere the birds return to their summer breeding grounds.

Migration among fish

Long-distance migratory journeys are also undertaken by certain species of fish either for the purpose of feeding or of reproduction.

The Atlantic salmon (*Salmo salar*) spawns[1] in the freshwater rivers and streams along the northern Atlantic coast. The young stay in the breeding grounds for a number of years, then swim down to the sea and live a marine existence for a variable number of years. Eventually they return to the same stream in which they themselves have hatched, mate and the females lay their eggs. Their migratory journey may be two thousand miles long or more.

Little is known about the navigational methods of the salmon but it is believed that once they reach the coastal waters it is their sense of smell that aids them in locating the correct stream.

After mating and spawning in most species of salmon all the males and most of the females die. The females that survive return to the sea and may come back to spawn again several years later.

Summary

A very special form of interaction occurs between members of some species of insects, called the social insects. Various castes in a colony have different functions and are distinguishable on the basis of their appearance. A more flexible form of interaction occurs in higher mammals. Another interesting aspect of behaviour in some animals is that of migration. Examples are the migration of birds to the south for the winter and the migration of some fish back to their original spawning grounds for the purposes of breeding.

[1] *spawning*: the action of laying eggs by fish or frogs

Section 6. GROWTH AND REPRODUCTION

GROWTH AND DEVELOPMENT

By definition **growth** is the increase in the amount of living material in an organism. This may be due to an increase in the number of cells or the size of individual cells or the combination of the two.
A very special feature of growth is the **differentiation** of cells and organs to enable them to perform specialized functions. In fact, in multicellular organisms a mere increase in the size or number of cells would not contribute to true growth if the cells were all to remain in an immature, unspecialized state.

Mitosis

Increase in the number of cells is achieved through the process of cell division called **mitosis**.

EXPERIMENT TO OBSERVE MITOSIS

Note: the staining procedure for this experiment is a little time consuming and is best done by your teacher or a small group of more interested students.
Materials
onion bulb
saturated solution of p-dichlorobenzene
1 N Hydrochloric acid
two percent aceto-orcein solution
microscope, slides, coverslips
Method
1. Fill a 250cm^3-beaker with water nearly to the top and balance the onion bulb over the mouth, using toothpicks, so that only the bottom of the bulb is immersed in water.
2. Place in a dark spot for several days until roots begin to grow.
3. Cut off about half-centimetre lengths from the root tips with a razor and place in the p-dichlorobenzene for three hours at 12°C to 16°C. You can maintain this temperature by keeping the tube of solution in a container of cold water.
4. Transfer to a pyrex tube containing a mixture of aceto-orcein and hydrochloric acid in the ratio of 9:1.
5. Heat to boiling, pour into a shallow dish and allow to cool.
6. After cooling place individual root tips on glass slides and put a drop of one percent aceto-orcein on top of each.
7. Cut off the deeply coloured tip of the root and discard the rest.
8. Put on the coverslip and press against the slide to squash the

Fig.6.1

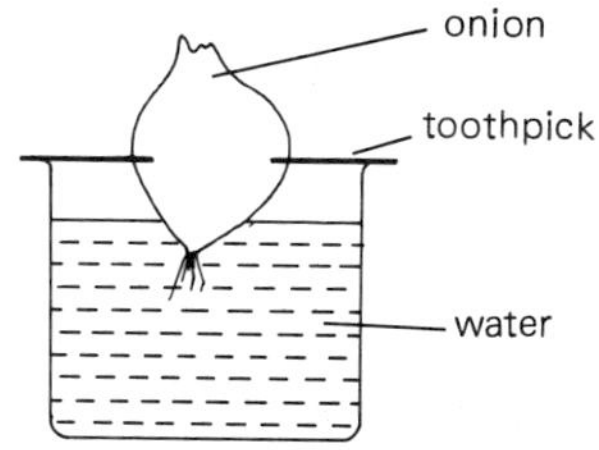

root tip. Remove the excess stain by blotting with a piece of filter paper.

9. Examine first at low then at high power under the microscope.

What do you see?
Can you spot rod-like structures in the nuclei of the cells?
Do the nuclei of the cells all look the same or are there differences?
Make simple drawings of as many different arrangements as possible.

Discussion

The threadlike structures that you see in the cell nuclei are the **chromosomes**. Encoded along their length is the set of instructions or 'blue-print' that regulates all the processes of the cell. Normally individual chromosomes cannot be seen under the light microscope because they are stretched out in a fine thread in the nucleus. During cell division the nuclear membrane disappears and the chromosomes coil up to form compact, rod-shaped structures that are easier to see.

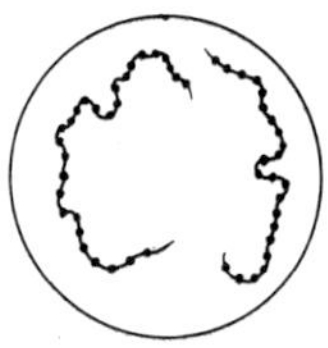

Fig.6.2 Diploid cell with one pair of chromosomes

What is the sequence of events occurring in mitosis?

Cell division is a smooth continuous process. However, for study purposes it is convenient to isolate a few individual phases much the same way as one can pick out individual pictures by stopping a movie film while it is being projected.

During the normal resting stage of the cell **(interphase)** certain preparations are already being made if the cell is to undergo division.

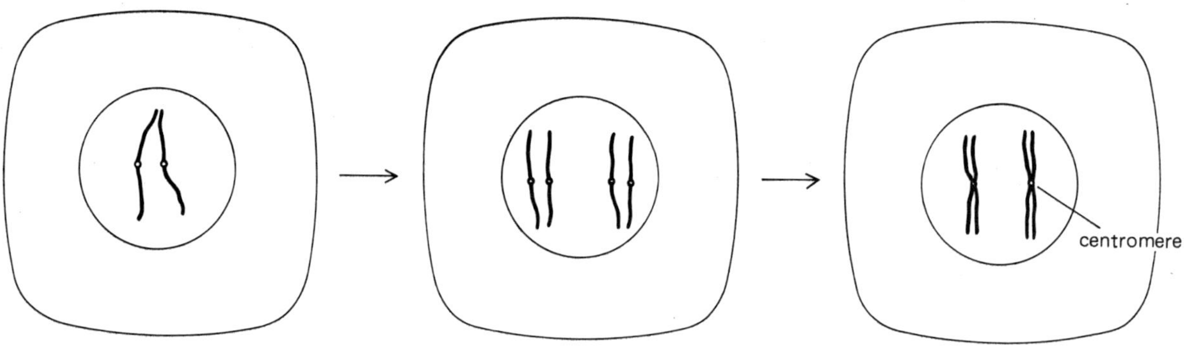

Fig.6.3 Chromosome duplication and joining of identical pairs of chromosomes

First of all chromosome replication takes place, that is, each chromosome of the cell directs the formation of a new chromosome exactly like itself, thereby doubling the usual chromosome number of the cell. The cell stores up enough energy to carry it through the process of cell division that can take anything from ten minutes to several hours. Also during this phase new cytoplasmic organelles such as mitochondria and chloroplasts are made so that after division there will be a certain minimum number in each new cell.

During the next stage **(prophase)** the chromosomes become even more coiled and the identical pairs of **sister chromatids** become

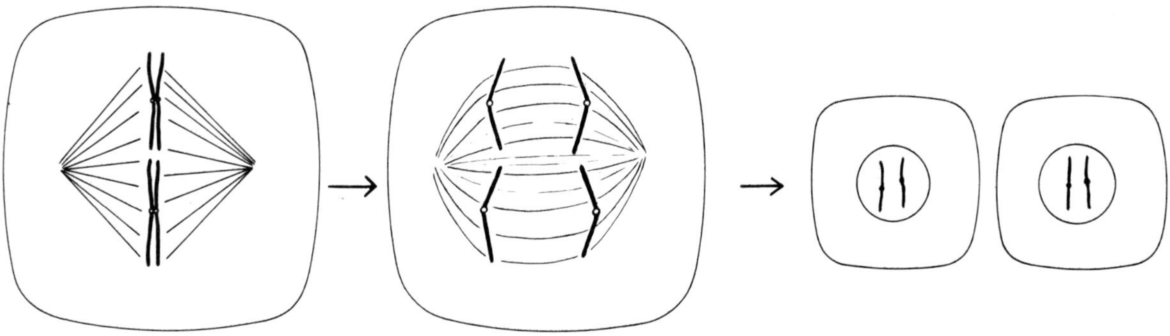

Fig.6.4 Division of chromosomes and cell contents to give two new diploid cells identical with parent cell

arranged side by side held together at a definite point called the **centromere**. This more compact arrangement of the chromosomes is necessary to keep them from getting tangled up and breaking as they move around the cell in the later stages of division. This is also the time of formation of the **spindle**, a system of long protein fibres spanning the cell from side to side.

During **metaphase** the nuclear membrane disappears and the chromosomes arrange themselves at the midline of the cell between the two **poles** of the spindle.

How does division of the cell take place?

The actual division of the nuclear material occurs during **anaphase** when the members of the chromosome pairs part company and move to opposite poles of the cell. Precisely what causes the movement is not known. Some scientists believe that spindle fibres act like tiny muscle fibres in pulling the chromatids along.

The motion of the chromosomes can be illustrated by a simple model made from a double strand of insulated electrical wire. Separate the middle portion of the wires as shown in the diagram below and tie a piece of string to each side. Slip an elastic band

Fig.6.5

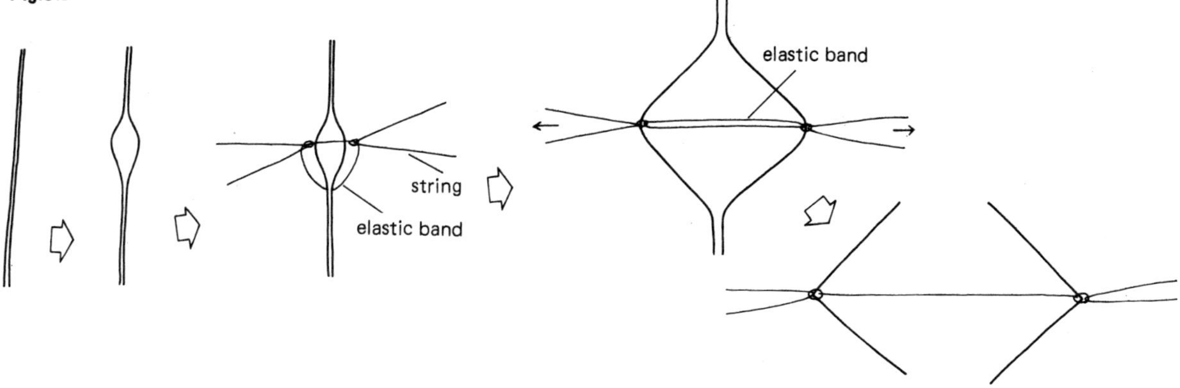

Fig.6.6 Division of cell contents in animals

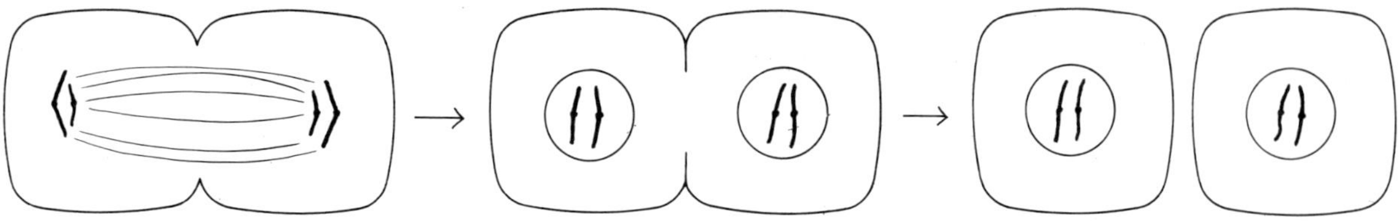

Fig.6.7 Division of cell contents in plants

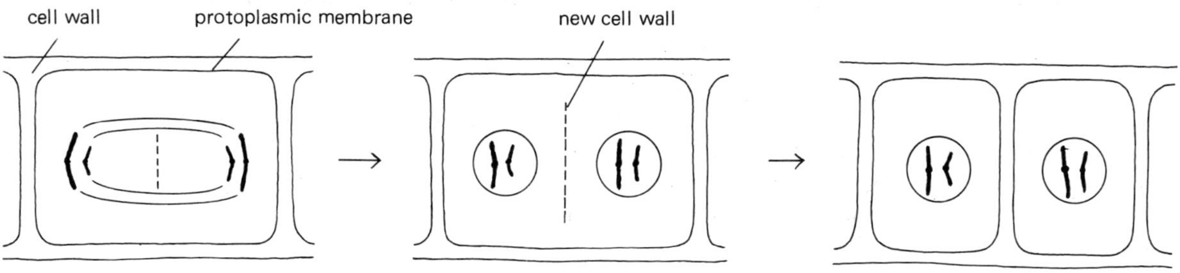

between the two ends of each string and slowly pull the strings apart until the wire splits in two. This gives you the basic idea as to how the chromosome pairs might separate and go to opposite poles of the cell.

After separation the chromosomes at the two poles become densely packed together and the nuclear membrane reforms. Meanwhile the rest of the cell divides into two parts. In animals this is achieved by a constriction of the cell membrane so that the cell becomes pinched into two. In plants a new cell wall starts to form in the middle of the cell.

The net result of mitosis is the division of the cell into two new **daughter cells** that have precisely the same chromosome constitution as the original, that is, they are both identical to the parent cell. Upon completion of the process of mitosis the cell returns to its resting stage.

The sequence of mitotic events described above is the general outline of the process. Close examination of the process would reveal many details that have not been touched upon. It would also show up the slight variations that exist between various species of organism.

Are there differences between growth in plants and in animals?

Although in both plants and animals growth involves cell division and cell differentiation, the patterns assumed by these processes are slightly different.

Growth in plants

Growth in vascular plants begins with the germination of the seed and continues throughout the life of the organism.
In all plants cell division is characteristically localized in specific areas called **meristems**. The principal areas of meristematic tissue are the **apical meristem** at the growing tips of shoots and roots and in the angle between the leaves and the main stem at potential points of development of side branches.
These meristematic areas are responsible for **primary growth**, that is, increase in the length of the shoots and roots.

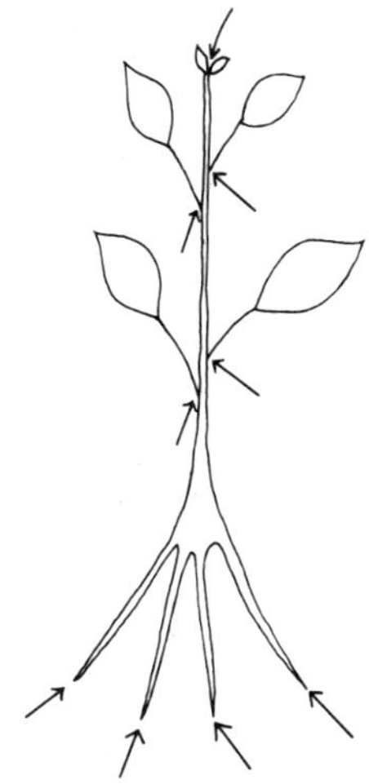

Fig.6.8 Sites of meristematic tissues

EXPERIMENT TO MONITOR THE GROWTH OF ROOTS IN A BEAN SEEDLING

Materials

several bean seedlings
thread
ink

Method

1. Mark the roots of several seedlings at equal intervals of about 2mm. The best way to do this is by using thread dipped in ink.
2. Place the seedlings between layers of moist blotting paper and observe for one or two days. Changes in the distance between the marks indicate the relative rates of growth of the various areas.

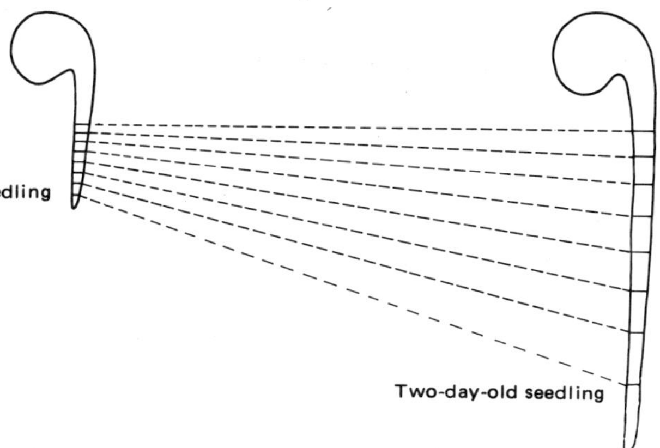

Fig.6.9

At what point does the greatest increase in length occur?
Do your observations agree with the theory of the existence of an apical meristem?
Draw a diagram of one of the seedlings at the outset and at the conclusion of the experiment.

Discussion

You will observe that the greatest increase in length between marks and therefore the most growth occurs in the section immediately behind the tip. The very tip of the root is covered by a **root cap** which protects against damage that might be incurred as the root pushes through the soil. The region of cell division, the meristem, is located immediately above the cap.

Fig.6.10 Growth of plant cell

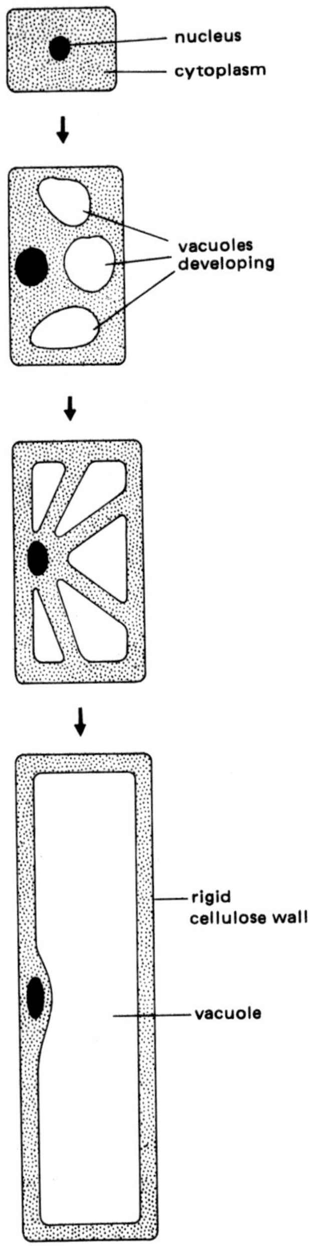

Further above are the **zone of elongation** and the **zone of differentiation**, the areas where cells increase in size and start to differentiate in preparation for some specialized function. There is no sharp distinction between the zones of elongation and differentiation.
Cell expansion takes place as a result of water uptake into the cell vacuole. Due to the increasing osmotic pressure the walls of the cell are pushed outward and the cytoplasm is forced increasingly towards the periphery of the cell. When fully expanded, most of

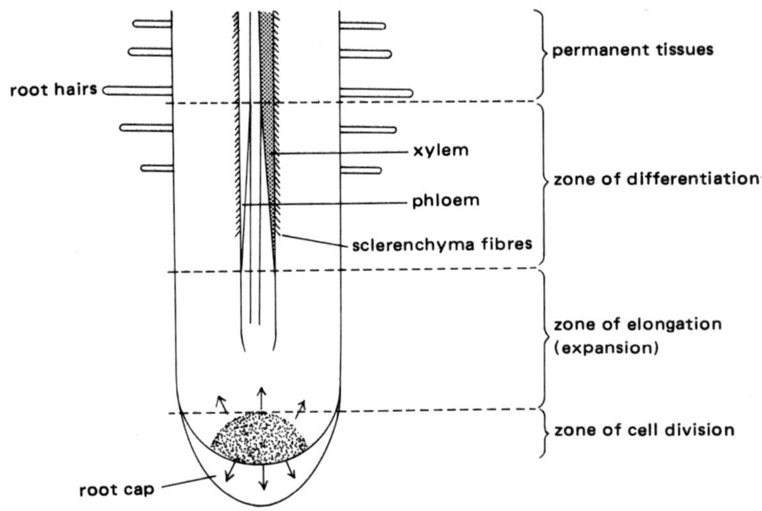

Fig.6.11 Growth of root in a flowering plant

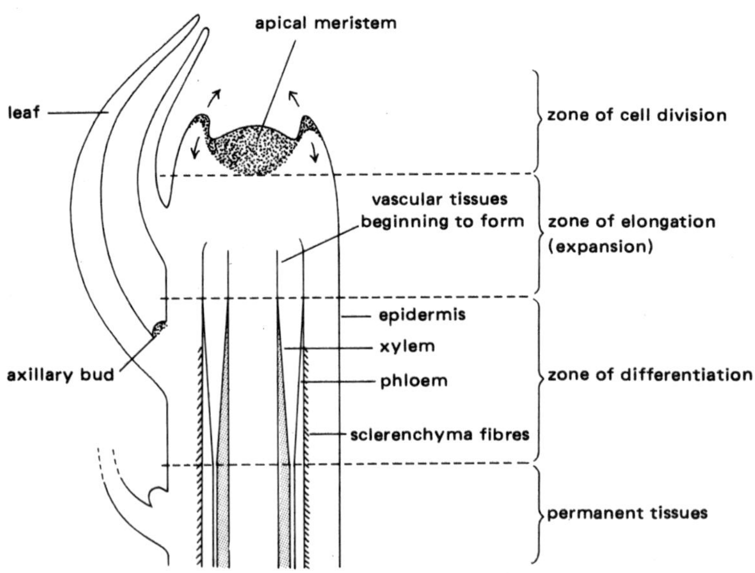

Fig.6.12 Growth of stem in a flowering plant

the space inside the cell is occupied by the fluid-filled vacuole. As the cellulose wall of the cells becomes thickened further expansion is prevented and the cell ceases to grow.

At the same time specialization for various functions begins. In the case of the xylem, for instance, the side walls become impregnated with lignin, a substance that makes them impermeable to water and the end walls begin to dissolve to leave a continuous longitudinal channel along the root or stem.

The organization of the cells and the zones of activity at the tips of shoots are very similar to that of the root tips except that there is no equivalent structure to the root cap. (Fig. 6.12.)

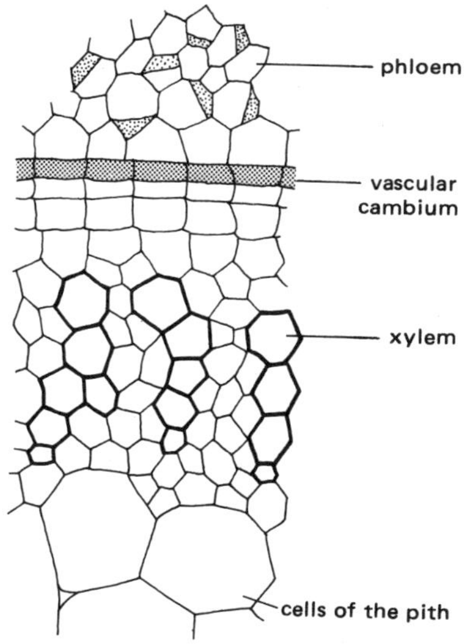

Fig.6.13 Organization of cells in stem of dicotyledonous plants

How is the girth of a plant increased?

In some herbaceous plants increase in girth occurs only as a result of the increase in size of the cells in a lateral direction. In others, however, it is achieved through the activity of the **cambium** resulting in lateral cell division referred to as **secondary growth**.

In both the stem and the root of dicotyledonous plants the cambium is arranged in a roughly circular pattern and new cells are produced by the cambium in both directions. The cells to the inside of the ring are the **secondary xylem** and those to the outside form the **secondary phloem**. The primary xylem and phloem are the tissues

Fig.6.14 Secondary growth in stem and root of dicots

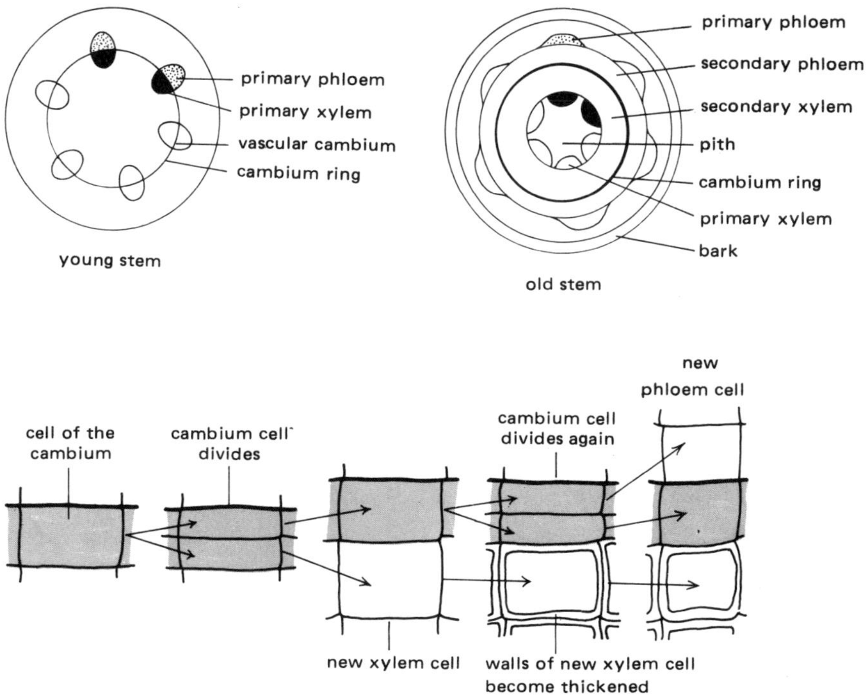

that are produced as a result of longitudinal cell division by the apical meristem. Since more secondary xylem than phloem is produced in the stem, the phloem along with the cambial ring itself gets pushed progressively closer to the outside of the stem.

In dicotyledonous woody stems the production of secondary xylem leads to the formation of **annual rings**. In the spring and summer when water is plentiful and the plant is growing rapidly the xylem cells produced are much larger than the ones produced during the relatively inactive autumn and winter periods. The alternate layers of **early wood** and **late wood** result in distinct rings representing growth in each successive year. Counting the number of annual rings provides a reliable indication of the age of a tree, while the thickness of a particular ring reflects the growing conditions of a particular year. A narrow ring is indicative of cold or very dry weather while a wide ring points to warm, moist conditions.

Fig.6.15

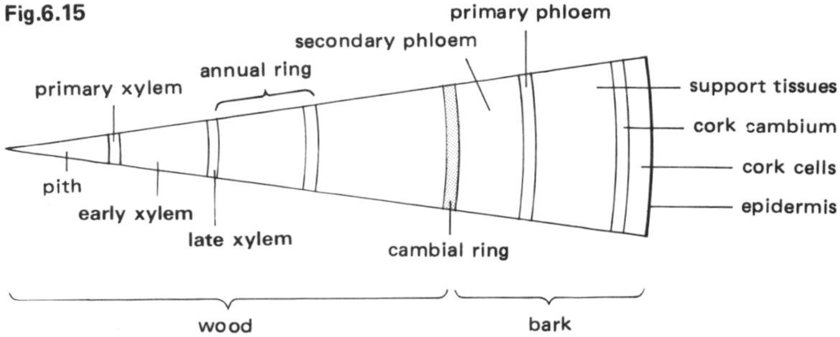

Scientists have gained much valuable information concerning past weather patterns in different areas of the world by examining the annual rings of some very old trees.

A second ring of cambial tissue found in dicotyledonous plants is the **cork cambium** situated on the outside of the phloem. This layer produces the protective layer of cork cells on the outside of the bark of a woody root or stem. These cells are impervious to water and air except for the scattered spongy pockets of cells forming the lenticels. (See p. 135.)

Plant growth is influenced by special plant hormones as discussed on p. 254.

The rate and direction of growth are also influenced by environmental factors such as temperature, light and the availability of nutrients.

What is the usual life span of a plant?

Some herbaceous plants, referred to as **annuals** remain alive for only a single growing season. Once the seeds have been shed the plant dies.

Other plants called **perennials** stay alive for a number of years, although in many instances the vegetative parts above the ground

may wither away during the cold or dry months.
Woody plants have much longer life spans. Some trees such as the giant redwoods on the west coast of the USA are believed to be over three thousand years old.

Summary

The process of growth implies not only an increase in size of an organism and an increase in the number of cells but also an increase in the degree of differentiation of the various cells. Through the process of mitosis a parent cell is able to divide and give rise to two daughter cells that are usually identical in every respect.
Plants have definite centres of primary growth called meristems where cell division is actively taking place. These areas include the tips of shoots and roots.
In addition, in many plants secondary growth is present due to the activity of the cambium.

Growth in animals

Growth and development in animals is triggered by the fertilization of the egg. Through a series of vertical and horizontal mitotic divisions the fertilized egg starts on its long process of development.
In animals there are no special areas of cell division corresponding to the meristematic tissues of plants and in animals growth takes place only during a certain period in the early stages of life of most animals. After this, what cell division there is is directed towards the maintenance of the individual in a healthy state. Some tissues such as the brain and heart lose their capacity for cell division altogether except in unusual instances such as the development of tumours. Bones are able to increase in length only while a non-bony group of tissues is present at the ends. As soon as this region becomes hardened, or **ossified**, growth ceases.
Many tissues retain the capacity for cell division in order to replace worn or damaged parts. Such is the case with the lungs and liver.
In still other tissues cell division continues throughout life. The outer layers of the epidermis are continually being sloughed off and are replaced by new cells originating in the lower regions. Blood cells are continually produced and destroyed throughout life.

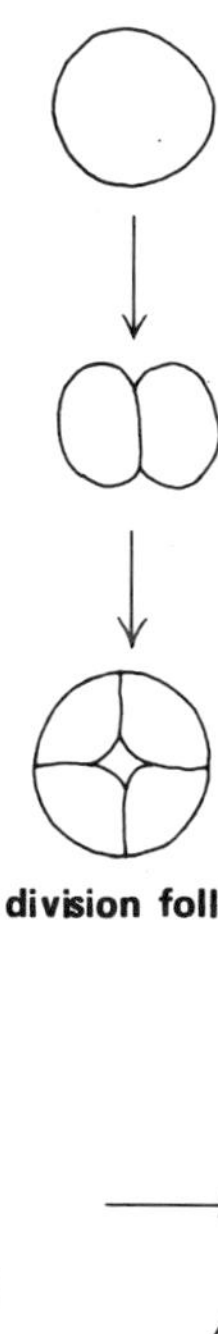

Fig.6.16 Cell division following fertilization

Tissue regeneration

Some lower animals possess quite remarkable powers of regeneration of damaged tissues. If a *planaria* is cut into several pieces each piece will regenerate into a complete animal.
Hydra and earthworms cut into two in a transverse direction will develop into two new individuals. Lizards and geckos at times shed their tails in attempts to escape from predators and are able to grow new ones.

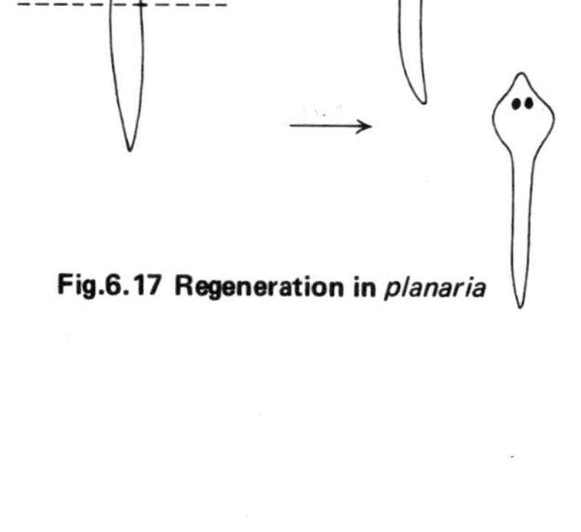

Fig.6.17 Regeneration in *planaria*

Growth of an embryo

The most rapid cell division and differentiation takes place during embryonic life. During the nine months of its development the human embryo grows from a speck hardly visible to the naked eye to the size of a newborn infant. From a single fertilized egg dozens of different cell types differentiate.

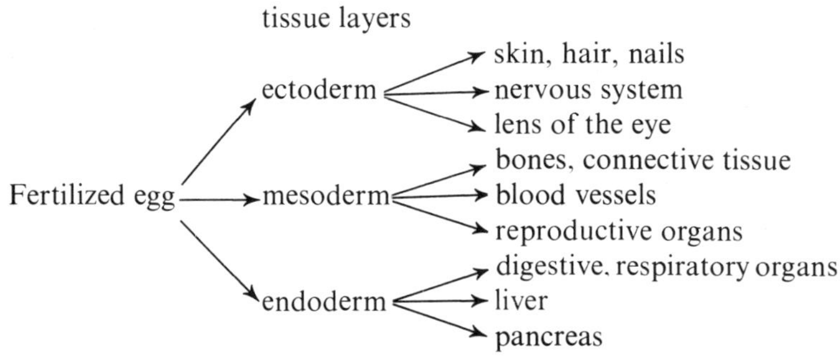

After birth, growth and development continue for at least another fifteen or sixteen years, under the direction of the genetic information encoded along the length of the chromosomes and under the control of hormones.

It is interesting to note the relative differences in the rate of growth of the various parts of the body. Fig. 6.18 shows the progressive changes in the proportion of the body parts as the infant develops into an adult. This is referred to as **differential growth** and is an important aspect of development.

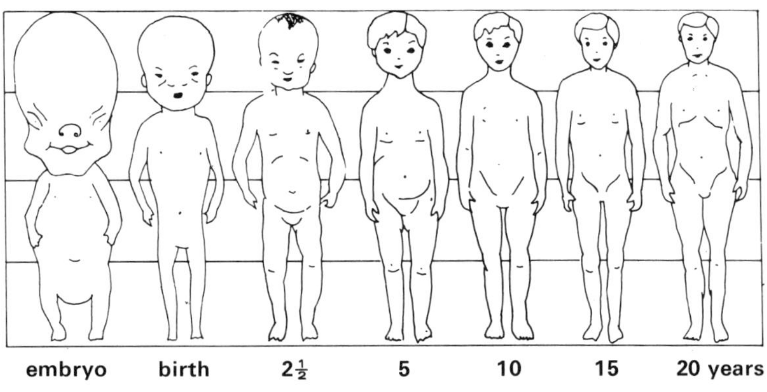

Fig.6.18 Diagrams of a human being at different ages showing approximate changes in proportion of body parts.

Metamorphosis

A special feature of development in most invertebrates and in some vertebrates is the process of **metamorphosis**. These particular animals develop from the fertilized egg into a **larva**, spend a certain length of time in this form and then undergo, sometimes very dramatic, alteration in body form to produce the adult animal.

Although the larval stage is intermediate in the development of the final organism most larvae are highly specialized creatures well adapted to the environment in which they live.
In some lower invertebrate species the larval stage is motile while the adult animal settles down in a fixed position.

Metamorphosis in frogs

The features of the process of metamorphosis can be studied by examining the stages in the development of the frog.
Mating in frogs takes place during March or April when conditions are suitably moist. The eggs are laid by the female and are immediately fertilized by the male who squirts his sperm on top of them in the water.
The eggs, collectively called **spawn**, are covered by a coating of jelly that keeps them together and gives some measure of protection against the elements and predators. The fertilized egg undergoes repeated mitotic divisions so that in a few hours, even though the size of the cell mass has not altered, the number of cells is greatly increased. Soon the cell mass begins to elongate, developing a distinct tail and a head equipped with external gills.
The fully formed larva emerges from the egg in about thirty-two hours. During its development it has been nourished by the yolk of the egg.
Immediately after hatching it attaches itself to a nearby water weed by means of a sticky secretion from a special mucous gland.
For the first day or two of its life the **tadpole** still feeds on the remains of the yolk that remains attached to its body. As soon as its mouth opens it begins to eat the microscopic plants that float by in the water. Between three and eight days after hatching the tadpole changes considerably. The external gills are replaced by internal ones, it becomes detached from the water weed and starts to swim around with the aid of a muscular tail similar to the way in which a fish does.

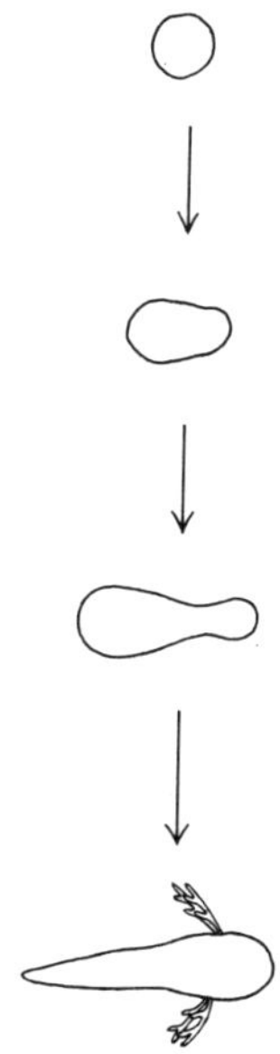

Fig.6.19 Tadpole hatching from egg

Fig.6.20

(i) 4 days after hatching

External gills shrivelling, blood flow in them becoming sluggish

Side view

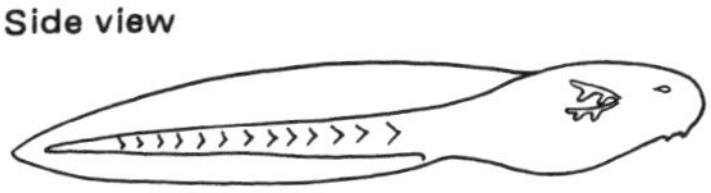

Operculum growing over gills

Dorsal view

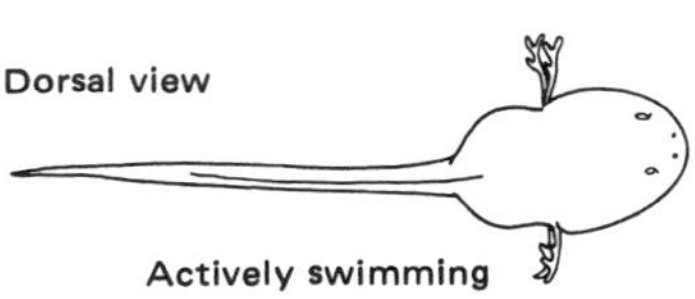

Actively swimming

(ii) Diagram showing how operculum grows over gills

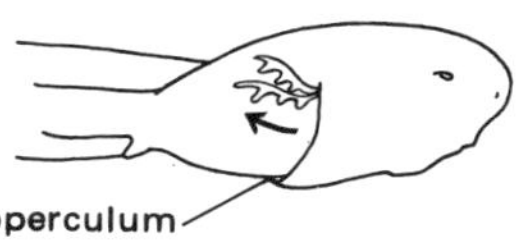

(iii) About 8 days after hatching

External gills and mucous glands gone: swimming vigorously

Remains at this stage for several weeks while increasing in size.

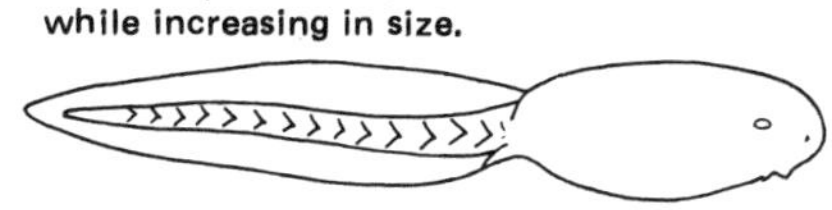

For the next two months it increases in size with little change in external appearance. After this time the processes leading to metamorphosis start to take place. Lungs begin to develop. Leg buds form at the spot where the back legs will be and the front legs begin to take shape under the operculum.

The diet of the tadpole changes too, from an entirely vegetarian one to an omnivorous one.

At about ten weeks the front legs break through the operculum. The tail becomes increasingly shorter as it is reabsorbed into the body and its tissues are used for nourishment. The eyes and mouth become greatly enlarged and in general the animal takes on a more and more frog-like appearance.

Fig.6.21

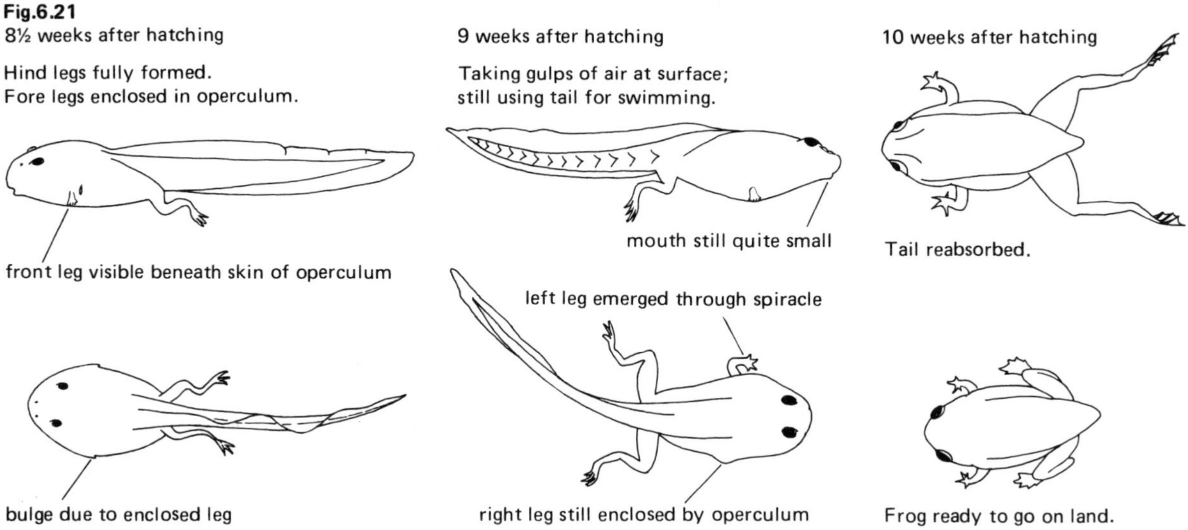

Metamorphosis in insects

Larval forms in insects assume a great variety of shapes. In some species a further stage is interposed between the larval and the adult stage. It is called a **pupa** and is found especially in instances where the larval and adult bodies are drastically different in form such as is the case of butterflies and moths. At the termination of the larval phase of development the organism is encased in a hard, shell-like structure from which it does not emerge until the adult body has been completely formed.

In mosquitoes, eggs are laid in the water and in some species they are supported on the surface by tiny **floats** placed on either side of the egg. After an incubation period of one week a legless larva hatches out. It has a distinct head, segmented body equipped with a **breathing tube** at the back. In order to breathe the larva has to swim to the surface, assume an upside-down position and stick the tube out through the surface of the water. While in this position it is able to feed on microscopic plants that float about, using the tiny brushes on the head to sweep the food into the mouth.

Since the body of the larva is covered with an inflexible cuticle increase in size can only take place after **ecdysis** which occurs four times within ten days. The last moult, instead of revealing yet another larval form, results in the formation of a pupa. The pupal form is shaped like a comma, is able to swim by flicking its tail and breathes through a tube located on the head but does not feed.

Within a few more days the adult body parts develop under the pupal case, the case splits open and the adult mosquito emerges.

The feeding habits of the mosquito are discussed on p. 91.

Fig.6.22 Photo and diagram showing life-history of mosquito

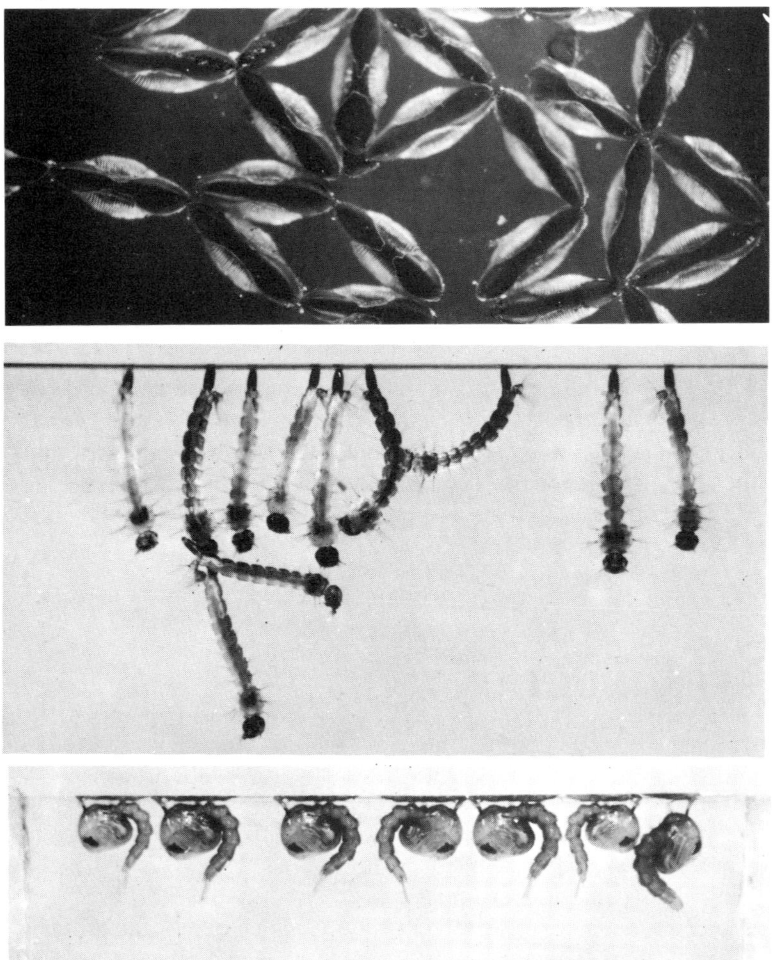

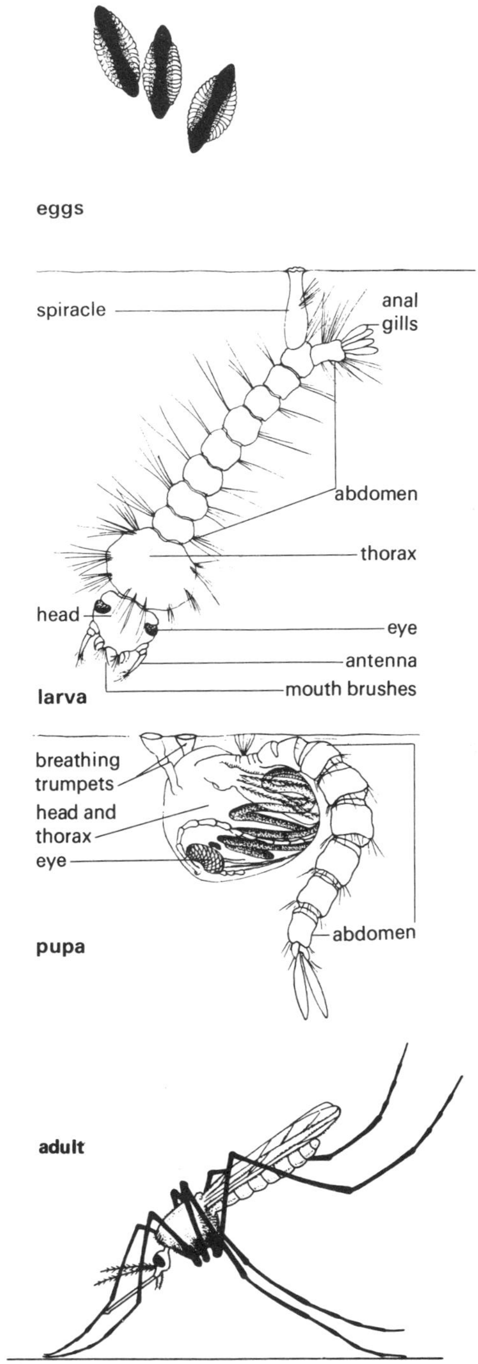

Suspended growth

Many organisms are able to enter a state of suspended growth or **dormancy**.

Among plants it is found in seeds, spores, buds, storage organs such as tubers and so on. In many instances dormancy is a way for the organism to survive adverse conditions such as drought or extreme cold. A thick outer coat usually develops around the structure in question to protect it from the external environment while cellular processes are carried on inside at an extremely slow rate barely enough to keep the cells alive.

Among animals dormancy occurs for instance at various stages in the life cycle of insects. The embryo of the tapeworm, for example, once shed from the original host, can remain dormant for up to a year and develops only when eaten by a suitable intermediate host.

A special kind of dormancy, **hibernation**, occurs on a seasonal basis in some higher animals. In mammals it has the advantage of freeing the animal from the almost impossible task of maintaining its usual high body temperature during the cold winter months when the food supply is inadequate. During hibernation the metabolic rate drops to a level that is just sufficient to keep the cells alive. At the end of the period the metabolic rate is gradually restored to normal levels and growth and development resume.

Summary

Animals have no special body areas where growth takes place. Most tissues divide and grow for only a certain period in the life of an animal. After that cell division occurs only for the purposes of repair.

Most invertebrates and amphibians assume several stages of development throughout their life. The egg hatches into a larva; in some species the larva turns into a pupa and it is only then that the adult form appears. The process is called metamorphosis.

Many plants and animals assume a state of dormancy at times of adverse environmental conditions.

REPRODUCTION

Although individual organisms of a species have a limited life span, the species as a whole is normally kept alive through the ability of individuals to produce new organisms of their kind, that is, to reproduce.

How are organisms produced?

There are two distinctly different ways in which plants and animals can reproduce. These are **asexual reproduction** and **sexual reproduction**. Asexual reproduction is simply an extension of the process of growth. Only one parent organism is needed and the new individual produced is usually an identical copy of the parent.

In the process of sexual reproduction the genetic material of two parents combine to produce an offspring with a new combination of traits that is different from either parent.

Asexual reproduction

Asexual reproduction is widely present among unicellular organisms and simple plants and animals. In unicellular organisms the process usually consists of **binary fission**.

What is binary fission?

Binary fission is simply cell division resulting in the production of two new, genetically identical individuals of the same size. The greatest advantage of binary fission is the prodigious rate of duplication that can occur. Under favourable conditions of temperature, humidity and nutrient supply bacterial cells, for instance, are able to divide at twenty-minute intervals. Since each new cell can produce two new cells which in turn produce two more each, the entire population is doubled every twenty minutes.

Fig.6.23 Increase in numbers through binary fission

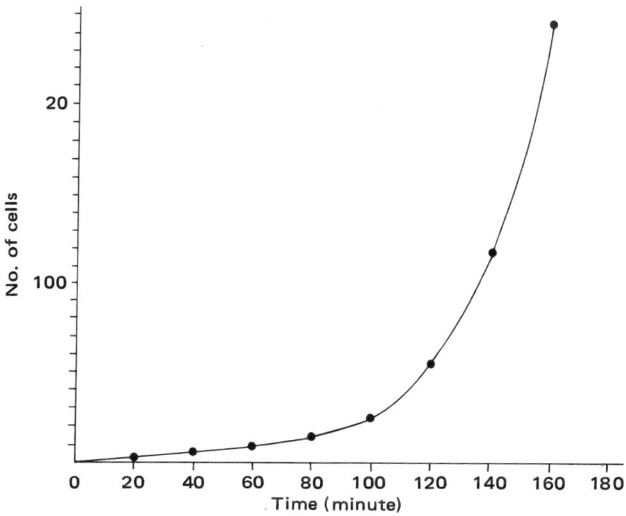

Fig.6.24 Production of new cells

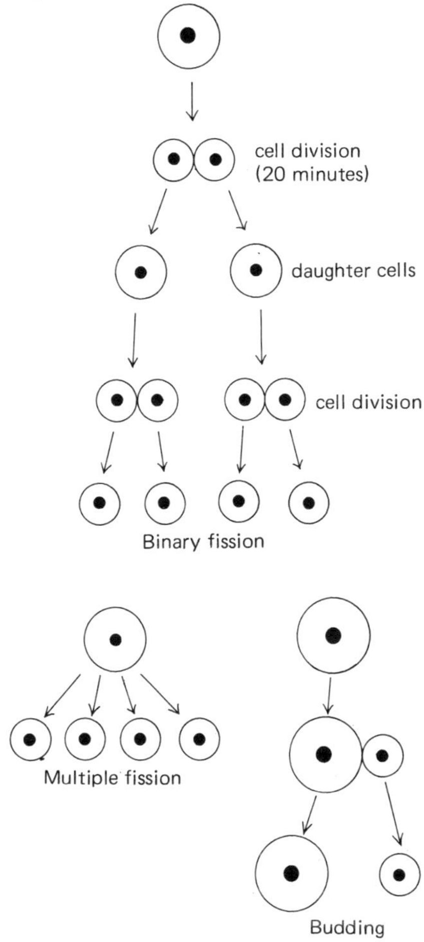

Even more phenomenal rates of reproduction can be achieved by organisms that are capable of **multiple fission**. In multiple fission the nucleus of the parent divides repeatedly and each new nucleus along with a small portion of cytoplasm breaks away to form a new individual.

Budding

Budding involves the development of outgrowths on the parent organism. In time these become detached to become separate individuals. The process is very similar to binary fission except that the new cells produced are much smaller than the parent. When budding occurs in multicellular organisms, the newly formed bud consists of undifferentiated cells which then differentiate into a fully formed copy of the parent before becoming detached.

Fig.6.25 Budding yeast cells

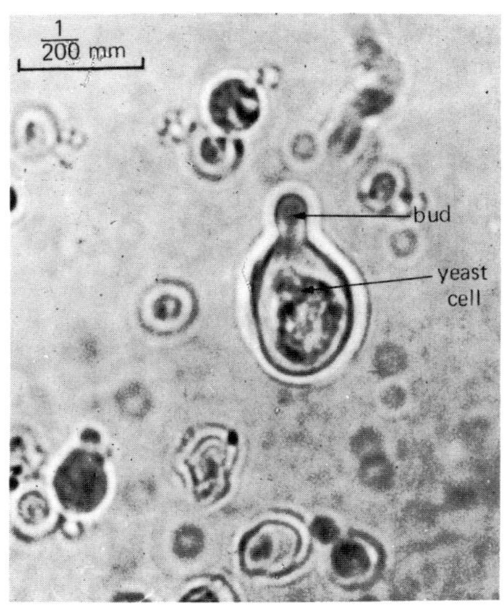

Spore formation

A more complex and lengthy form of asexual reproduction found in plants is **spore** formation. Spores are individual cells that are formed by cell division of the parent organism, usually inside an enclosing structure called a **sporangium**. When fully matured the sporangium ruptures and the small, light spores are carried away by the wind, water or animals. If a spore comes in contact with a suitable surface it germinates to develop either directly, or through an intermediate form, into a new organism exactly like the parent.
A typical example is asexual reproduction in the common bread mould, *Mucor*. Asexual reproduction takes place in the initial stages of the growth of the organism when conditions with respect to food and moisture are favourable.

Spore formation in Mucor

Long hyphae called **stolons** grow out of the mycelium at first vertically into the air, then, as they get longer, bending onto the surface of the food. At the point of contact with the food surface a number of hyphae are extended into the food, while others start to grow vertically upwards. The tip of each vertical hypha develops into a sporangium, and the contents become divided into numerous, multinucleated spores. The ripe sporangium is black in colour and a collection of these structures accounts for the black colour of the fungal growth. Once the development of the spores is completed, the walls of the sporangium break open and the spores are freed.

Fig.6.26 Diagram and photo showing sporangia of fungi

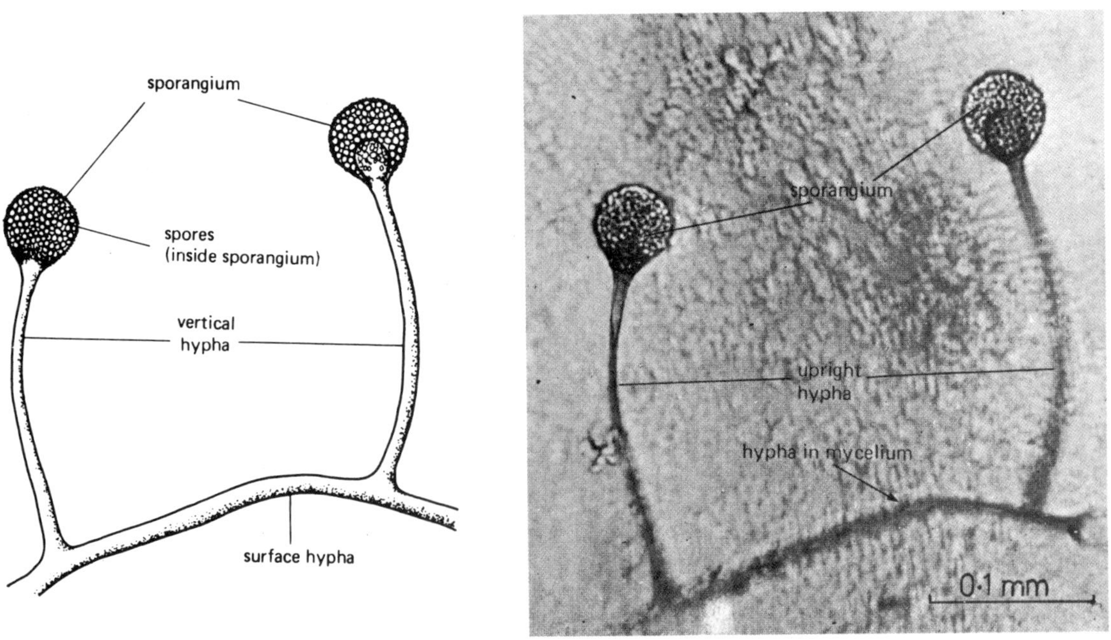

They are extremely hardy, resistant structures and are able to germinate even after several years of dormancy.

Advantages of spore formation over simple fission or budding.

Although spore formation is a more lengthy process and the number of individuals produced is not nearly as great as in fission or budding the great advantage is the possibility of dormancy. Although the parent organism may die due to lack of food or other adverse conditions the spores remain viable and germinate at such time as the conditions become favourable once more. Spore formation is the asexual equivalent of seed formation by higher plants.

Vegetative reproduction

Vegetative reproduction is another form of asexual reproduction found only in plants.
The vegetative portions of a plant are the roots, stems and leaves as opposed to the reproductive portions such as flowers. There are several types of vegetative reproduction depending on which part of the plant is involved.

Storage organs

New individuals may develop from underground storage organs that remain in the soil through the winter and start to develop the following year. Some of these storage structures such as the **tuber** of the potato and the **rhizome** of the iris and rhubarb develop from the stem while others develop from the root, such as in the case of the carrot.

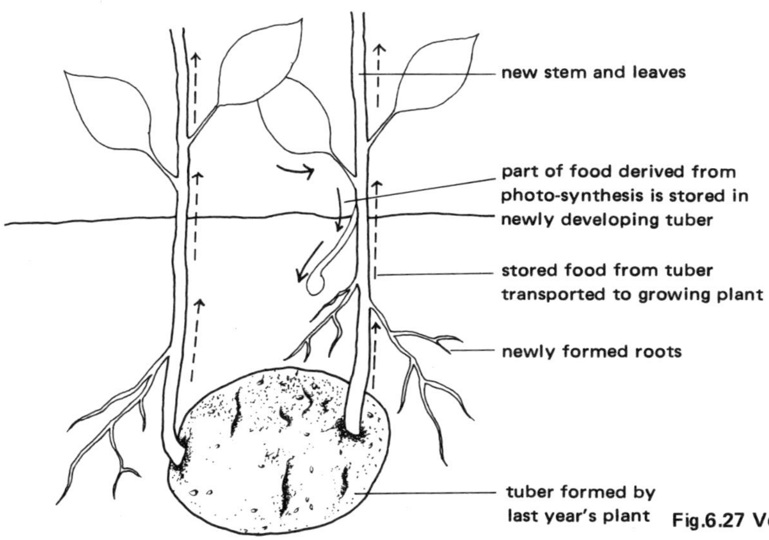

Fig.6.27 Vegetative reproduction in potato

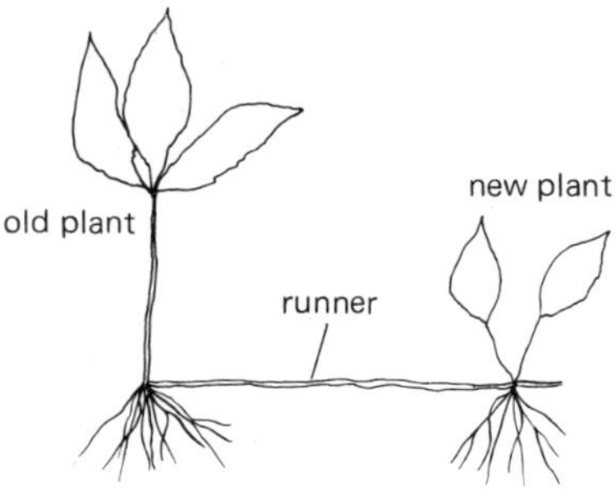

Fig.6.28 Runner of strawberry

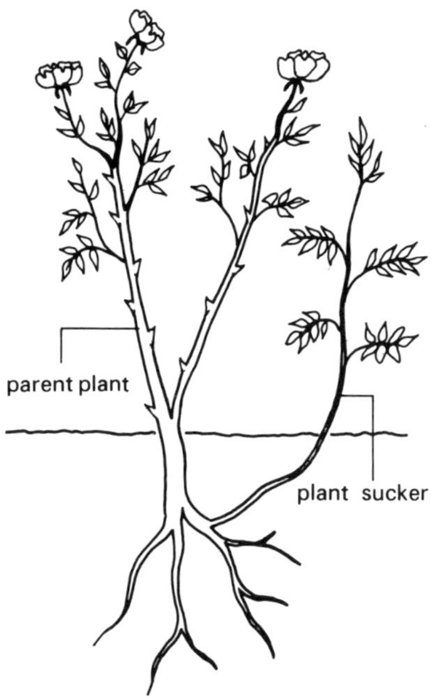

Fig. 6.29 Suckers of rose

Runners

A **runner** is a side branch originating from an axillary bud in the lower portion of the plant. It grows horizontally along the ground to some distance away from the parent plant then gives rise to shoots and roots. Each such rooted portion will become a separate plant as the runner withers away.

Suckers

A **sucker** is a short branch, similar to a runner but originating from the portion of the stem just below ground level. It grows out of the ground at an angle, develops roots and leaves at the apex and finally becomes detached from the parent plant. Suckers are found for instance on the rose plant.

In addition to the above natural means of vegetative reproduction, plants can be propagated by artificial vegetative reproduction such as stem cuttings. If a portion of stem from, for instance, a begonia plant is detached and placed in water containing suitable organic salts, adventitious roots will start to develop from the base of the stem.

Relative advantages and disadvantages of asexual reproduction

Asexual reproduction is very useful in that it is a rapid means of reproducing large numbers of new organisms. Since there is only one parent involved there are no problems associated with coinciding the activities of two individuals or the meeting of two reproductive cells. The main disadvantage is that there is no mixing of genetic material between two individuals and the new organism produced is almost always an exact copy of the parent. A plant or animal that reproduces exclusively by asexual means will be much less adaptable to new environmental conditions than one that is capable of sexual reproduction.

Summary

Asexual reproduction can take place through binary fission and multiple fission and budding. All three methods result in the production of a large number of new individuals in a very short time.

Among plants spore formation and reproduction by means of tubers, suckers or runners are also found.

Sexual reproduction

Sexual reproduction can be defined as any type of reproduction where there is a mixing of the genetic material of two parents.

At its simplest level genetic material is simply transferred from one organism to the other through a process called **conjugation**.

Conjugation

In *Spirogyra* adjacent cells of two different filaments form small protuberances that meet and fuse to form a tubular passage between the cells. The cytoplasm, which is usually arranged in a thin layer around the outside of the cell wall collects in the centre. The nucleus and chloroplasts cease to appear as separate identities. The entire cell contents of one filament pass into the cells of the other through the conjugation tubes. The two cell contents fuse and develop into a thick-walled **zygospore**. The cell walls of the filament break down and the zygospores are released, ready to develop into new filaments. The process of sexual reproduction therefore results in the death of both the parents in *Spirogyra*. This is not always the case however.

Fig.6.31 Sexual reproduction in Spirogyra

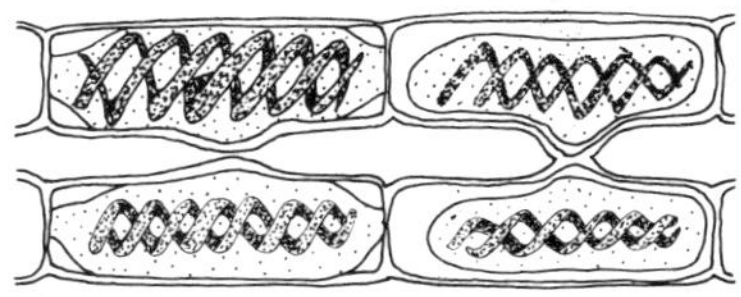

(i) Adjacent cells develop protuberances. Cell contents shrink and round off.

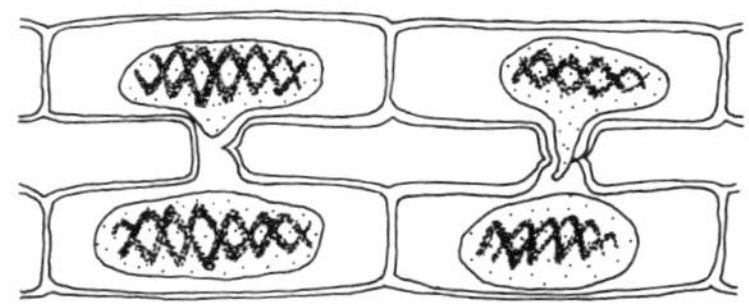

(ii) Protuberances meet and form tube. Cell contents from one filament pass into the other.

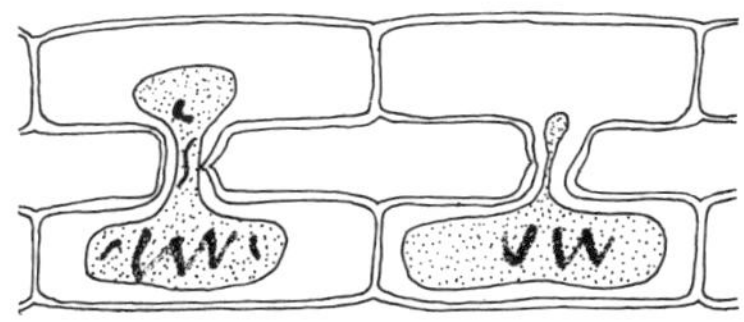

(iii) Cell contents fuse.

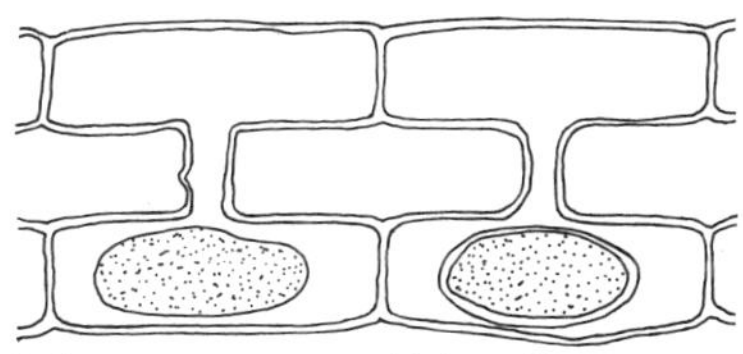

(iv) Zygote secretes thick wall. Old cell walls dissolve away.

Fig.6.30 Stereogram of Spirogyra cell in section

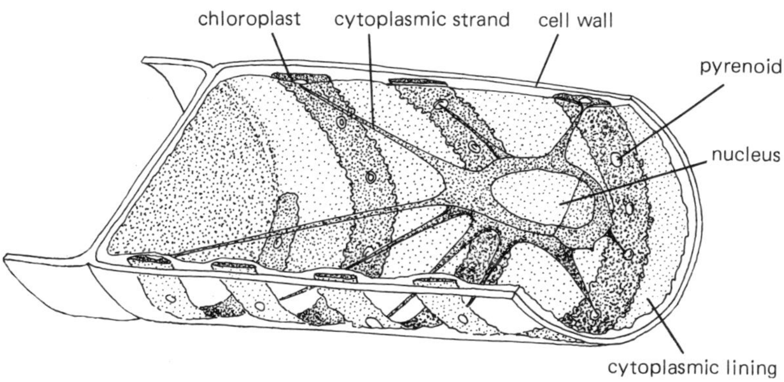

In *Mucor*, two developing hyphae that have grown out of different spores may sometimes meet and send out lateral branches that fuse. A new wall is formed between the side branch and the parent hypha while the middle wall where the fusion has taken place dissolves. The two nuclei fuse and a thick-walled zygospore is formed. The zygospore becomes detached from the parent hyphae and after a suitable dormancy period germinates to form a single vertical hypha bearing a sporangium. Spores develop, mature and proceed to produce new individuals.

Fig.6.32 Conjugation in *Mucor*

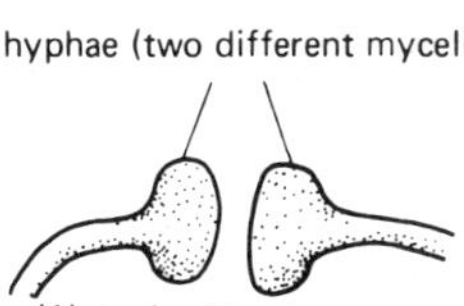

(1) ends of hyphae thicken

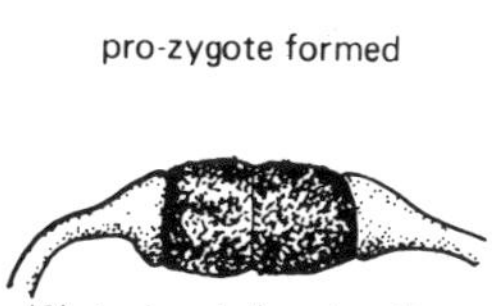

(2) two ends fuse together

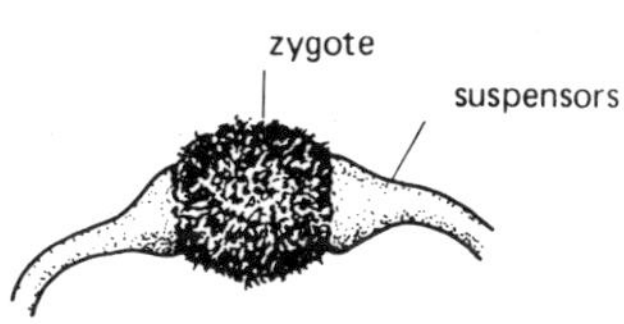

(3) zygote formed with thick coat

(4) suspensors shrivel and die away

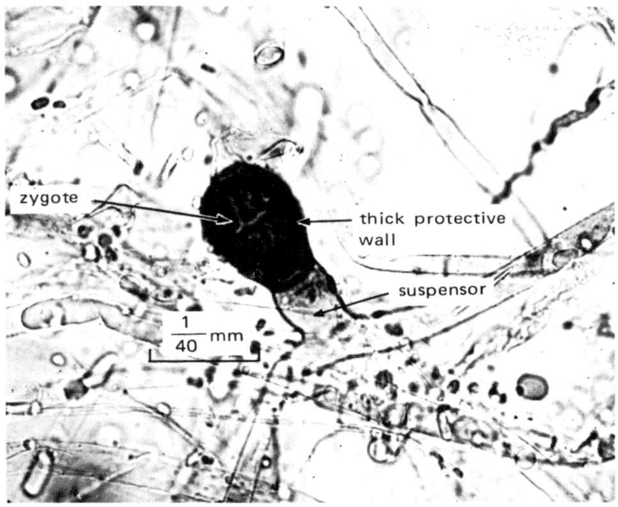

Fig.6.33 Spore formation in *Mucor*

Thus in *Mucor* asexual and sexual reproduction are linked in that both ultimately result in spore formation. The life cycle of the organism is shown in the figure below.

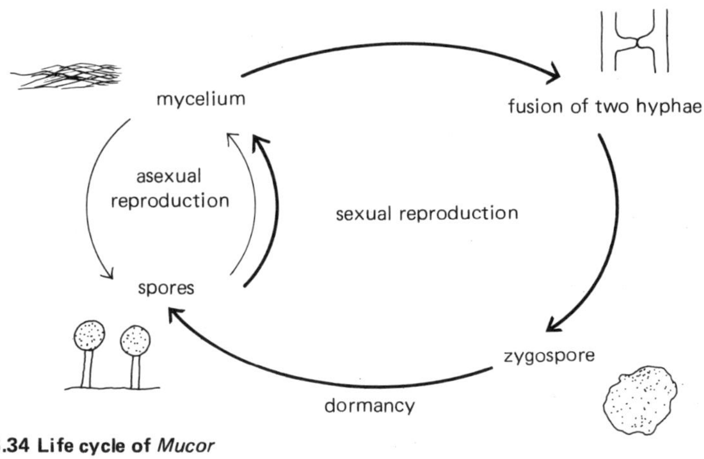

Fig.6.34 Life cycle of *Mucor*

Gametes

In most organisms sexual reproduction involves the union of special reproductive cells called **gametes**.

In more primitive species gametes are identical but gametes from the same individual will recognize each other and fusion between them will not occur. Some have the crude beginnings of separation into sexes. Although identical in every respect members of the population can be divided into **plus** and **minus strains**. Fusion is only possible between a plus and a minus.

Among animals the most advanced form of sexual reproduction takes place in organisms that show a distinct separation into two sexes and two distinct, fully differentiated gametes are formed.

How are gametes formed?

Gamete formation occurs through a process called reduction division or **meiosis**, resulting in the formation of cells that have only half the usual chromosome number of the particular organism.

Chromosome number

The nuclei of all **somatic** cells, that is, all body cells, each contain two sets of chromosomes that can be arranged in **homologous pairs**. These cells are referred to as **diploid** and their chromosome number is designated as **2n**. During mitosis chromosome replication occurs so that after the division is complete two new diploid cells are obtained.

If gametes were diploid, the union of two gametes would result in a new cell that has twice the usual number of chromosomes. In order to end up with a normal 2n cell after fusion, gametes must contain only half the usual number; that is, they must contain **n** chromosomes referred to as **haploid**.

Fig.6.35

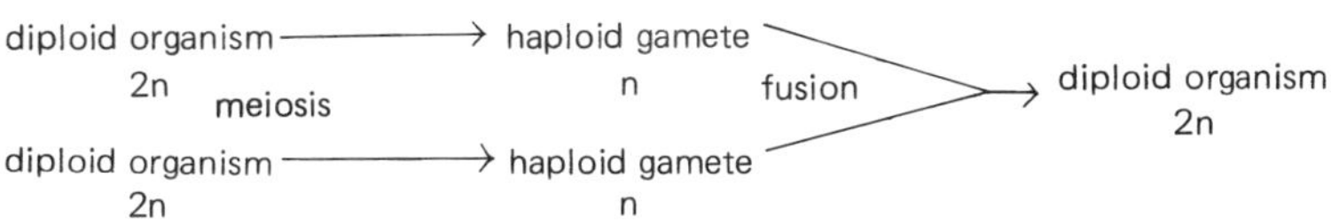

How does meiosis occur?

Meiosis consists of two successive cell divisions. In preparation for the first division chromosomes replicate in the same way as in preparation for mitosis. However, during meiosis homologous pairs of chromosomes come to lie side by side.

During the first cell division the homologous pairs move apart and migrate to opposite poles. Thus the resulting new cells produced will contain different genetic information as homologous chromosomes are genetically different.

It is during the time prior to the first division when the homologous pairs are adjacent that exchange of genetic information between them can occur. (See p. 316.)

During the second division the chromatids separate from one another to form a total of four haploid cells.

Fig.6.36 Comparison of meiosis with two consecutive mitotic divisions

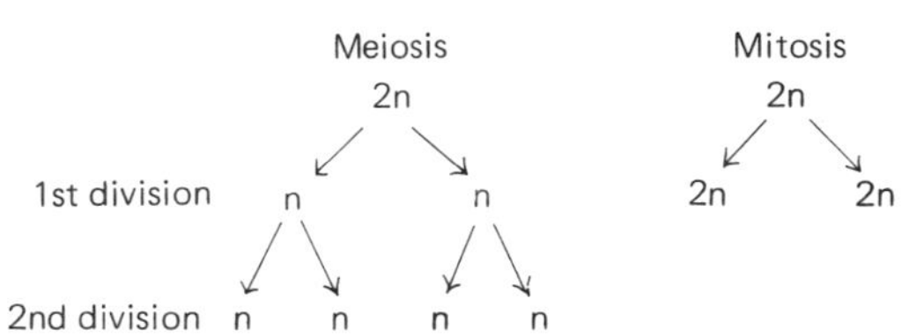

During the second division the sister chromatids making up each individual chromosome part company and two identical cells are formed.

When the male and female gametes fuse during sexual reproduction the normal 2n chromosome constitution of the cell is restored.

Parthenogenesis

Some invertebrate species, notably insects, are able to reproduce from the eggs produced by the female without fusion with a male gamete. This occurs only at specific points in the life cycle of the insect concerned. At other times normal sexual reproduction takes place.

Parthenogenesis can be of two kinds: haploid or diploid. In haploid parthenogenesis the eggs are produced by meiosis and the new individual produced will possess a haploid chromosome constitution. For example, drones are produced from the unfertilized haploid eggs laid by the queen (see p. 258). In diploid parthenogenesis eggs are produced by mitosis and the resulting adult has a diploid chromosome consitution.

Parthenogenesis seems to be half way between sexual and asexual reproduction. The species in which it occurs show a clear separation into two sexes and gametes are formed in the usual way. However, there is no fusion of genetic material between two separate organisms. The process is not well understood by scientists especially with respect to the stimulus necessary to induce the unfertilized egg to start developing.

Sexual reproduction in mammals

Sperm

Fig.6.37 The human sperm

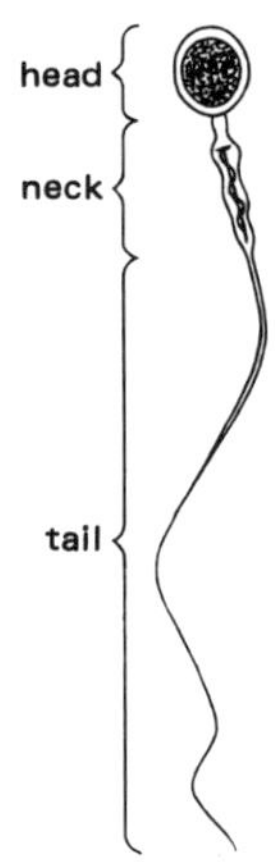

The head contains the nucleus and the neck region contains mitochondria necessary for respiration to make energy available for movement.

The male gamete, called a **sperm**, is a very tiny structure. The head contains the nucleus and to it is attached a tail that provides the sperm with a means of locomotion. By lashing from side to side the tail can propel the sperm in the liquid medium through which it has to swim to reach the female gamete.

Sperms are produced from special cells called **spermatogonia** in a special organ called the **testis** (plural **testes**).

Testes

Testes are paired, oval-shaped organs that at first develop inside the body, one near each kidney. Around the time of birth they move downward, leave the abdominal cavity to be held in two small sacs of skin called **scrotal sacs** outside the body between the hind limbs. If, for some reason, the testes do not descend the individual will not be able to produce viable sperm (i.e. sperm able to fertilize an egg). The crucial factor seems to be the temperature at which the testes are maintained. In the scrotal sacs the temperature is somewhat lower than 37°C; apparently mammalian sperms are not able to develop properly at body temperature.

Each testis is filled with numerous **seminiferous tubules** that are the actual sites of sperm formation. The sperms are collected by a series of tiny ducts that lead to the **epididymus**, the site of sperm storage. From there they pass into the **sperm duct (vas deferens)** and leave the body through the **penis**.

Cells located between the seminiferous tubules produce the male sex hormones that are responsible not only for the development and maintenance of the reproductive organs but for the presence of the **secondary sexual characteristics** such as body hair and deeper voice in humans.

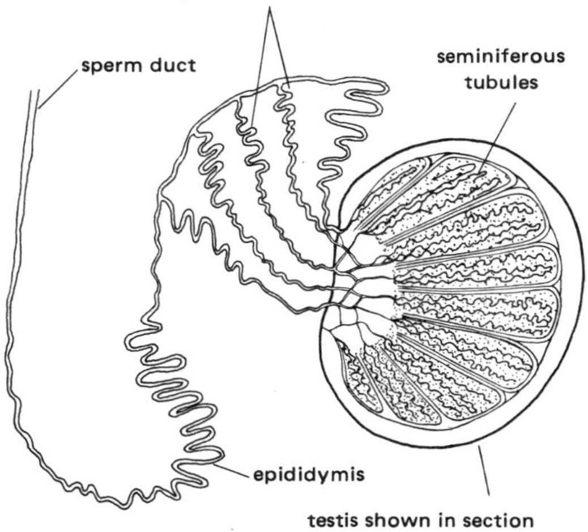

Fig.6.38 **Diagram to show relation of sperm ducts and testis**

Front view

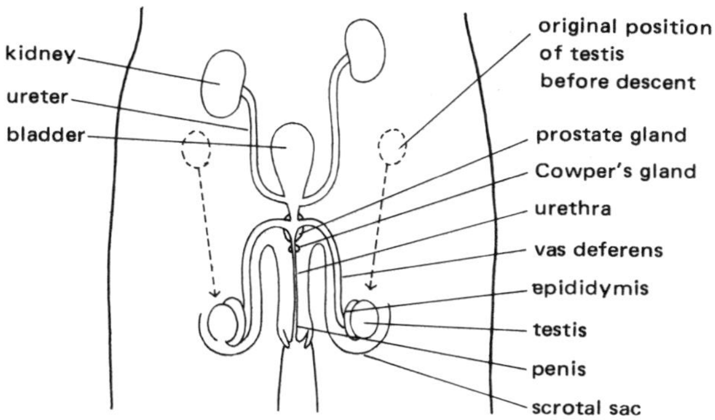

Vertical section

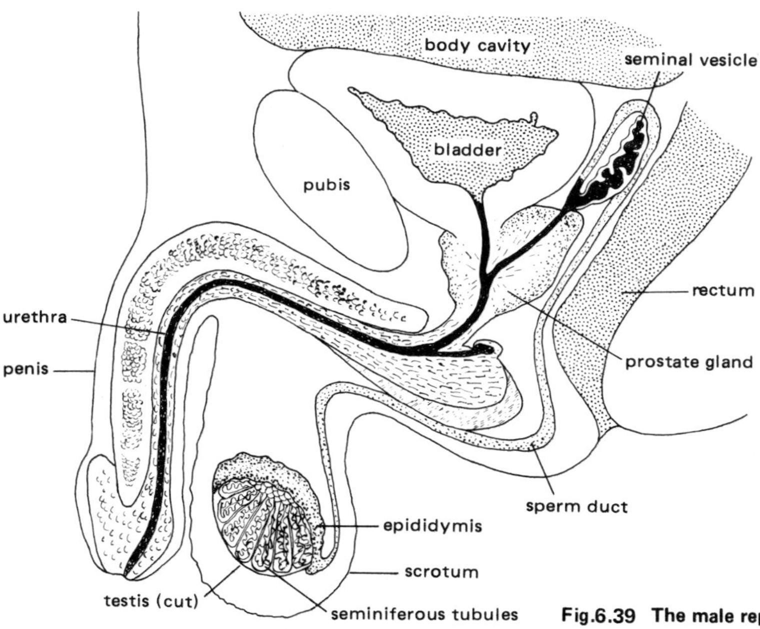

Fig.6.39 **The male reproductive organs and associated structures**

How do sperms get out of the body?

As a result of sexual excitation the blood supply to the penis is greatly increased causing the organ to become rigid or **erect**. Peristaltic contractions of the sperm duct cause the sperms to be pushed along the length of the duct past the **seminal vesicles** where various secretions are added. The mixture of sperm and secretions called **semen** is expelled from the body through a passage in the penis called the **urethra**. The process is called **ejaculation** and it occurs at the climax of the act of **copulation**, or sexual intercourse as it is more commonly called in humans. If you examine fig. 6.38 you will see that the reproductive system and the urinary system share a common duct through the penis. For this reason the male reproductive system is also referred to as the **urogenital** system.

In humans each ejaculation results in the release of between three hundred and five hundred *million* sperms. The number of sperms that are produced during the lifetime of a single individual is quite astronomical.

Sperms are produced continuously so that after each ejaculation the supply is immediately replenished. There are no cyclic alternations between fertile and infertile periods in the male.

Egg cells

Female gametes, called **ova** (singular **ovum**) or **egg cells** are much larger in size than sperms and since they are not motile their structure is much simpler. An egg cell consists of a haploid nucleus surrounded by dense cytoplasm and **yolk**. Yolk is a mixture of protein and fat that is intended to provide nourishment for the developing embryo. The amount of yolk depends on the details of the development of the new organism. In mammals, as we shall see, the embryo develops inside the body of the mother and receives nourishment from her. Thus there is no need for large amounts of yolk. The embryos of birds develop outside the mother's body and therefore all the necessary nourishment must be supplied by the yolk.

Fig.6.40 Diagram and photomicrograph of an ovum

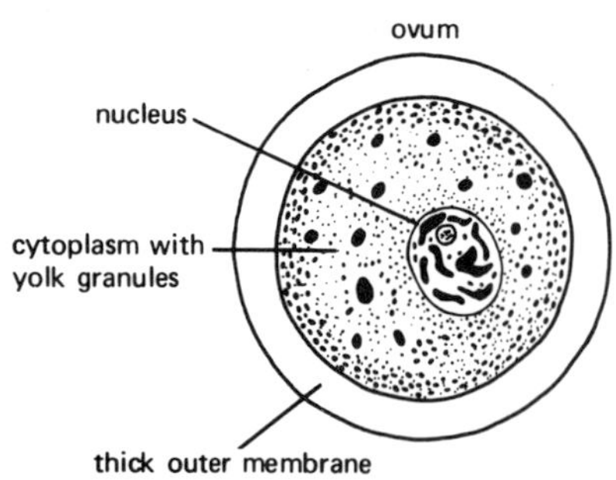

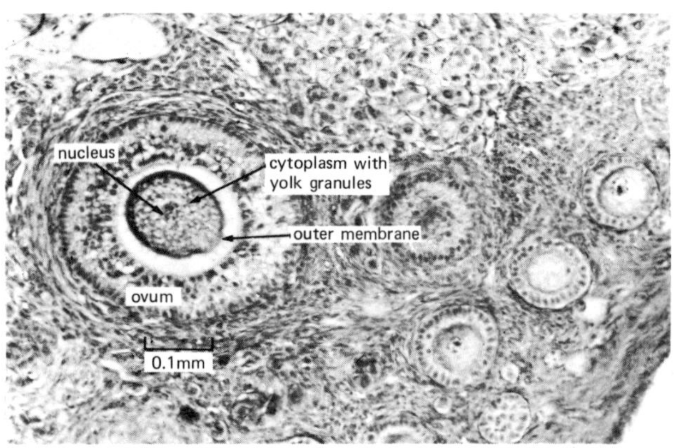

Where are the eggs produced?

Eggs are produced in small, oval-shaped organs called **ovaries** located below the kidneys. The walls of the ovary contain small fluid-filled structures called **ovarian follicles**. Potential egg cells develop during embryonic life and lie dormant until the age of sexual maturity is reached, in humans at about the age of twelve or thirteen. After this time every twenty-eight days or so a single egg in one of the ovaries completes its cycle of development and is released into the **oviduct**. The opening of the ovaries is not continuous with the oviduct but communicates with it through a funnel-shaped enlargement of the end of the duct (see fig. 6.41).

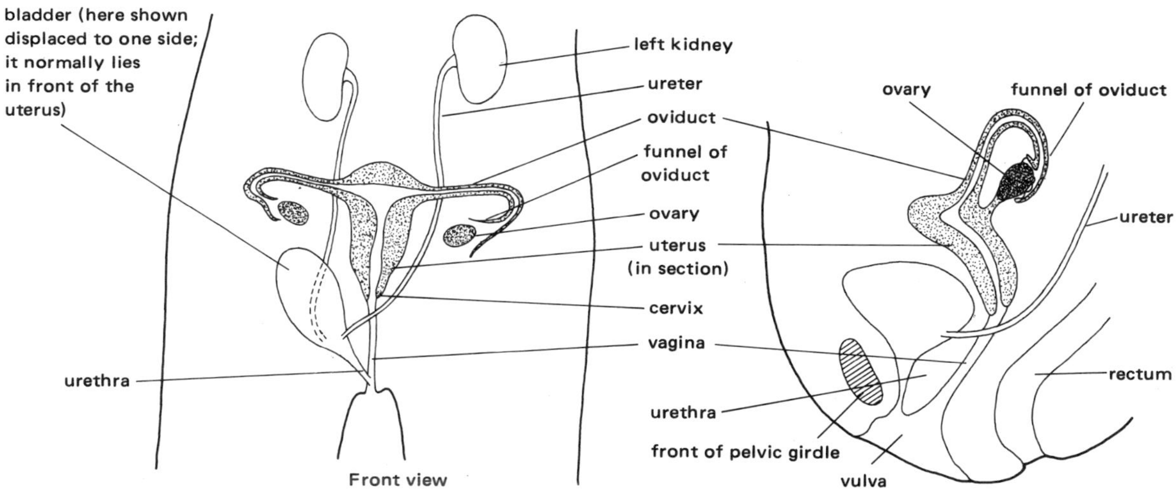

Fig.6.41 Female reproductive organs in human

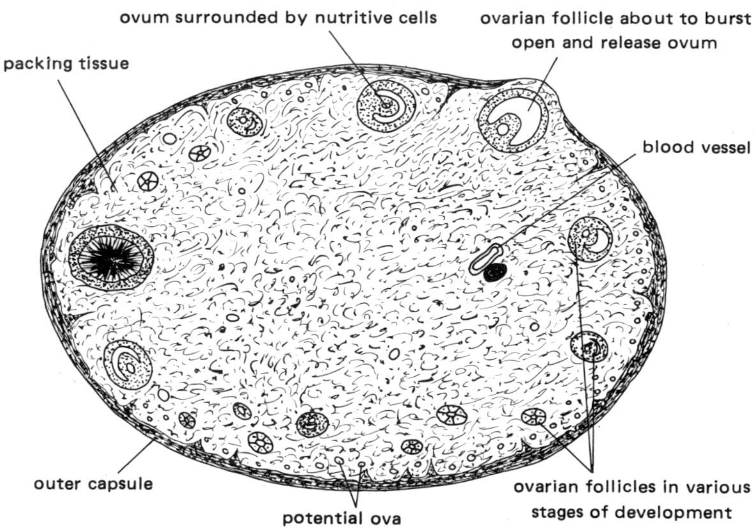

Fig.6.42 Section through an ovary

The maturation period of an individual egg is about twelve to fourteen days. After being released into the oviduct the egg slowly makes its way towards the **uterus**. The journey takes about ten days and it is during this period that the egg is capable of being **fertilized** by a sperm. At the same time the inner lining of the uterus prepares for the possibility that fertilization has taken place and that a developing embryo will be arriving.

What happens if fertilization does not take place?

Once the egg reaches the uterus it is no longer capable of being fertilized. At this point the thickened walls of the uterus intended for the implantation of the fertilized egg is sloughed off and the cellular debris along with some blood passes out of the body in what is called the **menstrual flow**.

When menstruation is completed, after about five days, the lining of the uterus heals and the cycle is ready to begin again.

This regular alternation of fertile and infertile periods is called the **oestrus cycle** and is regulated by the action of specific hormones. In some mammals the oestrus cycle only operates either once or twice a year during the mating season. In humans the cycles are continuous at approximately monthly intervals.

Fig.6.43 The oestrus cycle

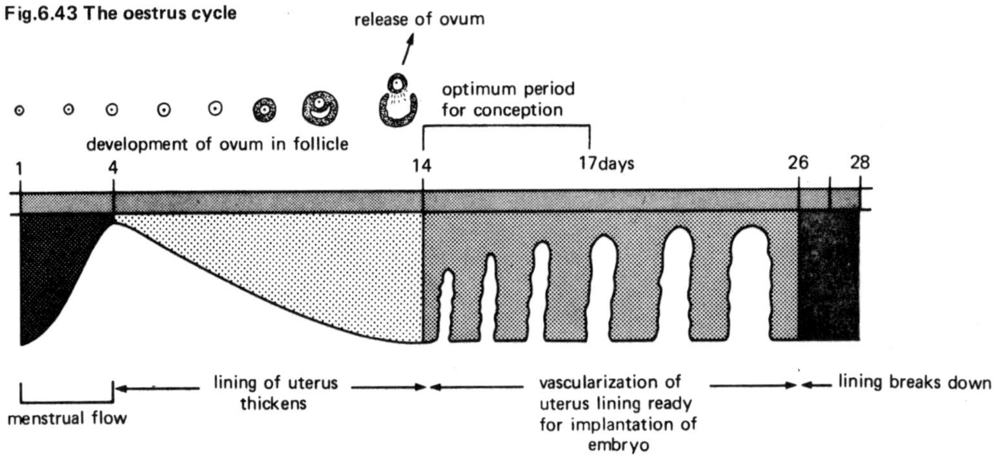

What is fertilization?

Fertilization is the union of the sperm and the egg and the subsequent fusion of the two nuclei to produce the **zygote**. It can take place either outside or inside the body of the female.

In species where fertilization is external mating usually consists of the male lying on the back of the female, stimulating her to release her eggs and at the same time ejecting the sperms on top of the eggs. **External fertilization** is found in many aquatic animals and in amphibians that lay their eggs in the water. It does not occur on land because the fertilized eggs would very quickly dry out and

die and because the sperm would have no liquid medium in which they could swim to find the egg.
On land the only suitable place for fertilization is the interior of the body of the female **(internal fertilization)**.

Summary

The simplest forms of sexual reproduction occur through a transfer of the cellular contents of one organism to another of its kind. The process is known as conjugation.
In higher organisms gametes are produced. By definition the gamete that is motile is the male while the stationary one is the female. Gametes are produced through meiosis, a process that results in the formation of haploid cells containing only half the usual chromosome number for the species.
Parthenogenesis is the development of a new organism from an unfertilized egg.
In mammals the male reproductive cells, the sperms, are produced by the testes and the female reproductive cells, the eggs, are produced by the ovaries. The union of the two gametes is called fertilization and the resulting cell mass is referred to as the zygote.

Details of fertilization in mammals

In mammals internal fertilization takes place during the process of **mating**, as it is called in animals, or **sexual intercourse** as it is referred to in the case of humans.
The penis of the male is inserted into the **vagina** of the female and upon ejaculation the semen is squirted up the vagina to the opening of the uterus. The combination of the various secretions of the female organs with the seminal fluid provides a liquid medium through which the sperm can pass to reach the oviduct.

Fig. 6.44 Sperms travelling towards oviduct

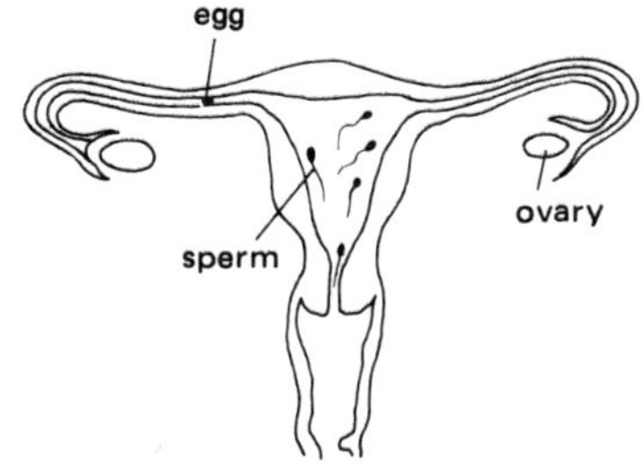

Fig.6.45 Fertilization of a starfish egg

(i) Sperms swim towards ovum attracted by chemicals diffusing from it.
(ii) One sperm touches ovum and sticks.
(iii) The nucleus of the sperm passes into the cytoplasm of the ovum.
(iv) A membrane appears around the egg and prevents any other sperms from penetrating it.
(v) The nuclei of the sperm and ovum fuse together.

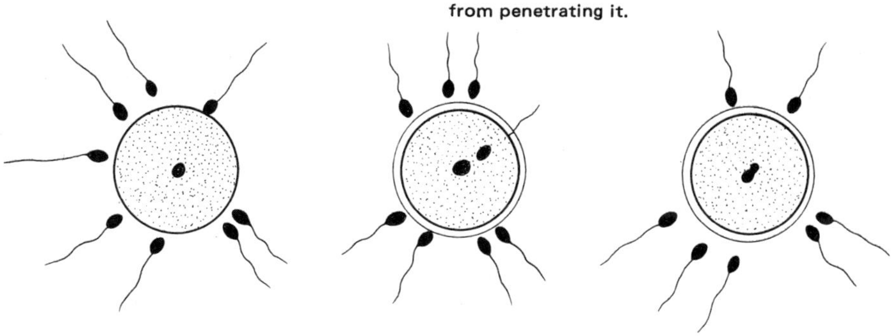

Fig.6.46 **Development of human embryo**

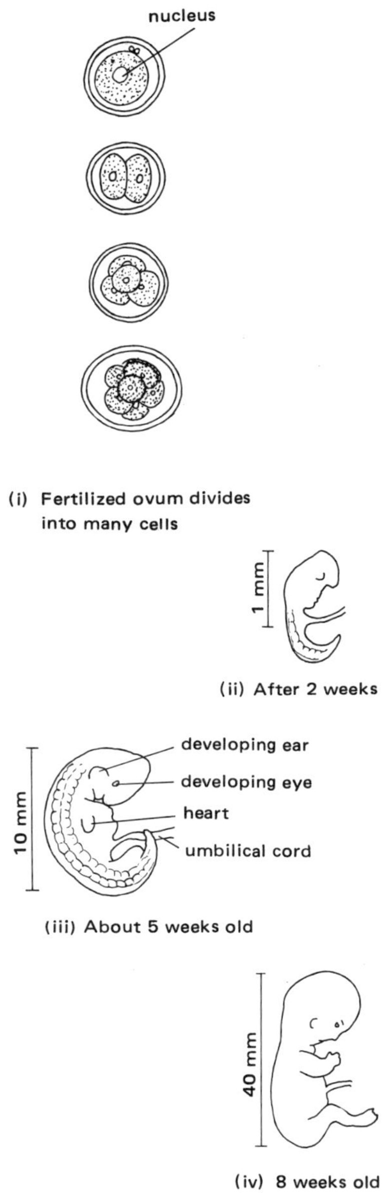

The total length of the journey is seven *thousand* times as long as the size of the head of the sperm. The entrance to the uterus is usually filled with a mucous substance that the sperms have to dissolve away before they can enter the passage. Furthermore, once released, a sperm is only able to stay alive for twenty-four to forty-eight hours. It is no wonder that so many sperms are necessary to ensure that even one will successfully reach its destination.

Doctors have estimated that when a cubic centimetre of human semen contains less than sixty million sperms, fertilization is almost impossible.

When a sperm does manage to reach an egg it sticks to it. The nucleus of the sperm passes into the cytoplasm of the egg cell and fuses with the egg nucleus. At the same time a **fertilization membrane** appears around the egg to prevent the entry of any other sperm.

What happens to the egg after fertilization has taken place?

After fertilization the egg is either covered by a hard or soft shell as in the case of insects, birds and reptiles, and passed out of the body, or remains inside the mother throughout the length of the **gestation period**.

In humans the fertilization of an egg is referred to as **conception**.

The development of the fertilized egg in mammals

With the fusion of the haploid nuclei of the two gametes the fertilized egg is restored to the diploid state. The zygote, as it is now called, undergoes repeated mitotic division to produce two, four, eight, sixteen cells and so on. All the while the cell mass continues on its way to the uterus.

Upon reaching the uterus finger-like projections from the zygote anchor the cell mass to the wall of that organ. These projections develop into the **placenta**, through which materials are exchanged between the body of the mother and that of the developing embryo. Connecting the embryo to the placenta is the **umbilical cord**.

How is the developing embryo nourished by the mother?

The circulatory systems of the mother and embryo are not directly connected at the placenta. Rather, exchange of materials between them takes place by diffusion. The circulatory system of the embryo is slightly modified so that the blood can pass from the umbilical cord directly to the heart, bypassing the lungs. In fact until the moment of birth the lungs of the embryo are completely deflated.

During the entire gestation period the developing embryo is supplied with oxygen and souble nutrients by the mother through the placenta and waste products of the embryo are eliminated by the same route. Fig. 6.47 shows details of the structure of the placenta.

How is the developing embryo protected from injury?

As a means of protection the embryo is surrounded by two separate layers of membrane: the inner **amnion** and the outer **chorion**. The interior of the **amniotic sac** is filled with a liquid in which the embryo floats around. This way, it is cushioned against any dangerous shock that might result from the movements of the mother.
To accommodate the growing embryo the uterus enlarges tremendously in size. In humans it goes from a normal size of about five cubic centimetres to between five thousand and seven thousand cubic centimetres depending on the size of the embryo. The human embryo is also called the **foetus**.

How long is the gestation period?

The length of the gestation period varies considerably from one species to the next. It varies from three weeks in the mouse to twenty-one months in the elephant. In humans it is nine months. The series of diagrams below summarizes the major stages in the development of the human embryo. Studying the development in humans is, of course, extremely difficult, as there are no opportunities for detailed experimentation. Much information can be gained, however, by examining the stages in the development of a chick embryo.

Fig.6.47 Transportation during gestation

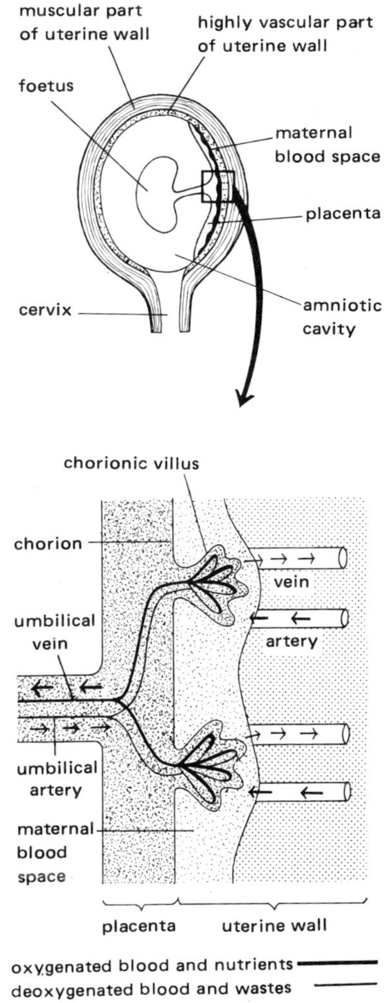

Fig.6.48 Growth and development in uterus

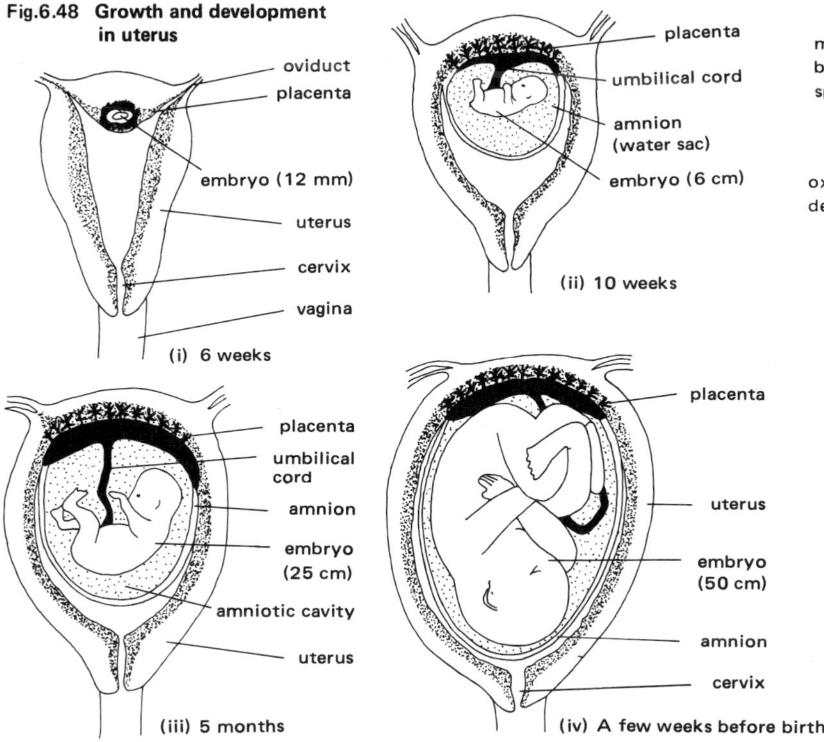

EXPERIMENT TO STUDY THE DEVELOPMENT OF A CHICK EMBRYO

Materials

Fertilized hen's eggs that have been incubating for one, three, seven and ten days.

dissecting instruments

warm salt water

hand lens

Method

1. Remove the egg from the incubator and place into a shallow dish lined with soft paper.
2. Carefully crack the shell in the middle of the egg and start to pick off bits of the shell to expose the interior. Try to remove the shell only keeping the membrane layer intact.
3. After you have made a fairly large window carefully cut the membrane around the edge and expose the developing embryo.
4. Observe carefully, make a simple drawing of what you see, and label it. Measure the length of the embryo.
5. Repeat the same procedure with the other three eggs. Free the embryo from the surrounding protective membrane and identify all the newly developing structures.
6. Compare the appearance of the developing chick embryo with the diagram of that of the human embryo.
7. If possible leave a few eggs until the completion of the incubation. period and watch them hatch.

In the case of birds, at the end of the development period the fully formed embryo pecks its way out of the shell with the help of a special egg tooth. In mammals at the end of the gestation period the embryo is 'born', that is, it comes out of the uterus of the mother through the vagina.

The birth of a human foetus

In preparation for birth the foetus changes position in the uterus so that its head is pointed towards the opening of the vagina. Rhythmic contractions of the uterus signal the imminent birth. The contractions, brought about by the action of the hormone oxytocin, become more and more frequent as **labour** progresses.

At some point the amnion bursts and the fluid contained in it escapes through the vagina. The opening of the uterus, the **cervix**, dilates to allow the head of the foetus to pass through. The uterine contractions become more and more rapid and vigorous until the entire length of the foetus is forced through the cervix and out through the vagina.

At this point the umbilical cord is cut and tied close to the body of the baby. Uterine contractions persist until the membranes that surrounded the embryo, referred to as the **afterbirth** have also been expelled from the uterus.

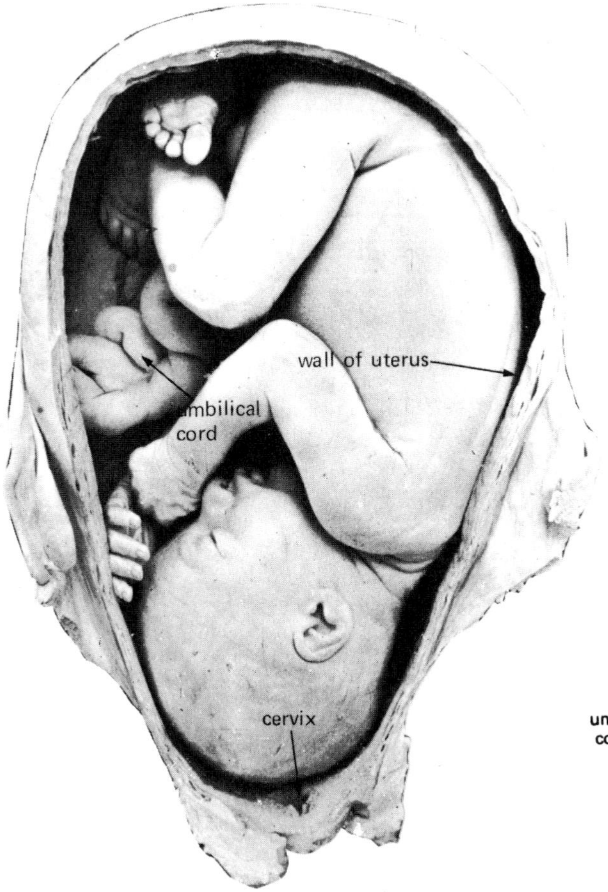

Fig.6.49 Human foetus just before birth

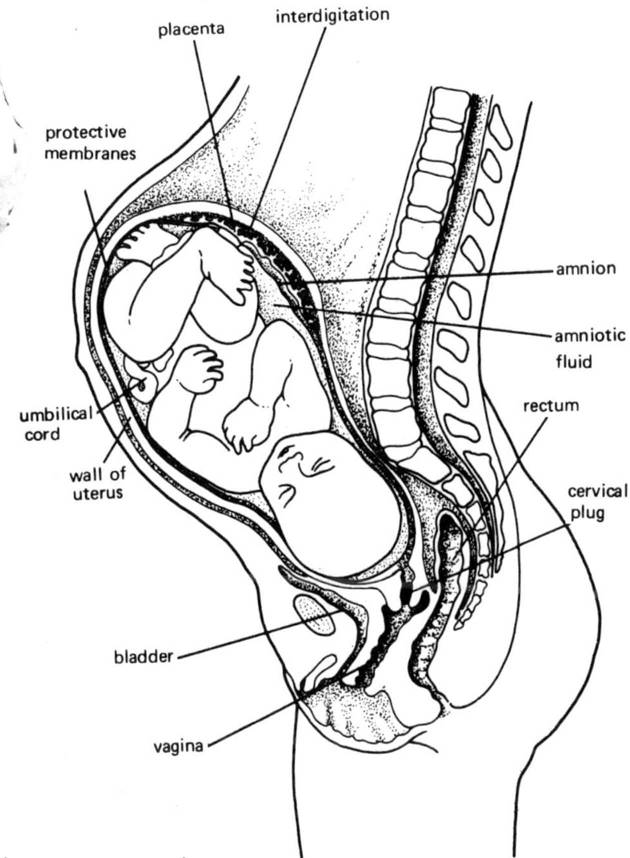

The moment of birth

The moment of birth is probably the most crucial one ever experienced in the life of a human. From a comfortable existence inside the warm body of the mother where food and oxygen are supplied automatically, the newly born baby is thrust into the cold, bright outside world. The life line to the mother is severed and the new human being is left to fend for himself.

At the time of birth many important changes take place in the body of the baby. The lungs must take over the task of supplying the body with oxygen so the circulatory system has to be modified to form a connection to the lungs. The opening that exists between the left and right sides of the heart during embryonic life must be closed to separate the venous blood from the arterial blood.

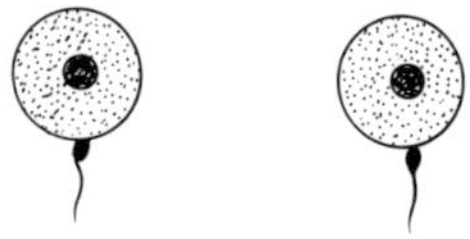

Fig.6.50 Fraternal twins from 2 separate fertilized eggs

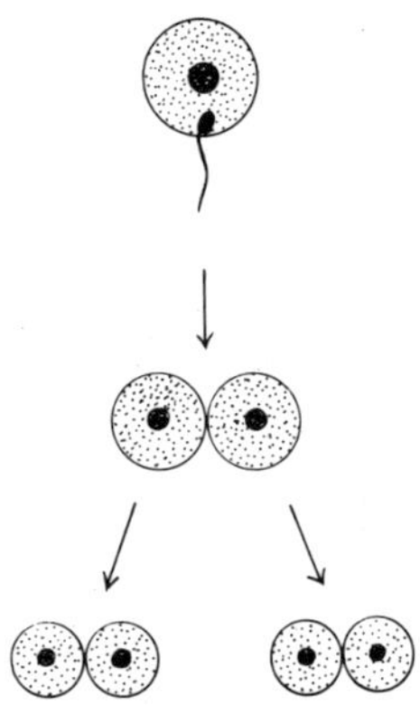

Fig.6.51 Identical twins from a single fertilized egg

Multiple births

In the section on the female reproductive system we said that in humans normally only a single egg is released from the ovaries at a time.
How then can we account for the birth of two or more siblings at a time?
There are two ways. At times it is possible for two or more eggs to be released from the ovaries at ovulation. The tendency for this to occur seems, at least in part, to be genetically determined. As a result the percentages of multiple births are different in various races and can sometimes be traced through the successive generations of a single family.
Twins resulting from the fertilization of two eggs by two separate sperms are called **fraternal** or **non-identical twins**. Fraternal twins are no more similar in appearance and characteristics than siblings born separately.

How do identical twins develop?

When the newly fertilized egg undergoes its first cell division, normally the two new cells stay attached and then proceed to undergo further divisions. At times, however, due to circumstances not fully understood by scientists, the two cells separate and each develops into an individual embryo leading to the birth of **identical twins**.
The cells of identical twins contain precisely the same genetic information since they both originate from the same fertilized egg. They are therefore always of the same sex.

Parental care

Do all animals look after their young?
The amount and type of parental care given to the young before and after birth varies among animal species. In almost all invertebrates and in most amphibians, fish and reptiles parental care is entirely absent. Eggs are either fertilized externally or, if internal fertilization occurs, they are laid and left in a suitable spot. After this the parents have nothing to do with them.
A notable exception among invertebrates are the social insects such as bees and ants. Among these groups the fertilized eggs and the developing larvae are cared for by the workers of the colony (see p. 256).
Among fish, the male stickleback builds an elaborate nest for the eggs and spends a great deal of time and effort protecting the eggs and the newly hatched young. Among seahorses the male incubates the eggs in a special brooding pouch in his body.
An even higher level of maternal care is shown by a few species of fish in which eggs are fertilized internally and develop inside the

body of the female. In general however, in these lower species parental care at best only extends to the end of the incubation period and after hatching the offspring are on their own.

True parental care is found in most species of birds that build elaborate nests to receive the eggs and where the male and female take turns incubating the eggs and feeding the newly hatched nestlings.

A special feature of parental care found only in mammals is the suckling of the young by the mother. The production of milk by the mammary glands is triggered by **lactogenic hormone**. The milk produced provides the young with a rich balanced diet.

The parental care given to young mammals continues for various lengths of time. In addition to feeding and cleaning the young it may include such things as elaborate training in hunting as undertaken by the large predatory animals and social training in higher primates and humans.

Fig.6.52 Structure of mammary gland

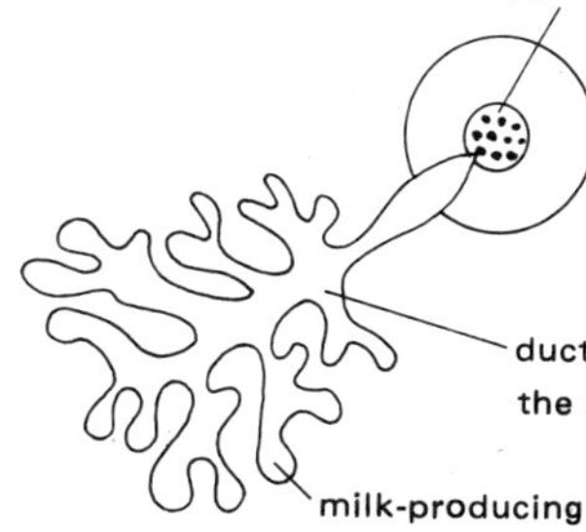

What is the significance of parental care?

It is obvious that the greater the degree of parental care prevalent in a species the greater are the chances of survival of the young.

As a general rule the disadvantages of the absence of parental care are offset by laying a much larger number of eggs. In aquatic animals and insects, especially if the eggs are fertilized externally, many thousands or millions of eggs are laid by the female in a single breeding season. At the other end of the scale in higher primates and humans where there is a high degree of parental care, ovulation usually results in the release of only one egg at a time.

Control of conception

Preventing conception while still being able to carry on intercourse is at times desirable for personal or social reasons.

Various methods of **birth control** are known. According to the **rhythm method** sexual intercourse is restricted to certain 'safe' periods in the female reproductive cycle. If you refer back to p. 286 you will see that the egg can only be fertilized during three or four days in every monthly cycle and fertilization is impossible the rest of the time. The determination of the safe periods, however, is subject to considerable error since monthly cycles are not always regular.

Insertion of mechanical barriers into the vagina or uterus to prevent the entry of sperms is also widely used. The **diaphragm** is inserted into the vagina to cover the opening of the cervix while the **IUD (intra-uterine device)** is inserted directly into the uterus. In recent years the use of the **contraceptive pill** has become widespread. The pill contains a hormone-like compound that prevents ovulation from taking place. It is the most reliable means of contraception available today. The disadvantages of the pill are that many women suffer from unpleasant side effects. A connection between the use of contraceptive pills and various diseases such as cancer has also been suggested although not proved.

Summary

In mammals fertilization occurs internally in the oviduct of the female. The zygote travels to the uterus and is implanted in the walls of that organ. Nutrients are supplied to the embryo by diffusion across the placenta and waste products are removed in the same way.
At the end of the gestation period the birth in mammals is stimulated by contraction of the uterus due to the release of oxytocin.
The degree of parental care given to the young varies among the different animal species. The highest degree of care is found in birds and mammals.

Sexual reproduction in plants

Animals that reproduce sexually possess specialized reproductive organs for the production of gametes. In plants a specialized part of the shoot, the **flower**, is modified for the purposes of reproduction. For the moment the structure of the flower and its function in reproduction will be discussed using a schematic diagram of a generalized flower. After this we will look at several flowers from plants found in Hong Kong.

The parts of a flower

The section of stem to which the flower is attached is called the **pedicel** and the thickening of the stem that forms the flower base is the **receptacle**.
From the receptacle arise the modified floral leaves arranged in a circular pattern of **whorls**. The outermost whorl, the **calyx** is composed of a number of **sepals** that are usually green but can be coloured. Inside these is a whorl of coloured **petals** making up the **corolla**.

Fig.6.53

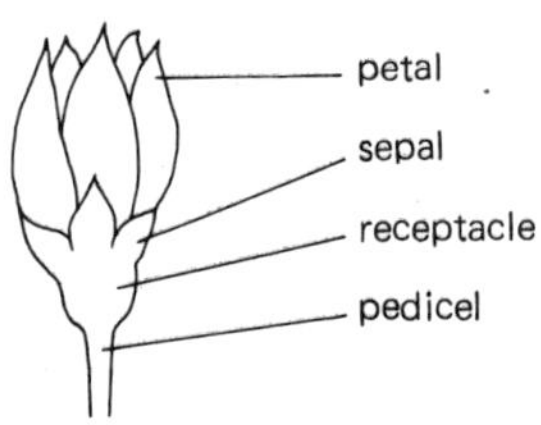

The **androecium** is the collective name given to the male reproductive parts of the flower. Recall that the definition 'male' derives from the idea that the motile reproductive cell is always considered to be the male and the stationary one the female.
The androecium consists of a number of **stamens** each made up of a slender supporting stalk called the **filament** and a terminal portion, the **anther**. The anther usually has two lobes and each lobe contains two compartments filled with the male reproductory cells called **pollen grains**.
The female reproductory organs are collectively referred to as the **gynoecium**, formed by one or more **pistils**, occupying the innermost

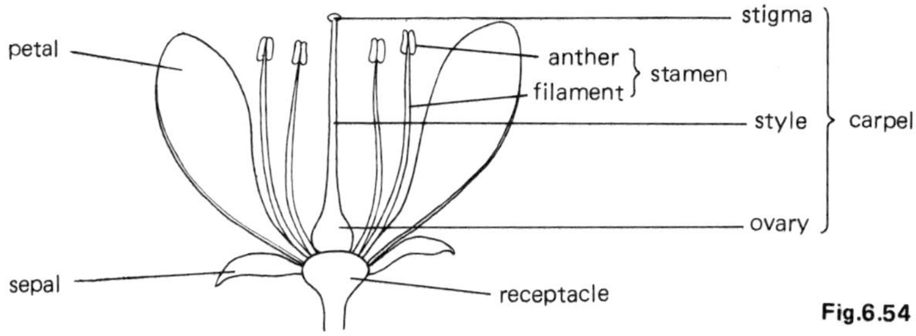

Fig.6.54

whorl. Each pistil in turn consists of one or more **carpels**. The swollen base of the carpel is called the **ovary** and it houses the **ovules**. The supporting stalk, the **style**, leads to an apical enlargement called the **stigma**.

Flowers vary greatly with respect to the number and the particular arrangement of the various floral parts. Flowers that bear both stamens and carpels, that is, both male and female reproductive organs are said to be **hermaphroditic** while those that have only one or the other are **unisexual**.

Among unisexual plants in most cases a single plant will bear both male and female flowers, but there are some species that are divided into distinct male and female plants in the same way as animals are divided into separate sexes.

EXERCISE

Using the accompanying generalized diagram of a flower examine as many flowers as are available and notice the variation between them. Fig. 6.56 illustrates the various receptacle types and fig. 6.58 the types of pistil. Fig. 6.59 represents the ovaries of various types of plant that have been cut open to reveal the internal structures.

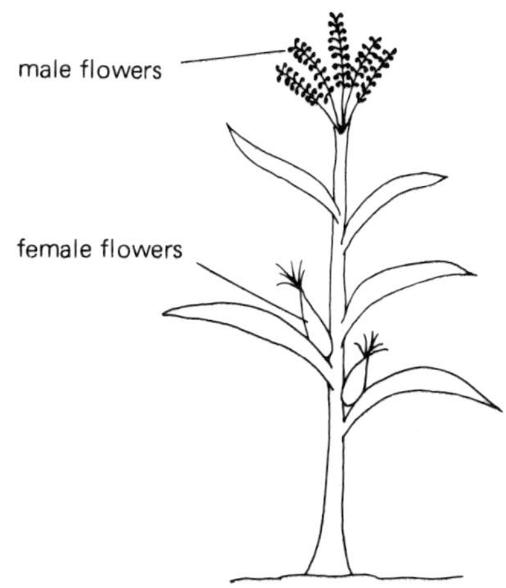

Fig. 6.55 Zea mays plant

Fig.6.56

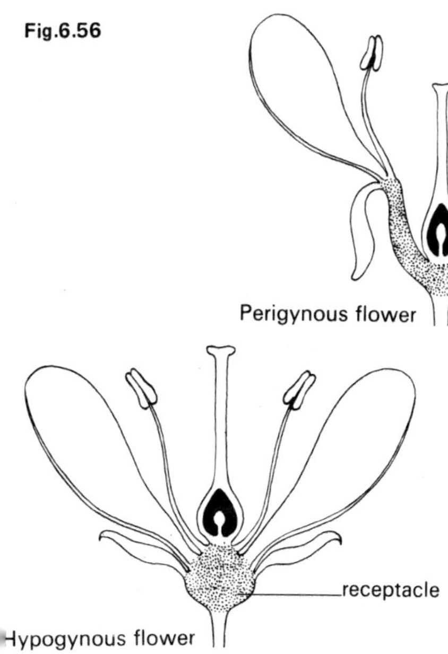

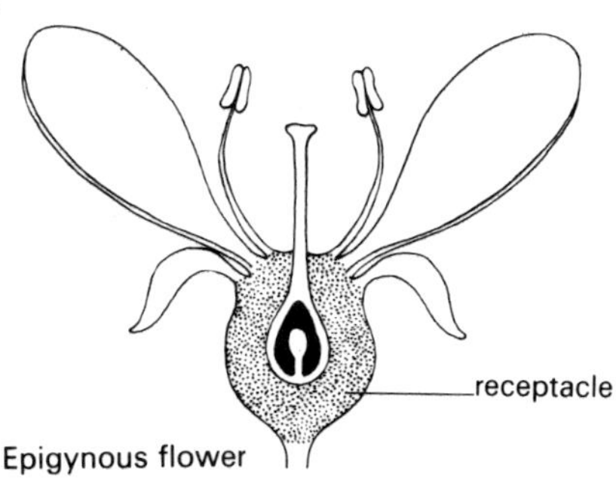

Fig.6.57 Typical stamen

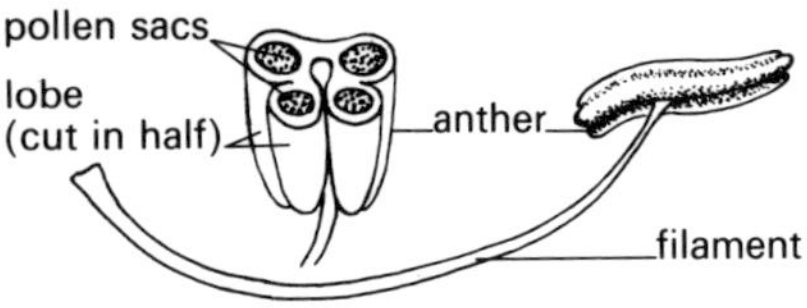

Fig.6.59 Different types of ovaries

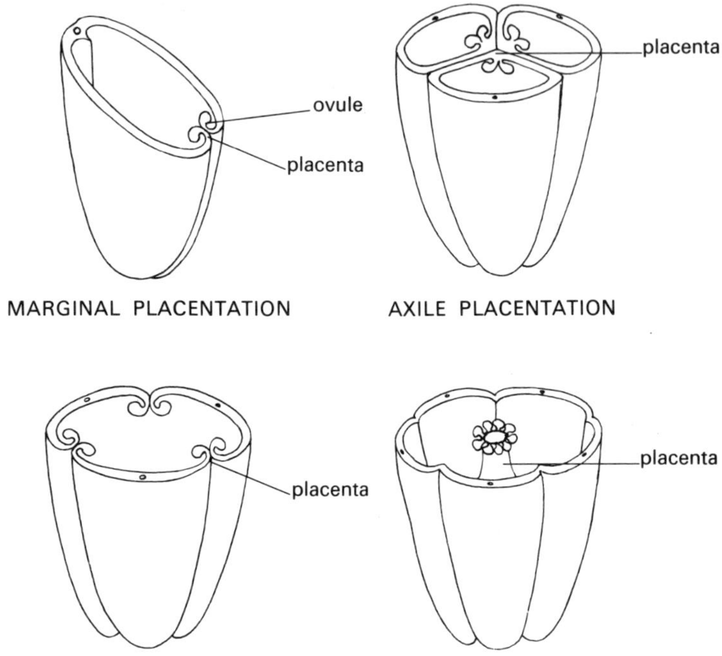

MARGINAL PLACENTATION AXILE PLACENTATION

PARIETAL PLACENTATION FREE-CENTRAL PLACENTATION

Fig.6.58 Types of pistil

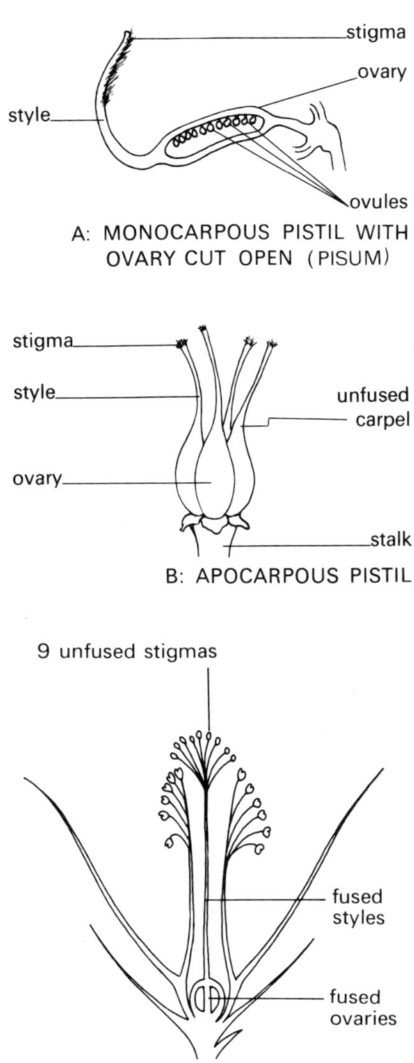

A: MONOCARPOUS PISTIL WITH OVARY CUT OPEN (PISUM)

B: APOCARPOUS PISTIL

C: SYNCARPOUS PISTIL (MALVA)

As you examine the flowers record your observations in a table such as the one below and make a drawing of each flower. Figs. 6.60–6.62 show some common local flowers that you might have available for examination.

Table of flower structures

NAME	Type of receptacle	No. of stamens	No. of pistils	Type of pistil	Type of ovary

Fig. 6.60 Helianthus (Sunflower)

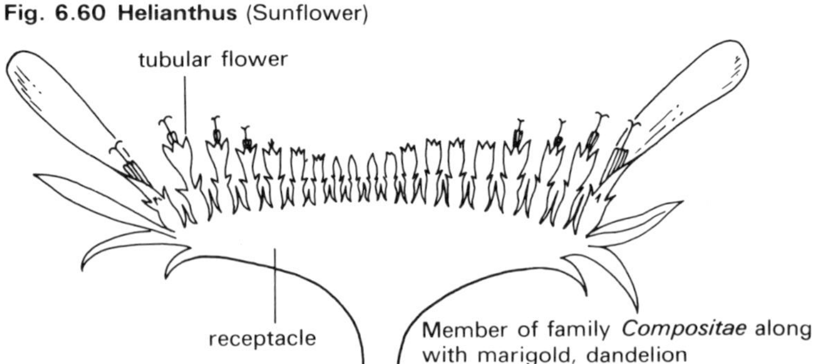

Member of family *Compositae* along with marigold, dandelion
What appears to be one large flower is a great number of small flowers
Each consists of a lower part containing the ovary and the upper part forming the anther

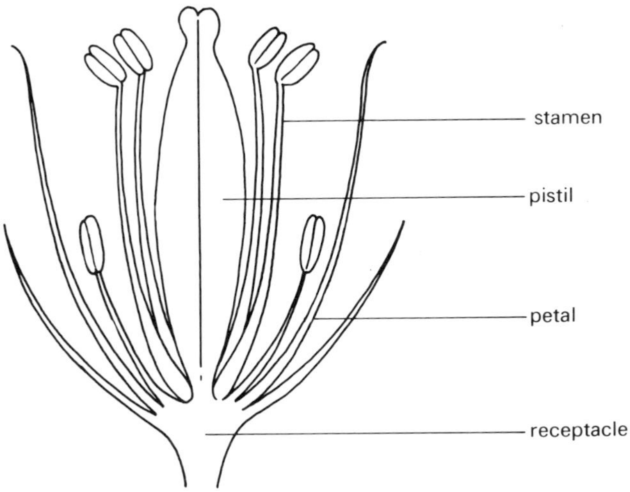

Fig. 6.61 Brassica
Hypogynous receptacle
6 stamens
Single pistil of 2 fused carpels
Axile placentation
2-celled ovary

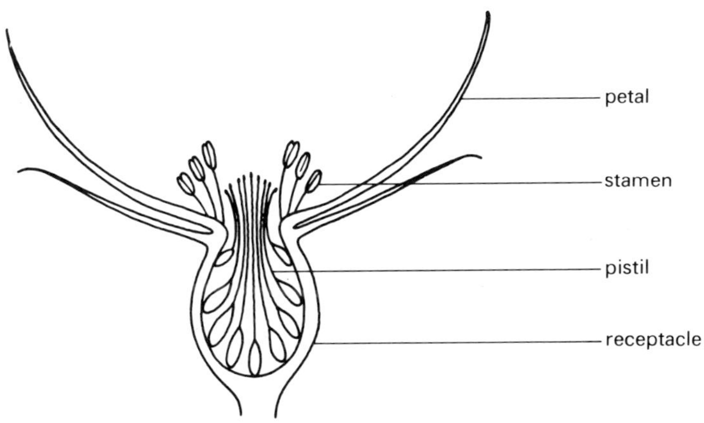

Fig. 6.63 Rosa (rose)
Perigynous receptacle
Numerous stamens (depending on species)
Carpels separate and numerous

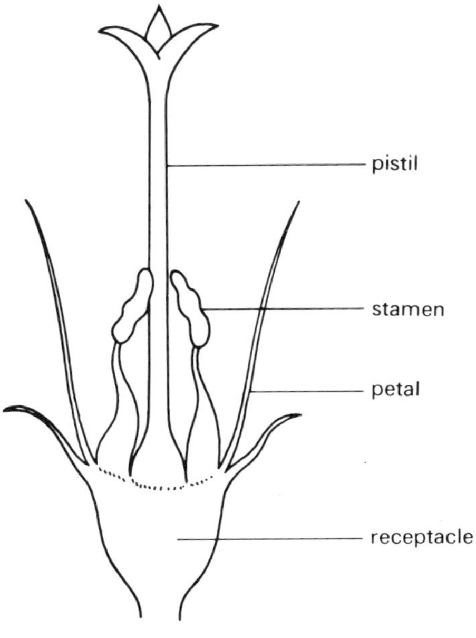

Fig. 6.62 Campanula (bluebell)
Epigynous receptacle
5 stamens
Single pistil of three fused carpels

How do the reproductive cells develop?

The development of pollen cells

Each of the pollen cells in the anther is at first filled with diploid **pollen mother cells**. The term 'mother cells' is probably an unfortunate choice to refer to the cells that will develop into male reproductive cells, but it simply means that these are the **precursor cells** from which the pollen grains will develop.
As a result of meiosis these diploid cells each give rise to four haploid pollen grains. Once the pollen grains have matured inside the anther, the latter splits open to expose the mature pollen.

Fig.6.64

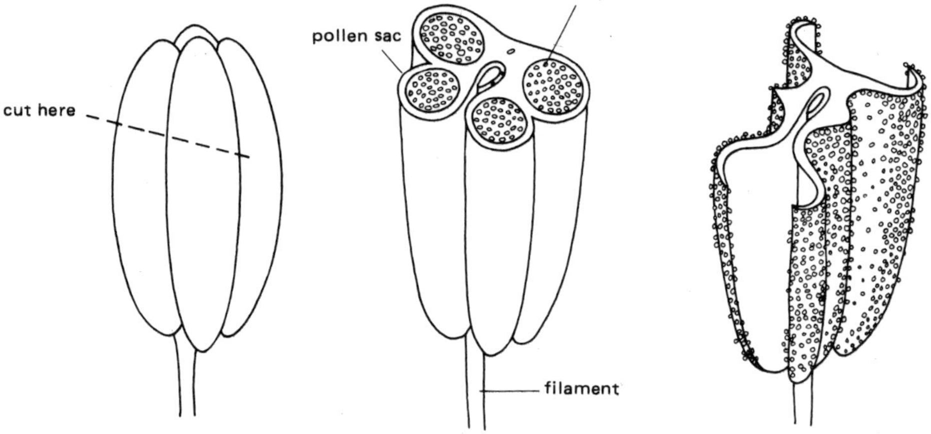

Structure of anther (top cut off)

Pollen sacs split exposing pollen

Fig.6.65 Egg cell inside ovary

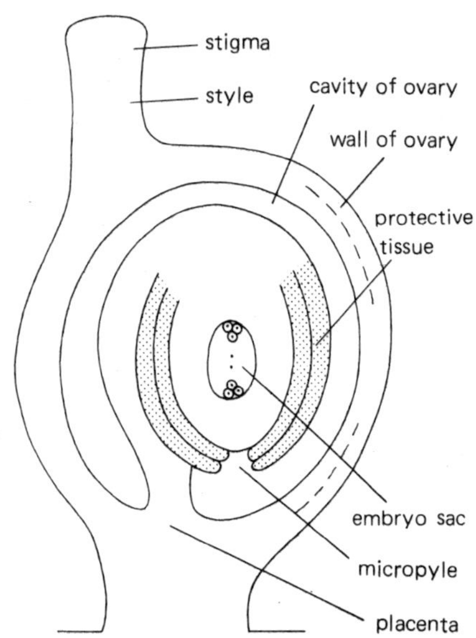

Development of the embryo

Initially the ovary is a hollow cavity containing one or more ovules that project into the cavity and are attached by the **placenta**. As development proceeds the diploid embryo mother cells, of which there is one per ovule, undergo meiosis to give four haploid cells. In most cases three of the cells degenerate while the fourth develops into an embryo sac containing a single egg cell and several other nuclei and accessory cells. The embryo sac is surrounded by several layers of protective tissue through which a tiny pore called the **micropyle** passes. This is the point at which the pollen grain will enter the embryo sac.

Pollination

Pollination entails the transfer of pollen from the anther of a flower to the stigma of the same flower or of a different flower of the same species. If the pollen grains fall onto the stigma of the same flower the process is referred to as **self-pollination**. As more often happens the pollen is carried by the wind or insects to the anther of another flower and **cross-pollination** is said to have occurred. In fact, in many plants pollen from the same flower is not effective in initiating the process of fertilization. Cross-pollination is preferable because the mixing of genetic material from different flowers and different plants results in the production of healthier progeny.

Fertilization

When a pollen grain comes into contact with the stigma it adheres to the sticky surface secretions produced by the stigma cells. Since the ovary containing the egg cells are at the opposite end of the pistil, for fertilization to occur the pollen grain must make its way to the ovary through the style. This is accomplished by the development of the **pollen tube** which becomes increasingly elongated until it 'grows' right down the length of the style and enters the ovule through the micropyle.

As the pollen tube penetrates down the style the nuclei migrate along so that they are always very close to the growing tip of the tube. When the centre of the ovule is reached the pollen tube penetrates the embryo sac, bursts open and the male nuclei are liberated. One nucleus fuses with the egg cell to produce a diploid zygote. The second male nucleus fuses with some of the accessory cells in the embryo sac to develop into the food storage tissue called the **endosperm**.

The ovule containing the zygote proceeds to develop into the **seed** while the surrounding structures of the ovary will develop into the **fruit**.

Fruits and seeds

There is tremendous variation in the structure of the fruit and seeds of different species of plant. It is always the seed that contains the fertilized egg cell from which the new plant will develop. The function of the fruit is primarily to protect the zygote.

Fig.6.66 Development of pollen tube

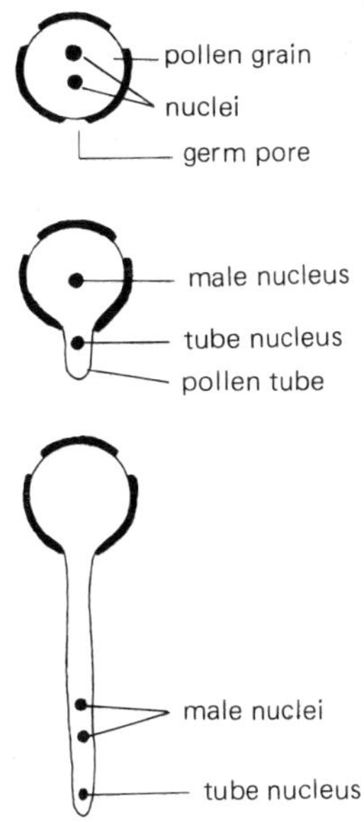

Fig.6.67

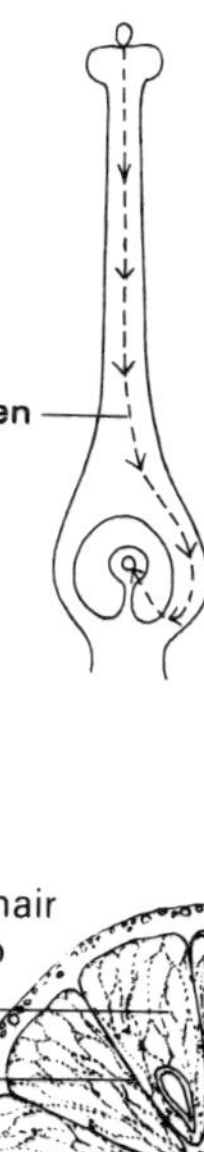

Fig.6.68

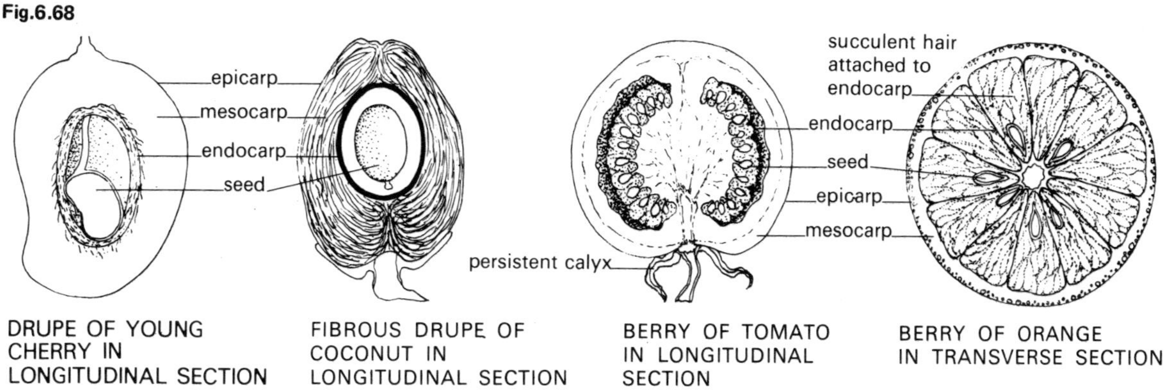

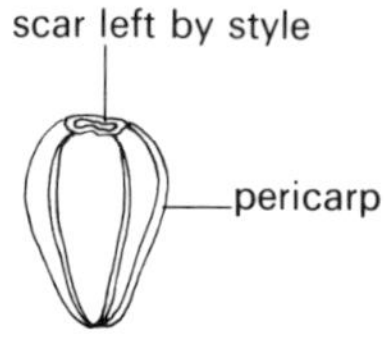

ACHENE OF
SUNFLOWER

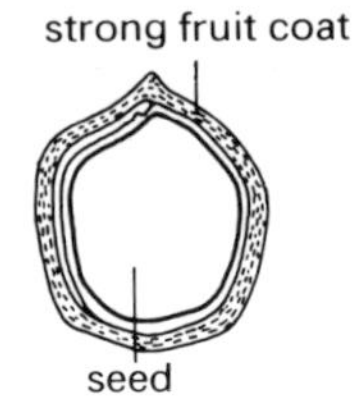

SECTION THROUGH
HAZEL NUT

CARYOPSIS
OF MAIZE

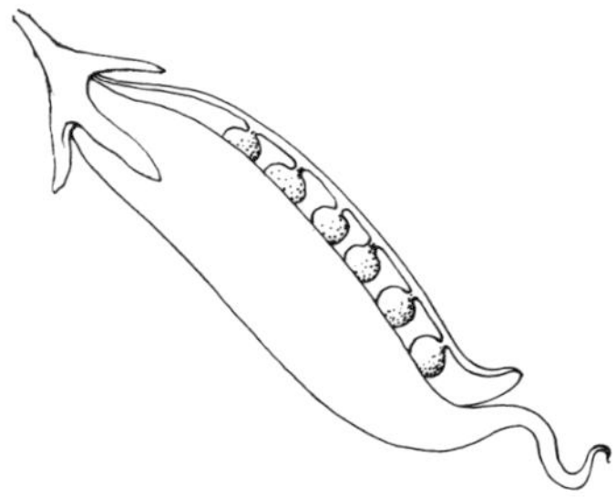

LEGUME OF
PEA

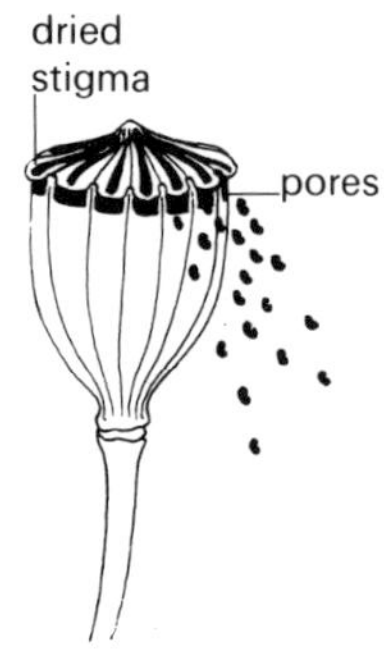

CAPSULE OF
POPPY

Dispersal of seeds

It is to the advantage of the plant species from the point of view of survival to have the seeds dispersed over as wide an area as possible. If all the seeds shed were to start developing very close to the parent plant the ensuing competition for light and raw materials would cut down the chances of survival of the seedlings.

In some instances only the seeds are dispersed while in others the fruits are dispersed.

Seeds that are dispersed by the wind are generally small and light. Some have wing-like structures or hairs to give added buoyancy. (Fig. 6.70.) In some species as the fruit ripens it begans to dry out. This puts more and more strain on the outer wall of the fruit until finally they split hurling the seeds away in all directions. (Fig. 6.69). Seeds can be dispersed by adhering to the fur of mammals. In some instances the fruit is eaten by an animal and the seeds are scattered.

Man is responsible for spreading seeds both purposely and inadvertently. In many instances crop seeds have been introduced into areas where they would not normally grow. Unfortunately many harmful plants such as weeds have also been introduced into new habitats along with some of the crops.

Summary

There are some plant species that are divided into separate sexes like the higher animals. In other species male and female flowers are present on the same plant. In most plants male and female

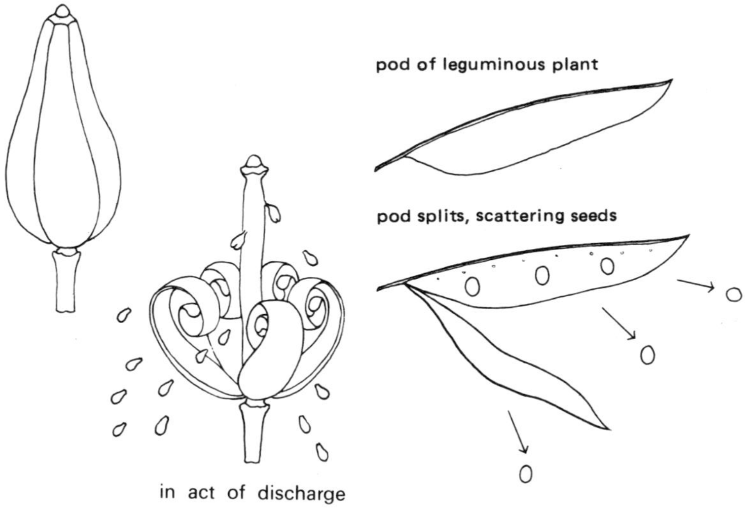

Fig.6.69 Seeds dispersed by explosive action

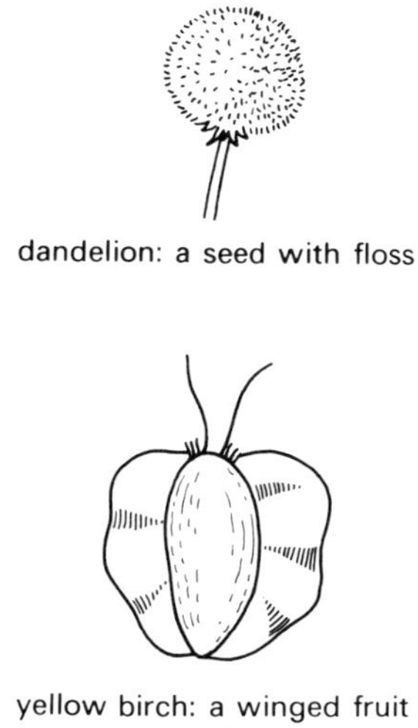

Fig.6.70 Seeds dispersed by wind

reproductive cells are produced by the same flower.
The male reproductive cell, the pollen, is produced by the androecium. The ovule is produced in the gynoecium.
Pollen is transferred from the anther to the stigma and then makes its way to the ovary by developing a pollen tube.
Fertilization occurs inside the ovary and the resulting zygote develops into the seed.

Seed structure

OUTER APPEARANCE

The following will be a description of the seeds of most of the common species of flowering plants. As with the structure of flowers there is some variation from one species to the other.
The seed is surrounded by a double layer of protective tissue called the **testa** and **tegmen** respectively, and jointly referred to as the **seed coat**. A small scar on the outside of the seed coat called the **hilum** marks the point of attachment to the fruit.

INTERNAL STRUCTURE

Inside the seed coat is the embryo which, upon germination, will give rise to the new plant.
The embryo is enclosed by the **cotyledons** or seed-leaves. In the case of **dicotyledonous** plants there are two (e.g. vigna) and in **monocotyledonous** plants there is one cotyledon (e.g. maize). In seeds where an endosperm is not present they may serve as a food storage organ (e.g. vigna). In many instances the cotyledon appears above the ground after germination, its cells synthesize chlorophyll and manufacture food by photosynthesis. As soon as the leaves of the seedling have developed the cotyledons cease to function and fall off.

Fig.6.71 Parts of a corn seed and embryo

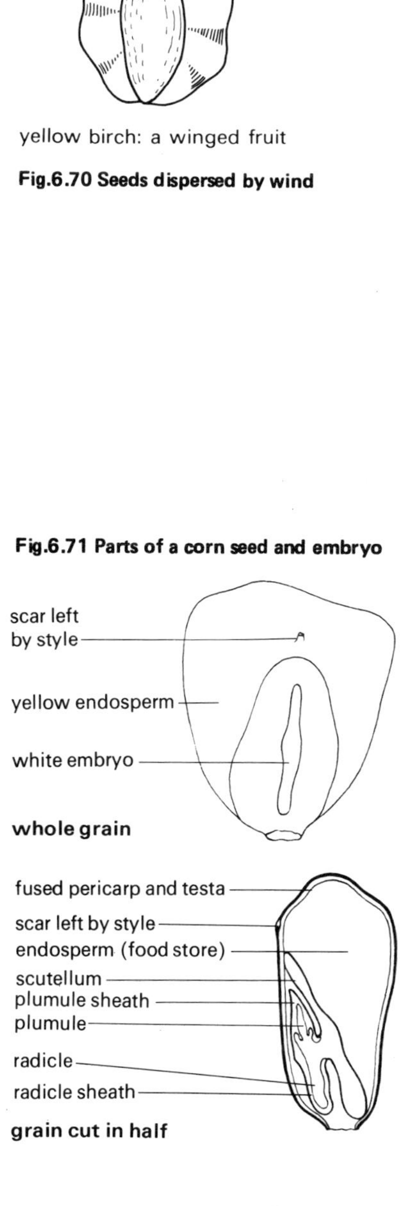

The embryo possesses distinct regions that will develop into the shoot and the root system of the new plant. The **plumule**, the embryonic shoot, is connected to the **radicle**, the embryonic root, by a short **stalk**.

Fig. 6.72 Seed of Vicia faba (broad bean)

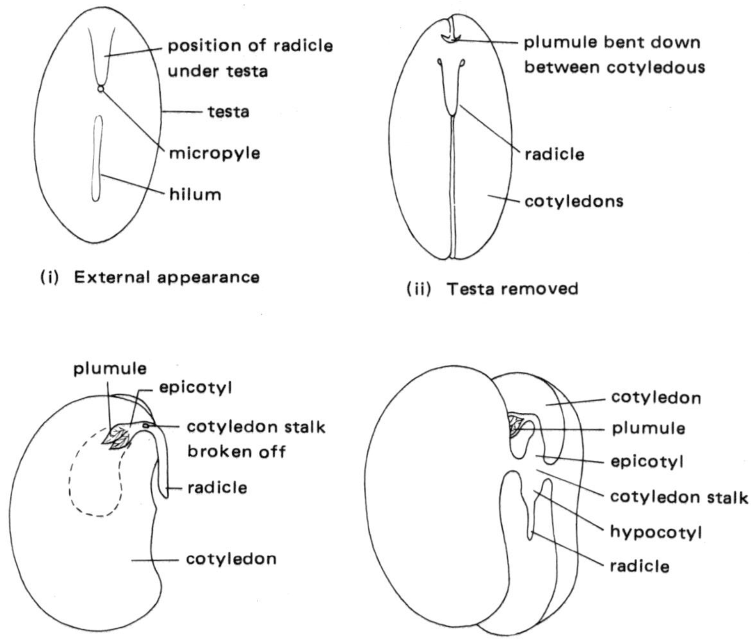

(i) External appearance

(ii) Testa removed

(iii) One cotyledon removed

(iv) The embryo plant

EXERCISE

Split open a cowpea and a corn seed; examine the internal structures. Compare the appearance of your seeds with that shown in figs. 6.71 and 6.72. Note that the bean is an example of a seed without an endosperm while corn does have an endosperm.

Dormancy

The time elapsed between the shedding of the seed or fruit from the parent plant and germination is a period of **dormancy**. Most seeds are extremely dry when they are shed, some containing as little as ten percent water. In this condition the embryo is alive but its chemical processes are carried on at an extremely slow rate.

The maximum length of dormancy possible so that germination will still take place depends on the species of plant. Some crop seeds such as wheat, if stored properly, will germinate even after fifteen years or so. In many tropical plants, on the other hand, germination must occur within a few days after the shedding of the fruit. In some instances there is no dormancy period at all and germination occurs while the fruit is still attached to the parent plant.

External conditions necessary for germination

EXPERIMENT TO FIND IF WATER IS NECESSARY FOR GERMINATION

Materials

Four small covered containers such as Petri dishes
seeds of pea or bean

Method

1. Label the containers A, B, C and D.
2. Soak some seeds in water overnight.
3. In container A place one third of the soaked seeds between layers of moist filter paper.
4. In B place also a third of the soaked seeds but do not moisten the blotting paper.
5. Place the remaining soaked seeds in C and cover with a layer of water.
6. In D place unsoaked seeds on dry filter paper.

Fig. 6.73

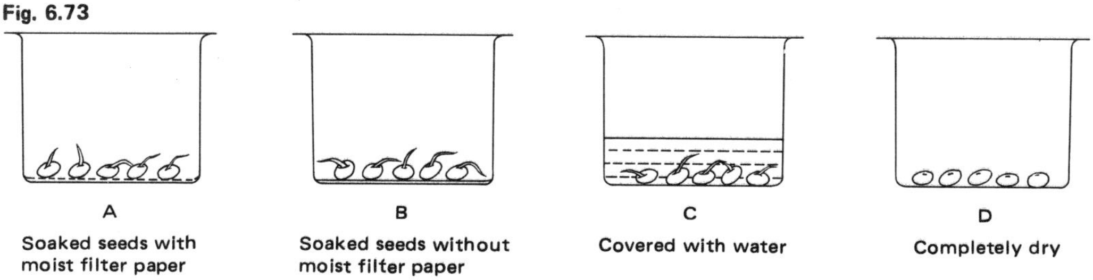

Make certain that the number of seeds in each container is about equal and that the containers are kept under the same conditions of temperature and illumination for a few days.

What difference do you observe between the seeds in the various containers?

Is there an optimum amount of moisture that is most suitable to ensure germination of seeds?

Why do you think water is necessary for germination?

Discussion

The seeds in container A are the ones that germinate properly. The ones in B may start to germinate but will soon shrivel up and die. Some of the seeds in C may start to germinate but most will likely rot due to excess moisture. The seeds in D will not germinate at all because they do not have any moisture.

From this experiment we can conclude that adequate water must be provided for seeds to germinate but excess moisture is as unfavourable as inadequate moisture.

Water is needed to soften up the seed coat and allow it to burst, releasing the embryo. Water is also needed by the individual cells in order for enzymes to function and chemical reactions to take place.

EXPERIMENT TO FIND OUT IF OXYGEN IS NECESSARY FOR GERMINATION

Materials

seeds of bean or pea
sodium pyrogalate solution
cotton wool

Method

1. Soak the seeds in water overnight.
2. Place the seeds in the bottom of two flasks between layers of moist filter paper.
3. Suspend into flask A a piece of cotton wool that has been soaked in sodium pyrogalate. Do not allow any of the solution to drip on top of the seeds.
4. Seal each flask with a rubber bung and leave for a few days. The effect of the sodium pyrogalate is to remove all the oxygen from the air in flask A. The air in flask B will contain oxygen.

Fig.6.74

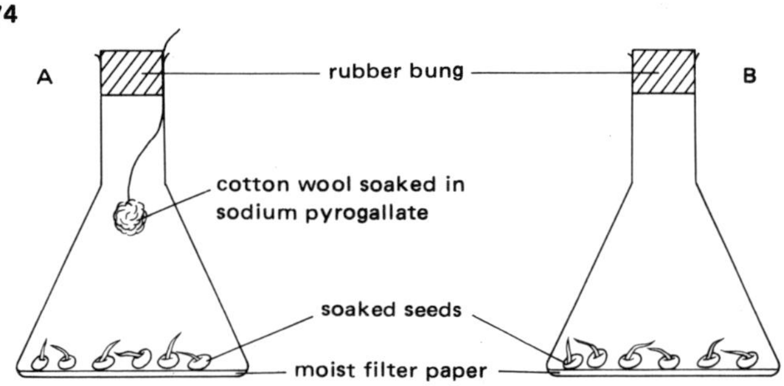

Do you observe any difference between the ability of the seeds in the two flasks to germinate?
Why do you think oxygen is necessary for germination?

Discussion

After a few days most of the seeds in flask B will probably have germinated but not any of the ones in flask A. This shows that germination cannot take place without oxygen.
The action of germination is a living process and as such requires energy. The energy is normally derived from the food materials stored in the seed and released through the process of respiration. Without oxygen no respiration can take place and the seed will not be able to obtain energy for its metabolic activities.

EXPERIMENT TO INVESTIGATE WHETHER TEMPERATURE AFFECTS THE GERMINATION OF SEEDS

Materials

pea or bean seeds
four small covered containers

Method

1. Soak the seeds in water overnight.
2. Place equal numbers of seeds between sheets of moist blotting

paper in the four containers. Label them A, B, C and D.
3. Place the containers in spots where the temperature varies from about 4°C to 45°C. For example, place A in the refrigerator at 4°C, B in an airconditioned room, about 20°C, C into a room where the temperature is about 30°C or in an incubator at 30°C and D in an incubator at 45°C.
4. Observe for a few days. Do not allow the filter paper to dry out.

What difference do you observe in the ability of the seeds to germinate under the various conditions of temperature?
Is a high temperature more favourable than a low temperature?
Why do you think this is so?
Discussion
The results of this experiment will show that germination is favoured by moderate temperatures. If it is either too hot (45°C) or too cold (4°C) germination will be impaired because the enzymes necessary for the living processes of the cells will not function efficiently. You will probably find that the seeds kept at 20°C will germinate the best. The optimum temperature for germination also depends on the normal habitat of the plant. Tropical plants will germinate better at higher temperatures, about 25°C or even 30°C. Temperate plants such as peas and beans do better at lower temperatures.

Fig. 6.75 **Stages in germination of castor oil seed**

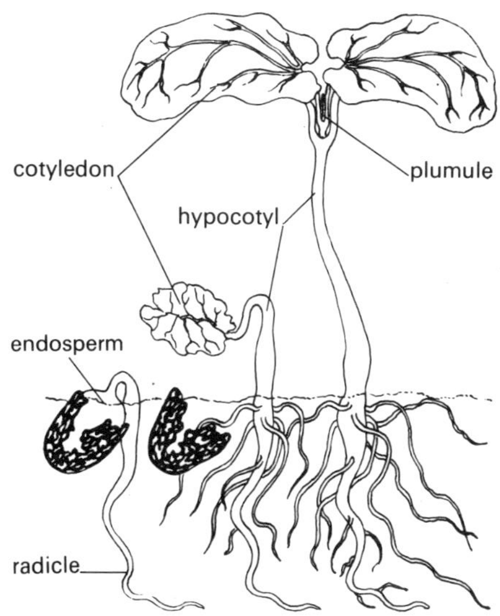

Sequence of events taking place during germination

EXPERIMENT TO EXAMINE GERMINATING SEEDS AT VARIOUS STAGES OF DEVELOPMENT
Materials
broad bean seeds or maize seeds
castor oil seeds or mungo bean seeds
two shallow planters
soil
Method
1. Plant about three dozen of each type of seed into separate planters in about two inches of soil. Water well.
2. Observe the planters for any signs of germination above the soil.
3. Every two days remove a few germinating seeds from the ground and examine carefully. Draw a diagram of each.
4. Measure the length of the shoots and roots.

What difference do you observe between the germination process in the two species?
Compare your drawings of the seedlings at different stages of development with those shown in figs. 6.75 and 6.76.
Remember that each plant is an individual living organism and therefore variations in appearance and rate of growth are likely to occur.

Discussion
In preparation for germination the seed coat absorbs water, swells and softens. The process of respiration is initiated and the energy

Fig. 6.76 **Stages in germination of maize grain**

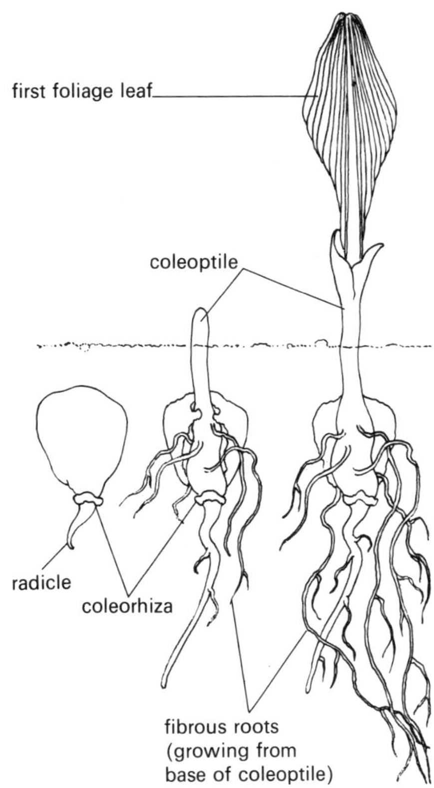

thus derived is used. The seed coat ruptures and the hypocotyl starts to emerge. In the case of some plants such as the mungo bean both the plumule and the cotyledons appear above the ground. This is referred to as **epigeal germination**. (Fig. 6.78).
In the case of some other plants such as the broad bean and the maize, the cotyledon remains inside the seed coat and only the plumule emerges. This is known as **hypogeal germination**. (Fig. 6.77).

Fig. 6.77 Hypogeal germination

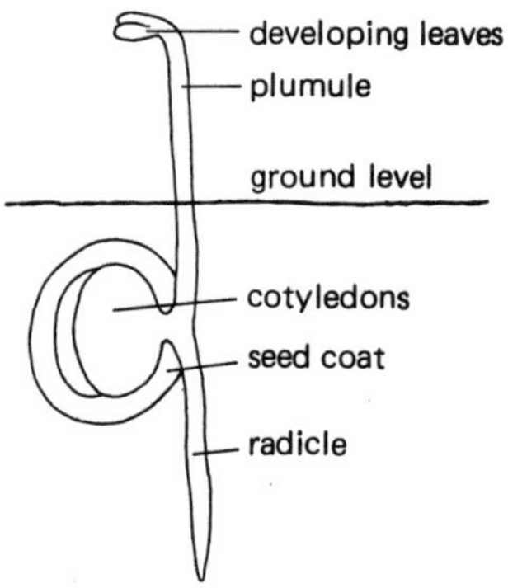

Fig.6.78 Epigeal germination

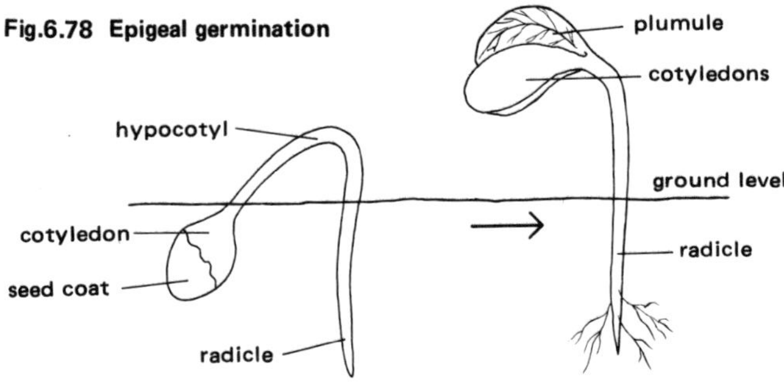

Summary

The seed is protected on the outside by the seed coat. In some seeds food is stored in the endosperm, in others in the cotyledons. The embryo proper consists of the radicle, stalk and plumule. The external conditions necessary for germination are adequate moisture, oxygen and a suitable temperature.
In epigeal germination the cotyledons appear above the ground while in hypogeal germination they remain below the ground.

Section 7. GENETICS AND EVOLUTION

GENETICS—THE STUDY OF HEREDITY

Although man had been interested in **heredity** for centuries, until recently the topic was shrouded behind a veil of superstition and old wives' tales. The first scientific study of the process of heredity was not carried out until the middle of the last century.

Principles of genetics

In 1865 Gregor Mendel, an Austrian monk, published the results of his experiments with cross-breeding different varieties of the garden pea. For the purposes of his investigation he classified his plants according to characteristics such as height, flower colour, seed colour, seed shape and so on. In each instance he chose plants with contrasting characteristics, cross-bred them and observed the distribution of the various features in the next generation. He was careful to start with **pure lines** of plants, that is, ones that kept the same characteristic through several generations of self fertilization.

Details of Mendel's experiments

Fig.7.1

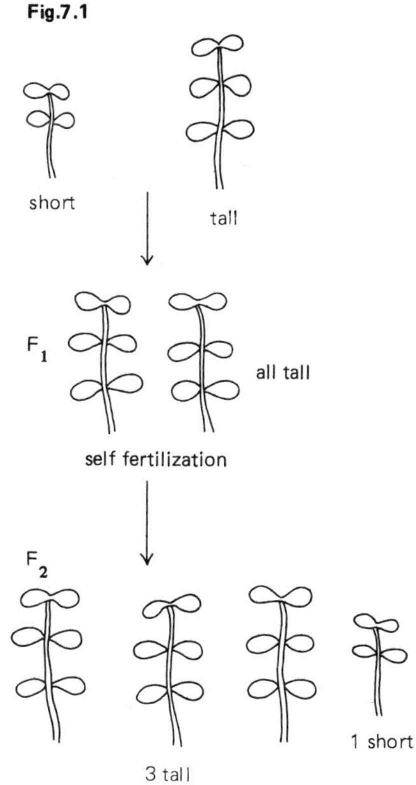

In a typical series of experiments he crossed tall and short plants by pollinating the ovules of one type with the pollen from the other. He found that he could open the buds of the plants and remove the stamens before the pollen seeds ripened. Then he would dust the pistil with pollen from the other plant type. To avoid possible contamination he kept insects away with the help of a fine net.

He planted the seeds thus produced and found that all the first generation (F_1) were tall. He then allowed the plants to be self-pollinated and found that the ratio of tall to short in the second generation progeny (F_2) was 3:1.

Mendel carried out similar experiments with different varieties of pea and found that other characteristics exhibited the same pattern of inheritance.

He came to the conclusion that the reproductive cells of the plant, that is, the ovule and the pollen grains must carry certain 'factors' that are responsible for handing on characteristics from parents to progeny.

Some factors, such as tallness, are **dominant**; the opposite trait, shortness, tends to be **recessive.**

He also suggested that factors are present in plant cells in pairs.

What led Mendel to these conclusions?

If you refer back to the table showing the cross-breeding experiments you will note that even though the entire F_1 generation is tall the factor for shortness must somehow be retained by the plants because it reappears in the F_2 generation.

Mendel explained those observations by postulating that each gamete is capable of carrying one factor for the determination of any given trait so that after fusion of the gametes two factors are present in each cell. Mendel's factors are today called **genes** and his conclusion is referred to as **Mendel's First Law**.

Mendel's first law

The First Law may be restated in modern terminology as follows: *Genetic characteristics are governed by genes that occur in pairs.* When reproductive cells are being formed the pairs separate with only one going to any individual gamete.

The process by which pairs of genes separate is called **gene segregation** and it occurs during meiosis. Recall that the second cell division in the process of meiosis results in the production of haploid gametes. Since a particular gamete only contains half the usual chromosome complement of the cell it follows that only half the amount of genetic information is being carried by the gamete.

Let us now review Mendel's cross-breeding experiments in the light of present-day knowledge.

An individual organism that carries identical genes for a certain trait on both its homologous chromosomes is said to be **homozygous** with respect to the trait in question.

The tall plants that Mendel started out with were homozygous for the trait. That is, if we represent the gene for tallness as T, the genetic composition or **genotype** of the plant is TT. The genotype of short plants is tt.

An individual organism that carries different genes for a given trait is referred to as **heterozygous**. An example of a heterozygous individual would be one with the chromosomes Tt.

Genes situated on corresponding homologous chromosomes but governing the same characteristics are referred to as **alleles**.

Fig.7.2

(i) Homozygous chromosomes for eye and hair colour

(ii) Heterozygous chromosomes for eye and hair colour

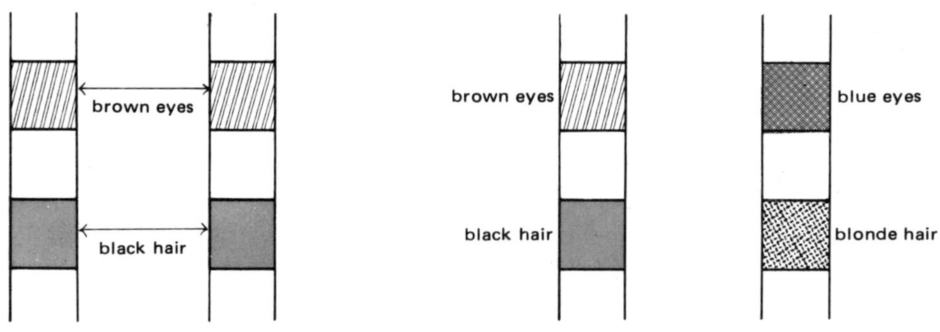

What happens if we cross a plant that is homozygous for tallness with one that is homozygous for shortness? The cross is represented diagrammatically below:

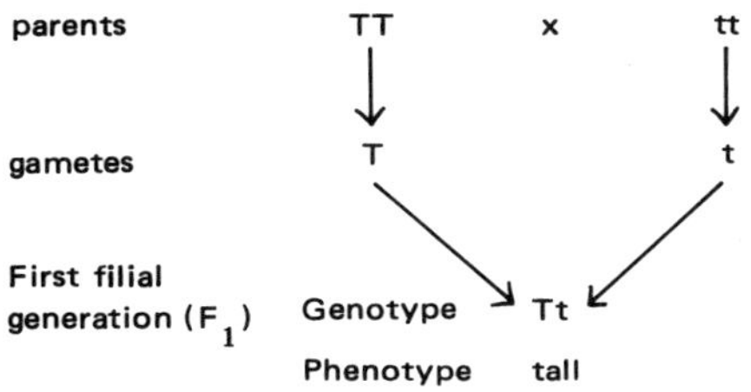

Fig.7.3

All of the plants produced in the first filial generation have identical genotypes of Tt. Although they carry the gene t for shortness they will all look tall. This is because the gene T is dominant over the gene t. That is, the **phenotype** of the plant will be tall. A plant that is phenotypically short must have the genotype tt.

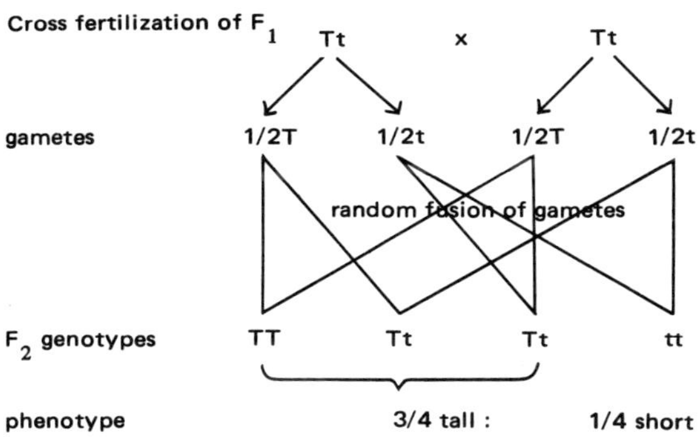

Fig.7.4

The ratio of genotypes obtained from self-pollination in the F_1 generation above is:

$$\tfrac{1}{4}\text{TT}: \tfrac{1}{2}\text{Tt}: \tfrac{1}{4}\text{tt}$$

The corresponding ratio of phenotypes is:

$$\tfrac{3}{4}\text{ tall}: \tfrac{1}{4}\text{ short.}$$

The above is referred to as a **monohybrid cross** because only one trait is involved (mono) and the parents possess contrasting characteristics with respect to that trait (hybrid).

Fig.7.5

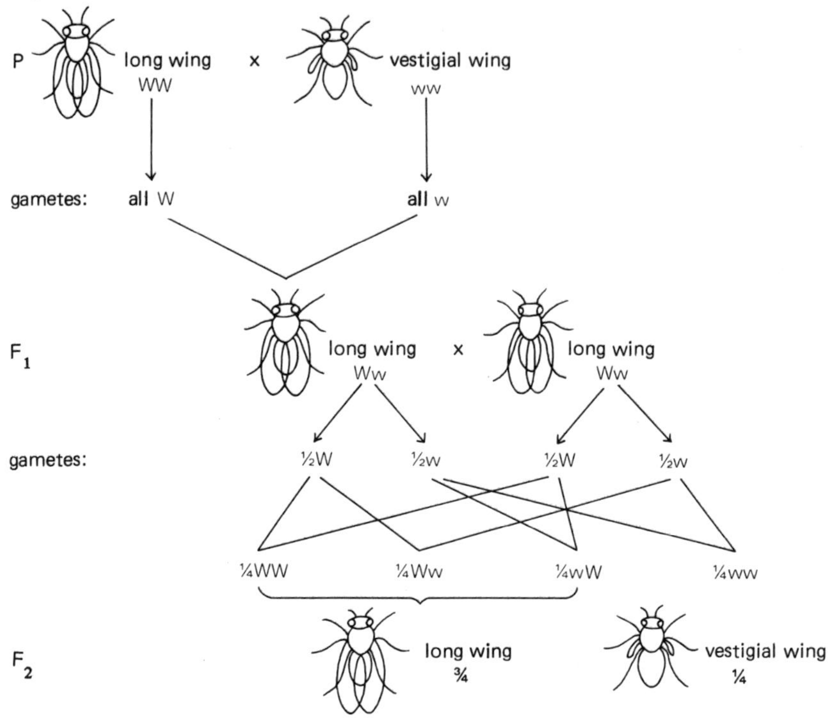

Does the inheritance of animal characteristics follow the same laws?

The same laws hold true for inheritance in animals as in plants. The animal most commonly used in genetic investigations is the fruit fly, *Drosophila*. Most flies have long wings that expand beyond the length of the body at the back. Some, however, have short, stumpy, so-called *vestigial* wings. If we call the gene for long wings W and the one for vestigial wings w a monohybrid cross between animals that are homozygous for these contrasting traits would be as follows:

Fig.7.6

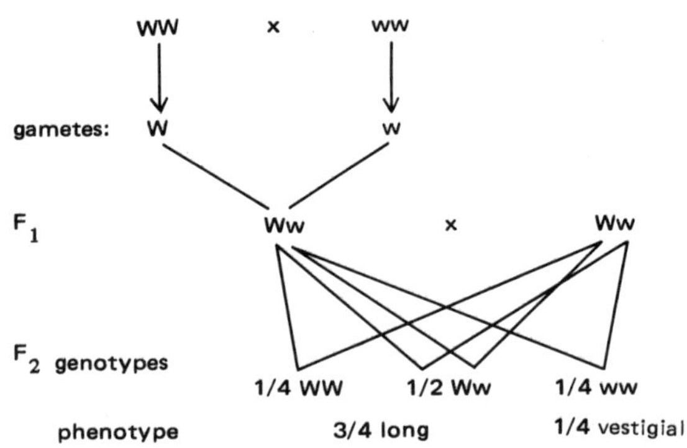

A very simple trait that you can use for testing inheritance in humans is the ability of a person to 'roll' his tongue. Fig. 7.7 below shows exactly what is meant by this. Can you roll your tongue? Stand in front of a mirror and see if you can do it.

EXERCISE

Ask at least one hundred of your schoolmates, chosen at random, if they can roll their tongues. Which group is in the majority: those who can or those who cannot do it?
Which trait do you think is dominant?
Try to trace the pattern of inheritance of this trait within your own family.
If the gene conferring the ability to roll the tongue is designated R and its recessive counterpart r, a monohybrid cross of these two genes can be plotted out as shown in fig. 7.8.
This pattern of squares is another method of representing the inheritance of various traits. The letters on the outside of the square represent the gametes while the ones inside the individual squares represent the genotype of the offspring.
Another easily detectable characteristic that is not shared by every human is the ability to taste the chemical phenyl thiocarbamide (PTC). You can soak pieces of filter paper in the chemical and place on the tip of your tongue.
Can you taste it?
The gene T conferring the ability to taste PTC is dominant over that for non-tasting, t.
Draw a chart to show the cross between two people that are both homozygous, one for T and the other for t.

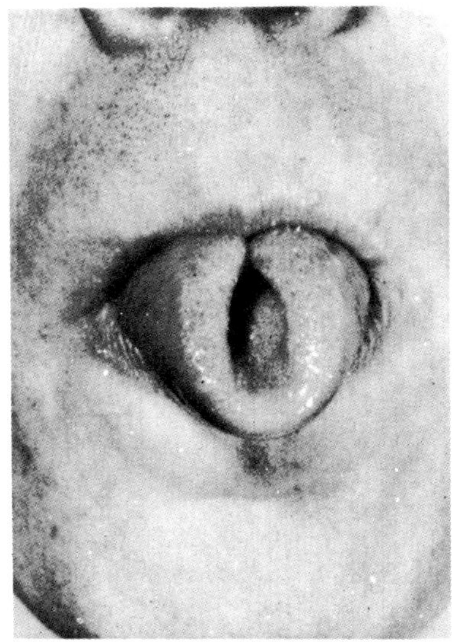

Fig. 7.7 Ability to roll tongue

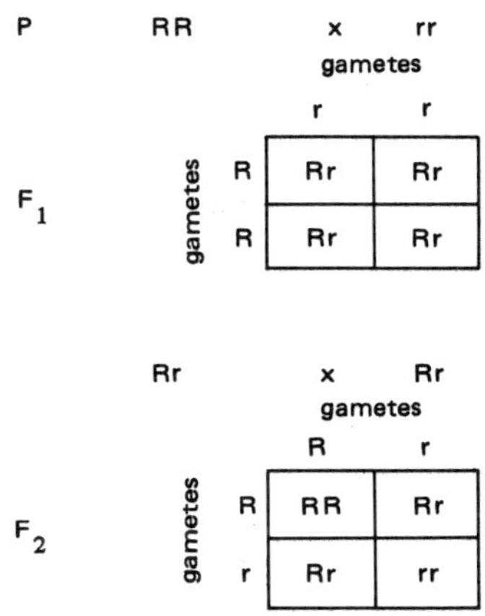

Fig.7.8

EXERCISE

Again, take a survey of at least one hundred students in your school testing their ability to taste PTC.
Do the results indicate that T is indeed dominant?
The examples that we have referred to above were all traits determined by the action of a single gene pair and there was a clear relation of dominance and recessiveness between the two. This is not always true, especially in the case of human inheritance. Many traits are determined by the action of two or more pairs of alleles and at times there is no clear-cut dominance. Conversely, a single gene pair may influence the inheritance of several different traits.
Sex determination involves the presence or absence of an entire chromosome.

Sex determination is humans

Humans have a total of forty-six individual chromosomes in their somatic cells. Of these forty-four are made up of homologous pairs while the remaining two are the **sex chromosomes**, designated X for female and Y for male (see fig. 7.9). A person who is phenotypically female will have two X chromosomes, while a male will have one X and one Y.

The diagram below depicts the pattern of inheritance of sex. Notice that the chance of a given offspring being male or female are fifty-fifty on a genetic basis. The fact that there might be more males or females actually being born in the world can also be influenced by their relative chances of survival as determined by other genetic traits.

Fig.7.9

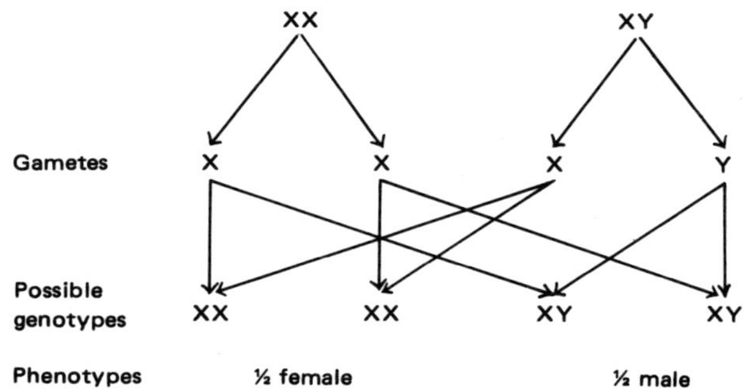

Family tree studies

How can human inheritance be studied in greater detail?

The study of inheritance in humans is understandably more difficult than in animals since scientists cannot cross-breed people.

In addition the time scales involved are extremely long. Humans do not usually reach sexual maturity until the age of twelve to fourteen and in most cases do not have children until at least the age of seventeen or eighteen. The best and almost the only method

Fig.7.10

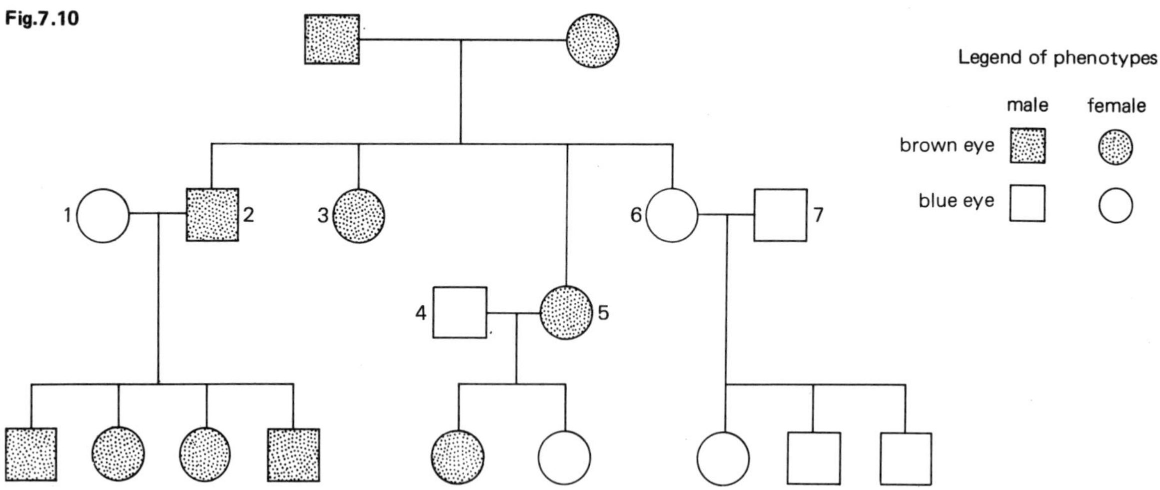

Fig.7.11

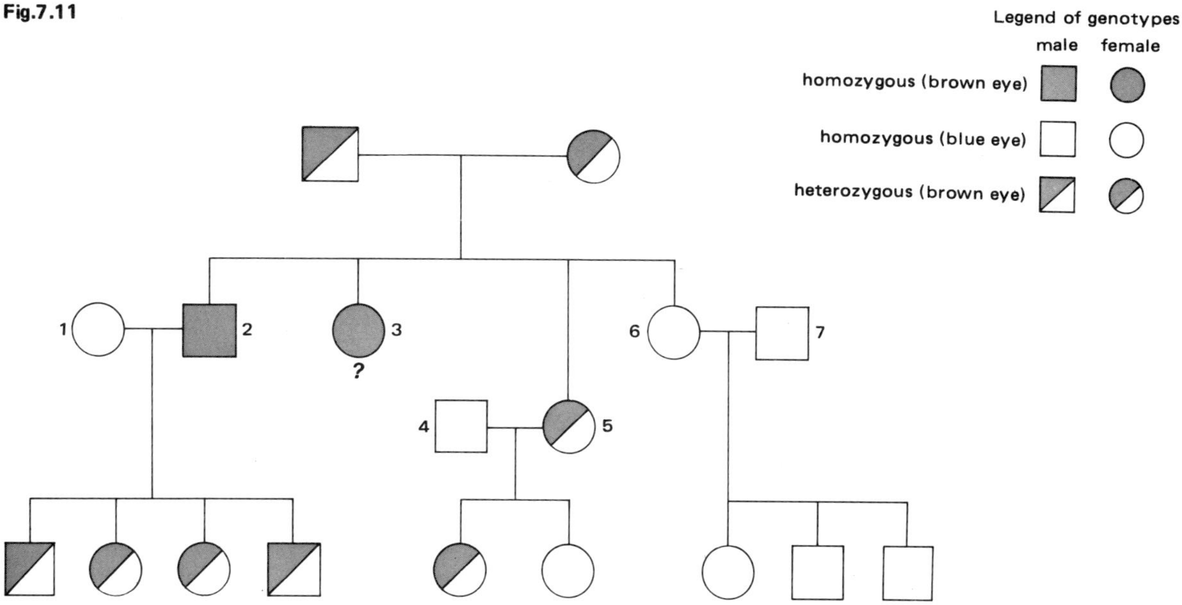

Note: since 3 does not have any offspring we cannot determine if she is homozygous or heterozygous.

Fig.7.12

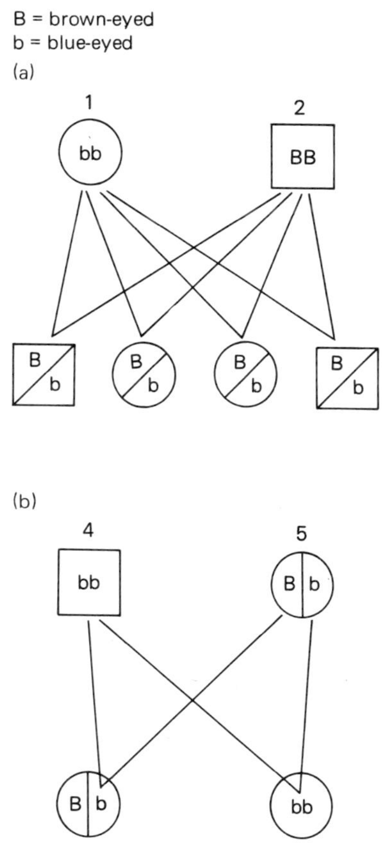

available is the study of family trees to trace the pattern of inheritance of some easily recognizable traits.

BROWN EYES VERSUS BLUE EYES

Fig. 7.10 shows the inheritance of eye colour within a certain family. How can we interpret this family tree in relation to the dominant or recessive nature of the genes for brown and blue eyes?

Parent 1 is blue-eyed and parent 2 is brown-eyed. Since all the offspring from these two parents were brown-eyed, the gene for brown eye colour must be dominant to that for blue. Parent 1 is therefore homozygous for blue eyes. In order to produce all brown-eyed children parent 2 must be homozygous for brown eyes. Further more, as indicated in fig. 7.12(a), all the children are heterozygous. In order to have both blue- and brown-eyed offspring the original parents must have both been heterozygous.

Parent 4 has blue eyes and therefore must be homozygous.

Parent 5 has brown eyes but since some of her offspring are blue-eyed she must be heterozygous (see fig. 7.12(b)). Since 6 and 7 have all blue-eyed children they must be both homozygous for blue eyes.

Fig. 7.11 shows the same family tree with the individuals designated as homozygous or heterozygous. Compare with the original family tree in fig. 7.10 and make certain that you understand how the two are related.

Fig.7.13

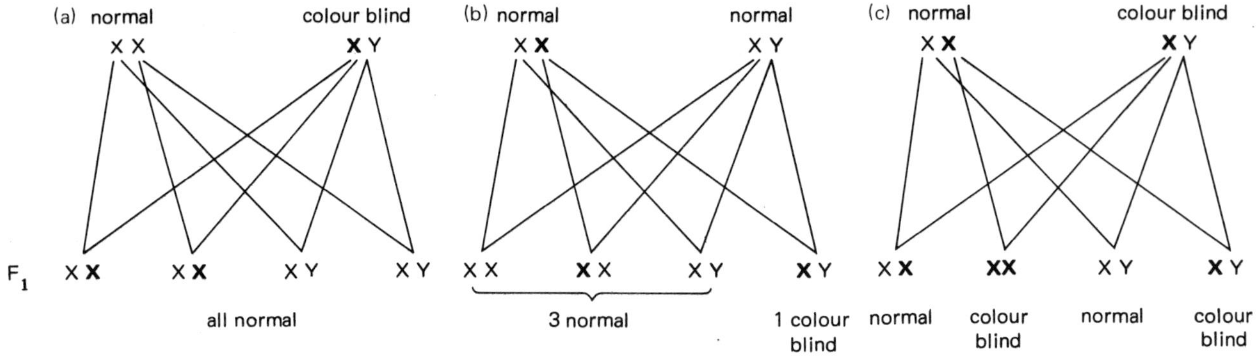

Sex linked inheritance

The two sex chromosomes in addition to their role in sex determination also bear along their lengths genes for other traits. In the section on vision we referred to the hereditary defect of colour blindness. The recessive gene bringing about this condition is carried on the X chromosomes. The incidence of colour blindness is therefore very much higher in males than in females.
Why is this so?
Since females have the chromosome constitution XX, if one of the X chromosomes carries a gene for colour blindness but the other is normal the person will have no abnormality of colour vision. That is, the normal gene on the other X chromosome overrides the effect of the defective one.
In the case of a male, however, there is no second X chromosome and the Y chromosome does not contain an allele for determining colour vision. A male with an X chromosome carrying the recessive gene for colour blindness will therefore possess the abnormality. Fig. 7.13 illustrates the pattern of inheritance of colour blindness. **X** carries a gene for colour blindness.
The offspring of a female with two normal X chromosomes and a colour blind male will all have normal colour vision but all the female offspring will be carrying the recessive gene. (Fig. 7.13(a).)
If a heterozygous female and a normal male have children half the male offspring may be colour blind. (Fig. 7.13(b).) A cross between a heterozygous female and a colour blind male can result in both colour blind males and females. (Fig. 7.13(c).)

Summary

The scientific study of genetics began with the experiments of Gregor Mendel.
Some of the most important principles of heredity are embodied in Mendel's First Law: Genetic characteristics are governed by genes that occur in pairs. Genes are derived from the organism's

parents, one coming from each parent. During meiosis pairs of genes are distributed to separate gametes (gene segregation).
Dominant members of a gene pair can exert their influence over genes that are recessive so that the recessive characteristic is not expressed.
Genotype refers to the genetic makeup of an individual while phenotype refers to the physical expression of this genetic makeup.
When two individual organisms with contrasting characteristics are crossed the resulting offspring is referred to as a hybrid.
An organism is homozygous with respect to a certain characteristic if the two genes governing that characteristic are identical. If the two genes are not identical the organism is said to be heterozygous.

Variation

If you look around you at your fellow human beings and at plants and animals you will undoubtedly remark on the amount of variation that exists from one type of living organism to the next and between individual members of the same species.
Every human being, for instance, is sufficiently different from other human beings to be recognized as an individual.

How does variation come about?

In the previous section we discussed the mechanism of gene action and the way genes are passed on from one generation to the next. If genes were always passed on according to this pattern and remained unchanged throughout the generations there would be very little variation between individual humans, plants or animals. There are, however, several known ways in which changes in genetic constitution do arise. During the process of mitosis and meiosis when chromosomes are duplicated and distributed to the daughter cells certain errors can slip in.
Any error occurring during the mitosis process in somatic cells is irrelevant from the point of view of heredity because somatic cells are not able to pass on their characteristics from one generation to the next. They can however, alter the appearance or character traits of the individual concerned. Errors occurring during meiosis and gamete formation are much more significant because there is a chance that the new combination of characteristics acquired as a result will be passed on.

What are the errors that sometimes occur?

The most common one, **crossing over**, is, in fact, so frequent that it can hardly be referred to as a mistake; it is more of a general rule in the process of meiosis. When the homologous pairs of chromosomes come to lie side by side in preparation for the first division of meiosis the chromatids of adjacent chromosomes sometimes cross over and break, then rejoin so that a section from one chromatid joins up with the chromatid of the other member of the homologous pair.

The mechanism of the process is illustrated in fig. 7.14. The consequences of crossing over on the selection of genes along the length of each chromosome are indicated by letters. Let us take Mendel's peas as an example with genes T and t representing tall and short plants respectively and Y and y representing yellow and green seeds respectively. (*Note:* yellow seed colour is dominant over green colour.)

Before crossing over the arrangement of genes along the two chromosomes was such that tall plants would always have yellow seeds and short plants green seeds (A). After crossing over two new combinations are obtained, namely, tall with green seeds and short with yellow seeds (B). Since the second chromatid of each homologous chromosome has remained unchanged the original combination of characteristics has also been preserved (C).

What is the significance of crossing over?

The mechanism of crossing over provides for a continuous reshuffling of genes within a population of living organisms. It therefore plays a significant role in producing variety among the individuals of a species. It does not, however, lead to completely new characteristics being evolved and for this reason does not play a major

Fig.7.14 Crossing over

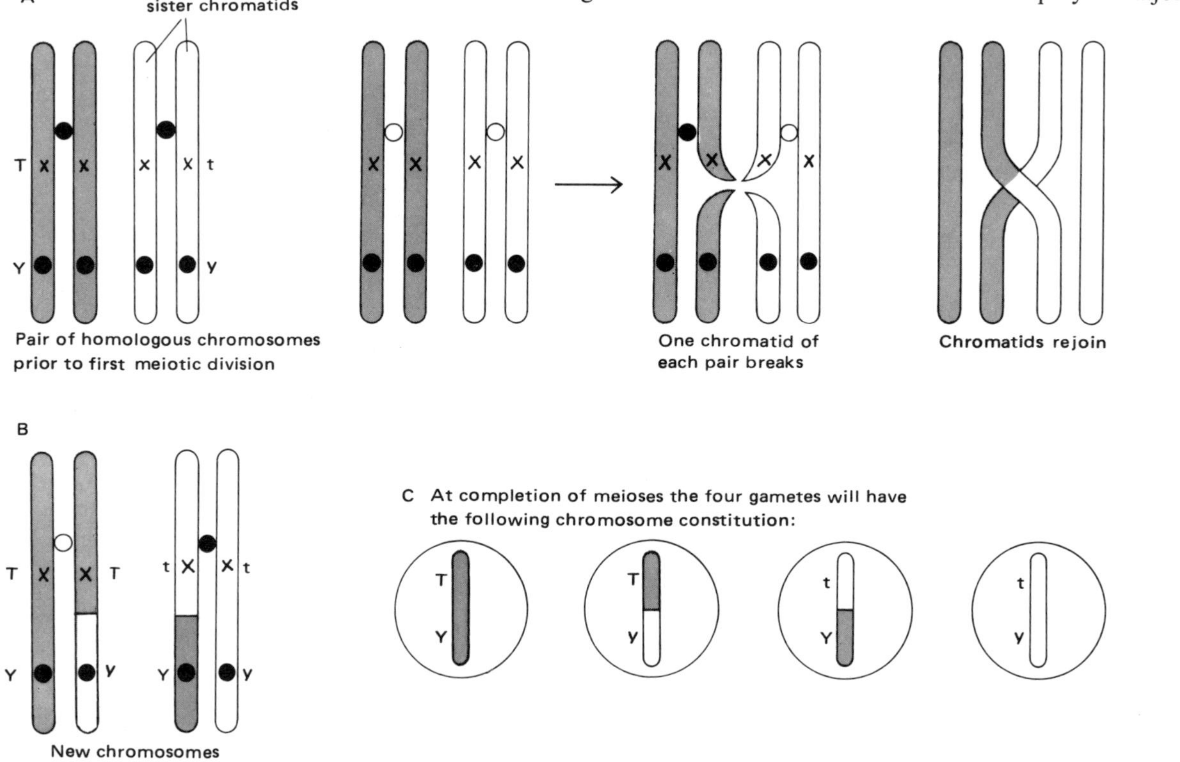

role in the long-term process of evolution. A much more important process in the long-term view is **mutation.**

What is mutation?

Mutation is a mechanism producing a change in the genetic material of a reproductive cell that will lead to the development of an individual with a characteristic strikingly different from the rest of the species. Such an individual is referred to as a **mutant.**

Mutant characteristics are generally recessive and they are transmitted according to the Mendelian laws of inheritance.

Mutations seem to arise spontaneously and once formed a mutant gene can be passed from one generation on to the next in the same way as any other gene.

Mutations are comparatively rare. In most organisms the rate is between one per thirty million gametes produced. The great majority of mutations are disadvantageous for the organism concerned. In many instances the gamete bearing the mutation will not be fertile, or if fertilization does take place the offspring will not survive.

There are two general types of mutation known, namely **chromosome mutation** and **gene mutation**.

Fig.7.15 Different types of chromosome mutation

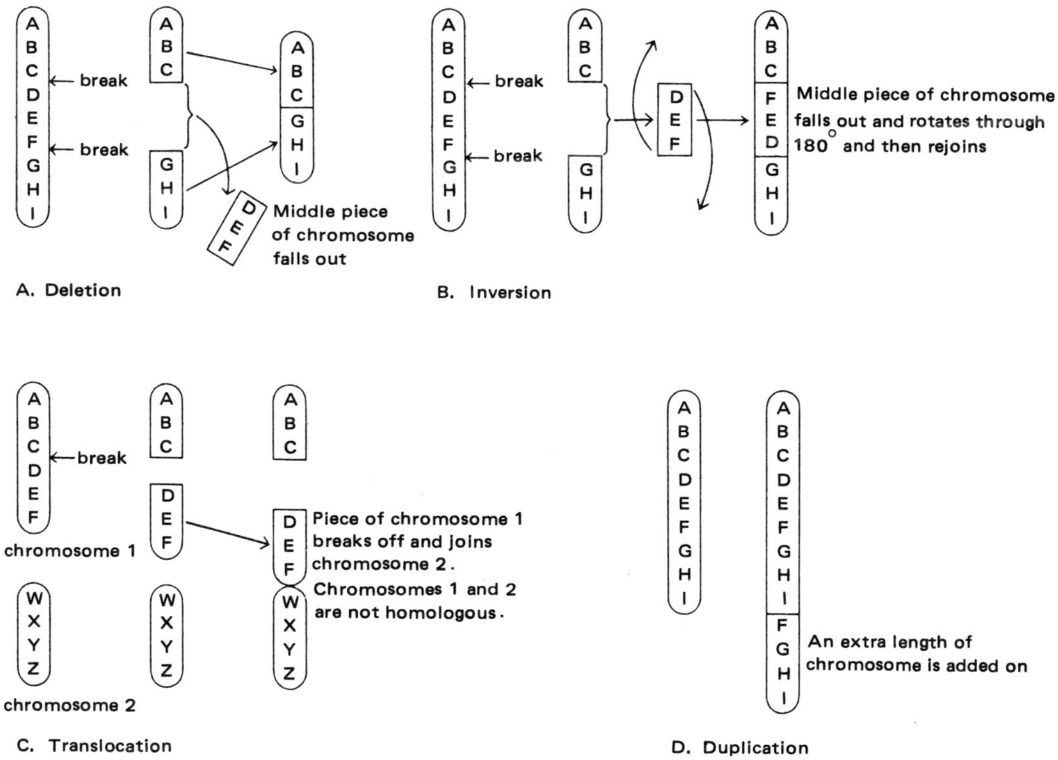

Chromosome mutation

Chromosome mutations are a result of errors occurring in the duplication or segregation of chromosomes during gamete formation. These errors include **deletion** of short lengths of a chromosome, **duplication** of a section of a chromosome, **inversion** of a chromosome section with respect to the total structure or a **translocation** of a small section from one chromosome to a different chromosome.

The addition or loss of an entire chromosome from the new cell through failure of the homologous chromosomes to separate is known to cause several abnormalities in humans. *Down's syndrome* is caused by the presence of an extra member of chromosome twenty-one in the cell.

Various sex anomalies occur when gametes either have an extra sex chromosome or lack a sex chromosome. In *Turner's syndrome* the individual has one X chromosome only. Such an individual has the outward appearance of a female but is incapable of producing fertile eggs.

Another error that sometimes occurs is the failure of homologous chromosomes to separate during meiosis leading to gamete formation. This results in the production of gametes that are diploid. If fertilized by a normal gamete the resulting individual will have 3n chromosomes, that is, it will be **polyploid**. (Fig. 7.16.)

Among plants polyploid individuals seem to be hardier than normal ones. Artificially induced polyploidy is one of the techniques used to develop new strains of crops in an attempt to solve the world food shortage. The condition seems more often than not to be detrimental in animals.

Fig.7.16 Failure of chromosome pairs to separate during meiosis

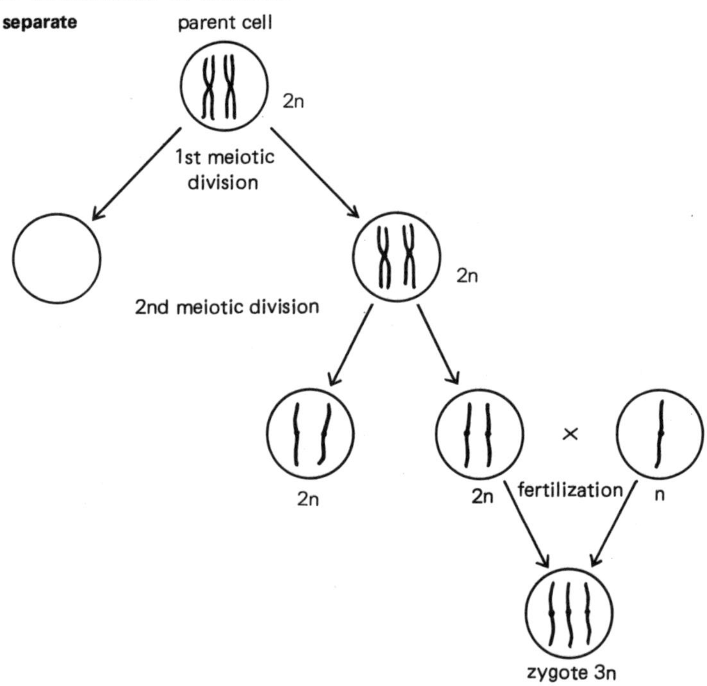

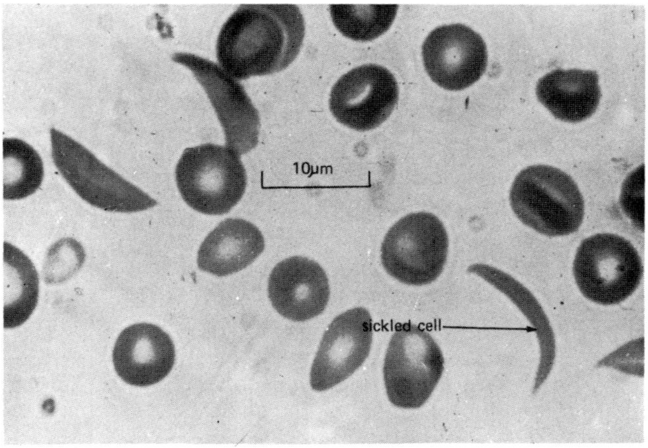

Fig.7.17 Sickled red blood cells

Gene mutation

Gene mutations arise as a result of chemical changes in individual genes. Chemically a gene consists of a certain sequence of organic molecules called **nucleotides** that are arranged lengthwise to form a chain molecule called **deoxyribonucleic acid (DNA)**. A chromosome is a collection of genes arranged in a chain.

The types of mutation that can occur in genes are similar to those occurring in chromosomes—such as deletions, inversions, substitutions etc. except that instead of an entire chromosome section, only one specific gene is involved.

For example, a condition called *sickle cell anaemia* in which the red cells are sickle shaped is caused by a mistake in one amino acid along the sequence of the protein molecule. This is very likely caused by a mutation in a single gene. Sickled red blood cells are impaired in their ability to carry oxygen and this leads to weakness, lethargy and, in extreme cases, to kidney and heart failure. The interesting point about the sickle cell gene however, is that it also seems to confer on its bearer a remarkable resistance to the disease malaria, a point that we will discuss shortly.

Natural selection

The process through which some genes are passed on and increase in frequency in a population while others die out is called **natural selection**. The basis on which natural selection operates is the survival value of the particular mutated gene. Some mutations are so disadvantageous that they are **lethal** to the mutant organism. That is, the individual will die sometime before reaching maturity and will therefore not have a chance to pass on the mutant gene.

Genes that are not lethal can still impair the organism's ability to adapt to its environment and therefore its chances of survival. On the other hand, the mutant may be better adopted to the environment than its fellows. In this instance the mutant and its offspring will tend to increase in number until the majority and finally the entire population possesses the mutant gene.

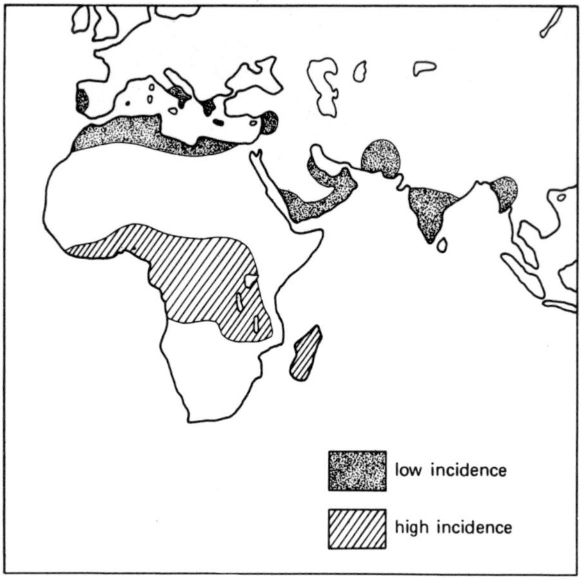

Fig.7.18 Distribution of malaria

Let us pursue this idea in greater detail.
A population of organisms living under ideal conditions, that is, plenty of food, favourable weather and the absence of predators, can increase in size indefinitely with no need for competition between individuals.
These ideal conditions very rarely, if ever, exist. In general a population is always faced with certain unfavourable conditions that limit its growth. These conditions include:

1. shortage of food,
2. lack of adequate light, particularly in the case of green plants,
3. predators,
4. lack of shelter,
5. disease.

All these factors play a role in limiting the size of a population either by increasing the death rate or decreasing the birth rate or both.
The better suited a member of the population is to its environment the greater its chances of survival, or as Darwin expressed it, the rule is the 'survival of the fittest'. A mutation that gives favourable traits increasing an individual's chances for survival such as resistance to a certain disease will have a better chance of being passed on than a less favourable one that will perhaps hinder an animal in escaping from predators.
Let us return to the example of the sickle cell disease referred to previously. Statistical studies have shown that the frequency of the sickle cell gene is much higher in populations in some African and Asian countries than in the rest of the world. (See fig. 7.18.) The reason for this seems to lie in the ability of the gene to confer resistance to malaria. In areas where malaria is not endemic sickle cell

Fig.7.19 Finches with different beaks adapted to different feeding habits

confers a definite disadvantage to its bearer, and the frequency of the gene in the population will not increase. In areas that are infested with malaria, however, the gene will increase in frequency due to its beneficial effects that outweigh the detrimental ones. There is also mounting evidence to show that the eradication of malaria causes the frequency of the sickle cell gene to drop.

Examples of variations between species

Repeated gene mutations will lead to the development of distinctly different varieties among species of organisms. Often these varieties will be found in different geographical locations or in different habitats in the same region. Charles Darwin in the course of his historic voyage on the *Beagle* came across over one hundred species of flowering plant on the Galapagos Islands that were not found anywhere else in the world.

Differences might also reflect variations in the diet of the animals. An example is the variety of finches found by Darwin on the Galapagos, each having a beak structure suited to its particular method of feeding. (Fig. 7.19.)

(a) Against a dark background

(b) Against a lighter background

Fig.7.20 Grey and black coloured moths

Natural selection at work

An excellent example of the process of natural selection at work is provided by the case of the peppered moth, *Biston betularia*. The original colour of this moth was greyish white—as the name suggests—so that it blended in with the light-coloured lichen on the bark of the trees where the moth rested during the day. For the first time in 1848 much darker coloured, almost black variants were seen in the region around Manchester, England. Records show that today almost the entire population of the area is made up of these black moths.

What caused the change?

Natural selection favoured the dark-coloured moths over the grey ones due to the need for protective colouring. Normally the birds that prey on the moths find it very difficult to spot the grey ones on the trunks of trees. However, with the advent of industrialization around the Manchester area the trees became increasingly covered with soot and grime. Suddenly the grey moths began to stand out against the trees. As a result of the previous mutations there happened to exist a black variety of the moth that had been at a disadvantage previously and was present only in very small numbers. During the late 1800's with the advent of industrialization these became more and more numerous.

Evolution

Natural selection processes such as the one discussed above are believed to be the basis for the process of **evolution** that has led to the emergence of the almost countless number of plant and animal species that are found in the world today.

Scientists are able to piece together the probable sequence of the evolution of various species from the evidence presented by fossil finds. Fossils from successive layers of rock strata have shown the development of the modern horse as shown in fig. 7.22.

The probable pattern of development of the various classes of chordate is shown in fig. 7.23. At almost every point of divergence there are fossil forms that are intermediate between the two classes. One of the most famous of the fossils is that of Archeopteryx, an animal with reptilian teeth and tail but also possessing feathers and wings and presumably the ability to fly.

Fig.7.21

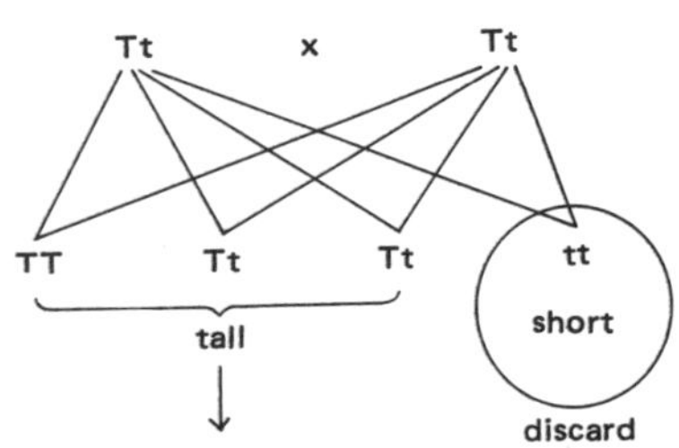

Artificial selection

Modelled on the natural selection process man has for centuries been practising **artificial selection** in breeding plants and animals.

Individuals possessing certain desirable characteristics are repeatedly chosen from a population and mated with each other. From among their offspring again the desired ones are selected. Gradually the frequency of the desired gene will increase until a pure breeding line displaying the characteristics in question is obtained.

In the case of a trait determined by a single pair of alleles, recall

Mendel's experiments with the peas (p. 307). If the tall plants are continually self-fertilized the frequency of the T gene in the population will steadily increase. This is the process by which various breeds of horse, cattle, dog and high-yield disease-resistant strains of crop have been developed.

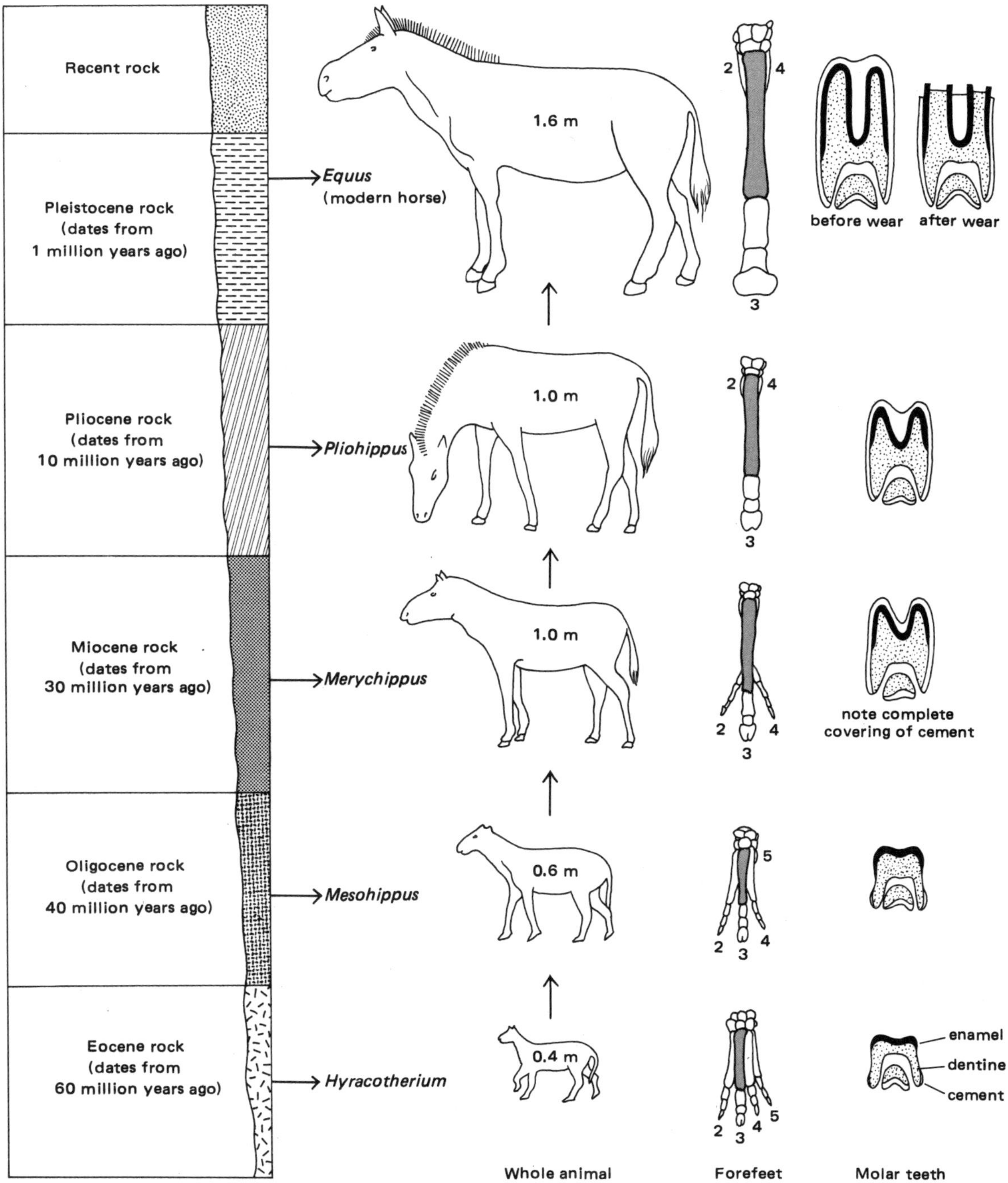

Fig.7.22 Evolution of the horse showing reconstructions of the fossil species obtained from successive rock strata

Fig. 7.23 Evolutionary tree for the chordates

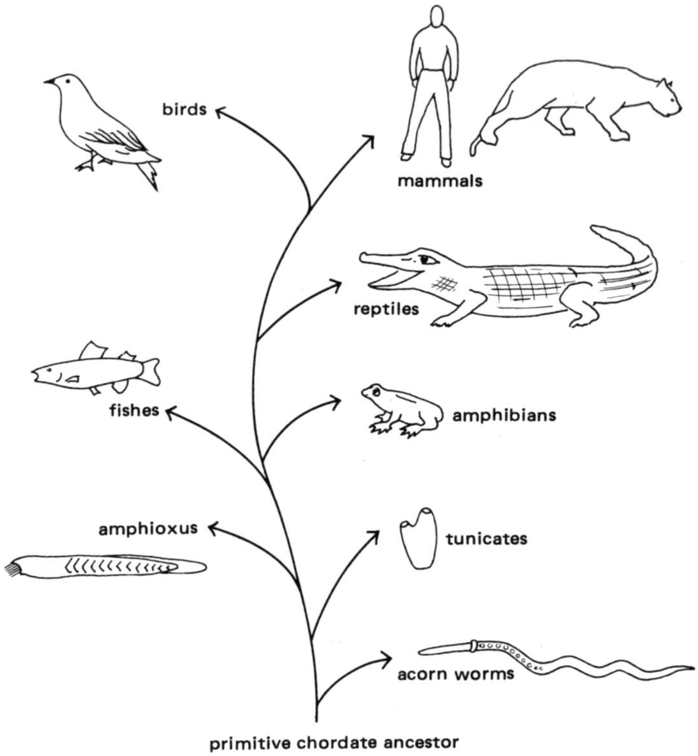

Heredity versus the environment

Environmental factors can also influence the degree to which an individual will be adapted to its environment. A type of crop for instance might have all the desirable genes to predispose it to grow into a vigorous healthy plant but if there is inadequate rainfall during the growing season its genetic potentials will not be realized. Similarly a genetic predisposition for exceptional intelligence in a human child will not develop unless the child is adequately nourished and his mind is stimulated by study and training.

Summary

Variations in the characteristics of organisms arise as a result of mutations. Processes such as deletion, inversion and duplication can occur among individual genes or entire chromosomes. Whether the mutant characteristic survives or not depends on the relative advantages or disadvantages conferred on the organism by the new gene. The process is called natural selection.

Natural selection is the basis of the process of evolution that has resulted in the development of the countless different species of plant and animal that are found in the world today.

Section 8. HEALTH AND HYGIENE

Micro-organisms

Any living organism that is too small to be seen by the naked eye can be called a **micro-organism** or a **microbe**. The group includes plants and animals and some organisms that cannot really be regarded as either. Some are useful to man, some are extremely harmful and dangerous.

Historical background

Due to their small size microbes could not be studied in detail until the last century even though their existence was first discovered in 1676. Until the middle of the last century it was generally believed that microbes arose spontaneously in decaying organic matter such as meat. This theory of spontaneous generation was finally disproved by Louis Pasteur. He was able to show that if all the living organisms in a sample of nutrient broth (similar to a meat soup) were killed by boiling, new organisms would only grow if particles of micro-organisms were able to enter the container from the air.

Bacteria

EXPERIMENT TO CULTURE[1] BACTERIA FROM VARIOUS SOURCES

Materials

five sterilized nutrient agar plates
microscope, slides, coverslips

Method

1. Find four possible sources of bacteria that can be used, for example, air, water, dirty hands, a person with a cold, dirt on the floor and so on.
2. Turn your plate upside down and without removing the covers make a note of the bacterial source you are going to use on the first four plates. Label plate 5 as the control.
3. To obtain bacteria from the air leave the plate uncovered for about fifteen minutes.

Bacteria from your hands can be obtained by gently touching the surface of the plate with a fingertip. Do not squash up the agar as you are doing this. To obtain bacteria from dirty objects touch the sticky side of a piece of Sellotape to the object and then to the

[1] *culture*: grow

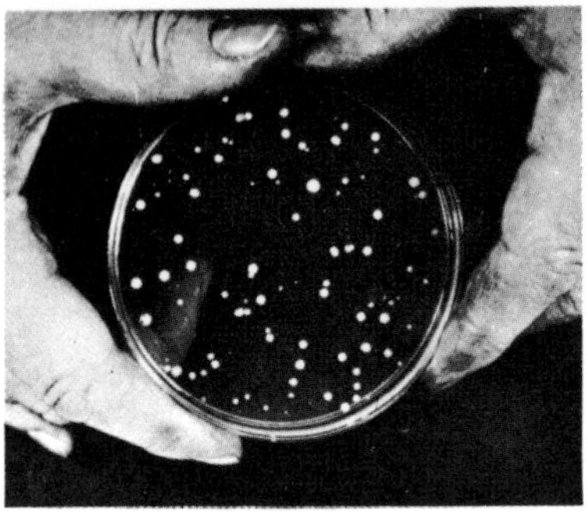

Fig.8.1 Bacterial colonies on an agar plate

surface of the agar. To obtain bacteria from water cover the top of the agar with a thin layer of water and leave for about fifteen minutes then pour off.

If any member of the class has a slight cold ask him or her to cough on one of your plates.

In every instance be sure to remove the cover of the plate only when you are ready to work with it and replace it as soon as you are finished.

4. Place the plates by a warm window or, if available, in an incubator at 37°C.

5. Observe for several days until you see evidence of bacterial growth.

What do the bacterial **colonies** look like?

Are they all the same? Do you get any growth on the control plate?

Why can you see the colonies although you were not able to see the bacteria you originally applied to the plate?

Warning: Do not touch the surface of any of the plates with your hands and discard the plates as soon as you are finished with them to avoid possible infections.

Fig.8.2 Various types of bacteria as seen under the microscope

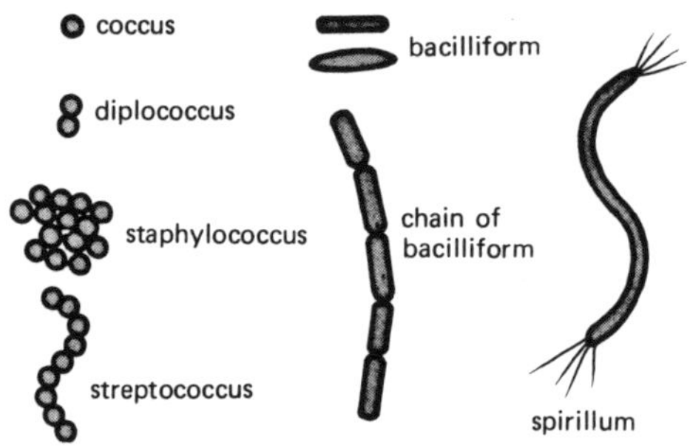

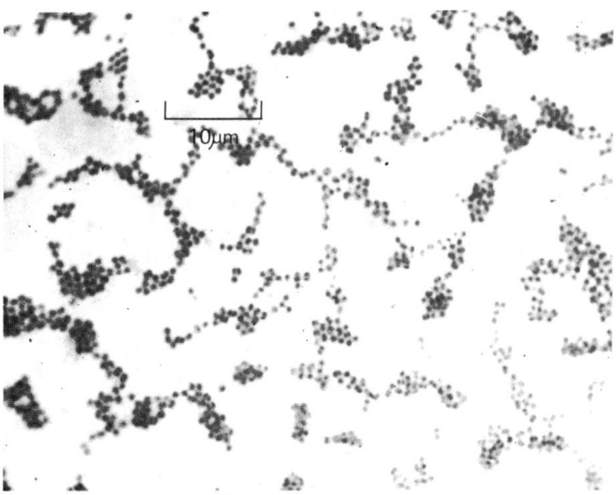

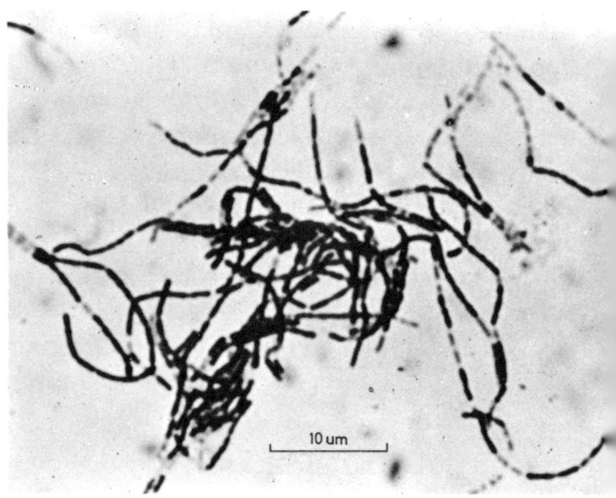

Discussion

What you are observing on the plates with your naked eyes are colonies of bacteria containing millions of individual cells. These have arisen through binary fission from the original bacteria that were transferred to the plate. The colonies appear as circular patches on the surface of the agar. They may be in various colours and sizes.

If a high-power microscope is available you can observe the bacteria and draw simple diagrams of the various shapes. To do this scrape off a little of the growth from the top of each of the plates. Place the scrapings on individual microscope slides in a drop of water, apply the coverslip and press down gently to distribute the cells more evenly. Observe first under low then high power. You will not be able to see the bacterial cells in very much detail because they are extremely small—0.2μm to 2μm ($1\mu m = 10^{-6}$ m). Some of the shapes that you might observe are shown in fig. 8.2.

Diseases caused by bacteria

Around the middle of the last century scientists and doctors began to associate various diseases with the presence of bacteria. Robert Koch studied the bacteria associated with **anthrax**, a disease that attacks and kills certain animals including cattle. He isolated some bacteria from diseased animals and showed that injecting healthy animals with the bacterial extract communicated the disease to them. The various diseases caused by bacteria are summarized in Table 8.1.

At about the same time surgeons began to realize that the extremely high incidence of post-operative deaths due to **septic** wounds were also caused by bacteria. A search was mounted to find chemical agents that could be applied to wounds to kill off these harmful micro-organisms. The first of these substances which became known as **antiseptics** or **disinfectants** was discovered by Joseph Lister. The chemical was carbolic acid.

Table 8.1 Summary of the most common diseases caused by bacteria

Name of disease	Symptoms	Treatment	Transmittance	Remarks
Bacilli are aerobic, saprophytic bacteria, usually rod shaped. They move by means of flagella and are very common in the air and soil. Diseases caused by various bacilli				
Anthrax	gastrointestinal disturbances	antibiotics	most common in cattle but can be transmitted to humans by inhalation	historical importance due to role in the early study of bacteria

Diphtheria	bacterial toxin attacks upper respiratory tract causing difficulty in breathing; heart and nervous system may also be affected	large doses of antitoxin and antibiotics	inhalation	immunization programmes have virtually stopped the disease in most parts of the world
Leprosy	affects nerves and the skin causing deterioration of tissues	previously thought to be incurable, can now be stopped even in advanced cases	direct contact with infected persons, usually due to crowded living conditions	still found in some parts of Africa and Asia
Food poisoning	diarrhoea; pain; vomiting; fever; in serious cases difficulty in breathing or even partial paralysis	*consult a doctor* as many types of food poisoning are fatal; treatment depends on the type of organism involved	contaminated food and the faeces of infected individuals	best prevention is the hygienic handling of food and adequate refrigeration in the hot months
Tetanus	muscle spasms; death due to respiratory failure	administration of antitoxin	spores of organism found in soil, manure etc and can enter the body through a cut or a scratch especially on the feet	immunization is the best preventive measure, booster shots must be given every 5 years
Tuberculosis	infection of the lungs leading to the formation of small areas of dead tissue called a *tubercle*; high fever and respiratory problems; can be fatal if not treated	antibiotics, lengthy period of rest in a pollution-free place to allow lung tissue to repair itself, attacks will usually recur	through contact with affected persons, through bacteria in the air and sometimes in milk from infected cows, intensified by crowded unhygienic living conditions and malnutrition	immunization is the best preventive method
Typhoid fever	high fever; rash on upper abdomen and back; serious diarrhoea with blood in the faeces; the site of infection is the lymphoid tissue	antibiotics	spread by contamination of food, water and milk—most common source of bacteria is a carrier who does not have symptoms of the disease	incidence related to efficiency of sanitation, vaccination can give partial protection but adequate hygiene is the best policy

Pertussis (whooping cough)	bacteria attacks the respiratory system causing difficulty in breathing and coughing; most common in children	antibiotics	highly infectious, transmitted by cough droplets and contaminated articles such as clothing	vaccination is very effective, attack of disease produces immunity, fatality rate very low. Concern about brain damage after vaccination
Streptococci are saprophytic or parasitic bacteria, usually attached to one another to form long chains. They produce a powerful exotoxin. Diseases caused by streptococci				
Bacterial pneumonia	Inflammation of the lungs with formation of a liquid in the alveoli; high fever	antibiotics	micro-organisms in air and dust	can be fatal in old or physically weak people
Scarlet fever	headache; sore throat; vomiting; rash on face, neck and chest; high fever	antibiotics	organisms carried in air and dust	rarely fatal
Tonsilitis	inflammation of the tonsils; high fever; sore throat	antibiotics	spread by coughing, spitting and objects handled by infected individuals	best protection is to stay away from people that have the disease, infected individuals should stay away from others while they are ill
Spirrili are spiral-shaped bacteria commonly found in water and organic matter.				
Cholera	toxin attacks the mucous lining of the gut; severe diarrhoea; painful cramps; total physical collapse;	antibiotics, strict isolation, saline infusions	spread by contaminated water, bad sanitary conditions especially in hot humid climates	high mortality rate, immunization is effective if booster shots are given every six months, strict precautions are taken against the disease at all sea and airports throughout the world
Meningitis	inflammation of one of the covering layers of the brain and central nervous system; severe headache; vomiting; fever and neck rigidity	antibiotics and steroids	spread through discharge from infected people as well as clothing, linens etc	various forms exist depending on the species of bacteria, important factor for susceptibility is fatigue

Fig.8.3 Binary fission in bacteria

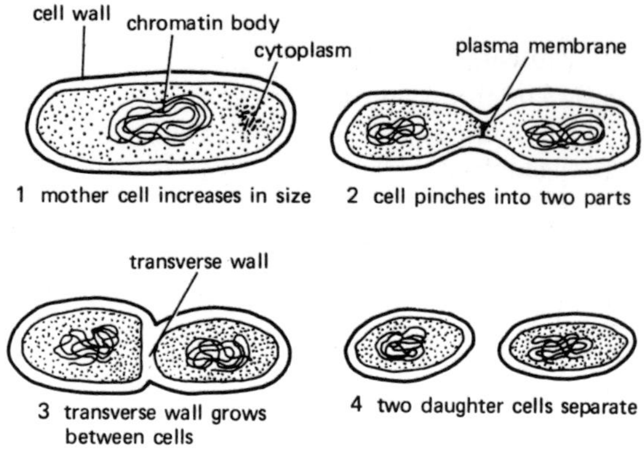

Reproduction in bacteria

Most bacteria are able to reproduce both by spore formation and through binary fission. Both the bacterial cells themselves and the spores are extremely small and light so that they can easily be carried by the movements of the air around us or stay suspended in liquids. In fact, bacteria are found in just about every conceivable spot around us.

Why do some bacteria cause diseases?

The harmful effects of bacteria in most cases are due to the toxic substances they liberate as by-products of their metabolism. These substances attack various parts of the mammalian body disrupting the activity of the cells and often killing the cells.
The toxic substances released by some bacteria for instance disrupt the temperature regulating centre in the brain causing fever (p. 161). Tetanus toxin affects the functioning of the central nervous system and quickly leads to death. The bacteria that causes cholera, *vibrio cholerae*, secretes an enzyme that attacks the mucous lining of the gut.
Saprophytic bacteria release toxic substances into the food they live on. *Clostridium botulinum*, the most dangerous of these organisms, found mostly in spoiled meat, releases a powerful toxin that can kill in minute amounts of 10^{-10} g.

Viruses

THE DISCOVERY

With the discovery of the role of bacteria in disease, it seemed that the riddle of infectious diseases had been solved. However, it soon became apparent that not all infectious diseases could be attributed to bacteria.
Infectious particles much smaller than bacteria were discovered in 1872 in the juice from tobacco plants infected with a disease that caused patches of dead cells to appear on the leaves of the plant.

Fig.8.4 Virus particles under the microscope

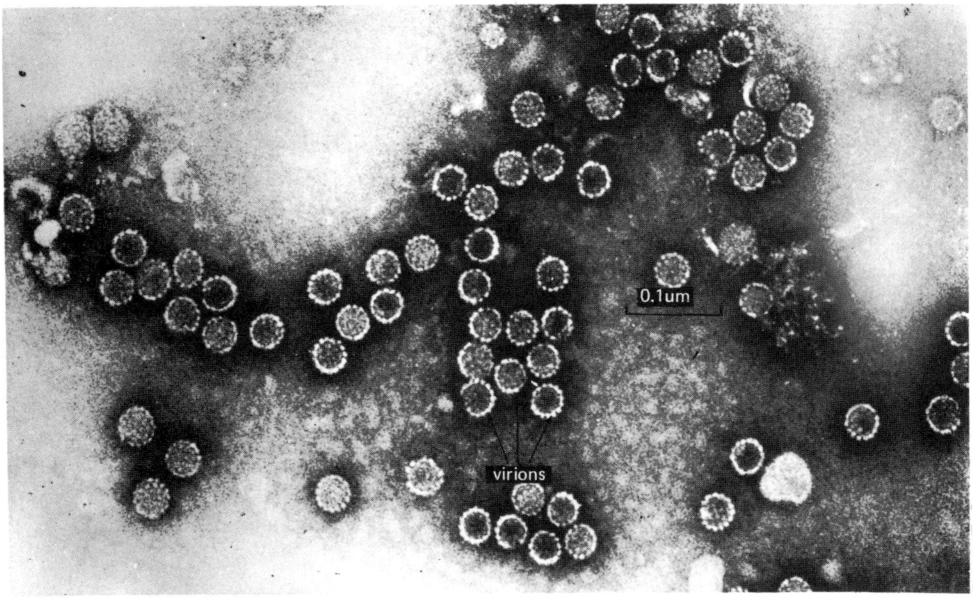

Table 8.2 Causative agents of disease

Disease	Transmission and infection	Spread in body
Influenza	Droplet infection attacks lining of respiratory tracts.	Spreads over surface of respiratory tracts only.
Common cold	Droplet infection attacks lining of respiratory tracts.	Localised on surface of respiration tracts.
Small pox	Droplet infection, direct contact. Enters mucous membrane of upper respiratory tract.	Spread by blood stream, attacks skin and mucous membranes.
Yellow fever	Mosquito bite. Multiplies in lymph glands.	Spread by blood stream to liver and kidneys.
Mumps	Droplet infection. direct contact. Multiplies in salivary glands.	Spread by blood stream to testes or ovaries, pancreas and brain.
Rabies	Infected dog bite. enters wound.	Spread by blood stream to central nervous system and brain.
Poliomyelitis (polio)	Transmission uncertain. enters by mouth. Primary multiplication in throat and intestines.	Spread by blood stream to central nervous system.
Infective hepatitis	Transmission uncertain. Contamination of food and water by faeces. Enters by mouth.	Spread by blood stream to liver, multiplies in liver causing cell destruction.

Fig.8.5

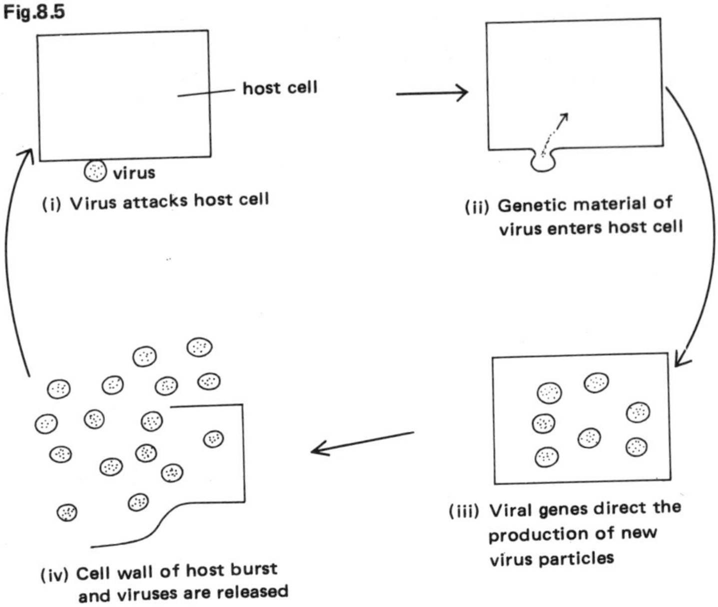

The particles were named **viruses** and the particular one infecting the tobacco plant became known as **tobacco mosaic virus (TMV)**.

Characteristics of a virus

A virus is the smallest and simplest of living organisms. In fact it is on the borderline between living and non-living things. For this reason we never refer to a virus cell but a **virus particle**.

All viruses are parasitic. Not only do they enter the cells of their animal or plant host but they take complete control of the cell so that it loses all identity with the host organism.

Fig. 8.5 shows the sequence of events in the infection of a healthy cell by a virus. In most instances it is only the genetic material of the virus that enters. It 'overpowers' the control mechanisms of the cell and makes use of the facilities of the host to direct the production of new virus particles.

Table 8.2 shows some of the diseases that are viral in origin.

Defence against harmful micro-organisms

It seems that everything in our environment is contaminated by invisible micro-organisms that are ready to do us harm if given the chance. How do our bodies protect us from these disease-causing **pathogens**? First of all it must be pointed out that only a very small percentage of all micro-organisms are in fact directly harmful to humans. The first line of defence against micro-organisms is the external barrier formed by the skin and mucous epithelium that lines the outside of the body. Under normal conditions the skin prevents the penetration of pathogens.

Micro-organisms are able to enter, however, wherever there is a break in the outer lining, for example, as a result of a cut or scratch. Once the organisms enter they become established and cause a localized infection.

The role of white blood cells

Chemical substances released by the organisms alert the body to the presence of the micro-organisms whether they are harmful or not and a counter-attack is quickly launched by special white blood cells called **phagocytes** (Greek: *phago* means 'to eat'). These cells are able to squeeze through the lining of the capillaries (amoeboid movement) and 'eat up' the invading organisms in much the same way as the amoeba ingests food (p. 88).

To bring more and more phagocytes to the area blood flow is greatly increased and the area becomes hot and red. The condition is known as **inflammation**.

Inflammation

Within the inflamed area a fierce battle is waged between the body's defence mechanisms and the invading organisms. The phagocytes attempt to engulf as many organisms as possible, while the organisms

Fig.8.6

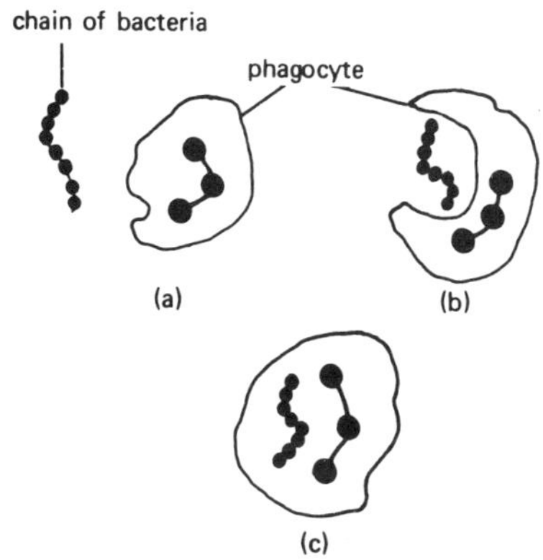

(a) the phagocyte near the bacteria
(b) the phagocyte engulfs the bacteria
(c) the phagocyte digests the bacteria

Fig.8.7 Phagocytes engulfing bacteria

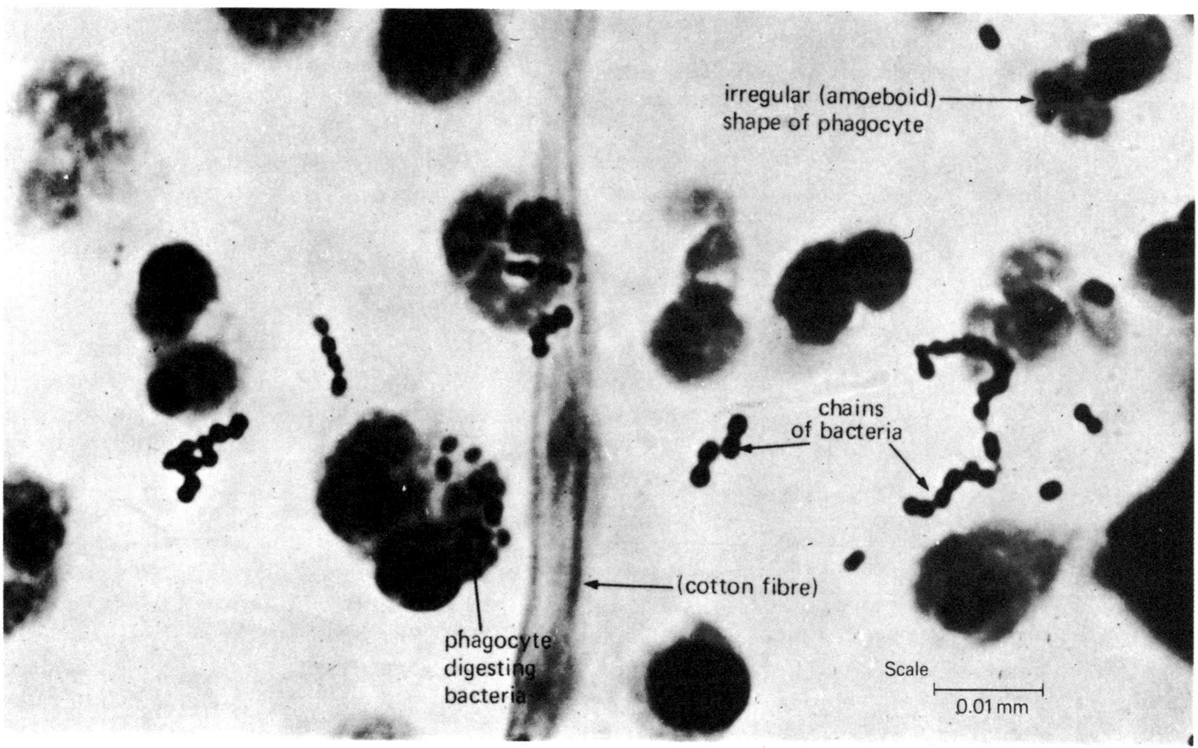

Fig.8.8 Structure of a pimple

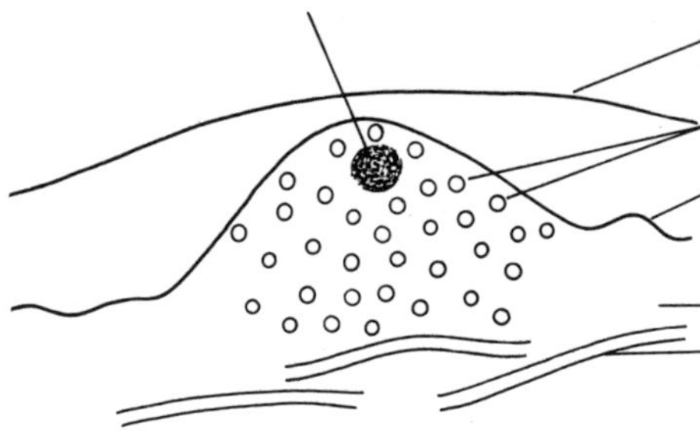

attempt to multiply as quickly as possible. Once inside the phagocytic cells the microbes are killed and dissolved away by the digestive enzymes of the cells. The process is suicidal for the cells themselves because they too will eventually be digested by the powerful enzymes. The accumulation of debris from the dead micro-organisms and white cells becomes visible as **pus** and the resulting pressure in the swollen area causes the pain usually felt. An example of a small localized inflammatory reaction is a pimple. (See fig. 8.8.)

Apart from eliminating as many of the organisms as possible the process of inflammation also seeks to localize the infection by sealing off the contaminated area.

What happens to the organisms that evade the local defences of the body?

Some of the microbes that escape from the area of the inflammation are likely to end up in the lymphatic system, being moved along by a stream of lymph towards the various lymph nodes. In the nodes there are numerous fixed phagocytes that attempt to engulf the invaders.

If the organism penetrates the blood stream the situation is much more serious due to spreading of the organisms to all parts of the body.

Antibodies

An additional line of defence available is the action of **antibodies**. An antibody is a specific protein that is able to combine with and neutralize a particular foreign substance called an **antigen**. The specificity of an antigen for an antibody is similar to the specificity of an enzyme for its substrate.

The mammalian body has a very efficient system for recognizing chemical substances that belong to itself and those that do not. As a general rule whenever a foreign substance gains access the body reacts by synthesizing an antibody for neutralizing this potentially dangerous substance.

The first time the given substance is encountered by the **immune system** the production of antibodies is initiated. Since the process is a lengthy one the invading organisms can usually spread through

a considerable area before the immune system is able to react to it. However, the second time the same antigen is encountered the antibodies are ready to pounce on it and eliminate it immediately.
This aspect of the body's defence system is made use of in the practice of **immunization** or **vaccination**.

Immunization

Immunization consists of introducing into the body a very small amount of a live infectious agent, or sometimes merely the non-living cells of the agent. In either case the vaccine is incapable of causing the actual disease but does stimulate the immune system to produce antibodies against it. If the same agent is ever encountered by the person again the antibodies will be ready to defend.
Today immunization can protect us against many infectious diseases such as polio, tetanus, smallpox, typhoid and diptheria, all dreaded diseases that before the days of immunization would cripple or kill thousands of people every year.

Drugs effective against micro-organisms

A certain group of drugs called **antibiotics** are effective against various disease-causing bacteria. The first of these to be discovered was penicillin made from an extract of the *Penicillium* mould. The substance has the ability to inhibit the growth of certain but not all bacteria. Other drugs such as streptomycin and aureomycin are effective against other different groups of bacteria. The best defence against viral diseases is immunization.

Reducing the chances of infection

By adopting a number of simple precautions for preventing the spread of micro-organisms it is possible to drastically reduce the incidence of infectious diseases. Especially in an area as crowded as Hong Kong these simple hygienic measures must be scrupulously observed to ensure our own personal safety and the safety of the community in general.

Personal hygiene

Micro-organisms accumulate on the surface of the body especially in such places as under fingernails and in folds of skin. Regular cleansing with soap and water kills these organisms and keeps the skin healthy.
Dust and dirt that accumulate in the pores of the skin weaken the skin's action as a barrier and as a means of regulating body temperature. Blocked pores can also lead to infections such as pimples.
Washing your hands before eating or handling food is also important. Teeth should be cleaned regularly to remove decay-causing bacteria.

A person who has some type of infectious disease should take every precaution to ensure that he does not hand the infection on to others. Sneezing and spitting, for instance, release literally millions of bacteria into the air and must be avoided.

Food hygiene

Most disease-causing bacteria are killed by temperatures of above 65°C. A heating process called **pasteurization** is used to make foodstuffs such as milk safe from these organisms.

Low temperature also reduces the activities of micro-organisms and therefore freezing or refrigeration will keep food safe for a certain period of time. Solid foods such as meat and fruits can be preserved by the addition of large quantities of salt or sugar. Under these conditions micro-organisms are inactivated or killed due to the effect of the high osmotic pressure around them which draws out large amounts of water from their cells. Foods such as pork and fish which may pass on various parasitic infections should always be thoroughly cooked to kill any organisms they might contain. Surfaces used for food preparation should be thoroughly cleaned after each use. If food particles are allowed to remain in crevices these provide an excellent spot for the multiplication of bacteria.

Waste disposal

Wastes should be disposed of into closed containers to keep out flies and other animals as well as disease-spreading organisms. Refuse bins should be regularly washed and disinfected. Wastes should never be thrown away on the streets or the beaches or in the woods. If you go out for a picnic carry your refuse back with you until you find a suitable container to dispose of it.

Medical attention

Fig.8.9 Yeast cells under the microscope

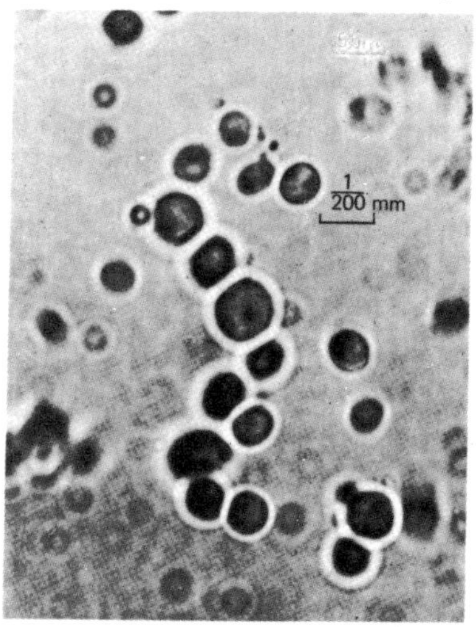

If you find that you have an infectious disease of some sort it is always best to get medical advice.

For the duration of the infection stay away from large crowds of people. Coughing and sneezing and spitting can release millions of bacteria into the surrounding air and should be controlled as much as possible.

Useful aspects of micro-organisms

As we have already pointed out only a very small percentage of micro-organisms are in fact harmful to man. Many are of direct benefit to us.

Yeast

Yeast, an organism that you are already familiar with, is one of the useful ones. On p. 115 when studying anaerobic respiration ex-

Fig.8.10 Production of CO_2 by yeast cells in fermentation

periments were done to show that under anaerobic conditions yeast cells produce carbon dioxide and alcohol as by-products of their metabolism.

The production of carbon dioxide is made use of in baking bread. If you were to make a dough out of flour and water only the resulting bread would be very dense and hard, not pleasant to eat at all. By adding a little yeast and sugar the carbon dioxide released from the yeast cells makes the bread *rise,* that is, the gas liberated makes air spaces in the dough. As a result the bread becomes soft and fluffy. Sugar has to be added as a food for the yeast. The sugar and yeast are usually mixed with a little warm water to make the temperature suitable for the yeast to start growing.

How do we make use of the alcohol produced by yeast cells? The production of alcohol by yeast is made use of in the making of wine and beer. In wine making the necessary yeast is already present in the skin of the ripe grapes and the sugar is in the grape itself.

For making beer the source of sugar is the malt made from germinating barley seeds and yeast has to be added.

In each case the mixture is allowed to ferment producing more and more alcohol until the alcohol content becomes so high that it kills off the yeast cells.

Antibiotics

Several antibiotics in common use today are made from extracts of different species of mould. The first to be discovered, penicillin, is derived from *Penicillium notatum*. The next discovery was streptomycin from a mould of the species *Streptomyces*.

Today many other antibiotics of fungal origin are known and all are effective against a different selection of bacteria, but never against all bacteria. The disappointing aspect of the use of antibiotics is the continual development of resistant strains of bacteria. Since bacteria are so numerous and multiply so quickly the chances of new resistant mutants arising during the course of a particular infection are very great. For this reason new drugs have to be developed all the time and the use of the drugs should be carefully controlled.

Summary

Pathogenic bacteria and viruses cause many diseases in humans. The body's defence system against invading micro-organisms is comprised of the barrier action of the skin, the action of white blood cells in the inflammatory response and the activity of antibodies.

Immunization can protect us against many infectious diseases. By following the various rules of hygiene we can prevent many dangerous micro-organisms from spreading.

Useful micro-organisms include yeast, used in making bread and alcoholic beverages and certain moulds that are used in the production of antibiotics.

Section 9. The Ecosystem

Ecology

What do we mean by the word ecology?

The word **ecology** was first used in the middle of the last century. It refers to the study of the interrelationships between different individual living organisms and between living organisms and the environment around them. It encompasses many diverse situations:
(i) the influence of climate on the growth of the fruits and vegetables we eat;
(ii) problems arising from large populations of people living in a limited area such as in Britain;
(iii) a factory dumping waste materials into the sea and causing a reduction in the number of fish that are able to survive;
(iv) an oil spill from a tanker that ruins our beaches.
These are all examples of the almost limitless range of interactions that can be grouped under the heading of ecology, or **environmental studies.**
These are not remote questions that are only of interest to specialists but ones which very intimately affect our daily lives.
The concerns of ecology are our concerns, the problems are our problems and the solutions have to be our solutions.

What is an ecosystem?

Ecosystem is the term applied to the total environment of an area including plants, animals, weather, supply of inorganic nutrients, and so on. In fact, all of the physical and biological components of the environment are regarded to comprise the ecosystem, such as:
(a) Weather
  (i) temperature
  (ii) water: both free water and atmospheric moisture (relative humidity)
  (iii) light
  (iv) gases: primarily oxygen and carbon dioxide
  (v) pressure
  (vi) wind
(b) Food
(c) Other plants and animals
  (i) competition
  (ii) predators
  (iii) parasites
  (iv) pathogens: disease-causing organisms
(d) Shelter (a place in which to live)

Why are the physical and chemical aspects of the environment important?

It is for the reason that these factors, to a large degree, determine the type of plant life *(flora)* and animal life *(fauna)* that can survive in an area, the numbers in which they are present and whether they will continue to increase in numbers or gradually disappear.

What are some of the important aspects of the physical environment that are significant in the study of ecology?

There are two *basic* types of environment in which living things are found, namely, *water* and *air*. These two media are very different in nature and therefore different in the types of organism that they can support.

Table 9.1

Comparison of Water and Air as a support for life	
AIR	*WATER*
78% nitrogen gas 21% oxygen gas	water with small concentration of dissolved gases from the atmosphere
extreme temperatures	more moderate temperatures
no solvent action	serves as a solvent and transport medium
low density (0.0013 at sea level)	higher density (approx. 1.0)
relatively small pressure changes with altitude	large pressure changes with depth
gives little buoyancy	gives a high degree of buoyancy and support
adequate light for photosynthesis	rapidly decreasing amount of light as depth increases
presence of wind	no wind but may be currents in the water
problem of possible water shortage	no water shortage, but may be osmotic problems

Physical aspects of the environment

Temperature

Living organisms have been found at various temperatures ranging from extremely low to extremely high temperatures. Within these limits every organism has an optimal temperature range in which it functions with the greatest efficiency, and a definite range of temperatures that it can tolerate while still remaining alive. The usual air temperature range within which most plants and animals live is 10°–30°C.

In their reaction to temperature plants and animals can be roughly classified as:

(a) Boreal: northern; species which can withstand cold, and are found in the extremely cold parts of the world.

(b) Temperate: species which live a cool to warm climate, and avoid both cold and hot extremes.

(c) Tropical: species found in the hottest parts of the world and generally they die if the temperature drops to about 15°C.

On a world-wide scale, the range of average temperatures between the polar regions and the equatorial regions is enormous. On land, temperature also depends on the altitude and in aquatic environments on the size and depth of the particular body of water in question.

On land there can also be a considerable difference in the amount of heat received by an organism within a rather short period of time. For example, on a hot, sunny day in the summer the difference in temperature between sun and shade can be as much as 10°C. The difference between sun and shade in water is much less, usually not more than 1°C.

Variations between day- and night-time temperatures on land can be as high as 17°C in many areas and in desert regions may even reach 40°C.

What about seasonal temperature changes?

There is a pronounced difference between water and land as far as the daily and seasonal variation in temperature is concerned.

Seasonal temperature variations are superimposed over those due to differences in latitudes and altitudes.

In tropical and polar seas the temperature between summer and winter shows a difference of only about 5°C. In temperate seas, however, a difference of 10°–15° or even up to 25° can be found. The temperature of sea-surface waters ranges from about 8°C in winter to 17° in summer round Britain, varying with latitude.

On land, tropical climates undergo relatively smaller seasonal temperature changes but in temperate climates differences range from 30° to 70° or more.

In tropical areas, in addition there are differences due to alternating wet and dry seasons.

Although the amount of heat coming from the sun may be the same, the presence of clouds in the rainy season will result in lower temperatures than in the dry season when there is no cloud cover.

As you can see all organisms must be able to survive considerable changes in temperature on a day-to-day basis and on a seasonal basis.

Plants and animals have various ways of adapting to these changes.

Can you think of some of these adaptations?

Here are some examples:

1. The wilting of plant leaves to avoid the direct rays of the hot sun (see p. 175).
2. Dormancy period of seeds to enable them to survive through the cold of winter (see pp. 273 and 302).
3. Hibernation among animals during the winter months (see p. 274).
4. Nocturnal animals that become active at night when the temperature is much lower and hide in their burrows during the heat of the day.

What are the temperature ranges found in the British Isles?

In Britain the temperatures range from a low of 4.5°C in January/February (mean monthly temperature) to a high of 17°C in July/August (mean monthly temperature). The highest and lowest temperatures recorded on the mainland are 38.1°C at Tonbridge, Kent (1868) and −27°C at Braemar in the Cairngorms (1895).

Light

Either directly or indirectly, light is necessary for all photosynthetic organisms and for most animals.

The light received by an organism must meet the following requirements:

1. It must be strong enough in intensity and long enough in duration to satisfy the needs of the organism concerned.
2. It must not be so strong that it causes harm to the organism.

Where does light come from?

The chief source of light available on the earth is the sun.

The actual amount of light from the sun that reaches a given environment depends on the location (e.g. latitude of the environment), the time of day, the time of year and other factors such as moisture and dust in the atmosphere and the presence of clouds. In addition the amount of light is affected by the presence of trees, shrubs, houses etc. that are in the area.

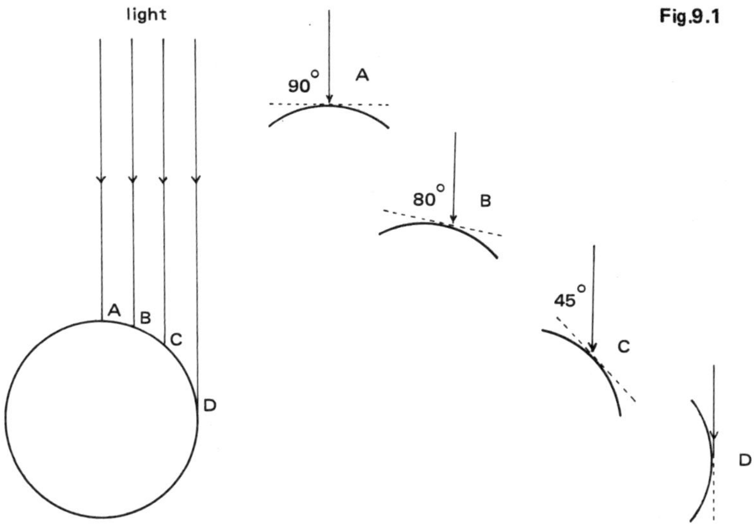

Fig.9.1

Why does light intensity and duration of sunlight vary with altitude and the time of year?

Variation in the amount of light from the sun versus latitude depends on the position of the sun relative to the earth. You have probably studied this topic in your geography classes but a quick review would probably be helpful.

The diagram below shows a light source such as an electric bulb and a spherical object upon which the light is falling.

Because the object is spherical the angle at which the light hits it is different at different points on its surface. At point A the light is shining directly on the surface forming an angle of 90° to the horizontal.

As we go from A to D the angle is gradually reduced until at D the light simply skims over the surface.

As the angle at which the light strikes the surface changes so does the intensity of light reaching the surface. As the angle decreases, more and more of the light is reflected and scattered.

This is similar to the case of light reaching the earth from the sun. Greatest intensity is obtained at points where the sun's rays are hitting the surface at an angle of 90°.

Due to the orientation of the earth with respect to the sun the area of the earth where the sun's rays are at an angle of 90° changes with the revolution of the earth around the sun. At the same time the number of hours of sunlight per day also changes.

This variation of light and therefore temperature conditions throughout the year makes possible the existence of some plants and animals in polar regions for at least a part of the year.

The above discussion dealt with light conditions on a world-wide scale.

Changing conditions in a particular environment

PLANTS

There is a high degree of specialization among plants and animals as to the type of light conditions that they find suitable for life. Some plants must grow in a spot that is fully exposed to the sun while others can tolerate a shady location with low light intensity; a few shade plants can actually be killed by exposure to very high light intensity and the high temperature this causes.

ANIMALS

Some animals become active during the daylight hours while others prefer to feed and move about during the night, but this is usually not a direct response to light but rather the avoidance of such predators as man which are active during daylight hours. But there are animals which are really nocturnal and have special eyes and other sense organs adapted for night life, for example, certain owls, bats and certain insects

Britain's average daily duration of bright sunshine varies from 0.5–1.5 hours per day in December to 6.0–7.5 hours per day in July. One days when the sun is actually hidden by cloud cover quite a lot of useful radiation still reaches the earth's surface.

Water

A large proportion of the weight of an organism is made up of water and all living things need water in order to remain alive.

Aquatic environments do not present any problems of water shortage but, as we shall discuss later, can cause difficulties with excess water flooding into an organism.

On land sometimes serious problems are associated with obtaining adequate water.

Where does water on land come from?

The chief source of water is rain. Rain is formed as a result of condensation of moisture in the atmosphere.

Condensation and rain are parts of the continuous recycling process of water, referred to as the **water cycle.**

The water cycle will be discussed in the next section dealing with the recycling of the various resources of the ecosystem.

What controls the amount of rainfall received by an area?

Due to the action of the winds and the influence of temperature conditions the amount of rainfall varies from one area to another on the surface of the earth.

In some areas of the world annual rainfall can be as little as 25 cm while in other areas as much as 2000 cm or more.

Even more significant are seasonal variations in rainfall. If rainfall in an area occurs during the growing season plants will be able to grow and thrive in large numbers. However, if the rain comes when the weather is either too hot or too cold for plant growth to take place, then most of the rain will be wasted.

The average level of precipitation in the British Isles

The climate associated with Britain is usually regarded as being equable and wet. It is influenced by the warm North Atlantic Drift and moist Westerly winds. The precipitation, which falls mainly in the form of rain, varies noticeably more as you move from one locality to another, than does the temperature. The average annual values for precipitation range from about 500 mm along the Thames Valley increasing to over 5000 mm in some parts of highland Britain. The average annual rainfall over lowland Britain is less than 750 mm. Changes in the topography are seen when comparing the two approximate areas of east and west, eastern England has less rainfall as it lies in a 'rain-shadow'.

As the region of highland Britain has cooler temperature, more of the precipitation falling here does so in the form of snow.

As a general rule for most of the country the months of February to April inclusive tend to be drier (on average) than the months found either side. The summer months of July and August tend to be fairly wet with drier conditions in September. Wet conditions begin again in October continuing for several months.

Water and the Aquatic Organism

When discussing aquatic organisms or specifically aquatic animals it is important to distinguish between those living in sea water and those in fresh water.

ANIMALS

Sea water is isotonic with the body fluids of most animals and therefore does not present any problems of osmoregulation.

Animals living in fresh water must, however, have special ways of keeping excess water out of their cells.

On p. 137 these special adaptations have already been discussed.

PLANTS

Plants living in fresh water generally have an internal osmotic pressure that is slightly higher than that of the surrounding water. As a result a certain amount of water is always entering the cells to satisfy the high water requirements of plants.

Some plants growing in sea water or on seashores need enormous internal osmotic pressures in order to ensure that water will keep entering into their cells. Seashore plants have an added complication in that at low tide in times of heavy rainfall they are growing in almost pure fresh water.

Life in the estuaries

A similarly complicated situation is faced by organisms living in the *estuaries*, that is, the junctions of rivers with the sea. In these locations there are wide variations in the salt content of the water due to the action of the tides. At low tide there is a lower salt concentration because water is flowing from the river out to the sea. At high tide the estuary is flooded with salt water.

These organisms must have a 'two-way' control of water balance. An interesting way of dealing with this problem is shown by various marine invertebrates living in shells. They simply close their shells very tightly at low tide to keep out fresh water and open them only at high tide when the salt content is adequate.

Land Organisms

Terrestrial animals face a much more serious difficulty in obtaining and conserving water.

They generally obtain water by either directly drinking it or deriving it from the plant or animal material they eat as food.

Some animals such as the frog and the toad have the ability to absorb water from damp surroundings through their skin, but they also lose water through their skin equally easily in dry conditions.

Certain insects, such as some moths, can satisfy their needs by the use of **metabolic water,** that is, water derived from the breakdown of food in respiration.

Problems of water loss

Avoiding excessive water loss is as equally important as obtaining water in the first place.

Water regulation by the mammalian kidney has already been discussed (see p.145).

Effective covering of the body surface with skin, exoskeleton or a layer of mucous secretion serves to cut down evaporation.

Many animals hide in burrows or holes in the ground during the day when the heat of the sun makes the air very dry and come out at night when the air and ground become damper.

In extreme cases of heat and drought certain animals go into a state of 'hibernation' known as **aestivation.**

Water relations in plants

Plants obtain water through their roots and therefore rely on soil water to stay alive.

The cuticle on the leaf surface helps to cut down water loss.

Desert plants such as cacti have very reduced leaves thereby cutting down their surface area exposed to the air.

Other adaptations for conserving water include folding up of the leaves under the scorching rays of the sun; having longitudinally rolled leaves; reduction in the number of stomata, and the presence of sunken stomata (see p. 154).

Gases

All living things require oxygen to stay alive. In addition most autotrophs require carbon dioxide and a few require atmospheric nitrogen. In most areas of the world there is a virtually unlimited supply of these gases in the atmosphere.

In heavily industrialized areas the balance between the various gases present in the atmosphere can be disrupted by waste chemicals that are discharged into it. For example, if a large amount of carbon monoxide is discharged into the atmosphere, the carbon monoxide will consume oxygen as it becomes converted to carbon dioxide.

$$2CO + O_2 \rightarrow 2CO_2$$

In seas and lakes supplies of gases, especially oxygen, are more limited and can vary considerably depending on the time and the place. Even at full saturation the amount of oxygen dissolved per unit volume of water is much less than that contained in the atmosphere. The oxygen supplies of bodies of water are replenished mainly by diffusion from the air, and as a result of activities of the photosynthetic organisms. Oxygen supplies are influenced by the balance between the other chemical substances found in the water. Dumping of waste substances alters the chemical balance and as a result can decrease the oxygen levels over a period of time.

At the present time we do not as yet really feel the effects of serious air and water pollution in Britain. However, increasing levels of industrialization and increasing numbers of automobiles could result in serious problems in the not too distant future.

Chemical substances

Autotrophic land organisms need certain chemical substances from the soil to use as raw materials in the synthesis of organic nutrients. The mineral content of the soil in a given area can therefore influence the distribution of plants, and thus indirectly the distribution of animals.

We have already discussed these important minerals in Section 1. In the following section we shall discuss how these important nutrients are recycled in the ecosystem.

Energy flow in the Ecosystem

Ultimately almost all the energy available on earth comes from the gigantic thermonuclear reactor, the sun. In the interior of the sun there is a continual conversion of hydrogen to helium accompanied by the release of tremendous amounts of energy in the form of electromagnetic radiation. This radiation is largely in the region of the visible spectrum.

Since the sun radiates energy in all directions the amount that actually reaches the earth is only a small fraction of the total. Almost half of that which reaches the earth is reflected back by the atmosphere.

Of the energy arriving at the surface of the earth a small percentage is captured by green plants through the process of photosynthesis. Various studies have indicated that the efficiency of green plants in capturing solar energy is only about 1.5% at the most. However, their efficiency in utilizing the energy that they manage to capture is about 75% depending on the particular plant.

What happens to the energy captured by green plants?

Part of the energy is used for the respiratory processes of the organism and part is lost through decomposition. Of the remainder only a small portion is utilized by the herbivores that eat the plant while the rest remains unused.

The portion of the energy that reaches the herbivores can in turn be subdivided into that used for respiration, utilized by carnivores, released through decomposition or remains unused.

The final links in the energy cycle are the decomposers.

The figure below shows diagrammatically the distribution of the energy of the sun through the ecosystem.

Fig.9.2

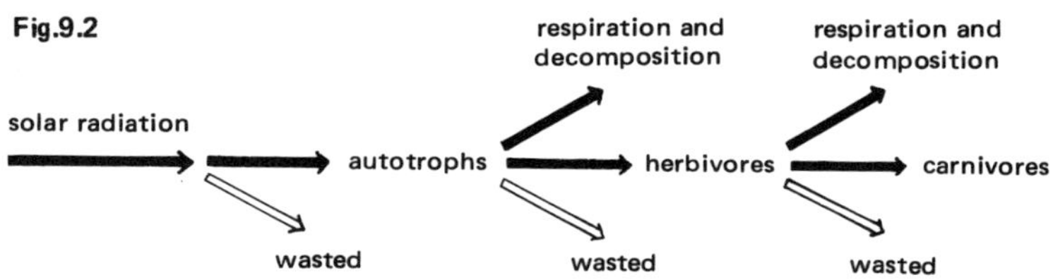

Nutrient cycling

Along with the transfer of energy from autotrophs to herbivores to carnivores there is a corresponding cycling of organic nutrients. The autotrophs use inorganic substances to synthesize organic nutrients. These nutrients are in turn consumed by the herbivores and carnivores and finally turned back into the original inorganic materials by the decomposers.

Fig. 9.3 shows the relationship of energy flow and nutrient cycling. Notice that the flow of energy is non-cyclic. Decomposers release a certain amount of energy-rich by-products such as methane (CH_4) gas. These gases are usually lost to the atmosphere. At times they do become trapped in underground pockets and serve as sources of natural gas.

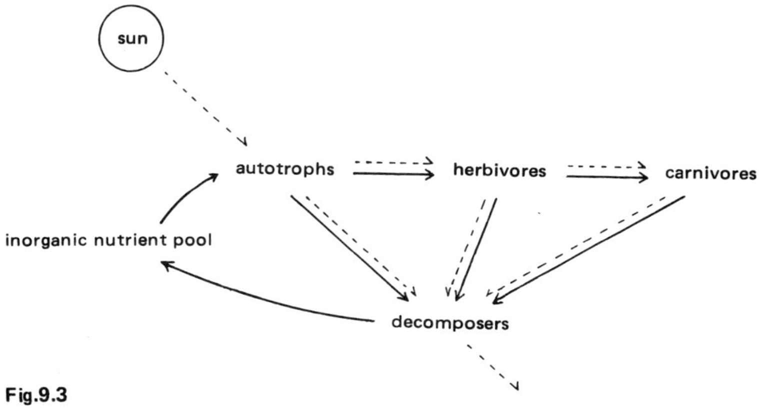

Fig.9.3

Carbon cycle

The source of carbon atoms for the synthesis of organic molecules by autotrophs is atmospheric CO_2. The ultimate source of CO_2 is limestone ($CaCO_3$) formed mostly in the oceans of the world. It is believed that there is a continual exchange of CO_2 between the atmosphere and the waters of the seas and the formation and

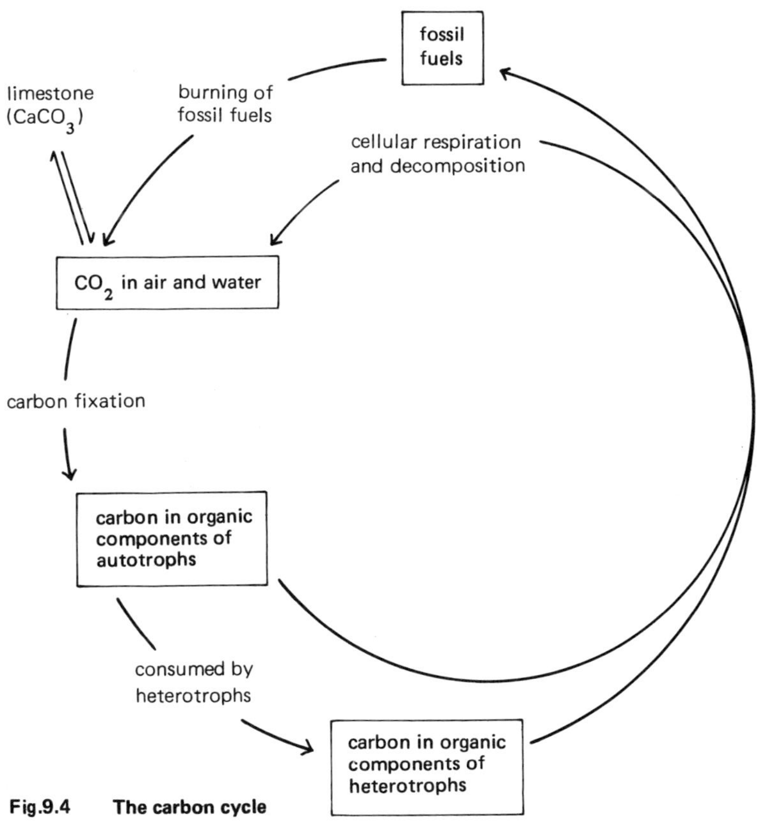

Fig.9.4 The carbon cycle

breakdown of limestone is the main means of regulating the atmospheric concentration of the gas.
With the increasing use of fossil fuels the burning of these fuels has become a very important additional source of CO_2.

How is carbon recycled?

Carbon fixation by autotrophs results in the synthesis of organic carbon compounds which are then consumed by the heterotrophs. Cellular respiration and decomposition reconverts most of the organic carbon to CO_2 except for the small amount that might be converted into fossil fuels. (See fig. 9.4.)

Oxygen cycling

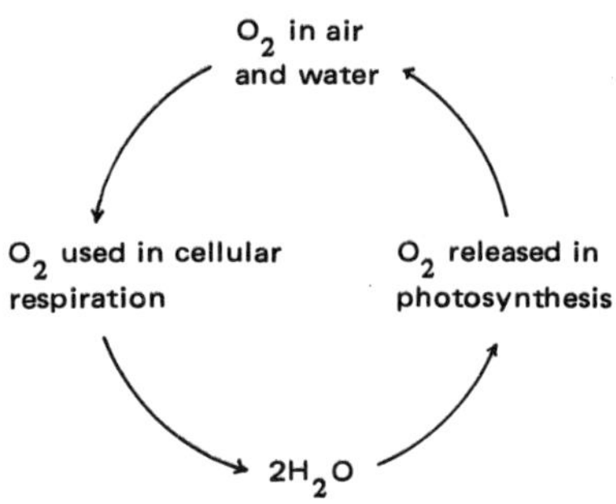

Fig.9.5 The oxygen cycle

Through the processes of respiration and photosynthesis the recycling of oxygen is closely linked with that of carbon.

Water cycle

Water is being continuously recycled both as a result of purely physical factors and due to the activities of living organisms.
Although the activities of heterotrophs also play a role in this recycling process the major effect of living organisms is that of the absorption of water and transpiration by plants.
Plants obtain water from the soil through their roots. To get enough water to all the cells of the plant there is a continuous movement

Fig.9.6 The water cycle

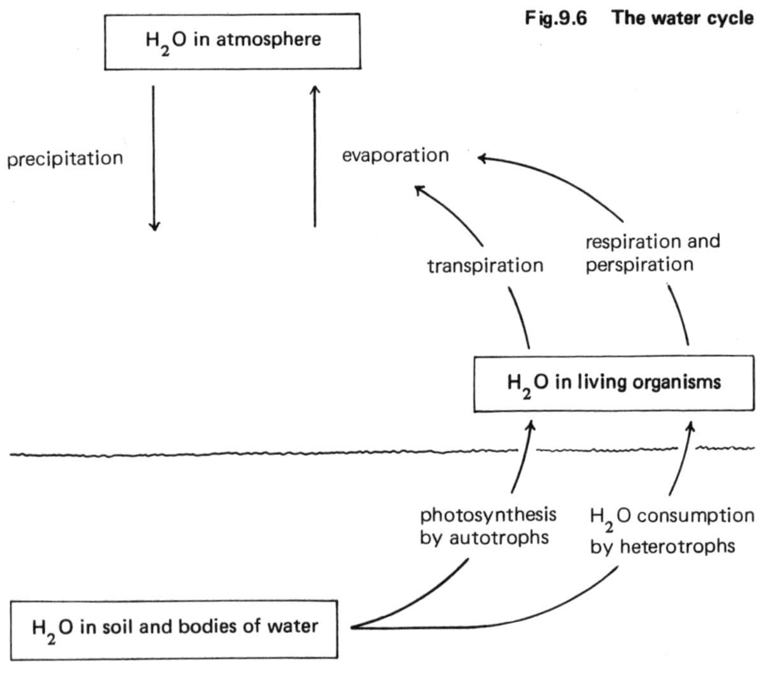

of water from the roots up through the stem and into the leaves. The force that causes this movement to take place is transpiration. (See Section 3.) The amount of water lost to the atmosphere due to transpiration is much larger than one can imagine. For example, a single acre of land covered with mature trees can transpire as much as 10 000 litres of water *per day!*

Nitrogen cycle

An essential component of the proteins and nucleic acids found in all living organisms is the element nitrogen.
The atmosphere is composed of 78% of nitrogen, thus there is no shortage of supply of the element. The problem is that most living organisms are unable to utilize atmospheric nitrogen directly. Green plants must have nitrogen in the form of nitrates, nitrites or compounds of ammonia while animals must have preformed amino acids. (See Section 1.)
For the above reasons the nitrogen cycle of the ecosystem is considerably more complicated than the other cycles.

What is the pathway of nitrogen recycling?

Direct conversion of nitrogen to nitrates occurs as a result of the action of lightning. The nitrates thus produced are washed into

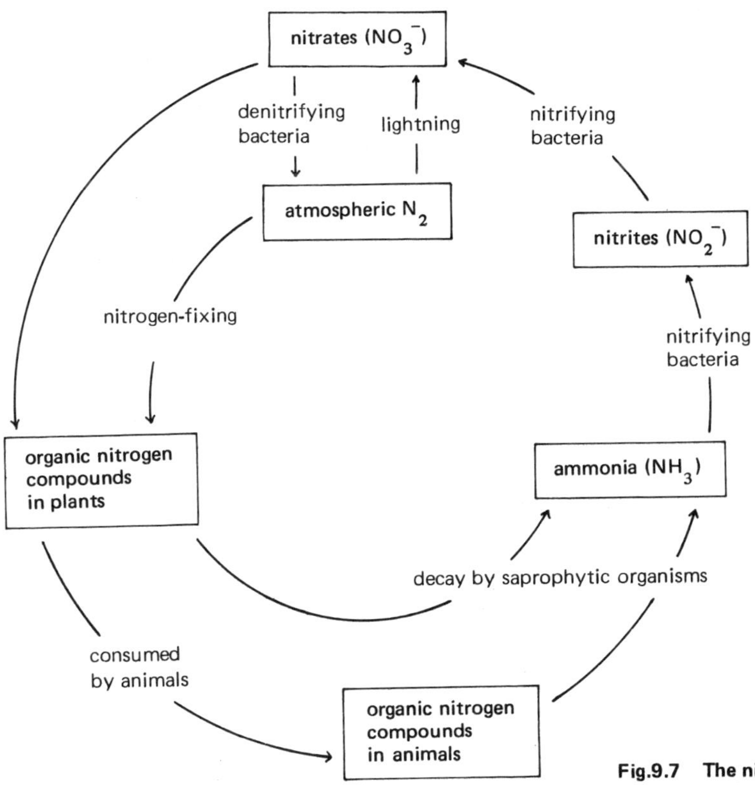

Fig.9.7 The nitrogen cycle

the soil by the rains where they can be used by autotrophic organisms. Nitrogen-fixing organisms are able to incorporate nitrogen directly into organic compounds. Denitrifying bacteria reconvert some nitrates to gaseous nitrogen.

The organic nitrogen compounds synthesized by autotrophs make their way up the food chain through the various levels of consumers. Eventually they all die and are decayed by the decomposers. As a result of decomposition the nitrogen-containing organic molecules are converted into ammonia. The ammonia is then converted into nitrites and nitrates by the nitrifying bacteria.

The operation of the natural nitrogen cycle is adequate in most areas of the world. In agricultural areas, however, the nitrogen removed from the soil is very great but there is little decaying material to replenish the supply and the process of natural decay is too slow to meet the demand for nutrients. In these areas nitrates must be added to the soil in the form of fertilizers.

Other nutrients

Similar cycles of nutrient consumption are found with other inorganic materials such as phosphorus, sulphur, potassium and sodium. As in the case of nitrates, supplies of any of these can become depleted so that they must be replenished through fertilizers.

Crop rotation

Since the nutrient requirements of various crops do vary in certain respects, planting the same crop in a plot of land year after year will deplete the soil of certain components. The inorganic materials returned to the soil as a result of decay of different plants will also be different. For example, the presence of leguminous plants will restore nitrogenous compounds to the soil.

For these reasons the practice of crop rotation is common in most agricultural areas. By changing the distribution of the various crops on the land from year to year a more satisfactory balance and recycling of nutrients can be achieved.

Biological aspects of the environment

What do we mean by biosphere?

The part of the earth and its atmosphere that is inhabited by living things is called the **biosphere.**

The biological aspects of the environment of an area, that is, the organisms that inhabit the place, can be collectively referred to as the **biotic environment.** Thus, the biotic environment of an organism is made up of all the other organisms around it with which it might establish a relationship.

What are the most common relationships that exist within the biotic environment?

Apart from autotrophic organisms, every living thing must feed on another living thing or its remains to stay alive.
This means that the numbers and types of organisms found in a certain area will largely be determined by the type and amount of food available for the organism.
By examining the relationship of 'who eats whom' in a certain area we can set up certain interrelationships between the living inhabitants of that area.

Food chains

With respect to types of feeding habits all organisms can be grouped into one of the following three categories: **producers, consumers** and **decomposers.**
The **primary producers** are the autotrophic organisms such as green plants that are able to synthesize organic nutrients from inorganic components. These have been dealt with in Section 1.
Organisms that feed directly or indirectly on the autotrophs are regarded to be consumers. Herbivores feed directly on plants and are therefore called **primary consumers.** They form the first link in the chain.
Carnivores or omnivores that eat the herbivores are called **secondary consumers:** larger carnivores that feed on the secondary consumers are called **tertiary consumers** and so on. Another way of looking at consumers is to regard them as **secondary producers** because they too add to the pool of organic material available in the eco-system.
If we group living organisms into a sequence depending on their feeding habits what we obtain is a **food chain.**
To give an example, a very simple food chain is: grass → cow → man
Another one is: plants → grasshopper → lizard → snake.
Fig. 9.8 gives further examples of food chains.
Food chains vary in length up to about six links, sometimes even more.

Fourth-order consumer	——	——	Sparrow hawk
			↑
Tertiary consumer	Merlin	Sparrow hawk	**Coal tit**
	↑	↑	↑
Secondary consumer	Tree sparrow	Thrushes	Lacewing larvae
	↑	↑	↑
Primary consumer	Caterpillars	Snails	Aphids
	↑	↑	↑
Producer	Green plants	Green plants	Green plants

Fig. 9.8 Examples of food chains in Britain

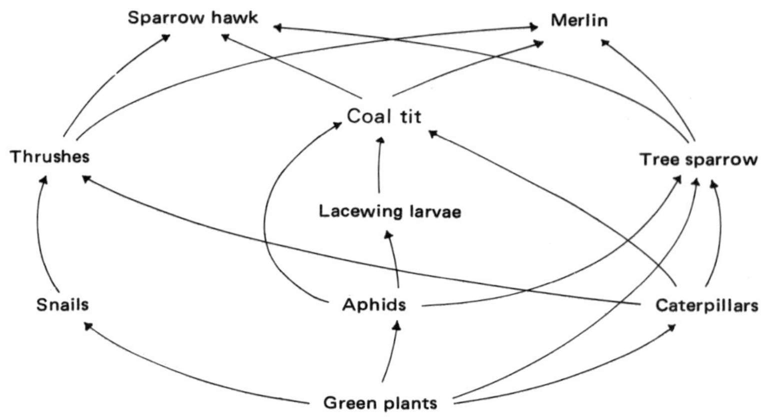

Fig.9.9 A food web made up of the food chains in Fig.9.8

Food web

At this point it may occur to us that very few animals feed on only one type of organism, so there should be branches in the food chain at various levels. In fact there are.

When we consider the interrelationship of an entire group of organisms in a certain habitat, we obtain a **food web.** The figure above illustrates the relationship between individual food chains and a food web.

As we shall see later many food webs are more complicated than the one shown.

Characteristics of a food web

A food web is not a static, unchanging relationship between individual members of the ecosystem but a dynamic, ever-changing one. The balance between the available food supply and the number of consumers that it is able to support is an extremely delicate one. In an unusually dry season the number of plants growing in a certain area might be considerably reduced. As a result, the number of primary consumers that this food supply is able to support will also decrease. In our example of food web for instance, the number of snails, aphids and caterpillars will decrease. It follows that the numbers of secondary consumers such as tree sparrows will also decrease.

If on the other hand, favourable weather conditions prevail and there is an abundant supply of green plants there will be a corresponding increase in the numbers of all the consumers.

What would happen if for example due to some disease all the sparrow hawks in an area suddenly died off?

By examining the food web you might predict a great increase in the numbers of coal tits crowding out any of the other consumers that feed on the lacewing lavae, aphids or caterpillars.

The intervention of man

Man has been responsible for upsetting the food balance in some regions of the world by various means. For example, the introduction into a region of a species of animal that has no local natural predator can have disastrous effects. This allows the number of these new species to increase almost indefinitely thereby crowding out all other species competing for the same food supply.

A particularly dramatic example of this type of situation was the introduction into Australia of the European rabbit in 1859. Since the rabbit had no major predators in Australia its number increased dramatically. Within a short time the spread of the rabbit posed a serious threat to the food supply of the sheep making sheep-raising, one of the country's major sources of income, very difficult.

In many places today the ecological balance of an area is being disrupted by the indiscriminate cutting down of trees and shrubs to obtain vacant land for farming or building purposes.

Clearing a piece of land causes a reduction in numbers of organisms at all the levels of the food chain. The ultimate result is the gradual disappearance of the large predatory animals that are at the very top of the food chain.

The balance between producers and consumers in a food chain is similar to a balancing act performed by a group of acrobats. If any one of the people in the act loses his balance the whole group will tumble to the ground.

Biomass

Biomass is the total mass of organic material contained in the organisms that comprise a specific section of a food web.

As we look at the higher levels of a food web both the total number of individuals and the total biomass decrease. Fig. 9.11 gives you an idea of the relative numbers of individuals in one of the food chains that we have been discussing. Because of the triangular shape of this type of diagram the figure is usually referred to as the **pyramid of numbers.**

Another figure that we could draw represents the relationship of biomass at the various levels. It is called the **pyramid of biomass.** The decrease in numbers is greater than the decrease in biomass due to the increasing size of the individuals at the top of a food chain.

Fig.9.10 Pyramid of biomass

Fig.9.11 Pyramid of numbers

What happens to the species that are at the top of each food web? And to the organisms further down that escape being eaten by predators?

When an organism at any point along the food web dies its remains serve as food for the many saprophytic organisms that are the decomposers of the ecosystem. Their critical role in recycling nutrient materials and making them available for further use has already been discussed on p. 348.
The interdependence of producers, consumers and decomposers can be summarised in the following diagram.

Fig.9.12

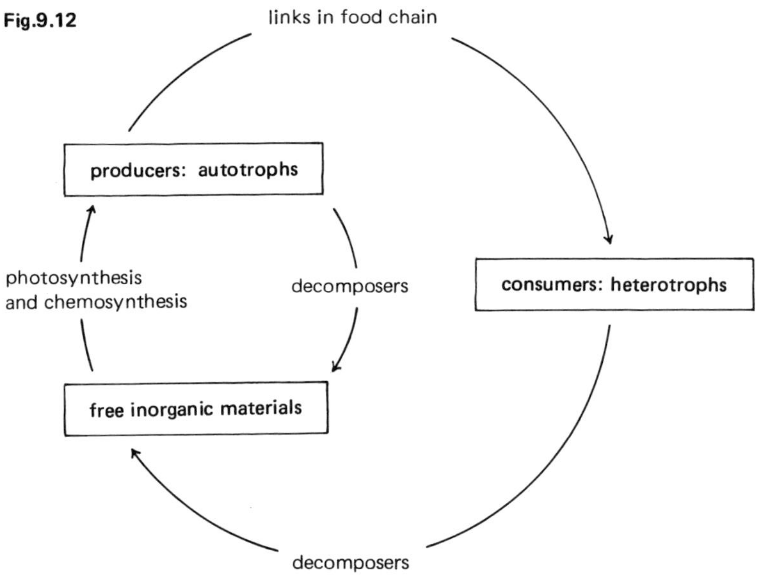

Competition

From the study of the characteristics of food webs the idea of the existence of competition among various organisms may have occurred to us. Individual organisms of the same species and organisms of different species that are at the same level in a food web are continually competing for food, shelter and the other necessities for survival.

COMPETITION AMONG PLANTS

Consider the situation of a population of plants on the same hillside or field.
All the individual plants must obtain their nutrients and moisture from the same patch of soil and they must all try to grow in a spot where there is adequate sunlight. If the number of plants is small, chances are that there will be enough nutrients to satisfy the needs of all. But gradually, because growing conditions are favourable, the number of plants will increase.

Although the plants are increasing in number the amount of nutrients available barely increases, if at all. Soon there will be insufficient supplies to satisfy the needs of all the plants. Overcrowding occurs and competition between individual plants will become even more intense.
At this stage, most likely the growth rate of all individuals will be reduced by some degree. Those that are not so well suited to that particular environment will gradually disappear. Over a period of time a new balance will be achieved and only the hardiest and best suited individuals survive.
An interesting illustration of the competition between plants can be observed in the area around a very large tree.
Find a suitable large tree and look at the plant growth around it. You will find that growth is reduced not only in the immediate area where the tree casts a shadow (competition for light) but in a larger area where the roots of the tree extend. This is due to competition for nutrients and water from the soil. As you look further away from the tree plant growth will gradually increase.

COMPETITION AMONG ANIMALS

Competition among animals of the same species and of different species is just as important. In general, the more similar two animals are to one another the more intense the competition is between them because their needs are very much alike. For this reason competition among individuals of the same species is the most intense of all, because their requirements for food and shelter are identical. In addition, they may also be competing for specific territory and for a mate.

OTHER KINDS OF COMPETITION

Another form of competition is between a predator and its prey. This type of competition, if kept in balance, is responsible for maintaining the numbers of both predators and prey at an optimal level.
For example, the tree sparrows that feed on the caterpillars help to keep the caterpillar population in check. On the other hand, since the supply of caterpillars is limited the number of bulbuls is kept in check due to competition for food with the tree sparrow.
The relationship between a parasite and its host can also be regarded as a form of competition. The dodder living on the stem of the host plant, or the tapeworm in the intestine of an infected individual are competing with their hosts for food in the same way that two predators will compete.

Succession—changing communities

Ecological communities develop very slowly from very simple

beginnings. New communities are continually being established; for example, on the hillsides after a landslide or in an area where the edge of the seashore has been extended by reclamation.

How does life get started in a new spot?

The way living organisms begin to appear in a certain area depends very much on the terrain and the type of soil. The first sign of life on a rough, rocky terrain such as that found on many hillsides in Britain is usually the **lichens**, although in the more polluted atmosphere of our towns lichens may look no more than a grey or greenish patch on a pavement or wall.

A lichen is the result of a symbiotic arrangement between a green alga and a fungus. The fungus is able to obtain mineral salts from the rock that it is attached to and water from the tiny crevices in the rocks. It also provides support by firmly anchoring itself to the rock surface.

The function of the alga, the green part of the plant, is to synthesize organic nutrients through photosynthesis.

Due to their mutual association the two organisms together are able to colonize and survive in regions where neither could live separately. Over a period of time the lichens break up the rock surface, dust and decaying organic materials can accumulate in the crevices and larger plants such as mosses and ferns, from spores that have been carried to the area by the wind, are able to gain a foothold.

At the same time various small consumers such as insects and many decomposers will start moving into the area.

With further development small shrubs and finally trees will begin to take root. The process is a very slow and very gradual one. Once a stable community is established there will be little change in the balance between the organisms unless a drastic environmental change such as a forest fire or prolonged drought upsets the balance. Under these circumstances, the community will fall back to a more primitive existence and start to evolve again.

In every instance of establishing a new community or restoring an existing one some organisms will at first prove to be more successful than others. Undoubtedly this is because they are most suited to the particular environmental conditions of that area. As more new species colonize the area some of the original ones may be crowded out and the pattern of the community changes.

The establishment of new communities and the changes taking place in already established ones are referred to under the term **succession.** The final type of vegetation that can grow in an area is called the **climax vegetation,** and its nature is determined by a series of factors, such as, climate (temperature, rainfall etc.), type and depth of soil, steepness of slope etc.

In Britain the natural climax vegetation is deciduous forest, but this can really only be seen in a few localities because most has been destroyed by man in the felling for timber and fuel and in the too frequent burning of the hillsides, both intentional and accidental. Normal terrestrial succession in Britain is **grassland,** through **scrubland** to **forest (woodland).** Any one stage in the plant succession is called a **sere,** and so a succession consists of a series of seres or **seral stages.**

The habitats

The various aspects of ecology discussed up till now have mostly been of a theoretical nature. Let us look at some of these aspects with regard to our local environment.

Where can we find evidence for the various types of interrelationships between organisms?

There are many different types of habitat in Britain but we shall consider only five which most of us can recognise. These are:
1. Grassland
2. Forest (woodland)
3. Freshwater
4. Marine soft shores (sandy and muddy)
5. Marine hard shores (rocky and boulder)

Habitat I: Forest (Woodland)

There is little remaining of the primative forest which once dominated our island some 2000 years ago. Most has been destroyed and the land used for agricultural purposes. Whilst large areas of land are still occupied by indigenous species they have been subject to some interference by man and therefore are said to possess a semi-natural vegetation. Our most extensive woodlands are Oak, but other types do occur, dominated by native trees such as Ash, Birch, Pine, Alder, and Beech. There is a marked vertical stratification of plants in response to light, wind, temperature, and soil conditions. The dominant trees forming a canopy layer; then a lower shrub layer; and a ground layer of herbs. Oak, Birch, Pine, Ash, and Alder woodlands may possess an extremely varied ground flora dependent upon soil conditions. In Beech woods the canopy can be so dense that the ground flora is severely limited by the lack of light. In such conditions saprophitic plants such as fungi and some orchids may flourish.

Habitat II: Grassland

As noted above, normal terrestrial succession in Britain culminates in forest; thus the majority of our present grasslands are almost entirely artificial, having been established by the clearing of forest by neolithic man, and maintained subsequently by the grazing of sheep and rabbits. The introduction of the myxomatosis virus in the 1950s in an attempt to control the rabbit population has had a marked effect on the stability of these grasslands. Many areas are now overun by shrubs and coarse vegetation: the tender shoots of which are no longer cropped by the rabbits.

During the last war much derelict land was cleared of trees and scrub, and weed infested grassland ploughed up; the land then being sown with superior strains of grasses and clovers. Nevertheless, most of our grasses are tolerant of adverse conditions and whilst some have lost favourable habitats to the demands of agriculture, the majority have persisted in the natural communities still available: heaths and moorlands, hedgerows and woodland, pond, lake and riverbanks, saltmarshes and sand dunes.

Habitat III: Freshwater

There can be few of us who are not familiar with one type of freshwater habitat or another: whether it be a clear, fast flowing mountain stream, a stagnant pond, a road-side ditch or an ornamental lake in a city-centre park. Each will possess a variety of plant and animal species, some of which may be characteristic for that type of water. The importance of such information is undeniable although it is only during the last few years that the value of our freshwater reserves has become an issue with which we can all identify.

Habitats IV and V: Marine Habitats

Marine habitats on the sea-shore (littoral zone) are two basic types: hard-shore of bare rock surfaces and boulders, and soft-shore which are essentially sand and mud beaches. The sea-shore habitat is a hazardous one in that the wave action can be very violent and damaging to the plants and animals living there; and also at low tide these aquatic plants and animals are exposed to the drying effects of wind and sunshine, and to very high surface temperatures in the summer time when the sun is shining.

Thus the algae that grow on the beaches are usually found very firmly attached to rock or boulder surfaces and so resist the dislodging effect of waves. However, they are not able to withstand the exposure to sunshine and the resulting desiccation during the warmer months.

Some of the animals that survive in this rather hazardous habitat have structures which allow firm attachment to the rock surface (such as limpets, barnacles, chitons). Others live in the crevices in the rocks, or on the sides, back and sheltered from the wave-action and excessive sunshine.

On the soft shores the animals tend to burrow into the sand or mud to avoid both wave-action and solar radiation.

The plants which grow at the back of the beach are essentially the same for both soft and hard shores.

Habitat IV: Soft Shores (Sandy and Muddy)

Sandy beaches are usually made up of fragments of very hard rock, generally quartz: fragments originating from softer rocks would soon get reduced to the size of mud particles. Nevertheless, because of their small size, water is retained between the sand particles by capillary action and this has a number of effects upon the animals living there: they are still effectively in water after the level of the water has fallen and salinity and temperature within the sand are little affected by changes at the surface. Wave action can, however, churn up the surface layers, thus sand is not a stable medium. On the other hand muddy shores do tend to be physically stable and there is an accumulation of the finest particles of both inorganic and organic material. The physical stability enables animals to safely build permanent burrows, but the presence of organic material is both advantageous and disadvantageous. It represents food for many animals but its decomposition results in the removal of oxygen from the mud producing anaerobic conditions at any marked depth below the surface.

Habitat V: Hard Shores (Rocky and Boulder)

Rocky shores are characterised by waves that crash against them, with the wind blowing the spray high up the shore. These places are said to be exposed. The fauna and flora have to be adapted to withstand the force of the waves and various degrees of exposure. The animals found on rocky shores, such as the bivalves, barnacles etc. all have some means of holding on to the rocks to keep from being washed away.

The only plants to be found on hard shores in the littoral zone (between low and high water marks) are a few species of grass on the upper shore and algae on the mid and lower shores.

The plants found at the back of the beach on rocky shores are very similar to those on soft shores.

GLOSSARY

active transport: passage of solutes or water across a membrane in a direction that is opposed to the osmotic pressure

adenosine triphosphate (ATP): an energy-rich organic molecule

aerobic respiration: the release of energy from organic nutrients through a process of complete oxidation making use of oxygen and releasing all the available energy

alimentary canal: the complete digestive system of an animal

anabolism: building up of large organic molecules from smaller ones

anaerobic respiration: incomplete oxidation of organic nutrients, without the use of oxygen and releasing only part of the available energy

antibiotic: a chemical that destroys bacteria

antibody: a specific protein synthesized by the body to neutralize foreign substances (antigens) such as bacteria or viruses

antigen: any substance that is regarded by the body as a 'foreign' material and against which antibodies will be made

apical dominance: suppression of the growth of side branches due to a chemical substance secreted by the apical bud

appendicitis: inflammation of the appendix due to infection

articulation: movement of one bone relative to another

atrophy: an unused skeletal muscle becoming weak and reduced in size

autotroph: a living organism capable of synthesizing organic molecules from inorganic raw materials, i.e. a primary producer

balanced diet: a daily intake of all necessary nutrients in the required relative amounts

basal metabolic rate: the minimum rate at which the body uses energy simply to stay alive

calorimeter: apparatus for measuring the energy content of a substance by determining the heat liberated when it is burned

cancer: unrestricted multiplication of cells to produce a continually spreading abnormal growth

carbon fixation: production of sugar from CO_2 and hydrogen in photosynthesis

carnivore: an organism that feeds on animal flesh only

catabolism: breaking-down of large organic molecules into smaller ones

catalyst: an agent that speeds up a chemical reaction but does not itself take part in the reaction

chemosynthesis: the synthesis of organic compounds using energy obtained from the oxidation of inorganic compounds such as hydrogen sulphide or iron compounds

chitin: a hard plastic-like material found in the outer covering of insects

chlorophyll: green pigment found in the chloroplasts of green plants; plays a role in trapping the energy of sunlight for photosynthesis

chloroplast: cell organelle found in green plants and containing chlorophyll

chromosome: a structure in the nucleus of cells carrying genetic information

circulatory system: a transport system carrying gases and nutrients throughout the body of an animal

commensalism: a form of symbiosis where one partner benefits from the relationship but the other remains unharmed

connective tissue: a type of tissue in which the cells are spaced very far apart and the space in between is filled with a matrix, e.g. bone

dark reaction: second phase of photosynthesis, the synthesis of basic carbohydrate units from carbon dioxide and hydrogen

deamination: removal of an amino (NH_2) group

deciduous: having leaves that fall off in the autumn and grow again in the spring

dentine: non-living interior part of a tooth, between enamel and pulp cavity

dentition: the complete set of teeth of an animal

diaphragm: sheet of elastic tissue separating the thoracic cavity from the abdominal cavity in mammals

dicot: (dicotyledonous plant) a plant in which the embryo is enclosed by two cotyledons or seed leaves

diffusion: the movement of substances from an area of high concentration to an area of low concentration

digestion: chemical breakdown of food material to a form that can be absorbed by the body

diploid: containing 2n chromosomes, the usual number in a somatic cell

disaccharide: a sugar molecule formed from two basic sugar units joined together

ecdysis: moulting, shedding of the exoskeleton to allow for increase in size

ectoplasm: the clear, semi-solid cytoplasm at the surface layer of an amoeboid cell

emulsion: a suspension of droplets of a liquid in another liquid

enamel: hard, non-living outer covering of a tooth

endocrine gland: a ductless gland from which the secretion passes directly into the blood stream

endoplasm: the granular, more fluid cytoplasm found in the interior of an amoeboid cell

endosperm: part of seed specialized for food storage

epidermis: the outermost layer of living cells in a plant or animal

essential amino acid: an amino acid that cannot be synthesized by the human body

exocrine gland: a gland from which the secretion is led away through a duct

fatty acid: molecule with the general formula R-(CH_2)nCOOH

fermentation: anaerobic respiration by yeast cells

fertilization: union of the male and female reproductive cells to produce the zygote

fungus: a non-green plant that obtains nutrition from dead and decaying organic matter

genotype: genetic composition of a plant or animal

genus: a grouping of organisms that are closely related to one another; corresponds to the first of the two words in the scientific name

germination: the beginning of the development of the embryo inside a seed to produce a new plant

glucose: grape sugar; one form of hexose

grana: disc-shaped membrane structure in chloroplast, containing chlorophyll

haemolysis: bursting of a red blood cell

haploid: containing n chromosomes as in a reproductive cell

herbivore: an organism that feeds only on plant material

hermaphrodite: producing both male and female reproductive cells in the same individual organism

heterotroph: a living organism that uses preformed organic materials as food and builds them up into more complex molecules, i.e. a secondary producer

hexose: six-carbon sugar $C_6H_{12}O_6$

holozoic: dependent on preformed organic compounds as food

homeostasis: the tendency of living organisms to maintain a constant internal environment in the face of changing external or internal conditions.

hormone: chemical messenger produced in one part of the body that can influence and regulate a metabolic function at some other part

hydrolysis: splitting of a chemical bond followed by the production of one molecule of water

hydroskeleton: body support formed by having a layer of liquid in the interior of the body surrounded by layers of muscle to keep the fluid at a high pressure

hypertonic: having a higher solute concentration relative to another solution

hypoglycemia: abnormally low blood sugar level

hypothesis: a theory that is proposed on the basis of preliminary experimental evidence but not proven conclusively

hypotonic: having a lower solute concentration relative to another solution

immunization: injection of a small amount of an infectious micro-organism to stimulate production of antibody
in vitro. in an artificial system designed to simulate conditions in a living organism
in vivo: in a living organism
inflammation: the reaction of living tissue to injury, infection or irritation characterized by swelling, redness, heat and pain
ingestion: the process by which animals take food into their body cavity
inorganic: not containing carbon in any form other than CO_2 and carbonates
intercostal muscles: muscle connecting the individual ribs
invertebrate: an animal without a backbone
isotonic: having a solute concentration equal to that of another solution
isotopes: two or more forms of the same element differing only in atomic mass
ligament: flexible attachment between bones
light reaction: first phase of photosynthesis where water is split into hydrogen and oxygen using the energy of sunlight

malnutrition: deficiencies in the required nutrients especially vitamins and proteins due to improper diet
mesentery: membrane holding the large and small intestine in place against the body wall
mesophyll: layer of cells under the epidermis in the green leaf
metamorphosis: a very marked change of form during the development of an animal, e.g. from larval to adult form in the frog
mitochondrion: cell organelle serving as site of respiration
monocot: (monocotyledonous plant) a plant in which the embryo is enclosed by a single cotyledon or seed leaf
monosaccharide: a sugar with a single basic sugar unit
mutualism: a form of symbiosis where both partners benefit from the relationship

negative feedback: a system in which a certain change in one direction produces a reaction in the opposite direction
nitrification (nitrifying bacteria): the oxidation of ammonia (NH_3) to give nitrites such as nitrous acid (HNO_2)
nitrogen fixation: the direct incorporation of atmospheric nitrogen into organic compounds
nutrition: the processes associated with obtaining the organic and inorganic materials necessary for the survival of a living organism

omnivore: an organism that feeds on both animal flesh and plant material
organic: containing carbon in forms other than CO_2 and carbonates
osmoregulation: maintenance of the correct concentration of water

inside a living cell

osmotic pressure: the pressure caused by having two solutions of different concentration on either side of a semi-permeable membrane

ossification: conversion of cartilage to bone

parasitism: a symbiotic relationship in which one partner benefits and the other is harmed in some way

peptide: short chain of amino acids

phenotype: physical appearance of a plant or animal

photosynthesis: synthesis of organic sugar molecules from inorganic raw material using the energy of sunlight

pigment: a chemical substance that absorbs certain wavelengths of the visible spectrum and therefore appears coloured

plasmolysis: cell membrane of a plant cell pulling away from the cell wall towards the interior of the cell

pleural membrane: membrane around the lungs

pollination: transfer of pollen to the stigma of the same flower or another flower

polysaccharide: a long-chain molecule made up of many monosaccharides

portal vein: passage leading from the region of the small intestine to the liver to carry absorbed nutrients

potometer: instrument to measure the rate of transpiration by a plant

proprioceptor: one of the senses that gives information about the position of various parts of the body

protein: long chain of amino acids

pulp cavity: innermost part of a tooth containing living cells, nerves and blood supply

radioactive: capable of emitting radiation by the breakdown of atomic nuclei

respiration: oxidation of organic molecules to release energy

secrete: to pass a chemical substance, e.g. an enzyme, from the inside of a cell to the outside

somatic cell: body cell (as opposed to a reproductive cell)

stoma (pl stomata): opening in the surface of a leaf for the purpose of gas exchange and transpiration

species: a name that specifies a living organism; corresponds to the second word in the scientific name

symbiosis: a situation where one organism lives in or on the body of another and obtains nutrition from the other

triglyceride: a fat or oil made up of three molecules of fatty acid and one molecule of glycerol

variegated leaf: a leaf with patches of non-green cells

vertebrate: an animal that has a backbone

INDEX